A THOROUGHLY CANADIAN GENERAL:
A BIOGRAPHY OF GENERAL H.D.G. CRERAR

PAUL DOUGLAS DICKSON

A Thoroughly Canadian General

A Biography of General H.D.G. Crerar

UNIVERSITY OF TORONTO PRESS
Toronto Buffalo London

© University of Toronto Press Incorporated 2007
Toronto Buffalo London
Printed in Canada

ISBN 978-0-8020-0802-2

Printed on acid-free paper

Library and Archives Canada Cataloguing in Publication

Dickson, Paul Douglas, 1963–
  A thoroughly Canadian general : a biography of General H.D.G. Crerar / Paul Douglas Dickson.

  Includes bibliographical references and index.
  ISBN 978-0-8020-0802-2

  1. Crerar, Henry Duncan Graham, 1888–1965. 2. Canada. Canadian Army – History. 3. Generals – Canada – Biography. I. Title.

  U55.C73D53 2007   355.0092   C2007-900285-4

University of Toronto Press acknowledges the financial assistance to its publishing program of the Canada Council for the Arts and the Ontario Arts Council.

University of Toronto Press acknowledges the financial support for its publishing activities of the Government of Canada through the Book Publishing Industry Development Program (BPIDP).

This book has been published with the help of a grant from the Canadian Federation for the Humanities and Social Sciences, through the Aid to Scholarly Publications Programme, using fund provided by the Social Sciences and Humanities Research Council of Canada.

*This book is dedicated to my parents, Douglas and Betty Dickson.
They encouraged my love of history in myriad ways.*

Contents

Acknowledgments ix
Introduction xiii
Abbreviations xxi
Maps xxv
Map Credits xliv

1 Hamilton Roots 3
2 Baptism of Fire 25
3 The Killing Ground 46
4 Learning the Game 69
5 Stagnation 86
6 The Politics of Preparedness 100
7 Limited Liability War 118
8 Chief of the General Staff 137
9 Hong Kong and the Politics of Army Expansion 157
10 Father of First Canadian Army 174
11 Preparing 1st Canadian Corps 184
12 Dieppe 198
13 Replacing McNaughton 211
14 Corps Command in Italy 226

15 Taking Command of the Army   237
16 First Canadian Army and Overlord   260
17 The Normandy Campaign   283
18 The Learning Curve: Totalize and Tractable   304
19 Coalition Battles   321
20 First Canadian Army and the Scheldt   337
21 The Rhineland Offensive   360
22 Veritable: Crerar's Battle   381
23 The Final Campaign   401
24 Casting the Postwar Army   422
25 Fading Away   442

Notes   467
Bibliography   543
Index   559

Illustrations follow page 380.

Acknowledgments

Many people have contributed to the development of this book, directly and indirectly. It began life as doctoral dissertation examining Crerar's professional education and experience to March 1944, a study that was guided to completion by Ron Sunter, Terry Crowley, and, in particular, Terry Copp. Terry Copp has been an ongoing source of advice and support. He taught me much about how to be a historian. He was always willing to respond to the requests for help, even ones out of the blue from a grad student just starting his master's. I am thankful as well to the Department of History at the University of Guelph, which provided generous support for a number of research trips to Ottawa and office space when I needed a spot to finish the dissertation and much of the subsequent draft. University of Guelph historians Eric Reiche, Jamie Snell, David Murray, Cathy Wilson, Richard Reid, Susan Armstrong-Reid, and Gil Stelter were equally generous with their time and encouragement.

James L. Stokesbury and Barry Moody of Acadia University were also sources of guidance, in both my undergraduate and graduate studies. Jim's death following a car accident deprived Acadia of one its most inspirational teachers. He is missed.

The dissertation was fleshed out into a biography with the support of a post-doctoral fellowship in military history from the Department of National Defence's Directorate of History and Heritage, a fellowship held at the Laurier Centre for Military, Strategic, and Disarmament Studies, and, in part, a Social Sciences and Humanities Research Council of Canada Post-doctoral Fellowship. I gratefully acknowledge their support. Over the course of those fellowships, as well as during the writing of the dissertation, I learned much from Stephen Harris, Norman Hillmer, J.L. Granatstein, John English, Roger Sarty, John Hilliker, A.M.J. Hyatt, and Serge Bernier even if I did not always take full advantage of all the advice they had to offer. Friends and colleagues have also contributed to the project over the years, sharing ideas and research as well as support. Thanks go out to Dean Oliver, David Lenarcic, Geoff Hayes, Mike Bechthold, Hugh Henry, Mark Cortiula, Barb Mitterer, Scott McLean, Kristopher Churchill, Andrew Nichols, Galen Perras, Jock Vance, and Greg Donaghy.

Research is, of course, a collective endeavour, requiring the support of many people across a number of institutions. I would like to thank the archivists at the Library and Archives Canada, and I hope these acknowledgments are published before the name of the archives changes yet again. They were always helpful and those who have used archives overseas appreciate how user friendly and inexpensive is our national archive. I was particularly appreciative that, as a grad student on a limited research and travel budget, the reading room was open for twenty-four hours, and they let me rest my head on the desks. In Canada, I also received assistance from the Massey Library, Royal Military College of Canada, in particular Benoit Cameron; Queen's University Archives; the Archives of Ontario; Special Collections at the Hamilton Public Library; Ontario Hydro Central Records and Archives; and University of Toronto Library Archives. In the United Kingdom, I found the Public Record Office became progressively more efficient and easy to use. Equally helpful were the staffs at the Imperial War Museum, and Liddell Hart Centre for Military Archives, at King's College, London. Research at the IWM, in particular, is a real pleasure.

I was also fortunate to discuss General Crerar with family and others who knew him. I would like to thank the following for their insights and time: Margaret Crerar Palmer and H.Z. Palmer, Peter Crerar, Mr and Mrs P.T. Nation, G.E. Beament, Richard Preston, Henri Tellier, Trumbell Warren, Finlay Morrison, and Jeffrey Williams. Terry Copp and Jack Granatstein generously shared interviews with me. They, as well as Dean Oliver and Geoff Hayes, also shared research materials with me at an early stage of the study. I tried to reciprocate where possible.

The final manuscript benefited from the reviews and comments on conference papers and articles from the people already mentioned as well as a number of patient, if long-suffering, readers and commentators. The manuscript was also improved by the thoughtful comments of two anonymous reviewers for the University of Toronto Press and the ever-patient History Editor Len Husband. My thanks as well to UTP's Frances Mundy.

Finally, some formal acknowledgements are in order. I gratefully acknowledge permission from the Vaniers for the use of the G. Vanier Papers at the LAC. I acknowledge the permission of the Trustees of the Liddell Hart Centre for Military Archives, King's College London for permission to use the Alanbrooke papers. The maps are reproduced with the permission of the Directorate of History and Heritage and the Minister of Public Works and Government Services. Any mistakes or omissions are mine alone.

Introduction

General H.D.G. 'Harry' Crerar fought in, led, or was responsible for most of the defining moments of the army's history during the first half of the twentieth century. He was almost killed during the Second Battle of Ypres. He was a gunner, helping to secure victory at Vimy Ridge. He was a senior staff officer, helping to plan the offensives at Amiens and during the Hundred Days. He was the primary architect of First Canadian Army. As Chief of the General Staff, he advised the government to dispatch troops to Hong Kong. He campaigned for Canadian involvement in the Dieppe Raid. Briefly led a corps in Italy. Assumed command of the army during the Normandy Campaign. Played a controversial role in the Scheldt Campaign. Commanded a combined commonwealth army during the Rhineland Offensive, the largest ever commanded by a Canadian. And was feted as the liberator of Holland. He made mistakes in judgment, but he learned steadily from experience. During the Second World War, Crerar occupied, and often defined, the Canadian army's senior staff and command appointments: Senior Officer, Canadian Military Headquarters; Chief of the General Staff; General Officer Commanding, 1st Canadian Corps; and finally General Officer Commanding-in-Chief, First Canadian Army. No single person did as much to shape the Canadian army during the Second World War. Yet few remember him now.

Even at the height of his career, Crerar was an obscure figure to the public. 'One of my frustrations as a war correspondent ... in the last European episode,' remembered Ross Munro in a *Toronto Star* obituary for Crerar, 'was my inability to get to know well the Canadian army commander, General Crerar ... It was "H.D.G. Crerar" and never "Harry."'[1] He was described in 1945 as an example of what hard work, virtue, and modesty can achieve – a 'thoroughly Canadian general.'[2] Crerar would have agreed with that characterization of an exemplary Canadian life. Describing himself in a postwar interview, he said, 'Generals are pretty much like other people.'[3]

Crerar left no memoirs, declining offers to publish them on the grounds that he could not break the trust or betray the responsibility of his former position as a government servant. Rather he wanted his professional papers, particularly those from the 1930s, published. His wife, Verse, was the only person to whom he fully revealed himself; his letters to her have unfortunately – but deliberately – not survived. He did leave behind a vast correspondence, although much, but not all, of it was guarded and circumspect. He saved everything and before his death ordered it organized chronologically, thematically, and alphabetically, more telling about the man and his aspirations than some of the contents themselves.

The primary focus of this biography is Crerar the soldier, not Crerar the family man. Crerar was a devoted husband and father, but his relationship to the army was almost as strong. Crerar's life and his concept of himself were, from 1919 at any rate, inextricably bound up with the evolution and growth of the Canadian army as a profession and his place within it. And thus the members of his Canadian army 'family' are at the centre of this version of his life.

Crerar was born in Hamilton, a second-generation Scot, his Canadian and Scots heritage residing comfortably together. In some ways, he was imprisoned by the circumstances of his birth. He was far more ambitious than was seemly in Victorian Canada, and was raised in a family, or at least by a mother, who exalted public service that she defined and measured by the ideals of British imperialism. In consequence, he presented a public face of selfless civic virtue; the tension between his public face and private self showed itself in his professional life when his career prospects slowed, and was more consistently evident in his relations with children. He loved his children dearly, and lectured them endlessly; nothing extraordinary about that, but much of his advice centred on mastering selfish instincts, and the pop psychologist in me suspects that this was the result of a lifetime of not always practising what he preached.

Crerar's life spanned a period of dramatic social and political change. He was never fully comfortable with the mass democratization of Canadian society during the first half of the twentieth century, fearing as he did the consequences of poorly informed choices. Although he was raised in a comfortable upper-middle-class environment, Crerar's world was much changed by the two world wars, and like many of his contemporaries, he struggled to adapt to the broader changes in Canadian society and the international order. While he blamed the expansion of the franchise for destroying the national outlook of politicians, he had a middle-class faith that the problem was rooted in the failure of the newly enfranchised to understand their civic responsibilities. Education, in the broadest sense of the term, was the answer. A civic religion replaced the Christian ideals imparted by his mother. The army was the main vehicle for spreading the gospel. The nation was maturing in the first fifty years of the twentieth century. Crerar was part of a generation of Canadians who had to first define and then redefine what it meant to be Canadian. Intellectually, he mirrored Canada's own evolution from British dependency to ally; emotionally he was a British Canadian, although during most of his lifetime, the hyphenation would have been unnecessary. In the 1930s, he described himself as a 'British subject, and a Canadian national'; these were not incompatible.

Crerar served with great distinction in the artillery during the Great War, a branch that won acclaim in a corps that won no small number of accolades itself. Following the war, he pursued a career in the Permanent Forces, enduring two decades of frustrated hopes and aspirations in the 'stagnant backwaters' of the interwar army. These frustrations were exacerbated by the failed hopes for more attention to defence issues and army expansion that he expected after the First World War and the failure of successive governments to improve the military in general, and the army in particular, in response to the heightened international tensions that characterized the 1930s. The dominant figure in the Canadian military during that period, General Andrew McNaughton, wanted educated and talented soldiers to form the basis of a professional force.

From 1935 to 1938, Crerar held a series of senior General Staff appointments, including the influential post of Director of Military Operations and Intelligence. During the Second World War, on the strength of ability, hard work, vision, extraordinarily well-placed friends, and limited competition among the small pool of trained senior officers, Crerar rose rapidly, successively occupying – and often defining – the positions of Senior Officer, Canadian Military Headquarters;

Chief of the General Staff; General Officer Commanding, 1st Canadian Corps; and finally General Officer Commanding-in-Chief, First Canadian Army. He retired in 1946 to spend time with a family that had largely subordinated their lives to his military career.

Crerar chose the army as a career, not as a life, but when he had a real choice in 1919, he chose it over other potentially more lucrative pursuits. To understand that is to understand what he wanted to accomplish during his years of service. His goals for the army were forged by the contrast between the invigorating environment of the Canadian Corps in the First World War and his frustrating experiences in the interwar army. In 1919, he saw the army as a respectable profession and institution within Canadian society. As the promise of his first years as a professional soldier gave way to the political and economic realities of the interwar period, his main goal was to reestablish, as he saw it, the professionalism of the army and reaffirm its position in Canada's society and political system. These goals and experiences informed his wartime policies towards army expansion, organization, training, and ultimately command. Because he came to see the army as a civic institution, it was on these terms that he understood, if imperfectly, its relationship with the society that spawned it and the government that directed it. After the Second World War, he wanted his speeches and papers to be examined and published by a diplomatic or political historian; he felt it was in these fields that their long-term value lay.

As a commander he was a cold and remote figure. On a personal basis, he was warm, even kind. His nickname 'Uncle Harry' reflected both the generation gap between Crerar and his subordinates – he was fifty-six when he assumed command of the army – and the type of relationships he cultivated. Crerar's personality informed his approach to his career: self-disciplined and hard working. He expected no less from subordinates, and family. The Chief of Staff at First Canadian Army, Major-General Churchill Mann, summarized Crerar's approach to command and life: he was a man whose 'personal creed seemed to be to lead, to set an example, never to spare himself, never to take personal advantage of his rank but never to tolerate less than maximum effort from any of his close subordinates.'[4]

Crerar was singularly unconcerned with the public spotlight, an unusual trait in generals and one that left many believing that he was not a leader. Crerar never aspired to be a charismatic leader; he led by example and when forced to drive, he 'drove hard.' He repeated this as an axiom of command. He understood his limitations, perhaps too well, and to his credit did not, in command, try to be something he was not.

His stiff formality masked a self-conscious, sometimes under-confident man. Immaculate grooming, bordering on fussy, reinforced a stodgy image. He had a slow and methodical manner of speaking: prosy, 'rather as if he was teaching a rather dull class.'[5] He explained himself at length, a habit that brought him some success in a politically stifled interwar army, which often found that its only means of expansion and development was on paper, but was not welcome in operational command. Neither was Crerar physically imposing. He stood five foot eight inches, an average height, had a slight build, but was fit. While he enjoyed and he sought out opportunities to go sailing, fishing, horseback riding, and walking, his competitive nature led to numerous small injuries that would plague him over the years. Few hints of the ambition and emotion that drove him came from his flat, sometimes sardonic, expression; to those who did not know him, he could appear pompous rather than reserved. His soft blue-grey eyes were a reminder of the more genial character that emerged in lighter moments and among friends. A narrow face, hawkish nose, neatly clipped moustache, and unassuming chin served to complement an aristocratic demeanour. He looked more like a kindly 'renaissance prince' as one author noted, but he perceived himself as a Canadian man of affairs weighted down by his noblesse oblige.[6]

How best to examine Crerar as a general was, and is, a difficult question. Crerar's 'practical patriotism' infused his career, and life. Professionalism also influenced Crerar's behaviour, but it did not determine it. Personal ambitions played a crucial role. So too did the Canadian military's position within Canadian society and politics. The country's, and consequently the government's, ambivalence towards the armed forces was an important aspect of Crerar's story, and, if public recognition is any measure, is still. And the two world wars are what make that ambivalence, and Crerar's response to it, important on a larger stage. Canada's coalition experience was also a key part of the story. Command in modern coalition warfare required a diplomatic and political acumen, as well as a heightened understanding of the implications of advances in communications, logistics, and weapons technology. These realities also imposed limits on Canadian generalship. Finally, a good general in any army required intangible qualities, the product not of education, but of genetics – the ability to inspire men and shape operations; this marks the difference between a commander and a leader. To reconcile these themes and measures, this study examines Crerar through his intentions, objectives, and the results. What was possible must be compared to what actually happened, a balance struck between what was accomplished and whether it could have been accomplished in a more effective manner. Crerar as a general emerges from an examination of the interaction of character, personality, the evolution of the army, and the context within which he worked, in war and peace. Crerar as a person emerges from the examination of his aspirations, experiences, failures, and successes.

Canadian generalship does not lack critics, only studies. Biographical studies of Crerar are limited to one chapter in J.L. Granatstein's *The Generals* and the details that emerge in John A. English's *The Canadian Army and the Normandy Campaign: A Study of Failure in High Command*. In *Warrior Chiefs: Perspectives on Senior Canadian Military Leaders*, Dean Oliver provides an insightful chapter on Crerar's treatment by historians, concluding, fairly, that he has to be evaluated within his own 'rules of engagement.' C.P. Stacey's characterization of Crerar, scattered through two of three volumes of *The Official History of the Canadian Army during the Second World War*, and in subsequent works, is favourable, not least because Stacey appreciated the obstacles facing the Canadian army during the Second World War.

Crerar also figures prominently in biographies of his peers and subordinates. Dominick Graham portrays Crerar, perhaps not unnaturally, as the yin to General Guy Simonds's yang in *The Price of Command: A Biography of General Guy Simonds*. John Swettenham's three-volume biography *McNaughton* is generally favourable towards Crerar, although it shares its subject's view that Crerar benefited from both McNaughton's patronage and tutelage. The former is evident, but the latter is less clear. Important details on Crerar and his professional growth, and collaborations, are found in the memoirs of colleagues and subordinates like Chris Vokes, *Vokes: My Story*, Maurice A. Pope, *Soldiers and Politicians: The Memoirs of Lt-General Maurice A. Pope*, and Lester Pearson's *Mike*. These should be used with some caution, or least in conjunction with their papers and letters where available. Some insights can be also gleaned from those who were more junior, notably *The Memoirs of General Jean V. Allard*, but Crerar usually emerges as a distant, if paternal, figurehead.

Most studies focus, not surprisingly, on his tenure as army commander or his role in specific events. His generalship and influence have been dealt with in varying degrees of detail and accuracy. These interpretations are examined in more detail throughout the text, but a selective survey of the works on these topics suggests the breadth of his involvement in Canada's military history in the first half of the twentieth century. His role in attempting to bring the harsh light of reality to Canadian defence and foreign policy in the 1930s did not go unnoticed by scholars: James Eayrs in *In Defence of Canada*, volume 1, *From the Great War to the Great Depression*, and volume 2, *Appeasement and Rearmament* records many of Crerar's achievements, particularly those during the late 1930s as he fought to prepare Canada's defence establishment for the looming war. Stephen Harris's *Canadian Brass: The Making of a Professional Army, 1860–1939* provides some additional and important insights into Crerar's role.

Crerar's tenure as Chief of the General Staff has largely escaped attention, except for C.P. Stacey's *Arms, Men and Governments*. The one notable exception to this was his role in the decision to send two brigades of Canadian troops to Hong Kong. Generally, the treatment of Crerar's decision has ranged from Stacey's and Granatstein's considered assessment of the contemporary difficulties facing the political and military leaders to Carl Vincent's indictment of Crerar's negligence in *No Reason Why: The Canadian Hong Kong Tragedy – An Examination*. J.L. Granatstein's opinion has most recently been proffered in *Canada's Army: Waging War and Keeping the Peace*. The decision has rarely been viewed in the context of his goals as CGS.

The scholarship on the Dieppe Raid is voluminous, and Crerar has not escaped notice or censure. Again, Stacey provides a balanced account in the official history. Notable as well are Denis and Shelagh Whittaker's *Dieppe: Tragedy to Triumph* and Brian Villa's *Unauthorized Action: Mountbatten and the Dieppe Raid*. Crerar played an important part in securing Canadian participation in the raid. On that there is agreement. There is less agreement as to whether this action demonstrated incompetence or was understandable in the context of the period. In contrast to the literature on Dieppe, his role in McNaughton's removal has received relatively little attention, although more of late. Swettenham's work reflects McNaughton's own limited understanding of Crerar's actions in his removal. Granatstein, on the other hand, is blunt in *The Generals*, describing Crerar as underhanded and a backstabber.

The Canadian performance in the northwest Europe campaign, from Normandy to the liberation of Holland, has its fair share of critics, with

Crerar receiving some, but not all, of the criticism. Montgomery biographer Nigel Hamilton asserts in his three-volume *Monty* that Crerar was both incompetent and overly nationalistic, the latter a preoccupation that was a source of constant aggravation to Montgomery. Hamilton's opinion becomes harsher by the third volume, and his tone more shrill, reflecting Montgomery's. John A. English suggests in his study of the Normandy campaign that Crerar did nothing of note, and simply parroted Montgomery and Simonds. Some more dated critiques suggest Crerar, and hence his army, was ponderous and overly cautious, in effect slowing down (particularly in September 1944) the more flexible and speedy British senior command, surely a first. Hubert Essame and Eversley M.G. Belfield, in *The North-West Europe Campaign, 1944–1945*, and L.F. Ellis, in *Victory in the West*, volume 2, are representative of British historiography. Denis and Shelagh Whitaker, in *Tug of War: The Canadian Victory That Opened Antwerp and Rhineland* are more balanced but tend to reflect Simonds's view of the campaign. More favourable is Terry Copp and Robert Vogel's assessment in their *Maple Leaf Route* series, as well as in Terry Copp's subsequent books and articles on the campaigns in northwest Europe, *Fields of Fire* being the most recent. Copp's work, supported by recent studies by Stephen Hart, *Montgomery and 'Colossal Cracks': The 21st Army Group in Northwest Europe*, demonstrates that the Canadian forces did very well in very trying circumstances.

Some recent scholarship, foremost Dean Oliver's chapter on Crerar in *Warrior Chiefs*, has also highlighted the point, as Crerar himself did, that First Canadian Army was ultimately measured against the reputation of the Canadian Corps during the Great War. It is safe to say that, in the eyes of historians, and somewhat unfairly, FCA and Crerar were not able, in ten months of operations, to emerge from the shadow of that reputation, forged as it was over three long and bloody years. This reflects more on the historiography of the Canadian Corps, which tends to skim over the difficult years before Vimy Ridge.

J.L. Granatstein has written that Canadians get the generals they deserve. Not always; sometimes they get better ones. Crerar was a better general than he has been given credit for, and, like First Canadian Army, he learned steadily from his experiences from the Second Battle of Ypres in 1915 through to his command of FCA in the final campaigns of 1945. His adaptation to the changing nature of warfare, and his country, over the thirty years of his experience is at the centre of this study.

Abbreviations

ADC	aide-de-camp
ADPR	Assistant Deputy Public Relations
AEAF	Allied Expeditionary Air Force
AG	Adjutant-General
AGRA	Army Group Royal Artillery
AOC	Air Officer Commanding
AQ	army quartermaster
ASSU	Air Support Signal Units
BEF	British Expeditionary Force
BGS	Brigadier, General Staff
BRA	Brigadier, Royal Artillery
C-in-C	Commander-in-Chief
CAC	Canadian Armoured Corps
CAPF	Canadian Army Pacific Force
CAOF	Canadian Army Occupation Force
CAS	Chief of the Air Staff
CBE	Commander of the Order of the British Empire
CBSO	Counter-Battery Staff Officer
CCRA	Commander, Corps Royal Artillery
CDA	Conference of Defence Associations
CE	Chief Engineer
CEF	Canadian Expeditionary Force
CFA	Canadian Forces Artillery
CGS	Chief of the General Staff
CIC	Canadian Infantry Corps
CIGS	Chief of the Imperial General Staff
CIIS	Canadian Institute of International Affairs

CMHQ	Canadian Military Headquarters
CNS	Chief of the Naval Staff
CO	Commanding Officer
COHQ	Combined Operations Headquarters
CRA	Commander, Royal Artillery
CRU	Canadian Reinforcement Unit
DA	Deputy Adjutant
DIGA	Deputy Inspector-General of Artillery
DMO and I	Director of Military Operations and Intelligence
DND	Department of National Defence
DSO	Distinguished Service Order
EA	External Affairs
FCA	First Canadian Army
FDP	Forward Director Post
FOO	forward observation officer
GHQ	general headquarters
GOC	General Officer Commanding
GOC-in-C	General Officer Commanding-in-Chief
GS	General Service
GSO	General Staff Officer
HQ	headquarters
IDC	Imperial Defence College
IODE	Imperial Order Daughters of the Empire
JAG	Judge Advocate General
JBR	Joint Battle Room
JIC	Joint-Intelligence Sub-Committee of the Chiefs of Staff
JSC	Joint Staff Committee
LOB	left out of battle
MGA	Major-General in Charge of Administration
MGO	Master-General of Ordnance
NCO	non-commissioned officer
NDHQ	National Defence Headquarters
NRMA	National Resources Mobilization Act
OC	Officer Commanding
PF	Permanent Forces
POW	prisoner of war
QMG	Quartermaster General
RA	Royal Artillery
RAF	Royal Air Force
RCA	Royal Canadian Artillery

RCAF	Royal Canadian Air Force
RCE	Royal Canadian Engineers
RCHA	Royal Canadian Horse Artillery
RMC	Royal Military College
RUSI	Royal United Service Institution
SASO	Senior Air Staff Officer
SCAO	Senior Civil Affairs Officer
SDD	Staff Duties Directorate
SHAEF	Supreme Headquarters Allied Expeditionary Force
SO, RA	Senior Officer, Royal Artillery
UCC	Upper Canada College
VCIGS	Vice Chief of the Imperial General Staff
VFA	Visiting Forces (British Commonwealth) Act

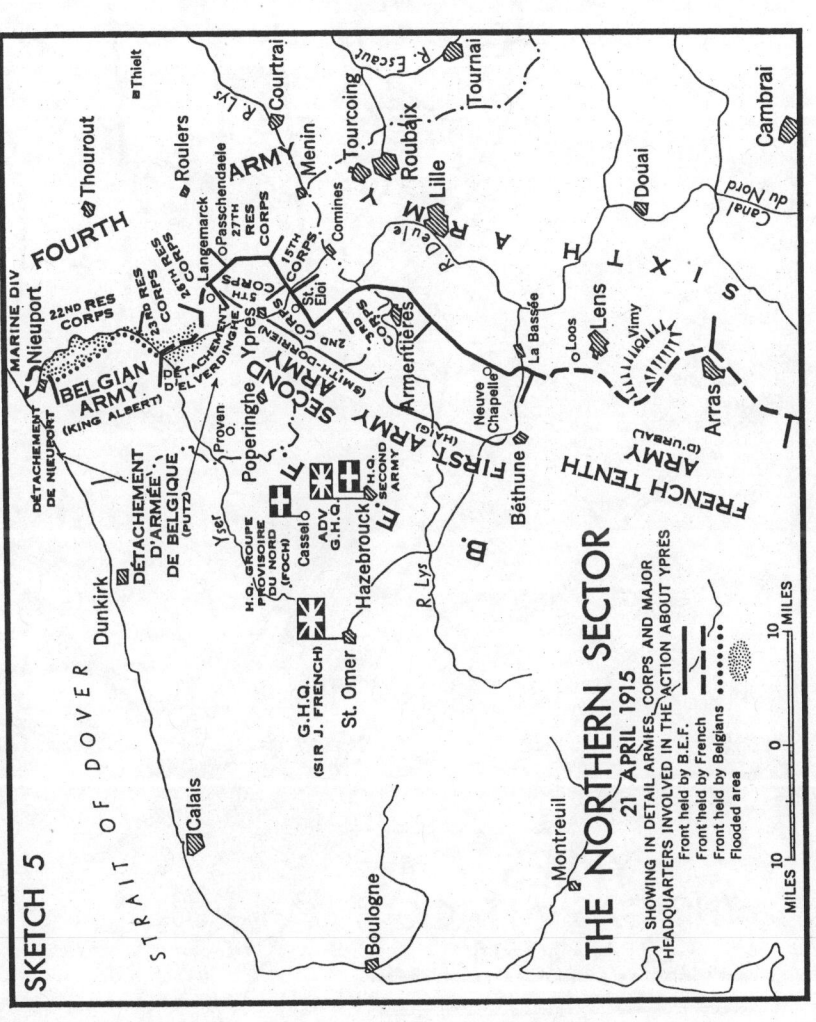

1. The Northern Sector, 21 April 1915
Source: *Official History of the Canadian Army in the First World War: Canadian Expeditionary Force 1914–1919*, p. 54, G.W.L. Nicholson, Department of National Defence, 1962.

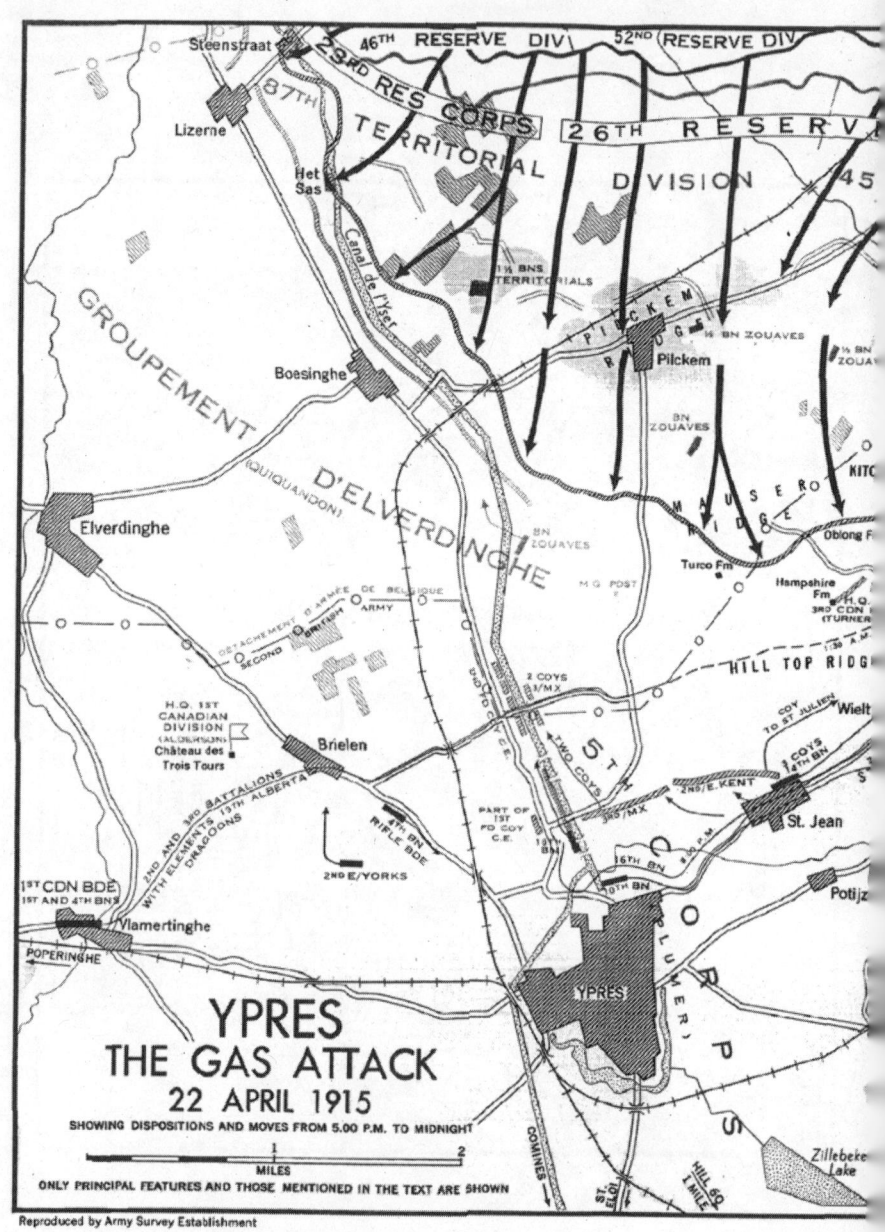

2. Ypres: The Gas Attack, 22 April 1915
Source: *Official History of the Canadian Army in the First World War, Canadian Expediti*

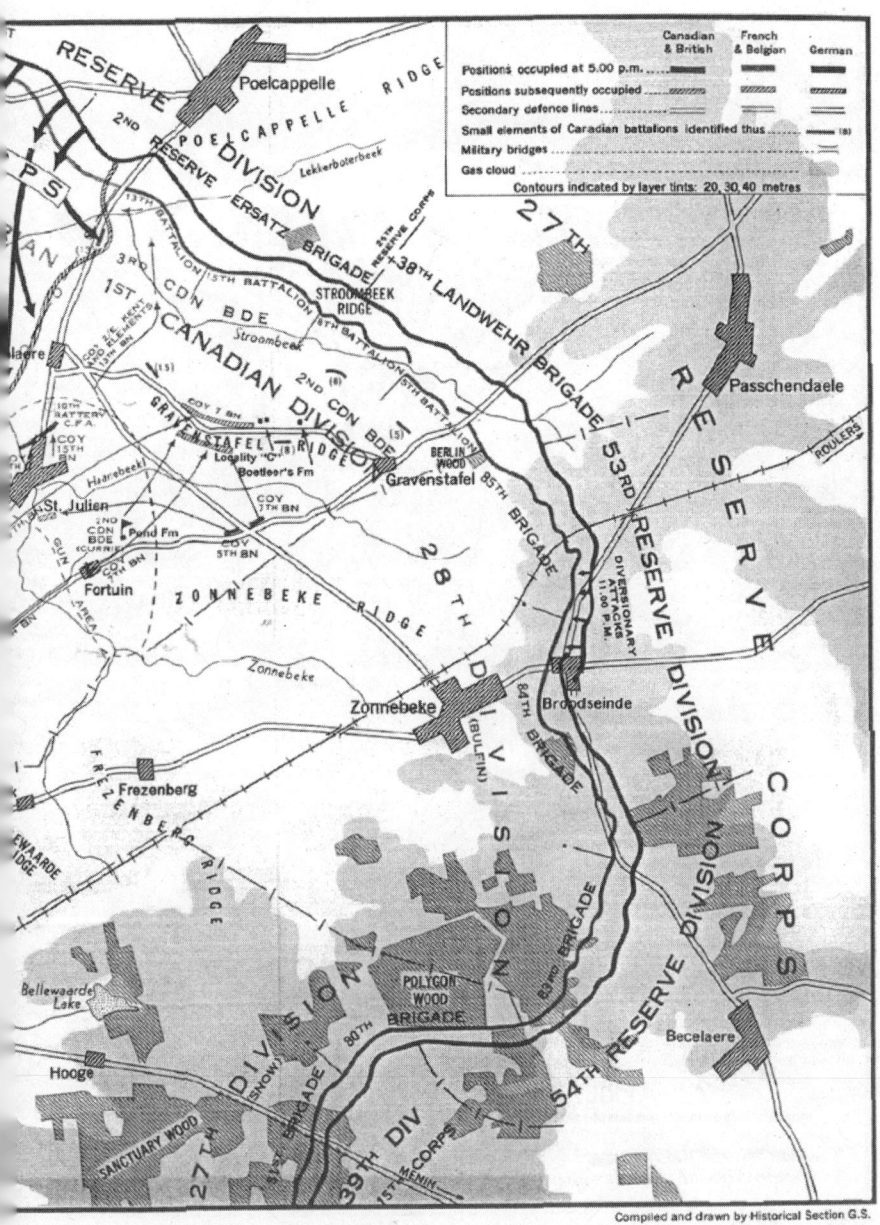

1914–1919, p. 66, G.W.L. Nicholson, Department of National Defence, 1962.

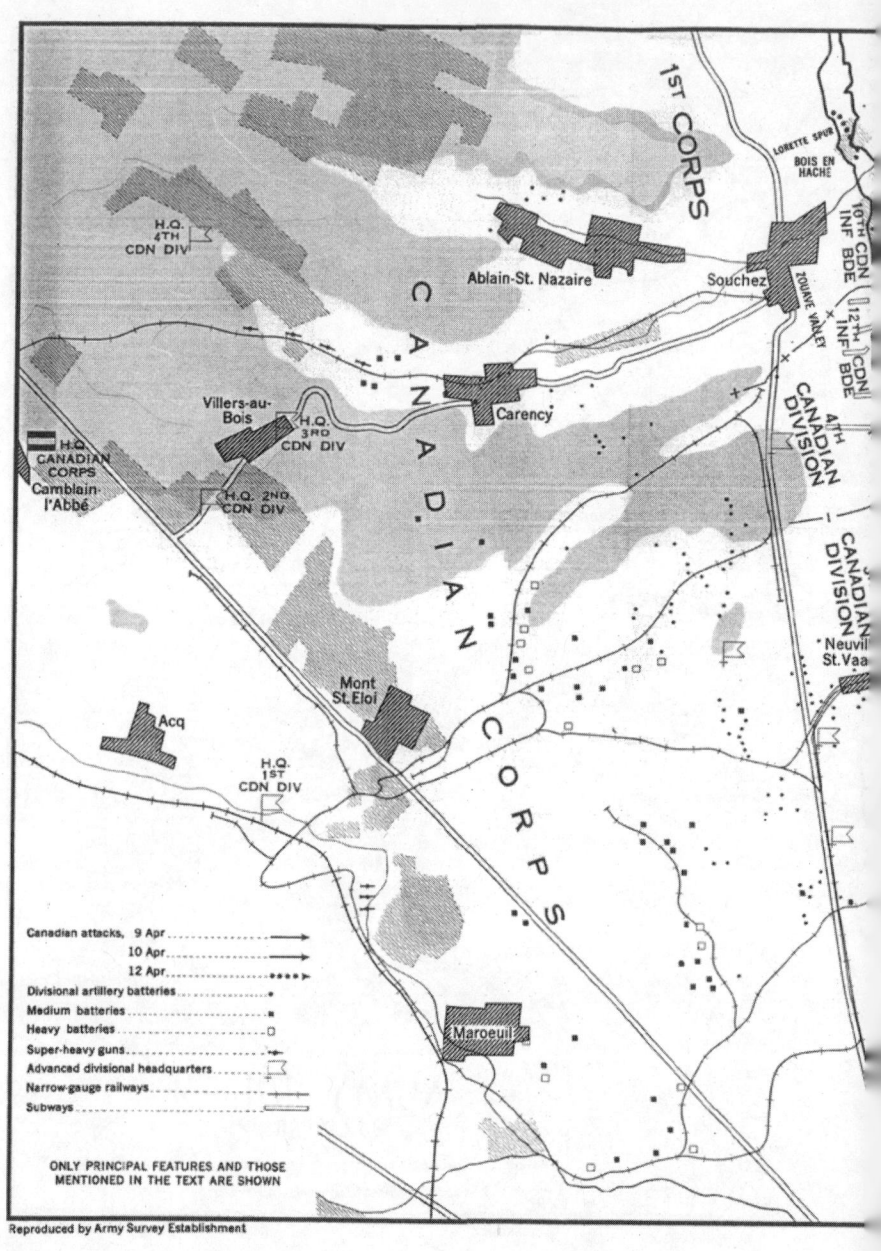

3. Vimy Ridge, 9–12 April 1917
Source: *Official History of the Canadian Army in the First World War: Canadian Expedit*

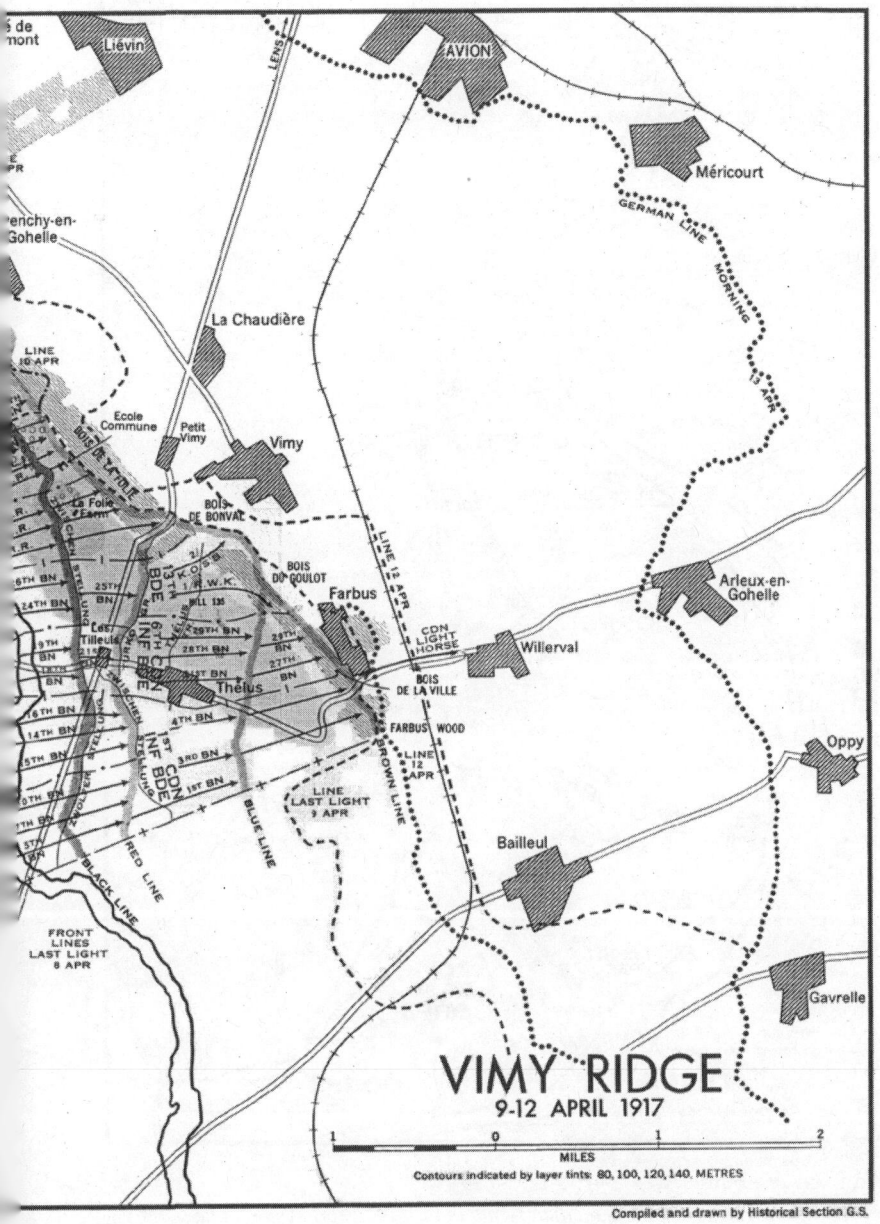

14–1919, p. 262, G.W.L. Nicholson, Department of National Defence, 1962.

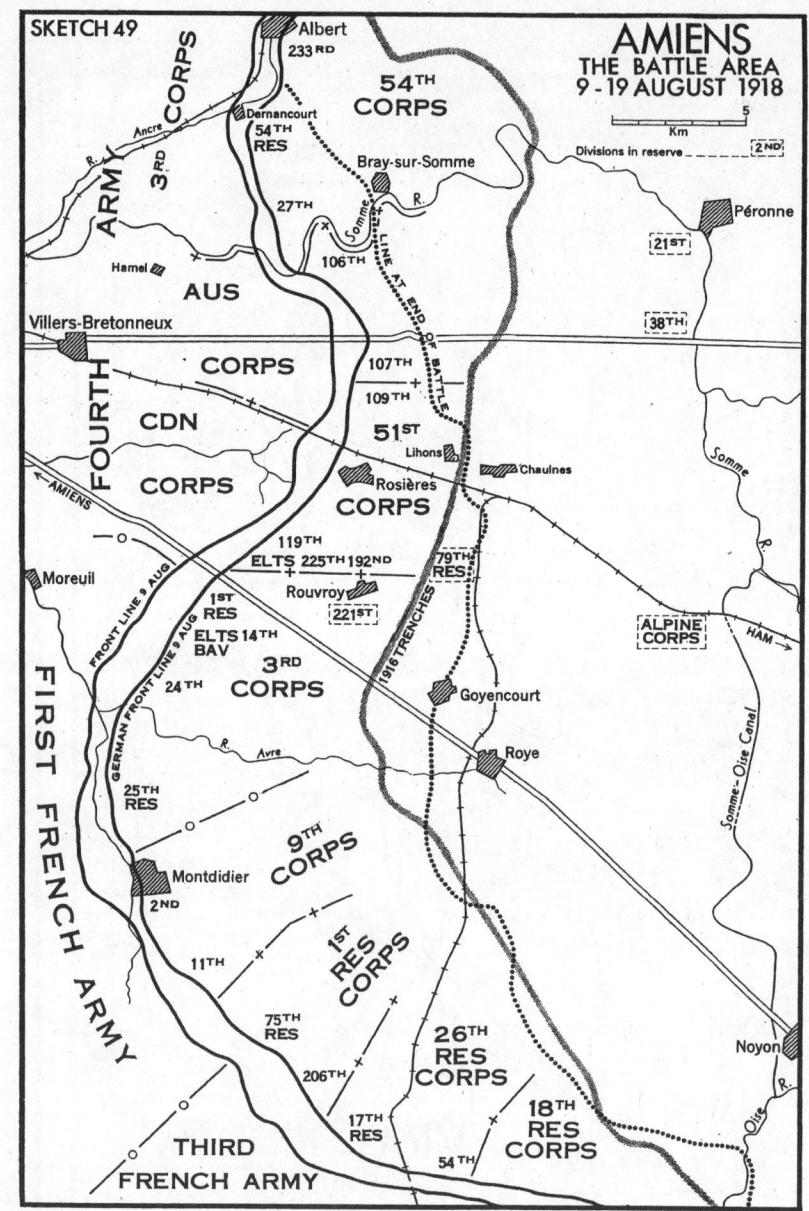

4. Amiens, The Battle Area, 9–19 August 1918
Source: *Official History of the Canadian Army in the First World War: Canadian Expeditionary Force 1914–1919*, p. 409, G.W.L. Nicholson, Department of National Defence, 1962.

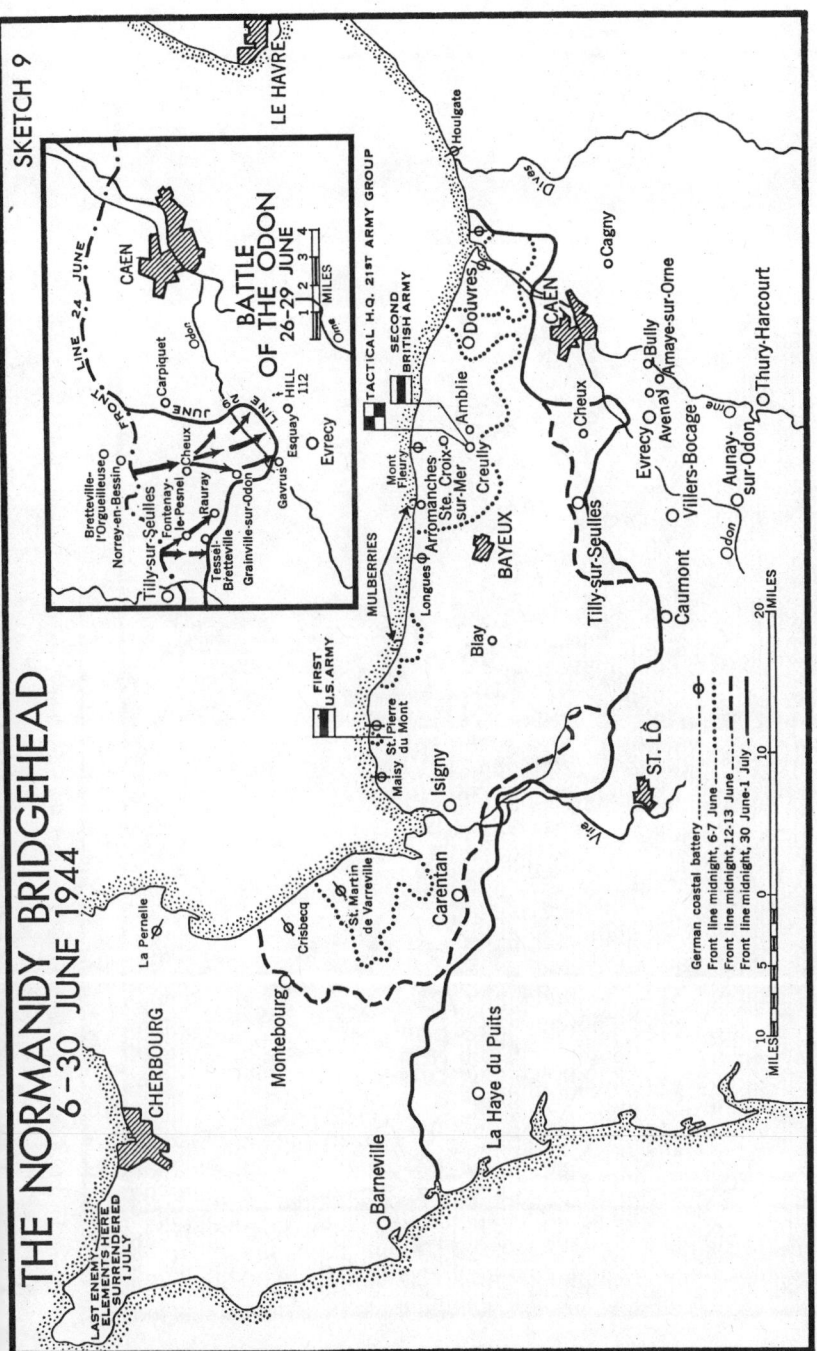

5. The Normandy Bridgehead, 6-30 June 1944
Source: *The Victory Campaign, The Official History of the Canadian Army in the Second World War, Volume III*, p. 148, C.P. Stacey, Department of National Defence, 1960.

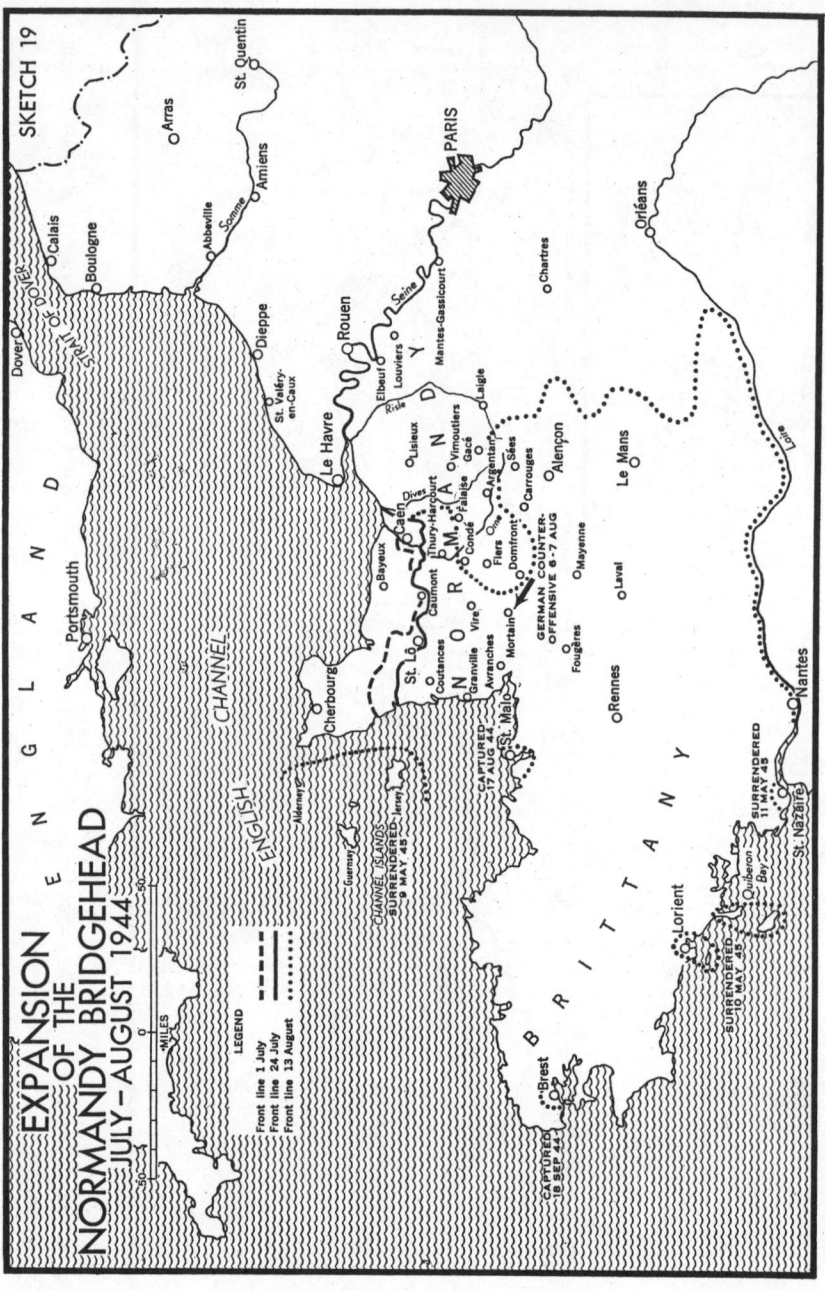

6. Expansion of the Normandy Bridgehead, July–August 1944
Source: *The Victory Campaign, The Official History of the Canadian Army in the Second World War, Volume III*, p. 253, C.P. Stacey, Department of National Defence, 1960.

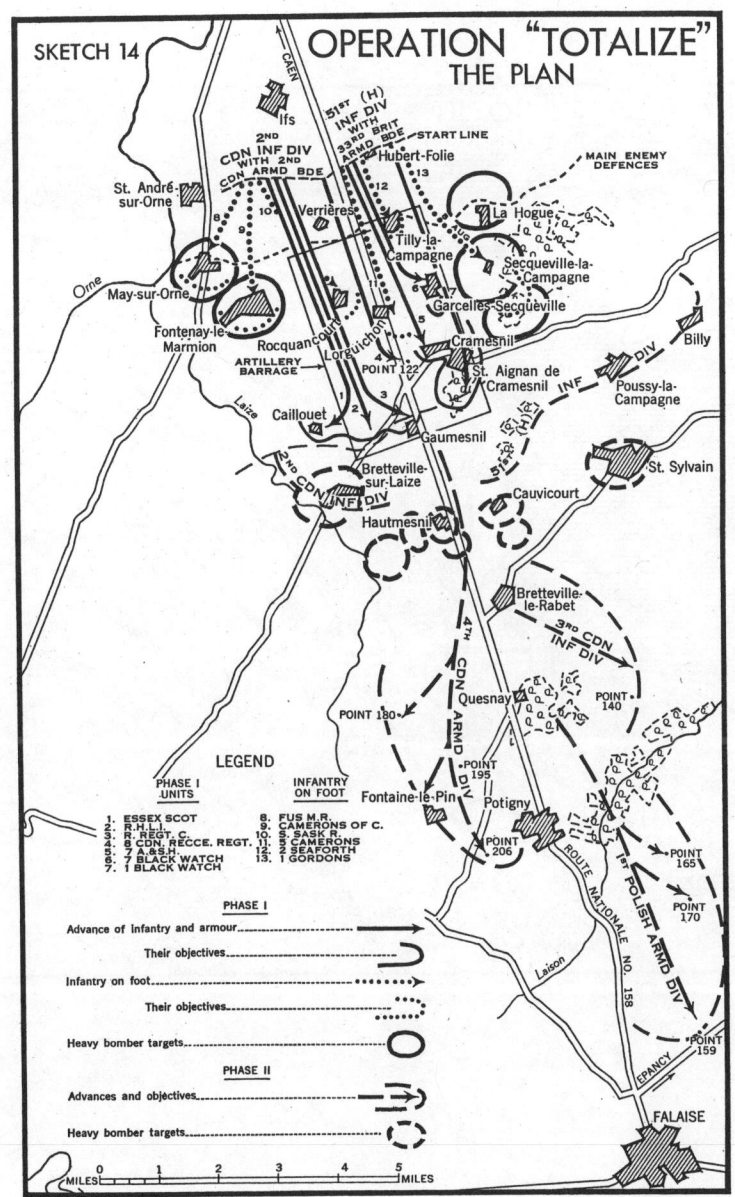

7. Operation Totalize: The Plan
Source: *The Victory Campaign, The Official History of the Canadian Army in the Second World War*, Volume III, p. 217, C.P. Stacey, Department of National Defence, 1960.

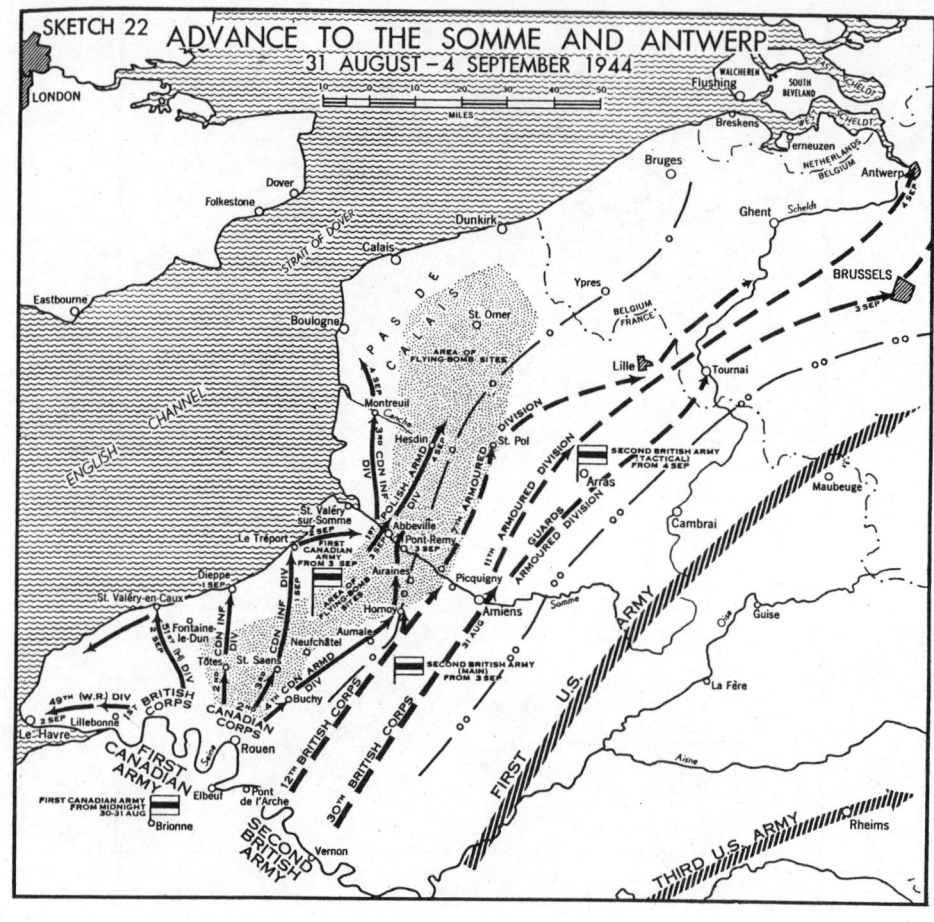

8. Advance to the Somme and Antwerp, 31 August–4 September 1944
Source: *The Victory Campaign, The Official History of the Canadian Army in the Second World War, Volume III*, p. 299, C.P. Stacey, Department of National Defence, 1960.

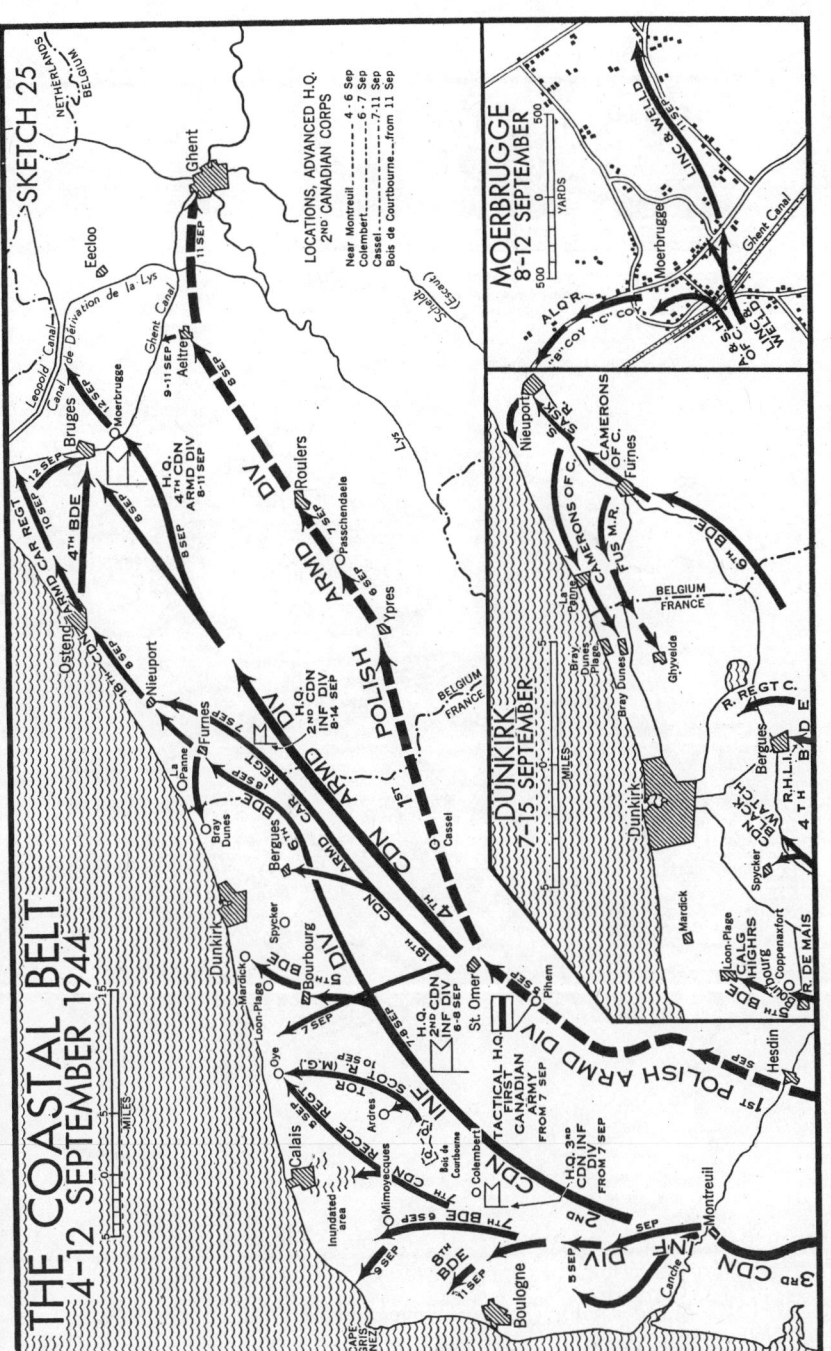

9. The Coastal Belt, 4–12 September 1944
Source: *The Victory Campaign, The Official History of the Canadian Army in the Second World War, Volume III*, p. 325, C.P. Stacey, Department of National Defence, 1960.

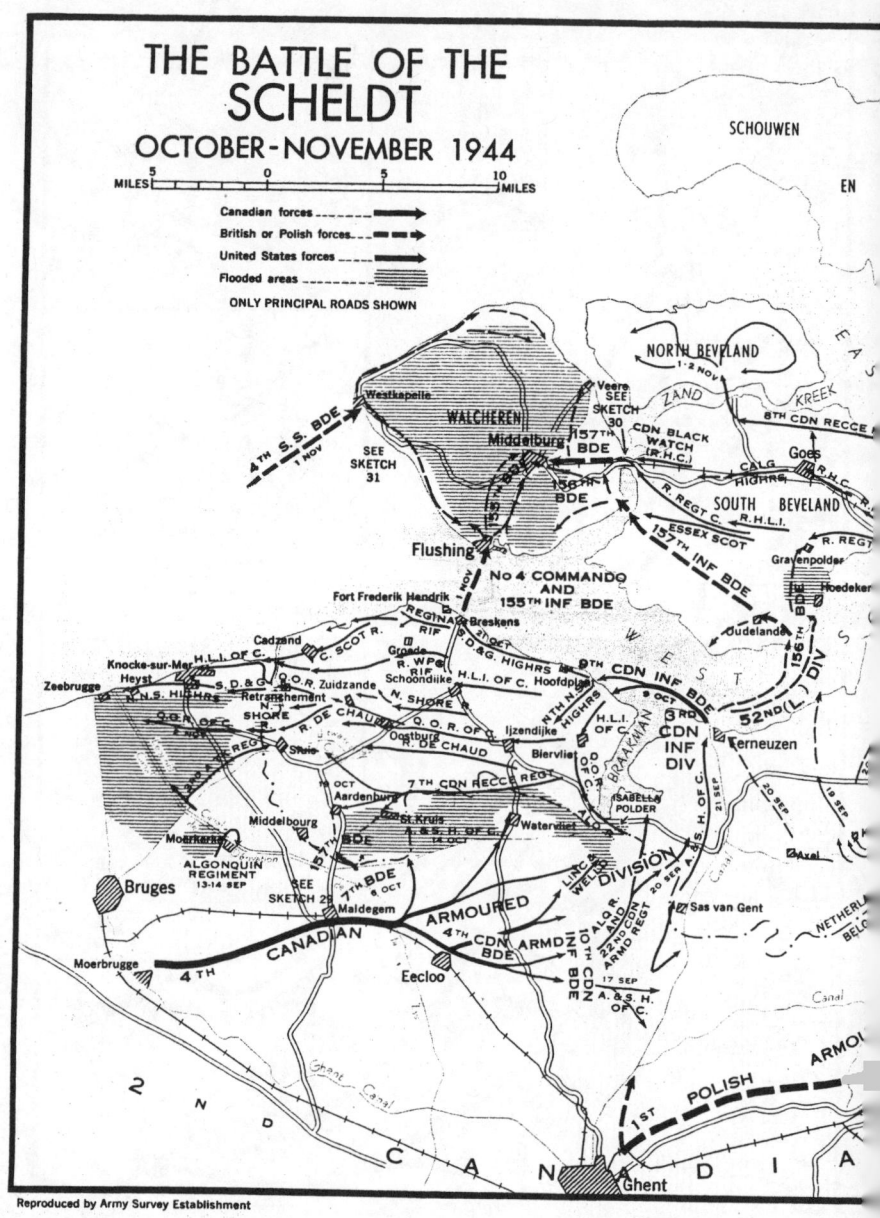

10. The Battle of the Scheldt, October–November 1944
Source: *The Victory Campaign, The Official History of the Canadian Army in the Second*

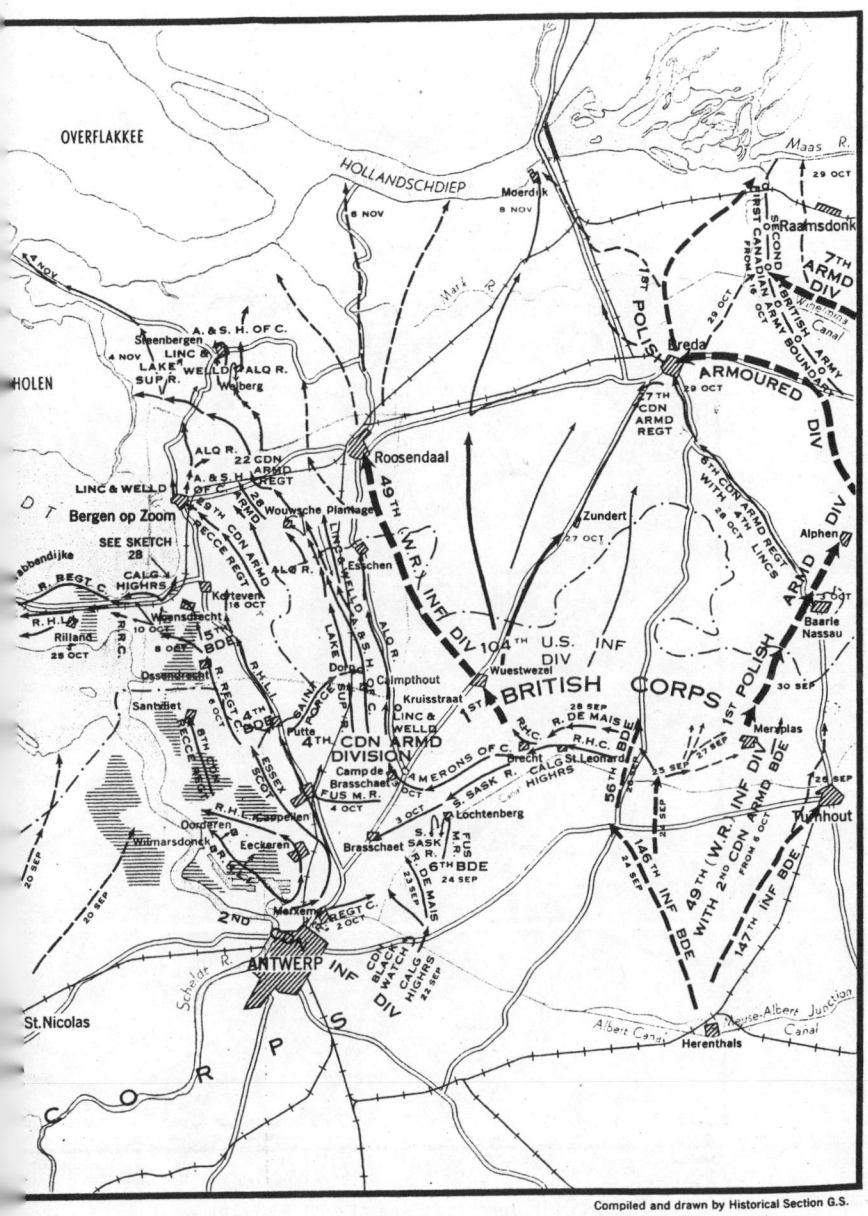

ume III, p. 424, C.P. Stacey, Department of National Defence, 1960.

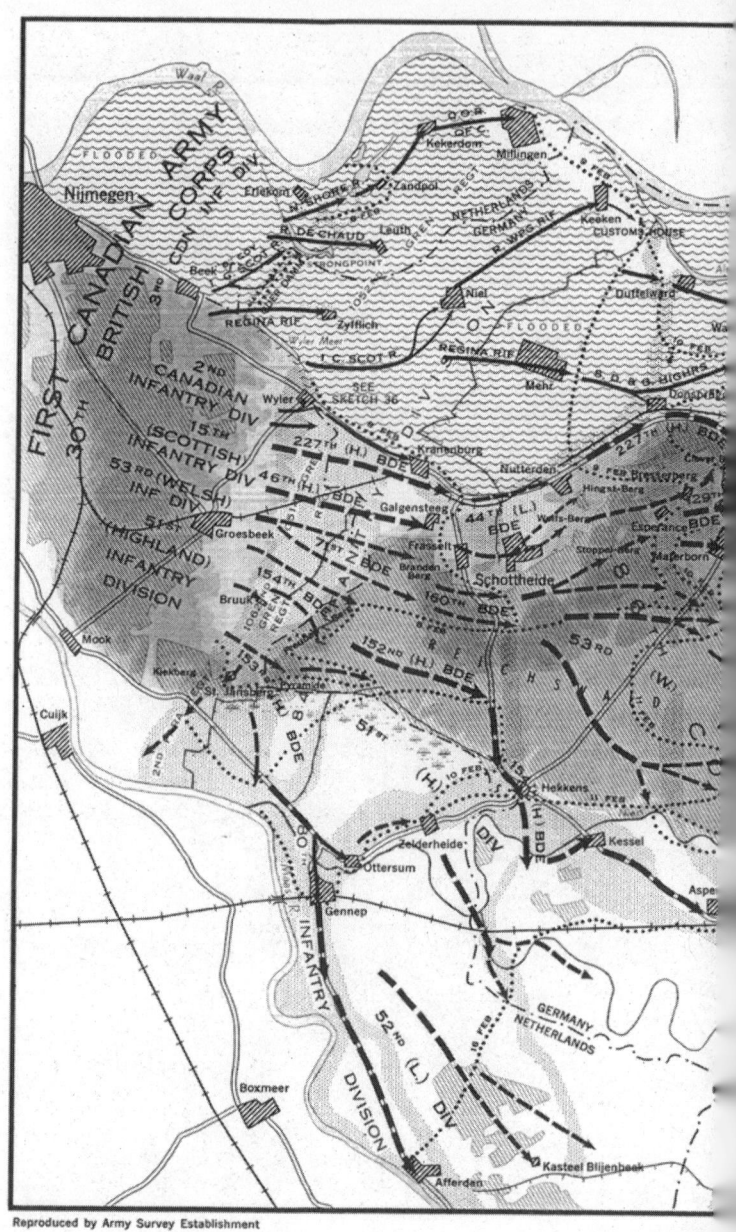

11. The Rhineland: Operation Veritable, 8–21 February 1945
Source: *The Victory Campaign, The Official History of the Canadian Army*, Defence, 1960.

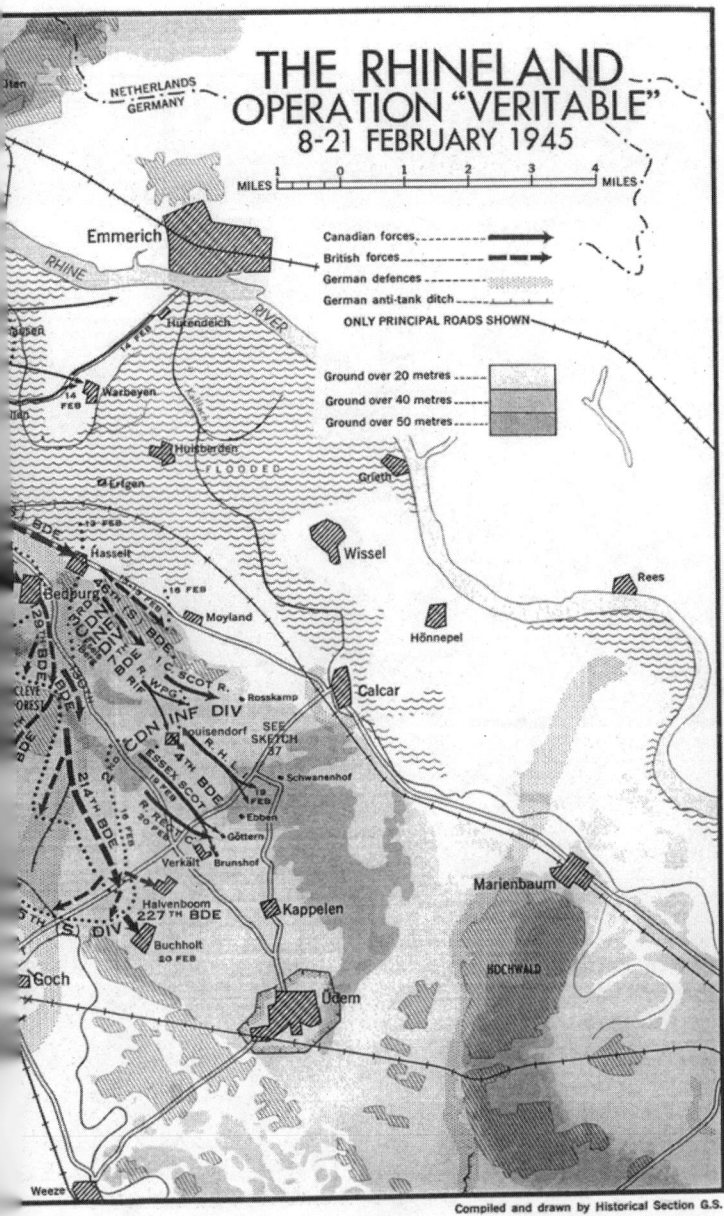

World War, Volume III, p. 523, C.P. Stacey, Department of National

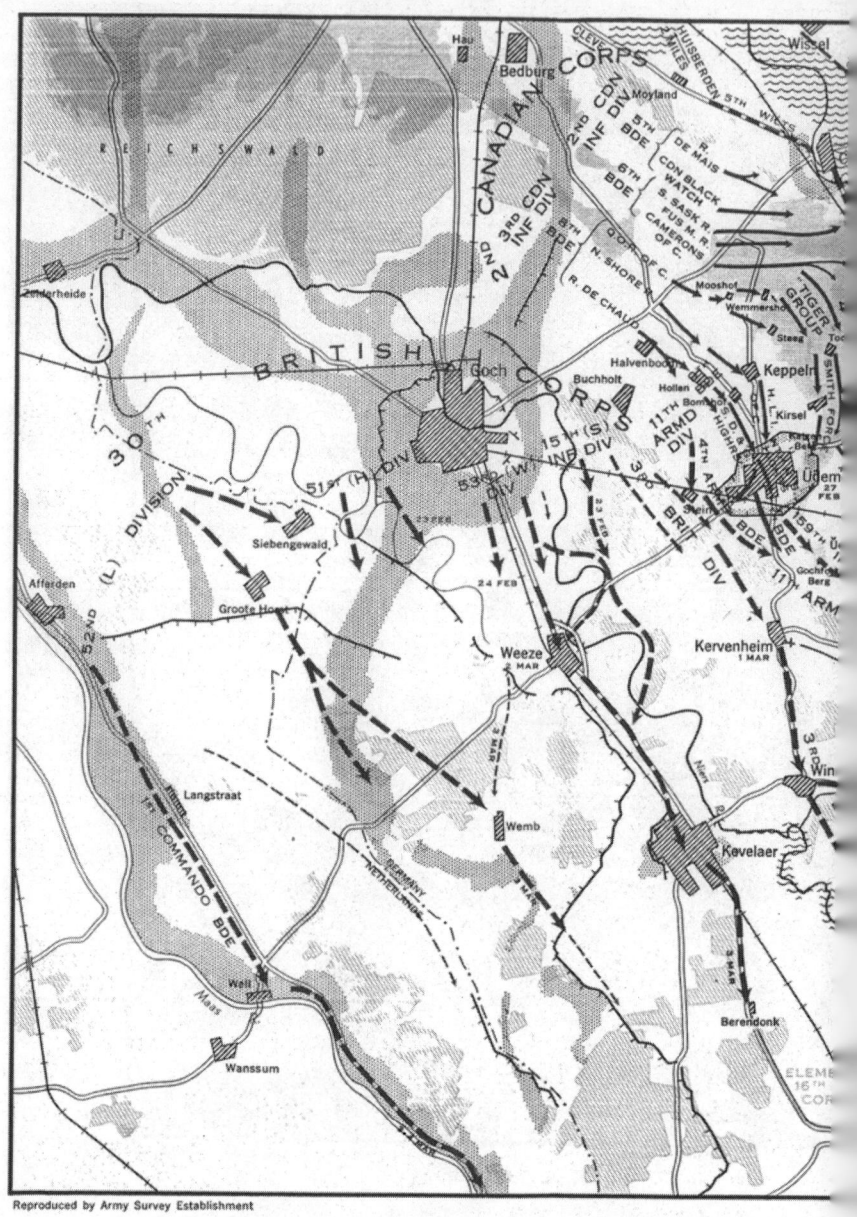

12. The Rhineland: Operation Blockbuster, 22 February–10 March 1945
Source: *The Victory Campaign, The Official History of the Canadian Army in the Secon*

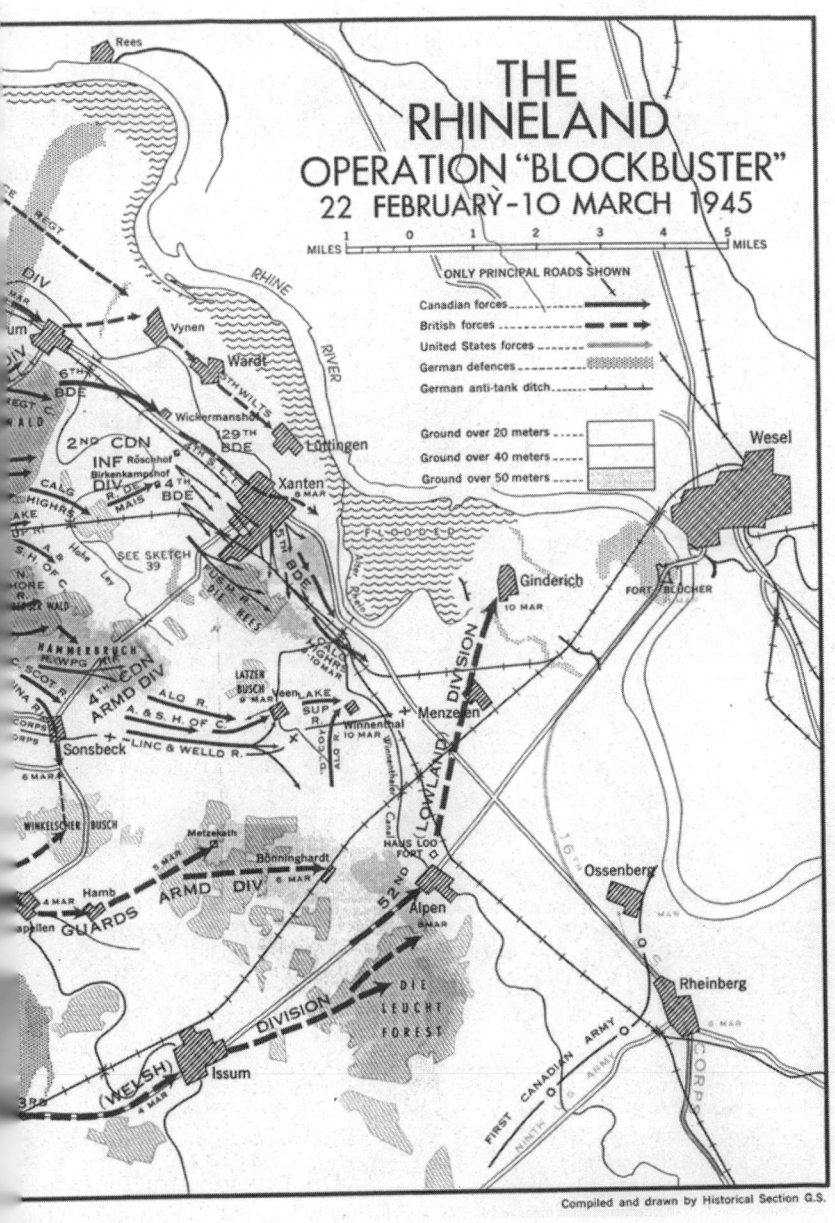

ume III, p. 490, C.P. Stacey, Department of National Defence, 1960.

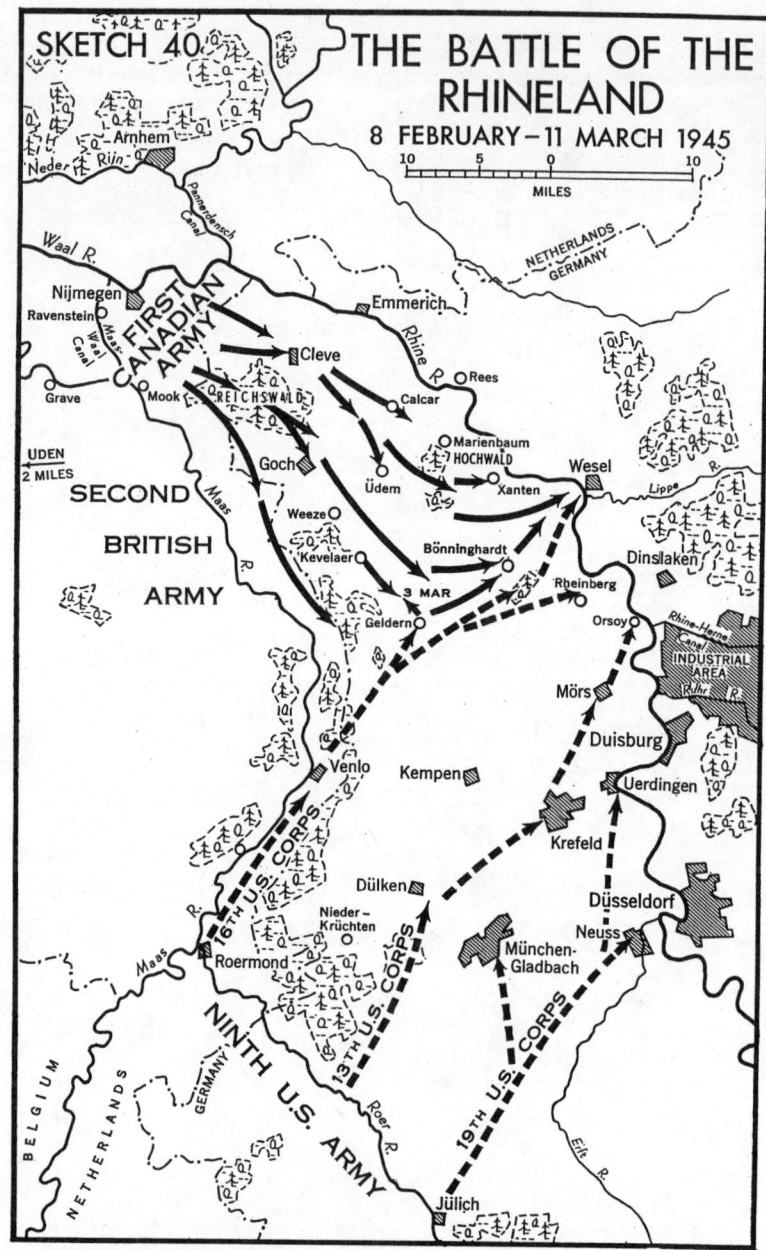

13. The Battle of the Rhineland, 8 February–11 March 1945
Source: *The Victory Campaign, The Official History of the Canadian Army in the Second World War, Volume III*, p. 518, C.P. Stacey, Department of National Defence, 1960.

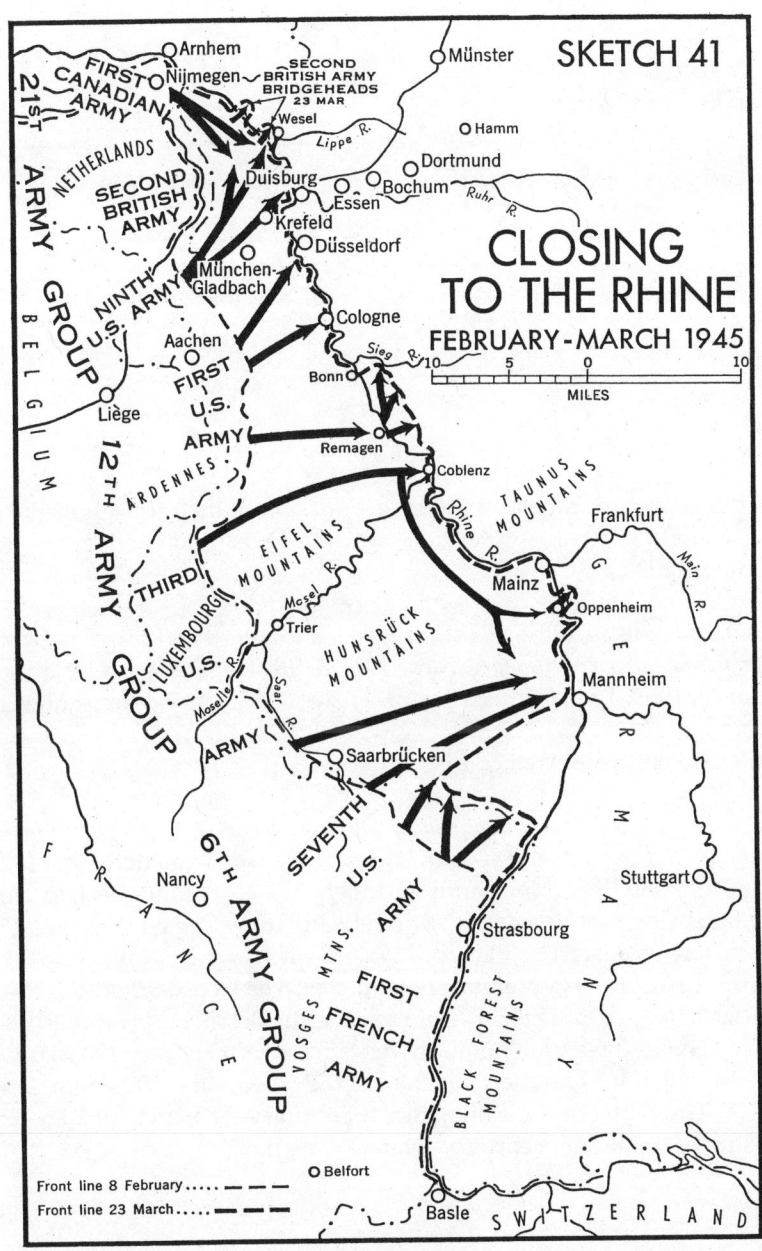

14. Closing to the Rhine, February–March 1945
Source: *The Victory Campaign, The Official History of the Canadian Army in the Second World War, Volume III*, p. 525, C.P. Stacey, Department of National Defence, 1960.

Map Credits

All maps are reproduced with the permission of the Minister of Public Works and Government Services and the Directorate of History and Heritage, 2006.

G.W.L. Nicholson, *Official History of the Canadian Army in the First World War: Canadian Expeditionary Force 1914–1919*, Department of National Defence, 1962: The Northern Sector, 21 April 1915, p. 54; Ypres: The Gas Attack, 22 April 1915, p. 66; Vimy Ridge, 9–12 April 1917, p. 262; Amiens, The Battle Area, 9–19 August 1918, p. 409.

C.P. Stacey, *The Victory Campaign, The Official History of the Canadian Army in the Second World War, Volume III*, Department of National Defence, 1960: The Normandy Bridgehead, 6–30 June 1944, p. 148; Expansion of the Normandy Bridgehead, July–August 1944, p. 253; Operation Totalize: The Plan, p. 217; Advance to the Somme and Antwerp, 31 August–4 September 1944, p. 299; The Coastal Belt, 4–12 September 1944, p. 325; The Battle of the Scheldt, October–November 1944, p. 424; The Rhineland: Operation Veritable, 8–21 February 1945, p. 490; The Rhineland: Operation Blockbuster, 22 February–10 March 1945, p. 518; The Battle of the Rhineland, 8 February–11 March 1945, p. 523; Closing to the Rhine, February–March 1945, p. 525.

A THOROUGHLY CANADIAN GENERAL

1 Hamilton Roots

I

Henry Duncan Graham Crerar was born in Hamilton, Ontario, on 28 April 1888. Canada was a few months shy of twenty-one years old. Sir John A. Macdonald was Prime Minister, and Queen Victoria, on the throne since 1837 and having emerged from her self-imposed internal exile, had already lent her name to the age. The spirit and circumstances of the age of Victoria into which Crerar was born were already well-defined: few doubted the authority of church, history, political institutions, tradition, or the importance of character, civic duty, and self-discipline. And if they did, most kept it to themselves. Victorian values, and the pursuit of them, as much as family circumstances, moulded and bounded Crerar. He would preach throughout his life, often uncritically, the virtues of the values taught him in his youth. Experience tempered his convictions, but he rarely doubted the adequacy of his late-Victorian values. The importance of his British heritage and what he believed it represented – civic virtue and an emphasis on courage, character, discipline, and duty – stood high among the primary values he inherited. Concepts like duty were concrete, not abstract. The individual was important, able to effect real change. Yet he was wary of human nature. Even after two world wars he could say to a reporter, without a hint of irony, that selfishness – individual and collective – caused wars. Like many Victorians, he reconciled personal ambition with duty by directing it, or convincing himself it was directed, towards the collective good. He didn't always meet his own expectations, but that was his measure nonetheless, for himself and others.[1]

The Hamilton of Crerar's boyhood was a community that, in its culture and social organization, was a microcosm of nineteenth-century urban Ontario and a stronghold of British-Canadian sentiment. In the last decades of the nineteenth century, Hamilton was a confident, growing, and prosperous community, the fifth largest Canadian city. The majority of the population was Canadian-born but of British stock. The population growth reflected the increased economic opportunity for the working classes. There was also a widening split, as result of this economic growth, between business and labour.[2]

Crerar's parents, Peter and Marion, were prominent members of Hamilton's upper class. Their families had well-established links to the business and political elite of Ontario and the country; they had only marginal ties to the military. Marion dominated at home. All who knew her attested to her forceful character and strong personality. Speaking to the Women's Canadian Club in 1945, Crerar admonished the women present to remember their influence: 'If my own experience is that of the average man, as I believe it to be, then on the women of Canada immensely depends the future position and progress of our country.' He credited his mother for his convictions about the importance of duty and responsibility.[3]

Privilege and tragedy characterized Marion Crerar's life. Marion Elizabeth Stinson was born in 1859. She had deep Irish-Dutch roots in Hamilton, a combination that contemporaries, who believed that ethnicity mattered, said produced her best qualities: 'an admirable blend of enthusiasm and practical perseverance.'[4] Her grandmother Margaret Stinson (Zimmerman) was descended from Pennsylvania Dutch loyalists. Her grandfather Thomas Stinson, of Irish-Scottish descent, emigrated following his father's death and the widespread economic dislocation that characterized Ireland in the mid-nineteenth century.

Thomas Stinson prospered in North America. Hard working and ambitious, he settled in Clinton Township in Upper Canada, where he met and married Margaret Zimmerman.[5] Margaret's poor health forced them to move to the 'healthier' climate of Hamilton, where he established himself in business with his brothers. Stinson's success provided his family with education and status, but this well-being was marred by the premature deaths of six of the family's nine children, one by suicide. An essence of tragedy permeated their lives, inspiring a grandson to record the sad tale in a fictional account entitled *The Pride of Margaret Alleyne, or Glimpses at a New England Family*. Stoicism became a family trait.[6]

Marion's father, John Stinson, was claimed by tuberculosis in 1865 and her mother, Emma Caroline Counsell (the daughter of prominent Hamiltonian Charles Owen Counsell), married William McGiverin, a Canadian-born merchant, three years later. McGiverin was also a member of the Church of England and his lieutenant-colonelship in the volunteer militia brought the family its first close contact with the Canadian military. McGiverin's stature meant continued social prominence, even after some financial difficulties in the 1870s. Marion had one brother from Emma's first marriage: Thomas Henry. Two younger siblings succumbed to scarlet fever before their second year of life in the fall of 1864. Two more children in the 1870s completed the family: Harold Buchanan and May. The former went on to become a prominent lawyer and a Liberal member of Parliament. He served under Sir Wilfrid Laurier, whom Peter Crerar greatly admired, and was minister without portfolio in Mackenzie King's government in 1924, sitting as member for Ottawa East. Between the McGiverins and the Crerars, the Liberal tradition was strong. The Stinsons were Conservatives.[7]

Soon after her mother remarried, Marion, her education at local private schools complete, was sent to school in England. Travel and education, according to her obituary, produced a self-assured 'woman of the world, cultured, broadminded and possessed of all the social graces.' In England, she married a wealthy young English professional, Cuthbert John 'Bertie' Ottaway, but their marriage was short-lived. In April 1878, less than a year after their wedding, Ottaway died of 'tubercular trouble,' leaving an eighteen-year-old Marion widowed and pregnant. A devout Anglican, she found solace in her church and community work. Sometime after the birth of her daughter, later Lady Lillian Beck, who remained in England living off a trust fund established by her father, Marion returned to Hamilton, where in 1884 she married Peter Duncan Crerar, a Scottish immigrant with a thriving law practice and growing business connections.[8]

Peter Crerar emigrated to Canada in 1879. His parents were Alexander and Margaret Crerar, farmers in Crieff, Perthshire, of above-average means.[9] Alexander secured solid educations for his children, in an area where poverty forced many to take their children out of school at any early age. John, born in 1836, was educated at the Madras College of St Andrews University in Glasgow. His younger brother Thomas completed his education, on what was described as a 'prestigious' Cunningham scholarship, at Edinburgh University. He became a prominent minister of the Free Church of Scotland as well as a respected linguistic and theological scholar. Alexander, named for his father, became a successful merchant for the West India company in London, while Graham was a prominent manufacturer in Glasgow. Peter was the youngest of the family, born in February 1859.

John was the first Crerar to move overseas – to Canada West in 1857, where family connections with an MP from Canada West secured him an appointment with the Bank of Montreal, and then encouraged a switch to law in 1866.[10] John married well – Jessie Anne Hope, the daughter of Senator Adam Hope – and he proved an exceptionally capable law student, winning the first law scholarship in each of his years at Osgoode Hall. He began his own practice in Hamilton in 1871. He was soon a prominent citizen in the self-styled 'Ambitious City,' winning high-profile cases, a patron of the arts, an actor, and a local politician. He was also a staunch Liberal.[11] John and his family had a high profile in Hamilton society, and were particularly famed for the genial atmosphere of their huge stone residence, called 'Merkworth House' after the fashion of the local elite to name their estates (Merkworth derived its name from an old Scots silver coin, the 'Merk.'). Family gatherings were events of enormous interest, reported keenly in the society sections of the local newspapers, an interest prompted by the cosmopolitan allure of their constant stream of British and Continental guests.[12]

Peter Crerar was born two years after John had immigrated to the United Province of Canada. Their parents died when Peter was young, and he was brought up in the home of his bachelor brother Thomas, a junior cleric in the Free Church. Peter practised the Free Church's version of Presbyterianism throughout his life, with a zest undoubtedly fostered by his brother. Peter also displayed a scholarly bent that matched that of both Thomas and John. He received his early education at the Crieff Grammar School and Dumbarton Academy, subsequently completing his formal education in Scotland with a scholarship, winning tenure at the University of Glasgow; he graduated with honours. The limited opportunities available to an educated professional in Scotland, contrasted with John's success, prompted Peter Crerar to immigrate to Canada, at the age of twenty.

Peter followed the standard set by his brother's achievements, demonstrating the ability and determination that would lead to his success in Hamilton's professional community. His academic abilities won him a number of scholarships while he studied law at Osgoode Hall. In 1883, four years after his arrival in Canada, he was called to the bar in

Ontario, having won the silver medal on the barristers' examinations, and became a partner in his brother's law firm – Crerar, Muir, and Crerar. Following John's death in 1904, Peter became senior partner and, joined by his nephew, T.H. Crerar, successfully continued the practice of Crerar and Crerar.

Quiet but firm, Peter established a prominent economic and social position in the city. He shared political and religious views with his brother John that did not fit the mould cast for the Hamilton elite, a homogenous group who were generally conservative and mainstream. Like his brother, Peter was described as a 'supporter of unrestricted reciprocity' and a free trader. His economic stance placed him in the Liberal party camp; he had a six-year term as president of the Hamilton Liberal Association, 1905–11. His solid, subdued support won, it was said, the confidence of his fellow Liberals and the respect of men of 'opposite political leanings.'[13] And while the city's social and economic elite supported the Anglican and Presbyterian churches, Peter attended the services at the Central Presbyterian, a church in which the congregation was, in the words of one Hamilton centennial assessment, 'in sympathy with those in Scotland who ... resented State interference in religion.'[14]

Peter Crerar's convictions did him little harm. He succeeded in commerce, on a scale that eluded his brother. He was drawn into business interests by his specialization in commercial and corporate law, and family ties. As Harry Crerar, among others, would later observe, Peter 'was always at hand with wise counsel and well thought out plans for action,' traits emulated, if not always shared, by his son. Peter became a director on the boards of numerous companies including the innovative Canadian Tungsten Lamp Company and the Ontario Lantern and Lamp Company. These directorships, in particular, revealed Peter's business acumen, as they were over companies characterized by enthusiasts as among the 'newest and ... largest industries in Hamilton.'[15] Peter Crerar's business activities soon overshadowed his legal practice to the point that in 1908 he turned down a judgeship because of his 'numerous commercial interests.' Peter also mirrored his brother in his philanthropic and cultural endeavours, acts that distinguished him from the mainstream of men of commerce but fit with the legal profession's sense of itself as a 'civilizing elite' in the frontier country.[16] This approach to life was evident in his son.

Peter's marriage to Marion Stinson in 1884 further secured, or reflected, his success. Together they became a force on Hamilton's social, cultural, and economic scenes. They were both described by contemporary authors as adherents of the 'older school of life and manners.' For the first decade and a half of their marriage, Marion's attention was devoted to her family. Harry was their first child; three siblings followed – Alastair, Violet, and the youngest, Malcolm, born ten years after Harry in 1898. Lillian, the child from Marion's first marriage, returned from England permanently in 1896 to join the family briefly before she married, in 1898, Adam Beck, a forty-one-year-old bachelor from London, Ontario.[17] Sir Adam and Lillian lived in London, where as a boy Harry would spend many summers.

Duty to monarch, country, and God were the main tenets of Marion Crerar's life; 'practical patriotism' marked the family's philanthropic endeavours in which she took the lead. She was deeply religious; she was also demanding and strong. 'We saw her pass through many trying experiences,' remembered the president of the Hamilton Mountain Sanatorium, 'yet she never questioned or doubted His dispensations ... To use her own words, she regarded life as a pilgrimage and looked forward to that City which hath foundation.'[18]

Imperial sentiments engendered by the South African War took her out of the home. Marion founded the Hamilton branch of the Imperial Order Daughters of the Empire (IODE) in 1900; she set the chapter's course as vice-regent from 1900 and as regent from 1902 to 1919, except for a brief hiatus due to illness in 1913–14. She also initiated the Hamilton IODE's battle against tuberculosis. 'No work more practically patriotic,' noted one of her obituaries, 'could be undertaken than the fighting of what is one of the insidious foes of national health and well-being.' Family deaths made her efforts both personal and urgent, but she was not alone in her belief that the physical and moral health of the people equalled the physical strength of the nation.

Her leadership in public health followed naturally. In early 1906 she was an original member of the Ladies' Auxiliary Board of the Hamilton Health Association, then in the process of establishing the Hamilton Mountain Sanatorium for Consumptives, a new instrument in the growing international anti-tuberculosis movement that was assuming crusade proportions in Canada, where the disease was the single most frequent cause of death. She soon formed a new chapter of the IODE to provide linens for the sanatorium. As the board's president until her death, Marion led its executive in the operation of the sanatorium.[19]

Peter was a strong supporter of Marion's work with the Hamilton Health Association, serving as an original member of the Men's Board and giving generously of his time and money; in 1906, he donated a recreation hall for patients at the sanatorium. Peter's role in the sanatorium was largely advisory, as was that of the Men's Board in general. Peter also contributed his time to the St Andrews Benevolent Society. Harry Crerar noted the roots of their success: 'They made a fine team,' a lesson that was not lost on him.[20]

Peter and Marion Crerar provided their family with all the social amenities that upper-class life in southwestern Ontario at the end of the nineteenth century offered. They lived in the most fashionable districts of Hamilton, close to the commercial centre – a privilege in a period before flight from the inner city was the rule. In the lavish furnishings and well-kept grounds of their family homes, the Crerars enjoyed the service of domestics and leisurely games of billiards amidst the gatherings of white-gloved women and brandy-sipping, cigar-smoking men.

Peter and Marion joined John and Jessie Crerar as prominent figures in Hamilton's high society. Peter was a member as well as a promoter of his brother's Garrick Dramatic Society. The family's support of theatre was extensive, and they often entertained visiting theatrical guests in their luxurious home, 'Dunedin.' Marion trained as a singer, and, while she never applied her talent professionally, her interest guaranteed a regular attendance at the opera. Travel, at home and abroad, was an important aspect of the family life. They visited the Crerars' ancestral home in Scotland on occasion and toured the Continent. Closer to home, the family maintained a summer getaway in the Muskoka region, a popular turn-of-the-century vacation area for Ontario's upper classes. Loon Island was the spot for many enjoyable summers filled with fishing, boating, and hunting. Harry Crerar's fondness for Loon Island and the Muskokas was a constant theme in his correspondence. His love of the sporting life came from his father, who was a member of the Royal Golf Society of Canada and the Canadian Association of Amateur Oarsmen.[21]

Marion's pre-eminence in the home and her dominant personality made it inevitable that her traits would leave the largest imprint on the Crerar family. Lillian and Vi inherited their mother's regal bearing and imperious nature, tempered by charitable personalities. Peter Crerar's impact on his family was subtler than Marion's. He remained a remote figure, although he fostered affection in his children and was, by all accounts, 'genial.' Crerar's quiet side was perhaps Peter Crerar's imprint. He may have hinted at his relationship with his father when years later he admonished his own son about his lack of communication. 'This may just be the indifferent attitude which sons occasionally show to their father.'²² Alastair was much more like his father – gentle, but resolute. Malcolm was the least like his mother and thus her favourite. According to all, he loved life, approaching it with a sense of humour and openness uncharacteristic of the reserved Crerar family. 'He was the one that really had many of the characteristics, more so than the rest of the family, that were ... attractive to other people,' his niece suggested, possibly echoing her father's reminiscence of his brother, whom she never met.²³

II

Only vignettes of Harry Crerar's pre-war life remain to help the historian understand him as a boy, yet some key themes are evident. Hamilton was important, always remembered as his home, and his mother was a major influence. 'Whatever I have accomplished,' he recalled on a visit to his hometown in 1945, 'I owe in the greatest measure to my early life in Hamilton, and, in particular to the influence and inspiration of my mother.'²⁴ He was intelligent and showed much 'promise,' but he did not stand out. His sensitivity to criticism later in life and his eagerness to seize every opportunity to teach his children – critiquing grammar in personal letters, for example – suggest a youth that was less exemplary than he would have liked. His parents clearly had high expectations. Harry too would have very high expectations of himself and others. He applauded achievement but was impatient with failure. Nevertheless, the young Harry Crerar was more adventurous and reckless, and less ambitious, than he later admitted. Reminiscing by mail with an old Hamilton girlfriend in 1945, he recalled, 'In the course of my amblings around the city, I actually passed the spot where, by bad driving on my part, I dumped you and I out of the sleigh.'²⁵ Crerar eventually adopted the family's constrained and serious character, but he was relaxed in intimate social settings, maintaining an informal contact with many close friends. His self-consciousness perhaps developed out of the contrast between his personality and the ideal of self-discipline. He preferred to mask his sensitivity.

Crerar never embraced his parents' faith or practised their observance. Journal entries from the First World War suggest that he appreciated the invigorating effect of religion and Christian martial songs, but after the war he did not attend church regularly, except when required by circumstances. The impression he left was that he viewed it as a vehicle for promoting certain values, but he did not accept it as a necessary source of spiritual inspiration. Later when his daughter developed negative views towards religion he expressed his concern, belabouring the error of her ways. Yet once he considered her an adult, these concerns lapsed. Crerar, and his family, preferred skiing to church.[26]

Crerar's early education was in private schools in Hamilton. In 1899 he left that city, with some hesitation, for Upper Canada College in Toronto. His mother gave him *The Words of the Son of God*, a daily meditation guide; 'This book,' she wrote, 'has been for 20 years my constant guide. On 1st January 1899 I give it to my oldest son Harry Crerar, with his Mother's love. *Read it daily.*' He kept it until he died; whether it inspired him is unknown.

Upper Canada College was the province's foremost private school, flourishing under the tutelage of George Parkin, the well-known educator and British imperial advocate.[27] While Parkin's reputation was the product of the fervour with which he promoted imperial federation between Britain and its Dominions, his early passion – his 'mission' – was education.[28] Parkin was preparing a generation of men who would lead and influence Canadians in the future. Upper Canada College was an institution that could serve Canada much as he perceived Britain was served by English public schools such as Eton and Uppington. The college would follow that model – it would train 'character not intellect.' Merit and education would create a responsible elite, ready to serve.[29]

Parkin had little direct contact with his students, but he spoke to them regularly on a variety of topics as well as on special occasions. The themes of his Prize Day Address in 1901 and other years reflected his obsession. So too did visiting speakers, distinguished men of letters, theologians, and the military officers who lectured to the boys on Sunday evenings. Formidable teachers such as Stephen Leacock and E.R. Peacock staffed the school. Parkin's colleagues did not all share his earnest Christian outlook or his imperial fervour, but they generally reflected his views on Canadian nationalism and the character-building potential of Victorian muscular Christian values.

Parkin also ensured a measure of influence by increasing the number of student boarders and instituting a policy of the masters living in residence. As surrogate parents, masters 'dominated the boy's lives and memories.'[30] Two masters were particularly important to Crerar: W.L. Grant and E.R. Peacock. Grant, who served as first head of history and geography and later became principal, was the son and heir apparent of George Monro Grant, a contemporary and imperial compatriot of

Parkin and one of the 'unchallenged leaders of the imperial movement in Canada in the 1880s and 1890s.' W.L. Grant did not mirror Parkin's earnest Christian outlook but he shared his faith in the imperial connection and mission. The main themes in the younger Grant's 'reformist' imperialist thought were 'social service and strength – an attitude of social responsibility and a desire to make Canadian society a place in which [everyone] had a chance to develop the best that is in them, and strength which would protect that society in a world of imperfection, anger, and unreason.'[31] Crerar maintained a steady, if formal, contact with W.L. Grant when the latter became headmaster at UCC. He remembered Grant with respect and spoke of him often, quoting his opinions on matters of imperial organization and education. Grant's practical approach to the subject of Canada's relations with the British Empire was reflected in Crerar's own pragmatic view on the subject.[32] Sir Edward Peacock was another master who shared Grant's affection for the British connection as well as his reasoned perception of the practical limits on any type of organization. Peacock opposed the idea of imperial federation as proposed by Parkin and others on practical grounds. In his opinion, the ties were 'historical and sentimental,' and the colonies would eventually be 'bound by ties of affection, habit and self-interest to the Mother country and other members.'[33]

Crerar would echo Grant's and Peacock's views on ties to Britain. In lectures, addresses, and letters, Crerar belaboured the benefits that Canada and the Empire could gain through a closer relationship based on an understanding and knowledge of both their shared and distinct pasts. Peacock's influence on Harry Crerar was lasting. The two maintained close ties for many years; in 1959, Crerar characterized him as 'the finest Canadian to have taken up residence in the UK ... his interest and kindness to his fellow Canadians in both the Great Wars was most marked.'[34] Crerar, and many other college alumni remembered Peacock with affection and respect. As a Sixth Form house master, Peacock initially had little contact with the young boarder. He was 'out of my orbit for about two years' as Harry recalled, until he found himself in Peacock's English literature class. Crerar retained Peacock's friendship for years, with the elder master maintaining a paternal affection and pride in his 'old boy.' During the Second World War, after one of Harry Crerar's frequent retreats to the Peacock residence to escape the pressures of his position, Peacock remarked on the visit in a letter to a close friend: 'I had General Crerar with me for two nights and had some good, quiet talks. A grand fellow! I'm proud of him, one of my old boys.' Crerar valued their companionship, visiting the Peacock residence in London whenever the opportunity presented itself. 'In 1910 and again in 1911 and 1912,' he later wrote, 'I visited London ... I knew ERP was then living there ... As I always liked him tremendously when a teen-age boy, I got in touch with him and saw something of him each time.' Crerar recalled, 'I found him most understanding and much enjoyed being with him.'[35]

Still, Upper Canada College was a mixed experience for young Harry. Stephen Leacock recalled meeting the newly arrived boarder. 'He wasn't feeling so good,' Leacock wrote, 'just sitting on the edge of the bed and looking downhearted.' To console him, Leacock spoke of his admiration for Hamilton. The mention of his home, Leacock noted, brought tears to Harry's eyes.[36] By Crerar's own account, his contribution to the college was not notable. 'Neither my scholastic nor sporting career at UCC,' he recalled, 'was such as to give marked satisfaction and pride to either parents or masters.' He was an enthusiastic and competitive participant in the school's sports program, a requirement for all the boys. Crerar's competitive spirit, and diminutive stature – he was short and slim – resulted in a broken leg in rugby football in his second year as a boarder and a fractured ankle suffered playing hockey the next year. He noted years later, 'Those accidents rather put me out of the running for the school teams'; they did nothing to dampen his spirit.[37]

Attendance at the most elite school in the province, if not the country, produced in Crerar – albeit many years later – a paternalistic outlook and a belief in the character-building value of a leadership-oriented education. The purpose of the 'basically classical' curriculum was to build fortitude and character through competitive exams, course work, and a weekly regimen of sports, drill; and lectures. It was a rugged, competitive, and regimented environment designed to harden boys who came from soft living in wealthier Canadian families.[38] The rooms were sparsely furnished, particularly when compared to the comforts of the Crerar home. Food was plentiful, however, and extras could be had for the right price. Despite the control exerted over the boys' lives, they managed to exercise a degree of freedom, initiating the 'first form' boys and creating a personal atmosphere in their rooms with posters and prints. Prominent in Harry's room were two large prints of the battles of the Northwest Rebellion.[39]

Crerar left UCC in 1904 for a year of study in Switzerland; in 1905 he took classes at Highfield College to improve his scholastic record for application to the Royal Military College of Canada (RMC). Highfield was a prominent Hamilton boys' school with a successful record of placement in the RMC, over half the graduates continuing their education at the college at one point. The schoolmaster, John Collinson, taught 'his lads to take it on the chin with a grin – and stick it'; he had known Crerar and his family for a number of years and developed a high opinion of his potential.[40] The school's popular cadet corps, attached to the Royal Hamilton Light Infantry, was an attractive feature.

III

Highfield's cadet corps, like that of other schools, was an institution designed to transmit military and patriotic values to the youth of Ontario. Crerar had few direct family connections to the military, with the exception of William McGiverin's lieutenant-colonelcy in the Hamilton militia and his service against the Fenians. His early years, however, were ones that saw a growing general interest in the military and military affairs in those parts of Canada sympathetic with the British Empire, while the South African War prompted a burst of activity within the Crerar family as his mother became more active with the IODE and local causes. 'Patriotism, discipline, subordination, order and a competitive view of human nature'[41] as well as bravery and courage were the traits believed to be imbued by military training. War was a test of courage and bravery, of individual and national mettle in an increasingly urbanized world that offered little opportunity for the demonstration of masculine ideals.

Raised in an environment where the victories of British arms in South Africa and Queen Victoria's 'Little Wars' brought the admiration of military skills and the values associated with them to new heights, it was not surprising that Harry Crerar was enamoured of this romanticized militarism from an early age. 'I was always interested in military affairs,' he observed years later. An accomplished rider, he also attributed his early attraction in part to his love of horses and horsemanship, affection fostered by Sir Adam and Lillian Beck's love of riding and personal stables. He found Sir Adam to be a somewhat austere individual but he remembered holidays spent in London as happy ones. In 1946 he noted, 'Before the last Great War, when I was a school boy and later a cadet at the RMC, it was here, in London, that I spent most of my holidays, and very happy ones they were.'[42]

After Highfield, Crerar entered RMC. Admission to the military college required candidates to write an open examination and produce a 'certificate of good moral character' to ensure the gentlemanly nature of cadets.[43] Peter Crerar dutifully fulfilled these obligations, writing to the Militia Council in April 1906 on his son's behalf while the minister of Hamilton's Christ's Church Cathedral, and the headmaster of Highfield performed the formality of attesting to the ongoing excellence of Harry's moral fibre.[44] There was no reference from UCC.

Crerar's three years at RMC were some of the most important of his life. The regimen of the college began to develop in him the discipline and the perseverance that marked his pursuits in the years to follow. An education at RMC did not limit Crerar's career choice to the military. It did, however, cultivate the grounds for, and plant the seeds of, a unique outlook on life.

Crerar's attendance at RMC, and his subsequent service with the militia, coincided with a period of relative dynamism in Canada's defence establishment. The first Militia Act of 1868 had confirmed the militia as the central element in Canada's defence, creating a volunteer Active Militia and a Reserve Militia, and dividing the new country into nine military districts to facilitate recruiting. It was largely a paper establishment, but grew, albeit slowly during the second half of the nineteenth century, as the British withdrawal of their garrisons, and commitment, forced Canadians to take some responsibility for their own defence. A permanent force, building on two artillery batteries, emerged by the early 1880s, even if their role was limited to training the militia. Substantive reform followed the election of Sir Wilfrid Laurier in 1896 and his choice of Frederick Borden as Minister of Militia and Defence – an inspired appointment reflected in his tenure to 1911 when Laurier was defeated – as well as his appointment of a series of energetic general officers commanding (GOC), later inspectors-general, foremost among them Colonel Edward Hutton. Defence expenditure rose steadily from $1.6 million in 1898 to $7 million by 1911. A short list of reforms included improved training facilities as well as a shift from drill to field exercises; better arms and equipment; the addition of medical, supply, transport, signalling, ordnance, and intelligence corps to the militia; the agreement to conform to British equipment and organization; and the takeover of British fortresses of Halifax and Esquimalt. The numbers of militia attending the annual camps grew slowly but steadily, from an average of 20,000 in the twenty years before 1896 to 25,000 in 1904. Within a decade, that number would double. All of these initiatives reflected a more assertive role vice the British, a reflection of a more mature relationship, and a tense international environment.

The establishment of RMC in 1876 was one of the early steps taken by the young Dominion to shore up its defences. It was to provide the Active Militia with an adequate supply of officers to lead and train its non-permanent equivalent, the titular backbone of Canada's defence. As befitted a developing country, the college curriculum was designed to educate engineers for civil as well as military careers.[45] There was very little change in the object of the curriculum in the years between the enrolment of first cadets, the 'Old Eighteen,' and Cadet 749. The 'Objects of the College' in 1907 prescribed that in addition to imparting 'a thorough knowledge of the military profession, and for qualifying officers for command and for staff appointments ... the course of instruction is such as to afford a thoroughly practical, scientific and sound training in Civil Engineering, Surveying and Physics.'[46] The college also offered some basic military training and a cursory introduction to the humanities. Tactics and military history were offered sparingly. There was no guarantee that cadets had a firm grasp of these subjects prior to admittance; while geography and the history of Canada and Great Britain from 1763 to 1901 were obligatory subjects on the entrance exams, 33 per cent was a pass.

The 'subjects of practical instruction' were a mix of athletics, drills, and exercises apparently designed with familiarization, and not expertise, as the goal. Proficiency in small arms was imparted through rifle and revolver practice. Infantry and artillery drills as well as equitation were the required military exercises, supplemented by a physical fitness regimen that included gymnastics and swimming. The college's military training and academic program compared favourably with its British counterpart, although the lack of a large permanent force for complementary staff and command experience was a weakness.

Academic pursuits at RMC imparted a high degree of respect for education among Canada's senior officers, including Harry Crerar, but an increased emphasis on formal military education was not enough to overcome the perception that intellect was secondary to character in a competent leader of men. Crerar's own conception of officer training would reflect this amalgam of beliefs on the value of a military education.[47]

While the college developed in its cadets the sense of fellowship deemed necessary to create a professional outlook, RMC's mission made it a popular institution for the English-Canadian upper middle class who desired for their sons a 'disciplined education' that included moral and physical conditioning as well as intellectual growth, although the latter was a bonus. Fees were sufficiently high (including the cost of uniform, tuition, and board, the annual fee was $300) to limit admission to those sons of the professional or business groups who desired such instruction; entrance requirements sufficiently low to see that they were not denied.

The historical tradition, the physical and cultural reminders of previous classes, the instructional staff – military and academic – as well as the administrative staff including the commandant, were drawn from the British military, with few exceptions. Quite naturally, their interpretations presented the cadets with an imperial perspective designed, consciously or otherwise, to strengthen the imperial connection and provide Canada with a group of imperially minded leaders. The Royal Military College developed a program to create a leadership cadre, not simply to train one. With Harry Crerar, it cemented a strong patrician approach to leadership and education.

The effects of RMC were evident from Crerar's record. He did not burst upon the scene at the college. The Descriptive Roll placed Cadet Number 749 as twenty-seventh out of the batch of thirty-five new cadets joining the college in August 1906. Admission itself was only slightly more difficult than in earlier years. The entrance exams, while requiring only a 33 per cent minimum grade, were duplicates from the British system, an approach that placed Canadian students at a disadvantage; English public schools often had preliminary examinations or special army classes to prepare their students for Army entrance examinations. Canadian schools sought to impart the spirit of militarism, not the practical aspects of the military. Nevertheless, it was in these aspects of the Royal Military College's curriculum that Crerar's aptitude for organization and reasoned, methodical, if linear, solutions began to reveal itself, under the pressure of a control that was at first externally, and later self-, imposed.[48] In his first year, Crerar climbed from twenty-seventh position to twentieth after the results of the June examinations were tallied. He did so mainly on the strength of a solid performance in the drill and exercise aspects of the program as well as in mathematics and French components of the first-year curriculum.

Crerar was slowly carried upwards in the class standings by the strong ability shown in practical applications and implementation. Given direction, he flourished. By the end of his second year, he had moved into fourteenth place, aided by the depletion of the class from thirty-five to thirty-one. It was, however, his evident abilities in the subjects of practical instruction (infantry and artillery drills, signalling, gymnastics, and target practices) that brought him recognition. In the theoretical subjects such as physics and the second-year mathematics course, his performance was not as impressive, but he showed a flair for the intricacies of applied sciences such as military tactics and surveying, as well as a fluency in French. In the engineering courses he was close to the bottom of his class. His efforts in his second year were enough to earn him the Canadian Artillery Association Badge and the rank of cadet sergeant of the first class, a standing below the battalion sergeant-major, but a college distinction nonetheless.

In his final year, Crerar finished ninth in the final set of examinations and thirteenth overall in a class of thirty cadets graduating. He left with distinctions in French, receiving the Alliance Française Medal as well as medals for equitation, artillery, and gymnastics. The artillery awards included the Ontario Artillery Association Cup in 1909.[49] His aptitudes revealed a learning profile that was strong in most applied sciences and systematic analysis, but that included an aversion to theoretical solutions, although not theory. His marks suggested a propensity for group-oriented action and discussion, and the implementation, if not the initiation, of ideas.

The unofficial education practices of RMC also left their mark. Like similar institutions, the college hazing system left the senior students or cadets responsible for certain aspects of disciplinary action among the newer recruits. The exercise of this authority was intended to foster responsibility among the seniors as well as to initiate the younger men into the 'new and more mature society of the cadet body' at the same time as teaching obedience and the realities of power to 'youngsters who had often been indulged.' It seems likely the latter goal was more often realized. Excesses during hazing became more common during the years that Crerar was a cadet. In 1906, the severity of the initiation practices prompted a commandant's investigation and led to enquiries by the Board of Visitors into hazing among cadets. A descriptive amendment to his record, written in 1921, noted that 'Colonel Crerar spent the year 1906 in doing all the funny things which a recruit is asked to perform.'[50] A few years later, the author added, 'He got his own back.'

Nevertheless, Crerar's agenda as commandant of the college in 1938–9 suggests that he deplored the excesses of the unofficial system while respecting the overall results. As commandant he attempted to 'persuade the seniors to abandon some of the "excesses" and "stupidities."' Crerar later believed that 'the object of the system of administration and discipline maintained at the Royal Military College [was] the inculcation of self-control and self-discipline and the progressive development of leadership amongst the Gentlemen Cadets.'[51] His subsequent addresses and comments to the senior classes emphasized the 'unique opportunity' given the cadets in their final year 'to develop the requirements of a leader' but cautioned that self-control was necessary to prevent excesses of any type. In the closing exercises of 1939, Crerar summed up the characteristics that he believed RMC had imparted to him and had facilitated his advance: '[The] early years of the Cadet's training at the RMC should impress upon him the virtues of intelligent obedience, reliability, personal smartness, mental alertness and physical fitness.'[52] This observation came after years of reflection. His most likely reaction while undergoing the process was that of a recruit who passed through eight years before him: 'At the time I suppose we thought this was the RMC that our predecessors had suffered in the same way, and that if we couldn't stick it we were no good.'[53]

Crerar was also at home in Kingston. Nestled on the shore of Lake Ontario, surrounded by the Thousand Islands, Kingston was a beautiful spot for any who enjoyed sailing and leisure. The harder elements of life at the Royal Military College were tempered by Crerar's enthusiastic involvement in the social and athletic opportunities the school provided; friendships were formed that carried on through two world wars. Control, a hallmark later, still took second place to the reckless sense of youthful indestructibility. A broken jaw following a wild toboggan ride down the slopes of Fort Henry was evidence of his enthusiasm. The photographic record reveals a cocky young man, slight but sturdy, pillbox hat tilted to one side. And he fondly remembered the pleasures of the college, where he 'turned out to be a better than average gymnast' and a ladies man; horseback riding and hours of sailing Kingston harbour were his main enjoyments.[54]

IV

When Crerar graduated from RMC in 1909 he was still a romantic. He entertained notions of a career with the imperial forces, a path chosen by many cadets concerned with promotion and seeking travel and adventure. 'In my final year at the RMC,' he recalled, 'I had strong desires to join a British or Indian Cavalry Regiment.'[55] A cavalry appointment was, however, a costly path and he was reluctant to remain too dependent on his family. 'It was a gentlemen's career,' he recalled, 'and cost accordingly. My dad would have had to foot the bills for the rest of his life.'[56] It was also likely that his thirteenth-place standing in the class was not sufficient to guarantee him one of the seven preferred imperial commissions offered to the college, only two of which were in his choice of arms.

The alternatives of either the Canadian Permanent Force or civil engineering were hindered by the limits of the three-year course at the RMC. It was not considered a thorough preparation for either the military or for civil engineering. The usual course of action for a cadet wishing to pursue a career in civil engineering was to continue on to university to obtain a degree. Financial considerations presumably dissuaded Crerar from pursuing either this path or a Canadian Permanent Force commission. Following a summer holiday in the Muskokas, he took some fatherly advice and joined the Canadian Tungsten Lamp Company of Hamilton as a superintendent.

For an ambitious young man on the lookout for a career, the Tungsten Lamp Company was a good start. It was a new and growing industry, employing over four hundred people by 1911. His first year was spent in the factory, a learning process of 'ten hour working days ... often with some overtime thrown in.' It was a working-class experience that he naively described as having given him a shared experience with the employees.[57] Rather, the year was an apprenticeship for the white-collar professional. The next year, Crerar, eager to 'be in the forefront of his vocation,' spent six months in Vienna 'learning more about the technicalities of manufacturing' the incandescent lamp.[58] He was not alone in seeking his fortune in pre-war Vienna, but he left no record to indicate if light bulbs were his only pursuit.

The idyllic nature of the pre-war years was shattered by the sudden and unexpected death of Peter Crerar in 1912 after a cranial aneurysm. Marion carried on, but it proved a severe blow to her already unhealthy condition.[59] Harry Crerar's reaction went unrecorded, but he missed, for the first time, the annual militia summer camp. He also moved to Toronto, invited by his brother-in-law Sir Adam Beck to fill the position of illumination engineer with the growing Ontario Hydro-Electric Commission, persuaded to leave Hamilton both because of his father's death and by the chance to organize and head a research division to test the performances of various types of illumination.[60]

Crerar's career prospects with Ontario Hydro were attractive. Beck was the chairman as minister without portfolio in the provincial government. Starting work, in the glowing words of a wartime company profile, 'with a basement bench as his sole equipment and with only a single assistant,' Crerar was the company's first research director. At that time, Hydro was completing the construction of a Toronto laboratory and storehouse on Strachan Avenue that would accommodate departments engaged in experimental and testing work.[61] Hydro employees later credited and praised Crerar for his contribution to organizing, choosing, and designing the laboratories and equipment.[62] He directed the expansion of the laboratory's activities until it included four separate laboratories to test aspects of the application and transmission of hydroelectricity. The actual expansion of the 'volume and variety' of work done was attributable to the rapid expansion of the commission under Beck.

Crerar's responsibilities at Hydro proved an eclectic mix. In addition to his duties in Toronto, he travelled across rural Ontario with Beck's Hydro Circus, a mix of exhibits designed to promote hydroelectricity. In the spring of 1913 he left for Europe in the company of the commission's chief engineer, Frederick A. Gaby. Gaby had joined Ontario Hydro in 1907 and, like Crerar, was now caught up in the vibrant atmosphere created by Beck's relentless pursuit of innovation and expansion. Crerar and Gaby were charged in early 1913 to inspect and investigate the state of electrical energy transmission and generation in Great Britain and Europe, particularly the 'methods of rural distribution rates and the success of such undertakings.'[63] A small scandal emerged with allegations of overspending on the 3,600-mile trip but they were later dismissed as originating with a disgruntled ex-employee.[64] Crerar remained with Ontario Hydro until the outbreak of war in August of 1914, balancing his work with an active social life in Toronto, when he was not overseas or in the Muskokas. A member of the Toronto University Club, he golfed at every opportunity; a frequent partner was a young law student R.J. Orde, a future Judge Advocate General.

Crerar's success did not completely eclipse his military ambitions – ambitions he later said he deliberately hid, adhering to the self-described practice of appearing keen for his curent appointment, even when he was not.[65] In 1909, upon graduation, Crerar took a commission as a lieutenant in the Non-Permanent Active Militia's 4th Battery, Canadian Field Artillery of Hamilton, which he obtained after six months as a reserve officer.

This was an attractive time to be a member of the Canadian militia as Laurier, and then Sir Robert Borden, continued to reform Canada's defence establishment, as tensions grew first between the United States and Britain, and then between the mother country and Germany. Sir Robert Borden's minister of militia, Sam Hughes, was an energetic and a particularly fervent advocate of preparedness for war. This attention, and the popularity of things military, was translated into better facilities, equipment, and training for these part-time soldiers than had been available in many years, if ever. The militia was also an important social institution, providing companionship with like-minded individuals. In a community like Hamilton, an officer in the militia was accorded a degree of respectability. In addition, Crerar's belief in service provided a strong stimulus to joining a militia unit. Despite being overseas for as many as six months out of the year, he was 'sufficiently keen on [his] militia work,'[66] and financially able, to return for the annual summer camp at Petawawa. The costs associated with militia training made this no small feat for the practical Crerar.

The greatest beneficiary of the reforms of this period was the artillery, already considered one of the most professional arms of the militia. The 4th Battery of Hamilton was one of those units whose records contributed to this achievement.[67] The 4th was reorganized in 1898 to form, along with the 7th from St Catharines and the 9th of Toronto, the 2nd Brigade. The battery's complement was increased from four to six more-modern guns. This reorganization was part of the new and energetic scheme of the GOC of the militia, Colonel Edward Hutton, to create a balanced 'national' militia, free of political influence. He reasoned that improvements in training would follow. The positive effects of the re-equipment and reorganization were strengthened by the establishment in 1905 of a central training ground at Camp Petawawa. This new facility provided the space and terrain necessary to allow more realistic combined arms manoeuvres as well as the firing ranges required by modern weapons.[68]

There was much room for improvement. Sir John French, the Inspector-General of the Imperial Forces, visiting Canada in 1910, delivered a highly critical report on the state of Canada's defence forces, commending only the results he observed at Camp Petawawa and RMC. Following Sir Robert Borden's election in 1911, Hughes, despite – or perhaps because of – a pronounced dislike of military professionals, was determined to do better.[69] He successfully fought for an increased share of the budget, better facilities and equipment, and an increasing number of men trained annually. By 1913, attendance at the militia camps had grown to 55,000.

French's report and Hughes's energetic presence produced practical, if limited, results, as reflected by Crerar's experience. In 1908, the 4th Battery was forced to miss the summer camp when a budget shortfall caused the cancellation of training, although the battery's records suggested there was less interest that year as well. In 1912, the 4th Battery, and indeed the 2nd Brigade, was out in almost full strength for sixteen days of training at Petawawa in early June.[70] The camp commandant, Lieutenant-Colonel Harry Burstall, a Permanent Force gunner, reported that the 'Field Artillery made good progress towards efficiency' and that 'all ranks were keen and hard-working.' He noted, however, that the engineering and cavalry units were hampered by the congestion of the 'Manoeuvre Areas.'[71] Limited space as well as personnel and equipment, shortcomings exacerbated by distance, remained constant problems. Brigadier-General William Otter, in his final report as Inspector-General in 1913, concluded that the militia, while improving, had not come far enough and that Hughes's influence continued to produce an amateurish and cronyish approach to the business of training for war.[72]

Despite the many deficiencies of the training for war, there were benefits, especially for the artillery. The large numbers attending the camp were exposed, if only briefly, to military administration, had contact with regular force personnel as well as other units, took part in some of the first large-scale exercises ever run in Canada, and were able to engage in long-range firing practice, with up to eighty rounds per gun. If this experience seemed to pale in comparison with the task that awaited them, it was more substantial than anything they had undergone before. Their inexperience may even have left them more willing to learn the new requirements of modern, industrial war. The summer before the war broke out in Europe, 'a force of more than 10,000 officers and men of all arms concentrated at Petawawa, where they carried out combined manoeuvres that came closer to approximating active service conditions than in any previous year in Canada.'[73]

Except in 1912, Harry Crerar faithfully attended these camps from 1910 to the summer of 1914.[74] His battery was consistently characterized as 'very good' and 'well above average' in efficiency, turnout of the ranks, and condition of equipment. The 4th's record, in fact, was exemplary. The numbers trained annually from Crerar's unit and 2nd Brigade, particularly among the officers, increased or remained steady from 1910.[75] Crerar was described in the annual reports as 'keen, active and energetic,' as were his fellow section commanders. The battery commander, Major H.G. Carscallen, was similarly praised as a 'very good and hard working' officer. A few years later, Crerar was described as 'one of the most popular officers of the old 4th field battery.' There was no doubt that he enjoyed the barrack's camaraderie of the camps.[76]

Crerar remained a subaltern with the 4th Battery until the war broke out, with the exception of 1910, when he served briefly on the regimental staff of 2nd Brigade as an adjutant to Lieutenant-Colonel J.H. Mitchell, a militia staff officer in whom Harry had very little confidence. The adjutant's position rotated between the officers of the three batteries composing the brigade and as such was not reflective of any special abilities on his part, except perhaps his training from the RMC. Crerar's poor relationship with Mitchell carried on into the war, and would deteriorate as Crerar demonstrated his lack of tolerance for incompetence – and how intemperate he could be in expressing his views.

Crerar's experience in the militia meant he would try to strengthen the ties between the citizen soldiers and the regular forces whenever he was in a position to do so, a tribute to his own pre-war experience. His sentimental ties to the militia, and RMC, were tempered by his family's hard-headed practicality and the ongoing tensions between the Permanent Force and the militia. After the war, Crerar measured the utility of the militia by its professionalism and how well it complemented the Permanent Force. The resulting decisions did not always endear him to the militia supporters. 'Civilization is impossible without traditions,' he wrote in the foreword to UCC's *College Times* many years later, 'and progress impossible without the destruction of those traditions.'[77]

2 Baptism of Fire

I

The Canadian response to Britain's declaration of war on 4 August was a quick and enthusiastic offer of an expeditionary force, gratefully accepted by His Majesty's government on 6 August. On the recommendation of the Army Council, Prime Minister Robert Borden's Conservative Cabinet authorized the raising and equipping of a contingent whose strength was set at 25,000 volunteers by an Order-in-Council on 10 August. Imbued with romantic notions of war, seeking adventure, or simply looking for three square meals a day, thousands of Canadians came forward.[1] Crerar and his brothers, only one generation removed from Britain, were among them.

The army's detailed mobilization plan was to recruit a contingent of 25,000 drawn from militia units across the country. Minister of Militia Sam Hughes scrapped this plan immediately, issuing instead, with the exception of artillery and other technical units, a call for volunteers, organized as the Canadian Expeditionary Force (CEF), and set the pattern that would characterize his approach to the war until his removal in November 1916: a celebration of the amateur over the professional, of the national over the effective, with the organizing principle being that all decisions ended up in the minister's office. Hughes's principles were summed up by British Secretary of State for War Lord Kitchener, who, when questioned a year later regarding his British 'New Armies,' replied, 'I prefer men who know nothing to those who have been taught a smattering of the wrong thing.'[2]

The individual volunteers who made up the First Contingent of the CEF would concentrate and organize at a new camp, Valcartier, another of the minister's creations that he was driving his contractors – political supporters all – to build just outside Quebec City.[3] To everyone's amazement, he succeeded. As one historian observed wryly, 'The role of the Militia units was restricted to recruiting and dispatching drafts of volunteers to Valcartier camp, where officers and men would be sorted out to form new battalions.'[4]

Hamilton's 4th Battery was one of the nine militia artillery batteries called out as a complete unit to form the artillery component of the expeditionary force, commanded by Lieutenant-Colonel Harry Burstall.[5] The mobilization order found Harry Crerar in Toronto. There was no doubt he would go overseas, and his brothers soon followed. He wrote years later that with his mother an 'ardent believer in the British Empire ... [it was] not a matter for surprise.'[6]

His immediate duties were two-fold. As second-in-command, Captain Crerar worked with the battery commander, Major H.G. Carscallen, and the three subalterns to hurriedly mobilize the 4th's men, horses, and equipment. Horses had to be found and reluctant owners persuaded to part with them. Finding equipment and uniforms was perhaps less demanding for the 4th than for some batteries; it had outfitted a full complement for the summers at Petawawa.[7] The task was completed within ten days of the mobilization order, the job made easier by the fact that the 4th volunteered 'to a man.'[8]

Crerar also began a journal, which he kept consistently until November 1915. It records the blur of events from Crerar's departure from Hamilton through his first months in command of the 10th Battery. The entries convey a range of emotions and circumstances – the tedium of daily routine, the nervous excitement and relief of battle, and the daily hazards of the trenches. Crerar observed some years later, 'It was written for "family" perusal' and mindful of the censor's wary eye.[9] There was an enormous disparity between what he encountered and what he revealed to his family. He was typical in that he was torn between attempts to conceal the reality of what was happening from the loved ones at home and the need to convey enough of that experience so they would understand all the same. Few soldiers revealed the horrors they encountered, the problem being, in part, as Paul Fussell has so aptly put it, the near impossibility of finding words to describe the 'indescribable.'[10] Crerar was nevertheless adept at recording his observations. Gruesome details were left out, but he was more than willing to paint a realistic picture – and as the battery's censor he was able to provide more information than most.

The entries suggest the transformation of an enthusiastic, almost cocky, civilian-soldier, proud of his Hamilton roots, into a cool and confident officer, appalled by the slaughter but resigned to its necessity. There is an evident maturation in the observations. The journal's emotional rawness and weariness reveal the effects of it having been written as events occurred; its dry humour reflects Crerar's understated personality.

Entraining the 4th Battery's men, horses, guns, limbers, and ammunition proved difficult, but the infectious excitement was Crerar's most prominent memory. Crowds gathered to see the trains pull away; the troops were cheered at every stop. 'I never saw such a crowd,' Crerar noted, 'and the few minutes we were there will long stay in my memory.'[11]

Crerar's second duty was personal but no less pressing: make permanent a relationship recently struck up with an attractive and fun-loving debutante, seven years his junior, Miss Verschoyle Cronyn. Verse, as she was known to most, was the great-granddaughter of the distinguished Church of England clergyman Benjamin Cronyn, famed as a pioneering bishop in Huron County. The Cronyns had prospered during their years in Canada. Verse's father, Benjamin Barton Cronyn, was a successful businessman in Toronto. His station allowed his daughter to live the life of the young socialite in the small closed society that characterized Toronto in the pre-war years.[12] Harry and Verse met and courted in this social circle. The emotions generated by his imminent departure prompted him to forge a permanent union.[13]

Events conspired to overtake Crerar's ambitious plans. A bout with typhoid ended any hope for a quick marriage ceremony, but he still hoped to marry before going overseas.[14] Amid the excitement and confusion of Valcartier, with the responsibility of preparing his battery for war weighing heavily on his shoulders, Crerar excitedly reported that 'his lass' had sent him news of her father's imminent, and apparently coincidental, arrival in Quebec City. He hoped the two could get together to talk matters over, as tradition and manners dictated. 'I do so want my friends,' he wrote, 'to know the reason of my happiness. I don't believe in hiding the particular light of my life under a bushel so to speak.' However, despite their best efforts, Harry Crerar and Benjamin Cronyn missed each other. Tracking Crerar down amid the newly constructed city of 30,000 proved impossible, and Crerar's telegram detailing their meeting place arrived too late. A lengthy letter was the only alternative.[15]

II

At Valcartier, as one oft-quoted gunner observed, 'Life was busy.'[16] However, the artillery mobilized 'with far less confusion than the infantry'; integrating a section from the 6th Battery of London, to expand the pre-war establishment of four 18-pounders per battery to the six guns per battery required for the war, proved the most disheartening task. 'Can't say that [I] think an awful lot of Scandratt [London officer] as a Section commander,' he wrote with ill-disguised contempt. 'Looks ornamental – but doesn't accomplish a great deal.'[17] The 4th Battery was re-designated the 8th Battery of the 3rd Brigade under the command of Crerar's pre-war 2nd Brigade commander, Lieutenant-Colonel J.H. Mitchell, whom he also held in contempt. He was not shy about this perception in his diaries.[18]

The war was still far away; training and administration were the main responsibilities. Citizen-soldiers and newly purchased horses had to be trained as a unit to make the battery truly mobile in more than name; the approach to training, as well as the particulars, reflected the distance. 'This afternoon I took out a "ride" of sixty men – and shouted myself hoarse at them – in an endeavour to instill some principles of riding into their heads, hands and seats. There were some funny ones – really it was very hard to keep a straight face and call them down.'[19] Other duties were more mundane; the men had to be paid, examined, inoculated, drilled, and drilled some more. Horses had to be fed and cared for. There were daily trips from the battery lines to Headquarters to the Ordnance Stores, drawing supplies as they arrived direct from the manufacturers to gradually complete the battery's supplies; the paperwork was endless. Major Carscallen's duties often took him to Quebec. The major's 'large mantle [was] cast on my shoulders,' Crerar noted, 'and a bit heavy I've found it, too.'[20] The dietary changes of army life took their toll on the battery: 'Practically all of us have had our internal workings disturbed – Storms, Scandratt and Hendrio have all been uncertain as to appearances and disappearances' – as did the cold, wet, fall weather; Crerar's personal fortitude earned him the title 'iron man.'

Crerar evinced a schoolboy pride in his Hamilton roots and military heritage. Although he derided the efforts of the London section, he was inspired by the results of the battery's efforts on inspection, impressed with the effort required to prepare, mount, and parade the battery.[21] The pomp and circumstance of the reviews and march pasts soon outweighed their usefulness, however, and the constant rain delayed drill and depressed morale. After two tiring and wet weeks in camp, he noted with exasperation 'another review – for Sam Hughes' benefit and for the moving picture operators. A damn nuisance and a waste of time.'[22]

The expeditionary force decamped on 25 September.[23] Anticipation ran high as the battery packed and prepared to leave. The departure began as darkness fell on the 25th. Only once the battery was safely aboard their transport ship did he find the time to record his impressions. Crerar was given the job of preparing the battery, as the paperwork required for the move quickly overwhelmed the 8th's commanding officer. The decampment was a memorable scene for Crerar.

> It was raining and cold which did not improve conditions. We paraded at 5 P.M. ... The RCGA band was on the job – and filled in the couple of hours of waiting before our departure by discoursing various popular airs – 'It's a long way to Tipperary' and 'Auld Lang Syne' being the most popular. It was quite a sight in the gathering dusk – the big bonfires of rubbish on the camp lines giving just sufficient illumination to see by. The rain pelting down and the broken clouds scooting by. At eight-thirty we pulled out ... It was very dark and impossible to see more than thirty feet or so ahead. The road, at any time, terrible – was on account of the rain, a regular mud hole and from the start we had our hands full to keep the battery intact.

Astride a nervous mare, which kept him from snatching any sleep, Crerar took up the rear of the brigade column, ensuring that the slower transport and ammunition wagons kept up the pace. He recorded the size of the 8th Battery as six guns, eighteen ammunition wagons, four transport wagons, one water cart, six officers, 187 men, and 183 horses. Through a cold and rainy night, with the aid of 'some hard work and strong language,' the battery column slowly wound its way along the muddy road towards the rendezvous camp at the Quebec City Exhibition Grounds, arriving at four in the morning to await the order to board ship.

The battery boarded their transport, the *Gambion*, without event, one of the few to do so. There followed several days of waiting as the expeditionary force was loaded onto the remaining twenty-nine transports. At anchor in the St Lawrence by nightfall on 1 October, the transports made their way to the rendezvous at Gaspé Bay, and from there, out to sea. The sight of the lead ship laden with cheering 'foot sloggers,' passing by as its band played 'O, Canada' prompted reflection. 'It's a beautiful Canadian day,' Crerar wrote 'and the peaceful look of the country makes thoughts of this business of war seem out of place.' Sam Hughes, passing through the lines of transports provided his final thoughts: 'Hughes was on this job in a steam tug this a.m., an impossible person truly – and crazy about "centre stage."'[24]

'Voyage without special incident' reads the 11th Battery's historical section's report of the crossing.[25] Crerar occupied himself with thinking up physical and drill activities to keep the men and himself busy, attending to the horses, and brushing up on his French. He took advantage of such training as was available, attending war games, lectures, and practical drills in small arms firing. He also reflected on the imminent fighting, his entries a mix of concern and bravado: 'Vaccination is the order of the day ... If they'd only produce some anti-toxin for bullets now, we'd be absolutely safe ... Revolver practice was held in the P.M. for officers. I made top score with seven hits out of seven shots – by Himmel, the Germans better look out when I come along.' Crerar was impatient for the end of the passage. The convoy was able to move only at the speed of the slowest transport – a pace that, as a frustrated Crerar noted in his diary, was 'largely a waste of time and particularly hard on the horses.'[26]

His brigade commander bore the brunt of his frustration: 'The Colonel has his usual mental indigestion,' he observed before the convoy was at sea, 'if his brain his sufficiently developed to have such a complaint. I'm afraid I don't relish the idea of Col Mitchell as our leader on active service. He's not big enough for the job.' Crerar's contempt was untempered by the fact that Mitchell was his superior officer. He wrote of the colonel's 'petty' behaviour towards the men during the voyage and consoled himself with the conviction that 'he [wouldn't] last long when he [was] under supervision in England.'[27]

The lead transports entered Plymouth Sound on 14 October 1914. The congestion of the port kept the 8th on the *Gambion* for six more anxious days. Orderly Officer Crerar had the unenviable task of escorting 200 men and officers on their first, and only, shore leave where all, 'with the aid of a thirst acquired from weeks of abstinence, hit the can pretty severely.' He managed, to his own satisfaction, to bring them all back. Relief came as the battery's men and horses were finally unloaded on the 19th.

III

Seven hours on the train and a twelve-mile ride brought Harry and the battery to Salisbury Plain. Anticipation ran high. 'It's a pretty country,' he observed, 'rolling plains with patches of woods and I'm mighty anxious to get our guns and work on it.'[28] The rain quickly dissolved that anxiety. Rain, mud, and cold were probably the most prevalent memories of the Canadian's extended ten-week stay on Salisbury Plain, hindering all work at hand. Daily training became impossible as the mud disabled horses, men, and equipment; living in tents, the troops found life miserable. Weather became a preoccupation. 'If a day comes along that is really fine,' he noted in December, 'I'll sit down and write an essay on it – until I do understand all days to be wet, this to be understood in the superlative.' He explained himself a few lines later: 'It really is too bad about the weather – you see I can't get off the subject but it does hinder our work so.'[29] Morale was further weakened, in his opinion, by the constant inspections, ceremonial reviews, and enforced temperance; the high proportion of British immigrants in the division exacerbated the situation, he believed.[30] Crerar nevertheless admired the men's 'grit,' observing with pride 'that in spite of wet clothes and wet feet the men are wonderfully cheery, their only worry being the delay before getting to the firing line.'[31] His concern for the men under his command was in direct proportion to the vehemence of his views of Colonel Mitchell's handling of the brigade. In one instance he arrived back from leave to find the division paraded for inspection in the pouring rain. To his amazement, 3rd Brigade 'alone' was without greatcoats, a responsibility he laid squarely on the shoulders of the colonel.[32] Common sense and discipline were his prescriptions for dealing with citizens turned soldiers. He had little time for superiors who did not meet his exacting standards, and he was not shy in sharing his assessment, albeit at this stage only with family.

Numerous obstacles hindered efforts to train the battery. In addition to the weather, scarce space and ammunition severely limited practice firing with live ammunition. The Canadian batteries were unable to fire until the fourth week of January 1915. Training was disrupted further by the reorganization of the battery ordered on 17 November by the British War Office after conditions in the early stages of the war convinced them that the manoeuvre of six guns was too great a responsibility for a major. Establishments were subsequently reduced to four guns per battery and four batteries per brigade; the 10th Battery was re-designated the 11th.[33] While route marches and manoeuvres emphasized equitation and driving, enhancing the ability to bring the guns smartly into action, the static warfare and terrible conditions on the Western Front would negate the utility of much of this training. More important was the constant rehearsal of gun-laying, loading, and firing, practised until it became second nature.

Morale remained the main preoccupation of the officers. Crerar evinced no disappointment at the imminent departure of the London section – 'We will have a purely Hamilton section, pretty hard to beat let me tell you' – and he did not appear particularly put out by the prospect of changing the unit designations on all equipment, given the concurrent gain in morale.[34] Instead he concerned himself with the more immediate needs of the newly designated 11th Battery, arranging 'sham' battles and lecturing to the men regularly. He also secured extra clothing and any small comforts that he felt would ease the position of the men. All were eager to see the front.

Crerar's morale remained remarkably high, despite the tedium of daily routine; the men inspired him, as did eagerly awaited bits of news from home. Soon after his arrival, he travelled to London but did not find what he was expecting. 'Got back yesterday for four days in London,' he recorded. 'A funny London, with many reminders of war about.'[35]

Christmas leave was uneventful. Crerar returned to find the battery packing under orders to move to new accommodations in private homes north of the camp. This welcome change in early January was met with 'relief and general thanksgiving.'[36] The enthusiasm engendered by the relative comfort of their new surroundings was heightened by rumours of the division's impending departure. Crerar noted that shortfalls in equipment were being made up and that maps of the Ypres area had been issued.

The long-awaited orders came 26 January 1915. The division was to be moved to the west-country port of Avonmouth by unit from 7 February. Four cramped and 'extremely rough' days at sea – during which one man and several horses were killed – brought the Canadians to the French port of St Nazaire, but there was no relief at the end of the voyage. A stevedore's strike forced the seasick men to unload their own equipment and luggage.[37] After a brief rest, forty-eight hours by train landed the weary battery near Hazebrouck, where it marched in a driving rain to its billets, some fifteen miles behind the front. Peeling off the clothes he had worn for a week, Crerar bathed and went to sleep to the flashes of searchlights and star shells and the sounds of the big guns in the distance.

The 1st Canadian Division found itself in reserve to the 3rd Corps, British Second Army. A deadlock had descended on, or rather created the giant siege that became, the Western Front following the climactic battles of September and October 1914. A series of entrenched lines now stretched over five hundred miles from the coast of Belgium to the

Swiss border. In early 1915, one Belgian army, the French Eighth Army, and two British armies held the northern section of the line. The British Second Army, commanded by General Sir Horace Smith-Dorrien, was flanked on the left by the French Eighth and on the right by the British First Army, commanded by General Douglas Haig. The Second's position extended some seventeen miles from the Ypres–Comines railway across the valleys of the Lys and the Douve to Bois Grenier, three miles south of Armentières. The Canadian division was placed in reserve of the 3rd Corps section of the Ypres-Armentières line, the beginning of a long and bloody relationship in the region dubbed 'Flanders Fields.'

The artillery component of the division, like the infantry, was given a brief period of indoctrination into trench warfare and conditions through attachment to a British division. From 17 February, the artillery brigades spent ten days gaining practical experience in the conditions of the front lines. Only a small number of men, however, were permitted to go to the front. Brigade commanders, battery commanders, and subalterns received the first chance.[38] In effect, this meant that the majority of the gunners would begin their first tour of duty in the lines without experience.

Crerar was not among those to make the initial trip to the lines. Much to his regret, captains remained behind, charged with the responsibility for the batteries' men and equipment. Time weighed heavily on his hands; it was not yet a luxury.[39] Living conditions were relatively comfortable. His needs were looked after by his 'man' Dodd, and he supplemented the bland 'bully beef, hard tack and desiccated vegetables' with purchases of biscuits and chocolate as well as eggs from the local farmers. 'We don't eat badly,' he observed, 'witness my breakfast: one orange, fried eggs, ditto potatoes, toast, butter, jam and tea.' Gunners generally had an easier life than the front-line infantry. One 4th Canadian Division gunner recalled the atmosphere:

> The general set-up for a battery in action was that the guns would be out in a field with the gunners probably in a billet, maybe an old barn or something, and the officers in a house sleeping on the floor. The food was excellent. We always had canned butter, jam, bacon, tea, the odd bit of meat. We didn't suffer.[40]

In these circumstances, the mundane became a source of humour and amusement. He had his hair cut 'pretty much to the bone': 'The effect is not becoming but at least I am not troubled with the necessity of brushing my hair, though on the other hand, I am no longer sure as to where

I should stop when it comes to washing my face.' The terrain left him cold, however: 'Gooey [and] sticky ... after I've been walking ten minutes, I have at least five pounds of [Flemish mud] on either foot.'[41]

The war was still abstract and benign. 'A lot of humorous incidents among the tragic ones,' he wrote, 'all indications of the savoury sense of humour of the Anglo-Saxon.' The Germans too were viewed with humour, approaching war with a professionalism that was, at this point, lost on the British and Canadians who persisted in viewing it as a sport: 'The German soldier appears to take everything so damn seriously – goes to bed and gets up to the sounds of "Deutschland uber Alles."' He had a poor opinion of the French soldiers and hoped his division would not be moved to a French trench: 'I have heard some pretty unsavoury tales of the condition of the French trenches ... They apparently are terribly slack as to sanitation, especially as regards the proper disposal of the dead, leaving them pretty well where they drop and so their lines are no bed of roses.'[42] In truth, in 1915, neither the French nor British constructed suitable trenches. They feared their troops would lose the offensive spirit. To be fair, senior officers also optimistically predicted that the man-hours necessary to properly construct trenches and defensive positions were wasted when they would not be used for very long. The trenches were as likely to be dugouts and ditches, conforming to the topography of the area and connected by sandbags. Even later, the mud and water table of Flanders defeated the efforts of both sides to dig too deep, and the trench systems in the Ypres Salient were consequently more unpleasant than most.

The surreal atmosphere of Crerar's first days on the Continent was magnified by the survival of some semblance of the local pre-war society. He commented on how little damage had been done to the area around Ypres in early 1915; farmers still tilled the fields, oblivious to the occasional shell. The characteristic architecture of the town, like the Cloth Hall, was damaged but still intact. Crerar found the local inhabitants a 'peculiar mixture,' their friendliness and gratitude in direct relation to their proximity to the front. 'It's a funny warfare,' he observed. 'One feels quite annoyed if the Germans start shelling during mealtimes and as a matter of fact, they rarely do – and five o'clock tea is vigorously observed by the English and German alike.'[43] Each morning, promptly at seven, the 'bearer of eggs' delivered four of them right to his dugout. The buildup was all around him. He watched hundreds of trucks and buses crowd the roads as men and material of the empire moved closer to the fighting, but observed that 'where the paint has worn thin, one can see such inscriptions as "Dewars White Label" and "Pears Soap."' He added, 'Wouldn't mind a bottle of the former right now.' Eager to be in the thick of it, Crerar had to content himself with snatches of what lay in store from those who had experienced the line and from rumours of impending moves. He belittled the danger, saying it was safe enough if one was careful and lucky, and amusing himself with the job of censor.[44]

By 3 March, the Canadians were assigned some three miles of front, and the field artillery moved forward with its affiliated infantry brigade. The 3rd Artillery Brigade was attached to the 3rd Infantry Brigade: the 48th Toronto Highlanders, the 91st Hamilton, the Royal Scots – 'a fairly useful collection,' Crerar observed. The batteries, including the 11th, were sent into action 2,500 yards from the front, while one was kept in reserve. Crerar saw the signs of the impending move as the roads became crowded with military transport, 'all headed the one way and comprising our Divisional Supply and Ammunition Columns.'[45]

On 2 March 1915, the battery was en route to the firing line. Supervising the positioning of the wagons, Crerar spent the next few days moving ammunition up to the battery. His excitement and fascination grew as the German shellfire burst close by and fellow officers of the battery recounted the hazards of duty near the front. He admired their courage and good humour in the face of danger; like most soldiers, he longed to be tested and not found wanting. For many at the front, their greatest fear was breaking under the strain of battle and through one's fear endangering the lives of others.[46]

Crerar was soon given an opportunity to prove himself. The British High Command planned to send Haig's First Army, on the Canadian right, to wipe out the salient centred on the village of Neuve Chapelle and the Aubers Ridge three miles beyond. This latter position dominated the British positions, and the Germans used every opportunity to make life unpleasant for the British troops, including directing their sewage into the enemy's lines. Forty-eight British battalions, supported by an artillery concentration that yard for yard would not be matched until Passchendaele in 1917, would attack on 10 March. The 1st Canadian Division was assigned the task of creating a diversion to stop the German troops in its sector from reinforcing the battle area.[47] The divisional artillery was instructed to engage obvious targets, but ammunition was to be carefully husbanded – a maximum of 180 rounds for the three batteries engaged – limits that would shortly prompt a political crisis in the United Kingdom.

Crerar spent the three days prior to the Battle of Neuve Chapelle in the infantry trenches obtaining a feel for the area that the 11th Battery was to cover – 'a useful experience ... one I won't forget in a hurry.'[48] He and his CO supervised the shoot in support of the British attack as the 11th engaged targets identified by an infantry observation officer. The battery functioned well, coming under only desultory fire from the Germans. The Canadian field artillery had no eighteen-pound high-explosive shells at this point, however; they, like the British army, were hindered by a shortage of shells, which persisted into 1916.[49] Nevertheless, the 11th and the two other batteries of 3rd Brigade together fired off 445 shells, 265 more than their allotment. It was, for Crerar, 'excellent practice' and an innocuous introduction to battle.[50]

The British offensive failed. After five days, and a missed opportunity to exploit one of the few complete breaches of the German lines, the British attack stalled in the face of stiffening German opposition and was called off. At a cost of 12,892 casualties, the gains were small, and the lessons learned would be relearned at even greater cost.[51] Crerar was impressed with the devastation wrought by the artillery fire – 'Every building was knocked flat as if it had been a house of cards' – and by the accuracy achieved by the battery guided by precision directions, the result of the innovations in the system of shooting by map.[52] Indeed, aspects of the battle portended well for the artillery and its proper application. Command and control procedures were refined to increase the accuracy and effectiveness of artillery fire: timetables were introduced, giving batteries prearranged objectives, and a beginning was made at directing shoots by map. However, deficiencies were evident. As noted by the artillery's official history, the 'operation emphasized the need for extending the scope of fire control at the divisional or higher level. Communications must be tremendously improved, and a greater use made of air observation. Above all was the need for developing an effective means of dealing with the enemy guns.'[53]

The Canadian division's infantry remained in the Fleurbaix sector of the front for two 'relatively quiet' weeks until it went into reserve on 27 March. The artillery was given no such respite. The 11th spent the several days after Neuve Chapelle on what seemed like 'a tour of Northeastern France in twenty four hours,' the highlight of which was an attachment to the British 8th Division. 'Quite a compliment,' Crerar observed, 'but still I prefer to fight with our own chaps,' a comment that reflected Crerar's ambivalent attitudes towards the British in person, although not in the abstract. At the end of the month, he recorded his feelings about the British officers: 'They are a funny lot, the English officers – I either find them tremendously to my liking – quiet keen chaps with abundance of humour and fellow feeling or else they are quite the limit – overbearing unintelligent snobs. There seems to be no half way house with them.'[54]

The Canadians' attachment to the Imperials was brief, and within a day an exhausted Captain Crerar led an equally tired battery back to its original positions.

Crerar's adaptation to the front was quickly characterized by the assumption of what one author has called the 'style of utter sang-froid,'[55] affecting an unflappable persona in the face of the dangers around him; as the casualties mounted, he tried to depersonalize the losses, but found it difficult.

> We lost many [at Neuve Chapelle] though in comparison, the number was not extravagant to the advantages gained and bigger losses inflicted – still, over five hundred officer casualties tells a pretty bitter tale. And there is no love lost between that Division and the Germans. The NCO telling the Major of the German counter-attack after the trenches had been stormed, said: 'We waited for 'em – smiling – covered up to our necks, and when they came in close, we gave it to 'em and piled the bastards up five deep' – not pretty or funny but just war.[56]

IV

The divisional artillery was moved northward to a new training area in the first week of April, near the ancient Belgian town of Ypres. Ypres and the surrounding area was one of the last pieces of Belgian territory still in Allied hands. The line surrounding the town formed a deep salient some seventeen miles long that bulged into German-held territory. Surrounded on three sides by German lines, the salient was as tactically untenable as it was politically important. The British Empire had gone to war for 'poor little Belgium,' and the German disregard for both the international law that guaranteed Belgium's neutrality and British strategic sensibilities that could not countenance a 'great power' so close to the channel. The salient was a potent symbol, as well as an important communication and supply juncture. The Allied High Command insisted it be held. The French Eighth Army had been responsible for the defence of the area since the liberation of Ypres in the fall of 1914, but at the insistence of French Commander-in-Chief General Joffre, the

British Second Army extended its section of the line north to include the Ypres Salient. The move began on 1 April 1915. It was the beginning of a long and costly relationship, for the British and empire troops would suffer over a million casualties holding the seventeen-mile stretch of front.

The infantry of 1st Canadian Division began its move to the salient on 14 April. Four days later, batteries of the 2nd and 3rd Brigades, Canadian Forces Artillery (CFA), replaced the French artillery. Crerar's brigade moved forward, surrounded by the departing French troops – 'sloppy little devils, the men – hairy faces and seemingly fairly old' – and billeted near the front at Poperinghe to await the order to take over the new section. A hasty review and some kind words from General Smith-Dorrien on the outfit's disposition and ability left Crerar and the brigade feeling 'rather chesty.' 'It's extremely satisfactory,' he noted, 'to feel that work has been appreciated' – a familiar refrain for the position-conscious and emotional young captain.

In sharp contrast to his desire for personal recognition, Crerar's distaste for publicity was evident. He commented on the publication of a letter from a fellow battery officer, Lieutenant Hendrie: 'I was amused at Hendrie's letter being published. His old man, the Hon. J.S. should know better. It's contrary to Army orders and good taste to publish a personal letter bearing on corps matters.' Concerned with the damage that could be done by indiscretion and false impressions, he launched into an emotional tirade: 'Such rot I never read before. About on par with the effusions of E. Barrieford Topp, special correspondent to the *Mail Empire*, etc I'd like to meet that little swine, but by the drivel he talks, he must be no nearer to the seat of the fighting than the Savoy Hotel, London.'[57]

Such distractions were soon far away. The German Fourth Army, whose objective was to eliminate the bulge in their lines to draw attention away from an offensive in the east, planned an assault to take the Yser Canal south to, and including, the town of Ypres, simultaneously using and testing the effectiveness of a new weapon, chlorine gas.[58] Four divisions were allotted the task of wiping out the salient. Their initial target was the French-held four-and-a-half-mile section of trench line that followed the rolling countryside from the Belgian lines near Langemarck to the Canadian positions along the Poelcappelle–St Julien road. On 20 April, a German forty-two-centimetre howitzer dropped a 2,000-lb. shell on Ypres, signalling the beginning of a general bombardment.

The 11th Battery moved forward in the thick of the German barrage on the twentieth. Crerar led half the battery's guns in column under shellfire through Ypres, successfully getting 'the guns in and teams out without any trouble' and retiring to the wagon lines and Brigade Ammunition column. Unfortunately for the Canadians, the French believed in lightly manning the front line and constructed their defensive works accordingly. This view came as a great shock to the Canadians, who found the trenches in a 'deplorable state.' The week before the German attack had been spent bringing the trenches up to British standards, a job made especially difficult by the mud, which prevented the men from digging down further than two feet. While the 11th's men at the front frantically constructed new positions south of Gravenstafel Ridge, Crerar worked to ensure the safety of the men and horses as shells rained down on the wagon lines 'fully a mile and three quarters from our own battery' but, because of the horseshoe shape of the line, they were 'quite as near the firing line as the battery itself.'[59] His responsibilities took him back and forth between the wagon lines and the battery's front-line position – a gruelling mile and a quarter through the mud and under fire, mainly on foot: 'One can't ride up to within a mile of the battery by day.'

The German bombardment caused a growing number of casualties. Death was still unfamiliar and Crerar was shaken.

> I was in Wipes this morning [the 20th] and before leaving tried to see Trum Warren and Bob Cory ... I couldn't find them and this afternoon I heard that Trum was killed during the shelling. Poor old chap – he was one of the best. It has made us all feel very blue ... It will take a lot to make me forgive those swine for killing Trum Warren. They've surely got a lot to answer for.

The 21st brought no respite:

> It was our turn today and Billy Young was plugged in the thigh by a rifle bullet ... They got all around the guns with their shells yesterday – one landed just five feet away from No. 1 and quite a few were dropping in the afternoon while I was up there. We are moving back into reserve tonight ... In a way, I'm sore about it, because we had registered their trenches so beautifully.[60]

It was a clear, sunny day on 22 April 1915, but there was no relief for the 11th. Crerar looked for alternative cross-country routes for the journey from the battery to its wagons and limbers, especially important in light of the impending relief of the 11th by sections of the 2nd Brigade's 8th Battery. He remembered, 'The enemy shelling of targets in the salient had noticeably increased during the previous couple of days and St Julien, through which my ammunition wagons and supplies normally passed enroute to the gun position, was becoming a place to avoid, if at all possible.'[61] Crerar was on the point of returning to the battery's wagon lines on the afternoon of the 22nd when he observed a greenish haze spreading 'along part of our front and to our left. A few minutes later, our eyes began to smart and our throats to choke and we understood.' He had encountered a small portion of the 160 tons of chlorine gas just released by the Germans into the light northeast wind; simultaneously, a call came in for intensive covering fire from the battery's forward observation officer in the lines with the 48th Highlanders. The attack had begun.

The return was harrowing. Eyes smarting and lungs choking for air, Harry sped off on his bike. At that moment the German barrage lifted from the French lines and concentrated its full might on the Canadians. 'It was Hell cut loose – that's all,' he recalled. Avoiding the village of St Julien, which was then going up in 'chunks,' he set out cross-country until he was forced back onto the St Julien–Wieltje–Ypres road, which was 'getting a lot of attention from the German artillery ... I had so many narrow escapes on my ride back that I haven't stopped marvelling yet.' Blown off his bike into a ditch by the concussion from one shell-burst within 'a couple of yards,' he was momentarily stunned but unhurt. He got underway minus a few spokes, but clutching a pebble that he kept for the rest of his life as a good luck charm.[62]

Crerar returned to find the teams hooked in, and the limbers, ammunition wagons, and all mounted men moved from their exposed position to the cover of a nearby ridge; the old position was already under long-range machine-gun fire. The new position, however, proved little better. The men of the French 45th (Algerian) and 87th (Territorial) divisions, many of them 'badly affected by gas,' had begun, he wrote,

> pouring over the next ridge [through the 11th's wagon lines] – regularly beating it I'm afraid and the German rifle fire came momentarily closer. Their planes were over head and their shell fire was all over them and us. As the shells caught up to us, I moved the wagons and teams slowly back – no flurry or excitement among our men at all and [I] kept sending orderlies [to try and establish contact with the battery commander].

I assumed that one of these successive orderlies would have the luck to get through and finally back to me.[63]

One did return, carrying orders to take up the gun limbers and move the battery to a position north of the village of Wiltje. Because the German attack had interrupted the relief of the 11th Battery, the left section of the 11th and the right section of the 8th Battery were fighting as a composite unit and would do so for the rest of the battle. Crerar was responsible for moving these sections, with the Germans less than a 1,000 yards off.

'We got orders to move the guns. We did – under shell fire.' Colonel Mitchell, the brigade CO, on instructions from Divisional HQ, ordered the harried batteries to withdraw. Driving the horses 'at the trot, and ... through heavy shell areas at the canter,' Crerar reached the Battery HQ near St Julien, losing one mounted signaller and his horse, both losses weighing on him. He found the battery cut off from its infantry battalion but 'very much in action,' although by later accounts to little effect, as they 'continued to fire to their front rather than engage uncertain targets.'[64]

Crerar's men worked through the night limbering the guns for the move. At dusk on the 23rd, they moved out along roads now congested with troops moving up and transports full of gassed and wounded men going back. It was nightfall before they reached their new positions near the GHQ Line just southwest of Wieltje. The situation was now so fluid that the 3rd Brigade's batteries were less than four hundred yards from the Germans, who were pressing down on an open left flank for which the guns were not sighted. A German attack in force over Frezenberg and Bellewarde ridges to the east caught the battery with guns just unlimbered. Small arms fire caused a number of casualties among the battery's horses, and it became obvious the position was untenable:

> There, we had another narrow squeak. The Germans attacked in force and got within a few hundred yards of us. It was a tense quarter of an hour – shell fire and rifle fire this time – the German flares lighting up the blackness. All our batteries had a number of casualties here. I don't think any of us expected to get through.

During a lull in the fighting the battery was ordered to a position west of Potijze, which they reached in short order.

Crerar took temporary command of the battery near Potijze, relieving the exhausted CO. He directed the fire of the battery for the next twenty hours continuously, through the night and into the morning of the 24th. It was frustrating, tough work. The battery was shelled from three sides and was unable to answer calls for help from the 15th Battalion of the 48th Highlanders, under gas and artillery attack as it defended St Julien.

Ordered to shift his unit by daylight, Crerar was forced to pass through Ypres 'chased up by shell fire nearly all the way' in search of a new battery position, only to have the order countermanded: 'It was a devil of a place to pass through. I went ahead with two men to try and locate the least dangerous route – an unenviable job – for the only way was to determine where most of the shells were falling. However, we got through – losing one man and a horse.'

The battery maintained its position at Potijze under constant shelling for another seven days, firing in support of the British, French, and Canadian counterattacks and breaking up German attacks. 'Shells came in from three sides here. Our position is fairly ploughed up with their holes – one, just ten feet from No. 1 gun is twelve feet diameter by six deep – yet our battery casualties have been wonderfully low to date. I wonder how long our good fortune will continue.'[65]

On 28 April, the Germans began shelling the position with a heavier weight of shell, adding to the strain.

> Have been shelled very heavily since yesterday afternoon – big fellows – coal-box type – coming over four at a time. The roar of their coming and the frightful concussion of their burst are mighty hard on us all, though our fortune stays of the best. Both my horses were wounded – though slightly, praise be. We are busy firing now as always have been for the last eight days.[66]

Locating the 11th's position, the Germans redoubled their efforts on the 30th. High-explosive 'coal-boxes' (from 150-mm heavy howitzers, known for their noise), 'Jack Johnsons' (named after the world heavyweight boxing champion of 1908–15), and 'plain brutes' ploughed up the area, and concussion shook the ground for a quarter mile, sending earth and shell fragments in all directions.

> The Germans seem to have an unlimited quantity of big guns and howitzers and they surely are not idle. They unfortunately have the battery

position located. It takes just plain 'guts' to fight our guns under the circumstances let me tell you. Half of us pull out to occupy new positions tonight. I stay to carry on with the remainder and follow tomorrow, God willing. I must confess, I'll be relieved when we arrive there safely – we've had a terribly nerve wracking ten days of it and a change will be a wonderful relief.[67]

Crerar retained a grim humour and pride about his experience in the face of the destruction.

It's extraordinary how one becomes [adept] in 'forecasting' shells. We know almost to a yard the line of flight of a shell by the noise it makes and consequently, can economize in the practice of ducking to a wonderful extent. We all have a profound respect for the 'Johnsons' – they are plain brutes. They generally come at us in fours – their concussion shakes the very earth for a quarter of a mile around and they send fragments of the shell to about the same radius. The base of one of the 17 inch shells after travelling about half a mile back from where the shell exploded in Wipes, buried itself 10 feet in a field not far from the line – it weighed 164 pounds – a disagreeable little souvenir all right.[68]

Relief came that same day. The exhausted British and French were determined to save their strength for the forthcoming Allied offensive against Arras, which would include a futile French attack against a German strongpoint on a ridge named for the village of Vimy. Recognizing the German artillery's dominance over the whole area as far as Poperinghe, the Allied commanders withdrew their forces to new positions on the old GHQ Line from Wieltje to Potijze and under Sanctuary Wood. On 1 May, the divisional batteries scattered around Potijze began their withdrawal. Colonel Mitchell ordered the batteries of 3rd Brigade moved west of the Yser Canal. It was welcome news.

'I really don't believe,' Crerar recorded in his diary on 29 April 1915, 'any of us expected to have endured a week of battle such as this one has been ... A good many thousands of us haven't but have been killed in the fighting of it ... The Canadians have made a name – a real name and have done one of the big things of the war.'[69] Crerar's diary entry captured the shock, horror, and pride felt by many of the survivors of the Second Battle of Ypres. The battle introduced the Canadians to the realities of modern warfare, with its immense capacity for death and destruction; 6,036 men, half the Canadian division's infantry, were casualties. Each of the three artillery brigades' losses of guns and horses were similar in proportion, although their men were spared the full enormity of the losses.[70]

The battery was blasted for several more days in its new positions; on 2 May, one shell exploded, Crerar recorded, 'about twenty paces from where I wrote. It rained dirt and shell splinters for ten seconds after that one struck.' It was his last entry for four days. On the 3rd, the Germans attempted one last assault: 'We had a tight half hour of it. The infantry couldn't stick it and had to pull back several hundred of yards but in the meantime our artillery had opened up such a rate of fire along their parapet that the Germans were held behind it and as soon as the gas dissipated, our chaps took up the ground again.'[71]

The wind had dispersed the gas, and the Allied artillery, including all the Canadian batteries, held the Germans to their parapets until the front lines were reoccupied. The fourth of May found Crerar rejoining the battery near Brielen – 'a relief, as in it we only were shelled from one direction.' The Canadian divisional artillery's support of British 4th Division continued, but over the next five days each battery was brought out of the line for some much-needed rest. Finally on 6 May, the 11th Battery was sent back for two days of recuperation.[72]

The strain of the constant exposure to shellfire and the unsettling effects of the huge casualties the Canadians had taken during the fighting at Ypres were evident. A few days after the 11th was withdrawn from the firing line, after an encounter with an acquaintance, serving with the 48th Highlanders, Crerar reflected on the battle: 'Was in Armetieres with Alex Mackenzie for a while yesterday. It has escaped wonderfully easily considering how close the Germans are and their usual idea of destroying everything in sight ... It's great to see an old friend these days, so many have gone on. There's mighty few of the original 48th left.'

News from home, while welcome, left him feeling melancholy. 'Felt quite homesick when [Adam] left,' he observed after the departure of an old friend. 'He was sort of a touch from another world and I am awake for hours thinking and wondering.'[73]

> It cleared a bit today and it's mostly warm and summer like. There seemed to be very little doing anywhere along the line but then there must be a reaction after three weeks of slaughter. I really can't see how it can last through the summer ... Still we expect action any moment. There's a certain tenseness in the air and troops are continually on the move.[74]

Although Crerar continued to write of 'finishing the job,' the bravado of the early weeks of the war was gone.

> The pity of this killing business gets me sometimes. War is so very truly hell and this yard by yard fighting finds it at its worst. The gains are so small when it comes to distance – it just resolves itself into a case of counting corpses, if we have fewer than they, it's a 'victory.' There is no romance in such as that. We'll beat them some day but they'll never be able to pay their just debt, the swine, not in this world anyway.[75]

The details of the Second Battle of Ypres and the Canadians' role in it are well known. It was a test of endurance and courage. It was a defensive battle, and the Canadians were applauded for their endurance. But mistakes were made. Hastily improvised frontal assaults were destroyed by machine-gun fire. Staff work was lacking, although in the end the Canadians, and British, held.[76] It was not until the crisis of the battle had passed that Crerar was fully aware of the important contribution that the Canadians and his battery had made to the outcome of the battle. For over a week the battery was in almost continuous action; he had little time for reflection. It was, however, an important turning point for Crerar. Before Ypres, his eagerness to be a forward observation officer was evident when he referred to it as the 'best job going.' Two months later, he 'would be more content if the Major would let me take my trick on that job [instead of my men] for it's not a very pleasant one under the circumstances [the unburied dead].'[77]

The battle was also Canada's baptism of fire. Canadians, at least those at the front like Harry Crerar, started to see the war, if not all war, differently after that battle. For Crerar, the romantic ideal was fading, although not the patriotism, replaced by both a determination to learn the art of soldiering and an intense hatred for the Germans – 'anything to kill is surely their motto.' By the end of 1915, Crerar's diary reflected his grim determination to see the war through to the bitter end.

3 The Killing Ground

I

The Second Battle of Ypres killed Crerar's romantic idea of war, but not his belief in the causes for which he was fighting. A taciturn and cautious Harry Crerar emerged from that battlefield. Steady promotion in the Canadian Corps artillery marked the next three years. Exposed to one of the most innovative branches of the corps, Crerar absorbed and applied the lessons revealed by the early engagements about the strengths and limitations of the artillery. He became an accomplished technician and staff officer, methodical and dedicated, but with a growing ambition. Yet he never forgot what was at stake, a belief confirmed by the cost of the next few years.

The battle was the beginning of over seven months of steady activity in the firing line for Crerar, fighting punctuated by only the briefest of rests. The Canadians remained in Flanders for another year. The Canadian artillery supported the British offensives at Festubert in May, Givenchy in June, and Loos in September 1915. The artillery shelled the Germans daily, and were shelled in return – registering for attacks, harassing repair parties, holding the Germans on their front while more serious operations were undertaken, or simply trying to inflict as many casualties as possible on the enemy. Through 1915, the German predominance in heavy guns continued while severe shortage of heavy calibres, confusion at the highest levels over the employment of artillery fire, and ammunition shortages as well as unreliability, handicapped the British and French.[1] In the firing line, the vulnerability of the Canadian eighteen-pounders and the men who manned them was pronounced and frustrating. Crerar observed that one could get used to the small shell but the high explosives were always 'nerve wracking.' The unit history describes the steady attrition of the battery.[2]

Crerar's increasingly haphazard and hurried entries into his personal journal reflected a new focus on the military as a profession, in part because it was necessary for advancement, in part to survive. He applied for a course in aircraft–artillery cooperation in April; using aircraft to find targets for the artillery was an innovation pioneered by the British. Counter-battery staffs did not standardize procedures until 1916, however. Crerar's professional development was still largely undirected at this stage. Idealism, not the ambition that marked later endeavours, shaped his actions. Approached informally soon after the Second Battle of Ypres about the 'permanent end of the game,' he was cautious, noting that while he would be hard pressed to refuse an advance in rank, he 'hated the thought of leaving the Hamilton crowd.'[3] Promotion interested him, but he declared his preference for a battery command over a staff appointment when both were presented as potential options.[4]

Despite, or perhaps because of, Crerar's preference, Colonel Mitchell recommended Crerar as an officer specially qualified for a staff appointment, and in mid-August, Crerar was attached to the Divisional General Staff 'for instructional purposes.' In the front lines and at brigade headquarters, he observed gun emplacements and communications, reporting his observations to the CO. Crerar did not record his reaction to Mitchell's recommendation, but on completion of his time as a General Staff 'learner,' Crerar was offered a choice of two positions – GSO 3 under Mitchell, or temporary command of the 10th Battery. He chose the battery over the faster track for promotion.[5]

Command of a battery, the 'fire unit' of a brigade, exposed Temporary Major Crerar to a new level of tactical and administrative experience. (Crerar had been acting commander of the 11th from 22 July when Major Carscellen became acting brigade commander.)[6] He was now responsible for fighting as well as the administration of the battery. All calculations, orders relating to firing, selections of battery positions, organization of observation posts and ammunition supplies, as well as communication and liaison with the infantry came under his purview.[7] In practice, this meant a great deal of time in the trenches, endless rounds of inspection of the firing line and forward posts, responsibility for morale, selection of subalterns, dealing with massive quantities of official inquiries brought daily by runners, and hastily answered field messages. The increased weight of his duties was also reflected in the rapid decline of both the quality and quantity of entries in the journal.

The records are scanty, but Crerar's command seemed to be characterized by thorough preparation, attention to detail, and personal care for his men. Crerar familiarized himself with his section of the front and brought the battery's position up to his standards. His notes and journal record his attention to detail. He noted that his unit's observation post was 'too prominent and tempting for the enemy artillery,' and moved it accordingly. He spent much of his time in the trenches 'getting the country in my mind' and getting to know the infantry on his front, a practice he continued and emphasized as the battery relocated over the next months.[8] He took great pains to perfect safe posts and to ensure the men's comfort, especially as the ground turned to mud with the fall rains. He tried to anticipate the difficulties that the knee-deep mud would bring and pushed the men to strengthen their shelters.[9]

Through the fall of 1915, in addition to a daily routine of shelling and being shelled, the 10th Battery was part of the recently formed Canadian Corps' effort to support the British offensive against the town of Loos, in support of the larger French offensive against Artois and Champagne.[10] The Canadians were fortunate to be spared heavy involvement in these ultimately fruitless attacks, but they were required to stage diversionary attacks and trench raids. The artillery was also called on for wire cutting and providing enfilade fire for the infantry raids. It was dangerous work, even during the routine periods. Crerar's dairy entry for 14 October illustrates the nature of the periods of 'quiet':

> Four days ago, we've moved from our old position near Plug Street [Ploegsteert], to this spot opposite Messines ... The few days have been eternally busy ones. I've been out observing fire or registering targets most of the time. Also locating observing stations and my nights have been interrupted by the fragment arrival of orderlies with memos as to plans for the next day ... [Yesterday] we shelled wire entanglements for an hour, then put H.E. into his trenches ... The Hun grew very excited ... so we dropped our fire onto his parapet again and let him have it for a few minutes.

He recorded many close calls as the Germans retaliated: 'A shell landed just the other side on a sand bag traverse which I was beside, covering me, and my telephonist and my maps with mud, but, happily, that was all.' The fall rains brought 'mud oozing up around ones ankles.' A court of enquiry held to investigate the suicide of a gunner from the 11th was given a passing mention, but, unable to recall the gunner's name, he characterized him as 'no-account.' Crerar was aware that the experience was hardening him. Late in September, he noted the 'awful rumpus' when a 'shell dropped in the next farm ... killing a man and the poor devils have all come in here to weep about it. Such is war – a year ago, I would have been horrified as it is I say "tough luck" and go on about my day's job.' He concluded the entry: 'It doesn't do to let one's mind dwell too much on the piteous side of this business.'[11]

Crerar's tenure as acting commander of the 10th Battery ended in the fall of 1915. On Major King's return, he relinquished his temporary rank, reverting to captain. He did so with regret. He was now supernumerary to the establishment of the 11th and was faced with the choice of retaining his rank and returning to the British Isles until employment could be found, or voluntarily reverting to a rank at which he could be absorbed. Rather than leave the front, he chose to revert to captain, but only after several days of great effort to ensure the retention of his seniority; a misprint in the *Gazette* that he had reverted in rank at his own request caused him considerable consternation. He was particularly concerned at how it would appear to his family.[12]

He made an impression in command of the battery. 'I am sorry to hear you are losing the 10th Battery,' wrote one superior. 'I know the work you put into the battery – and its results.' He was proud of it himself. He fiercely defended his battery's record, writing a lengthy refutation of an accusation that shells fired by the 10th had dropped short.[13] His command ended on 7 December 1915. Arrangements had already been made to place him on the staff as an adjutant to the OC, 3rd Brigade, but instead, after a seven-day delay in England trying to secure passage on a ship, he took a rare seven-week leave back home.[14]

Harry Crerar returned to Canada to marry Verse Cronyn. The news of his imminent arrival excited some interest in the society sections of the Toronto and Hamilton dailies as they announced the upcoming union.[15] It was nevertheless a subdued affair – simple but elegant, a fitting ceremony for this private couple. Archdeacon Cody of St Paul's Anglican in Toronto read the service on 14 January 1916. There were no attendants except a service friend who served as best man. After the ceremony, both families retired to the Cronyn home for a reception.[16]

Crerar had another month's leave in Canada before he and his new bride sailed from New York, a move that left the army temporarily unaware that he had come back at all. Verse stayed in England as a volunteer nurse, working at a hospital at Kingston-on-Thames; she went back only for their first child, daughter Margaret, to be born in Canada. Crerar returned to France on 22 February as an adjutant to the 3rd Brigade Headquarters, minus his kit, which had disappeared on the voyage. For the next month he was the office manager of the HQ.[17] The position fitted well with his organizational and administrative abilities, but he wanted a field command.

II

The reorganization and expansion of the corps infantry and artillery in early 1916 provided the opening he needed to obtain a command. Major Carscallen became commanding officer of the 9th Brigade in March 1916, leaving a vacancy at the 11th Battery, filled by Crerar on 25 March; Crerar also moved quickly to ensure that his seniority dated from August 1915. 'Otherwise,' he worried, 'my seniority would be very seriously affected. Juniors to me who have since been appointed would outrank me although I was senior to them some months ago.'[18] Reassured again, he held this position, with several important interruptions, until August 1917.

Major Crerar fought his battery through most of the important engagements of 1916 and 1917. The winter of 1915–16 has been characterized as one 'of relatively little activity'[19] in the Ypres Salient, a view the men who held the salient would not share. In late March the Canadians' section of the Ypres front became more active with the British decision to wipe out a German-held salient near St Eloi. The bitter and confused battles for the St Eloi craters, in which the artillery was able to offer the infantry little help, were followed by struggles over obscure pieces of ground whose names might have little meaning except for the lives they cost. On 2 June 1916, the Germans attacked the Canadian positions near Sanctuary Wood, virtually wiping out two Canadian units, and taking high ground designated only by its measure in metres above sea level. The corps commander, Lieutenant-General Sir Julian Byng, decided to mount a set-piece counterattack to retake some of the high ground. The battles for Hills 61 and 62 (Tor Top) and for Mont Sorrel, fought in the torrential rain and in swamp-like conditions, provided the classroom in which the Canadians began to learn the techniques that would bring them success later in the war. Rather than launching an immediate attack, the Canadian artillery took time to register targets, using new aerial reconnaissance, while the infantry methodically planned its assault. Byng gathered 218 guns, including Crerar's battery. The result was a success and a model for future operations.

Crerar's battery moved south to the Somme later that summer, leaving behind the mud and shattered remnants of Sanctuary Wood. During the summer and fall, he fought his battery through some of the bloodiest battles of the Somme offensives: Flers-Courcelette and Regina Trench were local attacks in support of the larger British attempts to break the German defensive line. Some could be characterized as aimless and wasteful, but the British and Canadians slowly learned the tactics, communication, and coordination necessary to achieve small operational victories. The German High Command felt the Somme was the graveyard of their army. The total casualties came close to one million dead and wounded, but led to a more intense prosecution of the war, not less. For Crerar, the only bright spot was the birth of his daughter Margaret.

Through 1916–17, the ammunition, armaments, and equipment available to the British and Canadians were catching up to the realities of the modern battlefield; the infantry was also reorganized and rearmed to better reflect the state of siege warfare on the Western Front. Many of the changes were initiated from the front lines as unit and formation commanders and staffs struggled to overcome the 'riddle of the trenches.' The Canadian Corps' artillery was particularly effective in adapting its role in the absence of any direction from the British High Command, making changes in its organization and command structure through 1916.[20] The Canadian Corps was the first to have a GOC, Royal Artillery, as a distinct command rather than as an advisor; artillery tactics were now defined by the needs of the infantry and technology instead of tactics conforming to the command structure. In addition to improving its infantry support role, the artillery gradually increased the quality of the fire-control techniques. Improvements were made in gun control, scientific calibration techniques, communication, intelligence-gathering methods, and target registration.[21] The Canadian artillery proved itself to be one of the most progressive branches of the Canadian Corps.

Problems remained, stemming from ammunition shortages and deficiencies as well as inexperienced commanders. Crerar recalled his experience on the Somme:

> I was commanding a battery at the Somme and the use of guns to cut wire at that time was very inefficient because we used the eighteen pounder

mainly. We cut it with a fused shell and if you didn't get your fuse to go off at the right instant in the air, you wouldn't get your bullets to come out the right place and it was very expensive in ammunition.[22]

The failure to cut the wire was also costly in men's lives. Close to 60,000 British and colonial troops were killed and wounded on 1 July alone, many as they struggled to find gaps in wire uncut and were decimated by German defenders, shaken but unharmed by the preceding week-long bombardment.

On his arrival at 11th Battery, Crerar brought in competent and familiar officers – not always an easy task, given the daily 'wastage'; by April 1916 he was facing a shortage of officers.[23] Bombardier James Logan, 39th Battery, attached to the 11th Battery in July 1916 as a learner, observed that the carefully constructed gun pits he found compared favourably, in his opinion, with those available elsewhere. Logan also noted that they were improved upon as the battery found itself in a better location.[24] At that time, techniques developed to enhance accuracy were quickly transmitted to the battery and brigade commanders, as were improved methods of positioning and construction designed to increase the protection afforded the gun crews. For his own improvement, Crerar took advantage of the relative quiet that characterized the front in the winter, as the corps moved north to the area in front of the village of Vimy, attending a five-week refresher Gunnery Course at Whitley Camp in England in February 1917.[25]

In March 1917, soon after Crerar's return from the Gunnery Course, the battery found itself facing the daunting defences of Vimy Ridge. The Canadian Corps' achievement in taking and holding Vimy in April 1917 is well known and was remarkable for a number of reasons, not least of which was the impressive coordination between the artillery fire-plan and the infantry's objectives. The Canadians succeeded where the French had failed, implementing the principle that 'the artillery conquers and the infantry occupies' through a precise and methodical plan of attack. This approach translated into a carefully registered and measured application of all the firepower at the corps' disposal, as well as some additional batteries from the British, to blast a path for the attacking infantry, neutralize hostile batteries, and break up counterattacks. The effectiveness of the plan was enhanced by the implementation of improved methods for location, accuracy, and communication and by the availability of the proper weight of shell. The battery's firepower improved when its complement of guns was increased to six guns in March, with the addition of a new section from the 54th Battery. The Canadians' preparations were also aided by the failure of the German Sixth Army defenders to fully implement the changes in defensive doctrine laid down by its high command. Secure in their success to date, and limited by topography, the Germans not only defended the forward slope of the ridge, but left most of the defenders in the forward lines, while the reserves were well back of the front lines. The Sixth Army commander was subsequently sacked.

The 11th Battery's role in the Canadian victory at Vimy began on 20 March with the scheduled thirteen-day preliminary bombardment. This was followed by an 'intensive phase,' more appropriately called 'the week of suffering' by the Germans, which lasted until the early morning hours of 9 April, the day scheduled for the attack. At zero hour, 5:30 a.m., all guns supporting the Canadians opened fire simultaneously, as the infantry moved forward under cover of a 'creeping barrage.' The effects of the fire had been impressive. The German infantry who survived were disoriented and unable to communicate with their rear lines. The defences had been largely neutralized. With 83 per cent of its guns destroyed, the German artillery was unable to counter the attack and its return fire was effectively neutralized, 'falling well behind the attacking troops.'[26]

'Well behind' the troops, some 3,000 yards behind the front lines, were the field batteries, however. On the second day of the attack, the plan called for the batteries to advance to the old German line. The 11th Battery was selected to be the first to advance after the infantry had taken their objectives. For ten days prior, working parties had filled in shell craters and bridged trenches in order to have roads built as far as the front line by zero day; on the morning of the 9th, immediately following the infantry advance, Crerar and the brigade working party began to construct a road onwards into the captured territory. The party came under heavy shellfire and suffered more than 50 per cent casualties; Crerar was untouched.[27] By noon, the battery's advance was stalled by the rain-filled shell holes. Crerar recalled,

> The actual bombardment with the heavier artillery used to plough up the country in a fantastic way ... We were due to go forward and there was no real enemy opposition at that time. The whole German area was so ploughed up and so full of shellholes, filled with water, that you couldn't move. I got my battery as far as No Man's Land ... We couldn't move, not even with eight horses.[28]

This was as intended. The attack's success had been due to the fact that the objectives were limited, and achievable.

Registering the guns, the 11th fired instead a protective barrage as the infantry consolidated its hold on the ridge. In the early afternoon, Crerar was in the forward lines with the new brigade commander, Lieutenant-Colonel E.W. Leonard, reconnoitring the area for gun positions. Leonard, returning to order the batteries forward, was wounded by shellfire en route and died a few hours later. His death left Crerar as the senior officer of the brigade and the last of the original officers who had left Canada in 1914. In April alone, the 11th suffered thirty-four casualties; it would lose another twenty-two dead and wounded in May.

Crerar was appointed acting brigade commander, with the rank of acting lieutenant-colonel.[29] He commanded the brigade for twenty-one days. Working under the future chief of the Imperial General Staff (CIGS), Alan Brooke, then Senior Officer, Royal Artillery (SO, RA), Crerar was given responsibilities that included the allotment of tasks to his batteries as per the instructions from division or corps and the organization of the overall tactical scheme of artillery support for the infantry. He commanded the brigade through the second stage of the battle for Vimy Ridge, the assault on the Pimple, and in the 1st Canadian Division's attack on Arleux, part of the British Third Army's continuing offensive against Arras. Enemy shellfire, gas, and wet weather took their toll; the 11th alone lost one third of its establishment during the period April to August 1917.[30] His command brought him a Mention in Dispatches; in June he was awarded the Distinguished Service Order (DSO) in recognition of his work during the battle.[31]

IV

The year 1917 proved a turning point for Crerar. He later recalled that by late 1916 or 1917, he was considering the postwar option of 'going regular.' He claimed he was prompted by dissatisfaction with the unscientific employment of the artillery and the desire to make a greater study of gunnery.[32] He also realized that staff rather than command provided the faster track for promotion and learning. Consequently, Crerar began sounding out the divisional staffs regarding vacancies on staff from September 1916, and in that pursuit took an even stronger interest in his seniority and position vis-à-vis those around him. In April 1917, 1st Canadian Division's CO ranked him as the third of four men recommended for possible vacancies as brigade-majors.[33]

The shortage of qualified Canadian staff officers ensured that staff work was the fastest route for promotion. Only twelve Canadians had passed through the Staff College by 1914. British staff officers filled the senior staff positions of the corps for the first two years of the war. By 1917, there was a call for increased Canadian staff, although it was recognized that the senior positions should go to the most competent, regardless of nationality. As part of this Canadianization of the staff, specially qualified officers were selected for the wartime staff courses at Camberley or attached to formations for staff instruction as understudies. By 1917 the selection was rigorous and thorough, based on competence and talent.[34] Attendance at the Staff College marked an officer for the senior staff positions.

Crerar returned to his battery briefly in early May; on 22 May 1917, he departed for the seven-week junior staff course in England to learn the intricacies of administrating a combat unit and turning an offensive plan into a practical and coordinated set of dispositions and objectives. He returned to his unit on 11 July; it had only just been moved from support of 3rd Canadian Division to a quieter position following an intense bombardment that had killed several men and destroyed its position. Within three weeks he was recommended as Brigade Major for the newly formed 5th Canadian Divisional Artillery.[35] After a brief stint with the 4th Divisional Artillery as a learner, he was ordered to join the 5th Division in England.

Crerar arrived in England just as the news came that his younger brother Malcolm had been killed on 3 August 1917. Malcolm had taken a commission in the Royal Artillery but, to his brother's disappointment, had found the Royal Flying Corps more suited to his adventurous personality. He died in a plane crash while posted to Palestine. He was barely nineteen. Malcolm's death proved a devastating blow for the family and one from which his mother, active at home with volunteer war work, never recovered. Crerar never visited his brother's grave, rarely spoke of his death, or referred to him in any available correspondence, perhaps a measure of the impact that it had on the Crerar family; in 1958 he asked for pictures of the grave from a colleague on a peacekeeping mission. They were some of the few photos saved for his personal papers. Marion Crerar, her home already open for convalescing soldiers, redoubled her efforts; she worked with the Red Cross and, through the IODE, opened and staffed a diet kitchen during the influenza epidemic of 1918. When in 1918 Alaister John was severely wounded, Marion's already failing condition was aggravated beyond recovery. It was also no coincidence that Verse returned to England and spent the latter part of the war as a nurse for the Voluntary Aid Detachments. It would be trite to suggest the family pulled together and persevered, but one piece of evidence, contained in the Christmas card sent by Marion to Harry in 1917, the first Christmas without Malcolm, suggests the Crerar's view as the war ripped apart their comfortable pre-war world. It reached Crerar in France in early 1918, as a German offensive loomed. It contained a patriotic poem entitled 'Fight On.' The last three verses have a meaning that went beyond the front lines: 'While I can stand and fight / I fling defiance at them as I cry / Capitulate? Not I.' Twenty-two years later, he would find reason to repeat that sentiment.[36]

Crerar remained Brigade Major – considered 'the most important staff officer ... able to handle the responsibilities of the G, A and Q branches'[37] – of the 5th Divisional Artillery until June 1918; he made his mark. A notebook in which he penned or typed information on the organization, administration, and composition of the divisions and its artillery exemplified his thoroughness: supplies of artillery ammunition, road spacing for movement, suggested formats for orders and appreciations – no detail was too small, and he carried it with him always.[38] Upon his arrival in England in August 1917, preparations for the move overseas were already underway. Crerar took over amending the orders of his commander, Brigadier-General W.O.H. Dodds, and reiterating the CO's demand for strict adherence to the schedule.[39] As the divisional artillery arrived in France, Dodds and Crerar made it clear that they would run a tight and efficient unit. Informed that the men were exploring the possibilities of their new billets in various states of dress, Crerar sent the message from the Commander, Royal Artillery (CRA) that 'immediate steps be taken to correct any such irregularities.' Crerar characteristically reminded his men of their social responsibilities: 'It should be drawn to the attention of all ranks ... that they are the representatives of the 5th Canadian Division in France, and that their responsibilities with regard to setting a standard in smartness and soldierly bearing must be ever before them.' The 5th quickly gained a reputation for efficiency.[40]

More practically, he continued to insist that the men maintain discipline and remember the training received in the United Kingdom as they were introduced to the front, including carrying their clumsy box respirators and paying attention to the careful construction of gun positions. 'Will you please impress upon your battery commanders,' he wrote his brigadiers, 'the importance of facilitating by all possible means the installation of anti-gas defenses at the Battery positions.'

Crerar also took the time to pass on his own ideas for various items, including the construction of gun pits. While such admonishments to remember their training were doubtlessly unappreciated by the ranks, he remembered his experience in Flanders.[41]

The 5th served a brief apprenticeship with the veteran units of the 2nd Canadian Divisional Artillery before moving into positions on the Vimy-Lens front in early September. The 5th's inexperience saved it from the costly and hellish fighting at Passchendaele, where his old battery endured 110 casualties in two months of fighting. It was, instead, attached to several British divisions for relief duties, rejoining the corps on its return to the Lens-Arras front in mid-November.[42] For the remainder of the fall and early winter, the corps' main task was the construction and strengthening of the defensive positions allotted to the corps infantry and artillery. Crerar's duties as Brigade-Major ranged from the overseeing of reliefs and interchanges, to the creation of defence schemes, to position of the batteries.[43]

Through the fall and winter, Crerar's position and activities brought him into frequent contact with men who would have decisive impacts on his career. As the Brigade-Major, he worked closely with his 'opposite number' at Corps Headquarters, the Staff Officer, GOC, Major Alan F. Brooke. Brooke was one of the group of exceptional British staff officers serving with the Canadian Corps at the time, and his contribution and abilities would be remembered 'with respect and gratitude' by most. Brooke was also demanding and suffered fools not at all. During the Second World War, he would characterize Canadian national feelings as 'child-like,' and, in some ways, he wasn't far off the mark. Brooke's initial contacts with Crerar were through the latter's divisional defence schemes, which were circulated as normal procedure to Major-General Edward Morrison, now the General Officer Commanding Royal Artillery, Canadian Corps (GOC, RA) and his staff. Through the fall of 1917, Crerar's detailed, prescriptive, and thorough defence schemes gained him the respect of Brooke, among others. The early schemes incorporated the most recent thoughts on the role and positioning of the artillery, including an emphasis on intelligence gathering and the maintenance of lines of communication to pass the information up to Corps HQ and to the infantry. Here perhaps his recent experience as a battery commander was important; it was a novelty among many of the senior artillery staff officers.

Brooke appreciated Crerar's efforts. On receiving one plan from Crerar, Brooke observed that he 'thought it was a most excellently put together ... and I am certain that [the general] will be delighted with it.'[44] This was praise indeed from Brooke. The respect the two men held for each other laid the basis for a friendship that grew as they 'tramped and reconnoitred ... [the] division or the corps front' in the desperate part of the front in which the corps wintered. Similar characteristics complemented the respect. Both were energetic and capable of painstakingly detailed work. They were also impatient with those they perceived to be of lesser abilities and both were reserved to the point of shyness. The result of these shared experiences and characteristics was a relationship that lasted beyond the war and into the next.[45]

Crerar's professional knowledge and approach were enhanced by his contacts with the experienced 'Brookie.' Crerar's growth, as well as the 5th Divisional Artillery's enlarged responsibilities in the corps' artillery defence system along the Lens-Vimy sector, was reflected in the increasingly elaborate defence schemes he produced through December and January. He standardized and simplified procedure, without sacrificing technical detail. The schemes doubled in length by January 1918 as Crerar used the stability accorded by this relatively static period to refine the effectiveness of the artillery's attempts to subdue the German guns. Crerar's inclination was to carefully detail organization to maximize efficiency. He pressed for standardization of test signals and code words. But Crerar's efforts were not always welcome; his attempt to extend the uniformity of signals along his immediate front was rebuffed early on by his British counterparts in the 11th Division.[46] However, he insisted on a uniformity of equipment in observation posts and a strict adherence to procedures such as the synchronization of watches and standard precautionary measures. He hoped to promote a rapid system of gathering, analyzing, and disseminating intelligence on the enemy's batteries, with the ultimate goal being the fulfilment of the Canadian artillery's policy of 'aggressive defence.'[47]

The directives reflected the centralization and concentration of firepower as the artillerymen implemented the increasingly scientific and technical methods used to locate and destroy the German artillery. But Crerar was practical as well. He set down a rigid set of parameters within which his brigade and battery commanders were to exercise their own initiative in response to the needs of the infantry and their presumably more up-to-date intelligence. The conditions under which the 5th Divisional artillery worked were to be controlled as far as possible through standardization, regulation, and continuous communication between staff and batteries, infantry and artillery. The official history of the artillery commented on both the high morale and initiative of two of the 5th's batteries, the 55th and the 66th.[48] This method would be characteristic of Crerar's approach to command.

Crerar's professional growth in 1917 was also demonstrated in his work on the organization of the two medium and one heavy trench mortar batteries of the 5th Canadian Divisional Artillery into 'counter-mortar' batteries, creating an important supplement to the division's firepower, one that gave immediate and close support to the infantry. During his brief ten-day attachment as a learner with the 4th Canadian Divisional Artillery HQ, Crerar worked with Lieutenant-Colonel Andrew 'Andy' McNaughton, the Canadian Corps Counter-Battery Staff Officer, to organize the six-inch Newton batteries of the Trench Mortar Brigade into an effective counter-mortar unit for use in the attack on Lens in August 1917. McNaughton was an engineer by trade and at heart, and he had the drive and intelligence to make empirical study a defining feature of the corps artillery. McNaughton had developed sound-ranging techniques to fix the positions of the German mortars, and communications were established in order to quickly concentrate 'intense fire on the enemy mortars at the moment of attack,' techniques that found widespread acceptance in First British Army.[49]

In 1918, prompted by a desire to neutralize the increasingly heavy and effective German mortar fire directed at the 5th's batteries, Crerar applied the successful counter-battery organization of the 4th Canadian Divisional Artillery HQ and Corps' HQ to the under-used mortars of the 5th. He quickly improvised a unit 'through a bit of organization and by "scrounging" and borrowing signals equipment and personnel to establish the necessary communications.' By his account the experiment was successful, and the Canadians found themselves in a position 'to concentrate fire from several ... mortar positions on any enemy mortar position within a few minutes of it opening fire.'[50]

Crerar's was a constructive use of a weapon treated as the 'Cinderella' of the artillery and the infantry. The infantry did not like the mortar. Cumbersome and inaccurate, it drew heavy enemy fire down on the infantry because of its proximity to the front. The British never fully exploited the potential of the Stokes mortar, which was the mainstay of the trench artillery, despite, or perhaps because of, the German and French enthusiasm for the weapon's effects. Similarly, the artillery considered the medium and heavy mortar too unwieldy for the semi-mobile warfare that characterized fighting in the latter half of 1918. At higher levels, advocates of the use of new technology to break the stalemate supported the mobile trench mortar but met with some resistance from a traditional school of thought that remained committed to the infantry supported by rifles, machine guns, and artillery. In static conditions, however, the mortar proved to be a welcome addition to the firepower of an artillery brigade, except where the prejudice against it was too deeply ingrained. Crerar did not share this perception and recognized that, if properly organized and under the proper conditions, the mortar could make a useful contribution to the effectiveness of his divisional artillery. The 5th Divisional Artillery remained in the forefront of mortar use; Bill Rawling notes that they 'illustrated the trench mortars potential [in May 1918] by making it more mobile.'[51]

Crerar's work on the counter-mortar organization brought him closer to Andrew McNaughton. He was constantly on the lookout for new techniques and equipment to improve the artillery's effectiveness and encouraged, or demanded, an innovative spirit among his subordinates. Crerar knew McNaughton before 1917, but it was Crerar's study of the counter-battery organization that brought the two together. McNaughton was impressed with Crerar's work on this project, and the respect was mutual. Crerar was struck by McNaughton's approach and his dedication to trading shells for lives, although he was less impressed with his organizational and administrative abilities. He credited McNaughton with many of the developments in counter-battery work in the corps, noting some years later that 'the development – to the highest degree – of Counter-Battery work was entirely due to McNaughton. "Dinky" [General Edward] Morrison, though admirable in other respects, was "Boer War" in matters of gunnery techniques.'[52] Their efforts in early 1918 marked the beginning of a long friendship; McNaughton's confidence in Crerar's abilities would be an important element in his career advancement.

Crerar impressed other officers as well. 'Major Crerar is an excellent Brigade Major,' wrote Brigadier Dodds in February 1918, 'and should make a good Staff Officer, RA.' Subsequently, Crerar was recommended for attachment to Corps Headquarters as a staff learner when a position was vacated. He was also considered for command of a brigade in May 1918, but was not required.[53] Staff appointments were assigned normally by seniority, except in the case of the Staff Officer, Royal Artillery, which was the key artillery staff position at Canadian Corps Headquarters.[54] In June of 1918, Brooke, now a lieutenant-colonel and the Staff Officer, Royal Artillery, was promoted to GSO 1, a counter-battery appointment, on the staff of Lieutenant-General Sir Henry Horne's First Army. His replacement was Major Don A. White, DSO, the first Canadian to hold that post and a friend of Crerar's from RMC days; White had graduated second in his class, and his reports characterized him as an officer of 'marked ability.' Although Crerar's career would eclipse White's, they remained close through two wars.[55] Since May, White had been seconded as a learner to Brooke, but he lacked Brooke's experience. Wrote one staff officer to Brooke, 'There are many people in your Corps who want you back badly.' He added, 'They are cute people these Canadians.'[56] In June, White was ordered to take the Senior Staff Course at Cambridge before he took up the appointment.

Crerar was subsequently recommended as White's replacement until the latter returned with his staff qualification. As Crerar remembered, 'The Allied intention was to delay the big-counter offensive until the spring of 1919 and Canadian Corps had been informed that no major operations would be required of it during the summer of 1918.'[57] Under these circumstances, it was assumed that Crerar's tenure as Acting SO, RA, would be a useful, and none too stressful, experience.

Crerar arrived at Canadian Corps Headquarters on 21 June 1918 as an understudy to Brooke and White before both men left for their respective appointments. Brooke, in particular, eased Crerar's immersion into the staff work required at the corps level. Crerar was generally responsible for preparation of the orders and plans of battle to implement artillery support for the corps as laid down by Morrison, an old-school artilleryman who gave his staff great leeway and little direction; Brooke, for one, was unimpressed with him.[58] Crerar was also responsible for training and the administrative aspects of movements. Given the relative autonomy, coordinating the divisional artilleries, exclusive of the heavy guns, for an offensive was a difficult task in the best of conditions, even for experienced staff officers. In the summer of 1918, however, the Canadian Corps was preparing to enter a new phase of semi-mobile warfare that demanded speedy planning and quick execution. Crerar was simultaneously overseeing the reorganization of the corps artillery, a change prompted by GHQ of the British Expeditionary Force (BEF), to give it the flexibility and mobility needed for open warfare.[59] McNaughton and Brooke encouraged and supported these changes. Brooke, however, left on 3 July and White relinquished his post to Crerar three days later.[60]

Crerar made a contribution to the Canadian Corps artillery reorganization; in particular, he advocated for the adaptation of lighter mortars for mobile use against trench targets, 'leaving available for more remunerative purposes the medium and heavy howitzers which might otherwise be employed.'[61] The effectiveness of the trench mortars was increased by deploying them on mobile platforms and by organizing the establishments for trench mortar brigades in each division. By the end of the summer, the establishments were set up to provide immediate support for the infantry, and they rendered, in the estimation of the official historian of the artillery, 'particularly effective service against machine-guns threatening to hold up the advance.'[62]

The Canadians' efforts reflected changes in German defensive doctrine as well as changes in the strategic situation on the Western front. The German spring offensives had run out of steam by June 1918. The new Allied Commander-in-Chief, General Foch, executed an inter-Allied counter-offensive in July, the success of which forced the Germans to retreat. The Allies seized the initiative. Encouraged by the confidence of the fresh American troops and the successes of new weapons and tactics, Foch turned his attention to the Amiens salient created by the Germans' first spring offensive. While the Allies used new technology like the tank and came close to a combined arms operational doctrine, artillery and the maximization of firepower in support of the infantry remained the key to their success in 1918.

The Allied High Command planned to wipe out the Amiens salient in a joint Anglo-French attack, the British assault was spearheaded by the Canadian Corps and the Australian Corps under the control of General Sir Henry Rawlinson's British Fourth Army Headquarters. On 29 July the Canadian divisional commanders were informed that they were to prepare for an offensive, on 8 August. On 30 July, the corps began moving to the concentration areas some three miles south of Amiens. The staffs had one week to prepare the corps for its role in the operation.

The Amiens offensive proved a heavy responsibility. The artillery was charged with neutralizing, although not destroying, all enemy batteries as the troops advanced. Crerar's coordination of the movements and distribution of sixty-eight field batteries of artillery, organized in a comprehensive fire-plan, was essential to the success of the operation. There were numerous challenges. No shots were fired to register and calibrate the guns; surprise was an important element of the operation. Instead, the muzzle velocities were set using a French method called screen calibrating, and reset by taking bearings on surrounding points –

an accurate but exhaustively detailed process. These were then coordinated into the overall fire-plan.[63] The deployments and plans had to be further coordinated with the Counter-Battery Staff Officer and the two staff captains of the Canadian Corps Royal Artillery Headquarters.[64] Intelligence gathering was particularly important. The Canadians were in new and unfamiliar territory. Successful dispositions and movements depended heavily on accurate information on the terrain and road network that characterized the fourteen miles of the Canadian front and the German artillery dispositions. Planning was further complicated by the necessity of organizing a plan to retain control of the artillery while allowing its advance to support the infantry and break up any attempted German counterattacks. Once the battle began, the dispositions and movements were decentralized and became the work of the divisional or brigade HQs. Overall direction remained crucial and required constant gathering and evaluating of information on the progress of the infantry. A scant six days was available for Crerar to prepare the field artillery for its role in the Battle of Amiens. Communication methods were tested to their limits.

At 0420, on 8 August 1918 a massive barrage signalled the beginning of the operation. Its success allowed the Canadian infantry to quickly overwhelm the enemy's forward areas. By the end of the day, led by the Canadians and Australians, the extent of the Allied breakthrough and the numbers of prisoners and guns taken prompted Ludendorff of the German High Command to dub the 8th 'the black day of the German army.' The success was the result of many factors: the extensive use of massed tanks, airpower, surprise, the weakened morale of the Germans, and the bravery and increased firepower of the Canadian and Australian infantry. The artillery, however, was one of the decisive factors in the initial successes, a fact confirmed by the Canadian infantry's encounters with the dazed and demoralized German infantry and the German artillery shattered by the Canadian counter-battery effort.[65]

Crerar looked back on his role with pride and if it was not, as he remembered, 'quite the heaviest Artillery job of the war,' it was a testament to his professional growth and skills.[66] The success was a team effort. Crerar, McNaughton, Morrison, and Fetherstonhaugh ('Fether') were all dedicated and competent officers, their professional relationship dominated by an innovative spirit and dedication to their craft. Crerar's apprenticeship with Brooke was also crucial. 'I am quite sure that I could not have carried out my part in arrangements for that great offensive,' recalled Crerar, 'if it had not been for the professional assistance given me by Brookie ... and, in particular, the clear memoranda and notes on artillery planning requirements, at the corps level, for a full-scale and hastily executed surprise attack.' Brooke gave Crerar more credit, visiting on the 14th to congratulate him on 'the success of his artillery plans.'[67]

The Battle of Amiens officially ended on 11 August, but the Allies maintained their offensives, keeping the Germans off balance. The advances of the 'Last Hundred Days' – through the Drocourt-Quéant Line, the Canal du Nord, Cambrai, Mont Houy, and Valenciennes – involved some of the heaviest staff work of the war as well as some of the heaviest casualties. Crerar's last task as SO, RA was the preparations for operations against the Drocourt-Quéant Line. The battle devolved into a 'succession of individual heavy blows supported for the most part by artillery barrages,' fifteen in all. To the credit of the corps and the artillery, the Germans withdrew across the Canal du Nord, conceding the line to the Canadians. The end of the battle was followed closely by White's return on 9 September, signalling for Crerar the beginning of a welcome two-week visit to his wife in England.[68]

Crerar's reports on these operations illustrated his grasp of the artillery's dilemma as they adapted to the semi-mobile and open warfare of the summer of 1918. 'Amiens,' he recalled, 'was the first experience I had in the Canadian Corps of a vast and I thought wonderfully improving change in tactics.'[69] The main problem, as Crerar saw it, was the creation of a command and control system that allowed the artillery to concentrate the guns under corps or divisional command during the preparation and break-in phases of the attack, or as needed during an offensive, while simultaneously facilitating a rapid decentralization to operate with the infantry and to increase their firepower to overcome strong points. To 'allow the greatest possible freedom of action to Battery Commanders and to junior officers commanding detached battalions' during open warfare, he advocated attaching a specially trained and selected section of field artillery to an attacking infantry battalion, affiliating the remainder of the field artillery battalion-by-battalion and brigade-by-brigade through combined HQs. These, with the heavy artillery, retained under corps control, could be concentrated as necessitated by circumstances under control by the battalion or infantry brigade commander. Elasticity, rapid devolution of command, effective communication with the infantry, and the need to increase the firepower available to the infantry were the principles that he believed should govern the employment of the artillery in this period of open warfare. Logistical questions were not addressed, although some potential problems were anticipated.[70]

An urgent request from HQ, Canadian Corps, to 'return to his unit immediately' interrupted Crerar's leave in England.[71] He returned to find the Corps HQ preparing for an assault on the Canal du Nord. The artillery operations for this offensive were particularly challenging for the staff because of the constricted area and the shifting nature of the infantry attack. The official historian of the artillery succinctly described the main staff problem, observing 'the limited communication available at the time imposed the necessity of working out beforehand in considerable detail the planned movements of every battery ... A plan that was to exploit the terrain for the advantage of the infantry had of necessity to be complex.' Crerar responded to this challenge with a barrage map that was described as a 'masterpiece' for its simple presentation of the complex and intricate fire-plan required to coordinate the employment of all the field and heavy artillery available in the Canadian Corps; simplicity of planning was important to Crerar. He had some problems with McNaughton's penchant for complex plans.[72] The result was another important success for the corps.

Crerar remained as a staff officer at Corps Headquarters through September. McNaughton's promotion in mid-October to GOC, Canadian Corps Heavy Artillery, opened the position of Counter-Battery Staff Officer (CBSO). On 24 October, as the Canadian Corps began preparations for its next operation, Crerar assumed the appointment and subsequent promotion to substantive lieutenant-colonel. A modification in the chain of command, however, at McNaughton's behest, altered the independent status of the CBSO, subordinating Crerar to McNaughton as the new GOC, Heavy Artillery. McNaughton argued that under the conditions of moving warfare, the functions of the heavy artillery officer and CBSO became essentially the same. Previously both reported directly to the GOC, RA. The new arrangements eliminated one level of administration by combining the two functions in one office, but McNaughton may also have been trying to avoid the acrimony that developed between himself and the former GOC, Heavy Artillery.[73] Despite the extinction of the position as a separate command, the CBSO remained an important staff appointment, responsible for the collection of intelligence, advising the GOC, RA, on counter-battery requirements and the implementation as well as coordination of the counter-battery harassing and destructive fire.[74]

Crerar's only substantial operational test as CBSO was the Battle of

Valenciennes on 1 November, a battle characterized by the coordination of all arms that resulted in a cheap victory for the corps. It was, however, remembered by the artillerymen as a battle dominated by the guns, the last effective showcase of the properly employed capabilities of artillery in 1918. It was described by McNaughton as 'one of the best examples of the employment of masses of artillery in the intimate support of infantry.' He felt it exemplified the long-standing policy of the Corps Commander – to pay the price of victory, as far as possible, 'in shells and not in the lives of men.' Crerar later marked this passage of the report as particularly important.[75]

Crerar controlled a third of the heavy guns to engage their German counterparts and break up enemy counter-attacks; he was also charged with disseminating intelligence throughout the corps. The effectiveness of his work can be measured by the fact that Crerar's forty-nine guns, working closely with air reconnaissance, destroyed 110 German pieces and prevented any concerted enemy counter-attacks.[76] This was the last operation for the counter-battery organization. The next week and a half was characterized by hostile shelling 'far below normal.' The German artillery fire ceased altogether at dusk on 10 November and was not resumed. The war was over. On the 11th, Crerar and his staff captain, Arthur Anglin, made the short ride into Mons with the leading company of the Princess Patricia's Canadian Light Infantry. They were thronged by cheering inhabitants, enjoying for several days the hospitality of a Madame Saliez; in April 1945, at the end of a second world war, she wrote Crerar reminding him of the armistice: 'I have not forgotten you.'[77]

As active operations ended, Crerar had one major task left to complete. McNaughton's organization of the Counter-Battery Office was an important accomplishment, the result of years of experience and experimentation. Crerar was concerned 'that lessons learned therefrom in Counter-Battery Work, if now unrecorded, might possibly be forgotten.' To forestall that possibility, he prepared a memorandum titled 'Organization and Procedure of Counter Battery Office, Canadian Corps Artillery.'[78] Running to twenty-five pages of primary text and forty-six pages of appendices, it represented the evolution and development of four years of counter-battery practice in trench warfare as well as the last four months of open and semi-open warfare.

The memorandum reveals a picture of the Great War that was different from the vision of 'men stripped to the waist serving guns recoiling from the two hundredth round of a barrage programme, or plodding in lines behind shell bursts through an endless expanse of mud that came to typify the war.'[79] The predominant image was that of a thorough and innovative professional force, dedicated to the preservation of lives through application of accurate intelligence, science, and all-arms cooperation. It also illustrated Crerar's strengths as a technician, administrator, and tactician. Crerar reported on the importance of the use of aircraft, in bombing and strafing roles, as auxiliary weapons in close conjunction with the Counter-Battery Office. Control and accurate intelligence were key to the initial application of overwhelming counter-battery fire; devolution of command and communications with the front lines were the elements emphasized during the crumbling process or after a breakthrough. Perhaps most important was the point that detailed and thorough staff work before the battle was just as important as what happened after the fighting began. It represented an accurate estimate of the sum of the artillery-based doctrine that had won the war for the Allies, although it ignored some of the tactical innovations used by the Germans in the last year of the war. It was well received by the British, Canadians, and Americans. McNaughton observed, '[GHQ appreciated the report] and I think you have let things off very well indeed. And the information should be of great help in the study of the Science prior to a future war.'[80]

Crerar also suggested refinements to McNaughton's organization as reflected in the latter's 'Notes on the Work of a Counter-Battery Office.' Crerar's comments grew from his experience with the open warfare of the last months of the war. The sum of his experience was summed up in his critique of McNaughton's notes.

> It should be emphasized that elasticity of methods and procedure is of the essence of effective Counter-Battery Work ... While the two extremes of procedure [should] be indicated in the Notes on Counter-Battery Work under Trench and Moving Warfare conditions respectively ... yet experience suggests that in six months time the changes in the general situation would be so great as to necessitate the whole procedure being revised and thought out afresh.

Flexible staff and command arrangements were equally important. Staff captains were to be kept informed of all developments so that they were capable of fulfilling the CBSO's duties if the need arose. Crerar viewed the staff as agents of the commander as well as advisors. He also indirectly criticized too slavish an acceptance of doctrine as an end in itself rather than a means to an end.

Crerar's experience with the artillery was critical to his decision that he could make a career of the military, that it might merit the description *profession*. From 1917, his actions were predicated on his hopes of pursuing a career in the Permanent Forces. The logic of the artillery work appealed to his predilection for methodical and tidy solutions. Conversely, he emphasized the importance of personality and personal relations in processing information and maintaining effective lines of communication.[81]

Crerar's wartime experiences also shattered his romantic and amateurish notions of warfare. The personal cost of war was heavy. Crerar lost his younger brother Malcolm, one of the brightest lights in the family; among his militia compatriots, he was, by 1916, one of the few surviving originals from the Hamilton artillery battery. When the Hamilton battery arrived at the train station in 1919, even Crerar was shocked to see how few of those who had marched off in 1914 had returned. He was silent on the rull effects of these deaths, preferring to relate only the light 'choice bits' of his experience to those who asked. His daughter recalled that the Great War was rarely discussed, even among immediate family. But the war cast a long shadow.

4 Learning the Game

I

At war's end, Crerar's future was determined by financial and family considerations: his daughter, Margaret, was born in 1916; his youngest brother was dead; his elder brother, John, had been severely wounded; and his mother was dying. There was truth in Cynthia Asquith's observation that with the war over, people now had to face an awful fact: the dead were not just dead for the duration of the war, but were gone forever. Crerar had not yet decided to make a career in the army. While Crerar was still overseas, Sir Adam Beck made overtures to the Minister of Militia at Argyle House, General S.C. Mewburn, on Crerar's behalf, indicating that Ontario Hydro was 'extremely anxious' for Crerar to resume his former duties. Crerar's pessimism regarding the possibility of obtaining a position in the postwar Canadian army prompted him to reluctantly accept this course and 'buckle down to civilian work.' Taking advantage of his privilege as a lieutenant-colonel, he formally, and informally, initiated the proceedings for demobilization from the Canadian Expeditionary Force.[1] Following a brief hospital stay, he obtained his release and was struck off the strength of the CEF on 24 March 1919. His final report judged him to have been an 'all around capable officer who has made good in every capacity.'[2]

Marion Crerar's death in May 1919 dramatically altered Crerar's ideas about the future. She left a relatively substantial estate that provided her children with small annuities of several thousand dollars each. With this financial backing, Crerar was able 'to think more of what I'd like to do and less of what otherwise I might be compelled to do.'³ Crerar was devastated by his mother's death; his children remembered he would often speak of her. He now, however, had a choice to make. What was Verse's position? Army life was hard on wives and families. 'She would have liked a simpler life,' recalled her daughter. But, in the 1920s, few wives made those decisions. 'It is a great help to a man,' Crerar counselled his daughter years later, 'if his wife will discuss, quietly, and helpfully, with him, his plans and intentions. At the same time, I believe that when it becomes clear to a husband that he could only be happy if he occupies himself in a certain way, then his "woman" should back him without stint, so long as the partnership is considered to be worth the trouble.'⁴ Both thought it was. Crerar quickly sought Andrew McNaughton's assistance in obtaining a position with the Permanent Forces.

Crerar was happy to return to the army. He found life in the military satisfied his sense of public duty and his social nature. He respected his superiors. The Chief of the General Staff, Major-General James MacBrien, 'was a man [he] admired tremendously.' Crerar recalled that his 'influence on my life [was] very great.⁵ In the early 1920s, the army staff was tiny – there were eight positions on the General Staff, ten under the Adjutant-General, and seven in the Quartermaster General's branch – and what little movement there was in the 1920s was usually lateral. Crerar's entrance into the army was nevertheless a career move, dependent on obtaining a satisfactory position, rank, and financial return to justify the change of vocations, because he was now a father and husband. These were recurring themes throughout his professional life. Crerar professed a desire for a 'turn at regimental work ... after two years staff,' but McNaughton directed Crerar's attention to an opening on the staff of the Deputy Inspector-General of Artillery (DIGA).⁶ General Sir Arthur Currie and those of like mind, including McNaughton, were anxious to retain as much expertise as possible in the postwar army.⁷ He instructed Crerar to write the Inspector-General directly, assuring him that the request would receive sympathetic consideration from Major-General E. Morrison, the former GOC, RA. 'Will be very good to have you here,' McNaughton added. 'Lots of interesting work in sight.'⁸ McNaughton steered Crerar in the direction of the artillery. 'I saw Andy,' Crerar's contact at Militia Headquarters wrote, '[and] as regards jobs outside the artillery, he doesn't think there is anything that would interest you.'⁹

Crerar was appointed to the Royal Canadian Artillery at the rank of temporary lieutenant-colonel and, in March 1920, appointed Staff Officer, Artillery, to the DIGA. Crerar's position was ambiguously defined as a 'combination of Director of Artillery and Staff Officer, Royal Artillery,' an appointment normally responsible for inspection of artillery and ordnance. The responsibilities that emerged, however, included the reorganization and administration of Permanent and Non-Permanent Militia and Royal Schools of Artillery.[10]

Crerar's appointment was part of a larger policy of retaining Canadian Expeditionary Force personnel in the services following the First World War. For the army, the immediate postwar objective was to cement the professionalism that had emerged during the war through increased educational opportunities and to disseminate the experience of a core group drawn into the Permanent Forces from the Canadian Corps. While the policy laid down for selecting staff officers confirmed the hegemony of the CEF – the number one criteria was satisfactory overseas service and experience – in practice, removing the 'deadwood' was a slow process. At the top levels, movement was quicker; most of the senior army staff in 1922 were veterans of the CEF. Nevertheless, the different experiences of the staffs and the divisions over appointments ensured that a consensus on the army's role in postwar defence policy making would be difficult to achieve.[11]

More important, the substantial growth in Canada's military anticipated by Currie and others did not materialize. In the atmosphere after the 'war to end all wars,' the government's attitude towards defence policy, and expenditures on defence, was 'defence against whom?'[12] The hopes raised by the professionalization of the Canadian Corps devolved into a scramble to rationalize a permanent establishment of 10,000 and an inflated paper organization of fifteen divisions, potential 'aids to the civil power.' The most important change, although the benefits were not immediately apparent, was the creation in 1923 of one Department of National Defence from the three separate departments.[13]

Through the interwar period there was a running internal debate over the army's position within the state and its role in policy making. There was no consensus on that issue among the senior officer corps, but this was partially a product of the focus on the battle between the Deputy Minister G.J. Desbarats and the Chief of the General Staff, Major-General J.H. MacBrien, over internal policy-making prerogatives. This debate overlapped with the destructive inter-service rivalry between MacBrien and the director of the Naval Service. It was hoped that the integration of the three services into one Department of National Defence would provide 'more effective military advice ... more economically,' but this expectation was destroyed by the struggle to define the hierarchy among the three service chiefs. The main focus of the struggle at this level was who should render advice to the government, rather than the form that advice should take.[14]

The reorganization of the artillery advanced smoothly, but was hampered by the absence of experienced officers and money for training, equipment, and facilities. Civil unrest shaped the immediate distribution of the artillery's resources. Ten batteries of six-inch trench mortars – sixty in total – and ammunition were distributed to the districts on Morrison's orders. Crerar recalled four years later without a hint of irony that this was done so that 'in the event of more serious developments of the late Winnipeg trouble, and interference in railway communications, the local Loyalist Defence Organization would have a weapon which could reduce any Communist stronghold with a minimum of delay.'[15] They were still scattered in 1925. Training, despite Crerar's promises, was limited.

Crerar proved a capable peacetime officer. 'Crerar ... worked like a beaver at his job,' recalled Brigadier R.J. Orde. 'His whole heart was in it and he showed a great deal of intelligence in handling his work. There was no trouble at all with him.'[16] He began to practise the habits of a man determined to get ahead. Files were organized and history books were collected. He started to keep a notebook of sayings, and 'bits of prose or poetry, which caught [his] imagination ... and seemed to offer help, and guidance, in tackling the daily problems of life.' He arranged them under headings that spoke to his values and his goals: *probity, candour, uprightness*, and *bravery*. He kept the notebook for years. 'Civilization,' he recorded under *progress*, 'is impossible without traditions, and progress impossible without the destruction of these traditions.'[17]

His manner was still rough. A year into his appointment, he recommended changing the Royal Canadian Horse Artillery (RCHA) to facilitate more efficient training, reasoning that the Permanent Force Horse Artillery's instructional role was limited because of the Non-Permanent Force's concentration on the more affordable field artillery. The idea was initially accepted by Morrison, but was later overturned by McNaughton on the grounds that the actual establishment did not justify the designation of either horse or field artillery. He recognized that sentiment played a part as well. Forced to concede the issue, Crerar remained convinced that greater efficiency could have been obtained from the Permanent Force for training purposes,[18] but he as yet lacked subtlety in gaining his objectives. Nevertheless, his work gained respect at Militia Headquarters. 'In his position [as Staff Officer, Artillery, he] has shown marked ability in organization and training duties,' commented Morrison in Crerar's confidential reports for 1920 and 1921, concluding that his record remained undiminished.[19]

II

The route to promotion and senior positions lay with further staff training at the Staff College at Camberley in England. Every year, two Canadians were selected. In the spring of 1921, Crerar applied to the Militia Council for one of two vacancies. To expedite matters, Sir Adam Beck approached Prime Minister Arthur Meighen, asking him to consider Crerar's application.[20] Meighen passed the matter along to Minister of Militia Hugh Guthrie, who presumably spoke with his military advisors. Guthrie was a capable, fair, and careful man – 'He never blotted his copy book,' recalled Orde.[21] Subsequently, Guthrie advised Beck that it would not be to Crerar's advantage to take the Staff College Course in 1921 as he was two years underage and had not taken the preparatory course at the Royal Military College. Denied the fast track, Crerar expressed 'a willingness to take this preparatory course,' which lasted for four months.[22] In 1922 Crerar successfully completed the entrance exams, characterized as 'tough and comprehensive,' to gain admission to the Staff College for January 1923.[23]

The Staff College's main purpose was to qualify students for Grade 2 staff appointments. For instructional purposes, the sixty students in attendance were divided by year into a senior and junior division. To build team spirit, each division was subdivided into 'syndicate' groups, which changed periodically to expose the students to as many members of the Directing Staff as possible; there were six syndicates in Crerar's junior division.[24] Instruction was given through lectures, conferences, indoor exercises, and 'practical work on the ground.' The syndicates also travelled to the Continent to observe and report on military and defence issues.[25] Derided as 'a highly cultivated place where the atmosphere [was] pleasant and the food very good,' where horsemanship counted for much, the college depended on the quality of the other Staff College students and instructors for its impact. In the years immediately following the war, there was a nostalgic atmosphere surrounding these activities.[26]

Curriculum content and form was more a product of the commandant and Directing Staff than War Office policy. The Directing Staff was a mixed bag during Crerar's years, but some stood out. The appointment of Major-General Edmund Ironside, a leader with a reputation for innovative and unconventional thought, as the college's new commandant in 1922 heralded a fresher approach to teaching. Ironside brought to the school as a chief instructor the military theoretician Colonel J.F.C. Fuller. Described as 'perhaps the "profoundest intellect which [had] ... been applied to military thought in this century,"'[27] Fuller was renowned as a tactician. He was also a pioneer in the study of war as a social phenomenon. This original, if eccentric, thinker joined such leading lights as the future Chief of the Imperial General Staff (CIGS) Alan Brooke and Ronald Adam, the pre–Second World War Deputy CIGS.[28] There remained those who, as characterized by Brooke, 'revolved round details and frequently lost the wood for the trees,' but the staff was composed of many who would make their mark and attain both high command and good reputations in the British army; the two were not always synonymous.[29]

Ironside was not complacent about the Staff College's objective. 'Staff work in the war was not good,' he commented in his introductory message to the junior division in January 1923. 'In fact, our staff work was often inferior to the French and German.'[30] The first-year curriculum was theoretically designed to teach the requirements of divisional and cavalry brigade staff work; the second focused on staff work at 'corps, the cavalry division and ... Army and GHQ.' The continued emphasis on studying cavalry divisions suggests that some of the old traditions maintained their sway. Indeed, each candidate was required to have at least one horse.[31] At the same time, the Staff College also drew on the Royal Air Force Staff College, the Air Defence School, and the Aldershot command to undertake cooperative exercises.

In practice, the curriculum was generally innovative. The commandant and most of the directing staff had experienced the fighting on the Western Front, and incorporated their experience and the personal lessons they drew from the war. In 1923–4, the staff officer as the servant of the troops was the predominant theme.[32] The directing staff's contribution was most evident in the content of the first-year curriculum. 'We soaked up every detail of the old famous battles,' Crerar recalled. 'We made advanced studies of command and tactics.'[33] Foreign travel by the syndicates to the Continent to study some phase of the Great War and the strategic circumstances of the European countries reinforced the program.[34]

Generalizations about the influence of the Staff College on Crerar are difficult to make. Crerar saved his notes and lecture materials. These and the reports to Defence Headquarters, written jointly by Crerar and Georges Vanier, the other Canadian student, suggest that Fuller's tactical, strategic, and training theories made the strongest impression on Crerar. By his second year, he was able to step back from the immense detail thrown at him and distill some principles. Reporting to Ottawa helped. In the abstract, the notes and reports mirrored Fuller's emphasis on restoring mobility to the battlefield and his desire to radically rethink the relationship between weapons and tactics by function. From the lectures and subsequent second-term outdoor exercises, Crerar reported that the tank scheme, characterized as one of the most important of those conducted, demonstrated that the tank's mobility must be fully exploited. In his opinion, this entailed freeing the tank from its infantry protection role, resolving the problem of maintaining close support by the infantry for mop-up and consolidation, concentrating and positioning the armour to secure room for manoeuvre, motorizing artillery to protect the tanks, and increasing the mobility of logistical and communications echelons.[35]

Crerar's lectures at RMC in the late 1920s and his addresses during the 1930s reflected these lessons. Following Fuller's reasoning, he suggested that the armies of the future would be small, professional, and mechanized, their speed and firepower greatly increased by airpower and improved communications – an interesting observation counter to many who were fixated on the tank. It was a formula, seemingly proved by German successes in 1939–40, he would use to frame the army programs in 1940 and 1941.

Crerar would take a more pragmatic approach to the theory and practice of mechanization in the Canadian forces. He considered divisional organization as still an open question. He would be consistent in his advocacy that it was impossible for Canada to make a commitment to a particular type of organization.[36] Also predominant among the lessons he drew from his study at the Staff College was the importance of the psychological aspects of command and training. Reviewing an article titled 'Study of War by Junior Officers' several years later, Crerar suggested that the knowledge of human nature was as essential to a leader as an awareness of technique; only then could training produce the maximum capabilities of weapons and users, instilling a 'desire to accomplish.'[37]

It was Crerar's postwar view of the human condition that most strongly informed his views on leadership, however. It was a crude social Darwinism. Struggle, ambition, and strength were the principles of human life as he recorded them in 1923. He refined this view but never substantially changed it. Lecturing to an RMC military history class on the general causes of war, he proclaimed, 'Life is a fight (which you will find out later, if not already realized) to possess your individuality ... and war is but a phase of that primitive instinct which urges self-preservation.' 'It is the healthy basis,' he added, 'of every game – it forms the main spring of life ... When ambition ceases, when the struggle is abandoned, our usefulness in this world is over.' These beliefs informed his approach to his profession and leadership; to Crerar, aspirations to higher command were one mark of a military professional.[38]

The Directing Staff's emphatic lectures and addresses on the First World War as a total war, on the links between the political, economic, civilian, and military spheres, also left a durable impression. 'The morale of the civilian,' observed Ironside, 'is as important as that of the soldier.'[39] When each syndicate travelled under War Office auspices to European countries, they were encouraged to examine national characteristics. They travelled to Germany, Italy, Hungary, Czechoslovakia, and Austria, inspecting defence installations, meeting dignitaries, and exploring old battlefields. The vulnerability of the new Eastern European states made the biggest impression on Vanier and Crerar.[40]

Crerar emerged from the Staff College with a strong impression of its general function and a grand strategic perspective on its utility to Canada. He also secured personal ties to the British army establishment; he remained in close contact with many of his fellow students through correspondence and subsequent postings. Crerar observed that while staff training and knowledge of military thought were the main elements of the course curriculum, they were not its only function. 'From the point of view of Imperial Defence it is to my mind most important that the Dominions should not have separate Staff Colleges,' he noted in a toast to the Dominions at the graduating classes farewell dinner. 'If one thing above others requires unified teaching and inspiration it is staff training and military thought.'[41]

Crerar's fondness for Britain was strengthened by the life he found there in the mid-1920s. Camberley was located on the plains of the Berkshire countryside. The hedgerows and fences of the neighbouring farms criss-crossed the area surrounding the college. Relations between the officers and the farmers were cordial. Horseback riding, golf, and countryside tours were remembered with fondness. The six weeks between terms allowed the Crerars to travel. London and Sir Edward Peacock were close by. Crerar visited him often, eager to show off his family, now grown to four with Peter's birth on 1 July 1922. Crerar enjoyed the camaraderie of the school and the Brits during this sojourn. He liked socializing with his contemporaries; his daughter recalled that her father was 'gregarious ... he really liked parties and he loved dancing.'[42] Tennis parties and formal dinners were reminiscent of the Edwardian upper-class vision of pre-war Britain, a vision that the British, and to some degree the Canadian, army firmly clung to in the aftermath of the Great War. They entertained and were entertained, in turn. A handsome couple, they made many lifelong friends. Many would rise to prominence in the British army. He became a godfather to one of Richard Dewing's sons; Harry and Verse travelled to France with Chief of Staff MacBrien.

Army life, however, placed great demands on the families of serving officers. The pay, while relatively good in comparison to the average Canadian's wage, was also used to cover the extensive social life expected of an officer. The standard practice was to pay officers seconded to Staff College at the major's scale. Even though Crerar was senior to most of his colleagues, his yearly pay was reduced from $4,200 to $3,700. While in England, Crerar campaigned unceasingly for greater financial support. 'I feel very bitterly,' he wrote McNaughton in 1926, 'that the Department does not recognize the peculiar responsibilities I must accept as a Canadian at the War Office.'[43] Verse found the life of a military wife trying. She was a strong woman but found traipsing with two children in tow to sometimes 'dingy quarters' tiring, and the endless rounds of socializing placed more stress on her. She did not complain, but in 1926 the family moved out of London into the countryside where, Vanier noted, Harry would get in his 'weekend golf and thereby retain [his] good humour.'[44]

Crerar's performance at the Staff College was praised, but did not yet mark him as a rising star. He received a good recommendation from Ironside. 'An officer of solid and imperturbable character, of strong personality,' read the report, 'possesses marked powers of decision. In his work he is thorough but apt to be a trifle slow.' Ironside also noted Crerar's tactful and skilful handling of his fellow students, all juniors, and concluded that he was 'well suited for either command or staff.' While it has been observed that Canadian officers were not appraised as critically as their British counterparts, Ironside's report raised Crerar's status in Canada. Georges Vanier returned to Canada in 1925 and informed Crerar that Ironside's evaluation had been enthusiastically received.[45]

Crerar was scheduled to return to Canada and may have returned to labour in obscurity had not an unfortunate turn of events helped shape his career. The course planned for Crerar was a year of regimental duty to obtain some experience of the actual working of the Permanent Force in peacetime, followed by a position with the General Staff at Defence Headquarters.[46] The untimely death of the first postwar Canadian appointee to the War Office prompted the Chief of the General Staff to suggest Crerar as a replacement. Much to his surprise, he received a letter in late December warning him of his imminent posting to the War Office.[47] The posting was a two-year appointment as General Staff Officer, 2nd Grade (GSO 2) in charge of the 'section ... dealing with home defence.' His immediate superior was Lieutenant-Colonel Archibald Wavell, in charge of Military Operations (MO) 1 under the Directorate of Military Operations and Intelligence, the newly amalgamated directorate that inherited the strategic responsibility from the Dominion's section of the Imperial General Staff.

III

Attachment to the War Office was described as 'a less formal method of broadening the horizons of Canadian officers than enrolment in British Staff Colleges – but no less educational for its informality.'[48] Crerar made the most of it. After a four-month attachment to the Aldershot Command at the behest of the Canadian government to study the British system for training in individual and combined arms, he assumed his appointment. His main task was a responsibility for coastal batteries and their organization.[49] His position as the Dominion representative in the Military Operations section allowed him a perspective characterized as affording the 'widest possible insight into British imperial strategic planning.'[50]

Despite the financial concerns that accompanied the reduced allowances for a War Office posting – and Canadian officers serving overseas were not shy about voicing these concerns to the authorities in Ottawa – Crerar was pleased with his new position, not least because of the chance it afforded him to remain professionally active. 'As the first Canadian to take on a War Office appointment,' he later wrote, 'and carry out my responsibilities as a regular member of the General Staff, I realized my position to be somewhat exceptional.'[51] He also believed he was fortunate to be in Britain. Just prior to his appointment, he publicly – and tactlessly – characterized defence expenditures in Canada as maintained at a 'destructive minimum,' bluntly concluding that while there 'are eight principles of war ... In so far as Canada is concerned, her military organization has been rendered impotent to fulfil any one of them.' McNaughton confirmed Crerar's good fortune. 'You are lucky to be out of it,' he wrote, 'with an interesting job of work to do while the rest of us have to temporize and economize on every point of order to bring the Militia through this very trying period.'[52]

McNaughton was correct. The milieu of 'uncertainty and retrenchment' that characterized the immediate postwar years had not improved. Only a few hesitant steps were taken towards reshaping the army, the General Staff had no real voice in making defence policy, and attempts to do so were firmly blocked. Deputy Minister Desbarats watched closely for any infringement on his prerogatives on policy discussions. MacBrien made few challenges. He sought to enhance the army's standing as military advisors to the government and institutionalize its position through an interdepartmental committee modelled on the British Committee for Imperial Defence. But generally, initiatives on defence policy were not welcome.[53]

Crerar had a far different experience in the United Kingdom. Through 1925, the dual role of Canadian military representative and GSO 2 forced Crerar to balance operational specialization and a broader strategic perspective. His ability to excel at both slowly gained him the confidence of the exacting Wavell. 'Wavell had a glass eye but he didn't miss much,' Crerar observed many years later. Crerar's bold critique of War Office coastal defence policy in Ireland was well received by Wavell. 'It was of great value,' Wavell wrote McNaughton, 'to have a fresh and acute mind turned on our problems of home defence, problems that we have dealt with for so long that our ideas on them are rather stereotyped.' Conversely, his blunt assessments of the failure to properly allocate and organize responsibilities between regulars and territorials drew a furious reaction from the Western Coast commander, much to Crerar's astonishment; he tactfully rebuffed the arguments. Others, however, were impressed. The future Judge Advocate General Brigadier R.J. Orde, attached to the War Office in 1926, recalled that Crerar 'was a great student of military history and painstaking in every job he undertook ... He was highly regarded by all concerned.' Wavell's final report was glowing, noting that he was an 'excellent officer of very great ability. He is quick to grasp a subject, expresses him views very well and clearly and is full of commonsense ... I have formed a high opinion.' Two years later, when the War Office Standing Committee on Home Defence reported on the 'existing state of affairs,' many of Crerar's proposals on command reorganization were endorsed.[54]

Wavell nominated Crerar to sit on various subcommittees of the Committee of Imperial Defence and encouraged him to undertake several addresses on the development of closer military relations between the forces of the Empire.[55] In addresses to the Royal United Service Institution (RUSI) (later the Royal United Services Institute), subsequently published in the RUSI journal and the new forum for Canadian military discourse, the *Canadian Defence Quarterly*, Crerar promoted imperial defence responsibility and an increase in the number of points where, in a military sense, Dominion and British forces came together. He went as far as promoting limited interchanges between the Canadian militia units and Britain.[56]

Crerar proved an astute observer of Canadian sentiment towards the mother country. He conceded that imperial unity seemed lacking and that there were differing attitudes towards similar problems. He felt, however, that when war threatened, 'Imperial politics as in the past will operate on one straight forward line ... so our responsibility as soldiers stands clear against that day – to prepare the military machinery of the Empire for its highest effectiveness.' This was the central tenet of his approach to military preparation during the interwar period. In form, it never changed, but the substance underwent an evolution that mirrored Canada's own constitutional maturation.

In the mid-1920s, however, Crerar was an unabashed imperialist. In contrast to Prime Minister King's attempts to distance himself from imperial commitments, Crerar argued that it 'is not enough that the Imperial Forces should be allies. We must make them far more than that: they must be parts of one and the same Imperial Army.' There was sincere conviction behind these emotional statements. For Crerar, the large numbers of British officers who staffed Corps and Divisional Headquarters during the First World War stood as a prime example of the effectiveness and necessity of military cooperation. 'Speaking as an officer [of Canadian Corps],' Crerar wrote, 'I can say that we counted the British officers who served with us as part of our organization, and the Canadian formations as an integral part of the Imperial forces as a whole.'[57] He pointed fondly to the end of the war when the 'entire Empire was welded together as never before.' Swept along by such sentiments, in 1925, Crerar sent a letter to the *Morning Star* arguing that 'the British Empire ... owes a large measure of its vitality to the bond of race and sentiment.' Unrestrained, Crerar believed that when war came, Canada would fight as part of the Empire so 'the crime ... now being perpetrated was that of continued military unpreparedness.'[58]

Crerar's comments were noticed. Prime Minister Mackenzie King's government was anxious to avoid any imperial entanglements or commitments, military and otherwise. O.D. Skelton, the Under-Secretary of State for External Affairs, closely monitored all public talks. A talk on 'Canadian Defence Problems' to the Royal Institute of International Affairs proposed by McNaughton in 1927 prompted a flurry of correspondence between the Canadian High Commissioner Peter Larkin in London, McNaughton, and King. McNaughton cancelled the talk, but not before King had spoken to Skelton regarding the implications of such a talk. King praised Larkin for making enquiries 'when it was proposed that a member of the [Canadian] General Staff ... open a discussion on a subject which might well involve considerations of policy.' Skelton's appraisal was telling. While he believed that 'McNaughton is pretty careful' and he doubted that he 'would have stepped outside proper bounds,' he viewed Larkin's precautions as well advised. 'I noticed,' wrote Skeleton, 'an address in London a year or so ago by Colonel Crerar which was out and out advocacy of Imperialist policy in defence.' Skelton subsequently kept a watchful eye on Crerar. The publication of the address in *Canadian Defence Quarterly* suggested that other members of the army shared Crerar's view.[59]

Crerar's War Office duties were not limited to defence: they also involved him in the 1926 General Strike, a situation he characterized, quoting Winston Churchill, as 'akin to revolution.' The army's role in it was largely passive; given no special emergency powers, it was limited to protective responsibilities and troop movements.[60] Crerar's Home Defence Section, however, played an important organizational role. He was one of ten officers assigned to help administer government services during the shutdown in May. After the General Strike, he reported on the War Office Organization and its response to the strike. Notable among his conclusions was the view that military aid was a preventive measure, not a last resort.[61]

While he found the War Office 'an unwieldy and very slow moving organization,' Crerar came to appreciate its complexities. 'It took me some time to find out how I stood with the 'boss,' he recalled, 'and at least that time to get a reasonable grasp of my duties and understanding of the War Office machinery and duties.' His tenure there introduced an element of bureaucratic acumen that would serve him well in later positions.[62] He was anxious to return to Canada, however, and he quietly initiated enquiries regarding his future employment. In March 1926, Vanier wrote Crerar of a discussion he had had with McNaughton: 'McNaughton ... informed me that the War Office had sent in one of the finest confidential reports he had ever seen on your work and that he had shown it to Sir Arthur Currie ... Don't worry about your future in Canada.'[63] Emboldened by the favourable impressions forming in Canada, Crerar wrote McNaughton stating his preference for a staff position in Ottawa, based on his present experience, ambition, and a desire to 'help in making the Militia a really good show.' His request was underscored by the qualification that he would accept regimental duty 'for a while ... [if] it is in accordance with the wishes of the Chief and yourself and not brought about by some external pressure or internal intrigue.' Crerar also made it clear that if regimental duty were in the future, he wanted to undergo a battery commander's course in England 'to make a useful show of the battery.' On his own initiative, he visited the appropriate training centres for artillery cooperation and anti-aircraft gunnery.[64]

IV

Crerar's appointment to the General Staff was delayed at the behest of Chief of Staff Major-General MacBrien. Crerar was instead appointed the Officer Commanding (OC), 'B' Battery, Royal Canadian Horse Artillery, upon his return to Canada. His War Office experience and reports were not overlooked. He was allowed to forego Senior Officer's School, having held lieutenant-colonel's rank and the result in part of glowing praise received from his superiors at the War Office.[65] This might have been a missed opportunity, as the postwar Senior Officers' School in England has been characterized, with some reservations, as both a 'comprehensive and challenging' tactical fitness course and useful in the absence of collective formation training in Canada or an equivalent institution to critically evaluate tactical proficiency.[66] Nevertheless, following War Office reports that Crerar was thoroughly fit for a lieutenant-colonel's command, the Chief of Staff and McNaughton filed recommendations that he be developed for General Staff employment as soon as suitable vacancies occurred.[67]

While he awaited a staff vacancy, Crerar assumed command of 'B' Battery in April 1927. The battery, like most, was hampered by outdated equipment, a succession of mediocre commanders, reduced numbers, and indifferent training. With a core of excellent subalterns that included future Canadian army officers Guy Simonds and G.E. Beament, the battery had great potential, which Crerar's professionalism and zeal were able to unlock. He brought the battery to a 'very high state of efficiency and discipline.' Simonds later recalled that he tried for three years to rid the battery of an ineffectual sergeant-major under a lazy commander but that after a few weeks under Crerar's 'scrutiny' the man was replaced.[68] Crerar's CO, Colonel H.E. Boak, nevertheless tempered his personal commendation, officially appraising Crerar's command of subordinates and his attitude towards superiors with a minimalist 'good' and commenting that despite the progress Brevet Lieutenant-Colonel Crerar had made to 'learn his new work ... [he required] at least another year of duty before he could be considered a thoroughly competent peace-time battery commander.'[69]

Crerar had eight months to familiarize himself with the peacetime Permanent Force. In October 1927, he was informed of his appointment as Professor of Tactics at the Royal Military College as of January 1928, an appointment likely made to keep him out of Ottawa.[70] Like National Defence Headquarters (NDHQ), the army staff was fractured along several lines. This schism was most evident in discussions on defence planning and the defence schemes between the Director of Military Operations and Intelligence Brigadier J.M. Sutherland-Brown, and McNaughton, the Deputy Chief of the General Staff. There was little consensus on what role the headquarters should be playing in the overall defence establishment.[71]

The danger of losing a promising officer to the collective 'rot' that forced the cancellation of the 1927 field exercises and threatened to erode the 'army's remaining expertise' was recognized by the new Chief of the General Staff Thacker ('he kept the General Staff out of mischief ... a nice fellow to have around' recalled one officer) serving his interim appointment, while Brigadier McNaughton, the Deputy CGS, was readied for the post.[72] It was also possible that McNaughton was trying to protect Crerar from the controversies swirling around the headquarters. Accordingly, Crerar was appointed to instruct at RMC, a plum position that fitted with the college's mandate to beef up the effectiveness of its curriculum.[73]

Crerar didn't view it this way. He believed an 'ungraded' appointment was a demotion and a comment on his abilities, particularly as he had been led to believe that a staff appointment was imminent. He wisely vented his anger in a rough draft; at home, the children were warned to stay out of his hair. He wrote to friends at defence headquarters, sending copies of recent appraisals to complement his desire for redress. While insisting that he liked the work of a lecturer, he protested that the rank associated with his new position suggested that he was not regarded by his superiors 'as worth while as [he] used to be' and that other, less objective, factors were involved. He suggested that 'in general interests, apart from my own, the case should be investigated.' Crerar's overreaction and tendency to self-pity were not unusual. 'He rather underestimated his ability,' recalled Orde. 'Sometimes he gave me the impression that he needed a boost to deliver the goods.'[74]

Calmed by reassurances from his superiors that the appointment was not a demotion, Crerar settled into life at RMC. Teaching tactics, strategy, and international affairs, as well as command of a company of cadets were the chief responsibilities of his appointment. Crerar proved a straightforward and effective teacher. He drew on his knowledge and love of history to illustrate the broad principles of war as presented in the Field Service Regulations. He emphasized the importance of powers of decision and simplicity in planning. This latter characteristic shaped his promotion of the direct advance over other forms of attack as offering the best chance of decisive victory. This principle would shape his approach to battle, if not always his profession.[75]

'Gentlemen cadets didn't take tactics terribly seriously,' recalled Brigadier G.E. Beament. 'A lot of it was tactical exercises without troops.' He concluded nevertheless that Crerar was a popular teacher, an assessment borne out by the accounts of other cadets and Colonel C.F. 'Consie' Constantine, the stern, athletic, and physically imposing commandant. Constantine praised Crerar as an 'excellent disciplinarian and organizer ... demanding strict adherence to orders and regulations but ... sympathetic to the [cadets] ... in whose interests he spared neither his time nor energy.'[76] Cadets remembered him for the consideration he showed his subordinates. Brigadier H.A. 'Sparky' Sparling recalled that Crerar as his company commander got the commandant's permission to 'let the senior class come to his house for beer in the evenings. He told the class even if he wasn't there they could help themselves.'[77] He recalled Crerar's thoughtfulness; others remembered him as strict and hard-nosed.

The academic life appealed to Harry Crerar's less ambitious side. The Crerars had 'first-class quarters in the College grounds, with a good garden.' As he described it to a Staff College friend, 'There [was] riding, swimming and gym for the youngsters, and inexpensive golf and tennis for us, plus all the sailing and boating we wanted. And there were excellent summer holidays, which thrilled my lazy spirit.' This ended when Crerar was ordered to report to Ottawa in May 1929. He left so abruptly that he had to have the examination papers of his 1st and 2nd Class forwarded. The class remembered 'Uncle Harry' by making him one of two honorary members. 'In many ways,' Crerar recalled, 'we hated to leave the College.'[78]

5 Stagnation

I

The promise of the early 1920s gave way to the 'stagnant backwaters' of the 1930s. The darkening international situation contrasted with the government's cautious approach to preparing the country for the storm that might soon break. A frustrated Crerar, convinced by the mid-1930s that war was on the horizon, tried to prepare the army and the country. Faced with public indifference, political hostility, interdepartmental rivalries, and hampered by his own inexperience, the first half of the decade was a difficult learning experience in the politics of defence preparedness.

Crerar's teaching career ended abruptly when Andrew McNaughton was appointed Chief of the General Staff (CGS) at the beginning of 1929. 'After many years of waiting,' McNaughton wrote in reply to Crerar's letter of congratulations, 'we will now be able to get on with some of the ideas which brought you and I into the Permanent Force on re-organization after the War.'[1] McNaughton's was a two-tiered agenda based on changing the civil–military relationship through enhancing, and institutionalizing, the army's influence on defence policy. This required an increase in direct access to the minister and government, and to this end the new CGS fought for the creation of several forums where advice could be rendered. Staffing the headquarters with officers both capable of making a contribution to policy, and willing to do so, would improve the substance of that advice. Crerar recalled, 'He wanted someone to get down to real consideration of the defence problems of Canada and to produce for him the results of his appreciation.'[2] It was not enough to improve access to the government; meaningful advice had to be rendered.

McNaughton's task was not easy. Initiatives on defence policy were not welcome. When the Canadian Infantry Association approached the Minister of National Defence J.L. Ralston – a hard-working and earnest Nova Scotian – to encourage the formation of some sort of parliamentary body to discuss defence issues, Desbarats cut them off at the knees: 'This is a matter for Parliament to decide.'[3] Thacker, reflecting his distaste for politics, had acquiesced in Defence Minister Ralston's request that the position of Chief of Staff be changed to Chief of the General Staff; Thacker also reconstituted a Militia Council, which elevated the Adjutant-General (AG), Master-General of Ordnance (MGO), and Quartermaster General (QMG) to a nominally equal position with the CGS by giving them the right of access to the Minister.

With McNaughton's appointment, greater influence in defence policy formulation became a key objective. Thacker's changes had diffused the authority that McNaughton wanted, and also made it, in his view, more difficult to speak with one voice on policy – the one voice being McNaughton's.[4] From the perspective of influencing defence policy, the army's main problem was political: the issues they addressed and the limitations they needed to overcome to influence policy required political – not just bureaucratic, personnel, and administrative – solutions. It was here that McNaughton's work was focused. He took several steps to alter the political landscape.

McNaughton was the voice and public face of the military during 1930–5. Prime Minister R.B. Bennett recognized his pre-eminence among the service chiefs. It was suggested that the new Minister of National Defence, Lieutenant-Colonel D.M. Sutherland, did little but 'read pulp magazines all the time.' The CGS bypassed both the naval chief and the Senior Air Officer and spoke directly to the Prime Minister; he also resolved the issue of the Deputy Minister's 'undefined position of control' by ignoring first Desbarats and then his successor, Colonel L.R. LaFleche, who was thoroughly disliked by all at army headquarters.[5] None of these changes were formalized, however, despite attempts in 1932 and 1933. How much his approach helped in the long run is questionable. The dependence on personalities – his, the Prime Minister's, and the Defence Minister's – was evident in 1935 when the government changed.

The army's ability to influence policy changed with McNaughton's appointment, but their legitimacy would ultimately be rooted in the substance of their advice. This meant new blood. The paradox presented by the surfeit of senior officers past their prime and the small number of senior positions was one of McNaughton's first problems.

Including the Chief of the General Staff, there were four senior Defence Council positions in 1930; thirteen military districts offered district officer commanding positions. At NDHQ, the General Staff's directorates and GSOs who staffed them provided twelve positions for officers ranking brevet lieutenant-colonel and above; the only other senior post was commandant of the Royal Military College. And junior positions were not abundant. From a low of forty-eight in 1929 to a high of sixty-nine in early 1939, the army section in the Wood Building at National Defence Headquarters in Ottawa remained small.[6]

Quantity was not the only issue. Burdened by a heavy administrative load, the army HQ staff was a mixed lot. 'There were many noble souls,' recalled Orde, 'elderly officers ... who though kindly seemed to have their brains in their feet instead of their heads.' A graduate of the Imperial Defence College in 1931, Orde, like Crerar, symbolized a generational rift that centred not just on age, but on education and experience as well. Small numbers exacerbated this rift. Resources were equally scarce. The Director of Military Operations and Intelligence (DMO and I), Sutherland Brown, also served as the departmental librarian, purchasing books and circulating news clippings.[7]

McNaughton fought to create movement in the upper echelons by retiring senior officers. Progress proved difficult. In June 1930, McNaughton, supported by the military members of the Defence Council, pinpointed one cause of the 'congestion of [the] senior ranks' as the tendency to extend the tenure of DOCs beyond the normal period of ten years. He recommended that if these officers could not be appointed to the Defence Council when their terms expired, then the solution was 'retirement to pension' rather than extension of tenure. There was agreement in principle, but in practice the application of this policy proved next to impossible. In 1931, eight positions were up; six were extended. In 1933, eleven positions required a change; five were extended and four officers shuffled to different military districts. Only one officer was retired.[8] Another problem was that the General Staff, like its counterparts in other government departments, was small and unfamiliar with the requirements of public policy formulation, much less the expertise required of a professional armed force. Creating a core of General Staff officers to undertake an appreciation of the defence policy of the country was thus slow.

Still, within two years, the primacy of operations and intelligence within the GS was at least established. The Directorate of Military Operations and Intelligence became for the next decade the driving force behind McNaughton's and his successors' efforts. Its importance resulted from a combination of responsibilities and personnel. Other sections were reduced in status – for example, the head of the Geographical Section was reduced in rank relative to the operations and intelligence sections.[9] In a HQ weighed down by its administrative burden, the DMO and I was one of the only directorates whose task – planning for and preparing the army (on paper at least) for war – was possible and attainable. For the most part, the work of the NDHQ staff was 'routine' and administrative. The work of the Directorate of Military Training was characterized as 'dull' and ineffective, fiscal limitations taking their toll.[10] DMO and I, in contrast, was characterized as one of the most exciting directorates. Colonel H.H. Matthews was Crerar's immediate superior. He succeeded Sutherland Brown as the Director MO and I in 1927, bringing his expertise as acting director but not necessarily fresh insights. He did, however, share McNaughton's belief that changes to Canada's mobilization plans were necessary and was willing to consider policy initiatives.

The 1930s thus dawned with some promise, although the political environment remained complex. Politically and constitutionally, Canadian governments sought greater autonomy from Great Britain. The military, however, remained dependent on the British for organization, training, and equipment, and correctly assumed that Canada would fight with the British in the event of a European war. Facilitating the transition from subordination to cooperation would prove difficult in the political climate of the 1930s, but it was the underlying theme of defence preparations. In addition, the absence of a realistic defence policy created a vacuum that exacerbated the army's struggle to define its role and legitimize itself to the Canadian government and public in order to advance preparations.[11] The Depression imposed severe economic constraints. The government was less interested than the public, which was not interested at all, in spending money or time on defence issues.

Crerar was an important player in McNaughton's strategy, and he quickly grew into his job. Crerar was appointed GSO 1 at the Directorate of Military Operations and Intelligence, a position he assumed on 1 May 1929. Crerar concurred with McNaughton that administration was a burden to the stretched staff. He immediately requested a military clerk and increases in civilian clerical staff to free him to consider more substantive issues, demonstrating how basic the staff's needs were.[12] He gave the impression of taking things in stride, complementing

McNaughton's 'impetuosity' and tendency to have many irons in the fire. Indeed Crerar was a picture of calmness, but he sometimes pushed himself to the detriment of his health. Admitted to the Ottawa Civic Hospital for an injured knee in 1931, twisted while skiing, he was discharged at his own request. 'Patient anxious to return to office on crutches,' read the doctor's report. 'Movement of joint should be avoided.' Two years later, the stress of his job was causing acute indigestion and insomnia.[13]

Crerar's responsibilities in the operations section were centred on conceiving options and bringing order to the country's preparations for war: producing paper schemes for mobilization and memoranda summarizing Canada's strategic positions from the Arctic to the Panama Canal as well as the impact of international developments on Canada. He was involved with most work of the tiny DMO and I office, as well as that of the GS. He was secretary to the Joint Staff Committee, comprising the CGS McNaughton, the CNS Commodore Hose, and the Senior Air Officer, Group Captain J.L. Gordon. He joined the Interdepartmental Censorship Committee established to draft regulations for wartime censorship. In addition, his intelligence duties included liaison between National Defence and External Affairs. He also assessed information received from UK military attachés posted throughout the empire.[14] By 1931, Crerar's memoranda – some under the signature of Matthews – on the needs of Canadian defence and the direction it should follow had McNaughton's full attention; militia reorganization became an important goal, anticipating what all believed would be Canada's main military commitment – an overseas force.

To that end, Crerar prepared the skeleton plan for reorganizing the militia and a memorandum justifying the reorganization of the Non-Permanent Active Militia in light of the evolution of the political and strategical environment of 1919–30. He argued that the 'existing Militia organization was radically incomplete.' Defence against the United States was no longer an issue. There were only two 'military contingencies which Canada must face': an overseas empire war and defence of Canadian neutrality in the event of a U.S.–Japanese conflict.[15] Despite Defence Minister Ralston's approval of the change to the basis of army planning – from home defence against the United States, to participation in an overseas empire war – this analysis of the changes in the international security environment was necessary, in part because of the resistance anticipated from the members and commanders of the militia units earmarked for disbandment or conversion. The memorandum, for general staff consumption, also warned against early distribution of these intentions before the details had been approved: 'Premature knowledge amongst Militia units of intended changes,' cautioned Crerar, 'would create unnecessary and objectionable difficulties.'[16]

Crerar's role in McNaughton's plans in the late 1920s and early 1930s marked the true beginning of his expertise in international and inter-imperial affairs. McNaughton encouraged his staff in this direction. Crerar was predominant among them, serving twice on the executive of the Ottawa Branch of the Canadian Institute of International Affairs (CIIA).[17] Responsible for extracting pertinent information from Department of External Affairs memoranda on disarmament, the League of Nations, and Canada's relations to the Commonwealth, he found that the breadth and depth of his knowledge grew quickly. The army was starved for experts on international affairs and Crerar was becoming one.[18]

The rigours of public lecturing and memo writing were tempering Crerar's views on a number of issues. His perspective on the imperial relationship changed substantially, at least on an intellectual level. In public speeches and correspondence, he placed the Canadian militia's international responsibilities firmly in the context of the constitutional and imperial developments of the 1920s. He echoed the pragmatic view that emerged from the 1926 Imperial Conference and the Balfour Declaration on the autonomy and equality of the Dominions and Great Britain. Militarily, the concept that Dominion provisions for local defence constituted imperial defence became an accepted principle.[19] Crerar believed that Canada's first line of defence was Britain, not least because the country benefited immensely from being able to draw on British military resources and institutions. Recognizing that obtaining British recognition of the benefits of equality was also important, Crerar pressed hard, particularly on an unofficial level, for more personal interchanges with the British army, worried that the window was closing.[20]

Involvement during a year and a half with the interdepartmental subcommittee formed in 1931 to examine the implications of the Statute of Westminster on the military relations between Britain and Canada served to deepen Crerar's appreciation for the changing relationship with Britain. He was concerned that as legal ties no longer existed, the 'future co-operation on the part of the armed forces' might be endangered. Crerar concluded that it was 'vitally important that the necessary reciprocal legislation ... be enacted.' He was correct. Canada's small forces required the assistance of a major power. From his perspective, Britain remained the logical choice.[21] The Visiting Forces Act was the legislation that subsequently framed the new military relationship.

Crerar believed that the public needed to be educated on the changes. 'The relations between the Governments of the Empire,' he observed in a review of the *Journal of the Royal United Service Institution*, 'are an approximate reflection of the views of the people electing them ... it profits little to discuss the improved machinery for the co-ordination of imperial defence until the demand ... has been created.' The problem, he concluded, was how 'to convince the layman that close co-operation is required.'[22]

Despite his interest in international affairs, Crerar identified his own fortunes and aspirations with the Canadian military. McNaughton was less sure. In 1931, he suggested that Crerar's future lay in the diplomatic field rather than the services, a suggestion that seemed rooted in McNaughton's determination to foster stronger links with External Affairs. McNaughton went as far as proposing a specific assignment – a diplomatic position in Washington under Bennett's brother-in-law Bill Herridge – an indication that he had discussed it with others.

Crerar wanted to stay in the army. He responded with a lengthy and reasoned defence of his decision. He was concerned over the financial and career implications of switching professions at the age of forty-four, particularly with two children in school. He continued,

> I feel that what I have to give, in a constructive and national sense, is bound up with the defence forces of Canada – and my ambition lies in that direction. I want to improve my knowledge of things military and the inter-relation of those things with national and international affairs so that some day, say ten years from now, I will be fit and wanted for the job you now hold.[23]

Crerar's ambition evolved into a concerted effort to indirectly effect change in defence policy. War and its roots in society were subjects of passionate interest that raised for Crerar fundamental questions about human nature, international relations, and societal responsibility. The importance of these ideas to Crerar were such that he felt his greatest contribution to Canada's defence was his talks on these themes during the interwar period. In this, Crerar was not alone. Through the 1930s, the middle echelons of the GS established a growing network of contacts with luminaries at External Affairs like Lester Pearson and with influential foreign policy observers such as Escott Reid, national secretary of the CIIA, and Professor F.R. Scott of McGill University. They debated the issue of Canada's political and international obligations in forums such as the CIIA and local regimental and service associations. Crerar also joined the Canadian Political Science Association and the Canadian Military Institute. Despite his dislike of public speaking, he addressed these forums whenever possible. Unofficially, he circulated confidential General Staff memorandums to his growing network of contacts in External Affairs and the CIIA. These papers were designed to show that military personnel were considering their roles in a larger context and pressing for Canada to accept the international responsibilities of nationhood. He advocated the maintenance of the informal and flexible commonwealth connections over the formality of the League or proposed commonwealth constitutional machinery.[24] These themes were in tune with the new breed of middle-echelon civil servant in External Affairs who viewed the government's foreign policy as timid: Pearson observed that there was very little in papers with which he did not heartily agree. Reid, albeit later in the decade, perceived that a central element of the CIIA's agenda was to 'popularize' its program and reach a wider audience.[25]

Work on disarmament also brought Crerar into contact with future luminaries such as Norman Robertson and cemented friendships with Pearson. In 1932, Crerar was appointed as the military technical advisor to the Canadian Delegation to the League of Nations' first, and largest, World Conference on Disarmament in Geneva. 'He will be able to do excellent work there for Canada,' Georges Vanier wrote McNaughton. As a member of the working subcommittee instructed to prepare briefs for the delegates, teamed with Pearson and Norman Robertson of External Affairs, Crerar had voiced his scepticism. 'Armaments are the effects, not the causes of political disagreements,' he observed to Brigadier J. Sutherland Brown. 'As regards our own show, it is quite certain that any figures which might conceivably be adopted will be away beyond any that our present organization requires.'[26]

His experience in Geneva did nothing to dissuade him from this viewpoint. Accompanied by Verse, on her first lengthy trip away from her son, he was in Europe from April through July. In his view, the debates were 'fruitless' until the former enemy powers were released from the armament restrictions imposed upon them by the Treaty of Versailles. In fact, 'each discussion seems to indicate a closer political alignment between those ... powers and Italy.' He returned home, his stock rising as his contribution was described as 'masterly,' but convinced that nothing would come of disarmament.[27] He was right; the conference ran until May 1934 but achieved nothing. Adolf Hitler was appointed Chancellor of Germany in January 1933, then withdrew from the League of Nations and the proceedings almost immediately.

Disarmament and international relations continued to occupy a significant position on Crerar's agenda both officially and through the addresses and talks aimed at educating the Canadian public. He continued a steady interchange of views on international affairs with Reid and Pearson. McNaughton encouraged Crerar in this direction, anxious that he 'help along [the army's] good relations with the "diplomats."'[28] This concern underlined the shaky relationship between the military and those whom James Eayrs characterized as the 'attentive public' – academics, intellectuals and interested citizens – whose negative views on things military were aggravated by the inability of the senior command of the military to share sensitive information. To this end, he and others on the General Staff tried to provide their views in more discreet ways.[29]

McNaughton also encouraged the establishment of the Conference of Defence Associations (CDA), to promote militia reorganization and professionalism but also to have an effective defence-policy lobby group. McNaughton and Crerar both played roles in framing its agenda but were warned off too blatant a use of it for policy changes in 1932 by the minister D.M. Sutherland and by the hesitation of the CDA itself to involve DND in policy questions.[30]

II

Crerar also worked to maintain and develop his knowledge of current tactical and operational debates. Enhancing the effectiveness of the army as a fighting force, even through debate, was important. His efforts in the realm of international affairs detracted from his ability to do it all, but he worked harder than most. First, Crerar introduced War Office administrative procedures to his directorate, improving the ability of the small staff, in the opinion of his superiors, to meet McNaughton's increasing demands. He also earnestly attempted to keep abreast of developments in technology and British operational theory. His interest in field and regimental work was marked. In 1930, he persuaded McNaughton to grant him permission to fly to Nova Scotia to observe the army exercises, participating in an 'unofficial' capacity.[31] In early 1933, Crerar promoted the idea of initiating short-term overseas attachments for militia officers, to expose them to the collective training denied them in Canada. Dissuaded by McNaughton, who feared a negative political reaction, Crerar nevertheless encouraged the non-permanent militia to retain such ambitions.[32] Similarly, he took a limited interest in Canada's service journal, the *Canadian Defence Quarterly*, regularly reviewing for it the contents of Britain's *Journal of the Royal United Service Institution*, and serving as a referee for the quarterly's annual essay competition.

Crerar was generally cautious about new operational and technological developments. He believed the first step for Canada even to attain military adequacy was the reorganization of the non-Permanent militia to reduce it to a realistic and equipable size. Crerar accepted mechanization as the future trend in warfare. He urged readers of the quarterly to study Liddell Hart's pieces on mechanization in the *Journal of the Royal United Service Institution*.[33] Crerar, however, was uncommitted to any particular organization and tactical doctrine that might integrate the new mobility and firepower provided by tanks and armoured vehicles. The role of air power was another area that was marginalized in the debate.[34] In Canada, he did little to advance the debate beyond emphasizing the study of the broad principles of war. Crerar had a fuller appreciation of the navy and air forces than many contemporaries, including a CGS who believed that the Canadian navy was a drain on defence expenditure.[35] He saw little reason to change his opinion on the need for a broad outlook through the 1930s. 'There is no trend in service thought which holds more important promise for the future,' he observed in 1933, 'than its ever-broadening interests ... A great deal of this improvement must be put down to the drastic education of the Great War. Even the private in the trenches learned that the chances of adequate artillery support ... and the problems of war were not restricted to the battlefield.'[36]

Crerar's ambitions coincided with his interests. He set his sights on the Imperial Defence College, attendance at which was characterized as 'sure a sign as any of eventual high command.'[37] If education at the Imperial Defence College (IDC) became for many a prerequisite for promotion, it also whetted the appetite for a more formal role in policy. From 1930, Crerar pressed McNaughton to nominate him, prompted by frustration with the 'chronically slow' promotions. 'Although I have been lucky in my staff appointments,' he noted to Robert Haining, 'I have yet to obtain my substantive Lieutenant-Colonelcy ... with a brevet of fifteen years standing.'[38] His requests took on a greater urgency following the death of a newborn child in May 1933. Verse and son

Peter, in need of new surroundings, left that fall to join Peg in England, where she was attending boarding school. 'I feel, too,' he observed, 'the need of a change and rest.'[39]

The glacial rate of promotion, symptomatic of Canada's interwar permanent forces, was not a reflection of the assessments of his performance.[40] 'Competent to assume the duties of a Director at NDHQ,' recommended Colonel Matthews in 1931, 'and very suitable for selection to attend the Imperial Defence College.' McNaughton confirmed this assessment.[41] In 1932, he described him as 'one of the best' officers in the Permanent Force. From this point, at least, McNaughton and Matthews pressed for his promotion and advancement. Highly favourable reports on Crerar's performance in Geneva, particularly given the apprehension that arose when the delegates learned McNaughton was leaving, confirmed Crerar's selection to attend the IDC in 1934, the eleventh Canadian to do so.[42]

III

Situated in the heart of London, the Imperial Defence College was founded in 1927, to address concerns over the service, economic and political cooperation, and coordination difficulties that emerged during the First World War. Turning out senior commanders was not its mandate; rather, the college was established to foster a greater understanding of the higher direction of war and facilitate cooperation among the services and civilian departments responsible for defence. Students were from the fighting services and the civil service. The curriculum focused on the organization of the services; economic, financial, and industrial resources of the empire; and the interrelationship of foreign policy, national policy, trade, and strategy. Of the thirty vacancies, twelve were reserved for students from the Dominions and India; Canada could send two but did so only three times prior to 1934 (1927, 1931, and 1933). Lasting one year divided into three terms, IDC's course grouped the students into syndicates of approximately five each, teaching them through conferences, lectures, written exercises, and visits to service camps. Each term dealt with strategic problems affecting imperial security in Europe, the Middle East, and Far East respectively, with specific analysis of the strength and weaknesses of the empire and its most likely antagonists.[43]

Generally, the curriculum complemented Crerar's own perspective on the major lessons of the Great War. Yet while it did nothing to dissuade him of the importance of the imperial connection, the narrow

British perspective that he encountered disturbed him. Crerar promoted the evolution of a Canadian defence policy that 'was supplementary to, but not incompatible with, the British imperial doctrine of which it is part.' The foundation for this perspective on imperial defence was the 1926 resolution, which, in his view, stated that 'the defence of the Empire was a matter of mutual concern for all its Governments in which ... local defence was accepted as a primary responsibility. All other matters: communications, similarity of organization, equipment, etc, etc follow naturally from its application.'[44]

Crerar's shift in perspective, and the tension between his emotional attachment and pragmatic understanding of the new realities of Canadian autonomy were illustrated by his revisions to drafts of addresses in 1934. Lecturing on 'Canada and Imperial Defence,' Crerar pencilled out references to 'the Mother country,' replacing it with 'Great Britain' or 'United Kingdom.' Other modifications included substituting 'chapter in British history' for 'chapter in our history.'[45] As he recalled a few years later, 'I preached *hard*, standing on the one safe plank of "adequate local defence."' While it probably meant wasted resources, he reasoned that, 'if carried out, even partially, it would at least result in adequate provision for mutual military action when the crisis comes.'[46]

The reports on Crerar's work and capabilities were very enthusiastic. Unofficially, the Adjutant-General was informed that IDC's Commandant characterized Crerar as popular and 'among the first three of the twenty-six at the College.' The confidential report at the end of the year confirmed this view:

> An earnest and clever student of all aspects of inter-Imperial relations and of foreign affairs. His quiet determination and sound analysis have much impressed both staff and students by which he has done much to emphasize (without veneer or respect for conventional attitude) the true position of Canada in defence matters ... A very pleasant demeanour. In my opinion he has all the attributes for high command.[47]

Praise from a senior British officer almost guaranteed Crerar's appointment as Director of Military Operations and Intelligence on his return to Canada in 1935.

IV

After the personal difficulties of 1933, Crerar and his family returned to Canada in 1935 refreshed and eager. While in England, they had lived twenty miles south of London in a cottage bordered by a nine-hole golf course, a garden, and tennis courts. 'Verse who had not been very well when we arrived,' he reported, 'got back to form quickly and the youngsters enjoyed the country life very much during their holidays.'[48] The family had travelled extensively during the breaks, and Crerar had enjoyed the opportunity to show his children the British Isles, from Scotland to Jersey.

The time in the United Kingdom was a sharp contrast to the stagnant professional atmosphere that greeted him on his return. McNaughton, attempting to negate the effects of the Depression that had prompted Bennett's government to ravage the Defence Department's budget, had compensated by emphasizing the military's civil role and continuing with attempts to increase the military's influence in defence policymaking. The public works approach had not improved the army's efficiency; training, modern equipment, and establishments were in disarray. Similarly, movement on militia reorganization was slow.[49] The promise of the early 1930s had soured into the 'stagnant backwaters' – Crerar's phrase – of the interwar period. The darkening international situation contrasted with the government's cautious approach to preparing the country for the storm that might soon break.

Crerar took up his appointment as the Director of Military Operations and Intelligence soon after his return from the United Kingdom. The DMO and I began to assert itself after 1935 under Crerar's directorship. A critical addition was Major Maurice Pope, characterized by all who worked with him as possessing one of the finest minds and sharpest pens in the army. He had acted as interim DMO and I in 1934, and like Crerar, was an example of the new breed of army career officer: educated and eager to play a role as a professional public servant. Pope was a few years Crerar's junior and, a veteran of the war, had followed a similar path: Staff College in 1924 and a year and a half with the Directorate of Staff Duties at the War Office from 1931 to 1933. More important for its influence on their approach to defence policy in the 1930s, they shared attitudes and aptitudes in the province of higher defence policy and international relations.[50]

Their actions were framed by a dramatic change in British defence policy, which reflected the situation in Europe. Under Adolf Hitler, Nazi Germany was rearming, and the Italians were eyeing Abyssinia; in the Pacific, the Japanese were becoming bogged down in China. The League of Nations was helpless, and hapless. British Air Chief Marshal Sir Edward Ellington underlined the shift when he reminded

McNaughton in February 1935 that while defence preparation had been governed by the policy that 'we need not expect a major war within ten years of the date when the Estimates were prepared ... the rise of the Nazis in Germany has led the Government to rescind this rule, and we are now seriously preparing for war.'[51]

In the face of the deteriorating international situation, the DMO and I pressed for more effective defence preparations, which meant changing government foreign and defence policy and the military's role within it. 'We cannot indefinitely continue,' Crerar wrote Lester Pearson in the summer of 1935, 'to have the cake and not eat it.' Fresh from the IDC, Crerar was eager to encourage interchange; his enthusiasm sometimes eclipsed his hard-earned political insights. In February, he urged McNaughton to convince Bennett to visit the college when he was in London. 'There is no reason,' he noted, 'that the IDC should be suspected of ulterior designs.' He would learn.[52]

From 1935, Crerar and Pope pressed forward on a number of fronts. They re-established the General Staff's defence priorities in successive papers on Canada's defence requirements. Defence Scheme No. 3, which Pope had begun to revise in 1934, quickly became the centrepiece of army mobilization planning. Indeed, the army planners had little doubt that through this scheme they were preparing an overseas force.[53] There was, however, much to be done. Prominent goals included advancing the scheme for reorganizing the militia, establishing firmer liaison with External Affairs, exchanging information with opposite numbers in the British War Office, and, most important of all, changing government policy on defence preparations.

Progress was slow for a number of reasons. In April 1935, a ruptured appendix hospitalized Crerar. It nearly killed him, although he made only passing reference to it, but he remained sidelined until mid-May. Meanwhile, the Bennett government, an election looming, temporized on militia reorganization. The Prime Minister's reading of the changing fortunes of the Conservative party prompted him to replace McNaughton as CGS with the former Quartermaster General, Major-General E.C. Ashton, in June 1935, a change that some, including Crerar, feared would hurt the army's standing.[54] The Italian invasion of Abyssinia and the election of the Mackenzie King Liberals in the fall of 1935 were the final developments in an unsettled year.

6 The Politics of Preparedness

I

The imminence of war shaped the second half of the 1930s. Crerar produced some astute assessments of the deterioration of the international situation and its probable consequences. Still, these translated into only modest gains in preparedness, particularly for the army, and fed an atmosphere of distrust and anxiety at the headquarters. External Affairs remained a major obstacle to further defence preparations, even as Mackenzie King slowly recognized the volatility of the situation in Europe and the Far East. Crerar emerged from these struggles a much shrewder political operative, but still frustrated with the slow progress in defence preparations and his career. He would later suggest that he was close to resigning over the glacial movement within what he would characterize as the 'stagnant backwaters' of the interwar army.

For the Directorate of Military Operations and Intelligence, the new Chief of the General Staff was, in some ways, an improvement. Although he was viewed as hard-working and diplomatic – 'a pearl of great price' – Ashton's policy objectives as CGS were largely derivative; in 'The Requirements of Canadian Defence' he signalled that he intended to pursue the agenda started by McNaughton. Ashton reiterated McNaughton's parting description of the sorry state of Canada's defences and added his own list, including details on the lack of mechanical transport and comments on the failure to build up any industrial base to equip the military. However, in contrast to McNaughton's political connections and support within Bennett's government, Ashton was not overtly political and he gave the department's policies a politically neutral feel.

Crerar would come to appreciate Ashton's gifts. During the war, Crerar would recall that during the 1930s Ashton 'gave honest advice and upheld the right.' He believed, and tried to gain public recognition for the belief, that the Canadian army's relatively smooth mobilization in 1939 was 'in great part due to the efforts of Ashton during his tenure as CGS.' Another important change in 1935 was the appointment of a new minister of national defence, Ian Mackenzie. Orde described him as a 'genial chap [who] had a high powered motor car' and who sat at Defence Council meetings 'looking like a Buddha,' leaving the substance of military policy to his advisors. He established a good relationship with Ashton, and proved responsive to the army's needs. His support and sympathy were important.[1]

Ian Mackenzie was astonished at the 'atrocious condition' of the country's defence forces; he responded to Ashton's admonishments by approving a seven-division militia reorganization plan.[2] Eager to follow up on this success, Crerar and his staff at DMO and I became more aggressive, swamping the minister with memoranda on their interpretations of international events and their implications for defence policy and Canada. These were also sent to EA personnel and other observers of the international scene, in the belief that the 'isolationist nationalism' that characterized their foreign policy reflected disillusionment with the League of Nations. It was hoped that they could be convinced that the future of Canada's foreign and defence policy lay with Britain.[3]

Public discussion and debate on defence policy were not forthcoming. And there were limits to how far Crerar could comment on public policy. By 1935, all references to policy and international affairs in statements by Permanent Force officers had to be cleared with the CGS. Crerar encouraged others to speak out where he, as a government servant, could not. 'Should you succeed in securing some private individual,' he wrote Alan Plaunt of the Canadian Institute of International Affairs, 'who possesses the ability ... to bring a sense of realities to bear in public consideration of these questions, you will undoubtedly be accomplishing a real service to the state.' General Staff officers also approached the CDA to bring more political pressure to bear on the government to establish a Canadian Defence Committee. Crerar spoke openly of the military's support for such a committee, stating that the government was holding back, not the department, as had been assumed earlier. That higher authorities sanctioned this approach is a reasonable conclusion, since the CGS vetted all public statements.[4]

Even with a receptive minister for national defence, progress was uneven. Approval for the General Staff's priority on an overseas expedition was not forthcoming, although the King government's ambiguous foreign policy proved beneficial for the army's plans for defence policy.[5] The 1936 budget provided for a small rise in defence spending. The importance of interdepartmental cooperation also seemed to have been recognized as the government approved the formation of a Canadian Defence Committee. The department also established a Sub-Committee on Supply, with some cooperation from the Department of Trade and Commerce.

The militia was also reorganized, at least on paper. This was no small task, given the resistance at the local level and the political pitfalls.[6] The plan for militia reorganization was reflected in Defence Scheme No. 3, the mobilization plan for an overseas expeditionary force; Pope and Major Elliot Rogers, GSO 3, deserved credit for much of the detail. Crerar proved sensitive to the need to obtain the support of the District Commanding Officers to implement it. When local commanding officers continued to resist changes, Crerar responded with 'soft' tactics, which presumed that the resistance was due mainly to 'a misunderstanding of the object in view.' He issued a confidential memorandum on the new imperial priorities of Canada's defence policy as interpreted by the army's General Staff, which concurrently undercut the raison d'être of a number of units. Some at NDHQ were harder to bring on side. It took until late 1937 to convince Director of Military Training and Staff Duties George Pearkes to help 'sell' the scheme by providing whatever assistance he could.[7] Results were soon forthcoming.

External Affairs was a tougher nut to crack. Skelton was already wary of the military or, more precisely, wary of their interpretations of international developments. The newest appointment to External Affairs was Loring Christie, whose job description read, in part, that he was 'serving as the Under-Secretary's closest colleague on questions of war and peace.' Christie, characterized as cold and overly logical, saw little reason for Canadian involvement in what he dismissed as 'European Affairs.'[8] Crerar felt him out, by sending him a memorandum on 'The Higher Direction of War, with Particular Reference to the British Empire.' Christie gave it a frosty reception, dissecting it with characteristic bluntness. Although Crerar received positive responses from Pearson and Escott Reid, Christie's reply awoke Crerar to the full extent of resistance in the upper echelons of External Affairs, particularly important given Christie's position as the 'first point of contact with the armed forces.'

More interchange of information did little to dispel the suspicion of the General Staff's motives. Crerar was buoyed by Pearson's positive responses, but grew concerned over Christie's influence at External Affairs. 'I admire his brain,' he observed to Pope, 'but his reasoning is cold and his conclusions ... always seem to ignore the human factors. He is, I consider, a "super-isolationist," and I am not at all happy about the effect his advice may have on his department.'[9]

Nothing worked. Skelton treated a proposal in September 1936 for filling Canada's vacancy at the IDC with a civilian official with disdain.[10] A few months later, when Crerar attempted to establish intelligence links with the military attachés of the British Embassy in Washington and promote firmer exchanges of information with the British army, he suggested that all such information pass through External Affairs. While he did not want the information subject to their veto, he hoped it might give them the military perspectives and '[serve] to torpedo the misconception ... prevalent in official circles ... that our personnel ... are inclined to leave our Canadian diplomatic organization in the dark.'[11] To counter the impression that the military was too imperial-minded, dependence on Britain was presented, correctly, as increasingly a function of necessity for a profession constrained both fiscally and politically; the use of British military expertise was the logical alternative to total stagnation.[12] This conclusion had the fortunate coincidence of being true.

Crerar placed great faith in this open flow of information and was encouraged by the results, even though his faith was misplaced. His friendships with his War Office counterparts, many of whom were colleagues from the Staff and Imperial Defence College, increased both the flow of military information to Canada and the points of contact between the forces. Mirroring McNaughton's official and unofficial liaison letters, Crerar stressed that Canada needed War Office strategic intelligence summaries as well as equipment lists and contact directories.

If ignored by Skelton, the army's assessments of the international situation and Canadian defence requirements caught the Prime Minister's attention. King was not oblivious to the dangers of Nazi Germany. Mackenzie King finally read McNaughton's parting assessment of the state of Canada's defences, minimized by O.D. Skelton, in August 1936; he was greatly disturbed. Hard on heels of the King's reading of McNaughton's assessment, Cabinet approved the Canadian Defence Committee. It was composed of the Prime Minister, and the ministers of justice, finance, and defence; it provided a forum to bring together the government's military advisors – the Joint Staff Committee, organized in 1927 – and the ministers. At its inaugural meeting, the service chief's presentations were the centrepiece. King was impressed by the members of the committee. Their conviction that public opinion would draw Canada into any major war in which Britain was involved and their assessment that Britain's foreign policy was returning to its more traditional balance of power and away from commitments of the League of Nations were far more accurate than EA's assessments. And it increased the government's and the military's trepidation at their inability to prepare for that future war in Europe. They also revealed an appreciation for the changing relationship with Britain and its implication for defence policy that sometimes escaped their EA counterparts.[13]

The Joint Staff Committee, the three senior officers of the services, and Crerar as secretary followed up in September 1936 with a paper entitled 'An Appreciation of the Defence Problems Confronting Canada, with Recommendations for the Development of the Armed Forces.' Written by Crerar, it has been characterized as 'among the key documents of Canadian history' for its forceful and insightful assessment of the international situation in 1936 and Canada's place within it. Crerar had expressed these opinions for years.[14] Although the document's impact foundered on the proposed costs of rearming, its arguments served notice that the military's analysis was important, if not politically desirable.

While King and Ian Mackenzie proved receptive to the military's arguments, political expediency and financial considerations set definite limits on what they would do. After much debate, despite Mackenzie's best efforts and the rare occasion of King defending the 'brass hats' in Parliament, the defence budget was reduced from the staff's estimate of $65 million to $36.2 million for 1937/8. Construction of Pacific coastal defences was approved, but the Atlantic Coast would wait until 1939 – an emphasis Crerar later said was 'due to a political rather than a military appreciation.' The army was relegated to third priority among the services. Most importantly, the government publicly denied that the services were preparing for an overseas force, forcing the army to re-address its preparations in light of home defence requirements.[15]

Subsequently, Crerar organized a subcommittee of the Joint Staff Committee to examine coastal defence construction, the Coast Defence Construction Committee, chaired by Director of Engineering Services Brigadier E.J.C. Schmidlin.[16] While examining the defences of the east coast in the fall of 1936, Crerar organized a series of confidential lectures to provide the militia officers with information on the General Staff's defence policies and shore up support for reorganization. The first was an address to the Halifax Military Institute scheduled for 26 November 1936. Crerar spoke from notes based on his JCS memo on the defence problems confronting Canada; afterwards he spoke informally on the possibility of war with Japan. Two days later, a sensationalized version of the confidential address appeared on the front page of the *Halifax Chronicle*; the headline screamed 'Canada Must Fortify Pacific Coast against Japan' while the subheading read 'General War Is Probable.' The article emphasized that Crerar and others were in Halifax carefully inspecting its defences; the inference was that war was imminent and that Canada would be bound to follow Britain's lead.

The political volatility of such assertions was clear. That summer many English dailies had slammed Ian Mackenzie's denunciation of visiting British statesman Viscount Etibank's criticism of Canada's 'weak defence policy.'[17] The General Staff, anxious to remain on good relations with a nervous government, printed a denial and launched an investigation to discover the leak. Crerar issued a formal apology to the Japanese ambassador. He was already in trouble for allowing some articles critical of Canada's defence preparedness to appear in *Canadian Defence Quarterly*. The minister and his deputy minister demanded full reports to arm themselves against possible criticism. It was a tempest in a teapot; there were no rumblings in Parliament, but the CGS cancelled Crerar's subsequent engagements and Adjutant-General Major-General C.F. Constantine barred all Permanent Force officers from making public references to defence policy and international affairs.[18]

Crerar labelled the file 'the Halifax Incident.' It illustrated the staff's delicate position. There was a difference between public expositions of policy and obtaining a position in shaping defence policy. 'I fully realize the ideas underlying the decision to issue these recent instructions.' Crerar wrote the CGS after a request to speak to the CIIA. 'It strikes me, however, that the full effect of this ban in Institute "circles" may produce reaction from influential members which may have unfortunate results all around.'[19] Had Crerar gone too far? Perhaps. His public addresses, intended to influence the policy debate, could too easily be construed as policy pronouncements, a point that he was slow to learn. The reaction from Defence Headquarters prompted Crerar to temper his public pronouncements and quickened his desire to bridge the gap between External Affairs and the military. 'I rely on you,' he noted to Hugh Keenleyside of the Department of External Affairs after some observations on military developments, 'to protect my "anonymity" securely. After the Halifax episode my very existence requires me to be eliminated from public consideration!' An article appearing in *Saturday Night* in late February, by an author using the euphemism 'Rideau Banks' and entitled 'Shush on the Empire!' also questioned whether it was playing too large a role in policy. Crerar reacted quickly, penning a memorandum to the minister, refuting the main points of the article. It was a sign that not all agreed with the General Staff's policies or approach.[20]

II

Skelton and Christie used the occasion of the Imperial Conference in May 1937 as the pretext to assert their prerogatives as the main interpreters of international affairs for Mackenzie King. They feared legitimizing the army's voice in defence policy, insisting that it should have no say in policy whatsoever. The catalyst for the decision was a UK Chiefs of Staff Sub-Committee of the Committee of Imperial Defence briefing paper, circulated to Ottawa, which advocated a centralized imperial defence and foreign policy. Pope and Crerar were wary of the political damage that might be caused by this 'bad' diplomacy, although Crerar viewed the Imperial Conference, and the preparations surrounding it, as an opportunity to promote discussion of defence policy and organization. In a memorandum to the JSC soon after the New Year in 1937, Crerar had anticipated that it was 'not unlikely that at the Conference efforts may be made to concert joint plans against the contingency of a major war with Germany.' He warned that it was 'even more unlikely, however, that the Canadian government will evince any desire to commit itself in advance.' Information sharing was the best he hoped for. He also achieved another important objective when, at the conference, the position of the RCAF vis-à-vis the other services was raised and the Air Staff Senior Officer's elevation approved in principle.[21]

The Chiefs of Staff briefing paper, and the JSC, prompted a furious reaction from Skelton and Christie. Christie first questioned the propriety of the document itself: 'Is it for the military staff to expound policies?' His answer was unequivocal: despite the fact that he acknowledged the interrelationship between foreign affairs, defence, and constitutional questions, he observed that it was for the civil arm of the government to lay down policy and 'then for the military to submit military plans accordingly.'

As a result, Crerar warned his British counterparts that few service personnel would be present at the conference.[22] He was visibly relieved when a few weeks later he was chosen to supervise the work of the subcommittees and write the memoranda. Lester Pearson, at the High Commissioner's office, was similarly relieved, writing tongue-in-cheek, 'I hate to think of the three chiefs of staff being let loose among the denizens of Whitehall without your expert guidance,' he wrote in March. Crerar set sail with Verse and Peter that April.

At the same time, Christie and Skelton told the Prime Minister that the British information on Canadian defence preparations came from the official 'liaison letters' between Defence Headquarters and the War Office, the details of which Crerar had given Christie early in 1936 to promote better relations. Subsequently, after consultation with Ian Mackenzie, the Prime Minister limited the flow of information and allowed External Affairs to control the tap. King set the tone at the conference, warning his defence chiefs and Crerar, who seemed to the PM 'anxious to put forward a programme with the British officials' that the last session's defence program had been intended to blunt further requests for the year. Skelton 'carefully instructed' the JSC and Crerar 'as to the necessity of avoiding any conversations with [their] "opposite numbers" ... which could be interpreted by them as being in the nature of a military commitment.' Crerar noted, as one example of 'how far this was carried,' that they were told they could 'not even discuss the steps planned by the United Kingdom for the protection of Newfoundland,' despite the obvious implications for Canadian defence. In case there was any doubt, he sat with Ian Mackenzie and went through the draft statement line by line, deleting 'any reference whatsoever to Empire Defence, even as regards consultation for cooperation.' Crerar nevertheless felt that some movement towards cooperation had been made, although the grounds for his optimism were obscure.[23]

Ashton's approach over the next year and a half was thus informed by both Germany's expansionist policies and by the new information practices. Skelton and Christie became more obstructive, delaying the interchange of information, ignoring requests from the NDHQ to transmit letters, or withholding their approval. They resisted the General Staff's attempts to establish interdepartmental subcommittees modelled after Britain's Committee for Imperial Defence. And, after a promising start, the Canadian Defence Committee stopped meeting in 1937.[24] Skelton and Christie kept the army at arm's length from any policy discussions.

Though slated for a new appointment, Crerar was retained in his position in response to the setbacks.[25] Official initiative for change was generated by the DMO and I's office. Crerar and Pope, perceiving the establishment of defence committees as a first step to high-level reorganization, prepared a comprehensive memorandum detailing a Canadian organization for the 'Higher Direction of National Defence.' They submitted it to the minister in March 1937. It was revised several times, but its basic recommendations on the establishment of subcommittees and the need to bring the service chiefs into defence policy making were unchanged.[26] The resistance of Skelton's External Affairs precluded any action in 1937.

Such steps as could be taken were. To overcome External's close scrutiny of the liaison letters, Crerar sent sensitive information to the War Office regarding coast defence via personal and secret letters to the British Military Attaché in Washington.[27] Defence Scheme No. 3 was modified to present the overseas force as a 'mobile force,' mainly for home defence, unequivocally the government's first defence priority. It was qualified by noting that an overseas war was the more likely scenario of the two, and the framework for expanding the expedition to seven divisions remained intact.[28] Crerar and Pope recognized the problems of justifying equipment procurements purely on the basis of home defence, and, proceeding on the assumption that they were preparing for an overseas war, they urged Ashton to present his case on the broad needs of mechanized operations. Ashton initially declined; successive memorandums on the requirements of Canadian defence placed direct defence of Canada as the first priority.[29] However, the two divisions designated for defence were also equipped – on paper at least – and organized for a major war abroad. Ian Mackenzie approved the new emphasis on home defence, but accepted the army's desire to prepare for every contingency in detail, and in principle. The Prime Minister also appears to have supported this practice, although it is unlikely he realized the extent to which army planning emphasized the importance of an overseas force. Indeed, he vehemently denied, on behalf of the Minister of National Defence, the ex-mayor of Montreal Camillien Houde's assertions in a federal by-election campaign in January 1938 that the army had 'secret plans to send five army divisions wherever necessary for the defence of Empire.'[30] Crerar, like others, denied that the army was preparing an expeditionary force. He felt there was 'much virtue, and no vice' in using British organization and doctrine, reflecting on the difficulties produced by a government policy of autonomy that precluded the cooperation that was the foundation for the military's professional status.

The British military did nothing to ease the evolution towards cooperation. In his personal correspondence – of which only extracts were saved – with his War Office counterpart and IDC compatriot Colonel R.B. Partiger, Crerar continued to suggest that informal visits from senior British officers returning from the East might be a means of circumventing government restrictions and simultaneously facilitating the transition from subordination towards cooperation. Few senior British officers, Crerar argued, had any knowledge of Canada's new constitutional, and domestic political, position. Partiger, obviously uncomfortable with the idea, preferred 'semi-official' visits; Crerar persisted through 1938, but with little success.[31] The British military's lack of sensitivity about or even awareness of constitutional changes was a constant source of irritation. Crerar and others perceived that their assumptions about Canada's contribution hurt, by alarming King and External Affairs, and cooperation was hindered.[32]

III

In the heated atmosphere of defence policy wrangling in the late 1930s, Crerar's political antennae were becoming acute. He promoted cooperation with the U.S. military, in part to overcome the perception that 'Whitehall was calling the tune.' He observed, 'for when Washington and London think alike we, in Canada, must think the same way, only more so.'[33] Promoting defence preparations was not easy, and could take on comical overtones. In October 1937, Crerar applied to the CGS for permission to discuss the organization of Pacific Coast defences with service authorities in Washington. He was not permitted to make a direct approach. Instead, while ostensibly on leave in late October 1937, but with permission to informally discuss the proposals, he and Verse 'motored to Washington for a fortnight.' While in Washington, he made 'the acquaintance of a number of U.S. army people,' exchanged information with the American War Department, and spent time with the British Military Attaché to coordinate plans with their proposals for defence of Juan de Fuca Strait. His report, delayed only by a three-day stop to visit his sister in New York, on the necessity of coordination prompted Mackenzie to allow 'confidential' talks between the service chiefs.

The lack of progress in Canada was highlighted by his observations on the deterioration of the international scene. His assessments, some gathered during sojourns overseas, were not encouraging, but were good. McNaughton's emphasis on an educated officer willing to undertake policy assessments had paid dividends: personnel at DMO and I evaluated the international situation more accurately and more realistically than did their counterparts at EA. Crerar's insightful analysis of Nazi Germany in 1937 is a case in point. While at the 1937 Imperial Conference, Crerar persuaded the CGS that the opportunity to visit Germany should not be lost. Using Sir Edward Peacock's name to open doors, he talked to businessmen in Hamburg and Berlin.

On his return he reported his observations, illustrated by some remarkable photographs. While he was critical of the organization of the higher levels of German government, noting for example that numerous parallel organizations were responsible for foreign affairs, he concluded that Germany was a 'highly dynamic nation, determined before long to break its present bounds and consequently, increasingly dangerous to European, and indeed, to world peace.' He pointed to Austria as an imminent target of Nazi aggression. He qualified this point by observing that, given the artificial nature of the Italian-German alliance, Mussolini's support was needed before this step was taken. Crerar drew the conclusion that Italy, Germany, and later Japan had no common interests on which to base their alliance; Germany, he maintained, was the real danger. Privately, he was 'both impressed and depressed with what [he] saw.'[34] Other studies and memoranda proved remarkably accurate. In October 1937, he forecasted that despite the problems in Europe, and the imminent danger to Austria and Czechoslovakia, there was little danger of a 'Great War' involving the United Kingdom and British Empire. 'We may get through the next year,' he concluded, 'or even the year after.'[35] In contrast, Christie's assessments of the deterioration in German–Czechoslovakian relations blamed the 'clever intriguer' Benes for isolating his country and drawing Britain closer to war.[36] Whatever the relative merits of their arguments, the response to the actions of External Affairs shaped the GS's agenda and increased its desire to have its professional voice legitimized.

The root of Crerar's frustration was in the inability of the General Staff to translate assessments of this nature into defence policy. This frustration was exacerbated by the lack of professional prospects. In the fall of 1937, upon learning that a peer eight years his junior had been promoted to full colonel, Crerar wrote, 'I am in my fiftieth year,' and the 'time during which I can apply the knowledge I have gained through the somewhat exceptional military education which has come my way can not be long, in the nature of things.' Within his directorate, he made some progress and was able to concentrate on preparing for war. A GSO 2 was added and, more important from Crerar's perspective, the pressure on the director was relieved by the appointment of a permanent secretary to the JCS. The DMO and I also initiated a board of officers to determine what sort of educational material was available in the districts; the replies suggested that most were pre–First World War War Office issue.[37] Still, the limits to what the DMO and I could achieve were real enough.

Part of the problem was structural. In mid-1937, Crerar initiated a study of the organization of the Department of National Defence that was directed at correcting what he and Pope perceived as an unnecessary encumbrance in the form of a 'civilian ... Chief of Staff' – the Deputy Minister. At the root of the argument was the belief that 'professional advice is tendered to the Minister by a non-professional official.' While the paper was aimed at altering the organization at the headquarters, it also harshly criticized the 'mediocre quality' of the collective output of the staffs at National Defence and bemoaned the lack of movement on tactical doctrine, equipment, and administrative organization. The author, most likely Pope, blamed the problems on the absence of a clear government policy and the fact that the service's main duty had been 'peace-time' administration. Yet there was an undercurrent of dissatisfaction with their superiors and some of their peers. The Adjutant-General was the butt of humour when he issued a memorandum on bow ties and mess kit. The DMO and I also found itself part of an ongoing debate when tension arose about training on Sundays. Crerar's incursions into Pearke's directorate sparked some animosity. The criticism of both the Permanent Force and the government that was implied in the document prompted Crerar to decide against circulation, but he drew the conclusion that the malaise informing defence policy and the services stemmed from both the personnel involved with, and the organization for, higher defence. There was truth to such a view.[38]

Some refinements in organization were effected, but while the practice of direct access increased under Ian Mackenzie, the organization remained unchanged. Years later, Crerar maintained that he was close to resigning over the stalled implementation of the interdepartmental subcommittees and the obstruction the military encountered, but he did not and, despite the frustration evident in much of his correspondence, he persevered and attacked the problem where he could.[39]

In September 1937, the King government reduced the militia estimates for the 1938/9 fiscal year to $16 million from a projected $18 million; the army was asked in June 1938 to find further reductions. Only the war scare prompted by the Czechoslovakian crisis in the fall of 1938 allowed them to raise their estimates. In March 1938, a Standing Interdepartmental Committee on Defence Coordination, representing fifteen departments, and chaired by the Deputy Minister of National Defence and supervised by Pope, was established. This move, as well as the subsequent development of subcommittees on censorship and other aspects of defence organization, was viewed as a major triumph. Crerar later observed that he believed that his efforts in initiating the organization of these interdepartmental committees did 'more for "Defence," both local and Imperial, than all my other activities in this job [DMO and I] put together.' Why? '[We] have, at last, succeeded in getting all Government departments actively concerned in their national responsibilities for war.'[40] Guardedly optimistic in the spring of 1938, he concluded that 'John Q. Public is at last getting behind the move for reasonable and efficient means of defence.' As a result, he wrote, 'defence preparations in this country are at least under way.'[41] For Crerar, recognition of Canadian defence obligations was the first step towards military preparedness. He insisted to his less constitutionally aware British counterparts that local defence was the first obligation of imperial defence and that all ends could be served from this start. Crerar and his counterparts were not oblivious to the needs of modern warfare, but were handicapped by political and financial restrictions: in the 1936–7 defence requirements, the army asked for provisions to obtain 312 tanks; by 1937 it had enough money allotted to buy nine and was begging the government for more.[42]

IV

The ebbs and flows of Crerar's professional life were mirrored by his personal life. For the Crerars, life was much better than for most Canadians during the first years of the Depression; his daughter remembered the 1930s as 'idyllic' and 'surreal.' Verse's happiness was Harry's priority; they shared a love of fishing and tennis. 'Peggy is a débutante and Peter is at boarding school,' he wrote in 1935. 'I occasionally annoy Verse by telling her that she will be a grandmother in a couple of years.'

Verse was strong, if more reserved than her husband, but had to be, given her husband's sometimes headstrong personality. Home was his sanctuary; his children were instructed that nothing said at the table was to leave there. Although Verse was unhappy with the constant moves – she wanted a home of her own – her main preoccupations were her children, the need to find suitable domestic help, and retaining a semblance of home life. Their social life was busy and they were remembered as great entertainers. Despite some temporary reallocations, Ottawa was home and their circle of friends tight. Ottawa was a small society in the 1930s, the army even smaller, and arguably more insular. The society circles in which the Crerars moved was small enough to temper the difficulties of maintaining a stable social life. It was like a merry-go-round, recalled Peggy Crerar Palmer: you always ended up with some of the same people.

Crerar numbered some colleagues – military and political – among his close friends. The Pearsons and McNaughtons were frequent visitors. He kept close contact with his U.K. friends, even as they scattered around the globe to safeguard the empire's interests. His remained close to his Hamilton cronies; he discreetly helped many from his old battery, providing financial and professional help. Yet his closest friends were not in the military, but from UCC and RMC, as well as Ottawa neighbours, who were also part of the small stratum of society that provided Canada with her professional and political class. Irvine 'Ike' Perley-Robertson, a prominent Ottawa businessman, married to the daughter of the former Conservative minister Sir Robert Perley, was his 'best friend' and fishing partner. Ken Greene, Perley-Robertson's partner and a veteran of the CEF, was well known in Liberal circles; after the Second World War, he received plum diplomatic appointments as High Commissioner in Australia and Consul General in New York. An avid golfer, he was a close confidant. Harry was very close to his brother John, also in Ottawa. Crerar seemed to identify with, even need, friends outside the military. The Crerar of the 1930s was remembered by one Ottawa newspaperman as more of a 'civil servant' than a soldier. While Crerar would have used the term *public servant*, he would have been happy with that description.

The summers were important to Crerar. They rented cottages, alternating between Vi's entertainment at Loon Island in the Muskokas and time with the Cronyns and Boswells at Lake Simcoe. Aunts, uncles, and cousins often brought the numbers to thirty or more. Summers with his sister were formal: tea times in the tea room, semi-formal attire at lunch, and formal dress for dinner, a reminder of his parents' family life that Crerar could not completely emulate. Crerar's passion for golf as a distraction grew. There were limits to its palliative effects; he was said to be unapproachable after a bad game. He read mysteries and Civil War books to fall asleep at night. Photography became another distraction.

Harry Crerar was also learning the art of parenting. He was a demanding father. He expected close to perfection, his daughter recalled, and if he didn't get it you knew about it. He was a believer in bringing home the consequences of actions. He gave his children, and wife, an allowance and expected them to live within their means. When Peg produced an overdraft while in boarding school, he was quick to deduct the cost from her monthly allowance. When he sent the message, he was terse: 'This a business letter, so I am having it typed.' He kept a careful watch on her friends and boyfriends. He cared deeply about his family. Despite his admonishments about money, and the sometimes pedantic rants, his letters to friends were those of a proud parent, filled with wry observations on the trials and tribulations of child–parent relations. His files are full of apologetic letters to the organizers of regimental dinners and the international associations which he put so much stock in, as he begged off because his sister was visiting or a child was celebrating a birthday. He tried to use his connections to secure Peg a plum summer job at the Library of Parliament, but she struck out on her own. 'Peg is now a "working girl" and assists Mr John Powers, Photographer,' he wrote Lester Pearson at Christmas 1937. '[She earns] a modest emolument (which she promptly spends on self adornment!).'[43] Peg's friends remembered his interest in her life, and when she turned sixteen, he relaxed his grip, but not his interest, considerably. Peter too found him exacting, perhaps as a male more so, and was closer to his mother, but remembered fondly their travels and summers at his aunt's. His father watched closely as Peter adjusted to the rigours of boarding at Upper Canada College and eagerly anticipated his return during the holiday; he kept his friends well informed of Peter's progress. In both children, he valued above all bravery and responsibility; his values were 'traditional' in the sense that they were not transitional. Peggy recalled his disgust with popular trends like the esteem-raising rhyme, 'In every day, in every way, I am getting better and better.' Self-respect, not self-esteem, was his central aim for his children, and for himself. Through the 1930s, his children's growth only underlined his own age and modest career advancement.[44]

By 1938, Crerar was ready for a new appointment. Commenting in December 1937 on a recent shake up at the War Office, he noted, 'The

Lord knows a bit of movement in our own Permanent Force is long overdue.' He wasn't optimistic, contemplating at least another year at the DMO and I. He was actively seeking other opportunities within the military. While in England in May 1937, he discussed with Richard Dewing the possibility of a teaching post at the IDC. The War Office hoped to appoint a Dominion officer. According to Dewing, Crerar was one of two candidates being considered to fill an appointment, when a sudden vacancy required someone immediately; Dewing took the position. Through 1938, Crerar was favoured to be the first Dominion officer to hold the post.[45]

Instead, Crerar was posted, as the CGS's second choice, to RMC as commandant effective August 1938. That summer, Major-General T.V. Anderson, described as a 'likeable fellow ... who had to move along well-defined paths,' replaced Ashton. Before Anderson was appointed, he was screened by LeFleche, who had 'pointed out to him that there were too many instances of thoughtless talk or action as well as of lack of loyalty to their seniors on the part of Departmental personnel particularly on the part of Permanent Force Officers.' Anderson appeared to agree, leading the Deputy Minister to conclude, 'I am convinced that, if he succeeds General Ashton, he will do his utmost to assist me.' Other changes followed during the fall of 1938. Major-General H.H. Matthews was appointed Adjutant-General effective 15 August, and Major-General W.P. Elkins became MGO, effective 9 November 1938.[46]

Crerar was happy for the change after 'nine years of paper.' The commandant of RMC was an appointment characterized by Ashton as 'one of the most important and responsible positions for which we are required to provide.'[47] For Crerar, the promotion to temporary brigadier was welcome; so too was the change of venue.[48] His tenure was marked by its temporary quality, not least because Crerar's view of the college was framed by the imminence of war and his work on the mobilization plans. Following the Munich crisis in October 1938, he recommended that the college's role during a war be set down. He suggested that after the two senior classes had been recruited, RMC should produce Permanent Force officers for all three services throughout the war. His recommendations were not acted on, but suggest his frame of mind. Similarly, Crerar pressed forward on several fronts for better relations with the Non-Permanent Militia.[49]

He remained active in defence preparations. During the winter of 1939, he spent, by his own account, three days a week in the capital. In March 1939, Anderson requested his recommendations on a memorandum titled 'Preparation for War' and to flesh out the AG branches' priorities for implementing Defence Scheme No. 3. The final version reflected British views on mechanization as well as their ambivalent approach to the organization of armour. He concluded that the greatest obstacle to the implementation of any mobilization or defence plan was the lack of adequate staff and resources, a problem that his temporary allocation to HQ highlighted.[50]

Crerar keenly followed developments in Ottawa, applauding the news of Ian Mackenzie's informal restructuring, which allowed the chiefs of the staff direct access to the minister, and enabling them to avoid the Deputy Minister, the universally disliked LeFleche. Crerar was optimistic that this signalled a new respect for the military's voice within the civil–military relationship, but it was short-lived.[51] A steady unofficial correspondence kept him well informed. He also applauded any and all attempts to wake Canadians to defence issues. He joined the Kingston branch of the CIIA. He also encouraged the immediate publication of *The Military Problems of Canada* by a young scholar, C.P. Stacey. 'Whether or not readers agree with his conclusions,' he wrote the CIIA, 'his study is bound to create a healthy interest in Canadian defence policy and that interest is indeed needed.'[52]

Crerar did not ignore the college. He was a popular commandant, who was well liked by the cadets and who liked them. On weekends, he entertained the cadets at his home. When he and his wife came to RMC, recalled former senior cadet Lieutenant-Colonel P.T. Nation, they brought a greater sense of warmth to the commandant's house. Verse had improved the house within weeks of moving. The family fit in well. When Brigadier R.T. Bennett's brother was killed by lightning, recalled the former cadet, Crerar took the time to talk to him.[53] That same paternalism infused his ideas of education. He took a firm stand against hazing, viewing it as an example of a lack of the control he prized in himself and others. He was also active on the college's behalf, using his friendship with his former Rockcliffe neighbour Norman Rogers, the Minister of Labour, to press for improvements to the grounds and infrastructure surrounding the college. In the summer of 1938, he initiated a calendar to 'correspond to the calendars issued by Canadian universities,' to give parents and cadets a complete picture of the college.[54]

Crerar too had a clear idea of the value of a combined military and civil education. Debating the point with Terry MacDermot in the spring of 1939, he described the advantages that RMC training offered young Canadians: 'It tends to produce men able and willing to accept responsibility in the administration and control of others.' He realized that while this trait was not universally accepted as a positive one, in 'a practical sense ... the wheels within a family, institution, group, or nation just wont [sic] go all around at all unless there is some organization of leadership and control. Complete individualism means complete selfishness – and that will get the world nowhere but into trouble.'[55] Here too was a neat summary of RMCs impact on him. His addresses to the cadets stressed the importance of character and control.

Kingston proved an important reprieve for the whole family. The fall of 1939 would mark an abrupt change in their lives, and lifestyles. At RMC, life had a timeless quality: Edwardian formality was the order of the day; calling cards, teas, and servants were typical adjuncts to everyday life. Crerar kept a record of the number of people entertained and the types of entertainment, whether lunch or simply 'refreshments'; the number was in excess of 1400. While he fussed over expenses, pleading a 'Scotch conscience if I did not,' he took great pleasure in it. For Peggy, returned from boarding school, Kingston the university town was remembered as a whirlwind of dances and boys, and one boy in particular: Zouch Palmer.[56] Perhaps the highlight of his term was the royal visit in the spring of 1939. Fort Henry and RMC were scheduled as part of a Canada-wide tour, although Crerar was anxious enough to suggest that the royal couple's visit be unofficial, 'for whatever arrangements I could make would produce more criticism than popularity.' The visit was a success, however. He used the opportunity to extract funding for improvements to the grounds, from the Minister of Labour. He felt justified by the enthusiasm with which the royals were received. 'The visit of Their Majesties to Canada,' he wrote on 14 July 1939, 'brought all the latent patriotism and adherence to the Empire to the forefront.'

> Our 'isolationists,' always few, but vociferous and sometimes importantly placed, have been pushed aside ignominiously. No sensible person now in Canada, or elsewhere, doubts the attitude and action of Canada should the next 'Great War' break out. And God knows it does not look as if we can avoid it much longer.[57]

7 Limited Liability War

I

'It will be a long war, or series of wars, and Canadians (and Americans too) will need to put every ounce into it,' observed Crerar in 1939. To him, a large army effort was a foregone conclusion. He was also convinced that Canadians would quickly rally to Britain's side. These assumptions, and the memory of the problems during the First World War, shaped his goals when he was sent overseas to establish the Canadian Military Headquarters in London. Freed, or so he thought, from the constraints imposed both by Mackenzie King's fear that speaking of war would make it so, and the rivalry with External Affairs, he was soon disillusioned by the government's hesitant approach to preparing for war and had to relearn some of the hard political lessons of the 1930s. Still, Crerar never doubted that, as in 1914–18, Canada needed to field a large army as its primary contribution to winning the war.

The German army drove across the Polish border on 1 September 1939. Two days later, the British Prime Minister Neville Chamberlain announced that, for the second time in a generation, Britain was at war with Germany. France was left with no choice but to declare war that same day. Mackenzie King promised to let Parliament decide the timing of Canada's entrance into the war, a symbolic but important gesture; the declaration of war came on 10 September. The Armed Forces were already on alert, and a designated 'Canadian Active Service Force' was organized by an order-in-council issued on 1 September. Numerous precautions had already been taken such as the cancelling of leave for all members of the Permanent Force as of 25 August. Even earlier, on 1 August, a tentative list of the officers who would constitute the staff of the 'Mobile Force' was circulated. As of 1 September, a 'state of apprehended war' existed.¹ In sharp contrast to the haphazard mobilization at the start of the First World War, the army stuck to the plan as outlined in Defence Scheme No. 3. If it was still ill-equipped and poorly trained, it was not poorly organized at the General Staff level. In response to the order-in-council, National Defence Headquarters issued General Order No. 135 authorizing the complement of the 'Corps of the Active Militia' and notifying all units and staffs so designated. Crerar was selected as Brigadier, General Staff of the Corps.²

Crerar expected to play an important role in the war effort. To his surprise, and horror, his name was accidentally left off the final list for those designated to go overseas. Major-General H.H. Matthews, now the Adjutant-General, immediately telephoned to assure Crerar that the omission was an error.³ Crerar, not one to leave his career to others, quickly launched a flurry of correspondence to ensure his position in the Active Service Force. A letter was sent to Major-General Anderson, the Chief of the General Staff (CGS), 'reminding [him] of [my] existence and asking that [he] not forget the somewhat special military experiences and qualifications [I] possess when responsibilities are being allotted for Active service.'⁴ On the same day, Crerar responded to Matthews' call, asking him to ensure that a correction appeared in the orders. As added insurance against a reoccurrence of what he feared was a deliberate omission, Crerar rushed a brief note to Ken Greene in Ottawa asking that he mention Crerar's name in 'non-service' (Liberal) circles. 'A year away from Ottawa,' he added, 'has placed me a bit upon the side lines and it may be that my qualifications will not be remembered when Ministers get around the Cabinet table.'⁵ The responses were immediate, and reassuring, as all noted that men with Crerar's capabilities were going to receive key positions in the near future. Still, Crerar's confidence could still be easily shaken.

The government's decision to send only one division overseas in 1939 eliminated the need for a Brigadier, General Staff of the Corps – the appointment envisaged for Crerar. By mid-September, however, he was slotted to go overseas as BGS of the 'Overseas Headquarters.'⁶ Once informed of his appointment, Crerar wanted personal assurances from the CGS that Verse would be given sufficient time and money to relocate and that the family would be reimbursed for the money sunk into the commandant's house in anticipation of a longer stay. He also requested an immediate promotion to major-general. 'All the British officers who were my contemporaries at the Staff College and Defence

College, of real capability, are now Lieutenant and Major-Generals,' he noted. 'My present [grade], on my arrival in England, will be a definite handicap in my dealings with them and in fulfilling my responsibility to Canada.' Events would prove him correct. Anderson tactfully rebuffed him, however. He agreed in principle, but noted the tensions that would arise if Crerar were promoted so quickly over others senior in rank. Instead, he held out the promise of future promotion.[7]

Through September, Crerar's position was as unsettled as the college's. In an official note in late August, Adjutant-General Matthews requested the names of recent graduates who had refused Permanent Force commissions upon graduation. The uncertainty was evident, however, as he penned a personal letter to Crerar on 28 August noting that a decision on offering commissions to the present 1st Class was being delayed 'in the hope that if some agreement is reached in Europe, even temporary, we might avoid disturbing the college work.' He nevertheless cautioned that should 'Canada order mobilization ... the college will no doubt be placed on a different basis.'[8] Once war was declared, Crerar pressed to ensure a central role for the college and its graduates in staffing the officer corps.[9] He received many enquiries and offers of service. One he would remember was a letter from an academic requesting information regarding a job 'in the present emergency.' He could offer the writer nothing at this early date, but he later called on a young C.P. Stacey to record the army's history. On 11 September, Crerar made what he presumed would be a final plea on behalf of RMC to the Minister of Labour, friend and neighbour Norman Rogers, asking that in 'the midst of ... this emergency you will not forget the present and future requirements of this institution.'[10]

Policy for the use of RMC cadets was soon determined by the decision to dispatch an expeditionary force. The British government indicated that it 'hoped for a large Canadian effort on land'; King hoped that a large industrial effort, combined with the training of aircrew under the British Commonwealth Air Training Plan, would suffice. The army's submission of a detailed proposal for an expeditionary force caught him by surprise, and horrified Skelton and Christie, confirming their worst fears. Public opinion was nevertheless strongly in favour of dispatching a force overseas. On 11 September, Rogers addressed the issue in the House of Commons; on 19 September, the government announced its decision to send one division to the United Kingdom and to raise a second division for home defence.

On 21 September, Crerar was called to Ottawa by Anderson 'to draw up a policy for the college.' In a session with Matthews, a former commandant, Lieutenant-Colonel Ken Stuart – Crerar's choice as the future commandant – and the CGS, the decision was made to commission the top two classes and to allow the first and second years to continue until the spring of 1940, when they too would be offered commissions. The college would then close as a cadet school and 'all officers would come from officer corps training units.'[11]

Still wary of political interference with officer selection, fearful of a repeat of Sam Hughes's patronage appointments twenty-five years earlier, Crerar intimated to the Adjutant-General that there would be trouble from cadets, and their well-connected parents, if 'recommended 2nd Class cadets applying for P.F. [commissions] ... find they are unable to obtain them because these, in the meantime, have been given to others who are not so highly qualified.'[12] In the hopes of impressing upon the government the importance of RMC's role, Crerar also invited Rogers, now Minister of National Defence, to attend the October graduation ceremony, an invitation gratefully accepted.

Crerar revealed the details of the mobilization policy in a farewell address to the college on 11 October. The sentiments he expressed foreshadowed his pragmatic approach to the war effort: 'There will be changes, with little respect for honours and customs, [but] each class must face its new responsibilities and privileges.' He concluded with the news that he had received orders to report to Ottawa. As he completed his speech the senior class 'marched off the square escorting the colours – every cadet in the class to accept a commission in His Majesty's Forces.' It was, in the official historian's words, 'a moving address.'[13]

II

Crerar was due to leave for Ottawa on 14 October 1939, a move he had suggested to familiarize himself with the new mobilization plans before embarking as advisor on army matters to the Canadian delegation proceeding to England to confer with the British and other Dominion delegations about coordination of the war effort. On the termination of that conference, Crerar was to remain in England as the senior officer of a Canadian Staff Headquarters to be formed in London 'in anticipation of the arrival of units of the 1st Division.'[14]

There was no firm departure date. Crerar knew only that he was to be the military advisor to the Canadian delegation, but little else. He arrived in Ottawa on a Sunday, 15 October, hoping to have several weeks to acquaint himself with the 'proposals under discussion concerning the despatch of Canadian Troops overseas.' He reported to the CGS the next morning, only to be told that the delegation was to set sail in a few days. The next four days were a frantic rush to gather information on 'the approved or anticipated policies of the four branches of the Army Staff of the Department.[15] Crerar met with Norman Rogers and O.D. Skelton. He was also able to meet with the heads of each branch of the staff, and finally with the head of the Canadian delegation, the Honourable T.A. Crerar, Minister of Mines and Resources. As a result of his discussions, Crerar prepared a memorandum on the 'Higher Organization for War' that included his proposals for the overseas headquarters. The proposals were informed by his First World War experience, which had demonstrated that without a clearly defined role, a political administrative headquarters could hinder as well as help the overseas forces.[16] Foremost in his thoughts was the fear of the evolution of an Overseas Ministry of Canada and its staff into a parallel army that might became 'more of a barrier than a link between the two vital centres of the Canadian military effort, i.e. the Department of National Defence in Ottawa, and the Canadian Corps in France.'[17] At the same time he urged flexibility, to avoid problems arising out of rigid interpretations of responsibilities and prerogatives. While still Senior Officer of what would become CMHQ, he characterized the HQ as the 'overseas military portion of the Department of National Defence' and emphasized the importance of maintaining a relatively autonomous position.[18] He clearly believed that the civil authorities should not hamper the military professional in the execution of war policy. He therefore pressed for policies and prerogatives that would establish the pre-eminence of the Senior Officer, CMHQ, and the General Officer Commanding (GOC) of the overseas forces in army policy making. He anticipated that the operational HQ would spend the war in France, involved in operations.

Crerar's final preparations were personal. He discussed with Verse her determination to join him overseas. He also instructed his bank on what to do with his finances in his absence; he left a 'memo' for Verse detailing her monthly allowances and those for the children. The day before he left he prepared his will. Fifty-one years old, a trim 150 pounds, his hair still brown, if somewhat less obvious, he said goodbye to Ottawa.

Through the end of 1939 and into 1940, Crerar was able to achieve his agenda, partially by design and partially because of the situation arising out of the distance between DND and CMHQ. He had three immediate goals: to establish CMHQ's headquarters and organization, to negotiate for quarters and equipment for the 1st Canadian Division, and to fulfill his role as special advisor to T.A. Crerar and the Canadian delegation. They were complementary. Crerar had been a welcome addition to the delegation; his opposite number at Canada House, Lester Pearson, described him in his diary 'as of yore, serious, hardworking, capable.' Pearson came to respect Crerar's views on the establishment of a Canadian military headquarters. Crerar also established a good working relationship with the Canadian High Commissioner, Vincent Massey – 'his desire and mine are for a very close measure of collaboration, as close as National Defence in Ottawa will permit,' noted Massey in his diary – and was able to convince T.A. Crerar to back him as he pressed his suggestions home.[19] After ensuring that Lieutenant-Colonel E.L.M. Burns – an acerbic, unsmiling, but gifted young protege – was preparing the accommodations and equipment for arrival of the 1st Division, Crerar held discussions with Massey and T.A. Crerar on the subject of the proper shape of the headquarters. Shortly afterwards, he recommended an organization modelled after the military establishment of National Defence Headquarters, with four staff branches, one 'redesignated' Canadian Army Staff. He tried to establish it as the non-political link between DND and its overseas forces. It would be associated with, but not responsible to, the High Commissioner's office.[20]

Crerar's ambitious goal also anticipated a much larger Canadian army effort than envisaged by the Canadian government and its External Affairs advisers. The plan was rejected, but Crerar was not deterred and pressed his conception of CMHQ's status on a cooperative Vincent Massey and T.A. Crerar. As the King government awaited advice on the structure to adopt overseas, T.A. Crerar followed up Brigadier Crerar's cable with the recommendation on 30 October that anything 'resembling Argyll House Organization in last war should be wholly avoided,' a conclusion that the cautious Mackenzie King fully agreed with. The minister also concluded that Canadian Military Headquarters 'should form part of the High Commissioner's organization and that its principal duties would be to give advice on questions of policy and to conduct liaison between National Defence Headquarters in Ottawa, the British War Office and the senior Canadian military commander overseas,' thus keeping it strictly under civil control.[21] This approach was viewed as a step forward as messages on military policy continued to go direct from External Affairs to the Dominions Office; Crerar and the High Commission received them a few days later. Small steps were evident. Crerar secured Massey's help, and that of his new flatmate, Pearson, in establishing the headquarters for his staff on the second floor of the Sun Life Building, conveniently close to Canada House on Trafalgar Square, but removed from it. The government reluctantly approved the move.

Crerar continued to build the headquarters from the ground up, establishing it along lines that anticipated a large army effort. He was aided by the absence of any clear boundaries. Until procedures and needs were clear, he looked to the British War Office and Vincent Massey for any additional help. The original staff were few but skilled. Colonel P.J. 'Price' Montague, a militia officer with a 'keen legal brain' but inclined to be suspicious and jealous of his prerogatives, was appointed Assistant Adjutant and Quartermaster General. Crerar also secured for his organization the intellectually gifted Burns, and one lonely stenographer. He was soon coordinating all military liaison, with the military advisors to the HC working through him. There could not be two separate lines of communication between NDHQ and its overseas forces.[22] The overseas HQ's separate identity was acknowledged in mid-November by the official authorization that the staff organization would be known as Canadian Military Headquarters. By December the government outlined the position and duties of the Senior Officer and CMHQ vis-à-vis Canada House, the War Office, and the newly arrived GOC, 1st Canadian Division. Responsibilities and relationships were loosely defined, but one point was clear: policy would be decided in Ottawa, and the High Commissioner, with his link to External Affairs, would remain the 'channel for communications on high policy between the Canadian government and the Canadian field commander.'[23]

'Harry is much disturbed,' wrote Pearson, 'because messages on military subjects go direct from External to the Dominion Office and we receive copies from the latter only a day or so later.'[24] At Crerar's urging, Massey telegraphed Ottawa regarding what he perceived as a problem, but with little effect.[25] Still, Crerar established direct lines of communication between the Department of National Defence and CMHQ on matters of detail in organization, administration, and training. Crerar, as Senior Officer, also wanted to provide military advice direct to Massey, 'as required.' Communications on policy between DND and the GOC, 1st Canadian Division, would go through the High

Commissioner. Massey seemed content with this situation, 'assigned' an important role and happy to be consulted but removed from the policy side.[26] Anderson responded by reminding Crerar that his task was, in fact, to provide information to the High Commissioner, not advice, on matters of military detail. That was where the issue stood into 1940.[27]

Crerar's relationship with his British counterparts served to confirm his position. Richard Dewing was Director of Military Operations (DMO), and Crerar's old Staff College commandant, 'Tiny' Ironside, had been appointed, against his better judgement, Chief of the Imperial General Staff (CIGS). Crerar proved cautious in his dealings with old friends – declining to lodge with Dewing lest it seem he was 'in [the] pocket of the DMO' – but he was able to use his friendships to facilitate better communications between the Canadians and the British War Office. He sometimes overstepped his boundaries – Dewing noted in his diary in late November that 'some people (Massey really) had felt that [Crerar] had abused his position by asking Tiny direct for AA guns for Halifax' – but no damage was done.[28] However, Lester Pearson's observation that military 'discussions and negotiations with the United Kingdom were greatly facilitated by the close personal relations established and maintained by Canadian Military Headquarters with the British Defence Services' makes the point. The British agreed. 'Having Harry here at head of the Canadian Mission during the past months,' wrote Dewing in his diary upon Crerar's departure, 'has been the best possible insurance against any serious misunderstanding between Ottawa and the War Office.'[29]

Good results were forthcoming in reduced administrative problems and friction as well as the eventual implementation of regular intelligence reports and appreciations, furnished first monthly and then weekly to NDHQ, by the War Office. This was the direct result of negotiations between Crerar and Dewing, a solid benefit, given the absence of any Canadian intelligence-gathering or -appraising apparatus.[30] By February 1940, a system was in place: the information was passed along to CMHQ, assessed and organized by Burns, approved by Crerar, and forwarded to NDHQ. The control of such intelligence once again reinforced CMHQ's position as an important forward echelon of NDHQ. On the negative side, it created a dependency on British intelligence assessments.

Crerar placed great emphasis on maintaining solid relationships with the British. He attempted, for example, to distance himself and the

Canadian delegation from 'representations' by the Australian and South African delegates that 'defence preparations being undertaken by the BEF are inadequate and are not being pressed forward with sufficient energy.' On hearing of the consternation this caused among the senior commanders of the BEF, Crerar 'drafted [a] letter to General Ironside disclaiming any personal responsibility for criticisms of BEF.' At T.A. Crerar's request he included a sentence indicating that the minister agreed.[31] Brooke noted in his diary, however, that the War Office view on prosecuting the war gave him the impression that 'whilst concentrating on ensuring that they are going to win the war in 3 years time from now, they neglect to realize the dangers of losing it this year!'[32]

Public rapprochement was an important factor in quelling potential problems arising out of McNaughton's sometimes forceful stance on autonomy. '[McNaughton] is explosive in his criticisms ... damns people like Ralston ... was embarrassingly indiscreet about the High Commissioner whom he doesn't like and calls him "a little popinjay,"' recorded Pearson in his diary in December 1939. 'Half the politicians in Ottawa he thinks are crooks and half the War Office over here, nitwits.'[33]

Crerar knew well the quirks and vanity of his long-time superior, but was glad to have him there. Both Crerar and McNaughton were vigorous in their pursuit of British recognition of Canada's autonomous position. In general, the relationship between the British and Canadian forces was defined by two related events: the First World War and the Statute of Westminster's Visiting Forces Act. The latter recognized as constitutional law what the Canadian Corps asserted in the former: the right of Canadian forces to choose the nature of their relationship with the United Kingdom, and, as it turned out, any allied nations. The Visiting Forces (British Commonwealth) Act of 1933 (VFA) was the military corollary to the 1931 Statute of Westminster, which redefined the constitutional relationship between the Dominions and the United Kingdom. The act defined the legal relationship between the Canadian military and that of the other commonwealth countries. Its main points reflected the complexity of recognizing the autonomy of the Canadian military at the same time as the forces of the two countries were tied together by organization, equipment, training, and doctrine, not to mention a shared heritage – a particularly critical component of an army organized around the regimental system. In retrospect it was a remarkable document in that it allowed for the complete integration of two, or more, independent military forces.

The act defined two possible relationships into which the Canadian military could enter with their commonwealth counterparts: 'acting in combination' and 'serving together.' The first prescribed a unified command structure, and essentially created, for operational purposes, one force. In many ways, it was simply a continuation of past practice and as such it retained the same degree of ambiguity toward the relationship between the national government and its army in the field when it served as a component of a larger force. Serving together recognized the evolution of the relationship: in practice it defined a coalition partnership of two independent forces. While the responsibilities of the command structure in both scenarios were relatively clear, the accountability of the Canadian commander was implicit rather than explicit; indeed, it did not define the relationship between the civil and military authority. When under higher British command, he was subject to 'the powers of command as if he were a member of the home force,' but the established precedent was that the senior Canadian officer was answerable to the Canadian government for all operational commitments.[34]

These details were hammered out in the first years of the Second World War. The ambiguity of the act left to the Canadian senior command a great deal of independence to define their own relationships with the British and the Canadian governments. Both McNaughton and Crerar recognized, and believed in, the value of the British connection. However, the strength of that belief was not static; familiarity did, to a certain degree, breed if not contempt then at least suspicion. McNaughton and Crerar interpreted the VFA as creating a two-fold responsibility for the senior Canadian commander to the Canadian government and the British commander-in-chief. They considered, however, that they were accountable only to the former.[35]

The British (and the Canadian government) did not always appreciate these changes and it often required gentle reminders that the Canadian forces were independent. The high-strung McNaughton was not so gentle, however, and while the British got the message, the resulting acrimony would work against him. Crerar could be high maintenance, but he was also more diplomatic. His tact stood him in good stead with the British authorities, a fact vital to his future.[36]

III

In the winter of 1940, questions about the VFA and even CMHQ were academic. During the 'Phoney War' period, the Canadian government's war policy, shaped by King's fear of a repetition of the political divisions of the First World War, promoted an industrial and agricultural effort. Canada's military contribution would be limited to training aircrew, supplemented by a small, token navy and army contribution. Poland's rapid fall, and the subsequent quiet in Western Europe, did nothing to dispel this policy. In contrast, Crerar envisioned a greatly expanded army effort. First, and foremost, he believed the best effort was the maximum six-division expeditionary force described in Defence Scheme No. 3. Second, his assessment of the course of the war suggested that large ground forces would be the decisive element in achieving victory. He also had a definite sense of the historical and professional importance of reviving the Canadian Corps. He thus requested additional commitments from the government for army units and formations wherever possible.

Soon after his arrival in England, Crerar had pressed both the War Office and NDHQ on the question of the non-divisional troops necessary to form a balanced corps, whether Canadian or otherwise. In an early appreciation of the war situation in November 1939, he hinted at the need for an early dispatch of a second Canadian division. Assuming the accuracy of War Office estimates that the Germans outnumbered the Allies by a third on the ground, Crerar observed that the Allies needed troops now, even while he noted that the 'long term significance of the Empire air training scheme should be fully appreciated.'[37] To emphasize his point, he noted that the Australian and New Zealand response to this information had been to cable for the immediate dispatch of more troops. He concluded his message by noting that the War Office was also pressing for the despatch of a second Canadian division; there was no immediate reply.

Crerar also tried to secure his own position. His quest for promotion had not subsided after Anderson's rebuff in September. In November 1939, T.A. Crerar wrote to Norman Rogers urging that consideration be given to adjusting the ranks of Crerar, Montague, and Loggie, recognizing they were 'at a disadvantage in talks with British or Dominion Officers.'[38] The strength of Crerar's personal relationships with his War Office counterparts obscured this problem. Similarly, McNaughton dispatched a telegram urging an improved rank for the positions of Senior Officer and several of the subordinate officers. Crerar was also active on his own behalf, pointedly recording any problems that arose between the War Office and himself, as well as McNaughton, as a result of the disparity in rank. The War Office, in fact, raised questions regarding

Brigadier Crerar's and McNaughton's direct access to the CIGS. As late as April 1940, officers at the War Office continued to be upset 'because General McNaughton [took matters] up direct with the CIGS.' Crerar made it clear that this was an issue between the representatives of two national governments.[39] Crerar was finally promoted to Acting Major-General, effective 15 January 1940, but he remained sullen. 'I suppose,' he wrote McNaughton, 'that the "acting rank" arrangement is the best that Defence Council feels it can do – though the inference is that the job merits the rank and not that I deserve it by the way I have done the job.'[40]

The promotion of Colonel V.W. Odlum to major-general and his appointment as GOC, 2nd Canadian Division, provoked outrage. When Rogers visited in April 1940, Crerar vented his frustration to the minister. He was angry that Odlum, with no service since the First World War, was given the divisional command he wanted.[41] Others shared his distaste for the political nature of Odlum's appointment, and his position as successor to McNaughton for a corps command. McNaughton had not been consulted, and Rogers intimated that Odlum had been appointed partially to counteract the 'feeling in Canada that professional soldiers were getting too many senior appointments.'[42]

Crerar equated Odlum's promotion to a testament of the minister's confidence in his abilities and his performance thus far. He noted that the responsibility 'which Odlum has been given, which I hoped against hope to get – is a straightforward and simple matter compared to the Command and Staff work I must do.' Yet, he continued, not only was Odlum a higher grade, but Crerar feared that the acting rank he had been given indicated that he was still slated for the appointment of Brigadier General Staff of the as yet unannounced Canadian Corps. This appointment would entail a demotion, a move that Crerar argued would not only be impossible for him to accept, but one he somewhat disingenuously observed would be difficult to undertake 'as [the] last few years experience have [not] fitted me for staff.' He concluded with a request that he be given 'a permanent rank as Major-General or better' and that he be granted command of a division. 'God knows, I have better qualifications than any other officer, except McNaughton, for the latter.'[43] This point may have been accurate, but it was undermined by the self-serving, and false, equation of the administration and supervision of cadres of reinforcements with divisional command.[44]

Crerar was also active in pursuit of greater decision-making powers for both himself and McNaughton. The matter became intertwined, in his view, with the reorganization that was occurring at CMHQ as command procedures and organization were brought in line to reflect the growing responsibilities of the headquarters in 1940. Preparations for the arrival of Active Service Force units ostensibly remained CMHQ's main responsibility. Increasingly, however, the liaison among CMHQ, the War Office, NDHQ, and GOC 1st Canadian Division on policy and administration matters ranging from command control to financing consumed most of their time. The decision to place reinforcement units and those not attached to either Canadian division under the command of the Staff Officer, CMHQ, meant further responsibility for maintenance, training, and, after a great deal of acrimonious debate, financing of all 'undetailed' units in the United Kingdom.[45] This reorganization was not completed until the early summer of 1940, when the fall of France added weight to Crerar's arguments.

Crerar was, in part, fearful of the potential cost of delays in communication. Initially, he was sensitive to the limitations of time and distance. In reality, however, Crerar begrudged the compromises necessary to slowly gear up the Canadian war effort. Crerar urged the minister to come and see the problem for himself.[46]

From Crerar's perspective, the situation degenerated at a rapid rate. Replies to his requests for personnel were delayed by DND – an aggravating occurrence, given the pace he set for CMHQ's expansion from a staff of 87 army personnel and civilians in December 1939 to some 900 personnel a year later.[47] He was particularly exasperated with the delays directed at men or policies that he personally recommended. In an effort to keep them in touch with developments in England, while concurrently impressing them with the soundness of his recommendations, Crerar also increased the flow of information to both the CGS and the minister. Still not convinced that this effort was sufficient, Crerar made personal entreaties to the CGS, 'demi-officially' as he termed it, on the need for quicker responses to urgent cabled requests.[48]

Part of the problem was personality. 'It [was] obvious that McNaughton and Crerar were of quite a different school of thought than was Anderson,' wrote Maurice Pope in 1944. Both sides insisted on seeing problems from their own perspective. Anderson, however, was not a wartime CGS. A 'gentle, likeable fellow,' he was characterized as a procrastinator to a 'certain extent' who had to move along 'well defined paths,' none of which were evident in Ottawa during the Phoney War period.[49] The NDHQ was also sensitive to the accelerated and increased chances of promotion for overseas personnel. The CGS finally instructed that individuals recommended for appointments not be mentioned by name in official telegrams and letters to the department. While Crerar pointed out, quite correctly, 'that this instruction is likely to produce very square pegs in round holes,' he seemed satisfied that preferences could be indicated in unofficial communications. Nevertheless, the delays continued to vex him. When his attempts to build up the headquarters staff were questioned by the Adjutant-General, Crerar responded by calculating the excessively long hours his HQ staff were working.[50]

Equally frustrating were the time consuming discussions over the financial responsibility for Canadian non-divisional units. This emerged as a particularly important issue, linked as it was to the question of the formation of a Canadian corps and ultimately Canadian autonomy. Through February and March 1940, Crerar and Pearson acted as intermediaries while Canadian and British officials debated who should pay for the equipment of non-divisional units, even after the Canadian government insisted that they were under the command of CMHQ. McNaughton tried to play the War Office and Ottawa off against each other, in anticipation of the formation of a Canadian corps; Pearson felt he was 'treading on dangerous ground.' For Crerar and Pearson it became a question of national autonomy, although the latter was conscious that there was nothing to be gained and good will to be lost if the British attempted to 'slide out from under the agreement.' Before the Canadian government was aware of the problem, Crerar and Pearson began a series of personal meetings with British officials. The Canadian position soured some British officials, however.[51]

Mackenzie King's announcement in Parliament on 25 January 1940 that the 2nd Canadian Division would be sent overseas '"as soon as possible"' aggravated the situation. Crerar believed that this announcement carried with it 'the implied formation of a Canadian Corps' and 'the imminent placing of the non-divisional troops under Canadian Higher Command.' Crerar wanted to begin immediate preparations for the staff organization and requirements of CMHQ in anticipation of future responsibilities.[52] The Canadian government, however, was in the middle of an election campaign and had not authorized a corps. Treasury officials continued to balk at the costs. They said no. The government authorized discussions only on the basis of what was already committed, aggravated by the 'tendency of its generals to anticipate events.' Only after the election of 26 March 1940 did the government devote its full attention to the matter of a corps.[53] The government opposed an overseas ministry, but intended to maintain direct civilian control through a system of regular ministerial visits. The first was arranged for April. As it turned out, the visit of Rogers in April and May 1940 provided the opportunity to speed implementation of these policies. The Minister of National Defence, in meetings with Massey, the Canadian senior commanders, as well as War Office officials, informed them that he was empowered to discuss the formation of a Canadian corps of a maximum of two divisions plus ancillary troops. McNaughton and Odlum agreed with this estimate, and while this was the consensus, Crerar's notes indicate that there was considerable discussion of the issue. With expansion in the offing, Crerar voiced his desire for a field command in personal discussions with Rogers in April.[54]

Crerar also pressed Rogers to approve his plans for expanding CMHQ, a proposal Ottawa strongly resisted, given the shortage of suitable staff officers. Elkins concluded, 'The proposed expansion appears to be based on the assumption of an expansion of our Military Forces Overseas, which present policy does not envisage.' Rogers, reluctant to approve the expansion outright, supported the principle that the GOC Commanding Canadian Forces in the theatre of war 'should have the final word in recommendations to the Department of National Defence regarding operations, organization, appointments and military business generally.' While large changes could not be undertaken without DND's approval, the opinion of the senior officers overseas would clearly carry more weight. Crerar's conception of the Senior Officer at CMHQ who oversaw policy and liaison, and generally supervised all aspects not under the purview of the GOC, had come to fruition with the minister's approval of the reduced establishment.[55]

CMHQ now reflected Crerar's 1939 proposals. Crerar as Senior Officer could concentrate on policy. His tenure as SO was a success. There were hallmarks of his later approach to command. He established a no-nonsense relationship with his subordinates at CMHQ, but one conducive to a strong working team. Brigadier Burns remembered him 'as a man who liked his subordinates [like himself] to get things done quickly, with not too much chat about it. Although he did not exude warmth and magnetism, he was a man of determination, of will ... Towards me he was understanding, helpful and generous.' Crerar was a patron to many, staffing CMHQ with competent professionals like Burns – who Crerar considered one of the finer intellects in the army – Chris Vokes, Maurice Pope, and Price Montague. He campaigned ceaselessly to have their, and his own, expenses met, arguing that life in London required considerably more money than in Ottawa. With solid ties to his superiors, subordinates, and peers, Crerar was able to make CMHQ function relatively smoothly.[56]

IV

Crerar's requests for staff support took on a new urgency with the German invasion of Norway in April 1940. Nazi successes only reaffirmed his conviction that this would be a long war, requiring every ounce of effort. When the fighting began in earnest, the inability of the overseas high command to commit the Canadian forces became a real liability in the eyes of the military professionals. McNaughton provoked the first explicit challenge to this policy, committing Canadian forces to the British Expeditionary Force that was sent to the aid of the Norwegians. Thirty hours elapsed between the time of commitment and the receipt of news by the Department of National Defence, a move that earned McNaughton a stern reminder from the minister that such commitments were to be cleared with him.

McNaughton was loosely within his rights as a designate of the minister to order Canadian troops 'in combination' with British units, but the main issue for Crerar and McNaughton, however, was one of government confidence in the advice of their military professionals. The situation had developed with a startling rapidity. The British were impressed with McNaughton's speedy response. Dewing noted that 'Andy played up magnificently, took responsibility of accepting, came up to War Office that afternoon ... and got right down to working out all the details.' The atmosphere in London promoted such actions, an atmosphere that Ottawa had yet to understand.[57] McNaughton's reaction to the minister's rebuke indicated that his personal sensibilities were also involved.[58] Nevertheless, neither side had anticipated events enough to organize a means of reacting to what could not have been a totally unexpected situation. A National Defence Headquarters that was desperately stretched and directionless did not alleviate the problem. Victor Sifton, with the *Winnipeg Free Press*, commented to Grant Dexter on the disorganization apparent at NDHQ and the need for a strong Chief of Staff to reorganize Canada's defence effort. Crerar believed, correctly, that the problem was 'the centralized system of Governmental (or financial) control in force in Ottawa.'[59]

The importance of Crerar's efforts was magnified by the German successes on the Continent. In early May, Crerar and Rogers, while concerned about Allied preparations, had been reassured by visits to the Maginot line that they would have some time to prepare. On 10 May

1940, the German army invaded Holland and set in motion Operation Sicklethrust, its planned assault through the Ardennes. Within days, despite sometimes fierce resistance, the Germans were across the Meuse and their tanks were heading for the coast. The fragile Anglo-French command system, and psyche, could not react quickly enough.

In the middle of this crisis, Crerar retained a remarkable faith in the ability of the empire to rise to the occasion. He had always believed that when war came, the Dominions and Britain would speak with one voice. On 26 May, the final paragraph of his cable to the CGS describing the situation at Dunkirk read, 'The military situation may well appear to be much worse before it unquestionably becomes much better but from the information and knowledge obtained I believe that the surmounting of our present awe-inspiring military difficulties is mainly a question of moral courage and determined action.' On 27 May, the British began to evacuate their troops through the port of Dunkirk; Crerar cabled Ottawa that the evacuation would have to be restricted to personnel. On the 29th, he cabled the CGS that it appeared that the bulk of the British Expeditionary Force might be lost.

On 1 June, the *Times* published a letter, accompanied by a poem written by Pauline Johnson entitled 'Fight On,' received by Crerar during the Allied crisis in the spring of 1918, a period of crisis for the Crerar family. While the author used the pseudonym 'A Canadian,' it was Harry Crerar.

> Time and its Ally, Dark Disarmament,
> Have compassed me about;
> Have massed their armies and on battle bent,
> My forces out to route.
> But though I stand alone, and fight and die,
> Talk terms of peace? Not I!
> They've torn my flag to ribbons, but in rents,
> It floated above the height.
> Their standards shall not crown my battlements
> While I can stand and fight.
> I fling defiance at them as I cry:
> Capitulate? Not I!

'It seems to me,' he wrote, 'that such is the spirit in which the Empire peoples should face the present crisis.'[60]

Worse followed. On 17 June 1940, Philippe Pétain, the Great War's 'Saviour of France,' asked Hitler for an armistice. That same day, the

Canadian Cabinet War Committee authorized a bill 'providing for the general mobilization of human and material resources' – the National Resources Mobilization Act. Meanwhile, Crerar dispatched a 'long cable' to the CGS 'summarizing present situation as between CMHQ and NDHQ, the necessity for swift co-operative action and some possible ways of achieving this,' one of which was the establishment of a broader basis of authority for the overseas command. He noted that he had not discussed the proposal with McNaughton, and although he was technically truthful, Crerar dissuaded McNaughton later that same day from sending his own telegram so as not to 'suggest collusion.'

Crerar did not record the fact that a week earlier he had been concerned enough about Anderson's direction of NDHQ to prepare a personal letter for Norman Rogers on the same subject. Counting on the discretion of a trusted friend, Crerar did not mention the letter to either the CGS or McNaughton. Rogers's tragic death in a plane crash – 'His death,' Crerar wrote, 'has left me with a strong sense of deep personal loss and ... I shall miss him tremendously for professional reasons' – on the very day Crerar wrote his letter forced him to address the matter to Roger's successor, J.L. Ralston, the former Minister of Finance and a man with whom Crerar had only a passing acquaintance, as a minister during the 1920s. Crerar did not share McNaughton's dislike of Ralston, but he was no more than an acquaintance. Obviously unsure of Ralston, Crerar took pains to explain his actions. 'I have no liking for those who ... tend to use other than the regular ... approach,' he observed '[and] I realize I am "cutting corners" on Anderson in doing this. I feel, however, that direct speech with you is the only way in which I can get my thoughts before you.'[61] Crerar emphasized the obstruction that he perceived was hampering the successful organization of the overseas effort. He included the letter he had written for Rogers, but elaborated on the key points in the covering letter sent to Ralston. He played to Ralston's military background: 'I know from your own experience, you would agree that responsible men in close contact with the military requirements of the troops who are doing the actual fighting (providing such men are worthy of trust) are best able to define those requirements.'[62] Establishing his point, Crerar moved in for the kill: 'If these views are accepted ... it is evident that your primary and immediate advisors on CASF operations and requirements in this theatre of operations must be the GOC Canadian Forces and the Senior Officer of this Headquarters ... Time, space and the rapidity of events prevent this function from being performed by the [Defence Council].' Crerar recommended that requests from overseas get first priority of consideration by the Defence Council and the minister. Further, he felt that 'certain of the Branches of the Department ... are inclined to argue against my proposals, rather than find reasons to support them.' He implied that the Adjutant-General was the source. There were grounds for concern: communications on policy were very slow, if not deliberately obstructionist.[63]

Crerar's direct communication with the minister was concerned with establishing his predominance, and that of McNaughton, as the government's chief military advisors. For Crerar, it was clear that 'war policy must be determined on the advice of the experts who were at the top of the services.'[64] Should he have communicated directly with the minister? Probably not. Did he feel it was critical to bring some order to Canada's war effort? Absolutely.

There is no record of any reply from Ralston. Earnest, principled, and a slave to detail, the minister, having just reluctantly switched portfolios on 13 June, was concerned with the preparation of his final budget before officially assuming his duties on 5 July. By that date, he had confirmed Crerar's appointment as the new Chief of the General Staff. Anderson's belated reply, however, promised speedier responses and gave the senior officer the wider authority that Crerar had been seeking.[65]

DND's change of heart was prompted by the German successes in the Low Countries and France. The intervening period was one of intense activity as the British Isles prepared for an anticipated German invasion following the rapid defeat of France. In late June 1940, unaware of his own impending appointment, Crerar was pressing his old friend Lieutenant-General 'Dick' Haining, Vice-Chief of the Imperial General Staff, to make full use of Andy McNaughton's abilities by appointing him to command a combined British and Canadian corps. While there was a touch of loyalty involved in this request, it was also obvious that Crerar considered himself next in line for divisional command upon McNaughton's promotion and that he wanted to see a Canadian corps organized as quickly as possible, given the government's authorization of 17 May. He did not inform McNaughton of his initiatives and conversation with Haining, although the two met briefly the next day.[66] The British authorities in the War Office, however, were not as keen on a corps as Crerar. On 27 June, Dewing suggested that McNaughton be advised that 'the project was by no means "firm."' In fact, the proposed British Corps, the 7th, was not officially authorized until 21 July and the Canadian Corps (later 1st Canadian Corps) would not be established until 25 December 1940.[67] By then Crerar was in Ottawa.

8 Chief of the General Staff

I

On 26 January 1942, Prime Minister Mackenzie King announced to the House of Commons the government's intention to establish in the coming year the overseas First Canadian Army, comprising two corps. The announcement was greeted with only a smattering of applause, suggesting the House's disapproval of yet another addition to Canada's ground forces. The army program speech was partly the victim of domestic politics. Presented to Parliament, and the country, in defence of the government's wartime record and timed to diffuse criticism of the plebiscite to free the government from its no-conscription pledge, the announcement also followed hard on the heels of the emerging political storm over the dispatch of Canadian troops to Hong Kong.[1]

The House's response accurately mirrored King's personal fear of the spectre of conscription raised by the opponents of the 'big army.' For a leader to whom the army represented most fully the political divisiveness of conscription for overseas service, the establishment of the First Canadian Army was an unexpected, but not inexplicable, reversal. Crerar returned to Canada determined to bring some order to Canada's war effort. And a key element of Crerar's goal as CGS was expansion of the army effort and creation of a more rigorous training establishment. The result, and a goal towards which the historically conscious Crerar was moving early in his tenure, was establishment of a First Canadian Army composed of two corps. That he was successful was the result partly of his own skills, partly the crisis following German successes from June 1940.

The fall of France changed the military's position within the government. The military's informal access to the government prior to the war was the rule after Canada's declaration of war on 10 September 1939, and throughout the Phoney War period.[2] Advice from the Chiefs of Staff was officially rendered to the civil authorities through the Defence Council: the Minister of National Defence, the Deputy Minister, the Chief of the General Staff, the Chief of the Air Staff (CAS), and the Chief of the Naval Staff (CNS), with Associate membership for the Adjutant-General (AG), Master-General of Ordnance (MGO), the Quartermaster General (QMG), and the Judge Advocate General (JAG). These associates weighted the council in the army's favour but also made it an unwieldy decision-making body. The minister had no mandate to report the council's decisions to the government, in any case. The council met regularly once a week after Canada declared war, but its influence remained marginal, if that, in matters of policy.

Defence-policy formulation was in the hands of the small enclave of ministers known as the Cabinet War Committee. The overall supervision of the war effort, and thus the policy-making power, was the responsibility of one of nine 'Committees of the Cabinet.' The Cabinet War Committee, which after July 1940 had a membership that included the three ministers responsible for the services – Minister of National Defence Ralston, Minister of National Defence for Air and Associate Minister C.G. Power, and Minister of National Defence for Naval Services Angus L. Macdonald – as well as the ministers for justice, finance, mines and resources, munitions and supply, and national war services, and the leader of the government in the Senate. However, the War Cabinet's composition was never fixed, and actual attendance depended on the Prime Minister's discretion and the issues at hand. Prior to 1940, the agenda was driven by issues and personality. Anarchy was the rule in committee discussions. Within this structure the Prime Minister's influence was usually decisive, and that, of course, was King's objective.[3] Mackenzie King's personal antipathy to military policies that he viewed as potentially divisive made this issue particularly important. The Cabinet War Committee continued to exclude the Chiefs of Staff – the Chief of the General Staff, the Chief of the Naval Staff, and the Chief of the Air Staff – from their meetings, a situation that did not formally change until June 1942 when they were invited to attend approximately two meetings a month.

The anarchy of Cabinet War Committee meetings was largely the result of Mackenzie King's aversion to formal procedure and organization, which he feared would reduce his flexibility and ability to set the agenda, thus reducing his control of government policy. The result, however, was disarray in the organization of the war effort. It took the weaknesses exposed by wartime expansion and the ambitions of A.D. Heeney, who became clerk of the Privy Council, to provide the impetus to organize and record the meetings of the Cabinet War Committee.[4] Beginning in May 1940, Heeney's implementation of formal procedures for discussion within the Cabinet War Committee was an important turning point in King's control of the war policy. Some of the control was removed from King's hands by establishing order and a set agenda. Nevertheless, there was still no strategic plan or military advice to guide the committee's defence agenda.

From a Canadian service perspective, the instability of the years 1940 through 1942 resulted in both great anxiety and great opportunity. The crisis in June 1940 accelerated every aspect of the Canadian war effort. The most important changes were the removal of the financial restrictions previously imposed on the military's expansion and the waning of the influence of the Under-Secretary of External Affairs O.D. Skelton. However, with the two defining elements of Canada's policy removed – fiscal restraints and doubts about the necessity of armed forces' commitments – an overall manpower plan and firm direction for expansion of the forces were now noticeably absent. The crisis-driven military expansion of the early summer of 1940 was not reconciled to any government policy beyond Mackenzie King's national unity, no-conscription agenda. This may have been a sound political strategy, but it was no policy for contributing to an Allied victory.

The crisis of Allied arms also prompted personnel changes at the highest levels. On 5 June, Ralston accepted the portfolio of National Defence. He was quickly educated about the inability of the CGS Major-General Anderson and the heads of the other branches to emerge from the lethargy of their pre-war existence.[5] Ralston expressed little confidence in the ability of the Permanent Force staff at NDHQ to create a policy or plan to direct the expansion of the militia. He quietly surrounded himself with civilian executive assistants, including the adamantly anti–Permanent Force newspaperman Victor Sifton, of the *Winnipeg Free Press*, and Colonel G.S. Currie. With the aid of men like Sifton, and excluding the Chief of the General Staff as well as the heads of the other army branches, Ralston began to consider policy for army expansion.[6]

The overseas forces were no less eager to shake up NDHQ. With the United Kingdom now the main theatre, relations between CMHQ, the overseas force, and Ottawa would be difficult unless all recognized the

GOC of the overseas force as a first among equals. German success had also destroyed any illusions that the Anglo-Canadian armies were prepared for modern warfare. In July 1940, McNaughton suggested that Crerar return to Canada as Vice-Chief of the General Staff 'so that first hand information [would] be obtainable regarding training and organization in light of [the] rapidly changing conditions.' He also suggested that Anderson be retired, a clear signal that Crerar was slated for the CGS. McNaughton also noted that Crerar's experience in England made him an ideal candidate. Ralston agreed. He promoted the idea to the Cabinet War Committee that 'certain changes that he proposed to have made amongst the higher officers of the General Staff ... would materially strengthen the General Staff.'[7] McNaughton, nevertheless, had his doubts whether the ministerial walls could be breached. 'He has been a tower of strength here,' McNaughton observed on Crerar's departure. 'I hope that he will be armed with sufficient authority to make his weight felt in the organization of military matters in Canada.'[8]

McNaughton needn't have worried. Harry Crerar was determined to use the window of opportunity afforded by the crisis to shore up the position of the army and of the other services. Crerar's agenda as CGS was shaped by his memories of the reputation of the Canadian Corps, his estimation of the deficiencies of the Canadian military establishment, and his experiences and observations of the British defence establishment to 1940. Crerar's long-term priorities included the introduction of the military professionals into defence policy-making – a continuation of the struggle for professional legitimacy that characterized the interwar General Staff. His short-term priority was to reorganize Canada's military machine and give it some direction; training, recruitment, supply, and organization had to be synchronized. The sum of these initiatives would be the First Canadian Army – to Crerar the next logical step and a key to ensuring the army's post-war position.

Crerar was unhappy to be recalled, convinced that he was entitled to a field command. Notifying the new CIGS, Sir John Dill, of the move, Crerar perceived his martyrdom clearly. 'My feelings about the appointment,' he wrote, 'do not really matter – there is no time for arguing personal preferences these days. Perhaps, however, the chance will yet come for me to command a Canadian Division.'[9] He tried to enhance this probability with McNaughton's support. 'I'm hot after the 3rd Division,' he wrote while en route to Canada, 'and count on you to help me. That alternative cheers me up.'[10]

Crerar quickly wired Anderson, declining comment on his proposed duties, but agreeing with McNaughton's assessment of the future position of CMHQ, as the United Kingdom was now the main theatre of operations and not simply an intermediate base. He then pressed for Price Montague to succeed him, citing the need for continuity and a replacement acceptable to McNaughton. Crerar also wanted to have an acceptable replacement; Montague was loyal to Crerar. Three days later, Crerar received confirmation of his appointment as Vice-CGS and of Montague's promotion.[11]

En route to Canada in July 1940, Crerar prepared a forceful memorandum for the Minister of National Defence that contained a statement of his objectives as CGS. He assumed that he was being brought back to Canada 'to undertake constructive action in respect to the development of its land forces.' Taking a characteristically broad view of 'constructive action,' Crerar produced a blunt assessment of the immediate and future needs of the Canadian military.[12] He wanted to clear house at DND, but he also believed that wartime reorganization should not stop with the measures necessary to win the war. If it did, it would be a wasted effort. He suggested that while the urgency of the situation did not permit immediate large-scale reorganization, greater efficiency could be obtained from the existing machinery by a wholesale removal of 'professionally unfit' Permanent Force personnel and the establishment of 'a well-balanced and properly co-ordinated Staff organization at the Department and in the Districts.' Determined to increase the efficiency of NDHQ, he was convinced 'from experience during the last nine months ... that there [were] definite opportunities to effect improvement.'

Crerar was equally committed to ensuring that when the war ended, the armed forces did not return to their previous state. 'We must not lose a moment,' he emphasized, 'in undertaking a thorough analysis of Canada's post-war military requirements and in planning a defence organization which will produce our future service needs with a maximum of efficiency and a minimum of expense.' The true depth of his feeling on this point was clear in the statements excised from the final memorandum. 'Even should victory be gained,' he wrote in the original, 'it is as certain as anything can be that ... the armed forces of Canada ... will not be allowed to slip back into the stagnant backwaters of their pre-war existence.'[13]

On his return, Crerar had the dual advantage of some prestige in the media and some government circles, as well as the fortune to have been junior enough to bear no responsibility for the disaster that was Canada's military policy before 1940. The *Globe*, for example, welcomed the 'fund of knowledge and experience' that he brought to his appointment; the *Kingston Whig-Standard* was 'enthusiastic in its approval.'[14] He would need it. In Ottawa, Crerar was confronted by the necessity of bringing some order to the war effort in general, and the military in particular. In early August, he wrote McNaughton and described the atmosphere he found in Ottawa: 'I found that as a result of rather a panicky outlook, the tendency here was to look inward and think in terms of strict "continental" defence.' '[The] pressure on the Government developed by recent events,' he observed in a letter to Lester Pearson, 'has completely blown off the restrictive lid on the Canadian military effort and, as a result, there has been a lot of wasteful and uncoordinated expansion.'[15] His remarks to *Winnipeg Free Press* journalist and Liberal insider Grant Dexter were less guarded. Crerar regarded 'the existing war organization,' Dexter noted, 'as most inefficient and unsatisfactory ... [He believes our] war effort largely botched.'[16]

Crerar was horrified to learn that Ralston was deciding policies that directly affected the military's responsibilities without any representation from the military staffs. There were rumours that Crerar threatened to resign if the matter was not corrected. He initiated daily morning meetings with Ralston, which remained the practice for the next year, at least. He began to discuss with Ralston each policy and practice in turn. Crerar believed that the policy of using volunteers for overseas service, and a mixture of volunteers and NRMA men for defence at home, was untenable in the long run. He also had before him, as the most recent example of the government's opinion of its military advisors, Mackenzie King's commitment to lease bases in Newfoundland to the United States without any consultation. The Chiefs of Staff protested the taking of such steps, with the obvious implications for the defence of Canada. The Chiefs were subsequently consulted on some, but not all, matters considered relevant, although King's antipathy towards the army's leaders never wavered. C.P. Stacey observed that while Crerar's advent as CGS and his exposition to the War Cabinet on the strategic situation in July 1940 strengthened the prestige of the Chiefs of Staff, retaining influence in ministerial circles remained a constant struggle in the face of the Prime Minister's disdain for his military advisors.[17]

From August 1940, Crerar's first concern – in addition to searching for a home, as it was 'time that Mum should have a house of her own'

– was establishing the parameters and policy for the army's immediate expansion, armament, and training. His pace was informed by equipment shortages and the enormous task that faced Britain and her Dominions in the summer of 1940 – staving off Britain's defeat and then turning to the offensive against Nazi Germany. 'I believe that I have been able to correct that defeatist attitude to a considerable extent both in the War Cabinet and publicly,' he wrote McNaughton in August, 'and as a result, during the last month or so the accent has been placed on the "fortress island" being our first line of defence rather than the Atlantic Seaboard.' Crerar's estimates were informed by British requirements and his own pre-war work on Canada's mobilization plans. The British Cabinet, acting on the recommendation of the War Office Land Forces Committee, authorized in September 1939 an army program of fifty-five divisions by September 1941, a figure that included fourteen divisions from the Dominions. The inability to supply these divisions later forced a reduction in this optimistic estimate but it was evident that the British, despite their vacillation prior to the war, were determined to commit large ground forces to the Continent, and the Dominions were an important component of this commitment.[18] In the summer of 1940, Canada already had two divisions overseas, and the decision had been made to form a Canadian corps. Expediency dictated that units already formed be sent overseas as soon as equipment shortages allowed. Crerar also persuaded Ralston to approve the establishment of the country's first armoured formation.[19]

Beyond these immediate conclusions, however, he maintained in his presentation to the Cabinet War Committee and in his first memorandum to the minister in September 1940 that it was impossible to accurately forecast the shape the army might take ultimately.[20] In his view, as presented in a memorandum to the government in September 1940, the object of Canada's long-term military effort should 'be to raise land and air forces until our total [allied] power is sufficient to over-balance that of Germany.' His work on the pre-war mobilization plan, Defence Scheme No. 3, in which it was estimated that Canada could raise six divisions for overseas service, framed his conviction that such a force was possible.[21] Equipment and manpower distribution would further define what was possible for Canada to do in 'furtherance of [the defeat of Germany],' but Crerar estimated that five to seven divisions, 'of which one or more should be armoured,' could be maintained overseas on a voluntary enlistment basis.[22]

Crerar had a much clearer, and more optimistic, vision of the size of the army than he publicly admitted; a two-corps army of six divisions was his goal. He fervently believed that in 'the final stages of the battle it [would] be action by the armies which [would] bring about the decision.'[23] This fact alone convinced Crerar that the army had a chance to emulate, and possibly supersede, the success and reputation of the Canadian Corps in the First World War. However, conscious of the political resistance to a large army commitment, he deliberately omitted any mention of the formation of a second corps or higher formations from the 1941 Army Programme. In an early draft of the program prepared by the Assistant Director of Staff Duties and submitted to Crerar on 13 September prior to submission to the Cabinet, several items caught Crerar's attention. One of the most important was a reference that hinted at a further expansion of the army organization: 'We should begin consideration of the formation of a second corps including 3rd and 4th Divisions plus an additional armoured division.' For the politically attuned CGS, this went too far. 'I would not mention a 2nd Can Corps at this stage,' cautioned Crerar in his critique of the proposal. 'That is for the future.'[24]

Privately, Crerar was already contemplating an army headquarters. Writing to McNaughton in August 1940 to congratulate him on his recent promotion to Corps command, Crerar observed, 'Shortly after the Canadian Corps is formed, and a going concern, your elevation to Army Command would, I believe give similar satisfaction to Canada, if that is of any interest to you.' He also hinted that he hoped the corps would leave the United Kingdom and find itself 'in some other area of operations where [it] can better demonstrate its fighting power.'[25] There was no record of McNaughton's reply, if any, and the subject, but not Crerar's interest, lapsed until the following year. For Crerar, First Canadian Army would become the vehicle to fulfil his postwar aspirations for the army. It would be the successor to the Great War's Canadian Corps. It was also a test of his determination to establish the Chief of the General Staff as the government's chief military advisor.

For the remainder of 1940 and into 1941, concerns over equipment shortages and confusion over the exact shape that Canada's army should take were paramount in Crerar's mind. He worked closely with Munitions and Supply to ensure that Canadian armament production and design was developing in response to the army's needs, the opposite having been a problem in Great Britain, and one coordination problem that Crerar addressed quickly. On 4 September 1940, he was able to write Pope that 'before many weeks I should be informed continuously not only as to the types and quantities of munitions required by the GS to meet the constantly changing operational programme, but also the forecast of deliveries of each of those items as calculated by the Ministry of Munitions.' He added that the procedures were those that they had been trying to establish since at least 1937.[26]

Crerar's inability, or unwillingness, to forecast accurately the 'final casting' of the army also reflected the confusion over operational doctrine that characterized British and Canadian thinking in the aftermath of the fall of France through to the summer of 1942. Crerar's suggestions on the organization of the future Canadian army stressed armoured formations as a means of creating an army that was less infantry-intensive but still packed a punch. He noted one serious problem with forecasting the shape of the army when he wrote that while Canada should send an infantry tank brigade before the end of 1941, 'the opinion is held in influential quarters of the British army that Infantry Tank units should be eliminated in favour of armoured formations.'[27] This uncertainty over the role of armour, reflected in the development of infantry and cruiser tanks organized in separate formations, plagued the British and Canadian armies until at least 1943.[28] Training, organization, and intra-service cooperation suffered in the absence of an agreed upon doctrine. The uncertainly over expansion of the infantry component of the armoured divisions, which went through several iterations between 1941 and 1944, would also contribute to manpower problems once the Allied armies returned to the Continent.

For the Canadian senior staff, the difficulty of estimating the size of the army was enhanced by the obscurity of the Canadian army's future role. As late as the fall of 1941, there was an evident dilemma over the number of support and line-of-communications units in the corps, centring on the specific requirements of theatres of operations in which the Canadians might see action. Crerar grew apprehensive about the growing 'tail' side of the corps, preferring to maintain a flexibility to allow its commitment in several theatres. McNaughton and Associate CGS, Pope advocated the maintenance, if not growth, of the organization, with McNaughton insisting that the corps be kept together until the invasion of Europe.[29]

In the long term, the biggest impediment to expansion was government resistance, led by Mackenzie King. Crerar recognized that the Prime Minister favoured a strong Canadian industrial contribution rather than a military one. The government's resistance to the formation of a Canadian corps in the spring of 1940 had also brought home to

Crerar the fact that the war had not changed the Prime Minister's outlook on the army. Privately, the CGS expressed doubts about King's leadership abilities, confiding to Lester Pearson, '[There is] a widely held conviction that Mr King's great abilities are not suited to the conditions of the world today ... It is a pity that a stronger opposition does not obtain in the House.'[30] Crerar, however, acquired a degree of goodwill from King during his first appearance before the War Cabinet Committee on 26 July 1940 by showing an appreciation for factors other than those of military necessity. Crerar emphasized that equipment shortages were more pressing than manpower needs, and by noting the importance of Canada's intermediary role between the United States and Britain, he promoted an idea favoured by the Prime Minister. King, judging the quality of his military advisors by their proximity to his viewpoint, liked the CGS's stance.[31] Nevertheless, King's antipathy was always reserved more for the army and its leaders than any other service, conjuring up visions of the First World War conscription crisis, which had divided Canadians along linguistic, ethnic, and regional lines. King repeatedly resisted a large army in Cabinet War Committee discussions. Privately, he railed against the General Staff and Ralston's support for their plans. 'Generals are invariably wrong,' the Prime Minister confided to journalists Bruce Hutchinson and Grant Dexter. 'All our generals were concerned about was to be in at the kill.'[32] There was some truth to this observation, but it reflected a particular twist in Canada's Second World War civil–military relationship, sharply tilted in favour of maximum civilian control: the generals proved, for better or worse, to be more determined to assert Canadian autonomy than the politicians.

II

Crerar's policy initiatives were complemented by his establishment of the CGS as the government's chief military advisor – a change he felt was critical for the long-term stability of the war effort. The key to this change was the assertion of the predominance of the General Staff Branch and the CGS at NDHQ. Crerar believed that the efficiency of the department depended on the subordination of the administrative branches of the army staff to the General Staff's operational branch – the organization that obtained in Britain. The United States Army completed a similar reorganization in February 1942, giving a single chief of staff 'indisputable control' to coordinate all army forces and activities, including those performed by the civilian secretariat. This stability afforded the Chief of Staff the ability to decentralize many details and focus on policy, planning, and strategic direction.[33]

In Canada, while nominally the CGS predominated, the heads of the other branches – the Master-General of Ordnance, the Adjutant-General, the Quartermaster General, and the Judge Advocate General had substantial influence on military as well as army policy through their status as Associate Members of the Defence Council. In 1937, Crerar had described the organization of the Defence Council as 'defective,' and he had recommended that the associate members be dropped to ensure equal representation for each service and to enable it to more effectively advise the minister.[34] Crerar's recommendations had prompted a minor crisis in the upper echelons of the department in 1937; while no formal change was made to the Deputy Minister's position, he no longer interfered with the CGS's access to the minister.

Crerar fired the first shot in the battle to subordinate the branches to the CGS, issuing in July a press release that defined the responsibilities of the General Staff and defined the CGS as 'charged with the coordination of the work undertaken by each of the four Staff branches of the Department.' Crerar quickly took up this refrain with the minister. At Crerar's request, following their first meeting in July 1940, Ralston loosely defined Crerar's responsibilities in a memorandum entitled 'Duties as Chief of the General Staff,' which charged him with the integration and general direction of the military policy of the General Staff Branch. Crerar's predominance was implicitly recognized through the directive that all general policies were subject to his approval or comment and the charge that he was to investigate and reorganize each of the branches in the interests of efficiency. These were the responsibilities that Crerar sought. Ralston, however, made no mention of initiating long-term changes, and he noted that, to save time, once policy was agreed upon, he would take up matters directly with the branch heads.[35] Crerar anticipated problems with the loosely defined responsibilities and informed the minister accordingly. In late July, he brought E.L.M. Burns back as a Special Assistant – later elevated to Assistant Deputy Chief of the General Staff – to analyze the organization and procedures. In the memorandum explaining the appointment to Ralston, Crerar observed that

> under the present established relationship of Military Members of Council, this action to investigate the activities of the other Branches by my nominee will not be well received by the other Heads of Branches. Nor can

the situation be definitely clarified until I occupy the same position to the Army Staff as the CNS and CAS does to the Staff of the other services. I recommend that this matter receive early consideration in the interest of efficiency and harmony.[36]

Ralston responded to Crerar's recommendations by removing the 'disproportionate Army representation' from the Defence Council in the summer of 1940 to make room for the two new ministers of national defence.[37] The council remained ineffective as a policy advisory body but its administrative efficiency increased.

As Crerar anticipated, the heads of branches resisted the proposed changes.[38] The response to the establishment of Crerar's Staff Duties Directorate (SDD) in the General Staff, with a mandate to coordinate business – such as priorities in issue of equipment, that affected more than one branch – and to essentially police the army branches at NDHQ to ensure that the policies were proceeding apace, was one of incredulity by the Adjutant-General Major-General B.W. Browne, and the Quartermaster General Major-General E.J.C. Schmidlin at Crerar's presumptuous interference.[39] This was, in part, a reaction to Burns, who seems to have put off Ralston, among others, with his combination of intellect and arrogance. R.J. Orde, the JAG, and long-time friend, supported change.[40] The SDD was a clear product of the Canadian experience with the British War Office, but one that was refined in light of Canadian needs and assessments of the effectiveness of the War Office operation. By early September, he reported to McNaughton that 'with the help of Burns, I now have the organizational future set-up of MGO, QMG and GS Branches all charted and approved by the Minister.' There was one holdout – the AG Branch: 'Perhaps this is due to the fact that there has been a tendency on the part of the head of that branch to resent any enquiry into it by me.' Crerar was typically mystified at resistance to his logic.[41]

Browne's antagonism was clear, and direct. A First World War veteran and a Permanent Force officer between the wars, he made no secret his dislike of what he considered encroachments on his prerogatives, the rapid advance of a junior officer, and perhaps, Crerar's appointment of gunners, engineers, and civilians to senior staff positions. One example suggests the nature of the relationship. Crerar sent a memorandum to the AG, QMG, and MGO in February 1941 suggesting that they establish a 'Follow Up' system to measure progress and ensure that plans were implemented to completion. Brown's reply was short and curt. 'I have no comment to make other than to state that there has been a [follow-up] system in all Departments of the [AG's] Branch since last August.'[42] The antipathy between the two remained strong through Crerar's tenure as CGS. Crerar recognized this fact and was largely able to circumvent and outmanoeuvre Browne with the support of the minister (who had a poor opinion of Browne's abilities) as well as that of Stuart and McNaughton. Crerar considered Schmidlin 'wooden' but he did little to resist the new order at NDHQ. The 'most controversial' appointments were those of Philip Chester and Victor Sifton – two civilians who assumed joint command of the Ordnance Branch until the end of 1940 when Sifton became sole Master-General of Ordnance. The appointment of two civilians caused the resentment of some military personnel, but Crerar noted in a letter to McNaughton that he was happy to have secured 'some outstanding man in civil life who would look at our problems in procurement in the broadest possible way.' He hoped that this would facilitate relations with C.D. Howe's 'dollar a year men.'[43] Victor Sifton was suspicious of Crerar's motives (despite the fact that Crerar had recommended him for the position) but indirect in his rancour, preferring to use his position as Ralston's confidant and former executive assistant to vent his frustration at what Sifton perceived to be Crerar's 'empire-building.' It was an opinion shared by others outside the General Staff, but not all. Crerar seemed unaware of Sifton's views, and during the summer of 1940 tried to enlist his support for the reorganization.[44]

Crerar was improving procedures and practices. He sought approval and advice for the staff of the SSD from the directorates within his branch and the heads of the other branches.[45] He was concerned with staffing NDHQ with the most competent men possible and facilitating cooperation at the highest levels. He appointed civilians to important positions, such as the Personnel Selection Branch, and supported others such as Sifton. Crerar's criteria for measuring their competency may be criticized as too theoretical and general, perpetuating McNaughton's vision of a 'military manager' that favoured gunners and engineers. Still, men such as Stuart and Pope were at the forefront of their profession and therefore positioned to enter senior staff positions as the army expanded.

By early September, Crerar was venting his frustration at the continued resistance to changes within Army Headquarters, arguing that the position of CGS should carry the rank of lieutenant-general. He drew on the example of the British Chief of the Imperial General Staff and cited the vast increase in the responsibilities of the position.[46] In early November, in the absence of any response, Crerar was moved to enlist the minister's direct support, urging him to send a memorandum drafted by Crerar, but over Ralston's signature, to 'help [straighten] out the present unsatisfactory situation.'[47] Ralston's response was verbal and went unrecorded. Nevertheless, it upset Crerar sufficiently to prompt another memo within hours of their conversation. Crerar implored Ralston to intervene, summarily stating, 'The nub of the whole matter is that the AG and QMG take the view that as Military Members of the Council, even though "junior" ones, the CGS should consult them before advising you ... I contend that the shoe is really on the other foot.' He went further: 'They should come to me willingly and support me loyally, as a team must support its captain if it is to play an effective game. They should not dispute or criticize my decisions or actions behind my back, although I would expect frank and friendly argument to my face.'[48] This position was hypocritical, given his propensity to use unofficial channels, and missed the point somewhat. Ralston was unmoved. Crerar periodically repeated his pleas for a confirmation of his position. He made it clear that he would accept the seniority of the other Chiefs of Staff, in recognition of the promotions of the CNS and the CAS, but that an equivalent rank was necessary for him to fulfil his responsibilities. His requests were repeatedly denied through the spring and summer of 1941.[49]

'I have left an atmosphere of comradeship and good team-work,' he wrote Pearson in July 1940, 'to enter one where my accelerated promotion has produced a certain amount of jealously and perhaps of intrigue.'[50] The prevailing impression left with Ralston and others by Crerar's attempt to correct the imbalance within the Army Council – the influence that Crerar's opposite numbers in Britain and the United States enjoyed through organization and sympathetic commanders-in-chief[51] – and the blunt methods he adopted, was that he was seeking personal aggrandizement as a virtual commander-in-chief. This perception was only enhanced by Crerar's domination of the selection of candidates for the senior staff positions created by expansion. Sifton, commiserating with Grant Dexter over the perceived idiocy of the General Staff in March 1941, observed, Ralston 'thinks Crerar is perhaps as good a soldier as we have available for the job in Canada but finds that he has very grave weaknesses of character. He is immensely ambitious and is constantly seeking to arrogate to himself the whole business of the department.'[52] These sentiments were reiterated by Ralston himself in conversations with Dexter and Sifton. Ralston was increasingly disenchanted with the forceful Crerar and, egged on by Sifton, adopted a cautious attitude towards Crerar's army and training programs.[53]

Dexter probably overstated Ralston's suspicions of Crerar. He gradually won over his minister. Ralston's 'anglophilic' attachment to the British Empire, his stubborn determination to ensure that the men overseas were the government's first consideration, even if that meant conscription, and his sense of responsibility to his portfolio enhanced his susceptibility to Crerar's arguments. Ralston's seemingly tireless schedule and inability to delegate responsibility further sapped his ability to resist his military advisors. And, in principle, he agreed with them. But perhaps most important was Ralston's own perception that he did not have the prerequisite knowledge to challenge the military professionals. Concerned over the General Staff's continual call for more men, an exasperated Ralston admitted to Grant Dexter in 1941, '[I am] minister but must act upon the advice of [my] staff of professional soldiers. Being a civilian, [I cannot] set aside [my] advisors simply because [I] disagreed with what they said. They knew; [I] did not know.'[54]

III

The first six months of his appointment were also trying for Crerar on a personal level. His family was scattered. A pregnant Peg and her husband, married earlier in what one correspondent characterized as the 'first Canadian military war wedding,' were in London as the German Blitz intensified and focused on the city. On 9 September, as the German air effort shifted from the coast to the dockyards, he wrote to McNaughton that 'it made one sick at heart to think of the damage which is being inflicted and the inevitable casualties to the civil population.' His personal correspondence reflected his fears for his daughter's safety. On 4 October, he wrote to Pearson thanking him for news of her health and recent visits with his son-in-law: '[We] continue to hope she will return before long to Canada where she can convert me to a grandfather midst less trying surroundings.' Pearson wrote him when Peg left the city, but the strain was still considerable, and became worse. The McNaughtons were on hand throughout.

He kept to a strict fitness regime, walking and jogging early in the morning, and tried to maintain a schedule at work. With Ralston's support, he tried to impose a sensible work schedule on his staff, encouraging them to take at least one day off a week, one long weekend a month, and no more then three late nights in the office a week. Crerar admitted to Lester Pearson that he met with only limited success, and that it 'has not affected [Ralston's] routine ... who comes back to the office practically every night and himself works until midnight.' By February 1941, Crerar had fallen back into a similar routine: 'I am at the office by nine o'clock and while I usually have dinner with Verse, most nights a week find me back at the office until close to midnight. It is a fairly trying routine ...' He read himself to sleep over books that dealt with 'sailing, either in salt water or fresh.'[55]

Like Ralston, Crerar was very hands on and detail oriented. Crerar kept up a steady correspondence to maintain confidence in what he was doing. The rancour produced by the reorganization of NDHQ was mirrored across the country in training depots and military districts. It was a critical time, and his personal stake as the Germans bombed London lent urgency to his activities. It was grey day in late September 1940 when Crerar submitted the Army Programme for 1941, which called for a Canadian corps of three divisions and an armoured brigade group; a fourth division and additional armoured forces would follow in 1941. He also proposed an extension of the training period of recruits to the Cabinet War Committee. Both proposals reflected a genuine belief that large ground forces, particularly armoured formations, were ultimately necessary to defeat Germany but they were also designed to have maximum appeal to the government. Ralston's wariness of Crerar had prompted a cool reaction to Crerar's tentative suggestion that changes were necessary to the National Resources Mobilization Act's thirty-day compulsory training scheme; Crerar subsequently assumed a more cautious approach to selling his army policies to the government. While he had concluded that thirty days was sufficient to make Canadians 'military minded,' it was insufficient time to train soldiers effectively or efficiently. Determined to extend the training period, Crerar tried a new tack in his second submission, emphasizing the requirements of mechanized war and remarked that 'at this stage nothing in the way of military training should be allowed to interfere with production.'[56] Similarly, in his presentations to the War Committee, Crerar again couched his proposals for expansion of the compulsory training period and the army program in terms guaranteed to appeal to King and ministers of like mind.

The trial undergone by Crerar's first program demonstrated the strength of government resistance to army expansion and what was necessary to overcome it. The CGS's program elicited an immediate response from the Minister of National Defence for Air who raised the issue of the proper emphasis of Canada's effort. Mackenzie King also made it clear to the Chiefs of Staff that he leaned towards the industrial and air effort and that the army program might require modification as a result of the 'increased contributions in the naval and air spheres.'[57] Crerar's presentation also prompted an apprehensive note in King's diary: 'Crerar ... and his group pressed very hard for an increase in the Army. Want to have a Canadian army serving in the Middle East, Africa and elsewhere. I feel we have to watch this particularly ... What men and money we have should be put to the best advantage possible.' The ministers, however, were impressed with the careful presentation of the army's case, subsequently requesting the CNS and CAS table similar programs.[58] The tabling of the General Staff's statistically backed program and arguments was decisive, particularly in the context of the reception of a carefully considered speech given by Crerar to the Ottawa branch of the Canadian Club on 23 October 1940, ostensibly to answer public criticism of the government's efforts. On the initiative of Ralston, hundreds of copies were issued to the press and to prominent Canadians while the Minister of Justice and the Minister of National Defence for Naval Services critiqued the drafts. It was the only speaking engagement accepted by Crerar that fall.[59] In this speech, Crerar was also trying to stir up public support for his approach and thus put pressure on the government. The Prime Minister's statements in Cabinet indicated that he was impressed with the emphasis in Crerar's speech on a balanced force and his disclaimer that 'the enlistment of large numbers of eager men is more quickly done than the less obvious, more complicated but equally essential action of gearing up industry to produce all the arms and equipment they need.'[60] The result was King's support for the extension of the training period, although he continued to voice his opposition to a larger army relative to the navy and air force. Ralston also championed the change, now convinced that 'four months was the minimum time within which trainees could be taught the fundamentals of soldiering.'[61]

The twin pillars of Crerar's army agenda were debated in Cabinet for several months, although the four-month compulsory training scheme was accepted in principle from late October. Ralston and Crerar left for Great Britain on 19 November and stayed until late January, to consult and collaborate with the U.K. government to 'ensure that Canada's participation represents the best team work we can devise' – a natural course, given the Canadian role in the empire war effort but one that was also a reflection of his modest confidence in his chief military advisor. The tension was heightened as he missed the return of his daughter: 'Verse is a bit upset about it, but Peggy is due to sail [on 11 November] and if she gets safely home, she can more than take my place in providing companionship in the home.'[62]

The imminence of the arrival of Ralston and Crerar prompted some discussion on the subject among the British. They wanted the maximum effort the Canadians could give, but wavered on the utility of simply dispatching ill-equipped divisions with no operational objective. The issue centred on the potential employment of the Canadian forces. In early November, a confidential memorandum was circulated through the WO outlining the position of the government on the Canadian formations. It noted that while two divisions were committed to overseas service, the 'Canadian government have not at present shown any inclination to send further divisions overseas, but it is understood that they would consider doing so if a suitable role could be found for them.'[63]

In response, a memorandum titled 'Possible Employment for Canadian Formations' was drawn up for discussion when the Canadians arrived. Far from home and provoked by 'inter-Dominion rivalry,' the 'Canadians in this country,' it began, 'are at present eating their heads off; it is desirable to give them some employment which would serve as an outlet for their energy.' Four possibilities were proposed: the Middle East; designation as an 'invasion corps'; 'irregular operations'; or a Home Defence role. Logistics and the fact of CMHQ were posited as arguments against the first; reality against the second. The third was dismissed because of the Canadian reluctance to take off the cream of their troops to form commando units, although it was noted that 'there are certain possibilities which may entail operations on the Atlantic sea-board in the fairly near future.' Home Defence was the best alternative, not least because the War Office believed, probably correctly, that the 'successful invasion of the United Kingdom would carry the enemy further towards victory than any other course of action open to him.'

Crerar's program already reflected what the British wanted from the Dominions: manpower to supply additional armoured divisions. In discussions with the British in mid-December, confirmed on 2 January 1941, he stated that equipment shortages would delay formation of additional Canadian formations, particularly the armoured division, but Crerar was confident that 'Canada could certainly provide more men for the armed forces.' The most immediate objective, he noted, was the formation of a corps of three divisions; the provision 'if the Government approved' was added to the second draft of the minutes. The British, anxious to facilitate the completion of an armoured division, asked that at least the personnel be dispatched no later than the autumn of 1941. If a tank brigade could also be raised without slowing the formation of the armoured division, 'this would be most welcome to the War Office.' A fourth division for dispatch in 1942 'might be borne in mind.'[64]

Following further talks with the British and visits to Canadian formations, the minister readily agreed to present to Cabinet a modified army program. That delayed the dispatch of a fourth Canadian infantry division until at least 1942 but promised an armoured division and 'possibly' an armoured tank brigade. He did this by cable in early January.[65] A considerable anti-army faction had built up in the War Cabinet in Ralston's absence, led by Angus Macdonald with the prime minister's full acquiescence, but Ralston returned on 24 January 1941 and four days later the army program was approved in all its essentials.[66]

Ralston's support for the army program was crucial to its success in Cabinet, but Crerar was gaining control over the substance of military policy. This shift was partially a result of the government's recognition that it needed to depend on the military's knowledge and expertise if the war was to be won, and partially tactics: Crerar understood that the government was now reliant on its military advisors. After Ralston's return from England, Crerar acknowledged the importance of his minister's allegiance. He realized that Ralston's support was the most important result of the trip. 'I must take my hat off to the Minister,' he wrote, 'for the way he backed my proposals up and got them through the War Committee.'[67] He also recognized a pattern of reactions to the army program and training scheme. '[They] required, firstly to be sold to the Minister and then to the Cabinet,' he observed. '[The] four month compulsory training took quite as much work and argument ... no doubt because there were more local angles to it.'[68] Similarly, Crerar noted the importance of British confirmation of his recommendations. 'The recent visit [to England] with my Minister,' Crerar wrote to an old Staff College friend, 'produced all the results I hoped and planned it would. The Development programme ... is now closely co-ordinated with the British programme.'[69] And the edge that his monopoly on statistics and projections gave him in the new procedurally organized Cabinet War Committee was not lost on him. In discussions of the committee – focused as they were on manpower – the carefully prepared statistics, programs, and appraisals of the General Staff gave the army an important tool in its fight to increase its influence and the size of its forces.

One sour note emerged from the trip to England: a confirmation of the disturbing news he was hearing from mutual friends on McNaughton's 'tired' and 'petty' behaviour. As Mike Pearson had written in September, 'I'm a bit worried about Andy – I think all his friends are. The terrific pace he is setting is showing.' He added, 'He should be forced to take a spot of leave before he cracks up.'[70]

9 Hong Kong and the Politics of Army Expansion

I

The Army Programme for 1942 was the culmination of Crerar's goals for the army. He steered it past the resistance of the Prime Minister and some of the Cabinet. Yet the most controversial aspect of his last year as CGS was his role in the dispatch of Canadian troops to Hong Kong. Although usually examined as distinct issues, the decision to send troops to Hong Kong and the selection of the units is better understood in the context of the second army program and Crerar's broader agenda as CGS. Combined with his strategic view of the benefits of sending Canadian troops to the Pacific as part of a larger effort at deterrence, the reasoning behind his recommendation is understandable.

Through 1941, Crerar increasingly played the role expected of a deputy minister, balancing departmental concerns with political interests. He gave a radio address in January 1941 aimed at providing the public with information on the direction of the war effort. One letter-writer suggested the address was 'universally approved and appreciated.' Crerar's imprint was apparent in a number of areas. The political and strategic consequences of policies informed his advice on questions ranging from the need to improve the road network with Prince Rupert in the event of a Japanese attack, to whether Canada should take over St Pierre and Miquelon. It was also a measure of the public and political atmosphere during 1941 as the Axis successes continued unabated. Crerar proved increasingly sensitive to the political and public repercussions of his policies as CGS as 1941 progressed. Public confidence was important to army expansion for recruiting purposes, morale, and, not least, political support. His influence within the Chiefs of Staff was high, but he failed to secure support of the coordinating bodies directed by the Prime Minister's Office that he hoped would centralize the national effort.[1] In the CGS's opinion, these structures would have firmly married the policy-makers with their military as well as economic and financial experts. Crerar remained committed to changes, although he worried that his ability to change the policy process to better reflect professional concerns was limited by his conceptions of training policy and practice. He wrote to Heeney, among others, to try and secure the support of the civil service.[2] He was conscious of the need to maintain a broad base of support for reorganization without slowing the momentum of his army program, or hindering his ability to properly train the army.

Still, training policies were contentious. Crerar's policy, focusing on individual and small-unit training rather than the more visible formation training, reflected current professional ideas as well as structural limitations. As in the British army, collective thinking and obedience remained the cornerstones of good training, if not good soldiering. Parade-square drill and proficiency levels were, at least, measurable standards. But Crerar's most effective achievements occurred at the policy, organizational, and administrative levels. He created the infrastructure necessary to train and organize Canada's army. He secured able assistants like Stuart and Pope – trusted subordinates who both took routine administration off his hands and made valuable contributions to policy. Crerar lost Burns, trying first to secure him command of the new armoured division, but then losing him in February 1941 to an appointment as BGS, 1st Canadian Corps. Still, these appointments decentralized the administration of the GS, freeing him to 'get out and about the country from time to time.' Through the winter of 1941, his activities ranged from admonishing district commanders about rumours of excessive drinking at training establishments to meeting with local businessmen to explain the army's approach to training.[3]

Crerar proved flexible when adapting policies that enhanced training efficiency and effectiveness. He introduced new methods to measure progress. He accepted British methods of personnel selection, which were strongly influenced by the psychological profession and, with the assistance of his Vice-CGS, brushed aside the objections of the Adjutant-General. Browne was told that a new directorate of personnel selection was to be established, under a civilian head, 'to develop a systematic program of personnel selection, ultimately classifying all men in the army, and seeking to identify potential officers.'[4] The establishment of the personnel directorate also illustrated the nature of Crerar's concept of officer material. The criteria for a professional officer were a mix of character, skills, and education. Equally important to 'professionalizing' the army, however, was a standardized, measurable procedure to procure these men. Form as well as content was a distinctive element in his vision of training. Corporate responsibility to the service professionals was secondary to efficiency and effectiveness.

Crerar centralized and standardized the training of officers and enlisted men, bringing a uniformity that he personally hoped would produce 'formations and units in Canada, that, on arrival overseas, will be ready to do a fairly good battle.' Officers would be selected from the ranks; duplication was to be avoided.[5] Officially, he tempered his objective, noting that his goal was to establish 'an organization ... to give that thorough basic and higher individual training which are essential before the more advanced forms of collective training are possible.'[6] At the same time, specialized training became a progressive part of the expanded syllabus. This was the method implemented by the American Chief of Staff George Marshall with some success.[7] The system also reflected the methods adopted by the British; individual training policy was centralized under War Office control, while formation training was the responsibility of commanding officers.[8]

The army basic training program was, by mid-1941, well organized and well administered, but the substance needed tweaking. This was largely a product of rapid growth as equipment shortages hampered training into 1943. Teachers had to be trained, facilities established, and men mobilized. The decision to extend compulsory training to four months entailed further complications.[9] As well, there were no facilities or equipment to undertake collective training. This unsatisfactory situation was exacerbated by the system of leaving collective training to the personal supervision, and abilities, of commanding officers. And, the lack of collective training was a liability to the army's public image in Canada.

Problems with individual training were also a result of the absence of a uniform operational doctrine to guide it. The British–Canadian failure to develop such a centralized doctrine increased the confusion that accompanied the expansion in 1941 and 1942. This situation was not unique to the Canadian army. The armies of all the major combatants went through periods of adjustment. Field exercises and manoeuvres in the spring of 1941, for example, 'brought to light grave deficiencies in the progress of training' in the American army.[10] The deficiencies in the Canadian system were not exposed until large-scale exercises in Britain in 1942 and through the realities of combat after mid-1943. Neither was the question adequately addressed by Crerar, who, immersed in questions of policy and organization, was barely able to establish training along lines that he considered progressive.[11] Similarly, officer training and selection was theoretical; in the absence of experience, it was assumed that the proper mix of character, education, and ability were suitable measures of competence. The syllabus and system were modelled on the 'progressive' system of the British as well as observations of the American army, neither of which had been effectively tested in battle. The assumptions about the adaptability of the Canadian soldier, officer, and other ranks to any situation, if given the proper background, were little more than Crerar's modern interpretation of the militia tradition of the citizen soldier.

Crerar implemented his ideas on training and recruitment with a view to public and political sensitivities. Yet he was prepared to support conscription, and even expected it. Crerar continued to envision an even greater army effort, as was evident in his reaction following the government's approval in April 1941 of the policy for basic training to mix General Service volunteers for overseas service and men conscripted under the National Resources Mobilization Act (NRMA) for home defence. While it was a logical move to standardize training, Crerar also noted with satisfaction that it would increase the pressure on conscripts to 'go GS.'[12] He was not oblivious to the political implications, but minimized the possible strains on national unity. This was why he initiated policies to secure French-Canadian enlistments and senior appointments for French-Canadian officers, yet it seems he never fully understood that French-Canadian hostility was rooted in more than a linguistic divide.[13] His statements on conscription also revealed that there was a growing disparity of views between the proponent of the all-volunteer army, McNaughton, and his one-time protégé. After the extension in May 1941 of NRMA service for home defence for the duration of the war, Crerar wrote McNaughton of the success and hinted at the possible long-term consequences:

> I believe that a high proportion of these twenty-one year olds will volunteer for overseas service ... All these represent several bites at the cherry – the cherry being conscription for overseas service anywhere. On the other hand, this progressive process is educating the public to what may well be

inevitable and I believe if this comes to pass, the final stage will be taken with a minimum of fuss by all concerned.[14]

Here he was wrong, although his acceptance of the inevitably of conscription is best understood in the context of ongoing German successes: Yugoslavia and Greece had just surrendered after painfully short campaigns. He genuinely believed that nothing short of an all-out effort would be required to defeat Germany or to prevent Britain's defeat. The pressure on NRMA men to go 'General Service' was great, but still there is no evidence he encouraged it in the training depots. He seemed to feel the men would do so of their own accord rather then 'be compelled to remain in service in Canada.'[15] Throughout 1941, his approach to policy formulation was informed by his perception of the crucial link between a public opinion, which through progressive education would bow to the inevitable, and government policy.

The training policy Crerar adopted – no large-scale formation manoeuvres would take place in Canada, because facilities were limited – combined with the inactivity of the Canadian troops, resulted in a sour media and public mood, one that the government and the military were hard pressed to quell. The Canadian army was a visible target for pro-conscriptionists and others who, not unlike Crerar, equated large ground forces with a commitment to total war.[16] Subsequently, Crerar bombarded Ralston with suggestions for establishing 'confidence in the direction of affairs of this department.'[17] Crerar's suggestion in the 1941 army program that the Canadian militia be renamed the Canadian army – characterizing the Permanent Active Militia as 'an awful mouthful' and Non-Permanent Active Militia as 'a horribly unwieldy and unattractive title' – illustrates the weight he attached to public perception.[18] His enlistment of the services of Charles P. Stacey to ensure that the exploits of the Canadian army were properly recorded was also a step in this direction.[19]

Volunteer enlistments remained reasonably good but were insufficient for the needs of the 1941 army program, prompting the first government-sponsored national recruitment campaign in May of that year. Despite a slow start, the drive was a success, netting over 48,000 volunteers, some 16,000 over the target.[20] Also in May, to the Prime Minister's horror, Ralston advocated greater activity for the overseas forces as one solution to the problem, a solution anticipated, if not precipitated, by Crerar. The journalistic rumour mill also had it that Crerar had urged the recruiting campaign on Ralston. 'I shall probably be sending you a telegram in the next day or so concerning the use of Canadians on "Commando" work,' Crerar wrote to McNaughton one day before the minister's representation to the Cabinet War Committee. He added, 'I feel it is in the interests of the Corps, if not the country,' as 'there is a not unnatural desire to see Canadians in the headlines these days.'[21]

Suspicions abounded in political circles about the direction of Canada's war effort and the limits of army expansion – and when they would be reached. Munitions and Supply Minister C.D. Howe was the most prominent of a number of ministers who believed Ralston was under the General Staff's thumb. Relations within his own department did not improve Ralston's mood. He resented Crerar's demands for promotion, purportedly stating that he despised the 'general staff from top to bottom.' Sifton rankled at what he perceived to be Crerar's vanity and machinations, suspecting, unfairly, that Crerar was deliberately sabotaging the recruiting campaign to ensure conscription. He also believed that Crerar, McNaughton, and Montague (Senior Officer, CMHQ) were involved in a nefarious 'plot to double the size of the army.'[22] Given Sifton's privileged position, his opinions, whether right or wrong, were bound to make an impression on the minister.

Crerar attempted to temper public criticism through a carefully orchestrated press campaign. In late June 1941, the CGS asked McNaughton to issue a press release stressing the positive results of the 'unspectacular but most necessary activities of our Basic, Advanced, Trades and Officers Training Centres and of my insistence on thorough section, platoon and company training being carried out before the more spectacular unit ... exercises are undertaken.' McNaughton obliged, with little effect.[23] Crerar also created, with more success, an informal network of journalists, editors, and educators, whom he implored to emphasize the positive aspects of the army effort and to keep politics out of 'technical and professional' decisions. In July 1941, sent a four-page plea to *Maclean's* editor Napier Moore to focus on his 'responsibility ... to render sincere and intelligent national service.' To that end, Crerar sent him his several pages of his reactions to a series of admittedly ill-informed articles, which were then appearing in the *Globe and Mail* attacking Canadian training practices.[24] Concrete results, however, were needed to dispel the malaise that was settling over the Canadian war effort.[25]

By late July 1941, Crerar was characterized by one observer as 'exceedingly worried' over the 'insidious' campaign of criticism, fearing it would shake morale, hurt recruiting, and destroy public confidence in the army.[26] That summer also saw one of his favourites, Burns, returned home in disgrace after some embarrassing remarks in his private correspondence to his mistress about the Canadian and British senior command. Crerar, not for the first time, put in a good word for him, and with Ralston's support, parachuted him into the senior administrative post at the Armoured Corps. His worries were not only professional. Peg and Peter were now at home. In the winter of 1941, Peg was involved in war work, after a prolonged bout of ill-health. Her husband was overseas, a separation her father described as 'pretty tough' and as trying as his own separation twenty-five years earlier. Because her husband's status was uncertain, she agonized over whether to go to England or stay in Canada. A sympathetic father took the time to compose a four-page letter to his son-in-law, discussing the postwar world and his place in it. Peter would matriculate in the spring and was considering joining the navy. His future weighed on both their minds. Crerar managed to get away for the occasional fishing trip or round of golf, and in July, three days at Loon Island, but often his leisure time was spent with colleagues and politicians as he campaigned for support. The Crerars also hosted large gatherings of staff members at home and the country club. His family, as ever, was a sanctuary, but he and they felt the strain of long days and extended absences. 'I only wish at this stage of my life,' he wrote his sister, 'I could take longer holidays and greater relaxation.'[27]

II

Crerar's perception of the prevailing public mood and his plans for the army provided the framework of expectations for the dispatch of two battalions of Canadian troops to Hong Kong that fall. In September 1941, the British government enquired if, in light of the what it perceived to be an improved strategic situation in the Far East, Canada could contribute 'one or two' battalions to bolster her garrison. The government turned to its CGS for advice. '[The] Canadian Army,' advised Crerar, 'should definitely take this on.'[28]

The tragic fate of the Royal Rifles of Canada and the Winnipeg Grenadiers in the battle for Hong Kong in December and their horrendous treatment at the hands of the Japanese following the surrender of the garrison would polarize opinion on the dispatch of the Canadians. The subsequent royal commission would question the soundness of

Crerar's advice and the state of training of the two battalions chosen for the expedition. Were Crerar's actions hasty and ill-considered? Historians such as Carl Vincent have said yes. Others believe the decision was understandable, if mistaken.[29]

Crerar's decision was made with a solid, if incorrect, understanding of the Far Eastern strategic situation, an understanding that reflected current British strategic thinking. Strategic intelligence gathering and assessment was almost beyond the ability of the Canadian army in 1941 but Crerar was familiar with the political and strategic circumstances of Britain's Far Eastern possessions. His senior staff positions on the General Staff in the interwar period required him to provide an ongoing analysis of Canada's political and strategic position within the commonwealth and the world. An attack on Hong Kong and the implications of an Anglo-Japanese conflict were prominent imperial defence scenarios that served as staff exercises at both of the institutional cornerstones of the Canadian army's professional education system – the British Staff College at Camberley and the IDC. Of course, Hong Kong's position changed from 1921 as the British reassessed their military relationship with the Japanese and their naval position in the Far East during the early 1920s.[30] The decision in June 1921 to fortify Singapore as the main British naval base, and the restrictions of the Washington Naval Treaty of 1921 forbidding the Pacific powers from upgrading the defences of their naval bases in the western Pacific, relegated Hong Kong to secondary status in the British imperial defence scheme for the Far East, not least because the Standing Defence Sub-Committee of the British Cabinet recognized the garrison's vulnerability to a landward assault. The strategic position of the outpost was further altered by the introduction of a 'period of relief' as an accepted strategic reality in planning for the defence of British possessions in the Far East. It was a recognition of Britain's inability in the 1920s to maintain a two-ocean navy.[31]

More influential on Crerar's assessment of the Far Eastern situation was his examination of Hong Kong in the context of imperial strategy when he attended the IDC in 1934. 'Exercise No. 3' reflected the 1934 reality of an increasingly aggressive Japanese policy towards China as well as Japan's growing estrangement from the Western nations as they expanded their possessions in China and increased pressure on British colonies in the Far East.[32]

Crerar's syndicate concluded that in the context of the requisite 'period before relief,' Hong Kong's position was precarious and that 'in the final event the security of Hong Kong rested with the British Main Fleet.' The key issues were defined as the necessity of retaining Hong Kong as a forward base of operations to exert pressure on the Japanese and to maintain British prestige in the area. Hong Kong's importance as a symbol of British power outweighed its vulnerability; indeed, its vulnerability underscored the trust in that perception.[33]

During the exercise Crerar also wrote an appreciation of a Pacific conflict from the Japanese perspective, with the combined economic, industrial, and financial strength of Great Britain and the Dominions; a comparative study was also made with the United States as a potential ally of the British Empire.[34] He concluded that Japan's only rational course was to avoid a war with this coalition, as it could not defeat it – an accurate assessment and one shared by the Japanese. When they launched their offensive in 1941, their goal was to create a defensive perimeter, not defeat the Allies. Cooperation in Anglo-American policy would, so the syndicate believed, overwhelmingly secure their positions against the Japanese, with the U.S. Pacific Fleet providing 'priceless' security for Hong Kong and Britain's other Far Eastern possessions.[35]

Accordingly, two assumptions informed Crerar's evaluation of developments in the Far Eastern strategic balance. Empire unity was critical to sustain Britain's ability to effectively counter Japan's growing naval strength, particularly following the lapse of the Washington Naval Treaty. He cautioned in 1937 that if empire ties weakened, 'then I think that a strong Japan would take full advantage of its world position.'[36] The second assumption was that while Hong Kong was vulnerable, the position of the United States was critical for the success of attempts at deterrence – or relief operations.[37]

Japan's expansionist policies in the late 1930s prompted the General Staff planners to rank second in defence priorities the maintenance of Canada's neutrality in the event of an American-Japanese war or her commitment in the event of an Anglo-American-Japanese conflict. Crerar, as the Secretary to the Joint Staff Committee and as DMO and I was an important architect of the priorities established by the General Staff. Canada could not avoid being drawn into a Pacific war in which Britain was involved, particularly as the 'Australasian' Dominions would fight.[38] Assessing the position of bases, particularly Hong Kong, in 1936, in a General Staff memorandum entitled 'Memorandum on the Possible Lapse of Article XIX (Regarding New Bases) of the Washington Naval Limitation Treaty,' the strategic position of Hong Kong was described as 'leaving much to be desired' if the status quo were maintained. However, an important proviso stated, 'Were there a definite alliance between Great Britain and the United States it is possible that this deterrent would more than compensate for the threat which new Japanese bases would constitute to Hong Kong.'[39] And Crerar was confident that the Americans would join the British in any hostilities with Japan, a confidence that grew through 1940 and 1941 as the United States became more embroiled in the struggle with Germany and Japan. The British Empire would have unqualified U.S. support 'before many weeks go by,' Crerar noted in confidential correspondence with Price Montague in June 1941.[40] He clearly hoped that war in the Far East might be avoided if the democracies showed their resolve.

In August 1941, as he prepared for the second round of army expansion, Crerar met with an old Royal Military College contemporary, Canadian-born Major-General A.E. Grasett. The Canadian government and Crerar were seeking concrete action to help dispel the malaise settling over the Canadian war effort when the question of the position of Hong Kong first was broached. Grasett was the former General Officer Commanding (GOC), British Troops in China, passing through Ottawa on his return voyage to the United Kingdom. Either innocuous or serious enough that the exact date of the meeting was not recorded, the discussions that took place between Crerar and Grasett took on a great importance after the fact. According to Crerar, the situation in the Far East and Hong Kong was broached in 'long discussions' between himself, Grasett, and Ralston. In the course of the conversations, Grasett forwarded the opinion that two additional battalions 'would render the garrison strong enough to withstand for an extensive period of siege an attack by such forces as the Japanese could bring to bear against it.'[41] This assessment confirmed the prevailing viewpoint, in some circles, of the viability of defending Hong Kong in the event of a Japanese attack.

Several years later, Crerar insisted that 'neither to myself alone, nor to the Minister and myself jointly, did Grasett then raise the question of obtaining these two additional battalions from Canada.'[42] The truth of this statement has been questioned in light of Grasett's subsequent suggestion to the British Chiefs of Staff that Canada might provide the necessary troops for reinforcing Hong Kong.[43] However, Ralston's cautious reaction to the British request in September suggests that the minister was not expecting this initiative, despite the fact that he met with Grasett in Crerar's presence. Irrespective, stated government policy, reiterated by the minister only weeks later in conversations with the British secretary of state for war, was that 'the Canadian government was fully prepared to sanction employment of the Canadian Corps in any military operations which the War Office might recommend.' In obvious deference to Mackenzie King's concerns, Ralston added that he 'did not wish this statement to convey the idea that the Canadian Government was pressing for the active employment of Canadian forces but ... that there would be no restrictive tendencies on the part of the Canadian government.' It would be surprising, then, if the deployment of Canadian units in some theatre of war had not, at least, been mentioned.[44] Indeed, in the circumstances, an initiative by Crerar or Grasett was unremarkable.

Grasett's subsequent suggestion to Churchill and the Chiefs of Staff that Canada might provide the additional troops he believed would secure Hong Kong for the 'period of relief' proved timely.[45] Months earlier it would have been dismissed. However, significant shifts in the diplomatic and military situation had taken place in the Far East and Europe during 1941, changes perceived through the filter of Britain's long-standing policy of deterring Japanese aggression and informed by Britain's determination to defend her possessions in Southeast Asia.[46] Crerar, like others, was focused on deterrence. Britain's chances of responding militarily to a major crisis in the Far East had decreased dramatically after the fall of France, the loss of the powerful French fleet, and the subsequent necessity of maintaining a presence in the Mediterranean on her own. Nevertheless, British political leaders remained committed to defending the empire in the Far East. In hopes of deterring rather than encountering Japanese aggression, their policy centred on the cultivation of American support, the maintenance of Chinese independence. and occasional shows of military commitment.[47] Doubts in early 1941 about the effectiveness of this policy were reflected in the oft-quoted Churchillian assessment of January 1941 that no troops should be sent to Hong Kong, given its precarious position and the imminence of a Japanese attack.[48] Even as Churchill proffered this opinion, however, he was convinced that greater involvement by the United States and her Pacific Fleet would provide sufficient military might to deter Japan from attacking at all.

By the summer of 1941, the British were optimistic that the policies designed to deter Japan were beginning to pay dividends. The joint American, British, and Dutch declaration of solidarity in mid-1941 was one result. The Americans began to reinforce the Philippines, moved the Pacific Fleet to Pearl Harbor, tightened their economic sanctions, and issued explicit warnings to Japan. The hardening of American policy towards Japan, and Roosevelt's enthusiastic support for Churchill's agenda at Placentia Bay in September, prompted reassessments of Britain's strategic position in the Far East.[49] Christopher Thorne's observation that, 'like [U.S. Secretary of War] Stimson, Churchill believed that a flexing of Anglo-Saxon muscle would keep the Japanese in their place,' reflects the sum of British calculations.[50] The Joint-Intelligence Sub-Committee of the Chiefs of Staff (JIC) reports for August and September, informed by self-serving racial comparisons, only confirmed this optimistic misconception.[51]

The British government, despite lingering concerns over American equivocation, responded by tightening economic sanctions against Japan and, at Churchill's urging, promising naval reinforcements in the form of HMS *Repulse*, *Prince of Wales*, and the aircraft carrier *Indomitable*. Ignoring doubts by First Sea Lord Sir Dudley Pound, Churchill was convinced of the effect such a squadron would have.[52] He believed that the conditions for providing an effective deterrent were in place and that Britain was required to show its resolve to the Americans and the embattled Chinese. Concurrently, strategic intelligence estimates, unaware of the impact on Japanese policy of the bloody nose inflicted by the Soviet Red Army on Japanese forces in 1938–9, indicated that the Japanese might turn north rather than south to take advantage of Russian weakness in 1941.[53] This new strategic intelligence, flawed though it was, was reflected in the British telegram of 1941 requesting troops from Canada for the garrison at Hong Kong.

The British government approached the Canadian government on 19 September, informing it of the favourable changes in the British assessment of its position in the Far East. Given these shifts, the British enquired if one 'or two' battalions could be provided 'from Canada' for the imperial outpost at Hong Kong. Implicit was that Canadian troops in Britain should remain untouched. The telegram stressed that the 'action would strengthen [the] garrison all out of proportion to actual numbers involved' and 'would reassure Chiang Kai Shek as to the "genuineness of our intention to hold the colony"' – an important objective, given that forty of the Japanese army's fifty-one divisions were committed to the Chinese theatre.[54] It did not mention that Hong Kong's status as an 'outpost' remained the same; rather, the telegram implied that Hong Kong's position was considered safer than in recent months. Finally, it implied that there was some urgency 'having regard to the political situation in the Far East.'[55]

The political implications of a refusal to dispatch Canadian troops to aid Britain were obvious. The arrival of the telegram found Ralston in the United States, thus the note fell under the purview of Associate Minister of National Defence Charles 'Chubby' Power. Power, in his testimony to the Royal Commission of Enquiry in 1942, recalled that upon receipt of the cable he immediately 'telephoned ... General Crerar and discussed the matter in a broad and general way.'[56] Power met with Crerar on the next morning.

As the government's chief military advisor, ambiguously defined as that position was, Crerar considered political and strategic factors as well as military ones.[57] King and Ralston may have resented their dependence on – and distrusted the motives of – their generals, but they needed them nonetheless.[58] Crerar, in his discussions with Power, noted that if a decision had already been made to reinforce the garrison, then the question of whether Canadian troops should be sent was ultimately a political, as well as moral, decision. Despite warning of the attendant military risks, Crerar recommended that 'the Canadian army should take this on.' Crerar believed that Canada had a moral responsibility to take the same risks as the British, and in this belief he was consistent. In June 1940, reacting to a suggestion that Canadian troops be spared a return to the Continent for political reasons, he wrote, 'In my view, and I believe the view of the Canadian Government, the Canadian forces now available over here should be regarded as available to accept the same responsibilities, however dangerous, as those which it was proposed to allot to similar British formations.' He would use the same logic when discussing Dieppe.[59] Regarding Hong Kong, Major-General Ken Stuart and Major-General Maurice Pope, the Vice-Chief of the General Staff and the Deputy Chief of the General Staff respectively, agreed that if some troops were to be sent, irrespective of Canada's answer, it was a political and moral question.[60] On 23 September 1941, Power submitted the British request to the Cabinet War Committee for consideration. A decision, however, was deferred until the proposal could be thoroughly examined by the General Staff and Ralston.

Because Ralston was in Los Angeles, a brief was prepared by the DMO and I as a basis for discussion with Crerar, giving the impression that the government had already approved in principle the decision to dispatch. Gibson related the Cabinet War Committee's preparedness to accept the proposal and the fact that the CGS saw no 'military risks in dispatching Cdn B[attalio]ns for this purpose.'[61] The first inference was incorrect and was absent from the DMO and I's draft memorandum revised by Crerar on the afternoon of the 24th.[62] Ralston nevertheless based his discussions with the CGS on the first brief and may have been labouring under the assumption that the War Cabinet had accepted the proposal. Following a conversation in the early evening of 24 September, during which Crerar reiterated his belief that the army could accept the responsibility, both were ready to promote the project.

Crerar believed the primary risk was the potential impediment to the organization of formations due for employment in the British Isles. The attendant military risks of sending troops to the Far East were implicit rather than made explicit. When questioned about a General Staff appreciation of the tactical situation of the Hong Kong garrison, Crerar observed to the Royal Commission, 'I was not asked by the Minister or anyone else for such a military appreciation, nor did I consider that in the setting of the British request that such a request would be made.' It was a policy decision.[63]

According to the testimony of the DMO and I and his senior intelligence officer, Lieutenant-Colonel William Murray, up-to-date information on the defences of Hong Kong was available at National Defence Headquarters, but no formal request was made for the information by the General Staff until after the dispatch had been decided upon. Neither was a military appreciation of Hong Kong's defences in the event of a war requested or prepared.[64] It would not have mattered. As the postwar CGS observed in 1948, 'There is nothing ... to show that the Department of National Defence had a staff which could work out the pros and cons of accepting this proposal ... the Canadian Authorities were completely dependent on information received from the UK.'[65] While the number of officers handling intelligence had increased from one in 1940 to seven in 1941, only one of them handled 'foreign intelligence.' This was an admission that it was beyond Canada's capabilities to start an intelligence assessment network from scratch.[66] It was impractical to expect that one could have been created, but it left Canada dependent on the British for information and, more importantly, assessments of that information. In the absence of an assessment of the merits of defending Hong Kong, Crerar's appreciations (and assumptions) and those expressed in the British telegram took on an even greater importance.

The government did not formally approve the dispatch until 2 October, but the selection of units was already underway. Crerar's choices for the units deployed to Hong Kong, the Royal Rifles of Canada and the Winnipeg Grenadiers, derived from the logic that informed his advice to the government – that war with Japan was less likely than previously thought, that Europe was the main theatre, and that their primary duty in Hong Kong would be to garrison it.[67] Crerar's memorandum of 30 September to the minister on unit selection emphasized two general points: that the units 'should be efficient, well-trained battalions,' and that the selection should not disrupt the training of the 4th Canadian Division, preparing for overseas service.[68] Crerar would not disrupt the organization of forces already slated for Britain, and the British did not want these formations broken up. Others, including the General Officer Commanding of the 4th Canadian Division, were of the same mind.[69]

Crerar's estimate that that hostilities with Japan were not imminent also informed his choice of regiments. He believed that, despite the assessment of the Director of Military Training that the two units were in need of 'refresher' training, they were by his definition ones of 'proven efficiency.' He assumed that the garrison duties in Hong Kong would not differ much from the Royal Rifles' responsibilities in Newfoundland or the Grenadiers' duties in Jamaica, observing that they were capable of 'upholding the credit of the Dominion' in 'a distant and important garrison.' He also believed that the men were of a high standard, based on information obtained from the unit commanding officers and on personal observation of the quality of the troops. Both battalions were among the most experienced of the available units.[70]

The measures of training efficiency applied in 1941 were different from those used later in the war; they had to be. In the summer and fall of 1941 the system was only beginning to show results. The decision to extend compulsory training to four months in January 1941 meant that the first troops to undergo the extended training program started on 20 March 1941.[71] Reliance on inexperienced unit and formation commanders exacerbated the problem. Crerar gave some indication of the generalities that characterized definitions of *well-trained* in the formative stages of army expansion in a comment he deleted from his testimony to the Royal Commission. 'As a commanding officer,' he stated, 'I would rather be in a position to select a number of partly trained volunteer reinforcements of superior type than be provided with an equal number of men who had completed their training but who might lack intelligence or the volunteering spirit.'[72]

Crerar also noted that the units chosen fulfilled a number of domestic political requirements. Attention was drawn to the fact that, in addition to representing two distinct regions, the Royal Rifles were from a French-speaking region. The unstated message, found in an early draft of the reasoning behind the selection, and one that confirmed his belief that hostilities were not imminent, was that the Rifles 'should serve in a theatre where casualties are not likely to be heavy or sustained.' The draft memorandum concluded, 'Clearly it could not long retain its character and identity in a main theatre of war for it could not be reinforced from its own territory.'[73]

Crerar's selection also indicates he believed that disrupting the expansion of formations earmarked for Europe was more dangerous than the garrison duties at Hong Kong. Visiting London in October 1941, he and Ralston were informed that in the opinion of the British Joint Planning Board, an inter-service strategic planning committee, any initial Japanese military action would be directed against Russia' and that, for offensive purposes, the 'retention of Hong Kong was stated to be of very great importance.'[74] War, however, seemed remote. The revised army program for 1942, submitted in mid-November 1941, reflected Crerar's focus on expanding the army for deployment against Germany and the optimistic assessment of the strategic situation in the Far East.[75]

Sending two battalions of Canadian troops, and later a brigade headquarters, was not going to deter the Japanese from going to war, but Crerar had long believed in the importance of a timely show of empire solidarity, particularly when combined with increased U.S. involvement and enhanced British naval strength to reduce the 'period of relief.' 'The proposed action,' Crerar observed, 'whatever the military risks of the enterprise, needed to be examined from the broad view as to its contributory value to the eventual winning of the war.'[76]

Should Crerar have made the potential risks clearer to the government? Yes, although he did so indirectly. However, NDHQ's assessment was unlikely to have been far different from the one offered by the British. It is also important to remember the urgency felt by all participants lest the chance to deter the Japanese and avoid a Pacific war fade. Crerar deleted several references to the urgency he felt was implicit in the British request, and explicit in the later requests, from his testimony before the Royal Commission. In one testy response to Drew, Crerar wrote, 'Special reports were not asked for [nor indeed could special reports of any value have been obtained within the time available].' The latter statement was not in the recorded testimony. Subsequent revelations indicate that the British were correct in their assessment of the importance of maintaining Chinese morale at this critical juncture, and thus tying down the bulk of the Japanese army, even if their intelligence miscalculated the magnitude of Japanese irrationality.[77] Crerar's that of assessment of Japanese intentions was no worse, and no better, than that of the British or Americans.

10 Father of First Canadian Army

I

Decisions highlighted by the tragedy at Hong Kong were secondary to Crerar's agenda in the fall of 1941. Working feverishly to prepare his army program for 1942, he built his proposals on an appreciation of the strategic situation as well as the crucial manpower estimates. With these assessments in hand, Crerar hoped to gain Cabinet War Committee acceptance of the program 'in principle,' and then seek confirmation of his appreciation from the War Office and McNaughton.[1] His goal was an army formation.

Crerar's fixation on public and political opinion during the summer of 1941 was shaped partially by the fact that he was trying to secure his position to launch the next army program in September 1941. At this juncture, the government was reluctant to approve more ground forces. Ralston's difficulties in gaining the War Cabinet's begrudging approval of a sixth division for home defence in the summer underlined the need for caution. King reminded Ralston and his cabinet colleagues that two principles governed Canada's military effort: 'It had been settled government policy to give priority to the Air Force, Navy and war industry,' and second, no commitment would be made to an army that could be maintained only through 'resort to conscription.'[2] Privately, King railed against the General Staff and Ralston's support for their plans, his view that 'Generals are invariably wrong' remaining unchanged.

Nevertheless, Ralston was successful, despite the Prime Minister's best efforts to defer the decision, using the army's manpower estimates – figures that none of the opposition could counter. Ralston, however, had initially tabled the proposals as the General Staff's and made no attempt to present them as initiatives with which he agreed – an approach indicative of the minister's state of mind. To secure King's support, dubious though it was, Ralston agreed to make no further commitments to army expansion.³

Conscious of the army's tenuous position among the ministers of the War Cabinet, the CGS was determined to maintain his solid relationship with McNaughton and the overseas forces – a difficult objective, given the growing disagreements over the organizational direction of the Canadian Corps as well as his doubts about McNaughton's temperament. Nevertheless, in a carefully worded 'personal, confidential and informal' letter to McNaughton, Crerar introduced the broad outlines of his 1942 army program. Prefacing his comments with the departmental appreciations that indicated that there was manpower enough for six overseas divisions and the two home defence divisions required by the agreements under the auspices of the Permanent Joint Board of Defence, Crerar observed,

> I believe that the numbers for the Army are there, without interfering with essential industry and other home activities providing the government takes the steps required to get these numbers into the Services.
>
> All the above leads me to the conclusion that providing the Government are prepared to face up to the financial and other strain, we should be able to reinforce the Corps during 1942 with not only 4th Division but another Armoured Division as well. This would result in too large a Corps but have you ever considered the pros and cons of a Canadian Army comprising 2 Corps each of 2 Divisions and an Armoured Division? ... I do not think the picture is an impossible one.
>
> I should add ... that all the above should be regarded as a personal, confidential and informal discussion of the future possibilities for no detailed study of what this would imply has yet been made and I have not put forward these suggestions, in even a tentative way, to the Minister.⁴

Crerar's intentions for 1942 were clear. He understood that for this round, manpower estimates would be the prerequisite for success, as training policy had been for his first army program. He undoubtedly believed the estimates, confirming as they did the maximum potential of the army as presented in prewar studies. He was also aware of the personal advantages. If the Canadian army expanded, he hoped to obtain early command of a division and someday succeed 'Andy as GOC Canadian Corps, when he went on to a higher post.' McNaughton, however, did not acknowledge Crerar's proposals, believing 'that an official proposition for 1942 originating in Canada might be expected shortly.'[5]

Crerar presented his proposed program to Ralston at the end of September 1941. Two aspects were notable. First was Crerar's provision that the 'plans for the army should be such as can be implemented with our present system of voluntary enlistment for overseas service.'[6] This position reflected Crerar's belief in the strength of the volunteer system, but was also meant for government consumption; Crerar was prepared to accept conscription. The second noteworthy element was the proposal for the eventual formation of a Canadian armoured corps and a Canadian army formation headquarters, comprising a total of six overseas divisions. The proposed program was tentative, dependent upon the outcome of discussions with the British and McNaughton.

The minister made no reply to the proposals. Rumours of the army program had circulated among Ottawa's inner circles for at least a month prior to the formal presentation of the program, but Ralston, although wary of further army expansion, was at a loss as to how to react. He believed, according to one observer, that Crerar had 'let him down,' but he was unable to counter the carefully prepared estimates and projections of the General Staff.[7] He decided to wait for the counsel of McNaughton and the British, sceptical enough of Crerar's interpretation to consider making the trip overseas without his chief military advisor. The minister also pointedly ignored a subtle warning from the Prime Minister that he should delay his trip to avoid contention with an increasingly irritable McNaughton, who had recently characterized Ralston as 'completely unfitted' for his responsibilities as defence minister. Ralston believed he had McNaughton's confidence.[8]

Crerar soon flew to England, a measure perhaps of the urgency he felt. An eight-hour overseas flight was still a novelty in 1941 and one that Crerar described to his sister as nearly 'record' setting and 'quite an experience ... [which] in spite of considerable discomfort, I enjoyed ... very much.' Once he was in England, events moved equally fast. Crerar proved adept at securing the allegiance of the War Office in his quest for an army headquarters over the next two months. In discussions with the CIGS, Lieutenant-General J. Dill, as well as a former Staff College friend the Adjutant CIGS, Major-General J. Macready, and the Director of Military Operations and Intelligence (DMO and I), Crerar placed his ideas on Canadian army organization before the War Office establishment. His war diary record of the conversations was written in such a way as to illustrate British support for Crerar's two-corps Canadian army, but on both occasions it was clear that he initiated the question of the organization of Canadian troops in the United Kingdom. Macready was passive in the first exchange, agreeing with Crerar's proposals. In the subsequent discussions with the DMO and I, again initiated by Crerar, he referred to 'Macready's view as to the composition and organization of the Canadian forces overseas.' The CGS found that the director, not surprisingly, 'thoroughly agreed with [Macready's] views.'[9]

McNaughton was not so easily convinced. His biographer believes that it 'may be doubted if McNaughton saw the creation of an army as [a] pressing need.' In the conversations between the minister, McNaughton, and Crerar on the future expansion of the army, no mention of an army headquarters formation was recorded in the existing transcripts, despite Crerar's initiatives upon his arrival.[10] On Ralston's return to Ottawa, he reported the British Secretary of State for War's suggestion that 'the most helpful addition to the Canadian forces overseas would be armoured formations.'[11] Ralston was also impressed by the 'extreme gravity of the whole war situation' and the maintenance demands in both men and equipment. He did not mention an army headquarters.

The proposed army headquarters was consequently excluded from the revised army program for 1942 submitted in mid-November. Crerar's program, however, continued to reflect his optimistic assessment of Canada's manpower. He prefaced his comments on the proposal with a chief of staff appreciation that reversed King's priorities, suggesting the 'maintenance overseas of as large an Army as can be developed without marked penalty to the expansion of our Naval and Air Services and the output of our war industries.' An argument followed for an additional armoured division and armoured brigade for overseas service, undoubtedly a reflection of the current state of opinion on the modest infantry support – one brigade – required in an armoured formation.[12]

The manpower projections and the army program again produced heated debates in the Cabinet War Committee and Cabinet circles, a contest exacerbated by the concurrent submission of the air and naval programs.[13] Despite omission of any reference to an army headquarters, the conviction among Ralston's confidants was that the General Staff's objective was a Canadian overseas army formation. Privately, the minister left the impression that his initial support for the army program was half-hearted and that he viewed it as 'a concoction of the brass hats.'[14] Further reflection on the manpower estimates provided by the AG's branch gave the minister pause. He had certainly overcome his doubts by the time discussions began in the Cabinet War Committee in earnest in early December, however; to King's dismay, Ralston announced his intention to back the army proposals to complete the six division force, including ancillary corps and army units, even if conscription were necessary.[15] His frequent references to the British sacrifices and war effort suggest the influence of his recent trip to the United Kingdom. Ralston may also have been moved by Crerar's appointment as GOC, 2nd Canadian Division, and his replacement by Lieutenant-General Ken Stuart, with whom Ralston had established an easier working relationship. Whatever the reason for his change of heart, Ralston's support of the program in Cabinet proved invaluable.

Crerar's appointment to divisional command was fortunate for his designs to establish a field army headquarters; it also fulfilled a long-standing ambition. The introduction of age limits for senior commanders, one of the few measures of command open to the inexperienced Canadian Corps, forced the retirement of Victor Odlum as GOC, 2nd Canadian Division. Such was the atmosphere of suspicion in Ottawa that overactive journalistic imaginations perceived the fixing of age limits as a 'move in [the] manoeuvre of militarists against politicians.' Dexter and Sifton saw sinister designs behind every move.[16] More important, the search for a successor was complicated by McNaughton's deteriorating health. Any appointee would have to be capable of assuming responsibility for the Canadian Corps. McNaughton's tireless pace and nervous energy had begun to tell on him many months earlier, a condition frequently brought to Crerar's attention by Mike Pearson.[17] The sojourn in Britain in October had brought the point home. McNaughton was reluctant to commence his sick leave until a suitable candidate had taken command of 2nd Division.[18]

Crerar pressed for consideration, securing Brooke's, McNaughton's, and Ralston's support. Brooke was enthusiastic: 'I had a long and useful discussion with [Crerar] about the future of the Canadian Corps,' he wrote in his diary in October. 'I do hope that they give him the 2nd Canadian Division.' He lobbied on Crerar's behalf.[19] McNaughton did not explicitly endorse Crerar to the minister but noted, after describing Brigadier J.H. Roberts as the best selection 'of the officers available here,' that 'consideration should also be given to Crerar' if he was fit and available.[20] Ralston, prepared to endorse Crerar, was apparently caught off guard by McNaughton's qualified recommendation. Before presenting the proposal to Cabinet, the minister wired back, 'Reference your 2081 assuming Crerar physically fit ... can I inform war committee of cabinet that you confirm verbal intimation to the effect that you would welcome this appointment?' A leisurely reply affirmed this view.[21]

The Cabinet War Committee approved Crerar's appointment on 19 November. Only then did Ralston solicit committee support for increasing the rank of the Chief of the General Staff to lieutenant-general, Crerar's goal since his appointment fifteen months earlier.[22] Divisional command forced Crerar to drop in rank, but Crerar would retain his seniority from the day of his appointment. As events turned out, it was a moot point. Crerar was appointed as CO of 2nd Canadian Infantry Division, but never assumed command of the division. He hoped first to gain experience in divisional command overseas, and had put pressure on McNaughton and Brooke to that end. Instead, in December 1941 he was chosen to replace Major-General George Pearkes as acting commander, 1st Canadian Corps, during McNaughton's extended sick leave, a displacement that Pearkes (and his biographer) believed was a result of Crerar's own machinations and influence as CGS. Pearkes recalled twenty-five years later that McNaughton had told him that he believed that Crerar should remain in Ottawa but barring this, Crerar should 'become a divisional commander before having a Corps.'[23]

Pearkes was half right. McNaughton was concerned about Crerar's lack of command experience. He was prepared to hand over temporary command of the corps to Pearkes and place Crerar in command of 2nd Canadian Division. Crerar was nevertheless McNaughton's choice for a permanent replacement. Lester Pearson recorded McNaughton's dilemma several months earlier as the corps commander pondered his failing health: 'He is quite worried ... as he is convinced that neither of his Divisional Commanders is quite up to the job of running the Corps. He thinks that Pearkes is a good soldier but of rather limited vision ... He feels certain that the only person who could take on the Corps if he had to leave would be Harry.'[24]

Ultimately McNaughton's poor health proved decisive. In mid-November, McNaughton was told to remain on medical leave for at least two months, until the end of February. This potentially doubled the period that Pearkes would be in command. Crerar would be subordinate to Pearkes for an extended period of time. McNaughton and Brooke, who was assuming the responsibilities of Chief of the Imperial General Staff on 1 December 1941, discussed this situation. Brooke backed Crerar. McNaughton subsequently wired Ralston on 29 November, observing that after further consultations with Brooke 'regarding command of Canadian Corps in my absence,' they had agreed that Crerar should take over acting command of the corps 'as Canadian Officer next in seniority to myself.'[25] Ralston confirmed Crerar's appointment; he would take over acting command as of 31 December 1941.[26]

As he prepared to go overseas, family issues also pressed on Crerar. Verse had anticipated following her husband to England, going so far as to drop her canteen activities and begin qualifying herself for 'possible active service,' presumably with the Red Cross. 'She has no intention of staying in Canada any longer than she has to,' Crerar wrote his sister. She did not go right away, however. His son had joined the army, and had in November 1941 been detailed to attend an Officer Training Centre in Brockville. His father was horrified to learn that his son had been sent to the OTC before he had completed his Advanced Training Centre course, where he had trained under the watchful eye of Tommy Burns. Crerar was concerned about the possible negative effects on his son; he was also fearful of the perception that his son had 'received special and favoured treatment.' After some discussion with Burns, he decided that interference would only make matters worse. Still, to friends and family, he wrote proudly that the army had done Peter 'a lot of good.' Zouch Palmer had also returned to Canada in November, and Crerar left for England knowing that his daughter was happy again. There was an inescapable sense of urgency during his last days in Ottawa. One of his final acts was to secure a new batman, Tom Macdonald, in a hurried interview in the CGS's office. 'The General ... put me at ease,' recalled Macdonald, 'but it was obvious from the beginning that he lived by the rules and that I would have to be on my toes at all times.'[27]

II

Happy to have obtained a field command, Crerar arrived in England on 23 December still determined to promote an army formation. He and McNaughton conferred with the Commander-in-Chief Home Forces General Sir Bernard Paget on the future organization of the Canadian forces. After Crerar outlined his program, he noted that it 'was before the Government and that while final approval had not yet been given, the proposals were receiving very favourable consideration.' This was, of course, an exaggeration – the program was being hotly debated. When asked by Paget what organization would control the units suggested in the army program then under consideration, McNaughton stated that he 'would prefer an Army HQ with two Corps.'[28] Despite a lukewarm reception by Paget for this idea, the GOC, Canadian Corps, subsequently cabled the same message to Ralston. Somewhat incredulously, the minister wired, 'This involves a somewhat imposing expansion in overhead and did not understand it had been advocated by you.'[29] McNaughton's advocacy, however, was secure and any doubts he had were stilled by the CIGS's stated support on 7 January 1942 for an 'Army Headquarters which will ... free the Corps Commander's hands for the job of commanding and training the fighting formations. That in itself is a full-time job!'[30]

There was truth to this view, but the key to this sudden spate of support for an army headquarters was Crerar's initiatives on his return to England, which coincided with the growing doubts about McNaughton's capabilities as an operational commander among senior British commanders and concerns about the unchecked growth of Canadian troops outside the corps purview.[31] Crerar cultivated the support of the War Office, persuading Brooke of the utility of a Canadian army formation in meetings in October and December in part because they viewed an army HQ as a means of removing McNaughton from operational command of the Canadian Corps. In discussions with Ralston in October, Crerar related opinions he had gathered from Brooke and 'other [War] Office officials' that McNaughton's best role was as a 'Force Commander' of two corps to take advantage of his scientific 'genius.'[32] Interviewed years later, Crerar recalled that Brooke, aware of the political implications of ousting McNaughton, broached the subject with Crerar and Ralston on the occasion of their visit to England in October and afterwards while Crerar was GOC, 1st Canadian Corps. Crerar later defended Brooke's actions, contending that 'most Canadians felt Brooke was right,' although Crerar tactfully steered clear of direct criticism.[33]

Doubts about McNaughton's ability as a commander as well as his health provided ample motivation for British support of the establishment of an additional force headquarters that would lessen, at least for the immediate future, McNaughton's operational responsibilities. Both Brooke and Paget, in their rationalizations to McNaughton, stressed that the administrative and organizational responsibilities should be the prime focus of the HQ, leaving the corps CO free to focus on training and operations. Brooke later observed that he was apprehensive about the time when the more 'drastic measure' of having McNaughton removed from command would come, suggesting that he viewed McNaughton's elevation as a temporary expedient.[34] This reasoning accounts for the lukewarm support given the idea of an army headquarters by Brooke. It was, however, no coincidence that Brooke's letter to McNaughton on 7 January 1942 suggesting an army headquarters followed on the heels of a lunch with Crerar that same day; their discussions centred on Crerar's ideas for the new 'Force Headquarters.'[35] The result of Crerar's initiatives was the British support for a Canadian army headquarters.

In an ironic twist, the British sanction secured McNaughton's support for the idea of an army headquarters. His endorsement, with its explicit statement of British concurrence, was then enough to sway a reluctant, and weary, Minister of National Defence. The Prime Minister recorded his observations on Ralston's condition: 'I am really deeply concerned about Ralston. He has become obsessed with the Hong Kong matter ... Looks much older and one can see is suffering intensely.' Shaken by the outbreak of war in the Pacific and the disaster at Hong Kong, he endorsed the proposal for the army headquarters.[36]

The program, including the proposal for an army headquarters, remained atop the War Cabinet agenda for several weeks. The Japanese victories in the Pacific, Ralston's threats of resignation, as well as reassurances from Crerar's successor as CGS, Lieutenant-General Ken Stuart, that 'the visible ceiling of army expansion' had been reached and that the commitments could be fulfilled through voluntary enlistments were enough to force King to concede the point. The idea of a sixth overseas division was dropped as a result of manpower anxieties, but Crerar got his army and second corps HQ, which were the important prizes from the standpoint of visibility and balance.[37]

The Canadian Permanent Active Militia, renamed the Canadian Army in 1940, had an authorized strength in 1939 of 4,268. The Non-Permanent Active Militia's authorized strength was 86,308. At its peak strength in June 1944, the Canadian Army had enlisted 495,073 men and women, organized into two tank brigades, eight divisions, two corps, and an army – a remarkable expansion by any measure.[38] The air force and the navy showed similar increases, all three services combining to put 1,086,343 men and women in uniform.

The fall of France was the catalyst for the army's expansion, but Crerar's agenda as CGS determined its shape. His success was due to his understanding that estimates of manpower were a trump card in Cabinet debates. Through his army program proposals, Crerar placed the army at the centre of the country's war policy. He hoped to emulate, and surpass, the reputation of the Canadian Corps and to prepare the ground for a professional postwar military force. But, first and foremost, he believed a large ground force was necessary to defeat Nazi Germany. He was right. Was Canada in a position to provide it to the war effort? Did First Canadian Army overtax Canada's manpower? The crisis of trained riflemen in the late summer and autumn of 1944 appears to suggest this conclusion, although the unexpectedly high casualty rates among riflemen, changes to the infantry needs of armoured formations, the growth of CMHQ, and the splitting of the army between two theatres probably did more to tax a delicately balanced system than the existence of the army headquarters and army troops themselves. And here too Crerar was a central figure, pressing for a large CMHQ and promoting the dispatch of a corps to the Mediterranean. The paradox facing Crerar and others was that as the campaigning on the peripheries grew in significance, and the probability of liberating northwest Europe remained remote (how remote in 1940 no one would have predicted), the opportunities for experience and even to contribute to operations would highlight the weaknesses they were meant to address. But that said, manpower, or rather the allocation and directed training of that manpower, was an issue for all of the Allied armies. Nobody got it right. Shortages of riflemen in 1944 reflected the changing nature of a global conflict and the reality that in 1941, the 'Allies' – until 7 December, Britain and the commonwealth, along with an invaded but not allied Soviet Union seemingly on the verge of defeat – did not know how to win it. And they were in danger of losing it.

11 Preparing 1st Canadian Corps

I

'On [my] arrival [in the] UK ... I had had no field command in this war,' Crerar wrote in 1946. 'It followed, therefore, that whatever conclusions I might personally reach as to changes in policy, organization and command in 1st Canadian Corps, it was necessary for me to delay action, whenever possible, until Lieutenant-General McNaughton returned and I obtained his approval or otherwise. I was very much in the position of a "locum tenens."' Crerar's candid avowal of his inexperience, and tacit admission of his insecurity as he began his tenure in command, was understandable in light of his rapid promotion. Indeed, while Crerar was assailed by self-doubt at the beginning of many new ventures, it was also true that as with most Canadian (and British and American) officers, Crerar was learning on the job. He did learn, however. His tenure was marked by important changes in the approach taken to train the corps, and credit for this was shared with Montgomery and Simonds. The most controversial policy was the decision to pursue operational experience through participation in the growing number of coastal raids. The Dieppe raid was the culmination of Crerar's campaign for this experience – a failed raid that became a driving force in his actions until the successes at Normandy two years later. Crerar was correct when he recalled the 'period January–June 1942 [as] one of the most trying and difficult periods of my professional life.'[1]

Once in England, Crerar felt handicapped by his sudden promotion to corps command. He seemed genuinely surprised, and even slightly distraught, at the idea that he would not have a chance 'to prove myself ... in command of a division.'[2] He was far more anxious about his new responsibilities than he was prepared to reveal. Without any previous command experience beyond the First World War brigade level, he was assigned the task of leading the largest tactical formation in the Anglo-Canadian armies. 1st Canadian Corps in early 1942 consisted of headquarters (HQ) staff, corps troops, and the 1st, 2nd, and 3rd Canadian Infantry Divisions, as well as, through late 1942, elements of 4th Armoured Division. The corps was rapidly expanding and there was a tremendous turnover among staff and experienced NCOs. Exacerbating the difficulties caused by this expansion – an expansion of Crerar's making – was the fact that the training agenda of the corps was in a period of sharp transition as the emphasis moved from defence against invasion to offensive training, when Montgomery became the Commander-in-Chief of South-Eastern Command.[3] Finally, it was unclear when, or for how long, McNaughton would return.

In contrast to the tempo enforced on the corps in 1942 and 1943, the headquarters was on the bucolic estate of Wakehurst Place, a Tudor mansion situated on 170 acres of Sussex woodland and given over to the use of the Canadians by Sir Henry and Lady Price. Its cultivated gardens, acres of weald, Tudor facade, and interior dominated by elaborately hand-carved wooden staircases and mantelpieces, boarded to protect them from the Canadians, provided Crerar little enjoyment except for his daily walks. The surroundings could not mask the atmosphere as Crerar had again entered a situation where his promotion resulted in resentment among subordinates like Pearkes. Crerar had to prove himself. He had desperately wanted a field command, just as the British and American chiefs of staff, Alan Brooke and George C. Marshall respectively, coveted field commands, expecting to be rewarded for their roles in creating their nations' armies; neither balked when it was not forthcoming.

Crerar did not immediately provide a clear direction for the corps, but he wanted to concentrate more attention on training than had McNaughton. Collective training in the Canadian overseas forces, like the British, was decentralized, and the onus for training practice was on commanding officers. The dissemination of the experiences of the fighting formations was similarly haphazard, although it was becoming more systematic. In February 1942 the War Office launched initiatives like the series called *Notes from Theatres of War*. There was still no mechanism for enforcing a uniform approach to training, and with no doctrinal theory to provide guidance, the responsibility lay with individuals.[4] Crerar set about gathering information, both general on operational ideas and specific to the corps. His earliest impressions on the corps' needs were formed from three main sources. First was the information obtained from the British and Canadian senior command, particularly Brooke and Paget, as well as Pearkes and McNaughton, prior to assuming command. Their main concerns were the weaknesses among the senior officer corps. There is ample evidence to suggest that the British were explicit in their criticisms regarding McNaughton's training and organization of the corps.[5] The second source was the conclusions drawn from a series of personal visits to units and formations in January 1942. This was gradually supplanted by observations and performance reports emanating from the successively rigorous exercises that became such a characteristic of Montgomery's South-Eastern Command. The third source was Montgomery's personal assessments of the Canadian Corps' staff and officers, a source of advice and strong opinion that, whatever its merits, was particularly important in evaluating command and staff at and below the brigade level in the early weeks of Crerar's command.

Crerar's initial contributions, however, were moulded by the presence of two people: Montgomery and the corps Brigadier, General Staff (BGS), Guy Granville Simonds. Montgomery's dynamic presence made itself felt immediately upon his assumption of command, the result in no small part of his determination to stamp his imprint on South-Eastern Command. Patronizingly self-assured, judgmental, brusque, and abrasive, Montgomery was also an efficient, knowledgeable, and effective military professional – an irritating combination of arrogance and ability that divided contemporaries and historians into two extremes of opinion. The split was exacerbated by Montgomery's habitual tendency, in the estimation of his biographer, to show 'favouritism towards some and excessive hostility to others.'[6]

C.P. Stacey relates that Crerar, enquiring about his new Commander-in-Chief, was told that Montgomery was 'an efficient little shit.'[7] Crerar was a little kinder but had him pegged: in 1943, he observed to Vincent Massey that 'Monty's [definition] of an army with good morale was an army commanded by Monty.' Still, Crerar had great respect for Montgomery as a professional.[8] Monty's relationship with Crerar became strained, but it varied in proportion to the degree of deference shown by the Canadian to the 'master of the battlefield.' If the early months of their relationship were calm, it was mainly because Crerar assumed the reins of power tentatively.

Montgomery's objective upon assuming command of the two corps,

12 British and 1st Canadian that constituted South-Eastern Command, was to instill a sense of urgency and professionalism in its troops and officers. He would countenance no resistance. Montgomery gave notice of his intention early in his tenure, retitling his new command 'South-Eastern Army' and inflating himself to 'Army Commander.' He hoped it would promote the 'offensive' mentality that his command should aspire to as well as ease the introduction of a standardized doctrine and practice of training. Pearkes, temporary CO, 1st Canadian Corps, was quickly irritated by Montgomery's interference, snap judgments, and patronizing attitude – aggravations that limited Montgomery's immediate impact.[9]

Nevertheless, Montgomery's influence was soon felt throughout the corps. Training Instruction No. 5 of 21 November 1941 prescribed a new level of intensity and realism, as well as progression, in unit training, beginning at the platoon level and culminating at the divisional level in May 1942. A battle-training area, the first, large enough for a brigade, was established on the South Downs in Sussex. The training directive used by the Canadians was the brainchild of Guy Simonds, a thorough and innovative professional in his own right. Nicknamed the 'count,' there was no doubt that a few officers left his presence white-faced and drained of blood. He put military effectiveness before nationalism, and for that reason alone would have stood higher than Crerar in Montgomery's eyes. But Simonds was also one of the best generals Canada produced. Simonds's training policy advocated the need for physical fitness, headquarters staff exercises without troops, and two-sided field exercises involving corps-size formations.[10]

Simonds was heavily influenced by Montgomery's thoughts on training. The latter's policies were spread throughout large portions of the retooled British army through the efforts of Alan Brooke when he was Commander-in-Chief Home Forces. Simonds absorbed Brooke's and Montgomery's realistic approach to training and attempted to spread it throughout the corps. He provided one of the few notes of continuity in the command and staff at corps HQ over the early months of winter 1942. Montgomery's nightly meetings with the three chiefs of staff of the army and corps HQs to 'coordinate' their staff work and ensure uniformity in training and implementation cemented Simonds's desire to adopt the progressive staff and unit physical training and exercises. Training Instruction No. 6, issued on 25 February 1942, reflected Montgomery's concerns with communication, locations of headquarters, need to seize the initiative, and cooperation – questions of control and movement that divisional exercises in 1941 had revealed were weak spots in 1st Canadian Corps.[11]

Training policy as prescribed by Crerar in successive circular letters followed the standardizing thrust of Montgomery's directives and informal comments. Crerar deferred to the training timetable laid out prior to his assumption of command, working closely with Simonds and relying, by his own admission, on the familiarity of his BGS, and Deputy Adjutant and QMG to ensure continuity until he felt he had learned the 'principle elements of the job.'[12]

Crerar's first weeks were spent familiarizing himself with his command, learning the topography, and meeting his subordinates as well as his superiors – time spent, by his own account, listening and 'learning their problems.'[13] A cautious evolution was evident. Crerar did not issue his first general circular in January 1942 until he had spoken with Montgomery and conferred with Simonds. He stressed the principle of preparing for the 'invasion battle' and harkened back to the example of the old Canadian Corps, 'a match for any several German Army Corps twenty-five years ago.' Attaining that standard would not be easy. In these aspects, his message was not original. Crerar's individual contribution was the promise of relative stability to 'give every opportunity to commanders of all grades to practice themselves ... and to staffs to secure that team-work which is essential to co-ordinated effort.' To assist in training, Crerar secured a number of experienced junior officers to act as 'junior umpires' for the unit and subunit phase of the training program.[14]

These were important provisions, recognizing that new training programs were not enough if they were undermined by the problems that accompanied the rapid expansion of the overseas forces, and by the inexperience of umpires, afraid or unable to impose a degree of realism on the exercises. Crerar gave every indication he was eager to facilitate the improvements in training and that he was willing to learn from the experience of superiors and subordinates. There is evidence that Simonds resented Crerar's appointment and his lack of experience, but the antipathy that was to develop between them was still muted at this point.[15]

Crerar differed with Montgomery on the issues of command changes as they related to the autonomy of 1st Canadian Corps within the British command – differences that deepened with minor disagreements over dispositions and training timelines. Montgomery's appraisal of the corps after Exercise Beaver in early January 1942 was Crerar's first formal encounter with his new CO. Montgomery's remarks were his usual blend of simplicity and hard-hitting criticism.[16] Four days later, Crerar gave Brooke the impression that he was 'delighted with all [Montgomery's] help and all out to play to the utmost.'[17] Montgomery's offers to inspect and appraise the units of the corps as well as his suggestions on the operational policy were also welcomed; the majority were implemented. The Corps Study Week, the timetable for completion of preparations for invasion, even the title and thrust of the 'Plan To Defeat Invasion' were faithfully adhered to. Uniformity of training, and to some degree organization, were the logical result of the fact that the Canadians would be fighting under British higher command and with British formations.

Crerar did not associate uniformity with the surrender of autonomy, nor was he willing to explicitly mirror Montgomery's approach to command. Crerar's determination to follow McNaughton's policy on the maintenance of Canadian military independence was implicitly signalled at a meeting between Crerar and Brooke on 7 January 1942, a move construed by Montgomery's biographer as 'one of his corps commanders complaining direct to the CIGS.'[18] Crerar's approach also eased the strains that characterized the relationship between McNaughton and Brooke. Crerar respected the British – in April, he would admonish his sister in California for her 'caustic and unpleasant criticisms' of the British Empire and Great Britain – but he was a Canadian national, and he knew his constitutional history.[19]

Brooke's account of Crerar's initial attempt to broach the subject of Canadian autonomy reflects Crerar's more temperate approach: he balanced the maintenance of good command relations with the assertion of his prerogatives as GOC, 1st Canadian Corps. Still, Crerar warned Brooke of the implications of the British treating Canadian officers, particularly senior officers, and units as if they were British. Brooke evidently felt that Crerar's warnings were worth passing on, if only because of the 'very touchy and childlike' nature of the Canadian soldier.[20] Brooke, albeit in a patronizing manner, took Crerar's warnings for what they were. Montgomery was put off both by Crerar's conferring with a superior as well as his assertion of autonomy. Indeed, he had already ignored similar warnings conveyed by Crerar in an earlier letter outlining his general policy on training.[21]

Montgomery's estimation of Crerar was not enhanced by his negative reply in this same letter to the suggestion that Canadian officers and NCOs attend further instructional courses. Crerar instead outlined his own conception of how 1st Canadian Corps was 'to reach the very high standard of training and effectiveness required of it.' He insisted that unit and subunit commanders have an uninterrupted period to plan and execute the progressive training program. To achieve this objective and benefit from British instruction and experience, Crerar requested 'junior umpires' to assist unit commanders. Unit training would continue until February. The emphasis on stability and decentralized training also fit with the role Crerar envisaged for himself, to set clear parameters for his subordinate but avoid being too prescriptives. He did not believe that a volunteer army could be 'driven.' It must be led, largely by example.

II

Crerar was also preparing himself to command the corps. His early practice was to establish himself as an example. He acted as a schoolmaster to his staff, testing their knowledge of organization, tactics, and procedure. Attempts by public relations to portray him as a man of action – the 'Hamilton Tiger' – were not successful. Immaculately groomed, bordering on fussy, with his prosy manner of speaking – 'rather as if he was teaching a rather dull class' observed one subordinate – it all reinforced a stodgy image. Crerar wasn't physically imposing at five foot eight inches but he was still fit. The narrow face had more wrinkles, but the neatly clipped moustache and unassuming chin complemented an aristocratic demeanour; he looked like a kindly 'renaissance prince,' as one author noted.[22]

Nevertheless, Crerar staff experience would serve him well. His first active participation in operational study as corps commander was in the Corps Study Week in January. In attendance were staff and commanders down to brigade level; it was, in theory, an intensive study of defensive and offensive tactics, inter-service cooperation and miscellaneous problems. 'The Problem of Cross-Channel Raiding,' which discussed the procedure for laying on a raid, was a significant addition. The staff exercises titled Beaver II and Victor Two followed in February, but Crerar's role was as observer, not participant. Further Beaver exercises through April and May were under corps direction, but the HQ's main exercise continued to be practice in speed of encampment and decampment. These exercises, conducted without troops, had an air of unreality, but seemed to have created a level of confidence and cohesion that was lacking prior to 1942.[23]

Crerar's growth in these months can be judged from his perceptions of command within the corps. Theoretical measures of command, shaped by the tiny pool of pre-war senior officers, predominated in the selection of the Canadian army's senior ranks. Technical education, staff experience, and character were the most important criteria for promotion during this period. Technical education was the province of the artillery and engineers, resulting in an early predominance of Royal Military College gunner and engineer alumni in the senior ranks of the Canadian army.[24] Crerar's emphasis on character, vision, and the sacrificial impulse as prerequisites for leadership qualified these criteria, but, in general, abstract theory dominated in the absence of operational experience. Performance in exercises was soon added to these measures for command.

Crerar's tact and restraint when replacing officers obscured his willingness to replace those who had not met his standards. He was too cautious for the immediate dismissals and personal attacks, often based on fleeting impressions, characteristic of the self-assured Montgomery. After assessing the potential strengths and limitations of his subordinates, he suggested the proper area where an officer's abilities could best help an expertise-starved Canadian army. 'He had a broader experience of life and human endeavour,' recalled his ADC, the future Lieutenant-General Henri Tellier.[25]

The replacement of George Pearkes illustrated the main elements of Crerar's standard in the early months of 1942. His main concerns, during discussions with Brooke and McNaughton over Pearkes's suitability for higher command, were his lack of foresight and broad vision, tactically, strategically, and politically. 'His disabilities,' Crerar wrote of Pearkes, 'are that his vision is narrow ... and finally he has no interest in long-term or larger policies.'[26] This quality was particularly vexing when Pearkes became the most obvious nominee for command of 2nd Canadian Corps. In principle Crerar believed that a commander or second-in-command was not fit for his rank if he was 'not trained or generally equipped to assume the duties of the next highest rank.'[27] In Crerar's view, Pearkes's failure to maintain a steady program of personal professional development weighed against him.

Personal integrity, stability, selflessness, and physical and mental fitness remained important measures of command ability. 'An officer must be a leader,' Crerar counselled his son Peter. 'You must always see to it that you do not yourself exhibit any [human] weaknesses and thus tend to lower the confidence of the men in your ability to lead them to success in battle as well as the higher things in life.'[28] In July 1942, he was concerned enough to suggest that McNaughton issue an edict regarding the importance of officers ensuring that their private lives were 'above reproach' and that evidence of 'grave social misconduct' should result in a court martial. Montague, among others, urged him to tone it down, not least because of the questionable legality of defining 'social misconduct' as a court martial offence. A tempered version went out to all. Individuals were also called up on the carpet. Crerar's cautions in the fall of 1942 to General Rod Keller, the CO, 3rd Canadian Division, about his drinking were a case in point; self-control had to be maintained, as not 'otherwise can a high standard of behaviour be demanded, as it should be, from other ranks under command.' Youth was also promoted as a hallmark of the corps. Until the Canadians were committed to battle, there was little else to go on.[29]

The operational expertise Crerar required of his commanders was still general, reflecting his own inexperience as well as that of the corps. He emphasized the importance of the offensive, a definite acceptance of Montgomery's admonishment that troops and commanders must obtain the proper 'offensive mentality.' 'The attack – dawn, day and dusk' was the first training priority in a March 1942 circular to all commanders; the night attack and the forced crossing of obstacles were second and third, while defensive tactics were a distant sixth.[30] In exercise Beaver III, Crerar criticized 2nd Canadian Division's Major-General John Hamilton Roberts both for organizing forward units in defensive postures rather than offensive ones and for hurried staff preparations for supporting firepower – an explicit critique of Roberts's handling of his HQ.[31]

Crerar was deliberate and considered in his application of criticism. He expected the same from those under his command. Crerar's evaluations suggest an appreciation for the strengths and weaknesses of the individual involved and the needs of the relatively small Canadian army. He judged the impact of the small cadre of Permanent Force officers replacing each other as potentially divisive; one consequence was that he supplemented most reports on senior officers with personal letters. In May 1942, he wrote a one-page defence of his critique of 2nd Canadian Division after the commander of 5th Canadian Infantry Brigade objected to his comments, concluding, 'You can accept as a fact that I enjoy congratulating people and dislike intensely the business of criticizing them.' The brigadier remained in command until February 1944.[32]

The strained relations between Crerar and Pearkes following the former's appointment to command of the corps suggests that Crerar's estimation of the closed nature of the Canadian army senior officers corps was correct. The relationship between Pearkes and Crerar deteriorated steadily until the establishment of First Canadian Army HQ and the imminent formation of 2nd Canadian Corps brought matters to a head. Crerar's doubts about Pearkes, mirrored by McNaughton and substantiated, if not increased, by Montgomery's bitter remarks, were forcefully presented in discussions with McNaughton in mid-April.[33] The clash that followed culminated in Pearkes's subsequent appointment to Canada as GOC-in-C, Pacific Coast, a transfer influenced by Crerar's recommendation that Pearkes be sent back to Canada as Inspector-General. Despite the shaky relationship, resulting from Crerar's suspicion of Pearkes's 'open subordination' and Pearkes's determination to maintain the independence of 'his' division, Crerar was reluctant to commit his opinions to paper; however, Pearkes's creation in December 1941 of a tactical exercise in which a 'staff officer fresh from Canada messed up a battle situation' was an example of how he demonstrated his displeasure.[34] Still, Crerar's emphasis on Pearkes's ability as a trainer, and Crerar's subsequent letter to Pearkes, were a marked contrast to Montgomery's sharp commentary: Pearkes would 'fight his division' bravely till the last man was killed, but he had no brains and 'the last man would be killed all too soon.' Montgomery's blunt assessments confirmed doubts already held by the Canadian senior command, but Crerar's evaluation was more conducive to securing the harmonious relations necessary for the 1st Canadian Corps to efficiently function as a national unit.[35] It was also an indication that the self-conscious caution borne of his lack of operational and command experience was coming to an end.

Montgomery's rigorous approach became evident in the training programs and exercises that culminated in May 1942 with Exercise Tiger, described by Montgomery as 'the most strenuous ever held in England.'[36] Crerar's contribution was to ensure that commanding officers had acquired the requisite knowledge 'to produce the desired results,' while stressing the importance of the commanders themselves being visible and actively inspecting units on the assumption that unit COs were the keys to the effectiveness of training policy.[37] George Kitching relates that upon assuming command of the Edmonton Regiment he requested the retention of two officers who had made Montgomery's 'doubtful list'; despite some hesitation, Crerar left the matter to Kitching's judgment.[38] Crerar himself practised an active schedule of inspecting units and headquarters. Nevertheless, the successive issue of 'reminders' to unit and formation commanders of their responsibility to train the junior leadership suggests that implementation remained difficult.[39]

Crerar was also an enthusiastic convert to battle drill as a means of teaching basic fire and movement tactics. Mongtomery felt that Crerar was too enthusiastic and cautioned him in March 1942 that it was not 'the whole art of making war.' The program was nevertheless spread throughout the corps; by April 1942, Paget had ordered the addition of a Battle Drill Wing to the Canadian Training School. Crerar's embrace of these realistic live-fire exercises was driven by the same impulse that involved Canadian troops in raiding activities. On 16 July 1942, he wrote his brother John, 'I am not sure what is allowed to appear in the press in Canada as I rarely receive a newspaper from my wife, but I think I can go so far as to say that we are using quantities of live ammunition and that unit and formation training which is now proceeding is about as close to the real thing as the absence of a physical enemy shooting back, will permit.' He noted that there had been casualties, but concluded, 'It is infinitely better to have a few of these in training than lose hundreds of lives through inexpert use of fire and movement.' A month later he ordered an increase in the emphasis placed on battle drill and physical fitness.[40]

In the spring of 1942, Exercises Beaver III, Beaver IV, and Tiger illustrated the gains made in the corps' objective of training 'all ranks up to that stage of mental, physical and professional fitness needed to engage successfully in offensive battles against the Germans.' Crerar described it to his brother as training on a 'grand scale.'[41] The Beaver program initiated a series of formation exercises designed to fit the commanders and staff from the divisional level down for large-scale offensive operations. Crerar stressed the importance of concentration, simplicity, and soundness in planning, and speed in execution, as well as echoing Montgomery's emphasis on the 'stage management' of battle – intelligence, positioning, control, and initiative.[42] '"Military knowledge, intelligent imagination, leadership and "drive,"' Crerar concluded in a catch-all manner, 'are essential to success in command.'

The formations involved, with the exception of the recently arrived 3rd Canadian Division, showed marked improvement in control and communications. The fitness level of the troops was much higher. In Montgomery's opinion, however, the exercises revealed that the divisional commanders were unable to seize the initiative and properly manage their brigades and battalions after the battle had begun. He was scathing in his criticism of Pearkes and the GOC of 3rd Division,

Major-General C. Basil Price, a Crerar recommended appointee. 2nd Canadian Division commander, Major-General Ham Roberts, was considered sound but not brilliant. Montgomery credited Brigadier C.C. 'Church' Mann for his contribution to Roberts's competent handling of the division.[43]

Montgomery's criticism of the divisional commanders contrasted sharply with his critique of Crerar's first exercise in handling the corps. Exercise Tiger, lasting from 19 to 31 May 1942, was fought as an 'encounter battle,' the object being the 'study of certain aspects of mobile operations between two forces where commanders have freedom of action and manoeuvre.' Montgomery, the director of the exercise, cited a further object as the 'study [of] the new model organization for armoured and infantry divisions.'[44] Crerar commanded 1st Canadian Corps, comprising two Canadian infantry divisions and a brigade from 2nd Canadian Division as well as 3rd British Infantry Division, 1st Canadian Tank Brigade, and one independent British brigade. It was a true test of the efficiency of Crerar's organization of the corps' HQ as well as his success in implementing Montgomery's training policy.

He was impressive. Montgomery praised Crerar: 'I would like to congratulate you on your handling of the 1st Canadian Corps in the TIGER exercise ... You did splendidly ... when I say you did well I mean it.' Montgomery also added praise for Simonds: 'And you have a first class BGS in Simmonds [sic]; I would like you to tell him I thought he was very good.'[45] Crerar himself brought attention to Simonds's importance at HQ 1st Canadian Corps, even after they had parted ways following the war.[46] McNaughton reported to the Chief of the General Staff that he was happy with 'the state of tactical training and endurance now reached by Canadian units and formations,' concluding that he was 'particularly pleased with Crerar's conduct of the operations of 1st Canadian Corps.'[47]

The best indication of the advances made by the corps HQ was in Montgomery's final remarks four days after the conclusion of the exercise. His most pointed critique of 1st Canadian Corps' command and control was its use of air power, both in planning and implementation. His harshest criticisms were directed at the divisional commanders and their failure to properly manage the battlefield.[48] The absence of any informal criticism channelled to Brooke – a favourite technique – suggests that Montgomery was pleased with Crerar's progress. Several months later, commenting on Crerar's attachment to Eighth Army HQ, Montgomery bluntly wrote to Brooke that while he was sceptical about

Crerar's present ability to handle a corps, he was 'really fond of him and he is very teachable.' He added, 'I fear he won't learn much from Andy.'[49] Battle experience soon became a 'fetish' for commanders like Montgomery. Crerar was also pleased with the results. On 3 June 1942, he wrote his brother, 'Your letter of the 22nd of April came in a few days ago in the middle of a very strenuous exercise ... , [which was], from the Canadian point of view, not unsuccessful.'[50]

The corps HQ improved in several areas of staff work, including traffic and logistical control, but 'Instructions to Staff Officers' issued to the headquarters staffs two weeks after the exercise indicates the corps commander's concerns, significant enough in Crerar's view that acknowledgement from each recipient, including staff officers of the services, was obtained and filed. The memo stressed Crerar's long-standing view of the staff as advisers as well as 'servants to the troops, not masters.' Staff were the eyes and ears of the commander. The instructions offered a clear explanation of Crerar's expectations as well as his experiences. With its emphasis on objectives and responsibilities rather than techniques, Crerar's memorandum suggests that the corps HQ needed to further refine the practice of staff work under a commander who was determined to lead rather than drive.[51] While his inclusive method of command did not endear itself to all, the results of Tiger and the impression left with senior commanders indicate that the corps HQ was responding to Crerar's steady hand.

The corps' advances in operational practice were not as impressive. It was apparent that the transition from preparations for the defensive to the offensive was incomplete. As Montgomery admitted before the exercise, 'Much practice will be necessary before we reach a final doctrine; and it will probably require the practical experience of battle to prove the right use of the new instrument.' He was speaking for himself as well. The characteristic dispersion and manoeuvre of the Eighth Army in the Desert War indicates that his theories on concentration and control were not widespread in the British army.[52] For example, Montgomery's insistence on centralization of artillery and administrative control under divisional and corps HQ was a main theme in the aftermath of Exercise Tiger. It had already been addressed from an organizational perspective in 1st Canadian Corps, although Montgomery's critique of divisional commanders suggests that implementation was scattered.[53] It was also obvious that the corps HQ was, like its British counterparts, only slowly coming to grips with organizing effective fire-support for the infantry in the offensive, hampered by inexperience and the rudimentary communications technology available to control air support.

Crerar impressed his cautions for thorough, methodical staff work on his HQ, perhaps to the detriment of encouraging initiative in the corps as a whole. Montgomery intimated that all of his commanders and staffs were still too slow to react to the modern battlefield, stopping to regroup and 'consolidate' – an ironic comment in light of Montgomery's own propensity for a tidy battlefield. Montgomery's didactic reaction was to discontinue the use of the word *consolidate* in South-Eastern Command, fearful of the resulting inaction and defensive mentality.[54] The army commander also implicitly pointed to the ineffective operational commitment and control of armour as a lingering gap in Crerar and the corps HQ's experience.[55] It was an indication that Crerar, the corps HQ, and the troops had come some ways. To his credit, Crerar proved eager to absorb the lessons of the first years of the war; dissemination throughout the corps, however, proved more difficult.

Enhancing the operational effectiveness of South-Eastern Command remained Montgomery's focus. He issued instructions for further unit training through August 1942. Crerar disseminated the content of the order as he called for 'a series of exercises for Divisional and Brigade Commanders and staffs ... based on the narratives and actual experiences of "Tiger" exercise.'[56] He emphasized the need to ensure that training policy was being properly implemented – no small change, as uniformity had been a weakness prior to his assumption of command. The repetition of the same theme in training instructions over the next three months suggests that while the participants might have appreciated Montgomery's animated presentations, broadening knowledge was not the same as changing behaviour. Crerar concluded with a cryptic reference to events that would cast a pall on achievements of the past months, but also accelerate the pace and intensity of 1st Canadian Corps training. 'We have done well, so far, in 1942,' he began, but before 'many weeks go by we may have full opportunity of proving whether that belief is fully justified. In the meantime we have no battle laurels on which to rest.'[57]

12 Dieppe

I

Crerar pursued another tack to make the corps more efficient. He wanted Canadian troops to be included in the increasingly ambitious raids on the coast of occupied Europe. Although not the only advocate of this policy, he was main Canadian proponent. The result was Canadian participation on the Dieppe raid in August 1942, the Canadians' first experience of combat in Europe during the Second World War. Crerar's role is clear enough. It centred on three issues: his persistent advocacy of the use of Canadian troops on raids; his involvement as GOC, 1st Canadian Corps, in the planning and execution of the raid, the latter including the selection and training of the 2nd Canadian Division; and his efforts in shaping the post-raid perspective. His approach to the issues was shaped by political and strategic considerations, the current state of operational thinking, and his goals for developing the army.

Prompted by the emphasis placed on raiding activities during the Corps Study Week in January 1942, in February Crerar instigated a campaign to involve units of 1st Canadian Corps in such raids. As his policy in May 1941 and the dispatch of troops to Hong Kong suggest, Crerar's advocacy of involving Canadian troops in operations was not new. He had supported McNaughton's drive in the fall of 1941 for Canadian participation in operations and to obtain more autonomy in committing Canadians to such actions.

By the winter of 1942, concerns about the lack of battle experience and the potentially harmful impact of the prolonged inactivity of 1st Canadian Corps strengthened Crerar's determination to see Canadian troops in action. While he was publicly optimistic regarding the high morale of the troops under his command, his observations on morale were couched in language that betrayed his uncertainty over the impact of further inaction. 'I find all ranks in fine fettle,' he wrote Allen Bill of the *Calgary Herald* in January 1942, 'with morale surprisingly high in view of the long period of stagnation here.' In this, and other correspondence, *disappointment, stagnation, sidelines* were the terms Crerar used to contrast morale with activity.[1] Concern over the negative effects of inactivity resulted in a memorandum to all commanders and commanding officers in the corps on the importance of maintaining discipline and morale.[2] Many senior officers believed morale was a serious issue, of no small importance to the future operational effectiveness of the Canadian forces.[3] This concern was not alleviated by the heightened awareness and reports, if not reality, of Canadian disciplinary problems in the harsh winter of 1941–2. McNaughton was not among those who troubled themselves over the morale issue or who believed that sending Canadians into action would resolve anything.[4]

Raids on the French coast by troops from South-Eastern Command were conceived, as early as September 1941, by the British as a means of maintaining the 'offensive spirit' and providing an 'outlet for the natural urge on the part of troops to undertake active operations against the enemy.' The scale was small – ten to twenty all ranks, led by junior officers, all of whom would be trained by combined operations. McNaughton, and later Pearkes as Acting CO of 1st Canadian Corps, welcomed the chance to get small numbers of troops some fighting experience. Montgomery encouraged specialized training for raids when he took command in November 1941.[5]

The intimations of the morale-boosting and information-gathering value of small-scale raids in January strengthened Crerar's resolve in the winter of 1942 to press for increased Canadian involvement in these activities. He wrote Montgomery early in February requesting that detachments from the Canadian Corps undertake a high proportion of the 'small raids across the Channel opposite the Army front.' His rationalization included strong references to the 'continued lack of participation' by the Canadians in operations and its detrimental impact on the professional pride of the officers and other ranks as well as the increasing difficulty of maintaining the 'desired keenness and morale.' The reputation of the corps, he explained, was at stake.[6]

Montgomery agreed in principle to Crerar's request, but noted that landing craft were in short supply and Vice-Admiral Lord Mountbatten's Combined Operations Headquarters had opted to use commandos rather than regular troops for raids; subsequently, 'raids by Home Forces [were] last on the priority list.'[7] Montgomery's noncommittal reply induced approaches by the impatient Crerar, both formal and informal, to the CIGS and the Commander Combined Operations through February and March.

Crerar's tenacious efforts to enhance the reputation, and profile, of Canadian troops were also informed by the concurrent domestic crisis over Hong Kong. On 10 February, he received an anxious telegram from Ralston indicating that he should make immediate arrangements to return to Canada to testify before the royal commission established to investigate the dispatch of troops to Hong Kong. Crerar believed his return would play into the hands of the government, who could accuse the Opposition of undermining the war effort. Similarly, if he did not return, the Opposition could claim the enquiry was incomplete.[8] Undoubtedly aware that it could effectively stunt his career, Crerar preferred to let the record speak for itself, and turned to Brooke for advice and support.

'The CIGS ... was very hostile indeed to the whole proposition,' Crerar observed. The secretary of state for war, Sir James Grigg, mirrored Brooke's hostility. The CIGS drafted a harsh rebuke to Ralston, chiding the minister for the 'intolerable' removal, without consultation, of a commander in whom he had confidence. Crerar managed to intercept this intemperate telegram but, over the secretary's signature, Ralston was advised that 'the general effect [of Crerar's removal] on the training of the Canadian Corps will be most unfortunate.'[9] The minister was upset at this admonishment, but replied that he would accommodate the needs of the overseas forces by delaying Crerar's return until the last possible moment. Dissatisfied with this reply, Crerar resisted, requesting either an immediate and speedy transfer of command to ensure continuity or that the minister rely on the record of his memorandums.[10] The situation remained unresolved through February and March. Only the combined opposition of Brooke, McNaughton, and Crerar overcame the minister's desire to have Crerar return to Canada. In the end, with some resentment, he submitted a written response to the questions forwarded by the commission. Near the end of April, he wrote his brother, with some relief and no indication of regret, 'The Hong Kong enquiry seems to be out of my way at last with the distraction that entailed.' He sympathized with Ralston's plight as the enquiry and political fallout dragged on into the summer. In July 1942, when

Ralston visited Crerar's son in a military hospital in Ottawa, he sent him a telegram of thanks, and noted to Peter that considering 'all that is on his mind, especially during this political attack concerning the Hong Kong contingent, I thought it was very decent of him.'[11]

The enquiry, and its potential domestic repercussions, may have influenced Crerar's perception of the importance of securing Canadian involvement in raiding operations. In early March, he pressed Brooke to promote Canadian participation in raiding activities; morale and pride were again his main arguments. Pressured formally, and through lunchtime harangues, Brooke set up a meeting between Crerar and Mountbatten; Simonds and the DCIGS Lieutenant-General Archie Nye also attended. At the conference Crerar argued that he found it 'galling' that the Canadians had been inactive for two years. He warned of the serious implications for morale as well as recruiting if some activities were not arranged. Against his better judgement, Mountbatten agreed to make an exception to his policy of using only commandos, provided that secrecy was maintained and that 'ample time should be allowed for proper organization and training.' He observed that 'no less than 100' troops should take part, landed by the recently arrived Canadian landing craft flotilla. Crerar 'readily agreed to these conditions.'[12]

II

Crerar's campaign to secure Canadian participation in raids began to pay dividends in April, a shift related to the CIGS's support in March, and Crerar's discussions with the Chief of Combined Operations (CCO) Mountbatten. Crerar's bargain with Mountbatten in early March for a small-scale raid had run into difficulties immediately. Through March and April, COHQ delayed and hedged on delivery of instructors and landing craft, and admitting Canadian troops to its training facilities. By early April, they were promising Simonds that shipping might be provided in mid-May or mid-June.[13] The only product of Crerar's work was a small raid on the village of Hardelot on the French coast near Boulogne proposed for mid-April. Fifty men of the 1st Canadian Division were involved but never actually got ashore, as a result of the incompetence of the naval officer in charge of the landing craft.[14]

At the same time, coastal raids were becoming an important element of Allied strategy through 1942. Despite the pressure from the Russians, the American Chiefs of Staff, and the British public, British military planners fought a rearguard action against a full-scale invasion of the continent through 1942. Coastal raids were thus a panacea for the difficulties faced by politicians, strategists, and trainers. Such was the case for Crerar, who was frank in his appraisal of the chances of Canadians seeing large-scale operational action on the continent in the near future, dismissing such notions as 'castles in the air' on more than one occasion.[15] Proposals for raids from SE Command and its corps HQs were called for in April, in anticipation of the 'raiding season.' The scale of attack in these raids gradually grew, the combined operations against Bruneval and St Nazaire overshadowing the intermittent, small-scale raids that Crerar originally envisaged as a proper morale booster and training ground for the inexperienced Canadians.[16] American Chief of Staff General George Marshall advocated commando type raids, following similar reasoning. The concept for – and in particular, the scale of – the Dieppe raid grew out of the desire to test new amphibious assault techniques and aid in training for the eventual Allied invasion of the Continent. In this sense it would also provide a sop to the American Chiefs of Staff and the British public's desire to launch an immediate assault on France as well as ease tensions with the Soviets. Tragically, the momentum for the raid took on a life of its own, career ambitions and institutional infighting becoming enmeshed with political, strategic, and tactical concerns.

Canadians were not involved in the origins of the raid or in the outline planning of the original raid, scheduled for July and code-named Rutter. The plan originated with Mountbatten and Combined Operations Headquarters in April 1942. Once Dieppe was chosen as the site of the raid, SEC was automatically responsible for its execution. Canadian involvement began with Montgomery's approach to Crerar in late April; Monty suggested that 2nd Canadian Division be assigned responsibility for the pending assault on Dieppe. The impetus for using Canadian troops had come from Paget, the Commander-in-Chief Home Forces, suggesting the influence of Crerar's lobbying efforts. Montgomery, displeased with the proposed composition of an Anglo-Canadian force, pressed for a homogeneous body, wanting to preserve unity of command and believing that the Canadian troops 'were those best suited.' Montgomery did not broach the subject with an annoyed McNaughton until 30 April, having already secured Crerar's nomination of the 2nd Canadian Division.[17] Montgomery's opinion was undoubtedly confirmed by Crerar's selection of the one formation in which Montgomery had evinced confidence only days earlier after

Exercise Beaver III, describing 2nd Canadian Division's Roberts as 'the best Divisional Commander in the Corps.'[18] Crerar's choice was limited by the doubts he felt about Pearkes, and the inexperience of 3rd Division.

Crerar's role in the Dieppe operation through to July 1942 was confined to initiating and overseeing the training of the 2nd Canadian Division and delineating the proper constitutional lines of command. Accordingly, for the former, Training Instruction No. 9 was issued on 30 April outlining advanced training in combined operations for formations starting with 2nd Canadian Division, a subterfuge intended to prevent 'dangerous speculation.'[19] Subsequently, the 2nd Canadian Division, less 5th Brigade, and the 14th Calgary Tank Regiment began combined operations training on the Isle of Wight. This ended Crerar's direct involvement with the training of the units; responsibility fell to Roberts, the divisional CO. Crerar was present at successive landing exercises, code-named 'Yukon,' designed to be dress rehearsals of the raid itself. Neither revealed significant problems with the troops, although doubts were expressed about the state of training of the naval support. Both Montgomery and Crerar reported themselves well satisfied with the results of the training. Concerns over ability of the naval units to perform their assigned task were quelled by the postponement of the raid and a second Yukon dress rehearsal with better results.

Constitutional concerns also surfaced. Montgomery planned to exclude McNaughton and Crerar from the Dieppe command centre at Headquarters No. 11 Fighter Group, Uxbridge – a stance supported by the British Home Forces senior command.[20] This position was clearly unsatisfactory. Crerar and Montgomery met, and had, according to Crerar, 'frank and friendly' discussions. Montgomery, Crerar observed, 'gained a wider appreciation of the issues that were at stake.' More persuasive was Crerar's statement that if the British insisted on treating the 2nd Canadian Division as another British formation, 'the issue would be raised to the highest political levels and that decision would go against the view apparently maintained by C-in-C, Home Forces and himself.'[21] Both Montgomery and Paget claimed to have gained a greater appreciation of the constitutional position of the Canadian military forces, although it seems doubtful that Montgomery ever appreciated frank reminders of anything. Hamilton's assertion that Montgomery perceived 'Crerar's pedantry [as] a form of "belly-aching"' was a more apt estimate of Montgomery's position. After several such incidents, Crerar came to the conclusion that, despite Montgomery's great abilities as a field commander, 'political relations, international or inter-Imperial have not been his study ... and these cannot always be reduced to that "forceful simplicity" which is his special genius in the matter of military operations.'[22]

The awkward situation of Canadian commanders waiting for an 'invitation' to observe a Canadian division in action was resolved by the cancellation and subsequent revival of Operation Rutter. Controversy surrounds the responsibility for renewing the operation, and the accompanying changes to the plan also became contentious, and more distinctly Canadian, issues. As noted, the Canadian senior officers were not involved in the initiatives and outline planning for the Dieppe raid. C.C. Mann, GSO 1 of 2nd Canadian Division, made an appreciation of the outline plan in mid-May, prefacing the paper by calling the plan 'almost a fantastic conception,' but, for reasons unexplained, concluded in favour of adopting it. McNaughton and Crerar, as representatives of the Canadian government, were entitled to reject the plan as unsound, but their acceptance of it was almost inevitable, given their continuing concerns over Canadian morale and the endorsement by senior British officers such as the Chiefs of Staff Committee and Montgomery. The main elements of the outline plan as adopted by Home Force planners and COHQ called for a frontal attack by infantry and tanks against the main beach at Dieppe, supported by two inner flank envelopments, and two outer flank attacks by British airborne troops. These were to be preceded by heavy bomber attacks on coastal targets as well as naval destroyer fire. Perhaps the most notable and pervasive aspect of the plan was intelligence staff underestimation of the defences facing the beaches.[23]

Before the project was executed, bombing of the port was dropped from the operation because of fears it might negate the element of surprise, impede the tanks, and be inaccurate. The decision was taken at a COHQ meeting in June, presided over by Montgomery, his postwar claims to the contrary, and agreed to by Roberts, who was swayed by arguments for maintaining an unimpeded path for his main fire-support.[24] The next substantial change took place after the cancellation of Rutter and its revival as Jubilee. This was the decision to place McNaughton in charge of the operation, replacing Montgomery as the military officer responsible for the conduct of the operation; McNaughton subsequently delegated military responsibility to Crerar on 27 July. Crerar made no direct comments on this change of command, although a week earlier he had written a letter to his brother describing in glowing terms the rigours of the new training regimen. Hong Kong was also on his mind, as he wrote in a postscript: 'I see that the case against George Drew has been dropped. It would have been poetic justice if he had been locked up and placed in the same cage as Camilien Houde from Montreal; he also made a subversive public statement!' In personal correspondence, he said little: 'My activities ... are not the kind of things one can write or talk about.'[25]

In consecutive meetings from 30 July to 2 August, Crerar met with Mountbatten, Air-Vice-Marshal Leigh-Mallory, Roberts, and Mann to discuss the naval and air plans; given its tentative status, the main subject was presumably the bombing. Crerar passed on Leigh-Mallory's views to Roberts, but they met twice more to monitor preparations. On 11 August, Crerar reported his comments to McNaughton: 'I ... am satisfied that the revisions made in respect to the previous exercise plans add, rather than detract, to the soundness of the plan as a whole. I am, therefore, of the opinion that, given an even break in luck and good navigation, the demonstration should prove successful.'[26]

Should the raid have been revived? And did it have a chance for success, whatever the changes? Most historians suggest not. Blame is levelled at McNaughton and Crerar for changes to the plan. No Canadian senior officer initiated the decision; it was, however, approved after the fact by Roberts and Crerar. Given that a massive increase in the bombardment at Normandy in 1944 barely dented the defences, it seems a fruitless debate. What is surprising is that officers like Crerar did not recall the lessons of the First World War and the importance of fire power.

Operation Jubilee took place on 19 August with devastating and well-known effects. Six thousand troops sailed from five ports along Britain's south coast: about five thousand were Canadian, the rest British, American, and French. They were supported by a small naval flotilla and a large air contingent. The attack was a disaster. By the end of the day, over nine hundred men were dead, almost two thousand taken prisoner, and the Royal Air Force had fought its biggest single day's battle of the Second World War. Correspondent Ross Munro in one of the last LCM's to land the Royal Regiment of Canada at Puys on the left flank, described one example of the landing:

> I recognized that things were pretty nearly disastrous as soon as we got within 100 yards of the beach. Our boat was in the last group of boats that went in and there had been about 400 Royals [who had] tried to get ashore

up until the point when we got there and our group of boats landed another 150 or so. It was just carnage ... the whole slope was just littered with khaki bodies of the wounded and killed Royals. It was unbelievable to see that gulch ... just covered with Canadians and ... the tremendous fire from the buildings and from the top of the gulch.[27]

The majority of contemporary Allied senior military command viewed it, or came to view it, as a tragic but necessary wake-up call for the Allies on the difficulties of executing an amphibious operation against a well-defended coast. The debate regarding its contribution to the eventual success of the invasion in 1944 continues today. How many lessons were learned is debatable, but it woke the Allies to one salient fact: landings were not assaults, and assaults required more than surprise to succeed. Crerar and McNaughton were, and are, criticized for allowing Canadian involvement, particularly given the changes made to the plan. In the contemporary context, however, it is difficult to refute their logic. Certainly the pre-eminent lesson, the need for 'overwhelming' air and naval bombardments, suggests that the main reasons for the senior British and Canadian planners accepting the weakly supported frontal assault was the widespread emphasis laid on tactical surprise and speed as the crucial elements in amphibious operations, as well as offensive operations in general – lessons drawn from the early German victories. Even for artillerymen like Crerar, the importance of firepower had to be relearned in North Africa.[28] Intelligence estimates of the weakness of the defences at Dieppe enhanced the belief that surprise would be decisive. And for an amphibious assault, a frontal attack was the only realistic alternative. The tactical and operation assumptions underlying the plan were shared by many Allied leaders and made a refusal to participate by McNaughton and Crerar difficult, if not impossible, particularly in view of Crerar's campaign for Canadian involvement. When he began to seek experience through coastal raids for Canadian troops, Crerar did not envision anything on the scale of the Dieppe raid; months of disappointed hopes and the size of raids increasing in proportion to their political impact lent an inexorable logic to Canadian participation.

It is also worth noting that the response of the troops at Dieppe suggests that the training syllabi disseminated by Crerar and Simonds were producing a general tactical proficiency, even if their effect for specialized tasks was limited. And the importance of that training can be overstated. Of 603 highly trained commandos committed to the assault on St Nazaire, 403 were casualties – a cost overshadowed by the positive results of the raid. No. 3 Commando's attack on the left flank of the Dieppe raid also suggests the limits of specialized training; No. 4 Commando's success suggests the importance of luck. By most accounts, the Canadian troops acquitted themselves admirably during the raid.[29] Significantly, Allied critiques of the troops during the raid, as represented by the COHQ reports on lessons learned, pointed only to gaps in specialized training for amphibious night operations, observing that training for specific tasks such as street fighting or attacks on battery positions should be carried out 'over similar ground and distances and under conditions of light the same as those which may be executed in the operation itself.' There was some criticism levelled by some naval personnel on the landing craft, but it was too self-serving to be definitive. In general, the report concluded that amphibious assaults required troops specifically trained for this highly specialized operation.[30] Still, the Canadians showed some proficiency in small unit tactics, particularly on White Beach and at Pourville. On White Beach, the Royal Hamilton Light Infantry, despite the murderous fire and lack of artillery support, showed initiative and tactical sense as it captured the Casino and used it to 'filter' small groups into the town.[31] The South Saskatchewans similarly disposed of pillboxes but were again disadvantaged by the disparity in firepower.

The tragedy at Dieppe also highlighted the importance of exposure to the conditions of battle. Visiting the wounded troops in hospital, and the returned troops throughout Sussex, Crerar suggested that morale had never been higher. It was a theme he took up in the personal notes written to the next of kin of soldiers he knew who had been killed in the raid. He believed that the soldier's were 'eager' to come to grips with the Germans as soon as possible. The lack of experience was a factor in the failure to achieve any significant successes compared to the scale of disaster; from that perspective, Crerar's attempts to obtain experience were correct. 'Canadians utterly lacked battle experience,' historian Desmond Morton has observed, 'even a. few veteran officers or sergeants might have spurred huddled, bewildered soldiers into action.' Others have alluded to that point.[32] The effects of inexperience on the final results of the raid can be overstated – the Royal Marine Commandos were also forced to abandon their attack by the fierceness of the fire – but in a perverse way, the impact of the Canadians' inexperience served to lend logic to the emphasis that Crerar placed on getting the troops in action. It would become a theme of increasing importance in Crerar's corps training policy.

The results of the Dieppe raid informed the direction of corps training policy for the next ten months. Crerar had already established an escalating series of exercises emphasizing infantry–tank cooperation, combined operations, individual weapons proficiency, and the importance of training junior leadership. Training at the operational level became the primary focus, although the massive casualties sustained by two brigades of 2nd Canadian Division forced their return to unit and individual training.

The implementation of the training policy as well as concerns about morale and discipline consumed Crerar's command. There was an enhanced inspection schedule and frequent circulars on the responsibility of each commander for disseminating the training policy established at corps HQ. This was an indication that not all corps directives on training were being used to full effect.[33] Significantly, emphasis on the development of a common doctrine on training methods was introduced as a 'principle of training' in October 1942 and reiterated in a training instruction in April 1943. Its absence was perceived as a persistent weakness in the training policy. Jack English has observed that the inexperience of unit officers in how to properly train troops diluted the effectiveness of the policies descending from corps HQ. The inability to fully disseminate the lessons of the first years of the war was a problem encountered by the British forces in general.[34]

There were notable exceptions to the apparent continuity in the content and syllabus of the training policy. Combined operations training and exercises were undertaken with a renewed emphasis on the lessons relearned at Dieppe, particularly individual and junior leadership initiative and the use of fire-support. Particular study and attention was to be given to the problem of beach landings, the establishment of beach bridgeheads, and operations on the scale of brigade and battalion groups against enemy-defended localities, especially villages and towns.[35]

The program begun in December at the Combined Training Centres confirmed the importance accorded these operations. Breakouts from, and expansion of, shallow bridgeheads were reaffirmed through the spring of 1943 as the most important subjects of 'special study' for headquarters staffs, undertaken concurrently with the regular signal and skeleton exercises.[36] This would prove contentious. Observes John English, 'The more time spent on combined operations training, moreover, the less there was available to practice open warfare.'[37]

The post-Dieppe emphasis on lessons learned and combined operations was in part a product of the perspective that Crerar placed on the results of the operation. In the immediate aftermath of the raid, Crerar believed, on the basis of reports by Roberts, that the strength of the enemy defences had been the main reason for the failure of the raid.[38] The faults in planning and execution emerged slowly, however, and were confirmed by the COHQ reports in the early fall. Earlier, McNaughton had wanted to prepare a statement for circulation throughout the corps on the story of the conception, preparation, and execution of the raid.

Tasked on 27 August 1942, Crerar cautioned that such a statement was 'more likely to be interpreted as an "apologia" than a frank satisfying explanation.' A more suitable alternative, Crerar suggested, was the preparation of a confidential memorandum for commanders and commanding officers 'sent out as a basis for preliminary study of this operation and as an immediate guide to training of all units and formations in Combined Operations.'[39] With McNaughton's permission, Crerar issued the preliminary report prepared by Roberts and indicated that a more detailed analysis of the requirements of a full-scale invasion would be forthcoming.[40] Subsequently, perfection of an amphibious landing combined operation became a favoured object of study for headquarters staffs. By August 1943, the 'Principles to Be Followed in the Organization of Fire Support for a Assault Landing' were distributed to all HQs in anticipation of exercises later that autumn. These principles reflected the determination, if not the reality, that lessons would be learned from Dieppe.

Crerar's personal feelings on the cost of the raid are difficult to discern. He never wavered, in any of the surviving letters and commentary, from the view that it was a tragic, but necessary, lesson. Yet he was closer to the men involved in the raid than might be expected from a corps commander. He knew many of the families of the men from the Royal Hamilton Light Infantry, which had suffered heavily; he wrote them all personal letters. He visited the casualties in hospital. And the only existing reference characterizing him as 'shocked' at anything was in reference to the extent of the casualties at Dieppe. In October, Crerar described to his sister his attendance at the investiture ceremony at Buckingham Palace where 'over a hundred officers and men ... who went over to Dieppe' received their honours and awards. 'It was a great thrill to see these fellows, most of them youngsters, get some outward recognition of the work they did on those beaches.' He talked to family friends after the ceremony and then sent telegrams to their spouses and families. In December, on learning the fate of another Hamiltonian –

Lieutenant Lew Counsell of the RHLI's – he immediately wrote his sister, 'I am so delighted that Lew Counsell [who had been reported killed] has been reported a prisoner.' A few weeks earlier, he wrote his brother, unintentionally reflecting on the strain: 'The results of the Press Photographers indicate very clearly to me that I can no longer get by as being in my forties for, what little hair I have left is greying fairly rapidly and the lines on my face are becoming obvious wrinkles.'[41]

Crerar took the view that, professionally, the raid woke the Allies to the difficulties posed by an amphibious assault. Despite Crerar's public and private assurances that the corps 'gained immeasurably from the wide-angle, long-term point of view,' not least because of the improvement in morale and fighting spirit, his concentration on amphibious assaults culminating in the cathartic pride he took in the assault techniques and tactics demonstrated in the Exercise Pirate of October 1943 suggests that Dieppe left a deeper imprint than he indicated. The assumptions underlying Pirate – that strategic and tactical surprise in a trans-Channel landing were impossible and even the weather might be against them – suggest that Crerar, among others, took a different approach to planning.[42] Mirroring feeling in the ranks, a more realistic tone was evident in Crerar's approach to training policy and exercises. This was reflected in his categorical, and ultimately successful, resistance to the GHQ, Home Forces conception of detaching and distributing 1st Canadian Corps troops for anti-raiding responsibilities and to subsequent reorganizations that would detract from the corps' ability to concentrate on training for offensive operations.[43]

Crerar's persistent applications from the fall of 1942 for operational experience for himself and staff under Montgomery's North African command – requests heartily supported by Montgomery – are further evidence of his determination to expand his professional study. Stymied, in his view, by McNaughton, who insisted that he stay with his command in view of pending operational responsibilities, Crerar secured a ten-day study attachment to the First British Army in Tunisia only after the 1st Canadian Corps was sent to the Italian theatre.[44]

13 Replacing McNaughton

I

Following the Dieppe raid, Crerar redoubled his efforts to train both himself and 1st Canadian Corps. His desire to see Canadians in action increased, mirroring that of Canadian politicians such as Ralston. This advocacy ruined Crerar's relationship with McNaughton, and he became involved in the British campaign to remove McNaughton from army command. Crerar was also chafing under McNaughton's tutelage. He disliked McNaughton's attempts to shield or distance him from the politics of high command, an aspect of their relationship since the 1920s. By 1943 Crerar believed McNaughton had to go, but his actions to achieve this removal were mainly behind the scenes. At best, they smacked of desperate indiscretion. In the end, it was a necessary, if distasteful, episode, made more so by the political manoeuvring, McNaughton's graceless exit, and Crerar's position as, and ambition to be, his successor.

By the winter of 1943, Crerar was anxious about his own lack of experience in high command. He was willing to drop in rank, temporarily, and take a division. On 20 September 1943, Crerar wrote to Montgomery, 'I have several times put it up to Andy that I should have personal experience ... I would like to test out [my] beliefs by practical experience. In fairness to those whom I might command in battle, it seems to me an essential personal preparation.' McNaughton brought the matter to the attention of National Defence Headquarters and Montgomery, but his support was half-hearted and he generally resisted Crerar's persistent applications from the fall of 1942 for operational experience for himself and his staff under Montgomery's North African command.

Montgomery supported the idea in principle, although as 1943 progressed, became increasingly non-committal.

McNaughton insisted that Crerar stay with his command in view of pending operational responsibilities, presumably the invasion of France. This was not an unreasonable stance on McNaughton's part, but Crerar was upset at, and possibly hurt by, this situation. 'I have been travelling around the country like never before,' Crerar wrote to his daughter in September 1943. 'Unfortunately, I have not succeeded in getting out of it, Andy having reserved these trips for himself.'[1] McNaughton also attempted to keep Crerar out of the policy disputes over army employment, protection that hurt his pride, and that Crerar came to resent as patronizing. 'Harry Crerar is absurdly isolated from high level conversations on army matters,' wrote Vincent Massey in 1943, 'and feels it.'[2] Their relationship was increasingly strained. Crerar was offended and seems to have believed that McNaughton was impeding his growth. It is possible there was an undercurrent of insecurity as well, with Crerar harkening back to McNaughton's suggestion in the 1930s that his protégé might be better suited for the foreign service.

Crerar's nerves were not helped by his decision in October 1942 that Verse should not join him overseas. 'Wives and war do not mix,' he wrote his brother in November, 'and the latter demands every ounce of my attention these days.' When October went by without a letter from Verse, he felt compelled to cable her. The decision for Verse to remain in Canada would be a source of tension throughout the war; he resisted her overtures to come to England, although it was a strain. 'From remarks that Verse makes in her letters, and from messages that reach me from others,' he wrote his brother-in-law in January 1943, 'it is apparent that she does not agree with my view.' Her close friend 'Flo' Gibson, wife of the future Minister of National Defence Colin Gibson, kept him updated on Verse's feelings. As late as February 1944, he responded to Mrs Gibson's Christmas card news, noting, 'I am so glad that Verse is getting more settled in her mind, and accepting, with less resentment, the situation we find ourselves in.' He attributed this shift to his grandson, describing 'Young Tony Palmer' as 'worth his weight in gold, by reason of the interest he affords my women-folk.' Crerar's letters to Peter reflected some of the stress. Through the fall of 1942 and the winter of 1943, Crerar admonished his son to choose a service, and to write more. Crerar's appreciation of family news from his sister, brother, and Peg was evident in his responses to their letters. Peter's arrival overseas in May 1943 was welcome. 'Keep in touch with Mum,' he wrote. '[She] now feels particularly lonely with both of us over here, and don't forget that I like to hear from you as well.' News from Ottawa was generally dispiriting. 'The bottom seemed to fall out of things,' wrote Maurice Pope in October 1942, 'when you pulled out less then a year ago.' Pope put it down to personalities at NDHQ, the country's acceptance of the war as routine, and the public anxiety following the Japanese attack on Pearl Harbor. He concluded that the public was in a 'very scratchy mood' as demands increased with 'little or nothing in return' as the Canadians stayed in England.[3]

Yet it was the deterioration of his relationship with McNaughton that cast the biggest shadow over the fall and winter of 1942–3. By March 1943, Crerar was convinced that his chief was 'difficult' and 'that as a leader of men he [had] grave defects of character.'[4] Others among the Canadian army senior command were similarly disenchanted with McNaughton. 'Ken Stuart [CGS] and the other Brass Hats dislike McNaughton intensely,' observed Ottawa journalist Grant Dexter. 'He treats them like office boys.'[5] Indeed, it was believed by some that McNaughton's ego had reached a stage where he 'wished to reduce in importance anyone collaborating with him and would endeavour to reduce their prestige.'[6] This perception was unfair, but the strain of fours year of work was showing. First Canadian Army Headquarters staff observed McNaughton's propensity to concentrate on minutiae to the detriment of operational training. The Brigadier, General Staff G.E. Beament characterized the army HQ, under Andy, as a 'war office of the country' rather than a mobile command HQ. McNaughton's relationship with the defence minister also continued to deteriorate. Ralston was angered by the shabby treatment he received at the army commander's hands, hearing rumours throughout 1942 that McNaughton was harshly criticizing him.[7] Canadian High Commissioner Vincent Massey was also ready to see McNaughton go, blaming him for the overexpansion of the army organization – ironic, given Crerar's efforts – and for what he felt were petty slights.[8]

There was much truth to such impressions. McNaughton's increasingly tenuous position in maintaining the Canadian army as a composite force for use in northwest Europe and the death of his son in June 1942 shook an already strained disposition. He became increasingly nervous and critical of the Canadian, and Allied, direction of the war. He also did believe that he was indispensable to the army effort.[9] Further, he suspected that Crerar, among others, was working against him after he received a transcript of conversations between Churchill and Ralston on the occasion of the defence minister's visit to England in the fall of 1942. Contrary to McNaughton's advice, Ralston advocated the use of Canadian troops at the earliest opportunity. McNaughton was not pleased and vented his displeasure on Crerar, who vehemently denied speaking 'out of turn.' He admitted that Ralston had asked his view on policies, but stated that he had 'turned the proposal down at once.' That seems unlikely. McNaughton was satisfied though and dropped the matter, but Crerar believed that McNaughton subsequently denied him his confidence.[10]

Despite protestations of innocence, Crerar was by the fall of 1942 fully at odds with McNaughton's policies on the employment of Canadian troops. 'Crerar ... is worried,' wrote Massey after a mealtime harangue as early as June 1942, 'about McNaughton's rigid attitude towards the War Office on subject of possible use in an Expeditionary force of a part of Canadian army.' The success of Montgomery's British Eight Army at El Alamein in October–November 1942, and the subsequent Operation Torch landings of American and British troops on the coasts of French North Africa on 8 November helped bring the issue to the fore. On 8 December 1942, Crerar wrote his brother, 'In spite of quite a lot of feeling on the part of all ranks concerning US troops "showing their stuff" in NW Africa before a large-scale opportunity has come to use, morale and discipline remain high and training is being pursued very energetically.' In January 1943, he noted that 'it takes all that I have to give to maintain that keenness on the part of the ranks ... I see comparatively little of Andy, who is much tied up with matters of higher policy and equipment, and am pretty much left alone.' Awarded a Companionship of the Bath (the highest level in the orders permitted by Canadian policy) in January 1943, he barely mentioned it, but the difficulties of maintaining morale were a constant refrain. A few months later Crerar told Massey that he disagreed with almost all of McNaughton's ideas about the army.[11] He nevertheless publicly defended McNaughton. Attempting to stop a tirade by former Prime Minister R.B. Bennett against McNaughton, Crerar took 'Bennett by both hands and looking at him with kindness said: "You musn't, you really must not – not to me."'[12]

Crerar was in a delicate position; torn between his concerns with the army's future and his loyalty to McNaughton, he could be excused venting steam to his friend Massey. His relationship with Ralston also appears to have improved as the defence minister made efforts to look in on Crerar's family, taking Peg to lunch, visiting Peter in England, and, over the course of the war, acting as a courier for the separated couple, with news and reports; Ralston and Crerar were also drawn together by a shared belief in what was best for the army. Ralston believed operational action was necessary for political reasons. However, Crerar also took up the refrain with Brooke about early use of Canadian troops and McNaughton's opposition to it; the CIGS blamed the Canadian government and McNaughton for preventing the dispatch of Canadian forces to active theatres. Brooke noted, that 'Crerar realized this concept must be broken down.'[13] Strong allies in Ottawa shared Crerar's views. Chief of the General Staff Lieutenant-General Ken Stuart invoked Crerar's observations that action was necessary for reasons of morale and battle experience. He mirrored Crerar's rationale, arguing that McNaughton was out of touch with the troops and that Crerar 'was nearer to them and understood them better.'[14]

Exercise Spartan, 4–12 March 1943, involving two armies and five corps, proved the turning point for Crerar and McNaughton. The purpose of the exercise was to analyze the problems of an army breaking out of a bridgehead secured on an enemy occupied shore. From that perspective, it was an apt test of Crerar's efforts to ensure that there was no repetition of the Dieppe raid. The troops were motivated: in December 1942 it was necessary to issue orders warning of the increase in the number of accidents that had occurred as a result of intensified sessions of hardening training.[15] In addition, despite the turnover among 1st Canadian Corps HQ personnel necessitated by the establishment of First Canadian Army and 2nd Canadian Corps, Crerar's corps HQ had continued to improve. The importance of the continuity provided by Crerar's command was particularly evident with Guy Simonds's replacement as BGS by Brigadier Churchill Mann, a Permanent Force officer of great, if erratic, intellect.[16] Conscious of the paucity of potential senior commanders, Crerar strongly urged McNaughton to appoint Simonds to command 1st Canadian Infantry Brigade, observing, 'I feel very strongly that owing to future contingencies, the sooner this officer is given experience that will fit him for higher responsibilities, the better all around.' Turnovers at all staff levels reached such proportions as to necessitate the reissue of Crerar's 'Instructions to Staff Officers' in October 1942.[17] To solve this problem, Crerar also instituted a constant regime of signal and model exercises with good result. In November 1942, he distributed an 'Aide Memoire for Orders' at the corps level designed to ensure consistency of format and method; notable was his emphasis on brevity and clarity, but also his admonishment that the issue of orders verbally (Orders Meetings) be limited, particularly if 'needless travelling on the part of Subordinate Commanders is the main result.'[18]

Crerar's understanding of the operational art was also maturing. His handwritten notes for discussion with his divisional commanders, dating from 1942, suggest a more sophisticated understanding of the commitment of a division into battle. Flexibility of organization was his number one general principle for success; surprise, concentration, all-arms cooperation, control, and rapid exploitation of success followed in sequence. His emphasis on flexibility reflected a belief that, to an extent, decentralization of command was the best method of achieving a breakthrough and maintaining the momentum of an offensive, whether against 'strong enemy resistance' or in a contact battle. His advice reflected the debate through 1942 between Montgomery and other British senior commanders in Home Forces over how best to sustain the tempo of operations. Decentralization 'encouraged initiative, [sped] up decisions and [made] for rapid action.' Generally, he believed that the divisional commander's role was prescriptive. Initiative shown by junior officers and subunits was important, but, like many contemporaries struggling with training in the absence of a collective operational doctrine, Crerar struggled with a dichotomy between addressing both the set-piece battles and the encounter battle. The necessity of creating training syllabi and distilling lessons lent itself to a prescriptive approach, so it is hard to be overly critical of Crerar's practice, particularly when doctrinal ideas were fluid, to say the least. It is safe to say that he still believed, for better or worse, that battles needed to be stage-managed, and his teaching reflected this ideal. For minor tactics, he embraced 'battle drill.' This was not an extraordinary approach in Great Britain in 1942–3 and could be defined as mainstream. Critics have suggested that the emphasis on control and centralization, based on timed artillery plans and stage-managed battles, negated the effects of tactical training, 'suppressing individual initiative.' In effect, it is argued that they produced soldiers, and thus battles, dependent on firepower, whatever the source, for success.[19]

Crerar's views on all-arms cooperation, and the integration of tanks and aircraft into battle also reflected his learning curve. He distinguished between the operational roles of 'army' (infantry) tanks and cruisers, stressing that the role of army tanks deployed in army tank brigades was to 'assist the infantry' and that the infantry 'looks after the tanks.' His emphasis on decentralization fitted perfectly into current ideas on the role of tank brigades. In the summer of 1942, armoured formations had undergone major reorganizations, with concurrent increases in infantry and artillery. Crerar's observation to his divisional commanders that armour and aircraft 'have restored mobility to the battlefield' but that they 'can never complete the victory by themselves' was thus unremarkable. Covering fire was essential for movement: 'Concentrated fire of artillery was a battle winning factor.' His was a view shared, correctly, by most British commanders.[20] Crerar's focus on operations, and operational flexibility, as well as his ideas on the respective roles of artillery, armour, and infantry suggest he had digested, partially at least, the lessons emerging from Africa and reflected current orthodoxy on unit and formation training: within a limited dichotomy, initiative and decentralization was encouraged, but communication, artillery support, and divisional control all pointed towards managed battles. In 1942–3, this approach was a tremendous improvement over what the corps had been doing in 1940–1.[21]

Crerar's handling of 1st Canadian Corps during Exercise Spartan reflected the work he had put into training as well the results of his own professional study. Brooke observed that Crerar had 'improved that Corps out of all recognition' and had put on a 'good show' during the exercise. Paget and McNaughton were similarly impressed.[22] Assessments of Crerar produced by CGS Stuart in March or April 1943 for Ralston were particularly overwhelming: 'Outstanding capable soldier,' he began, has 'made a high reputation in recent "Spartan" exercises and has been referred to as the outstanding leader shown up by that test.'[23] Crerar had benefited from Brooke's and Monty's tutelage. Despite Crerar's submission after his visit to North Africa that 'he saw nothing new in Montgomery's tactics,' he applied Montgomery's methods, as well as lessons learned from Brooke, to his own proficiency in the use of artillery. In April 1943, his training memorandum following Spartan stressed that battle drill should produce instinctive and 'habitual' responses to a variety of tactical situations. Battle conditions should be simulated as closely as possible. He qualified his emphasis on realism and physical fitness with a warning that such drills were means, not ends in themselves, a 'guide to action.' Crerar maintained the belief that the infantry and artillery predominated on the battlefield, and applied them in Exercise Spartan with some success.[24] His appreciation of the need for flexibility in planning to obtain 1st Canadian Corps objectives and the rapid forward advance of his corps despite initial disadvantages imposed by Exercise Spartan suggests that he had a firm grip on the operational use of infantry and artillery to ensure effective, if unspectacular, fire and movement.[25] But as Montgomery observed, Crerar needed experience in handling armoured formations.[26] Crerar demonstrated a practical ability to implement the professional methods and ideas he had been exposed to, and an ability to discern the weaknesses as revealed by the exercises. These concerns were subsequently reflected in the training syllabi of the corps.

The praise for Crerar's performance in Spartan was a sharp contrast to the opinions, some unfair, forwarded on McNaughton's handling of First Canadian Army. Similar charges were levelled at the other army commander, J.H. Gammel, but Spartan was the catalyst for destroying McNaughton's position.[27] Roundly criticized by Paget and Secretary of State Sir James Grigg, McNaughton's poor showing was the last straw for those who harboured doubts about his capacity to handle the army in operations. The depth of Crerar's own doubts is suggested by his attempts some years later to have McNaughton's positive comments on the Canadian army's showing in Spartan in the official history replaced by Paget's negative comments.[28] Grigg recalled that he and Brooke were 'appalled at McNaughton's indecision.' Brooke noted in his diary, 'McNaughton [proved] my worst fears that he is quite incompetent to command an Army!'[29] Crerar agreed with Paget's stinging assessment of McNaughton and 2nd Canadian Corps, which had been included at McNaughton's insistence, despite its inexperience (and because of it, a point many chose to overlook). In Stuart's report to the minister on the Canadian officer corps, he observed that there was 'a steadily growing feeling of doubt and loss of confidence in the Army Commander both in the Army in England and with the thinking public in Canada.'[30] Crerar's own concerns, discussed with Brooke earlier, were confirmed.

Following Spartan, Brooke became the main advocate of removing McNaughton, convinced that Paget 'was quite incapable of realizing how bad Andy McNaughton is!' and encouraged by the Canadian support for the idea. Crerar did nothing to counter the British campaign to unseat McNaughton that began shortly thereafter, despite some discomfort with the situation, and it seems likely that it was his advice that prompted Brooke to move cautiously among the minefields of Canadian army politics. Outside observers, notably journalist Grant Dexter in Ottawa, sensed a change was in the air: 'Watch Harry ... He was a regular Prussian and had gained immensely in prestige since going to

England. I rather thought, by the keenness of the praise [for Crerar], that McNaughton had better take a leaf out of Russian experience with timber wolves and begin throwing babies over the back seat.' Their relationship became the subject of much gossip throughout the army.

The exercise itself, and subsequent gossip, took a toll on Crerar. He was admitted to hospital for forty-eight hours with a bronchial infection just as the storm brewing over McNaughton finally broke. He also put more effort into seeing his son, who was then in the United Kingdom, insisting that they regularly take in a show together. However, he recovered quickly; within a few months he had offered C.P. Stacey the rights to all of his papers, anticipating that Stacey would write 'the most important military history of our times.'[31] He made extra efforts to get out among his formations and units. A stern reminder in early May 1943 to the commanders of 2nd and 3rd Canadian Divisions and 1st Armoured Regiment that dissemination of the lessons learned in exercises to all ranks was an immediate and pressing priority, underscoring Crerar's determination to train the corps to the highest possible level. There was also evidence of a continued concern for morale; at the end of May 1943, Crerar wrote his divisional commanders on the failure of a number of soldiers to salute during a visit to Brighton on the Sussex coast. He was concerned in case standards depreciated, especially, he noted tongue-in-cheek, in 'a place like Brighton.'[32]

II

Brooke and Crerar were aware of the political perils that awaited them, and proceeded cautiously. Brooke acted on the advice of Crerar, and later, Vincent Massey. He was careful to make it appear that Canadians initiated every step in the removal of McNaughton and took pains after the war to make it clear he had not acted alone. In the aftermath of Exercise Spartan, Brooke and Crerar deliberated on the best method of having McNaughton recalled without producing severe 'political friction between Canada and the United Kingdom.'[33] They were also conscious, however, of finding 'some job' for him to return to in Canada to ease the blow. Brooke wrote that he knew 'only too well what [McNaughton's] dismissal would mean to him.'[34] McNaughton's feelings became less important as he continued to resist the breakup of the Canadian army through mid-1943. Crerar felt that McNaughton was now 'unable to stand back and view the whole picture.' Brooke noted McNaughton's almost 'fanatic antagonism for employing any portion of the Canadian Forces independent from the whole.' Like Crerar, Brooke believed that the employment of a Canadian division was becoming an absolute necessity to 'provide an outlet to post officers and men to gain experience.'[35]

Brooke's dilemma in the spring of 1943 was how to split the Canadian forces against the wishes of the army commander, while ensuring Canadian command of First Canadian Army. If not, McNaughton, then who? Crerar was the obvious choice – if the HQ was not disbanded.

Brooke's first explicit action was in May 1943 at the Trident Conference in Washington, where he raised the question of McNaughton's physical and operational fitness with Stuart and Ralston.[36] In July, Stuart approached Brooke to discuss 'possible ways of relieving [McNaughton].' In this and later conversation, Stuart also suggested that splitting the Canadian forces between England and the Mediterranean would facilitate disposing of McNaughton. Brooke agreed that '[splitting the army] was the only way to save the outfit.'[37] On 10 July, Stuart brought McNaughton's failing health and his handling of the corps during the Spartan exercises to the attention of Ralston and King, through the Vice-Chief of the General Staff, Major-General J.C. Murchie. In response, Ralston intimated to King that he 'would like to see Crerar in command of Canadian Corps [sic].'[38] King's sympathies, however, were clearly with McNaughton, the anti-conscription nationalist who wanted to avoid commitments, and he treaded cautiously.

In August 1943, McNaughton's position was weakened during Ralston's trip to England to address the questions of command and employment of the Canadian forces. Crerar and Massey both indicated that they felt McNaughton might have to be replaced, Crerar obliquely ruminating, without mentioning names, about the ability of 'one individual effectively to do so many jobs – command, research and development, political functions and SCO.'[39] Brooke, encouraged by Massey to speak directly to Ralston and fired up following a heated confrontation with McNaughton after the latter's ignominious return from the Mediterranean, informally told the minister how 'nervous' he felt about McNaughton commanding in the field.[40] McNaughton himself dealt the final blow. Self-assuredly unaware of his precarious position, he met with Ralston on 5 August and took an unequivocal stance on further employment of Canadian forces in the Mediterranean. He questioning the minister's commitment to the Canadian army and berated his views on the employment of the army. In the circumstances, Ralston was remarkably fair.

The situation was more complex than simply the need to replace McNaughton. His removal was intimately tied to the question of what to do with First Canadian Army during the impending operations, which was tied to finding a successor acceptable to both the Canadians and the British. Brooke, in his discussions with the minister, had proposed dismantling First Canadian Army HQ as the most viable option. McNaughton and Ralston refused to consider this possibility. The 'national interest' required that FCA remain intact, and that a Canadian command it. McNaughton, not aware of the implications of the discussions, insisted he would resign if the army were split. Despite British reservations about the lack of command experience among the Canadians, he observed that by the time the army was committed to active operations, Crerar might have the requisite experience. 'It was frequently the case,' McNaughton testily suggested, 'that one man did the building and another got the benefit.'[41] Here then was a means to resolve several problems. They remained unsettled as King called Ralston home for the Quebec Conference.

In mid-August, while in Quebec, Ralston and Stuart once again related British doubts about McNaughton to the Prime Minister – convictions affirmed by Brooke in discussions with King at the same conference. In an important departure from earlier statements, Brooke enthusiastically endorsed Crerar, in a broad and unspecified manner, observing that he had 'the very highest opinion of Crerar. Could not have a better man. Would trust him in command anywhere.'[42] Only hours earlier, Stuart had told King that, in contrast to the British opinion on McNaughton, 'both Paget and Brooke were particularly enthusiastic about Crerar.'[43] King wrote in his diary, '[Ralston] indicated that Brooke had said he was trying to think of some position for McNaughton that would save his pride.' The presence of a viable alternative affected Mackenzie King's attitude. Mulling over the comparative estimates of casualties in northwest Europe and Italy, he was prepared to countenance the change in command and the dispatch of further Canadian units to Italy, despite his sympathy for McNaughton and reservations about Crerar's stance on conscription.[44] The government's decision to split the Canadian forces in the fall of 1943 signalled the end for McNaughton. The British Chiefs of Staff, led by Brooke, decided to send 1st Canadian Corps HQ, 5th Canadian Armoured and Corps troops to the Mediterranean. Brooke, in fact, felt confident enough to write to Montgomery, 'I think I have now got [McNaughton's] case settled.'[45]

III

The Canadian War Cabinet approved the dispatch on 12 October 1943, and planning for Operation Timberwolf began immediately. Crerar and the Corps HQ arrived in Algiers on 24 October 1943 in anticipation of the arrival of the rest of the Canadian troops. Crerar was ecstatic to leave England. In mid-September, he told his daughter that all 'dreaded' another 'winter of training, and retraining.' A few weeks after arriving in North Africa, he described his view of the final months in the United Kingdom: 'As the months turned into years and still we found ourselves in England ... [it was] becoming increasingly difficult to justify that sort of war to our friends and families in Canada.'

The employment of 1st Canadian Corps in Italy directly contradicted McNaughton's expressed opinion and brought the issue of the future of First Canadian Army and its commander to a head. Subsequent discussions through November and December between Ralston, Stuart, Brooke, Paget, and an increasingly obstinate and remarkably uninformed McNaughton, resulted in the decision to remove him from command. It was a sad conclusion to a distasteful process undertaken without McNaughton's knowledge. He knew nothing of the temper of the discussions until November, but he was well aware of the implications of the government's decision.[46]

The search for a successor occurred simultaneously, but was not a foregone conclusion. The appointment of a British commander or the dissolution of the army HQ remained as options, favoured by some British officers. If it was to be a Canadian, Crerar was the only viable candidate, although Guy Simonds's name had surfaced and Montgomery favoured his appointment in the long run. In November, when Stuart observed that Crerar was not 'fully battle trained' and thus unavailable until April 1944, Paget again proposed appointing a British commander – pressure that Ralston resisted. Paget then stated, according to Ralston's account, that 'he would accept Crerar any time he could come and that he was prepared to accept him as Army Commander without any experience in the field.'[47] But he wanted an appointment soon, and he was still prepared to press for a British general.

Ralston was determined to have Crerar, agreeing with McNaughton's observation that the appointment of a British general to command First Canadian Army, would mean 'that it would only be a Canadian Army in name.' While unfair in light of the fact that many British troops would serve in First Canadian Army, this comment aptly reflected the national feeling now attached to First Canadian Army. Two days later, on 10 November, Mackenzie King noted, 'There can be no doubt that Ralston and General Stuart have been a little over-anxious to get a change instead of allowing time to help bring this about.' He added, 'I think they have been most anxious to get Crerar in McNaughton's place.'[48] King's discomfort was only slightly eased by Chubby Power's unqualified support for Crerar: 'He felt sure the troops would prefer Crerar.'[49]

On 9 November, Stuart proposed a compromise on what Brooke characterized as 'the new set-up' of First Canadian Army. Some of the points were necessary changes to place First Canadian Army under command of the 21st Army Group. Stuart also agreed that a 'certain proportion' of the staffs of both HQ First Canadian Army and HQ 3rd Canadian Division would be British, and 'nominated by HQ 21 Army Group.' Finally, while Canadian commanders would retain the right of reference to the Canadian government, and the Canadian government retained the authority to appoint the commander, First Canadian Army, they agreed to 'consult the UK government in the matter.' These last concessions laid the foundation for Crerar's appointment. They could also be construed as small blows to Canada's policy of autonomy, but were, in reality, steps towards a more mature relationship: that of a coalition partner, able to make the compromises necessary to make the partnership work. They also indicated a lingering suspicion that HQ First Canadian Army needed careful support, a view that carried into operations. Brooke signalled his acceptance of the new arrangement on 12 November.[50]

Events moved quickly after that. McNaughton's increasingly erratic behaviour erased his political support. He attempted to lever Ralston out of power by telegraphing King that he had lost 'confidence in the Minister.' This proved too much of a challenge to the government's authority, even for the pro-McNaughton Mackenzie King.[51] McNaughton, faced with the inevitable, subsequently viewed Crerar as 'the only man we have.' By mid-November, if Ralston needed further convincing, Brooke was willing to support Crerar's appointment after he had a few months' experience in Italy.[52] When Ralston, with Stuart, travelled to the Italian theatre at the end of November to secure a tentative timetable for Crerar's return, he also canvassed more senior British officers for their opinions on Crerar. General Sir Harold Alexander, Deputy Supreme Commander Mediterranean Forces, 'spoke well of Crerar, liked him, and felt he would do well.' He agreed to try to get Crerar battle experience as quickly as was practical.⁵³ Montgomery's was the sole dissenting opinion. He stated unequivocally that he would not venture a recommendation until he had tried Crerar out in three or four battles, a position from which he did not waver.⁵⁴ Despite Monty's opinion, the endorsements from Brooke, Alexander, and Paget were enough for Ralston. On 29 November, he advised Crerar of McNaughton's situation and its possible effect on his future.⁵⁵

Crerar was prepared for this meeting with Ralston. An hour before the meeting, Price Montague had sent him a hastily pencilled note apprising him of the situation. Crerar proposed a restructuring of army and corps command, which went to the heart of the command and policy structure that had developed around McNaughton, often against Crerar's advice. Crerar elaborated on his ideas in a lengthy letter to the minister. What emerged was a formula that centred on the importance of Crerar remaining in command of 1st Canadian Corps until he had 'fought it successfully in action' and the necessity of changes to the relationship between CMHQ and First Canadian Army. Crerar observed that CMHQ should focus on policy, freeing the army commander to concentrate on operations, training, and organization. Crerar also pressed for Stuart's appointment as Chief of Staff, CMHQ, and in temporary command of First Canadian Army. He also insisted that Montague remain as Deputy Senior Officer. Ralston was left with the impression that 'Crerar [was] evidently nettled at idea of Stuart, his junior, in any position which might appear superior to him,' but for Crerar stability was the most important factor as he tried to minimize the impact of McNaughton's removal on troop morale and training. Crerar's willingness to consider a British appointee as temporary commander suggests that he was concerned for the well-being of the army.⁵⁶ The new Canadian army command and control organization was accepted. The final triumph of Crerar's ideas on army organization and staffing was the implementation of his suggestions for corps command.⁵⁷

Returning to England, Ralston considered the options before him. Crerar was 'rated high by UK officers who know him best.' Moreover, the development of the corps in Italy would not be unduly disturbed, given Crerar's and Montgomery's endorsement of Simonds as its future commander.⁵⁸ Neither did the British senior command feel that the immediate replacement of the GOC in Chief, First Canadian Army, was necessary, particularly in light of the indecision over the appointment of a Supreme Allied Commander. Ralston thus concluded that 'Crerar was the man, provided UK willing to take him.' Simonds could assume command of 1st Canadian Corps. Brooke and the VCIGS gave Crerar a formal vote of confidence, Nye commenting on Crerar's 'coolness and steadiness,' while contrasting the 'boldness of US and tendency, on other hand, of UK to depend on performance rather than take a chance on an untried but promising appearing man' decided the issue.[59] Ralston wired King of the final decision on 22 December 1943. McNaughton's retirement would be announced and Stuart would be appointed acting commander, pending the appointment of a successor.[60] Crerar would assume command of First Canadian Army in the New Year.[61] McNaughton returned to Canada, a bitter man bent on adding 'some scalps to his belt,' a threat that turned out to be remarkably empty except for his part in Ralston's resignation in the fall of 1944.[62] The British, with one significant exception, had faith in Crerar's ability and potential. Ralston still had reservations about Crerar's temperament and ambitions, but faith in his ability. Montgomery, however, continued to have grave misgivings about Crerar.

14 Corps Command in Italy

I

At age fifty-five, Crerar arrived in Italy to take the corps into operations, his first experience of operations since the First World War and, by the end of 1943, the primary purpose of his appointment. The course of operations in the Mediterranean, and Montgomery, conspired to prevent Crerar from obtaining operational command experience in Italy. He did grow, and helped groom the corps headquarters for operations. But Crerar's experience was limited to exercises and observations. These did nothing to dispel the concerns that swirled in some quarters, and indeed his clashes with Guy Simonds only furthered the impression that he was not up to the task of army command.

Montgomery's concerns about Crerar's suitability increased as they clashed in Italy. The corps HQ and 5th Armoured Division were unwelcome additions to the Allied forces in Italy. The decision for deployment was largely political, with the military considerations being those of the forces gathering for Operation Overlord in England, not those of the Mediterranean.[1] Montgomery made it clear how unwelcome the Canadian forces were on Crerar's arrival in Sicily on 29 October 1943, stating that another corps HQ was not required until the New Year and that the terrain did not permit the employment of further armoured divisions. Montgomery suggested that Crerar take command of 1st Canadian Division to gain operational experience. Crerar, pointing to the fact that he had shown a great eagerness in the past to drop in rank to gain experience, observed that his task was to 'get 1st Corps ... equipped and ready for operations at the earliest moment so that the prospect of putting 1st Canadian Corps into an operational role at the earliest possible date should not be delayed.'[2]

'For some reason – false pride perhaps,' recalled Major-General George Kitching, 'Crerar would not accept the idea of demoting himself.'[3] Kitching was wrong. One month earlier, Crerar was willing, eager even, to accept command of a division, regardless of questions of seniority; he had written to McNaughton and Montgomery to that end. Despite some hesitation, McNaughton twice proposed Crerar take command of 1st Canadian Division. In the first instance, Ottawa was opposed, as it feared the negative reaction to replacing Simonds. On the second occasion in late September 1943, Montgomery did not reply to McNaughton's request. By October 1943, the situation was 'changed materially' by the government's instructions 'to bring together all Canadian formations and units then in Sicily and Italy under my command in 1st Canadian Corps as soon as this could be done without embarrassment to field operations planned by higher command.'[4] Charged with such a responsibility by Ottawa, Crerar was no longer in a position to accede to Montgomery's wishes.

The uncompromising Montgomery continued to snub Crerar, however, their different personalities and styles of command exacerbating the problem. Montgomery emphasized the responsibility of the commander to create the correct 'atmosphere,' selecting subordinates, and keeping himself from becoming immersed in details, which in part entailed refraining from circulating detailed memorandums and orders.[5] Crerar's style in Italy was more pedantic and prescriptive. Complaints about the immense increase in paper that descended from HQ 1st Canadian Corps onto 1st Canadian Division were frequent, and not unfounded. 'Uncle' Harry was not considered totally responsible for this development, but as the GOC he set the tone. Immersed in preparations for his return to First Canadian Army, Crerar was perceived as more of a 'kindly figurehead' than a driving leader. Through the fall, the corps headquarters was remote, physically and mentally. Located in a partially destroyed villa on the northern tip of Sicily, it looked across the straits at the southernmost point of the Italian peninsula, a temporary clifftop 'home' Crerar described as 'beautifully situated, about 800 feet above the sea and with a very good view of Mount Etna when the clouds permit.'[6]

Though distant from his formations, Crerar spent much of November and December travelling and visiting the units. Peter was now in the Mediterranean, about sixty miles from his father. While Ralston was in Italy, they visited Peter's unit, 'in order that Ralston could see him and take first-hand word back to Verse.' He wrote proudly of his son as 'keen' and 'fit'; he experienced the same 'great satisfaction and pride' in the Canadian units. In his letters from the fall of 1943, there were few hints – and just those – that army command was a possibility; he indicated, a bit disingenuously, that 'my personal desire is to be left alone and permitted to command in action the troops which I have trained for these many months.'[7] He did want experience. But his greatest concerns were command issues, and the most serious, in his, and later Montgomery's, estimation was the infamous clash with Simonds in December 1943.

It was a dispute that was, perhaps, inevitable, but did not catch Canada's senior commanders at their best. It started innocently enough when Crerar obtained Simonds's permission to send a representative to measure the layout of Simonds's personal caravan so Crerar could build a self-contained accommodation that he hoped would enable him to observe the operations of various HQs without imposing on them – Crerar took such things seriously.[8] Discovering the officer in his caravan, Simonds tore a strip off him and sent the terrified captain packing. Crerar, sensitive to perceived slights, chose to view the issue as a 'personal discourtesy' and as an indication that Simonds's nerves were 'over-stretched and that impulse, rather than considered judgement, may begin to affect [his] decisions.'[9] Simonds responded in kind, and an acrimonious debate ensued, which culminated in Crerar initiating a discreet psychiatric assessment of Simonds.

The dispute had deeper roots: Crerar was, and had been for some time, judging Simonds's suitability for corps and possibly army command. The initial spark for Crerar's doubts came a few weeks earlier, with Simonds's quick-tempered judgment of the subordinates in his new command, 5th Canadian Armoured Division, particularly the divisional Commander, Royal Artillery, and his resolve to rid himself of this officer. The transit time between HQ 1st Canadian Corps in Sicily and HQ 5th Canadian Armoured had resulted in a breakdown in communications. Simonds subsequently removed his CRA, nominally before he had gotten Crerar's permission, and certainly before Crerar's caution on quick judgment that accompanied the permission was received. Simonds's abruptness with the corps commander's representative, viewed in light of previous warnings against ill-considered treatment of subordinates, prompted Crerar's admonishment and his questions about Simonds's mental health. Montgomery also recognized a problem. 'Simmonds [sic] is a young and very inexperienced Divisional general,' he noted, 'and has much to learn about command. He will upset his Division if he starts sacking the Brigadiers like this. I will of course hear the story, but Simmonds [sic] would be well advised to consult his superiors before he takes violent action in which he may not be backed up.'[10]

Crerar's main concern, particularly in light of his recent recommendation that Simonds be appointed GOC, 1st Canadian Corps, after Crerar returned to England, was that Simonds was becoming unglued under the heavy mental strain of fighting his division for the last six months. 'Should this, indeed be the situation,' Crerar wrote Simonds on 10 December, 'I would be extremely worried, for you are now reaching a position in the Army in which balance is becoming even more important to your future than brilliance.' Crerar reiterated the same concern to Montgomery, who characterized the problem as one of personality and naturally favoured his protege Simonds, observing that Simonds 'tried to go off the rails once or twice when he first went into action ... but I pulled him back again, and taught him his stuff.'[11] Privately, Montgomery interpreted it as the brilliant subordinate set upon by an envious superior.[12] His view only affirmed Crerar's assessment of Simonds's strengths and limits: 'Monty's primary interest is field command and not Canadian policies and business.'

Simonds's potentially 'disastrous' handling of the 'higher policy responsibilities of what virtually [was] an independent Canadian command' remained Crerar's primary measure for Simonds, and other senior staff and operational commanders. On 15 December, responding to Simonds's request to be relieved if his commander had lost confidence in his command ability, Crerar observed,

> I am sure you will realize that the removal of a Canadian Divisional Commander ... is a matter of widest interest and considerable national importance. The action is about the political and military equivalent of the removal of an Army commander in the British forces, owing to our differences in numbers. To elaborate ... the appointment of Brigadiers ... requires the approval of the Minister and the concurrence of the War Committee of the Canadian Cabinet. The 'firing' of Brigadiers is certainly a matter of significance to the government, even though I agree that the military situation may require such action to be taken in the field. The removal of a Major-General ... is a very drastic action, indeed, with national implications, some of which might have an important influence on the conduct of the war.[13]

Officers from divisional level on up were national representatives. They had to marry the political and military considerations that might arise. Operational proficiency was not the exclusive measure of ability, nor, given the position of the Canadians, could it be.[14]

That same day, Simonds penned an aggravated response to Crerar's cautions that set the stage for the final act. The subordinate's thinly veiled contempt was evident as he protested using any measure but operational effectiveness for the removal or retention of officers. He also revealed that he had nursed a resentment of Crerar since they were reunited at 1st Canadian Corps in January 1942, citing the groundless rumour that Crerar had sought his removal, an accusation for which there was no evidence. The belief that Crerar had initiated his transfer from 1st Canadian Division to 5th Canadian Armoured fuelled Simonds's anger; it was, in fact, McNaughton and Montgomery who initiated it in order to fit Simonds for corps command. Undertaking Operation Timberwolf without his knowledge proved to be the most recent irritant. The cumulative effect was Simonds's perception that Crerar revelled in this chance to 'administer a rebuke.'[15] Crerar's overwrought response suggests his astonishment and indignation; the tone of Simonds's letter prompted a five-page rebuttal and Crerar's consultation with his medical officers on Simonds's state of mind, as revealed through his correspondence. Crerar forwarded their assessments to Ken Stuart. Simonds was given a clean bill of health for operational command, but doubts remained about his capacity as an independent Canadian force commander. Despite these concerns, Crerar readily recommended him for corps command and later suggested to Mackenzie King, and in formal reports, that Simonds was the only logical choice to succeed him as army commander should he be killed or incapacitated.[16]

One contemporary recalled that 'Simonds from his 6'2" looked down on Crerar as a stuffy old man, while Crerar saw him as an upstart to be put in his place.'[17] The mutual tension in their relationship, although it can be overstated, began here. Indeed, Crerar generally took a kindly view of Simonds, as summed up in a letter on 10 December: 'He has made a very fine reputation as a Commander, but a bit of "ease off" would do him good. He is a highly-strung fellow, as you know, the responsibilities he has been carrying would worry him more than the average man. Things are now easier for him than they were and I hope that he will put a little more weight on and relax himself a bit.' Crerar's reaction suggests that he too felt the pressure of having his first major operational command placed on him, exacerbated by several bouts with dysentery contracted in October.[18]

II

Montgomery's explicit request that Crerar be replaced was one of the immediate repercussions of this argument. On 23 December, he suggested to Brooke that First Canadian Army command be given to General Sir Miles Dempsey, observing,

> The more I think of Harry Crerar the more I am convinced that he is quite unfit to command an army in the field at present. He has much to learn and he will have many shocks before he has learnt them properly. He has already started to have rows with Canadian generals under me; he wants a lot of teaching; I taught him about training; Oliver Leese will now have to teach him the practical side of war.[19]

He added, in an endorsement of Simonds, that as 'soon as they can produce their own general, then he takes over at once; until that time, give the Canadian army to Dempsey.' Monty also suggested that Leese return to England to take over Second British Army; Brooke ignored both suggestions.

Crerar maintained good relations with the majority of his subordinate commanders and staff. He remained too aloof and shy for them to warm to him, but he showed a personal interest in more than one that endeared him to many under his command. His relations with the British commanders in the theatre were mixed. Alexander seemed exasperated with the need to consider Canadian sensibilities, but respected his potential. Montgomery's successor at Eighth Army, General Sir Oliver Leese, Montgomery's personal appointee, was less impressed. Leese, described as 'a somewhat slow and unimaginative but competent general,' maintained a steady correspondence with his mentor, 'discussing tactical and operational questions at length in letters that were full of good sense and sound military judgement.'[20] No friend to Canadian senior officers, Leese was critical of 1st Canadian Corps HQ in the early stages. 'Harry Crerar ... is nice – and clever – but an academic soldier,' Leese wrote his wife in January 1944. 'I doubt if he is a commander in the field.'[21] He passed his opinions on to Montgomery. '[Crerar] commanded the 1st Canadian Corps for two years,' Montgomery smugly observed to Brooke in July 1944, 'and when it went into battle in Italy the Corps HQ proved to be quite untrained – so Oliver Leese tells me.'[22] Brooke never lost confidence in Crerar, or at least left it unrecorded.

Circumstances militated against Crerar obtaining the battle experience he so badly wanted, and needed. His primary goal was then to train a headquarters still in a state of flux. Crerar had expressed consternation in May and in August of 1943 at the turnover and level of experience of HQ personnel. The BGS who had replaced Church Mann was proving to be 'somewhat slow and unimaginative.' The same BGS put it more bluntly: 'We just didn't get along together.' And there were doubts about the other senior staff. Crerar subsequently requested Brigadier Charles Foulkes, CGS, First Canadian Army. McNaughton did not support that request, but in October of 1943, a new BGS, G.A. McCarter, was appointed.[23]

The turnover in the senior command and staff positions resulted in a recognizable lack of 'drive,' stemming from the inexperience and the uncertainty of newly arrived officers. They were eager – '[Canadians] are mad to get into battle,' wrote Leese – but not yet seasoned.[24] Crerar stressed this point in personal correspondence with COs and in formal memoranda.[25] In the absence of an experienced BGS, Crerar became increasingly absorbed in the details of preparing his staff and command for operations. The GSO 2, Royal Artillery at corps, remembered Crerar's 'meticulousness and discipline ... [he] was precise and knew what he was doing.' He admired Crerar's grasp of the function of artillery. While the influence of Dieppe was apparent in focusing the aim of operational training, Crerar's emphasis on artillery and firepower – the rediscovered queen of the Allied armies – reflected a broad continuity in his own thinking.[26] He issued Montgomery's respected memorandum 'Some Lessons Learnt during the First Two Years of War,' in October 1943, suggesting the state of command and training continued to be a concern, even as staff turnover slowed when the HQ moved to the Italian theatre of operations.[27] In December, in anticipation of forthcoming employment, Crerar issued further instructions on the duties of the staff and commanders at Corps HQ. The emphasis was not technical but rather procedural and mechanical. The GOC provided detailed information on implementing orders in the necessary detail.[28]

Alexander was slow to concentrate the Canadian forces. Transport shortages, strategic considerations, and British obstinance were working against deployment of the corps. Crerar forced the issue, obtaining transport for his HQ and corps troops. He then refused to part with it for Simonds's 5th Canadian Armoured, which was also finding itself a low priority for the British. Finally, he pressed Alexander and Leese for the rapid deployment of the Corps HQ.[29] Crerar exercised his most effective weapon – the potential damage to Canadian morale and commonwealth relations – with good results. On 12 January 1944, Crerar was informed by Leese of his intention to have 1st Canadian Corps relieve 5 British Corps. 1st Canadian Corps became operational on the night of 31 January–1 February 1944.

Crerar remained with the corps until 3 March 1944, but bad weather and an Allied focus on operations in western Italy prevented him from leading the corps in action. Crerar's letters in January and February indicated that he 'would have liked to be there a bit longer.' On balance, he proved a capable corps commander. He gained a good reputation for the organizational and administrative aspects of field command, but he garnered criticism for his immersion in detail as well as his obsession with correct procedural and disciplinary form. The latter was a result of an obsession with morale as well as a personal determination to present the Canadian army in a professional light. 'First Division veterans,' observes William McAndrew, 'preferred the casual professionalism of 8th Army.'[30]

Crerar's brush with operations was fleeting. On orders from Leese, he planned one major operation that was never undertaken. He continued to gather information on the tactics and operations of the Italian theatre, summing up his views from participating in the 13 Corps Study Period, running 1st Canadian Corps study weeks, and visiting operational HQs in an address to the commanders and staff of the Eighth Army titled 'The Principle of Effective Fire Support in the "Break-in" Battle.'

Observing that conditions in the Italian theatre were startlingly reminiscent of the First World War, Crerar advocated application of the advanced techniques of artillery and infantry control and coordination that were applied by the original Canadian Corps. Further, he emphasized to his divisional commanders, as he had to his Counter-Battery Staff twenty-five years earlier, the need for flexibility and adaptation to the changing circumstances of attack – strength must be concentrated and brought against enemy weakness whether led by infantry, tanks, or artillery. Others, although favouring mobile warfare, were coming to similar conclusions. Writing to his sister on 9 February 1944, Crerar described the operations in Italy: 'The weather has been pretty frightful at times ... The fighting has been tough also. The early sensational advances have given place to battle conditions which are so reminiscent of the last war that, to me, they are far from funny.'[31]

Crerar was subsequently criticized for a 'Great War' mentality, but this view overlooks two realities: the war of attrition that had developed in Italy and the highly successful operations that ended the First World War. Major-General Chris Vokes, GOC 1st Canadian Division, recalled that during one tactical discussion at Eighth Army HQ – it may have been Crerar's address – Crerar called for the use of Great War tactics to combat the conditions. Vokes claims Crerar's observation was greeted by an embarrassed silence from the British COs, who thought only in terms of mobile warfare. This commentary reveals more about the misconceptions about the final years of the First World War than Crerar's shortcomings. Crerar's 'old-fashioned' ideas on fire-support and movement were similar to those that the Allies would use to blast their way to victory. Discussions and demonstrations on 'fire support to achieve a break-in' were held in February. Soon, counter-battery and counter-mortar techniques and organization were reintroduced to 1st Canadian Corps, and questions of fire and support were addressed in the context of the specific conditions facing the Canadians. Crerar's approach was cautious, but he showed a solid appreciation of the problems facing his corps in the Italian theatre and respect for the manpower under his command.[32]

The practice of command also mellowed Crerar, to a degree. Previously criticized for an excess of paper, he issued the summary of points from 13 Corps Study Period to only the three senior commanding officers. Implementation and distribution were their responsibility, but Crerar added that the 'intermingling' of commanders and personnel of the assorted arms was an 'essential requirement.' The aim was to facilitate easy working relationships, mutual knowledge, and understanding, inspired by a common goal. This direction was formalized and reinforced by discussions of senior staff at corps study weeks.[33] Similarly, Crerar established a daily routine that was highly consultative by design, and made more so by his determination to spend several daylight hours establishing contact with the units and formation HQs under command.[34] He adhered to the use of paper as the best means of disseminating policy and operational lessons, but moved from this practice when it proved less practical in the Italian theatre.

Crerar was able to impress his stamp on the corps HQ, if not the units under his command. Well after he left, members of the senior staff kept him informed of the corps' actions, of which he 'was intensely proud.'[35] He was more remote to the soldiers in the ranks. This way of relating was mainly a product of his quiet demeanour and uncompromising particularism, which contrasted with the colourful Montgomery and the forceful Simonds. Crerar's weighty prose – Montgomery called him 'stodgy' – useful in peacetime, lacked the drive and simplicity to inspire his troops. As well, despite a tremendous faculty for absorbing new lessons, Crerar's focus shifted between the demands of the corps and the army as a whole.

1st Canadian Corps' subsequent performance provides some insight into how the HQ was developed under Crerar. Despite Leese's negative assessments, which were suspect not least of all because of his own mistakes, the corps performed solidly in its first operation in the Liri Valley in May, particularly in the assault phase. After the lessons were critically evaluated, the corps showed 'its prowess a second time in the Gothic Line battle.' The corps staff 'performed wonders,' administering the transfer prior to this battle and subsequently showed great flair operationally.[36] The training policy established under Crerar was continued through March and April as was the dissemination of the lessons learned through the HQ study weeks. Tempered by the experience of May and June, the corps HQ proved the equal, if not the better, of the British and American formations HQs in the Italian theatre.[37]

III

In February 1944, prompted by indications that 1st Canadian Corps would not be involved in major operations in the near future, and possibly by concerns about First Canadian Army's operational fate under a stewardship divided between Stuart and British military planners, Crerar pressed Stuart and Brooke to consider his return to England and involvement in planning for Overlord as quickly as possible. Stuart had no involvement in the planning, at his own request.[38] Brooke and Stuart both calmed Crerar, stating that his return in late March would provide ample time for him to assume his responsibilities. Brooke suggested that instead Crerar should 'make the most of the present period which is already all too short to fit you for the next job.'[39] Still untried, Crerar handed over command of 1st Canadian Corps to his chosen successor, Lieutenant-General Burns, on 3 March 1944.

On 16 March 1944, Crerar arrived in England, following stopovers to meet the Vaniers in Algiers and a brief tour of Gibraltar. Within hours of landing, Crerar began organizing his office; he ordered a new caravan and officer trailer, specially designed by his staff. It would serve as the Tactical HQ First Canadian Army, which was operational as of 9 March, and which he ordered to focus on Overlord under the direction of the Colonel GS G.E. Beament. Crerar also had brief meetings with Price

Montague and Montgomery. He attended a reception held by Eisenhower for his senior commanders; Montgomery and Brooke were conspicuous by their absence. Patton unkindly repeated the rumour that Montgomery declined Eisenhower's invitation because 'he could not bear to be second fiddle.'[40] Crerar, in contrast, was anxious to meet his Allied counterparts before his obligations to his HQ dominated his time.

The next day, he began a week's leave. 'I was tired [from the dysentery] and badly needed a rest,' wrote Crerar a week later. 'I spent several most enjoyable days as Margaret's [Wigan] guest, as one of a house party of half a dozen [including] a couple of my senior staff officers. For the last couple of days, I have been playing golf [and] staying with ... Sir Edward Peacock.' More difficult was the confirmation of the decision that Verse should remain in Canada. Crerar used his daughter to keep abreast of his wife's reaction – 'fine, but pretty disappointed at the breakdown of her chance' – but it was clear from his correspondence that he was anticipating the upcoming assault as the final stage of the war.[41]

Accompanied by the easygoing and popular former gunner Brigadier E.A. 'Ernie' Walford, who had held the senior administrative position of Deputy Adjutant and Quartermaster General (DA & QMG) of First Canadian Army since 1943, Crerar also used this opportunity to acquaint himself with the problems of his new HQ. Walford, as a long-serving officer on McNaughton's staff (he had been Assistant Adjutant and QMG of 1st Canadian Corps from 1940 to 1943), was well placed to brief Crerar on the obstacles that he faced as he took over HQ First Canadian Army.[42] Rested, if still tired, Crerar assumed command of First Canadian Army on 20 March 1944.

15 Taking Command of the Army

I

Crerar was well suited to the dual role he would play as army commander. He had a keen insight into the balance to be struck between his political and military responsibilities. His political acumen strengthened his nomination for army command, but the British, with one significant exception, also had faith in his ability and potential. Crerar took control of First Canadian Army before his return from Italy. He reviewed headquarters organization, sought (and gained) an operational planning role for his army, and attempted to divorce himself from the constitutional and political policy concerns that had, in his view, undermined McNaughton's position. Such a separation proved elusive; constitutional matters remained a constant point of irritation for Crerar, a distraction for which he was not blameless. Did this affect his ability to take control of and train his army? Not at this stage, but it added to the difficulties of his ambiguous role as an army commander under Montgomery's command, a situation exacerbated by Monty's attempts to diminish Crerar's role even further.

His immediate goal was to prepare the headquarters for its role in the upcoming operations in northwest Europe; to that end, he reviewed the administration and organization of the headquarters and acquainted himself with the staff. He also tried to impress his stamp on the headquarters – a difficult task, given McNaughton's personal popularity with the staff. With that in mind, and for public consumption, the March 1944 press announcements of Crerar's arrival pulled few punches. L.S.B. Shapiro characterized the HQ as a 'white elephant' under McNaughton and accurately, if incompletely, described his downfall as a result of differences of opinion with Ottawa and the War Office over deployment of Canadian formations. The press announcements also made clear the alternatives: disbandment and admission that Ottawa's military policy was 'faulty from its inception' or securing a commander of 'sufficient reputation' to satisfy the War Office and the man who had become for the commonwealth public the arbiter of generalship, Montgomery. Presumably the stark alternatives, and confirmation of Crerar's reputation, made the transition more palatable. His correspondence files indicate that many in England warmly welcomed his return. He was also encouraged by the Canadian government, particularly Ralston, and Vincent Massey to improve his 'noticeability as Army Commander.'[1]

The media campaign to raise Crerar's profile with the public struck a chord with some who had long been advocates of the necessity of a change of guard at HQ First Canadian Army, in particular those who had fallen out with McNaughton. The usual letters and telegrams of congratulations were mixed with queries regarding potential employment. Mike Pearson and Crerar had had minimal contact since 1941, but in March 1944, Pearson wrote Crerar a four-page letter, the first page praising the appointment, and the second devoted to pleas to find him some employ in First Canadian Army. 'I would certainly like to be somewhere else in the concluding phase of the war than Washington,' he wrote. It was an unintended comment on the divide in Canada's military establishment, and the kinship created by the time overseas: 'There will be a lot of people in Canada – those who know you best – who will feel that our Army, as it approaches the day of supreme decision, is in the best of hands.' Crerar gently dissuaded Pearson from pursuing an overseas appointment.[2]

Crerar was also concerned with 3rd Canadian Division's training for the D-Day landings, although he had no direct operational responsibility for that formation. Simonds, as 2nd Canadian Corps commander, took the lead in preparing the division for the post-landing operations. On 17 February 1944, he had issued a directive that outlined his operational policy, distributing it liberally throughout 21st Army Group.[3] The combination created a situation where the three Canadian formations in the United Kingdom were preparing separately for their immediate operational responsibilities, accountable to multiple authorities, and conscious of some as yet undefined point when they would be organized as one. Crerar retained, not without difficulty, overall responsibility for them. Crerar would be forced in the months ahead to confront the issue of responsibility for the Canadian forces fighting under 1 British Corps. In the circumstances, his ability to navigate these tricky, and unique, waters was remarkable. His focus was not on tactics; Simonds held up this end.

Meanwhile, Montgomery continued to fight a rearguard battle to either replace Crerar with Guy Simonds, or at least limit Crerar's command responsibilities. Crerar dined with Brooke on 29 March, who recorded the difficulties he had encountered manoeuvring McNaughton out of command of First Canadian Army, trying to give Crerar 'sufficient war experience' and getting 'Monty to accept him with very limited active experience.' He added, however, 'I have full confidence that Crerar will not let me down.'[4] That same day, Crerar met with Vincent Massey, who related that at the end of January he had been told by Montgomery that Crerar would return only after he was battle experienced, probably sometime in April. In the meantime, Montgomery was pressing Simonds to assume interim command of First Canadian Army; that move came to naught.[5] Montgomery did not mention his approach to Brooke in December 1943, an approach that marked the beginning of a long campaign to have Simonds take command of First Canadian Army.

Oblivious to this development, Crerar began the study of HQ First Canadian Army's role in the Normandy campaign. The Canadians' role was dictated by the plans recreated by Montgomery and his 21st Army Group on his return to England in January 1944. The 'Master' had, following a 'ruthless purge' of staff of his predecessor Sir Frederick Morgan, dismissed the assault plan as 'not a sound operation of war.'[6] The new plan for the invasion, Operation Overlord, envisioned a five-division landing on the beaches of Normandy: two American, two British, one Canadian, plus elements of three airborne divisions and armour. 3rd Canadian Infantry Division, commanded by Major-General R.F.L. Keller, and 2nd Canadian Armoured Brigade made up the Canadian assault force. They had begun training in July 1943. The Canadian units designated for the beach landings were 'in combination' with 1 British Corps. Second British Army, commanded by Lieutenant-General Miles Dempsey, controlled the entire British-Canadian force.

First Canadian Army would enter the battle in the second phase of operations, once a bridgehead was firmly established and Second British Army was off the beaches, likely within ten to twenty days of landing. As directed by a 21st Army Group planning order of 1 March 1944, it would 'assume responsibility for the left-hand sector of the bridgehead,' and, with one corps under command, advance eastwards to capture the ports of Whitstable (Le Havre) and Clarence (Rouen). It would, as operational circumstances allowed, assume command of 2nd Canadian Corps and continue to advance along the left flank of the Allied armies. Headquarters First Canadian Army was charged with two planning tasks: preparing the buildup priority tables, staff studies, and administrative instructions for the movement to the Continent of the headquarters and support troops; a study of the problems of capturing the ports of Le Havre and Rouen, Operation Axehead.[7] While the Tactical HQ worked on planning for the buildup, Axehead was the priority of the Main HQ.

II .

Headquarters staff was a relatively stable body of officers by the time Crerar took command in March. He had spearheaded a renewal of the headquarters while in Italy. Although First Canadian Army was effectively without an operational GOC from McNaughton's departure in December 1943, this omission was deliberate. The interim Commander Ken Stuart decided that, for security reasons, he should not be informed of the detail of the tactical plans for Overlord, and he was ill through much of January. Stuart was also following Crerar's direction, focusing on questions of policy in his new appointment as chief of staff, CMHQ, with a view to "streamlin[ing]' HQ First Cdn Army for its future operational role' by transferring certain duties to CMHQ. Stuart, acting as Crerar's proxy, ordered the First Canadian Army Chief of Staff to begin the stabilization of HQ First Canadian Army and to prepare it for operations.[8]

The winter of 1943–4 witnessed the emergence of a new spirit at army headquarters, the result of both new personnel and an operational goal. Chief of Staff Brigadier C.C. Mann was the newest among the senior staff, assuming his appointment on 28 January 1944. Crerar and McNaughton were responsible for Mann's rapid ascent.[9] Despite some confidence problems and an erratic personality, he renewed the headquarters with his vigorous no-nonsense approach and his clever wit. Crerar wrote of him in a personal note, 'Apart from my appreciation of his personal qualities, I am very glad to have him associated with me once more.' One First Canadian Army brigadier remembered the same qualities differently: 'He was the right hand man; he had "ten ideas" a minute and when they were good, they were very good.'[10]

Other senior staff had been with the headquarters for an extended period. Ernie Walford, as noted above, was the well-liked DA & QMG whose easygoing personality eased the sometimes difficult working relations between the administrative side and the operations side of the headquarters.[11] Colonel, General Staff G.E. Beament, the senior operational officer, was a sharp and blunt Ottawa lawyer before joining the army on the outbreak of war. He was an RMC graduate and had served with 'B' Battery in Kingston when Crerar was the battery commander. Beament had subsequently attended the Staff College, Camberley, assuming his appointment in November 1943. He was meticulous, but could be difficult to work with.[12] Similarly, many of the General Staff Officers 1 (GSO 1) were taken on through the late fall and early winter. Lieutenant-Colonel Peter Wright, GSO 1 (Intelligence), and Lieutenant-Colonel C. Archibald, GSO 1 (Operations), were among those who added to the stability of the HQ.[13] This group, although long-serving, were inexperienced, and required the leavening of a small cadre of experienced British staff officers, as per the agreement between Stuart and Brooke, foremost among them Lieutenant-Colonel J.R. Cochrane, GSO 1 (Staff Duties).

Prior to January 1944, the HQ was floundering, overstaffed, and without direction. Early in January, Stuart arrived at Headley Court to review the HQ's organization and operational responsibilities of First Canadian Army. He interviewed and examined the HQ with an eye to streamlining it for operations. Detailed reports and charts on commitments and organization were prepared by each section of the staff.[14] The unfocused nature of the activities of the HQ emerged as the main complaint of the staff, a problem exacerbated by the high turnover of personnel. The GSO 1 (Ops) summed it up best at the end of his report: 'There have been few Army exercises, negligible planning duties, and much routine detail.'[15]

The change of command and the dispatch of 1st Canadian Corps to Italy also affected personnel. In January 1944, a figure of 50 per cent was set as the maximum allowable percentage of British officers, and First Canadian Army was detailed to act 'in combination' with 21st Army Group. While the percentage of British officers on staff never rose above 14 per cent, the debates surrounding and the settling of First Canadian Army's status set the stage for further changes to the army headquarters personnel.[16]

Mann's first action as Chief of Staff was to gather all his GSO 1s and speak to them on the need to organize 'to be ready to fight.' He then met with each of them individually and discussed their roles at the headquarters. Captain George Pangman with the Canadian Planning Staff in London, under command of First Canadian Army, recalled that when Mann asked him what he did, the honest reply was, 'Nothing, Sir ... I came back from Italy two months ago and I've been enjoying myself in London.' The staff was eager for change. 'Under Andy,' recalled Brigadier G.E. Beament (then a colonel), '[we tried to convert] into a mobile army headquarters command that could move in active operations and continue to exercise its function ... we had some success but Andy didn't like it a damn bit.' Mann was interested; he hammered home the point in daily conference briefings with the senior staff.[17]

The first significant step was the creation of a Planning Section of the General Staff Branch, using the staff languishing in London and appointing Pangman as GSO 1. The Liaison and Training sections – previously forced to share staff despite the limits this restriction imposed on headquarters exercises, the provision of instructors, testing officers, and production of training directives for headquarters staff – were separated. Mann also added three officers to the Training Section, including a brigadier, to substantiate the changes. The Operations sections received two new positions. The most significant change to operations was the exchange of GSO 1, Lieutenant-Colonel J.R. Cochrane from Staff Duties (SD). The Air section remained essentially the same. No further changes were recommended for the senior staff.[18] Training, under Mann, continued to involve mastering routine work, but a stronger emphasis was placed on studying the lessons of current operations and exercises and creating a system whereby these would be readily accessible.[19] Routine administration was transferred to CMHQ. Reflecting the new thrust, revised Operational Standing Orders were issued for the Main HQ, the first such change since September 1943.[20]

Operational instructions from 21st Army Group HQ, as well as the imminence of Crerar's return, marked the beginning of a new round of changes to the HQ. Stuart had monitored Mann's progress, as well as that of Simonds, describing it as 'satisfactory.' He believed that planning for Overlord was well in hand and 'no cause for concern.'[21] To the Minister of National Defence, Stuart reported in March 1944 the invigorating effect that the new appointments at all levels 'with emphasis on youth and recent battle experience' was having on spirit and morale throughout the army. Satisfied 'that [the] McNaughton episode is over so far as the army over here is concerned,' Stuart believed that the 'peak [of morale would] be reached when Crerar is announced as army commander.'[22]

Stuart's observation was wrong on one account: planning for the Normandy operation was almost non-existent. Only after orders defining First Canadian Army's operational future were received from 21st Army Group was Mann able to begin the reorganization that culminated on 9 March 1944 with the creation of Tactical HQ First Canadian Army/84 Group RAF. First Canadian Army's role and its planning tasks for Neptune were firmly defined, as outlined earlier, and a greater sense of operational priority was restored. Planning for the Normandy landings became Tac HQ's responsibility. 'Neptune Directive Number 1,' dated 13 March, charged it with the responsibility for 'the movement of 2nd Canadian Corps' to the Continent, including the operational and administrative instructions for that move. Although under the Main HQ and the Colonel GS, Tac HQ's operations section functioned separately for the purposes of planning. Main HQ's planning priority was Axehead, training, and its own move to France.[23]

Training priorities were also more focused after 21st Army Group's issued its directive. 'Office Instruction Number 1' for the Tac HQ stated that representatives of First Canadian Army and 84 Group, RAF, were to work closely together in operational planning, a persistent problem according to Montgomery. To that end, G(Air) at Main HQ planned two training exercises in March designed to further air-land coordination and cooperation by having the air and army staffs work together.[24] By mid-March, HQ First Canadian Army had begun to tackle the problems associated with operations to break out from the anticipated Normandy bridgehead.

III

Crerar was determined to carve out a role for the army HQ, despite its marginal position in operational planning in the months leading up to D-Day. He assumed that First Canadian Army would be phased into the battle at an early date, in a logical order dictated by the necessity of grouping of all Canadian forces under HQ First Canadian Army. This reasoning informed his first assertions of the army headquarters prerogatives. Responding to requests from Simonds that two regiments of artillery, as well as various engineer, signals, and transport units be included in 2nd Canadian Corps Order of Battle, Crerar observed, 'In general, it is undesirable to decentralize Army resources to Corps under command until the situation indicates that there will be a definite operational or administrative need for such decentralization.' The army commander, Mann added, felt it was also 'undesirable' to decentralize any army artillery before arrival in the bridgehead 'as the situation may require the employment of all the Army artillery in support of another Corps already engaged while [First Canadian Army's] movement to the continent is still in progress.' This policy applied to all ancillary units.[25] Crerar's policy was logical, given that First Canadian Army was told by the C of S, 21st Army Group, that it might be 'required to assume command of 1 and 12 British Corps, making a total of three.'[26]

On his return from a week's rest, Crerar set the tone of his command with an early morning speech to the HQ staff on 31 March. Gathering the staff at a local cinema, he laid out how he expected the HQ to function, and, in general, the role he envisioned for each individual. Crerar began by attacking head on the question of McNaughton's dismissal from army command and the shock felt by many on the army staff. He reaffirmed his own loyalty to McNaughton, but, to his credit, implied that the circumstances of McNaughton's dismissal, while regrettable, were necessary. 'This Canadian Army,' he continued, 'which I have the high honour to command is his creation ... we will, none of us, forget the debt which we, Canadians, owe to him.'

Crerar then established his concept of operations, characterizing it in unspectacular and qualified terms:

> Given comparative equality in men, means and morale, it is approximately true to say that the successful waging of war is mainly a matter of more effective movement of military tonnage – military tonnage made up of men, their weapons, ammunition, motor transport, fighting vehicles and essential supplies of all kinds. The Commander who can move the right mixture of this tonnage, in the right amounts, to the decisive point, in the quickest time, and launch it in a manner unexpected by the enemy, has victory in his grasp.

This view was not completely wrong; neither was it a St Crispin's Day call to arms. It reflected his approach to command and the idea that the battle could be lost, if not won, before the first shot was fired.

Moving from the general to the specific, Crerar charged HQ staff with their duties as his eyes and ears, producing the information and intelligence that would be 'the foundation on which [the commander could] build up a sound and forceful plan which, if properly executed, [would] produce victorious results.' Crerar emphasized the importance of the rapid flow of information and paperwork. He also set out his belief that consultation would characterize his approach to command. Crerar expected 'constructive recommendations,' but weighed in against backbiting critiques and disloyal rumour-mongering. He charged that 'nothing but the best [was] good enough in quality, appearance and discipline of all ranks on Headquarters First Canadian Army.' They must set the example for the rest of the army.[27] There is no record of the response. Tired from the talk, Crerar spent the rest of the day answering personal correspondence.

Over the next weeks Crerar won over the staff with his determined efforts to make HQ First Canadian Army an active operational headquarters. He had a solid ally in Mann.[28] Other senior staff also appreciated the new regime and approach, even if they missed the familiarity of McNaughton. '[Crerar] had a loyal staff, a good working relationship [with his staff],' recalled Beament, 'but he never generated the same affection that McNaughton's warmth had generated.' Nevertheless, it was Crerar who 'cooperated very well ... in our endeavours [to become] a mobile army headquarters command.'[29]

Two changes were notable following Crerar's assumption of command: the relationship between CMHQ and First Canadian Army was altered, and the HQ increased focus on operational exercises, particularly Exercise Flit. The former prompted the first round of changes. In March, Crerar, in conjunction with Stuart, limited CMHQ's authority, successfully arguing that CMHQ was the 'rear echelon' of First Canadian Army as well as the 'forward echelon' of DND. The GOC-in-C reserved the right to approve all proposed changes to war establishments that had a bearing on 'the operational function and tactical performance of any HQ, unit, etc. in First Cdn Army' and, more important, the right to approve staff and command appointments in rank of brigadier and above *'throughout the Canadian Army Overseas'* [emphasis is Crerar's], as well as Grade 1 staff appointments in formations under his command. Crerar also recommended, and Stuart accepted, that performance in the field should henceforth be the main criterion for advancement.[30] In short, Crerar, while removing the administrative duties of the Senior Officer, retained substantial authority.

Changes to the HQ allotment followed suit. The most significant organizational changes reflected Crerar's concerns with effective procedure as well as the attempt to streamline the Operations branch. Staff Duties was organized as a separate section, responsible both to the Chief of Staff and the Colonel, GS.[31] This alteration was designed to facilitate the rapid movement of paper, ensuring that priority matters were addressed quickly. A variation on the U.S. and British models, the position of the SD Section gave it an authority that was absent in similar Allied organizations.[32] Channels of communication between the arms and the services were streamlined. Regular command channels were used, except for technical matters. The notable exception was the BRA, who, because there was no RA representative in HQs other than army, could communicate personally to formation commanders or through the staff. This recreated a semi-autonomous BRA, similar to that which was familiar to Crerar from the First World War.[33]

The most important change to senior staff personnel was the replacement of Cochrane, the British GSO 1 (Ops), by Lieutenant-Colonel W.A.B. Anderson, a Permanent Force officer with a great deal of experience on staff and a former personal assistant to Crerar. The circumstances of the replacement illustrate the nature of Crerar's command. The standing operational instruction orders regarding the functioning of the HQ and how to move the HQ in operations had been circulated after their issue in April. Cochrane reputedly wrote in the margins, 'I have never read such "cock" in my life,' and returned it to Beament. Cochrane's response was taken up with Mann, who passed it on to Crerar. He was not amused, and interpreted it as 'disaffection,' a danger to the smooth operation of his HQ. Cochrane, according to Anderson's recollection, was gone within an hour and Anderson, much to his dissatisfaction at not being able to go with his brigade into battle, was selected by Crerar to replace him. He assumed his post on 1 May. Crerar's response was telling: loyalty was of paramount importance to the smooth functioning of the headquarters.[34]

Training reached new levels of realism. For the HQ, the largest training exercise was Exercise Flit held 5–11 May at Box Hill, to 'practice deployment and [co-operation]' between HQ First Canadian Army and 84 Group, RAF. Though the Main and Tac HQs were to conduct operations and establish themselves only 'if operations progress[ed] favourably,'[35] Crerar stated that he 'intended to use his Tac HQ only on occasions when there [was] a need for it,' therefore he was anxious to personally 'try it out as a separate est[ablishment] on FLIT.'[36] Organization, communication, and movement were the focus. The exercise was a success, but several serious deficiencies were uncovered, most the result of insufficient practice that affected timing and coordination. Procedural problems also revealed themselves, particularly in the flow of crucial information between HQs. The failure to assign priorities or specific destinations to messages, especially routine contacts, and some needless duplication all reflected the anxiety and hurried exchanges borne of inexperience. The alterations were incorporated in a comprehensive memorandum on the organization and functions of the HQs staff.[37]

Through April and May, HQ First Canadian Army also initiated and oversaw training exercises for the formations under its command. In anticipation of Operation Axehead, 2nd Canadian Corps undertook a month-long exercise, Kate, designed to practise an assault crossing of a tidal estuary. Two corps HQ exercises were also planned for May. Simonds's corps was instructed to study, without interfering with the completion of Kate and other exercises, various tactical and administrative problems including 'a break-out battle, followed by a fighting advance to a topographical objective' some forty miles distant; 'assault crossings of rivers ... and the engineering problems involved'; and defending against determined enemy counterattacks and resumption of the offensive immediately afterwards.[38]

Crerar's hand was evident in some of the training initiatives undertaken for Axehead, based on lessons emanating from the Italian campaign. At the end of April, he consolidated the firepower under his command, directing the anti-aircraft and anti-tank units to prepare themselves to 'be able to take their place in an artillery fire plan, and fire indirect when, and if, required.' Crerar viewed this consolidation as a morale-booster as well as a means of supplementing the field artillery. Training, however, was shaped by the initiatives of the unit COs until the Canadian School of Artillery completed a set of standard operating procedures for gun drills, rules of ranging, and fire discipline.[39] Similarly, in late May Crerar pressed for the formation of Canadian Divisional Counter-Battery Mortar Staffs on the basis of 'experience gained in operations during the present Italian campaign.' This was a difficult proposition, requiring as it did an entirely new organization and increases in personnel.[40]

IV

The invasion was the main focus. Senior commanders and staff were treated to a series of assemblages of the key military players through April and May. The first was on 7 April 1944, with the dramatic launch of Exercise Thunderclap, Montgomery's 'run-in to the invasion,' at which he planned to 'put all senior officers and their staffs completely into the whole OVERLORD picture – as affecting the general plan, the naval problem and the air action.'[41] The meeting was held at St Paul's School, Monty's headquarters (and old school), and those in attendance remembered it affectionately. Montgomery's opening remarks, Bertram Ramsey's explanation of the naval plans, and Leigh-Mallory's talk on the air plans built the atmosphere to a crescendo; Bradley, Dempsey, and their corps commanders spoke in the afternoon. A rambling presentation by 30 British Corps CO Bucknall went on until Monty told him to 'bloody well shut-up,' sounding the one sour note. Churchill inspired all, despite a noticeably 'weepy condition.'[42]

Montgomery's conference set the stage for Crerar's most immediate, if indirect, training responsibility from April to June 1944: 3rd Canadian Division's state of operational readiness for its role in the Normandy landings. It appeared to some as his foremost priority. 'My recollection of Crerar during those months leading up to D-Day in June 1944,' recalled Beament, 'was that he was more concerned with the situation as it affected Third Canadian Division ... than he was with the army at large.'[43] This perception was not completely accurate, but Crerar did take an aggressive interest in 3rd Division's training and preparation, one that suggested he was influenced by more than just his normal command responsibilities. Dieppe weighed heavily on his mind. Crerar's cathartic pride in his contribution to 3rd Canadian Division's assault training, culminating in Exercise Pirate in October 1943 (he had outlined the fire plan and most of the elements of the all-arms amphibious landing in a detailed memorandum sent to Keller in August 1943) continued to inform his relations with the Canadian units earmarked for the D-Day landings.[44] With the exception of his involvement with Pirate, Crerar maintained some distance and concentrated on his own HQ and 2nd Canadian Corps. He visited 3rd Division units and attended training exercises; near the end of April, he also initiated periodic meetings with Major-General R.F.L. Keller, GOC of the division, as well as Simonds, 'that I may be kept well in touch with the activities and problems of your command.'[45]

Crerar's dealings with 3rd Division drew him, not unwillingly, into the policy and constitutional debates that swirled around the division as a result of the Canadian government's concerns for its troops, and its own political hide. As well, Montgomery persistently refused to recognize that Canadian formations could not be treated as British formations. Concurrent arguments regarding the army commander's position resulted in a constitutional battle of wills through May 1944, culminating in June, that satisfied Crerar and the Canadian government but left Montgomery even more convinced of the righteousness of his crusade to remove Crerar. The catalyst was the Canadian government's desire in April to obtain a formal statement from the army commander on the feasibility of the upcoming operation so it could issue formal instructions detailing Crerar's responsibilities to the government and the position of First Canadian Army within the British 21st Army Group as per precedent.

Crerar initially protested, feeling that the government's permission for Canadian involvement in the D-Day invasion was implicit in the decision to place First Canadian Army 'in combination' with 21st Army Group and, perhaps, fearing that King and Ralston were preparing a sacrificial lamb in case the worst occurred. A strongly worded reply from Ralston, however, moved Crerar to forward his assessment that he was 'satisfied that the tasks allotted ... in the forthcoming invasion of enemy occupied Europe, are feasible operations of war and ... are capable of being carried out with reasonable prospects for success.'[46] Crerar held this to be true, talking privately of his supreme confidence 'that [the] first assault' would succeed.

While Crerar, Stuart, and Ralston discussed the proposed operations, Crerar and Stuart came to the conclusion that formally establishing Crerar's position as a Canadian Army commander within the British 21st Army Group was necessary to 'strengthen [their] hands' in the event of problems with other Allied leaders. This concern appears to have been prompted by Montgomery's abrupt refusal to allow Mackenzie King to observe 3rd Canadian Division while it participated in the combined training Exercise Fabius, unless ordered to do so by 'higher authorities.' Montgomery reasoned that 'no "non-professional" people' should be about.[47] Crerar was already wary of Monty and suggested that the public and his subordinates would turn on him at his first failure.

Crerar and Stuart presented their concerns to Deputy Minister of National Defence G.S. Currie in late April, arguing that the Canadian army commander must be viewed as the CO of an Allied army. On 1 May, they cabled Ralston, urging him to formally draft instructions to that effect and that all Canadian formations be united under First Canadian Army after hostilities with Germany had ceased. Crerar also pressed Stuart, successfully, to follow the principle that only he, or someone directly responsible to him, could represent Canadian views to Montgomery and Eisenhower. The most contentious point was the difficulty of ensuring that Canadian commanders were informed of operations without prejudicing operational secrecy, but still in time to exercise their right to withdraw Canadians if they felt it necessary. Cabinet finally approved the instructions on 24 May, in what proved a timely move.[48]

Concurrent with the negotiations – and they were negotiations – surrounding the government's official instructions to their army commander, a minor crisis was developing between Montgomery and Crerar regarding Crerar's constitutional responsibilities for Canadians not under his immediate operational command. Montgomery was determined to assert his control over Canadian troops, while minimizing Crerar's operational command responsibilities. In part this move was due to lack of focus. On his return from commanding Eighth British Army, Montgomery was under a great deal more strain than he would ever admit. In December, Brooke recorded in his diary that 'Monty [was] tired out'; at the end of February, Admiral Sir Bertram Ramsay, the Allied Naval Commander for the Normandy landings, warned Brooke that Monty was 'wandering around visiting troops and failing to get down to basic facts.' 'Shall have to have him up again,' Brooke wrote, 'and kick him [sic] back side again.'[49] Montgomery's focus, however, was on the formations directly involved in the assault; First Canadian Army and Crerar were, through much of March, an afterthought. Montgomery and Crerar had a moderately testy exchange over Montgomery's distribution of a 'special letter' on army-air cooperation in which Monty outlined several points designed to achieve 'real unity' between an army and its supporting air force, including encouraging the proximity of HQs, and constant consultation and communication between HQs staffs.[50] Headquarters First Canadian Army, however, had already prescribed a program of close cooperation with its opposite numbers in the air force.[51] On 1 April, Crerar had directed that HQ 84 Group be physically joined to HQ First Canadian Army and a Joint First Canadian Army/84 Group HQ was 'under canvas' in Exercise Flit when Montgomery's missive was received. Crerar thus penned a testy reply to Monty, noting defensively that, since his return, 'great strides have been made in the desired direction' and that all points mentioned 'have had my attention and have been implemented to the extent that present conditions make possible.'[52]

There was already a degree of tension between the two when Montgomery blew a minor matter of constitutional procedure into yet another tedious, if necessary, battle with the British over the principle of Crerar's operational responsibility to the government for all Canadian troops.[53] An inspection of 3rd Canadian Division by General Dwight

Eisenhower, Supreme Commander of the Allied Expeditionary Force, without Crerar's knowledge, prompted Crerar to seize the opportunity of a prime ministerial visit in May 1944 to clarify the principle of his operational responsibility. Writing to Stuart, Crerar stressed that whether it was visits or operations, only he could represent to Supreme Headquarters Allied Expeditionary Force (SHAEF) or 21st Army Group the interests of First Canadian Army.[54] Crerar urged Stuart to use the Prime Minister's presence to clarify with the CIGS the 'proper procedure in these matters ... on the political level' and explain them to SHAEF. He wanted the 'special position' of the commander, First Canadian Army, cleared up before operations began.[55] To ensure that the message was passed to Brooke, Crerar arranged a private dinner with the CIGS on 16 May, their first since the end of March.[56] Although hesitant, Stuart wrote Brooke, noting, '[Crerar] commands the First Canadian Army and he is also the Canadian national representative in respect to all Canadian Formations and Units employed operationally in [the Western European] theatre even though some may not be under his operational command.'[57] Brooke readily agreed with the logic of the argument.

Montgomery did not. On 18 May, he orchestrated an informal luncheon meeting with the Prime Minister. Montgomery blindsided King, first praising Crerar, then noting that he required more experience and 'there were some things that he had to keep advising him on.' He recommended Simonds as Crerar's replacement and, as remembered by King, moved to his main point:

> [My goal] is to win battles and save lives. From that he went on to say that he hoped that so-called national considerations would not be allowed to override military considerations ... He said more or less directly that Crerar had kept asserting there were national reasons why such and such a thing should be done ... He said some [Canadian] officers had not had the experience that was needed for commanding [and] that it was dangerous to have lives of men entrusted to those who had not had the needed experience.

King's answer was ambiguous: 'I had from the beginning of the war insisted that no political considerations of any kind should be permitted to override a military consideration. Other things being equal, I felt that so-called national considerations should, of course, be taken into account at all times.' He pointed out that Canadian troops preferred to fight as a national unit, prompting Montgomery to press his advantage. He asked that if an emergency necessitated quick separation and amalgamation, he hoped King would 'back him up.' King's reply was non-committal. He gave no indication that he would back his own army commander against Montgomery.[58]

Crerar's broad national and political outlook on the army effort should have won King's Liberal heart. Only the day before, Crerar had spoken to the Prime Minister of the need to comb the various branches and arms of First Canadian Army for French-Canadian troops to ensure sufficient replacements to bring their number up to the sixty days requirements for the French-speaking regiments.[59] He justified it on the grounds that it was crucial both to avoid conscription of French Canadians and to forestall the breakup of these regiments. Crerar's commitment to this was such that he had authorized the Royal Montreal Regiment be taken on strength as First Canadian Army Headquarters Defence Battalion rather than agree to their being struck from First Canadian Army rolls. He feared the negative publicity.[60]

According to King, Crerar 'had said something to the effect that even if it might involve a little more loss of life it would save feelings ... in the minds of French Canadians.' This possibility seems unlikely but in contrast, King observed that Monty disagreed, stating that 'he believed French Canadians would prefer to have English speaking officers of experience if they felt certain that their lives would be better protected than simply to try to keep regiments wholly French Canadian.' Still 'deeply moved' from his meetings with the troops, King concluded, 'Montgomery's view is the one which is sound in actual battle,' although his political instincts would later tell him that Crerar's view was a more accurate gauge of French-Canadian opinion.[61]

The Prime Minister had, momentarily at least, abandoned his army commander. King reiterated his conversation with Montgomery to Crerar, and to the Cabinet War Committee on his return to Canada. King expressed some concern that the instructions to the army commander might conflict with the assurances he had given Montgomery. Ralston reminded him that 'since in our view Canadians fought better together, the concentration of Canadian formations was also a "military" consideration.' King conceded the point, and the instructions were approved.[62]

Montgomery, emboldened by his meeting with King – 'I like [King] immensely,' he recorded in his diary, 'and we had a great talk about his Canadians' – wrote to Stuart on 25 May, refusing to concede that Crerar had any operational responsibility 'for Canadian troops serving temporarily in another army.' Crerar would be treated like any other British army commander. He assured Stuart that Ralston and King agreed with his views. 'There is no doubt that the national and political feeling is very strong in the Canadian senior ranks,' he noted in his diary a day later. 'My view is that what people really want is victories.'[63]

Stuart was prepared to accept Montgomery's 'softened' position. Recognizing the modest support afforded them by King, he also expressed concern that Montgomery and the CIGS would lose confidence in their judgment if they appeared more 'constitutionally minded than [their] political masters.' Crerar, however, was unmoved. 'Quite apart from the specific instructions I have from the Canadian government in such matters,' he replied to Stuart, 'it is obvious that it can only be the senior Canadian Commander in 21 Army Group who *can* accept such responsibility' [Crerar's emphasis]. Crerar restated his admiration for Monty's 'great abilities and qualities as a Field Commander,' but concluded, 'Though in practice I expect to be treated, and behave, as any other Army Commander, in principle I ... am not. I am the Canadian Army Commander and, as such, am in a different category to the British Army Commander.'[64] Exactly.

Through June, Crerar pressed a reluctant Stuart to 'clear up' the issue with the CIGS and, through Brooke, Montgomery. Brooke agreed with Crerar, but Montgomery was already on the continent.[65] In practice, no major regrouping of Canadian formations occurred in northwest Europe, either with Canadian concurrence or against their wishes. In that sense, it was a waste of precious time and energy. There were more than simply command prerogatives at stake for Crerar. He continued to envision First Canadian Army as a national institution to promote Canadian unity and the army's profile.

V

The pull of policy and influence was irresistible to Crerar, but he had McNaughton's example before him, and maintained a focus on preparing the army for operations. If this was not a straightforward process, it was because the early months of 1944 were a transition period and because Crerar wanted to retain the ability to shape the Canadian army effort. The relatively small cadre of senior Canadian army officers made it inevitable that the army GOC in C would continue to exert an enormous influence on all aspects of command and organization in the overseas army. Similarly, an argument could be made that Crerar had to be kept abreast of all issues relating to the Mediterranean Force because manpower and command problems could affect First Canadian Army. There was, however, no obvious reason save respect for, and deference to, Crerar and his position to explain the continuous approaches regarding postwar policy and organization. For instance, Stuart approached him to secure both his confirmation and opinion on the appointment of a new commandant for the Royal Military College. In the midst of operations in August, Crerar was advising Stuart, at his request, on questions of appropriate dress uniforms and standardization of the use of flags for the cars of senior officers, an issue since May. The fact that he remained vexed by these questions suggests the difficulty of the Canadian army commander to focus completely on operations.[66] The ranks of the senior command and staff of the overseas army remained a tight club. Crerar stood at its pinnacle.

The exercise of Crerar's influence was most obvious in the operational commands from brigade through to corps. Both Simonds and Burns, on his recommendation, had been selected as GOCs, 2nd and 1st Canadian Corps, respectively. Crerar, in a letter to Stuart on 16 May 1944, and in conversations with the Prime Minister the next day, outlined 'his views concerning replacement of possible casualties amongst senior Canadian Comds, both as regards First Cdn Army and 1 Cdn Corps.' In April, he had solicited opinions on prospective divisional and brigade commanders, as well as senior staff officers, from Simonds and Burns.[67] Their opinions were important, but his own agenda also shaped his perspective on corps and army command. He had no hesitation in recommending that Simonds should take over the army in the event that Crerar should become a casualty. While he noted that 'both Simonds and Burns [were] capable of successfully filling the appointment of Army Comd,' he unequivocally told Mackenzie King that he 'thought Simonds should succeed [me].' In both cases, however, Crerar qualified his support: 'Of the two,' he wrote, 'Simonds would probably be more brilliant and show more drive in field operations.' Nevertheless, he added, 'Burns is the better balanced and looks further ahead.' In a similar vein, he told King that 'Simonds was a very good soldier, though he might not be the best man for post-war planning.'[68]

Policy remained an important factor in his recommendations. Crerar's views on potential corps' commanders suggested this view:

> Simonds and I are agreed that, as regards mentality, Foulkes possesses the necessary qualifications. On the other hand, he has not been tried out in

the field and though he certainly possesses the brain and the outlook, he may not show himself equipped with the necessary mental and moral stamina. I believe that Keller would make a two-fisted and competent Corps Comd in the field. On the other hand, while Keller's grasp of tactics and ability to command men are definitely good, matters of higher, and long-term policy lie outside his interest and this would be a serious handicap to a Cdn Corps Comd.[69]

The prerequisites of senior command in the Canadian army were the ability, and desire, to defend Canadian autonomy and place the army's effort in the broad national context.[70] As Keller would prove, policy skills and nationalism were not the best gauges of a commander's ability to withstand the stress of operations.

Crerar also made known his recommendations for replacing Keller and future divisional commanders; these were based on the advice of his subordinate commanders. The selections also indicate two other considerations that, in addition to either proven or potential ability, informed Crerar's criteria for promotion to brigade or divisional rank. One was Crerar's attempt to deal with the perception that the army's senior command and staff positions were dominated by artillerymen. Certainly, by 1944, this was not the case. While two of the senior command positions were held by the gunners Crerar and Simonds, as were some senior staff positions like the Colonel GS, First Canadian Army, the majority of senior positions were held by infantrymen: 1st Canadian Infantry Division's Major-General Chris Vokes was also commissioned into the RCE; 2nd Division's Foulkes had a commission with the Royal Canadian Regiment; 3rd Division's Rod Keller was from the Princess Patricia's Canadian Light Infantry; George Kitching of 4th Armoured Division had a pre-war commission in the Gloucestershire Regiment; and Major-General Burt Hoffmeister of 5th Canadian Armoured was a pre-war militia officer with the Seaforth Highlanders. By the end of the war, the infantry supplied twenty-two of sixty-eight officers of divisional command rank, compared to eleven from the artillery.[71] Nevertheless, Crerar was aware of the perceived imbalance – 'the first to twig to this,' noted his ADC – and tried to improve this situation.[72] It also remained a consideration once active operations were underway. In late August, responding to a recommendation from Simonds and Foulkes that a brigadier should be replaced, Crerar observed that he would support their recommendation and ask for a suitable nominee, but added emphatically, '*not* a Gunner Officer.'[73]

The second criterion that informed officer selection was the desire to bring French-Canadian officers into senior command positions. '[Crerar] was way ahead of others [in] being conscious of the French factor,' recalled Henri Tellier, and consequently 'he chose at least one bilingual ADC.' Crerar, despite his advocacy of the policy of promoting French-Canadians, remained a product of his English officer class with its prejudices regarding character and education. 'The civil educational system of Quebec does not tend to produce,' he wrote to Ralston in July 1941, 'in equivalent numbers to English-speaking Canada, the "officer-type" so essential to the purpose.'[74] However, he was not prepared to sacrifice his troops' lives to political expediency. By 1944, the search for suitable command material among the four French battalions was subsumed by the need for, and availability of, experienced officers. The pressure remained fairly constant, fuelled by the Quebec media.[75] Promotions remained slow; the CO of the Royal 22e Regiment Lieutenant-Colonel Jean Allard, who had come to Crerar's attention as a GSO 2 at HQ 1st Canadian Corps and subsequently been given a field command, was given 6th Brigade in January 1945.[76]

From May, as the organization and staff stabilized, Crerar imprinted his personal style on the headquarters. It was based on principles of management rather than leadership; procedure and communication were the keys to implementing his system. Responsibility was diffused among the staff, particularly the senior staff. After two weeks of observation, dissatisfied with the haphazard flow of information between himself and his senior officers, Crerar established the routine that, with a few essential changes, would serve him for the duration of the campaign. It was an effective routine, revealing a man 'governed by the clock.' The 'drill,' as laid down by Crerar, and related by Mann to the senior staff on 7 May, began with a briefing on 'the activities of the night, briefly and accurately,' over the phone, by the duty officer of the Army Operations Room as soon as Crerar awoke at 0700. This was followed by the twin pillars of the system: two early morning meetings, the first before breakfast with Crerar, Mann, and the DA & QMG Walford to apprise the C of S 'regarding anything of importance to be discussed at the morning conference,' and the second, the Chief of Staff's morning conference between Mann and all 'officers on "XO" list down to and including Grade 2 SOs.' For planning and efficiency purposes, this second meeting was broken down a week later into two meetings, with the pre-operational planning to include only GSO 1s, staff branch heads, BRA, CE, and the Operation's section heads. Following the C of S's morning conference, Mann and Walford 'if required' reported any important developments to the army commander. Breakfast was a quiet affair; Crerar, among others, often eating alone. Crerar, who believed it 'bad form' to talk over breakfast, set the tone. He categorically specified that no routine meetings should be held during the rest of the day – this was his time to visit the formations and units under command. His ADCs were familiarized with the headquarters layout and routine to provide the proper liaison.[77] Tellier recalled that Crerar spoke aloud as he planned or contemplated operational exercises both because it helped him think and so that 'if [Crerar became] a casualty ... [his ADC would] know what was in the mind of the ... commander at the time.'[78]

In the months before the headquarters became operational, Crerar also kept up a voluminous correspondence, remarkable both for its quantity and the amount of time devoted to it. He travelled by air, a method he would adopt during operations. He was fastidiously self-conscious, his ADC recalled, and 'he hummed away to himself as he worked, when he wrote reports and other papers ... he also had a noticeable, somewhat annoying habit of clearing his throat.' By 1945, that had developed into a cough so severe that it forced one of his aides out of the caravan, a product of his chain-smoking, which increased notably through 1944.

Reports from the C of S, GSO 1 (Int), BRA, CE, and DA & QMG at 1700 signalled the end of the working day, unless something 'of moment' emerged. A brisk walk followed one Scotch before dinner with 'A' Mess – usually an animated and wide-ranging affair, at least prior to July 1944 – and one Scotch afterwards. Crerar insisted that unless 'ops [were] active, the Army Comd will not take up business after 1930 hours and dinner.' He directed that the HQ staff plan their workdays on 'the basis of EARLY TO WORK and EARLY TO BED,' a view that could only increase his reputation as a paternal figure.[79]

Crerar's routine was rigid. Although his disciplined approach enabled him to consistently commit himself twelve hours a day, six days a week, over a six-year period – no small matter – when applied to both his professional and personal life, as almost everything was, as a matter of principle it created the largely inflexible and formal mindset that characterized Crerar's approach to matters of ceremony and propriety. Saluting and standards of dress illustrate Crerar's insistence on high standards for both, even after operations had begun. Near the end of June 1944, Crerar wrote to Keller, dismayed in case the 'tendency amongst troops ... to convey to all and sundry that they are ... "war-worn veterans"' took hold. He argued that 'thoroughly trained and "made" troops ... will maintain their long established standard of smartness, soldierly bearing and evident self-respect no matter how trying the conditions,' and that, if properly led, they would take great pride in doing so. 'Quite frankly,' he concluded, 'the bearing and turn-out of Canadian personnel and vehicles in the bridgehead are not above, and in a good many cases are below, the standard of British troops in 21 Army Group.' To reemphasize that he viewed this as a command problem, Crerar wrote Keller again on 3 July noting that while 'I do not wish to be unduly restrictive, it is important that the wearing of "non-regulation" clothing ... by officers, Canadian Army, be kept to appropriate time and places.'[80]

Crerar took great pride in appearance, believing that it reflected, and encouraged, personal discipline, morale, and self-esteem. In his case, it undoubtedly did. Others agreed. On assuming command of Third U.S. Army in January 1944, General George Patton asserted that the 'need for discipline overrides all other considerations ... perfect discipline and the outward evidence of it as shown in neat dress, personal cleanliness and shaving ... even in the heat of battle.' For Patton, discipline and adherence to regulations maintained alertness and morale.[81]

Crerar was no Patton. Crerar was without either Patton's experience in high command to substantiate his opinion or his flamboyance to temper the disciplinarian image.[82] To Crerar, soldiering was a higher civic calling, indicative of personal responsibility and pride. His words reflect the emotive power these concepts held for him. However, Crerar's view was not that of the average Canadian volunteer. He was the product of a closed society, in many ways out of touch with mainstream Canada, and no amount of success, paternal interest, or empathy would change that.[83]

Crerar's principled approach, while commendable in its aims, did not always endear him to his troops. Neither did it ease relations with his family. Verse Crerar still smarted from her husband's determination to set an example for his men by refusing to allow her to join him in England. Their grandchild in combination with Peter's renewed commitment to correspondence provided some solace and eased the strain. In England, Crerar was clearly relieved by the change. 'Mum seems well,' he wrote Peter in April 1944, 'and continues to be very enthusiastic about young Tony. I certainly look forward to seeing this young man one of these days. She also says that you have been writing often and that your letters mean a great deal to her, which is good to hear.' Peter's well-being and the ability to touch base with his son-in-law Zouch and 'interchange family news' also contributed to the relaxation of family tensions that played on Crerar's mind.[84] They were never far from the surface. When letters did not arrive from home as expected, particularly when he was in the theatre of operations, Crerar was disappointed and concerned. Crerar also sounded a jealous, if tongue-in-cheek, note, writing to his daughter in early May, 'Mum writes cheerfully and seems to be socially as gay as she wants to be. I note in her letters that Bill H. "wines" and "dines" her periodically, but I am glad to note that you ... figure in these parties.' After two and a half sometimes lonely years overseas, he found that his family was an important lifeline to the normality.[85]

Crerar held others to the same standards, refusing Ralston's request that Georges Vanier's wife accompany him in an inspection of the Van Doos, his old regiment, fearful of the 'precedent it would set.'[86] This visitation policy was broadened to include any unwanted visitors when operations began, an approach that did not always endear Crerar to his political masters. 'Chubby' Power dissuaded industrialist James Duncan of Massey-Harris from visiting Crerar, noting, 'He is, or thinks he is, an extremely busy man and would perhaps take it amiss if we were to ask him to do anything for what he will no doubt consider the furthering of mere civilian activity.' 'As you know,' Power added, 'Brass Hats are Brass Hats even in the midst of war.'[87]

16 First Canadian Army and Overlord

I

When C.P. Stacey drafted the official history of the Canadian army during the Normandy campaign, he described Crerar, prior to the employment of First Canadian Army headquarters in July 1944, as 'merely a spectator.' Crerar reacted to this view with unusual fervour. Detailing his activities, he concluded, 'I feel that I was something more than "merely a spectator," to be quite frank.'[1] He was right. But his operational role was limited, although still important. And again he faced major issues surrounding the seemingly interminable questions of the capability of Canadian senior command and their British doubters.

Montgomery orchestrated the final formal dress rehearsal for the senior command and staff of the armies in 21st Army Group on 15 May, a 'memorably frigid day,' at St Paul's School, London. As a prologue to Montgomery's talk, Crerar addressed his senior commanders on 14 May, repeating his views on the tactical principles that should inform First Canadian Army's approach to operations in a speech aimed mainly at newly arrived officers, of which there were a considerable number. He began by emphasizing the overriding importance of morale – 'a soldiery which knows how to fight, and believes ardently in the cause it is fighting for, will win, even if handicapped by inadequate weapons.' More hyperbole followed as he pronounced on the training and men of First Canadian Army; the conviction behind these words, however, was certain. Mental fitness, discipline, and the need for the officers to set an example for the rank and file were detailed in turn.

Crerar's discussion of tactical principles formed the bulk of the address. A mix of broad generalizations and clear insights into the nature of the operations the Canadians might face in Normandy, it was also a commentary on Crerar's own expertise and weaknesses. Crerar repeated Montgomery's emphasis on the stage-management of battle. In his discussion of the manoeuvre battles facing the Canadians, he limited his comments to generalizations on maintaining the initiative, references to an abundance of training in this area and 1st Canadian Corps' track record in Sicily, glossing over his own inexperience.

Crerar also pinpointed a possible gap in the training and preparation of his troops: 'It is quite possible, even likely that a situation will arise in which the particular problems of the First Canadian Army will be the development of a "Break-in" and "Break-Through" battle against organized and strongly held enemy positions. This problem is not so well known to any of you in training, nor in actual experience.' Referring to the experiences of the 'last war,' he maintained that the artillery-based tactics used by the Canadian Corps were still relevant to attacking defended positions. He advocated a short opening barrage, using all available weapons including anti-tank guns, mortars, and tanks themselves if not used in the assault, with the infantry deployed 'as closely as possible to the enemy FDLs.' He understood the limitations of bombardment and that the goal was to neutralize the defenders – the duration must be 'just sufficient to enable the psychological effects of heavy bombardment to take effect on the enemy.' A moving, continuous barrage should then carry the infantry into the enemy defensive positions from predetermined positions following a predetermined plan. He spoke of the necessity of integrating fire and movement, and infantry-tank cooperation, but left the tactics unexplained.[2]

Crerar grasped the nature of the fighting that the Allies could expect in Normandy. And he correctly foresaw some of the problems they would encounter. His omissions were significant as well. Exploitation and manoeuvre – tank-based operations – were not detailed. Tactical air support was also ignored. Crerar's knowledge of the operational art was certainly incomplete, a gap he acknowledged in a reference to Simonds that he was prepared to defer to the corps commander's operational experience in certain areas. It was an indication of how operations would be handled following his assumption of operational command in July. Still, Crerar contributed and proved capable of discerning and addressing some of the operational issues as they arose.

The Overlord finale on 15 May was characterized dramatically as Montgomery's 'Final Presentation of Plans.' The Allied political and military leadership sat on hard wooden chairs, assembled in a semicircle around a coloured scale model of the invasion beaches, and Montgomery. By all accounts, he inspired the assembled generals and staff officers numbering in the hundreds with his self-confidence and grasp of the strategic situation. Montgomery was not the only speaker – Churchill, Eisenhower, Ramsey, Leigh-Mallory all spoke, and even King George VI was inspired to give an impromptu speech – but the show was Montgomery's.[3]

The final meeting in the lead-up to D-Day took place when Montgomery invited his four army commanders to his HQ at Southwick on 1 June. Bradley and Patton arrived in the afternoon, and informally went over their plans. The official meeting took place after supper when Dempsey and Crerar arrived. Bets, a Montgomery hobby, were placed on when Germany would collapse; Patton declined to bet on this war, but predicted the next would be in ten years. Crerar, true to his nature, delayed his wager until 24 June, but in a fit of optimism predicted Germany would ask for an armistice by 1 September 1944. Patton recorded his impressions of the men and the meeting: '[Dempsey] is not very impressive looking, and I take him to be a yes-man. The Canadian is better, but not impressive. DeGuingand is very clever but is extremely nervous.' He concluded, tongue-in-cheek, 'Montgomery was very anxious to get the exact location of all command posts on D-Day, and also the succession of command down to, and including, the third generation.'[4]

D-Day's approach added pressure to address gaps in preparations for operations that remained in First Canadian Army and Crerar's command. He secured an aircraft to oversee the battle: 'In the last war,' he wrote Air Marshal L.S. Breadner, the Air Officer C-in-C RCAF Overseas, 'and in this ... I "bank" a great deal on direct, low-altitude, aerial reconnaissance by the Commander, or his representative, of the ground over which his troops must operate. As a result, I do a great deal of personal "checking" of the topographical advantages, or disadvantages, of the terrain.'

A spacious Vigilant aircraft provided Crerar with the all-around observation that he required. When the Vigilant he was using to visit his scattered units was abruptly confiscated for Eisenhower, Crerar was not impressed. He expressed his ire in a letter to Air Chief Marshal Sir Trafford Leigh-Mallory, who found him another aircraft. The transfer of 83 Group to Second British Army disrupted Crerar's careful plans. 'I have a strong personal and national desire,' he wrote to Breadner on 30 May, 'that the pilots who fly me, singly, or in the Anson with my senior commanders and staff should be Canadian.' With Breadner's assistance, he had a small RCAF section created within the Communication Flight of 84 Group. The sudden turnaround in personnel was not without problems, not least of which was Crerar's pained attempts to avoid causing any resentment among 84 Group pilots. The new pilot's unfamiliarity with Crerar's aircraft caused one crash landing that destroyed the pilot's nerves as well as his precious Vigilant, not replaced until mid-August.[5]

Planning for the breakout period was First Canadian Army's most immediate operational and planning responsibility. As such, it was the operation that involved Crerar most intimately at this stage. The Neptune Directive of 21st Army Group to First Canadian Army, as already noted, instructed the HQ, in addition to preparing tables for the movement to the Continent, to study the problem of capturing Le Havre and Rouen – Operation Axehead. The operation would involve a series of river crossings, with the most difficult being an assault across the wide tidal estuary of the lower Seine in the face of enemy opposition. As the river crossings were 'highly specialized Engineer problems,' special GHQ troops would be provided to the Canadians, but First Canadian Army was instructed to make sure that 'engineer units under your command ... undergo special training as early as possible.' The plans were based on the assumption that First Canadian Army would have two corps of at least three infantry and two armoured divisions at its disposal. First Canadian Army was also to plan for the possibility that a naval assault force might be available to provide a 'left-hook' – one of Montgomery's favourite flanking operations – to capture Le Havre, that one airborne division 'with appropriate airlift' as well as a regiment of special 'DD' amphibious tanks would also be at its disposal. More detailed planning instructions outlining the administrative restrictions arrived on 20 March 1944.[6]

Axehead, as the planning priority of the Main HQ, was a point of pride for a staff and army commander on the margins of the Neptune operation. As planned, the operation was based on the assumption that First Canadian Army HQ would become operational by at least D plus twenty.[7] Three major appreciations were drafted, the first in April and the final one in May; they differed mainly in their approach to the capture of Rouen as a prerequisite to the speedy capture of Le Havre. In the first 'Appreciation and Outline Plan,' dated 12 April 1944, the objective was 'the capture of Rouen and Le Havre at about D plus 90 in order to secure the use of the Port of Le Havre.' It was a conservative plan, but proved a more accurate appreciation of events as they developed than the second draft, altered at the request of Montgomery and his chief of staff, Major-General F.W. 'Freddie' deGuingand. In the first draft, Crerar asserted that the capture of Rouen and 'adequate crossings of the River Seine above Rouen' in conjunction with Second British Army were necessary to secure First Canadian Army's flank before 'advancing to the North.' The 'speedy capture of the port of Le Havre' would complete the operation, but the document cautioned that 'it may NOT be possible to accomplish its capture without a deliberate attack, requiring a number of days to prepare.' Crerar also 'opposed' the employment of a 'left-hook' Naval Assault Force and a diversionary Combined Operation against the coast as unlikely to produce results worth the cost in time and casualties. Dieppe's influence was obvious. Nevertheless, Crerar proposed that the Dieppe–Le Havre garrisons could be masked and slowly invested while a reconnaissance force pushed east, southeast, and north.[8]

In the covering letter that accompanied the first draft, Crerar also expressed reservations regarding the tactical situation anticipated by 21st Army Group in its appreciation on Axehead of 20 March, which assumed that the Germans would concentrate the bulk of their armour in front of the American forces threatening the Brittany ports.

> In my opinion, the more suitable and likely tactics of the German High Command would be to treat the threat to the Loire and Brittany ports as of secondary importance, and consequently to counter attack with maximum forces, and as soon as possible, the left sector, or Eastern flank, of the Allied bridgehead. It would appear inevitable that this bridgehead will require to remain the base on which the two armies in 21 Army Group will need to rely for a considerable period after their advance to the South and South East commences. A determined, heavy German attack ... would cut these two Allied armies off.[9]

Consequently Crerar suggested that First Canadian Army study 'the defence ... of the Eastern flank of the Allied bridgehead against heavy and determined German counterattack.'[10]

Commenting on drafts of the official history of the Canadian Army after the war, Crerar claimed that his reservations prompted changes to 21st Army Group's assumptions on how the battle in Normandy would develop. He was correct in that he and the senior staff at First Canadian Army appreciated the manner in which the Germans would react to the

Anglo-Canadian attacks on Caen, although the Germans were not able to mount a large-scale counterattack.[11] Montgomery, however, did not change his assumptions until forced to by the course of the battle. He believed that the bulk of the forces facing Second British Army and First Canadian Army by the time the latter was operational would be infantry. On 30 April 1944, 21st AG's intelligence officer, Brigadier Edgar 'Bill' Williams, responded to Crerar's query: 'Our main threat will be towards the Loire and how much the Canadian Army will have to face depends to a great degree on the success of the thrust South-East of 2 British Army with 8 Corps as its spearhead.' Monty did not change his view of how the campaign would develop.[12]

Chief of Staff deGuingand, although convinced the Germans would not have the strength to counterattack, noted that the possibilities suggested by Crerar 'could not be excluded,' and encouraged the Canadian headquarters to 'examine the sector allotted to the Canadian Army from the point of view of selecting ground most suitable for defence.' He also reemphasized the 'Commander-in-Chiefs intention ... to secure Havre by the quickest possible means.' Montgomery was reluctant to 'adopt any plan which necessitates the capture of Rouen as a preliminary to [the] attack on Havre.' He concluded by noting that Montgomery wished to 'discuss the whole problem with your Commander.'[13]

The problem was resolved in early May when 21st Army Group agreed that while Rouen should at least be masked, First Canadian Army could not attain both objectives. Montgomery directed FCA to Le Havre. Second British Army would have responsibility for the 'capture of Rouen and the establishment of a strong right flank.' This tactical conception, and the predictions it sprang from, informed First Canadian Army planning and intelligence assessments for Axehead. The majority of the intelligence information was supplied by 21st Army Group; First Canadian Army Intelligence staff sorted and assessed the topographical information and estimates concerning enemy strength for the commander's appreciation.[14] Detailed planning and training then devolved to 2nd Canadian Corps HQ and 2nd Canadian Division.[15]

Crerar and his headquarters staff were also intent on asserting overall army control of planning for the operation, partially as a result of deGuingand's exhortation that planning for the operation was too important to be left to a divisional HQ and that 'major river crossing ops planning should commence at an early stage on an Army or Army ops level.'[16] Crerar contacted Dempsey, hesitantly urging him to 'initiate the necessary "inspiration"' for 1 British Corps to begin deliberation of the 'tactical and administrative requirements which later might face them in Axehead.' He was more assured with 2nd Canadian Corps. A certain amount of tension between the two HQs was evident as Crerar and Simonds argued over details of the planning, disagreeing in June over the proposed employment of the airborne division and the degree of detail for which army staff should plan relative to the corps staff. The operation was formally cancelled in June as a result of the failure to take Caen in the first weeks, but it would influence the Crerar's approach to operations in September 1944.[17]

In contrast to the assurance he showed in handling high-level constitutional and command issues, Crerar was still unsure of himself in operational matters and thus of his overall authority in command. He was edgy and defensive; this response characterized his approach to problems that revealed themselves through May and June. In one unusual case, three weeks before the scheduled date of the invasion, Brigadier R.A. Wyman of 2nd Canadian Armoured Brigade and two of his senior staff officers were found drunk and talkative on the subject of pending operations by a local dairyman the morning after Wyman heard the news he had been awarded a CBE. Unsure whether to replace Wyman at this stage, Crerar referred the matter to Montgomery, stating that he would defer to his advice on whether to hold a general court martial or simply 'give [Wyman] a bit of my mind' – the decision depending upon whether Monty thought a change in command would 'have significance to impending operations.'[18] Montgomery replied unequivocally that 'unless such a change was *absolutely* essential,' any command changes 'would be most unsound.'[19] A delicate situation, but one the army commander should have dealt with. Crerar's reaction to the proposed addition of a second infantry brigade to the 5th Canadian Armoured Division in Italy indicated a similar hesitancy to commit where operational matters were concerned, as well as a caution about manpower.[20] Pressed by Leese, Alexander, and Burns, Crerar relented, as long as the change did not 'complicate the general Canadian reinforcement problem.'[21]

II

The D-Day invasion on 6 June was far more successful, and less costly, than was anticipated by even the most optimistic of planners. The 3rd Canadian Division on Juno Beach fought their way through largely undamaged German defences. Despite some traffic confusion on the beach, partially caused by Keller's decision to commit his reserve brigade, the Canadians secured a beachhead and, before returning to dig in, advanced inland farther than any Allied formation. The cost was still high: 359 dead and 715 wounded on Juno alone. The Canadian success was mirrored on the British beaches at Sword and Gold. Casualties were higher still at Omaha, but lower at Utah. The end of the day saw the Allies ashore and securing their bridgeheads; Caen was still in German hands and gaps existed between the Canadians and British bridgeheads. Much would now depend on the relative speed with which the Germans reacted and the Allies gathered troops and armaments on the beaches.

Crerar maintained his regular routine on D-Day, staying in his caravan to monitor the landings, spending the day busy with office work and meeting with Stuart. Neither his personal nor war diary records his feelings, and his personal correspondence lapsed until late June, by which time other issues predominated. Crerar's impression of the landings became clear the next day, when he took the opportunity to brief the senior officers of his headquarters. Standing at the front of the Crescent cinema in the town of Leatherhead near Headley Court, he told them of the success of the landings and what he believed it meant for Canadians:

> I think it is most important that, at this time, all of you should realize what a vital part the gallant and hazardous operation of the raid in force on Dieppe ... has played in the conception, planning and execution of the vast 'Overlord' Operation ... Until the evidence of Dieppe proved otherwise, it had been the opinion in highest command and staff circles in this country that an assault against a heavily defended coast could succeed with tactical surprise ... However hazardous the operation, it was natural and proper that after nearly three years of war without any fighting by Canadian troops, the responsibility for carrying out this essential preliminary to future large scale invasion would come to a Canadian division
>
> I will ... make it clear that from the study of [the Dieppe] experience emerged the technique and tactics first demonstrated by the 3rd Cdn Inf Div in 'Pirate' Exercise last October, and that this technique and these tactics, were adopted for the vast combined operation which took place yesterday.
>
> Although at the time the heavy cost to Canada, and the non-success of the Dieppe operation, seemed hard to bear, I believe that when this war is examined in proper perspective, it will be seen that the sobering influence

of that operation on existing Allied strategic conceptions, with the enforced realization by the Allied governments of the lengthy and tremendous preparations necessary before invasion could be attempted, was a Canadian contribution of the greatest significance to final victory.[22]

The success of the Normandy landings was a catharsis of sorts for Crerar. Lieutenant-Colonel Peter Wright summed up the feeling of the intelligence staff as they prepared for Axehead in much the same manner, observing, 'I have already prepared for one op with fellow Canadians and when it did NOT [sic] go as planned there were great criticisms of the preparations. Then as now those charged with the tasks spared nothing to do them well.'[23]

Crerar wanted to ensure that link was understood. Lunching with Brooke on 9 June, they devised a plan to publicize the relationship between Dieppe and the success in Normandy. Who broached the idea is not clear, but they approached a military correspondent with the *Times* to write an article bringing out the connection. Brooke made the necessary arrangements and, at Crerar's suggestion, the correspondent was put in touch with C.P. Stacey.[24] To further shape the record, Crerar also sent Brooke copies of his memorandum reports on Exercise Pirate from October 1943, noting that the technique and tactics were employed at Normandy and, with tongue only partially in cheek, 'I feel that whatever now befalls, I can be marked down for at least one worth while contribution to the winning of the war.'[25]

III

During his D-Day address, Crerar had observed that First Canadian Army would take over the left sector of the beachhead, 'our move over commencing fairly soon.' He clung to the prediction that the Tac HQ would be phased in on D plus ten. He naively maintained that if the 'C-in-C ... require[d] the Army Commander's presence before that time he [could] fly over and remain at the C-in-C's TAC HQ until D plus 10.'[26] Montgomery, however, did not want Crerar or his headquarters in Normandy. He was not pleased when Crerar and his party arrived before he had summoned them.

Crerar and his Tactical HQ crossed the Channel 'in considerable style' aboard the RCN destroyer HMCS *Algonquin* on the morning of 18 June. Crerar had personally secured the Canadian naval vessel from Percy Nelles.[27] Mann, Anderson, Walford, Brownfield (BRA), Wright, and Pangman, to Montgomery's evident surprise, accompanied Crerar, a sign that he believed HQ First Canadian Army would soon be operational. They established camp in the small village of Amblie, east of Monty's HQ at Creully.[28] After notifying Monty of his arrival, Crerar was driven to 3rd Canadian Division headquarters to meet with Keller. The next day Crerar met with Montgomery and rehashed their 'respective responsibilities.' Crerar noted that the 'C-in-C seemed satisfied that the "air was properly cleared."'[29]

Crerar spent the next three days familiarizing himself with conditions on the Canadian front and visiting his brigadiers. He found all in 'great form and good heart – full of confidence in respect to future operations.'[30] Tours of the beaches, 2nd Canadian Armoured Brigade, various HQs, and commanders down to battalion level, and observations of the Caen front filled Crerar's agenda over the cold and windy days of late June. He flew to the United Kingdom daily to stay in touch with his Main HQ. Crerar had also dined with Dempsey and the corps commanders, querying them on operations and problems encountered thus far.

Through June, the Allies built up their forces, slowed by the destruction of one of two artificial 'Mulberry' harbours by a storm on 19 June. The main problem was the steady buildup of German armour and defences in front of the Anglo-Canadian forces as they fought their way towards Caen. While the Americans moved through the bocage to the south, the Germans sent three more SS Panzer divisions to reinforce the three already facing the Allies. The long-anticipated counterattack signalled by the arrival of the armoured reserve did not materialize, but Montgomery's successes, limited as they were, in Operation Epsom at the end of June, drew the German armour north. The Canadians were making steady but costly progress, enduring casualties reminiscent of the First World War as battles for towns like Villers-Bocage became the Mount Sorrel of a new generation.

Crerar was understandably anxious to gather the Canadian forces under First Canadian Army, but Montgomery dashed his expectations on 22 June when, at a conference to discuss the postponement of Epsom, the C-in-C. told the gathering that 'owing to the delay ... in the "build-up" and in the capture of Caen, and the securing of the line of the R[iver] Dives to the East, it was necessary to phase back the arrival of the Canadian Army until this situation had been attained.' Second British Army should be brought to full strength and 'elbow-room' created before another army could be concentrated. 'In view of the existing circumstances,' Monty informed the group, 'it might well be the middle of July before the phasing in of the Cdn Army was completed.'[31]

Crerar was surprised. Montgomery gave him no warning, and Dempsey had only just told him of his eagerness to have another army take operational responsibility for the eastern flank. Crerar approached Montgomery following the conference to relate his disappointment at the delay and was brusquely informed that the 'Master' had only that morning reached the decision that one army commander 'should complete [the] ... expansion of the bridgehead.'[32] Monty was possibly correct, but he was not telling Crerar the whole truth. He had written Leese ten days earlier that he had 'grave fears that Harry Crerar will not be good; however I am keeping him out of the party as long as I can.' 'Georgie Patton,' he added, 'may be a bit of a problem when he comes into it!'[33] Montgomery was also more nervous about the course of the battle for Caen than he was willing to admit. On 25 June, he forbade the production of 'after action' reports, fearful that honest assessments of the problems encountered by the British formations in Normandy would cause morale to drop.[34]

Crerar followed up his discussion with a note stating that he appreciated the 'sound operational reasons ... for the delay [and hoped] for a speedy solution to [the] present difficulties.' In response, Monty requested a meeting at which he repeated his reasoning; he also told Crerar that because he did not need more armour, the 4th Canadian and Guards armoured divisions would be 'phased back.' However, he offered hope that 2nd Canadian Corps could soon be deployed and that 2nd and 3rd Canadian Infantry Divisions would be grouped under Simonds's HQ. 'Following arrival of 2nd Cdn Corps,' Monty noted, 'he would then bring in HQ First Cdn Army and Cdn Army Trps.' On 26 June, he confirmed this sequence, cabling his chief of staff in response to a query, perhaps on behalf of Crerar, that 'I am not going to have Canadian Army HQ over here with all its Army troops until we really have enough room.'[35] There the matter stood; Dempsey would control five corps, including 2nd Canadian Corps.

For the remainder of the month of June, Crerar restlessly tried to maintain a feel for the battle in the bridgehead.[36] Main HQ First Canadian Army, unable to follow the Tac HQ because of the weather (and awakened to their position by a sharp rebuke in early July from HQ 21st Army Group following a misunderstanding over when they were to arrive), was forced to re-establish at Headley Court. The course of the campaign and Montgomery's decision precluded a systematic approach to integrating Canadian units under FCA.³⁷ From his Tac HQ, Crerar made frequent recce flights over 3rd Canadian Division's front, arranged meetings with British and American formation commanders in order to 'pick up valuable information on recent battles,' and oversaw the establishment of Simonds's Tac HQ from 29 June. He made periodic reports to Stuart at CMHQ, and also kept a close eye on the performance of division and brigade commanders in the Mediterranean as well as the overall standard of discipline. Ongoing policy issues such as the argument over operational responsibility with Montgomery and war establishments continued to dominate his schedule.

Crerar's attempts to oversee the battle were complicated by two concurrent and intertwined crises of British confidence in senior Canadian commanders. The first problem was the growing British dissatisfaction with Burns as CO of 1st Canadian Corps in Italy. The second problem was prompted by British complaints regarding 3rd Canadian Division's Major-General Keller's competence and their desire that he be replaced as commander of the division. Crerar's responsibilities placed him squarely in the centre of these command problems, which were complicated by the fact that Keller was considered the most likely replacement for Burns.

Burns's problem with his British superiors was rooted in the British dissatisfaction with the formation of an operationally unnecessary Canadian corps in the Italian theatre; it was not the only problem, however.³⁸ The catalyst in June was a report by Oliver Leese, GOC Eighth British Army, and his schizophrenic approach to the Canadian Corps. On Burns's assumption of command, Leese had observed, 'He'll be very good,' despite characterizing some corps HQ staff personnel as 'old women' and 'classroom men.'³⁹ Through April and May, Leese evinced confidence in Burns, noting in his reports to the DMO Sir John Kennedy, 'The Canadians under Burns are developing into a very fine Corps. He is an excellent commander ... He also gets on better [than Crerar] with the Divisional generals.' Even as operations to break the Hitler Line and take Rome began, and the corps' inexperience made itself felt, Leese noted, 'They ... are improving daily.' He wrote Crerar on 28 May, praising the 'great achievements of the Canadian Corps under Burns in the recent battle.'⁴⁰ Nevertheless, some days after the end of the battle, Leese decided to pull 1st Canadian Corps out of the line and expressed some dissatisfaction with Burns to Alexander. Alexander related Leese's concerns regarding Burns to Brooke, observing that he felt that the Canadian Corps' commander was 'sadly lacking in tactical sense ... has very little personality and no, repeat no, power of command.' Alexander argued that this placed Leese in an awkward situation because his reservations denied him the full use of one corps HQ, leaving his army sadly unbalanced. Alexander suggested that the only alternatives were to replace Burns, although he knew of no suitable Canadians, or disband the corps, observing that with 'a Canadian Army operating in France I should think that Canadian national amour propre would be satisfied.'[41]

Alexander rarely had such firm opinions. Brooke believed he was a proxy for Leese and aimed his reply to Alexander in Leese's direction.[42] In some ways, Oliver Leese was the author of Burns's misfortune in that he had ordered the two corps to advance, as he admitted to Kennedy, despite the fact that the 'main obstacle in the Hitler Line has a very limited number of crossing places, and it proved very difficult to get divisions across quickly.' Both 13 British Corps and 1st Canadian Corps 'had difficulty getting across the Hitler Line,' he added. But in mid-June Leese also expressed the opinion that in spite of his reservations about Burns, with a new BGS, 'encouragement, teaching and training they will improve.'[43]

Brooke, however, was wrong. Alexander's proposal went much further than that written by Leese, who admitted, 'I realise there is no one who can succeed Burns' and thus have to teach him. Alexander wanted the corps dissolved; indeed, he had nursed a grudge towards the corps as strong as Montgomery's since its arrival in the Mediterranean. After being presented with a *fait accompli* with the Corps HQ's arrival, Alexander's mood was not improved by the pressure in January to get the corps HQ into battle to give Crerar some operational experience. Finally, his concerns about Burns's inexperience and his suggestion that Simonds take over were rebuffed.[44] Burns and the corps' apparent problems provided him with an opportunity to set things right.

Crerar had been kept apprised of 1st Canadian Corps operations. Burns gave him the 'inside dope concerning the performance of his senior commanders and staff.' Crerar also insisted on official and periodic reports from CMHQ.[45] When the issue of Burns's abilities blew up, Crerar's responsibilities required him to stay in England, so Stuart was dispatched in early July to the Mediterranean in response to Alexander's wire. In personal discussions on 2 July, and in writing, Crerar provided Stuart with the framework for his investigation. He discerned the roots of the problem: 'the Englishman's traditional belief in the superiority of the Englishman ... [and] the "military inconvenience," if nothing less, of restrictions on the complete interchangeability of formations, units, etc, under a higher command.' He continued: 'In practice, this means that no Canadian, or American, or other "national commander," unless possessing quite phenomenal qualities, is ever rated as high as an equivalent Britisher. It also means that, to a British Army Comd such as Leese ... the existence of a Canadian higher formation, such as a Corps, is a distinctly troublesome factor.'[46]

After noting that the existence of Canadian higher formations had troubled senior British commanders since the First World War, Crerar laid out Stuart's fact-finding agenda. Under no circumstances should the breakup of the corps be countenanced. Rather, Crerar noted, under the proper conditions, he would like to see it reunited with First Canadian Army. In addition to pursuing reunification of Canadian formations, Stuart should also evaluate whether Burns was as tactically and personally incompetent as Alexander and Leese believed or if the problem lay, as Crerar suspected, with Leese's shortcomings. Burns's subordinates should also be interviewed for their opinions. If Burns held their confidence, then Alexander and Leese must be persuaded 'to temper their present views' and perhaps strengthen Burns's position by the loan of 'one, or more, battle-experienced British Staff Officers.' However, if Stuart found Burns wanting and 'the joining of 1 Cdn Corps with Cdn Army ... impractical, then Keller is a prospective "bet."' Crerar, however, had reservations about Keller, noting that while he was 'the only battle-experienced Cdn Div Comd who would be considered for this ... I would like to see more of his work in the field before coming to a firm conclusion.' Crerar also warned that as a result of a 'change in Canadian high command ... The controversy in Canada [could be] acute and ... very far-reaching, indeed.'[47]

While Stuart journeyed to Italy to settle the issue, the British command in Normandy acted on the growing doubts they harboured regarding Keller. He had already garnered a bad reputation, with rumours circulating among his senior brigadiers that the strain of the Normandy battles was turning him to the bottle. Dempsey had also cautioned him on 8 June on 'the importance of getting his artillery and armour under control.'[48] The attack by 3rd Canadian Division against Carpiquet, poorly supported and ordered by 1 British Corps, on 4 July 1944 set the British in motion.[49] The Canadians captured the village, beating off 'several counter-attacks,' but were unable to secure the adjacent well-defended airfield, the real objective of Operation Windsor. 'On the RIGHT [the airfield] the operation was not well handled,' Second British Army GOC General Sir Miles Dempsey noted in his diary, only the second criticism of 3rd Canadian Division operations since D-

Day.⁵⁰ However, 1 British Corps GOC Lieutenant-General John T. Crocker responded to this incomplete success by writing Dempsey of his concerns about Keller. He credited Keller with the division's early successes, but observed that it had now 'lapsed into a very nervy state.' Allowing for the division's inexperience, Crocker nevertheless believed that Keller was not providing 'a steadying hand.' The CO, he continued 'was obviously not standing up to the strain and showed signs of fatigue and nervousness (some might almost say fright) which were patent for all to see.' The attack on Carpiquet only confirmed Crocker's doubts that Keller was unfit mentally and physically – 'he ... has the appearance of having lived pretty well' – for command.⁵¹ Dempsey agreed with Crocker's assessment – 'It will never be a good Division so long as Major-General Keller commands it' – and forwarded Crocker's letter to Monty. Montgomery also agreed and forwarded the matter to Crerar, but in an uncharacteristically diplomatic turn observed, 'I have given orders that no official action is to be taken ... [as 3rd Division] will be put into the 2nd Cdn Corps in a day or two and I would prefer that any official action ... should be taken by Canadian generals.'⁵²

Of course, Montgomery was clear that he expected the Canadians to remove Keller. On 7 July, he made this understanding known to Brooke in a long letter, which began with a diatribe against Eisenhower's failure to allow Montgomery to run the whole show, against Dempsey's failure to grasp the essentials of air power, and generally against all the inferior generals it was his burden to train in the art of war. 'I am not too happy about the Canadians,' he continued. 'Keller has proven himself to be quite unfit to command a division; he is unable to get the best out of his soldiers – who are grand chaps.' He was willing, however, to let the Canadians get rid of Keller themselves. Monty also used the opportunity to undermine Crerar:

> Harry Crerar once suggested to me that Keller would be the next for a Corps. The idea is quite absurd ... I fear very much that Harry Crerar will be quite unfit to command an Army; I am keeping him out of it as long as I can. He is a most awfully nice chap, but he is very prosy and stodgy, and he is very definitely not a commander ... He commanded the 1st Cdn Corps for two years, and when it went into battle in Italy the Corps HQ proved to be quite untrained – or so Oliver Leese tells me.⁵³

Leese's assertion was untrue. Crerar was reserving judgment, if at all possible, on Keller. It was a ridiculous charge in any case; several of

Montgomery's choices proved fallible when exposed in operations, including Lieutenant-General G. Bucknall, GOC of 30 British Corps. Brooke had no faith in Bucknall, and told Montgomery, who replied he 'had full confidence in him.'[54] Montgomery was also more generous with the replacement he chose for 7th British Armoured Division in August; he was given until mid-November, despite doubts about his capabilities, because Monty believed he should 'be given a fair trial.'[55] Even Dempsey was criticized.

Coming directly on the heels of the criticism of Burns, the British desire to remove another senior Canadian officer smacked of chauvinism, particularly to Crerar and Stuart. It also destroyed any chance of forwarding Keller as a potential replacement for Burns. The problem blew up on 9 July when Keller, unaware of the precariousness of his position, contacted Army HQ to report that he wanted the CO of 9th Canadian Infantry Brigade replaced, a move that still required ministerial approval. An exasperated Crerar moved quickly, but carefully. Crerar instructed Simonds to determine Keller's suitability for 'his high responsibilities as a Canadian Divisional Commander,' keeping in mind that 'Crocker's handling of Keller [may not have] brought out the best in the latter.' Once Simonds arrived at an opinion on Keller, he could take action on the 9th Brigade CO if, and only if, Simonds shared Keller's assessment. 'In coming to your conclusions,' Crerar concluded, 'you will ... give weight to the fact that neither of these officers ... has had previous battle experience – and that first experience has been about as trying as you can imagine.'[56]

Crerar's frustration with the British was more apparent as he related the latest twist to Stuart. 'While I have been most careful to avoid seeming interference in the present British-Canadian chain of command,' he wrote, 'I have something more than the impression that Crocker has not been beyond reproach, from the Canadian point of view.' He believed that Crocker tended to 'talk direct to the Brigadiers,' by-passing the Divisional Commander, in part, because 'Cunningham [the brigade commander] was the "white-haired boy" with Crocker ... before the assault.' Crocker's interference, Crerar implied, may also have been at the root of Keller's problems with Cunningham. And Crocker's failure to observe the chain of command was a sore point.[57]

The problem was potentially disastrous: the Canadian army was not in a position to replace two senior commanders. Simonds's report on his meetings with Keller and Cunningham served to exacerbate the precarious balancing act now forced on Crerar. Keller, surprised and upset when informed of the British opinion, responded that 'in any event he did not feel that his health was good enough to stand the heavy strain and asked that he be medically boarded as he felt that he would be found to be unfit.' A shocked Simonds convinced him to reconsider, but Keller's dejection served to confirm rather than dispel doubts surrounding his capacity for continued command. While Crerar felt that 'Simonds handled both Keller and Cunningham very sensibly,' and the problem was 'in better shape,' he noted to Stuart, 'I am not sure at all of Keller being able to last the course and I certainly would not now consider him for higher responsibility.'[58]

This might have proven a greater dilemma except that Stuart had sorted out the command problems in the Mediterranean along the lines that Crerar had suggested. In confidential discussions with Leese, Alexander, the COs of 1st Canadian and 5th Canadian Armoured Division, as well as the senior staff at corps HQ, Stuart was convinced that Burns should be given another chance. The senior Canadian commanders all 'expressed themselves as being quite happy to go into the next operation under Burns and all expressed confidence in his ability to make sound tactical decisions.' Stuart also pointed out to Leese that his 'first impression ... after the operation was that, in spite of the errors made, Burns could make a success of the Canadian Corps and you informed him to this effect.' Stuart charged that Leese's change of heart was puzzling. Following Crerar's lead, he chastised Leese for emphasizing personality over intelligence. Stuart observed that the corps had a new BGS and had had a chance to reflect on its experience, and all were anxious to resume operations. Leese was wrong, he asserted, if he believed the Canadians would be happy with a British CO. The bottom line was that Burns should be given another chance and the corps should be 'moved out of [the] present training area ... otherwise the morale of the Corps was apt to be adversely effected.'[59]

Crerar was relieved that Stuart had 'succeeded in pouring oil on the troubled Canadian waters in the AAI ... a most difficult situation which, incidentally, I believe is a passing one.' His faith in Burns was undiminished. Stuart, on his return to the United Kingdom, immediately flew to Normandy and was debriefed on the events of the past two weeks. He was back in London in time for dinner.[60]

Crerar would have been less satisfied if he had known that the successes were partially due to behind the scenes lobbying by the CIGS, efforts that were aimed as much at securing Crerar's position as they were at stabilizing the Canadian command. Brooke shared Crerar's concerns over the spate of criticisms of Canadian senior command; he also realized that they undermined Crerar's position by prompting doubts regarding his judgment, or, in Montgomery's case, confirming them. His determination to keep Crerar out of operations as long as he could was evident from his letter of 7 July. In response, Brooke admonished Montgomery, 'I am very worried about what you say about Keller of 3rd Can Div. It is evident that the Canadians are very short of senior Commanders, but it is equally clear that we shall have to make the best of the material we have.' Brooke noted that the Canadians would *'insist'* [his emphasis] on their own commanders. 'For that reason,' he continued,

> I want you to make the best possible use of Crerar, he must be retained in Command of the Canadian Army, and must be given his Canadians under his command at the earliest possible moment. You can keep his army small and give him the less important role, and you will have to teach him. We had the same trouble in the last war and had to replace Byng by Currie although the latter was a very medium commander.[61]

Brooke, as he often did, approached Monty with tenderness unwarranted by the situation. In a more strongly worded letter to Alexander, Brooke somewhat unfairly criticized Leese's lack of understanding of 'the true position of Canadian Forces, and conditions connected with their employment.' In Brooke's mind, the 'political and national feeling is so strong that it is quite useless going against it ... and it is up to us to *train* [their commanders] and make the best of them.' Burns should be given 'a *real* trial' and suitably trained for command of a corps. 'From what I hear from many sides,' he added, 'I am not convinced that this is impossible.' He went on to criticize Leese's command for an 'impression of stickiness and lack of thrust,' laying part of the blame at Alexander's door.[62]

Brooke's advances had their effect, although he did not know this for some days. Alexander and Leese were muffled. Montgomery backtracked, adopting an operational rationale for keeping Crerar's army out of the battle; nevertheless, his personal feelings crept into his justification.

> Do not worry about [the Canadians]. All Canadian troops are now under Canadian command ... It would be definitely wrong at this stage to introduce another army ... into the British sector ... When I hand over a sector to

Crerar I will certainly teach him his stuff, and I shall give him tasks within his capabilities. And I shall watch over him carefully. I have great personal affection for him, but this must not lead me into doing unsound things. I only wanted to make it clear to you that the Canadian senior commanders are not very good. They have some good officers, but their top commanders are bad judges of men – and Harry Crerar is no exception, and does not know what a good soldier is.[63]

IV

The gradual, and costly, enlargement of the Allied bridgehead in July prepared the way for First Canadian Army's deployment on the Continent. Simonds's Tac HQ opened at Amblie on 29 June; his Main HQ was stationed near Monty's Tac HQ at Camilly a week later. Commanded by Major-General Charles Foulkes, 2nd Canadian Division began its disembarkation two days later on 7 July. Caen became the central focus of Second British Army operations. After it fell to 1 British Corps in Operation Charnwood on 8–9 July, Montgomery's strategic purpose evolved to sustaining offensive operations to retain the bulk of the German armour on the Anglo-Canadian front, allowing the First U.S. Army to develop operations to clear the Cherbourg peninsula and break out to the Seine, west of Paris.

Montgomery issued a directive to this effect on 10 July. 'It is important,' it read, 'to speed up our advance on the western flank; the operations of the Second [British] Army must therefore be so staged that they will have a direct influence on the operations of the First [U.S.] Army, as well as holding enemy forces on the eastern flank.' The directive also described the future position of First Canadian Army:

> First Canadian Army will study to what extent command of this eastward front so transferred ... could be exercised at an early date with comparatively limited resources in Army troops. The result of these studies will be reported verbally to me; meanwhile no action will be taken as to phasing forward units of First Canadian Army HQ or Army troops until I have further considered the problem.[64]

The latter point was aimed at blunting Crerar's desire to establish his HQ. Montgomery had been spooked a few days earlier, on 3 July, by rumours that First Canadian Army's Main and Rear HQ had arrived in the bridgehead. In the early evening, he phoned Crerar and voiced his concern. A surprised Crerar promised to investigate and reported in a lengthy letter the next day that elements of the Main HQ, as part of the preparations for moving to the Continent, had simply notified 21st Army Group of their move to the marshalling area. Crerar felt it necessary to conclude with a confirmation that he was prepared to 'play the game,' a hint that Monty needn't be overly worried about Crerar asserting his prerogatives as Canadian commander – and that Montgomery was worried. Crerar confirmed this concern when the two met on 7 July to discuss the arrival of 2nd Canadian Division.[65] Following their meeting, Monty wrote his letter to Brooke noting his desire to keep Crerar out of the battle as long as he could.

Montgomery's directive came before Brooke's stern rejoinder and, with regards to First Canadian Army, was superseded by events. However, Operations Goodwood and the 2nd Canadian Corps ancillary Operation Atlantic, 18–21 July, materially changed the situation and marked the beginning of a new phase of operations that would, over the next month, destroy the German armies in Normandy.

Crerar had no direct responsibility for these operations. He met with Simonds several times to discuss issues of operational responsibility, 'tactical points,' and 'problems of Higher Comd.' It was evident, however, that Crerar was simply relating Montgomery's latest directive on the first, and he deferred to Simonds's experience. If his notes on these discussions are any indication, and they were admittedly written for government information, Crerar's main focus was the problems with Keller and Burns. Simonds focused on analyzing and overcoming the tactical problems encountered thus far in the Normandy battles. On 1 July he issued a 'Lessons Learned' memorandum for dissemination to his corps that underlined how to best effect the artillery-based operational methods used by the British army.[66] After the 2nd Canadian Corps took over a section of the line from 8 British Corps on 11 July and began fighting its first battles, Crerar drove across the fronts, observing the advances and visiting HQs. He felt further removed from the fighting without his Vigilant aircraft since the crash on 3 July.

Crerar still exercised his power of command in matters of troop discipline. In early July, concerned with the deportment of the Canadian soldiers he had encountered, he had warned Simonds and Keller to enforce regulations. On 11 July, he received an 'informal report' from the Senior Civil Affairs Officer (SCAO), First Canadian Army, on the conduct of troops, which implied increasing incidence of looting, theft, and 'misbehaviour towards inhabitants.' Crerar forwarded the report to Simonds, stressing the 'serious implications' of the problem and observing that he believed the root lay in 'poor control and administration by the Commander or Commanding Officer of the individuals involved.' He wanted firm actions taken against both.[67]

The disciplinary crackdown continued for several days. Two days later, prompted it appears by the 'exhaustion crisis' he saw developing as he visited Casualty Clearing stations, talked to the patients and COs, and had an evening discussion with his artillery commander, Crerar sent Simonds a copy of a letter previously sent to Burns. It detailed the army commander's views on the general problem of 'the natural, but in the circumstances of war, reprehensible objection of a small proportion of other ranks ... to risk death, or serious injury for their country.'[68] He included in this group the actions of 'desertion, self-inflicted wounds, attempts to be diagnosed as "exhaustion cases," V-D reinfection and so on.' To combat these cases, Crerar urged that discipline be tightened, punishment be severe, and all ranks be 'educated' that 'escapism' was 'a shameful thing.' In Italy, he had been shocked at the tendency to leave behind any soldiers deemed 'unreliable.' Following the battles of attrition in Normandy, and with Canada's manpower limits in mind after recent discussions on war establishments, Crerar was particularly concerned with limiting the number of men diagnosed with '"exhaustion neurosis."' Though he believed that a 'pretty high proportion of the cases' that were hospitalized were 'real nervous breakdowns,' he harshly attributed the neurosis to 'unstable mental characters.' He also believed that because it was 'not considered a disgrace to be an "exhaustion case"' it was a great temptation for slackers to 'seek this way out.' He urged that the 'administrative sieve ... be so close that the fake exhaustion case should be detected and held ... [and] suitably punished.'[69] Simonds, of like mind, responded with a crackdown and exhortations to greater efforts and discipline.

The senior commanders' problems were less easily redefined out of existence. Keller was now a marked man in the eyes of the Canadians as well as the British. The British tried one last time on 19 July to have him removed. While observing the 5 Canadian Infantry Brigade's attack on Fleury-Sur-Orne in Operation Atlantic, Crerar was summoned to Monty's HQ with the message that the CIGS would like to see him within the hour. Brooke, who was not aware that Stuart had resolved, at least temporarily, the situation in Italy, was determined to make progress in addressing these command issues. When Crerar informed him that Leese 'had agreed that Burns should be given' a second chance, Brooke expressed relief particularly since 'he gathered that ... Keller had not proved himself a suitable substitute.' Crerar promptly launched into a defence of the Canadian senior command. He pointed out the possibility that the British mishandled their commanders and the Canadian senior commands lack of battle experience was 'no fault' of their own – a backhand to McNaughton. He also voiced his disappointment, 'from the national point of view,' in the delay in transferring a sector to First Canadian Army, although he understood the operational reasons. Crerar probably suspected the other reasons. Brooke deflected this reproach, assuring Crerar that 'this difficult situation would not continue much longer.'

Following tea, Brooke departed. Montgomery, however, was not finished with Crerar. He showed him a memorandum he had prepared that raised 'directly with General Dempsey the continued fitness to command of Maj-Gen Keller, asking General Dempsey to obtain a report from GOC 2 Cdn Corps on this matter at an early date.' Clearly dissatisfied with Crerar's actions, Montgomery hoped to do something about Keller while Simonds remained under the operational command of Second British Army. In light of the operational situation, he noted that he was simply 'calling for this report in the normal way.' If both Simonds and Dempsey backed Keller, he 'would have nothing further to say' except that he was 'convinced that ... Keller was not up to the required standard.' Crerar concluded the meeting by admitting that while he could not object to Montgomery's methods, which were technically correct, only he could initiate any action 'that might be required' concerning Canadian command. That said, Crerar departed for his Tac HQ.[70] Crerar was not at this point predisposed to make allowances for the British.

As if to underline Crerar's broad-ranging responsibilities, the command problems were addressed simultaneously with the decision to establish First Canadian Army HQ. The next day, in the late afternoon, Crerar was summoned to Montgomery's Tac HQ so he could be given 'information and instructions concerning [his] future responsibilities.' Arriving by car, Crerar was forced to wait while until dinner was over before he was given the details of Montgomery's plans. The C-in-C stated that his strategy remained as stated in his 10 July directive – 'to secure and hold Caen and bridgehead east of the River Orne securely while US Army operates strongly Southward,' pivoting on its left to the south and east while clearing the Brittany Peninsula. 'To further this policy,' continued Montgomery, 'Second Brit Army would take over frontages now held by left two US Divs, of V Corps, commencing Sunday 23 July.' First Canadian Army would thus assume responsibility for far left flank with 1 British Corps under command, if possible, by noon on 22 July. The 2nd Canadian Corps would remain with Second British Army until present operations were concluded. The Tac HQ would remain small, with an increment of approximately one hundred personnel to make it operational, as Monty, 'in view of the very limited movement involved ... did not want any more Cdn Army HQ, or Army Troops, brought in than the problem presently called for.' A full-scale buildup would be gradual. The first operation would be 'to secure (or dominate) line of R Muance, R Dives and ... render Caen Canal of some use to us and deprive enemy of Cabourg-Houlgate utility.'[71] On 23 July, First Canadian Army, Lieutenant-General H.D.G. Crerar commanding, became operational.

17 The Normandy Campaign

I

First Canadian Army became operational at the beginning of some of the most intense fighting of the war in northwest Europe. The German armies in Normandy were disintegrating but continued to inflict heavy casualties on the Allies. With the German collapse in late August, the largely static conditions of the Normandy front rapidly devolved into a pursuit of the remnants of their armies. Crerar never grasped full control of the battles of August, in part because his experience was outpaced by the rapidity of events, and in part because, for better or worse, Montgomery (and Simonds) never loosened their grip.

First Canadian Army HQ became operational on 23 July 1944, commanding 1 British Corps. On 20 July, Montgomery and Crerar had outlined the procedure for preparing the headquarters for its introduction to battle. Clearly, the C-in-C remained leery of Crerar and his HQ. On the 21st, Anderson, Wright, and Pangman were sat down with their opposite numbers from 21st Army Group HQ and grilled to ensure they understood the basics of the task before them. 'Apparently we got good marks,' recalled Pangman. 'We became operational.'[1]

Crerar compared his first days as commander of an operational army to his early days as corps commander in Italy. On returning to his Tac HQ, he met with Mann and Walford to relate the timing of phasing in the rest of the headquarters. After the required personnel were flown in, arrangements were to be initiated to move the men and vehicles of 4th Canadian Armoured Division and complete the '1000 vehicle' buildup of First Canadian Army HQ. The 84 Group's Tac HQ was still in England and could not yet, according to Montgomery, be accommodated in the bridgehead. As an interim measure, two operations officers provided liaison with the Tac Air HQ of Air Vice-Marshall Harry Broadhurst's 83 Group, supporting Dempsey's army. They were informed of the situation the next morning. Early on the 21st, Crerar telephoned Dempsey to discuss the details of the proposed takeover; these were confirmed later in the afternoon over tea at Dempsey's Second British Army HQ.[2]

Crerar soon learned that his inexperience would work against him. On 22 July, following his discussions with Dempsey and Montgomery, Crerar prepared an operational and tactical directive for Lieutenant-General J.T. Crocker, GOC of 1 British Corps, a 'blood plain innocuous' document as described by George Pangman, which advocated a limited attack in order to partially fulfill Montgomery's operational directions of 21 July to 'ensure that all territory to the west of the river is dominated by our troops.'[3] Prefaced by a three-page summary of a German armoured division's analysis of its operational experience through most of June, it drew liberally on Crerar's 14 May address to the senior commanding officers and staff of First Canadian Army. Although many of the points made in May were relevant to the fighting encountered in Normandy, it was not the type of general tactical advice that an experienced commander would appreciate from an inexperienced colonial.[4]

Crerar informed the corps commander that First Canadian Army's immediate task, as outlined by Montgomery, was 'to advance its left flank Eastward so that Ouistreham will cease to be under close enemy observation and fire, and so that use can be made of the Port of Caen.' The directive also detailed the operational objectives Crerar believed necessary to secure this immediate objective: the approaches to the town of Troarn and the 'general line of the road which runs from Breville ... through Le Marais ... to the road junction of Le Petit Homme' were considered crucial; seizing Troarn and the high ground east of the River Dives, necessary to bring First Canadian Army right up to the banks of the river, were considered optional if they could be acquired with minimal casualties. Crerar believed, however, that the 'resources now at disposal [did] not permit any such large scale operation' as required by the latter objective. He sent Crocker several copies of this 'Tactical Directive' with the intent that it be distributed to his subordinates.

Crerar, slightly ill from a chill he had caught the previous day, and accompanied by Mann, visited Crocker's HQ to discuss the operation. He and Crocker, an experienced but 'stern and humourless commander,' had had problems in the past.[5] These were precipitated by the parallel development and testing of 'ideas on tactics, equipment and training' by Crerar's 1st Canadian Corps and 1 British Corps, commanded by Lieutenant-General G.C. Bucknall until Crocker's appointment in the fall of 1943. Bucknall, having been charged with training and equipping his corps for a seaborne assault and testing assault techniques, was already engaged in an informal rivalry with 1st Canadian Corps as it studied the same problems, which culminated with Exercise Pirate when Crocker took command. Whatever the extent of the rivalry, Crerar took great pains to secure credit for developing the assault techniques for himself and the Canadians, a factor that undoubtedly contributed to what Crerar described as the dour Crocker's resentment of the 'competition.'[6]

In the 1950s, Crerar asked Stacey to keep that episode out of the official histories, but noted that he believed that it made Crocker 'somewhat hostile to the idea of coming under my command in Normandy.'[7] Stacey and others observed, however, that Crerar's lack of operational experience in high command and his concerns over Crocker's handling of the Canadians also contributed to their strained encounter. Neither was 1 British Corps and its commander enthused over the arrival of the inexperienced army HQ, whatever its nationally. G.E. Beament noted that even from the staff perspective it 'was very rocky start with 1 British Corps.' He recalled that during this reasonably quiet period the corps would 'try us on [with] a series of questions, silly questions ... seeking an answer in the middle of the night ... It was really quite funny.'[8]

Crocker did not share his staff's sense of humour. He greeted Crerar's directive, and his arrival at his HQ, with disdain, informing an 'astonished' Crerar that the operation was definitely 'not on.' Crocker considered that neither clearing the enemy from the Caen Canal nor a small-scale attack with his limited resources would be useful, and would only result in unnecessary casualties. The resulting extended front, and Ouistreham, would still be within range of the German artillery and mortars east of the River Dives. In addition, the state of his divisions was such that he could not commit them to these actions. Crerar asked the GOC, 1 British Corps, to put his objections in writing and left.

Crocker reiterated his points in a written memorandum and requested that the proposed limited operation be reconsidered, stating that he was not prepared to take personal responsibility for carrying it out. As an alternative, he proposed a larger two-step operation on a divisional scale with full air and ground support to first capture Troarn and

Bures, followed with a set-piece advance on a broad front, supported by air, to the line 'Bavent-Gonneville-Merville, with exploitation to Varaville and towards Cabourg.' This plan was strange, in view of his description of the limits on his resources. And he did not explain how this operation to enlarge the bridgehead from the River Orne would remove his troops from dangers of enemy fire east of the River Dives unless he envisaged his 'exploitation' as a continuous advance, a movement that, by extending 1 British Corps front, neither economized forces nor supported the future operations as envisaged by Montgomery.[9]

Upon receiving Crocker's memorandum, Crerar sent it to Montgomery along with his own memorandum detailing his objections, in light of Montgomery's orders, to Crocker's operational proposals and a cover letter containing his interpretation of the 1 British Corps commander's actions. In essence, the army commander asserted that the limited operation would fulfill Montgomery's objective of freeing the Caen Canal and Ouistreham from enemy observation and fire; it was, in Crerar's view, 'obvious only a limited operation, and not a full scale attack involving a division ... can be attempted.'[10] Given that the 1 British Corps had just three infantry divisions under command – the 3rd Canadian (just out of Goodwood), 49th, and 51st – and could call on the 6th Airborne, it would presumably want air support. Crocker soon requested such support 'on the scale of "Goodwood,"' which involved almost 1,600 heavy bombers as well as light and medium aircraft. The operations Crocker envisaged were far larger than time or resources permitted.[11]

Crerar believed that more than disagreements over tactics and objectives informed Crocker's objections. 'Crocker gave me the immediate impression,' he wrote to Montgomery, 'at the commencement of the interview that he resented being placed under my command and receiving any direction from me.' He was unsure whether this 'attitude [was] personal, or because of the fact that I am a Canadian – but it certainly showed itself' in that Crocker was tactless and showed no inclination to discuss the operations with Crerar. His assessment was probably correct, but he overreacted, requesting that Montgomery replace Crocker with either Bucknall, his former GSO 2 at RMC, or Ritchie, a colleague from his War Office days in the 1920s, because he was 'quite convinced that Crocker is temperamentally unsuited to be one of my Corps Comds ... He does not like the position.'[12]

Montgomery immediately hauled Crerar up before him and, despite Crerar's characterization of Monty's 'very friendly and helpful manner,' told him that 'the situation had ... been caused by the manner in which [he] had handled an operational requirement with a somewhat difficult subordinate who had just come under [his] command.' Monty advised Crerar that he should seek to induce Crocker to 'see' his plans rather than order him to carry them out. He also made it clear that it was impossible to tie his hands operationally by transferring Crocker, both because of the potential problems that would result from the sudden change of command and because future operations might dictate that Crocker's corps come under First Canadian Army command, whether he was removed or not.

Montgomery was right, of course, and Crerar admitted that he 'had not given full weight to this prospective situation.' Still, he persisted in his view that Crocker would be a problem. When Monty suggested that the two meet and go over the tactical problem so Crerar could convince the British Corps commander to 'think [his] way,' the Canadian army commander resisted; rather, he asked Montgomery to convince Crocker to accept him 'wholeheartedly ... as his operational Army Commander' and to 'confirm ... that, in fact, what was urgently wanted was the clearance of Ouistreham and the Caen Canal from close enemy observation and mortar fire ... along the lines of my instructions to him.'[13]

Montgomery met Crocker, informing him that both he and his staff must be loyal to First Canadian Army and its commander. He told Crerar of his meeting by letter the next day; he also warned Crerar on several points regarding army command, points suggesting that Crocker's dissatisfaction stemmed from a perception that Crerar was overstepping his boundaries as Crocker's superior. 'An Army Commander,' Monty began, 'should give his Corps Commanders a task, and leave it to them as to how they do it.' He clarified his meaning two paragraphs later, observing that the army commander must 'stand back from the tactical battle; that part is the province of his Corps Commanders.' Montgomery made it clear that it was how Crerar had related his orders as much as the contents of the orders themselves that had caused the problem. He told Crerar he must cut down on paper in the field; he would get 'the best results' by dealing verbally with his corps commanders. 'I suggest it would be a good thing,' he continued,

> to tell Crocker that you sent him several copies of your Tactical Directive only in case he wanted to send them on to his subordinates ... I may add that the action that you took in this matter is definitely contrary to my wishes; I consider that *in the field* it is wrong to send tactical directives to

anyone except your immediate subordinates – so *they* are responsible to you, and *their* subordinates are responsible to *them*; ... If you inform Crocker as I suggest, I am sure it will help to ease the situation.

For emphasis, Monty repeated the message in a postscript. 'When an Army Comdr.,' he wrote, 'has only one Corps in his Army he will, unless he is careful, find that he is trying to command that Corps himself in detail; ... he has not enough to do, and he is inclined to become involved in details which are the province of his subordinates.' He concluded, 'It is not easy; but let us see if you can pull it off.' A handwritten addition with assurances that Crerar could 'pull it off,' asking that he take the advice 'in the spirit in which it was meant' and with hopes that it would not 'upset our friendship' suggested that Montgomery, or someone close to him, realized that he may have gone too far. In a hurriedly written note, Crerar replied that their friendship 'was never firmer.'

Montgomery disagreed. 'Harry Crerar has started off his career as an Army Comd,' he wrote Brooke,

> by thoroughly upsetting everyone; he had a row with Crocker the first day, and asked me to remove Crocker. I have spent two days trying to restore peace; investigating the quarrel, and so on. As always, there are faults on both sides. But the basic cause was Harry; I fear he thinks he is a great soldier and he was determined to show it the very moment he took over command at 1200 hrs on 23 July. He made his first mistake at 1205 hrs; and his second after lunch. I have had each of them to see me – separately of course.
>
> I have told Harry in quite clear terms that in my opinion the basic fault lies with him, in this quarrel. I have seen Crocker, and told him he must play 100%.

In a postscript appended to an enclosed copy of Crerar's response, Montgomery added, 'I hope this now ends the matter, and that Harry will sail ahead on an even keel!!'[14]

Montgomery missed two crucial points. First, the issue resulted from, and reflected, the ambiguities of Crerar's position as an army commander in an army group with a C-in-C determined to control operations and issue operational and tactical directives. Monty was able to exercise operational control through 21st Army Group's distribution of resources and formations to his respective armies (First Canadian Army and Second British Army), access to SHAEF, and command of 2nd Tactical Air Force. He was also personally inclined to seize control of operations with detailed tactical suggestions for operational responsibilities, nominally those of his army commanders; with Crerar, as already noted, he issued instructions on how to distribute orders. Dempsey's command was similarly interfered with; in the early stages of the Normandy battles, Montgomery strongly 'advised' Dempsey on divisional groupings within corps, divisional responsibilities and objectives, as well as which corps should lead attacks.[15] The Chief of Staff of 21st Army Group, deGuingand, wrote that Montgomery liked to control the battle, keeping a tight rein on his subordinates. He also observed that he had to allow Crerar, as a Dominion commander, greater flexibility in his army and formations.[16] That wasn't true.

Montgomery's initiatives in planning and strategy left the army commander with the responsibilities for control of the tactical air, administration, supply, and general tactical planning. Crerar wanted to work at this last level with his corps commander. Crerar sent the same tactical directive to Simonds; his emphasis on getting the infantry through the German's prearranged zones of defensive fire anticipated that 2nd Canadian Corps would soon be called upon to break the stalemate imposed by the enemy's 'well-prepared defences.' His modest efforts at tactical analysis were, however, stymied and chastised by both his superior and subordinate. Their reactions were one factor limiting Crerar's role in the operations of his army from the outset and would inform his approach for several months.

II

That Crerar was cowed by Crocker's reaction is surprising. His defence of his command prerogatives was characteristic, but his desire that Montgomery alone straighten out the situation was not. His reaction marked the beginning of a period in command during which Crerar's health caused his control of his HQ to slip slowly, but significantly. His reliance on Simonds and his staff for tactical and operational initiatives in the battles of July and early September has been well documented; Crerar's inexperience was credited as the main reason. While it was a factor, it was not the only one.

Crerar was not a healthy man. Severe anemia had resulted from successive bouts of dysentery. Two of these attacks had come while he was in the Mediterranean: the first in Sicily soon after his arrival, the second over the winter in Italy, the 'gyppy tummy' severe enough that he had elaborated on it in his correspondence, an unusual occurrence even for the fussy Crerar. The attacks in Italy had responded to the standard treatment of sulphaguanidine. In the middle of June, he was again racked by dysentery; this time it did not respond to treatment and it reoccurred at least five more times before Crerar was forced to give up command of the army. From late June, by his own account, he was bothered by abdominal pain and stomach distress. The severity grew and the impact was more marked as he noticed 'some shortness of breath on exertion, that he perspired easily on exertion, ... [experienced] an abnormal degree of fatigue and a necessity to drive himself to do work which should normally require ordinary effort.'[17]

Crerar's condition was aggravated by stress; chain-smoking replaced the briar, and he was given to uncharacteristic outbursts of temper. C.P. Stacey recalled seeing Crerar 'tear a strip' off his pilot for arriving late to shuttle the army commander to a conference. Stacey concluded from this episode that there was an 'element of terror' in Crerar's command style. Crerar's BGS related that during the first days of First Canadian Army's operational status on the continent, he was asked by the army commander to make an appreciation of the situation. Young and impulsive, Beament answered, 'Sir, I've provided you with all the necessary facts and I'm very happy to accept but it's always been my impression that the commander should make his own appreciation.' Beament recalled that his statement 'sent [Crerar] up like fireworks.' Ill, insecure in his position, and strained by his responsibilities, 'he was a pretty tense chap most of the time.'[18]

Though ill, Crerar put a human face on his command. He maintained a voluminous correspondence with both friends and colleagues. He also felt a fatherly concern for his subordinates, aides, and troops. When CMHQ Deputy C of S Montague suggested in mid-August that the groundwork had been laid for a long-overdue scheme for compassionate leave to Canada for long service men, Crerar enthusiastically supported it, although the impending reinforcement shortage delayed full consideration; in September, the situation had improved sufficiently for Crerar to press for an immediate analysis. 'GOC-in-C is anxious,' wrote Mann to Montague, 'that a detailed study be made at once in order that he may have a firm proposal for early implementation.' He hoped the first group could be home by Christmas. Later in the fall, he and Montague urged the cautious military members of the Army Council to increase the quota of men sent home to 450 from 250 a month; 450 was the quota when the scheme went into effect.[19]

Crerar's compassion was apparent on a personal as well as the policy level. He took the time in late August to dictate a letter to the mother of an American GI who picked him up when his jeep broke down, observing how proud she must be of her son. In December, a young soldier attached to his party was killed in an accident, a loss that prompted a letter to the soldier's family. He responded to most letters received from the public.[20] He also tried on occasion, with mixed results, to replicate the informality that marked the relationships between some commanders and their troops.

His insecurities were also evident. He bore grudges. George Drew, premier of Ontario by 1944, was refused permission to visit the two Ontario units in early September on the grounds that 'operations [were] far too intense and important for me to consider any visitors to Canadian Army.' His reasoning was logical and would have been persuasive had he not, the very next day, welcomed the idea of a visit from Vincent Massey, offering to put him up at his army HQ. Both Stuart and Massey saw the potential problems that would arise from Crerar's position and tried to change his mind. 'I may say,' wrote Stuart, 'that I have had a couple of most friendly conversations with Drew. I feel that the past is water under the bridge as far as he is concerned. He has spoken to a number of people here on the warmest terms concerning yourself and your accomplishments as corps and army commander.'[21] Crerar was unmoved, however, and suggested instead that Massey's visit be postponed and Drew's visit restricted to 'reinforcement units and recent battlefields.' Both came for abbreviated visits.

III

First Canadian Army operations for August 1944 were defined by the results of 2nd Canadian Corps Operation Spring offensive. Montgomery, in his directive of 21 July, planned to set the stage for another large armoured drive towards Falaise to draw the German armour to his flank and create a hinge for the U.S. First and newly operational Third Army under Patton to clear the Cherbourg peninsula and swing south of the bocage country towards Laval-Mayenne and Le Mans–Alencon. As outlined in a letter to Eisenhower on 24 July, Montgomery ordered Dempsey to first have 2nd Canadian Corps 'attack ... at dawn on 25 July to capture the area Fontenay le Marmion – Point 122 – Garcelles-Secqueville'; second, to attack on 28 July with the 12 Corps west of the Orne to capture the area Evrecy-Amaye; third, conduct an operation by the 8 Corps 'east of the Orne and through the Canadian Corps down the Falaise Road to cover the capture by the Canadian Corps of a large wooded area east of Garcelles.' This last was envisaged as a '"very large scale operation, by possibly three or four armoured divisions" on August 3rd or 4th.'[22]

Simonds had on 21 July begun preparations for a deliberate attack with the 'objective ... the high ground on either side of the Caen-Falaise road,' a prerequisite for implementing Monty's drive to Falaise. Operation Spring was designated to begin on 25 July, a complex three-phase attack begun under cover of darkness involving 2nd and 3rd Canadian divisions and 7th British Armoured Division. Its aim was to secure the high ground astride and including Verrières Ridge. While there is some debate whether Simonds designed it as a holding operation or a breakthrough, evidence suggests it was never meant to be more then a holding attack; whatever the corps commander's intentions, Spring was a failure and gained the dubious distinction of becoming the 'Canadian Army's costliest day of operations in the Second World War,' excepting Dieppe. It was Simonds's battle, and Crerar deferred to his judgment on its course, and ending.[23]

In light of Spring's failure to significantly alter the front line and the success of the American Operation Cobra, also launched on the 25th, Montgomery reconsidered his directive of 21 July outlining strategic policy on the Anglo-Canadian front. He concluded that the American success must be reinforced. To achieve this end, Monty directed that along 'the whole front now held by the First Canadian and Second British Armies it is essential that the enemy be attacked to the greatest possible degree possible with the resources available.' Second British Army would deliver the main blow.

The directive was vague in its description of First Canadian Army operational goals; Monty noted that resources were limited and that 'this may prevent the full implementation' of the operations east of the Caen Canal.'[24] Because Crerar had already based his assessment of 1 British Corps operations on the limits imposed by his resources, he interpreted Monty's observation as maintaining the status quo; he so informed Crocker, and planning continued at HQ 1 British Corps on this basis.[25] Events quickly outpaced the aim of the proposed operations. Montgomery, with Eisenhower's blessing, enhanced the scope of Second British Army's offensive directed against Caumont and pushed the attack date forward to 30 July. Eisenhower also urged the commander-in-chief to 'insist that the Canadians and Second British Army carry out their assignments with vigour and determination so that Bradley may bring your plans to full fruition.'[26]

Planning operations was one thing, achieving success another. The strength of the German defences had turned the Normandy campaign into one of attrition, comparable to First World War battles like Passchendaele in terms of the cost per yard of ground. What was Crerar's role as an army commander? Crerar, more so than his counterparts, took pains to study the German views on Allied tactics and circulated the captured German observations. His emphasis on surprise was one consequence of his study of the German evaluations of Allied shortcomings. More important, this approach reflected the climate of frank discussion and evaluation he tried to encourage; shortly after Operation Spring, First Canadian Army's Armoured Fighting Vehicle (Technical) Branch sought and received comments about the increasing unpopularity of the 'outgunned' Shermans. Considering that Montgomery had stopped the practice of after-action reports on the assumption that stating the obvious would lower morale, the importance of the support and encouragement of senior officers was critical. However, there was no one systematic approach to distilling lessons and disseminating them throughout the army. At one level removed from the armies were the Operational Research sections and groups, which studied, interviewed, and made recommendations for improving operational effectiveness. Staff and commanders of front-line units also shared ideas and experiences, informally and formally.[27]

New operations continued apace. Montgomery informed Crerar of his new intentions in a two-hour conference at 21st Army Group Tac HQ on the 29th. It relieved some pressure on the Canadian army commander, who was apprehensive about his army's ability to coordinate major operations before the end of the month while still integrating formations and units then coming under its control. 'I have been going through the second difficult experience in the last nine months,' he wrote his former DA & QMG at 1st Canadian Corps, Brigadier Jim Lister, on 2 August, 'of building up a Canadian command in the field under me.' He concluded that after two weeks, 'the HQ machinery is [now] beginning to work smoothly and effectively.'[28] But it was still very raw. Those army units that were on the Continent were still under command of 2nd Canadian Corps; the 2nd Canadian Army Group Royal Artillery, which had arrived in mid-July, is the example cited by Stacey. He also notes that First Canadian Army Signals was performing a variety of tasks. Most important was the unsatisfactory position of

First Canadian Army's air support, a point that Crerar made to Montgomery in their meeting. Second British Army's demands kept 83 Group so busy as to effectively leave First Canadian Army without any tactical air support until HQ 84 Group could be brought to the continent. He might have added, but did not, that the necessity of passing demands for air support from forward units to the fighter wings through Second British Army Air Support Signal Units (ASSU) undercut prompt support and relegated First Canadian Army's demands to secondary status. Following Crerar's complaint, Montgomery reluctantly promised to speed the transfer of the HQ to the continent; the group was not, however, fully operational until 12 August.[29]

At the meeting on 29 July, Montgomery directed Crerar to hold the German forces on the First Canadian Army front near Caen using all the means at his disposal, short of a major operation, to keep the bulk of the German armour away from Second British Army and First U.S. Army. The formations under Crerar's command were weary, but he did not argue. In a written directive, Crerar instructed Crocker's 1 British Corps 'by positive attack and deception' to give the impression of an imminent offensive. He also ordered Simonds, who would come under First Canadian Army command on 31 July, to prepare small-scale offensives that would give the same impression.[30] Further, although Monty had minimized the need for a 'large-scale effort,' Crerar instructed Simonds to 'draw up plans for an actual attack, axis Caen-Falaise, objective Falaise ... in about ten days time,' anticipating Second British Army's success in the operation to be launched on the 30th. The Canadian Corps' attack was 'to be carried out in great strength and with maximum air support.'[31] The 1 British Corps limited attack towards Vimont would serve to secure 2nd Canadian Corps' left flank.

The next day, 30 July, Crerar confirmed by phone his directive to Simonds. The Canadian Corps commander had already begun his appreciation of the difficulties; he informed Crerar that though the problem was 'tough, it could be well tackled.' He requested two more divisions, one infantry and one armoured as well as total air support for forty-eight hours. Crerar assured Simonds that Montgomery 'had intimated that "job" was on and [that] he [Crerar] would endeavour to get these forces.'

Two hours after Crerar's conversation with Simonds, Montgomery telephoned with the message that Second British Army's advance was making good progress. The C-in-C asked Crerar if he could hold 1 Brit Corps front 'with 6 Airborne Div and one Inf Div, and get two Brit Inf

Divs in reserve, west of Canal,' because he might want to 'very quickly' reinforce Second Army's success or 'start [an] important attack on Cdn Army front.' Crerar replied that he would try to arrange such a reserve.[32]

Crerar was already operating under the assumption that the Canadian army would be attacking within ten days.[33] Consequently, he quickly postponed Operations Rawlinson and Byng, and ordered Crocker to place 51 (Highland) Division and 3rd British Division in reserve. As a gesture of reconciliation, Crerar forwarded a letter describing the harmonious relationship of British formations under command of the Canadian Corps in the First World War. He spent the early evening reconnoitring the area south east of Caen by aircraft.[34] On 31 July, 2nd Canadian Corps, with the newly arrived 4th Canadian Armoured Division, Major-General George Kitching commanding, was brought under command of First Canadian Army. Crerar withdrew the exhausted 3rd Canadian Division, under pressure from the senior medical officer, for a week's rest. Crerar marked the day with an inspection of 4th Armoured divisional HQ and visits with the brigade commanders.

Simonds arrived at First Canadian Army Main HQ in the late afternoon of 31 July to brief Crerar on his plans for the upcoming operation, code-named Totalize. Simonds was determined to redeem himself following the failures of Spring. He unveiled a plan of attack that, if it can be faulted for too narrow a front, for erring on the side of complexity and for a fatal pause caused by Phase II's planned air bombardment on the 8th, was also an innovative attempt to breach two strong defensive lines. Simonds's conception, as outlined to Crerar on 31 July and detailed in a written appreciation dated 1 August, was a three-phase operation designed, in essence, to effect two breakthroughs. He asserted that the predominant concern was to handicap the Germans' 'strong defence in depth' consisting of machine guns, mortars, and anti-tank guns in carefully concealed positions that dominated the open country southwest of Caen. 'This defence,' he wrote, 'will be most handicapped in bad visibility – smoke, fog or darkness, when the advantage of long range is minimized.' Tactical surprise might be achieved 'in respect to time and method, but very heavy fighting must be expected.' However, 'overwhelming air support to destroy or neutralize enemy tanks, anti-tanks and mortars' might get the armour through, despite the loss of tactical surprise.' He concluded, 'It requires practically the whole day bomber lift to effect ... and if two defence zones are to be penetrated a pause with loss of speed and momentum must be accepted. It is considered that this may be avoided if the first zone is penetrated by infiltration at night but this can only be attempted with careful preparation by troops who are to do the operation.'

To fulfill his plan, Simonds requested three infantry divisions, two armoured brigades. and two armoured divisions; significantly, he also requested 'armoured infantry carriers to carry infantry through to deep objectives,' recommending that the armoured gun carriers – Priests – be converted for this purpose. In addition, he made use of the arsenal of Allied technology: 'one searchlight battery for movement lighting, if low cloud obscures the moon,' 'two squadrons of flails,' 'crocodiles to assist mopping up during the darkness,' 'the whole of the available air effort (heavy night and day bombers as well as tactical air forces),' and finally 'two complete AGRAs in addition to divisional artilleries and support of two additional AGRAs, one each with 1 and 12 Corps.' The use of heavy bombers at night and armoured personal carriers were the two 'features of marked originality.'[35]

Phase 1 of Simonds's outline plan called for two infantry divisions, carried in armoured personnel carriers, and two infantry brigades to assault the Fountenay-le-Marmion–La Hogue line under cover of night and without a preliminary artillery bombardment; instead, heavy bombers would 'obliterate' the surrounding area and the 360 artillery support guns would begin firing only after the attack had begun. Phase 2 of the preliminary plan would see an attack on the Hautsmesnil–St Sylvain position by one armoured and one infantry division begun after an air bombardment by heavy, medium, and fighter bombers; it was scheduled for the early afternoon, with the second bombardment designed to catch the German defenders by surprise. The third phase would entail exploitation by two armoured divisions.[36] This was the plan as outlined to Crerar on 31 July and 1 August.

Crerar recorded no qualms with this plan. His main operational responsibility was to secure the air support for Totalize. The tactical details of the operation were the prerogative of Simonds as corps commander. He had demonstrated an awareness of the issues; in his tactical directive of 22 July, Crerar, like others, had seized on the main problem facing the Anglo-Canadian armies: 'to get the infantry over and through the enemy's pre-arranged zones of defensive fire in the shortest possible time after the intention to attack has been revealed.'[37] Crerar made the same point when he wrote Simonds on the morning of 31 July to acknowledge receipt of his directives and to outline the agenda for the evening's meeting. The army commander characterized

Simonds's plan as 'excellent,' noting that 'good results' would undoubtedly follow 'if action is taken by your subordinate Commanders in accordance with them.' He was concerned with maintaining momentum, however. He instructed Simonds to be prepared to discuss 'in broad outline' the tactics he intended to pursue, as well as 'the particular technique.' He noted, 'I should like to know how you propose to secure continued drive in the attack, and the exploitation of success, wherever secured.'[38] Crerar later wrote Stacey and claimed credit for laying down 'the basic plan for Operation "Totalize,"' but this was an exaggeration. He did provide some broad insights, within which Simonds should plan, emphasizing, in part as a result of his evaluation of the German criticisms, the necessity of securing tactical surprise, while coordinating fire and movement.[39] These were important points, and it has been suggested that Crerar's 'relatively progressive firepower thinking' regarding a 'firepower oriented operational approach' would be adopted by 21st Army Group over the next six months. Still, Crerar was careful to give Simonds credit for the tactical planning. In the operational report to Ralston for the period 7–23 August, Crerar was more open: 'Detailed plan of attack was drawn up with very great skill by Lieutenant-General Simonds.'[40]

Immediately following the briefing by Simonds, Montgomery was on the phone to Crerar, informing him that 3rd British Infantry Division and 4 British Armoured Brigade were at the disposal of Second British Army as of 0700 hours the next day; he did not anticipate First Canadian Army operations beginning before the week was out but pressed Crerar to maintain pressure on the Germans to hold them on the Canadian front. The movement of German armour and infantry divisions to stem Second British Army's advance prompted a reiteration the next morning of the importance of keeping 'the Boche worried on our front.'[41] Despite the fact that units of 2nd Infantry and 4th Armoured Division had already launched two costly attacks on the well-fortified stronghold of Tilly-la-Campagne – and both divisional commanders were wary of the costly, limited attacks – the pressure from Montgomery and Crerar was interpreted by Simonds as necessitating yet another assault on Tilly. Initially Simonds was against this move, but after a call from Montgomery, he changed his mind, and 'prods' were ordered against points on the front. Crerar, when he transmitted the order, was working on the assumption, garnered from Simonds's verbal report on the morning of 1 August, that the attacks had 'gone well' and the casualties had been light; subsequently, Crerar took the initiative the next day, and upon learning of indications that several German formations were leaving the front, ordered both Crocker and Simonds to interfere with the reliefs of 9th and 12th SS Panzer divisions respectively.[42]

Crerar's determination to hit the enemy hard was also informed by the concurrent findings of an Anglo-Canadian-American Court of Enquiry (formed at his request) that on 8 June 1944 members of the 12th SS Panzer Division had murdered Canadian prisoners of war from the 3rd Infantry Division. He circulated the story to all commanders to be read to all troops in First Canadian Army. Although he directed that revenge 'must NOT under any circumstances take the form of retaliation in kind,' he stated that 'instead Canadian anger must be converted into a steel-hard determination to destroy the enemy in battle.' 'If any reminder was needed,' he concluded,' by any of us concerning the issues we are fighting for, and the evil forces we are fighting against, this has surely been provided.'[43] He did not need to remind 3rd Canadian Division veterans, engaged for weeks in their own personal and savage battle with the 12th SS.

IV

The situation in the bridgehead developed at a rapid pace in early August, forcing alterations in the Canadian plans. Operation Cobra had broken through the German defences on the left wing; as prearranged with Montgomery, on 1 August General Omar Bradley – mild, modest, but firmly resolved to maintain American interests – took command of 12th U.S. Army Group, composed of First U.S. Army, Lieutenant-General Courtney H. Hodges commanding, and the newly activated Third U.S. Army, commanded by George Patton, Jr. Avranches, 'the entrance to Brittany,' was in American hands, and Patton was pressing the armoured divisions of his VIII Corps to slash freely along the Brittany peninsula, refusing to be drawn into the methodical reducing of cities as proposed by Bradley and the Corps Commander Major-General Troy Middleton. The port of Brest's surrender freed Patton of the necessity of implementing the full-scale, set-piece reduction planned by corps HQ.[44] Similarly, Second British Army was making good, if difficult, progress towards Vire. On 2 August, Crerar described the progress and the Canadians' role, as he saw it at that point: 'We have been doing our full part in pinning down his three best panzer divisions in front of Simonds, so as to prevent them from taking an interfering part in the proceedings.'[45]

Crerar, meanwhile, had had time to consider Simonds's plan for Totalize. He made no direct comments, himself; rather, his concerns were apparent in a memorandum to Mann in which he laid down a planning schedule for developing the operation – he incorrectly called it 'Totalizer' – as a 'full scale air/land battle.' He directed that a conference be convened between himself, the AOC, Mann, the Senior Air Staff Officer (SASO), as well as his Intelligence and Operations (Air and Land) branch heads to discuss the proposed plan of operations. It was here, at HQ First Canadian Army and 84 Group level, that 'any basic confirmations, or amendments' to the plan would be made 'as discussion [indicated]' and here that the times to 'lay on' the components of the operation would be settled. Conscious of recent problems with the use of heavy bombers, Crerar use the conference to press for detailed and informed liaison between the air and army: the type of target and object to be attained by the bombing 'must be clearly indicated. Timing over target and duration of bombing settled. Distance from own Tps of different types of bombing – this connected with type bomb and fuse. Method of identifying target – visual, pathfinders and indicators.' Once the details were settled, Montgomery, Commander Allied Expeditionary Air Force (AEAF), and Bomber Command would approve them.

Most significantly, Crerar observed that the 'plan and method of maintaining [the] momentum of [the] Land/Air attack also requires settlement' and that he wanted it settled, along with the points he had outlined, by noon of 3 August.[46] He met with Simonds before noon on the 3rd but does not appear to have made any suggestions for changes to the plan at that time. He spent the rest of the day informally briefing his divisional commanders.[47] That evening, Montgomery, adapting his plans to take advantage of the unexpected success of the Americans, contacted Crerar at Main HQ First Canadian Army and informed him that Totalize was on. The C-in-C's formal directive, dated 4 August, detailed his intention to carry out a wide envelopment towards Paris by Bradley's 12th U.S. Army Group, masking the Brittany ports and forcing the Germans back to the Seine. The First U.S. Army was directed to swing eastward around the southern flank of the Second British Army, which would pivot on its 12th Corps southward and eastward. First Canadian Army was to launch a heavy attack 'from the Caen sector in the direction of Falaise ... as early as possible and in case not later than the 8 August' with the object of gaining 'such ground in the direction of Falaise as will cut off the enemy forces now facing Second Army and render their withdrawing eastward difficult – if not impossible.' The second object was generally 'to destroy enemy equipment and personnel, as a preliminary to a possible wide exploitation of success.' First Canadian Army was also to 'ensure that the front from the Cagny area northwards to the sea is held securely.'[48]

An informal meeting in the field on 4 August between Crerar, deGuingand, Mann, Beament, and Brigadier C.L. Richardson, BGS Plans, 21st Army Group, added nothing in the way of amendments to the plan. DeGuingand contented himself with stressing several administrative points and ensuring that Crerar was conscious of the importance of flexible inter-corps boundaries; he was. DeGuingand also asked what was being done 'in connection with progressively dislocating the enemy's administrative organization opposite 2 Cdn Corps front,' a question that prompted Beament to relate once again the dissatisfactory state of First Canadian Army's air support; army intelligence was developing a plan 'for this purpose but ... the project [was] considerably handicapped by [the] lack of air recce.' DeGuingand stated that First Canadian Army would now have first priority on the air group's resources – only three days before the assault was scheduled to begin – and would instruct Second British Army accordingly.[49]

Crerar was apparently dissatisfied with this situation, particularly as it limited his ability to influence the course of the battle through increased air support, but he preferred to focus on maintaining good relations with both 83 and 84 Group SAOs. This was demonstrably the case when, during the course of Operation Totalize, Mann wrote a memorandum, dated 11 August, to bring to Crerar's attention a 'practice that had apparently become [established] in the bridgehead which in effect [resulted] in the SASO 83 GP RAF becoming the adjucator of the military necessity or desirability of a particular attack upon a particular target.' Mann's frustration was prompted by the fact that he had to relay all requests for air support beyond the capacity of 83 GP RAF, through the SASO, who was at liberty to use his discretion as to whether or not to recommend further support from 2 TAF, affiliated at the army group level. Even if passed along, 21st Army Group HQ then prioritized the requests; it was not an expeditious process. As an example, and the catalyst for the memo, Mann and Beament had spent two hours attempting to order a medium bomber attack against a position that was holding up the corps' advance.

Mann thought the situation analogous to a Commander, Corps Royal Artillery (CCRA) questioning the necessity of supporting an attack after requests for artillery fire had been made and delaying action until it was too late. He implored Crerar to use his authority to have the terms of reference clarified and have superior authority define the 'procedure for applying the air weapon to its full capacity in furtherance of the C in C's strategic plans.' In his view, the casual practices that had evolved during the fighting to expand the bridgehead now threatened to sabotage the opportunities presented by the German collapse. 'At the present time,' he concluded, 'we can have harmony or efficiency, NOT both.'[50]

Mann hit on several crucial problems that hindered the army–air relationship throughout the campaign, and beyond. Air Marshal Sir Arthur Coningham viewed his 2nd Tactical Air Force as an independent force. This rendered the procedure for obtaining air support over and above the resources of the Army-Air Group more akin to an appeal than a request. The 2 TAF also chose targets that it assumed were important, and that it was capable of hitting with minimum risk to its pilots. First Canadian Army's difficulties were exacerbated by their reliance on Second British Army's 83 Group. Procedural problems were intensified by personality conflicts between the senior British and American army and air commanders. With no clearly delineated lines of authority or responsibility, several commands shepherded by strong individuals had evolved. The U.S. Strategic Air Forces and the British Bomber Command were commanded by Carl A. Spaatz and Sir Arthur 'Bomber' Harris respectively, both ardent proponents of strategic bombing as a decisive weapon, a strategic goal that they felt was hindered by supporting army operations. The tactical air forces (Ninth U.S. Air Force, the RAF's 2nd Tactical Air Force, as well as the Air Defence Command of Great Britain) were under the overall command of Sir Trafford Leigh-Mallory, who had made himself unpopular with clumsy attempts to seize control of the strategic bombing forces. Eisenhower had tried to tie these men to SHAEF, and ground operations, by appointing Air Chief Sir Arthur Tedder as his deputy. Despite Tedder's charm and good relationships with Spaatz and Harris, his authority was limited to coordinating the air forces. Coningham and Montgomery's antipathy has been well documented.[51] Tedder also disliked Montgomery, and the army in general.

Montgomery recognized a problem, but did little. During the battles in July, he had directed diatribes at Dempsey, who, in Montgomery's eyes, did not 'know a great deal yet about how to wield air power, and ... slipped up once or twice.' He added that 'Coningham knows this and will seize on an opportunity to make capital out of it.' Monty was correct; Coningham took every chance to speak out against Montgomery and Dempsey at SHAEF, his opinion reflected in his assessment of the campaign in early July: 'The army does not seem prepared to fight its own battles.'[52]

Mann recognized that the coordination problems between HQ First Canadian Army and 83 Group went deep, and were rooted in the mutual disdain that developed between HQ Second British Army and 2 TAF. His statement that the air force, when working in support of the army, was 'simply an agent whereby destructive projectiles are delivered into the enemy areas in accordance with the requirements of the army' indicate that he underestimated the necessity for friendly relations imposed by the command structure, and the need for the army to recognize their autonomy.

Crerar recognized the importance of interpersonal relationships; it was a central tenet of his career. Accordingly, he scribbled a hasty note to Mann: 'Fully agree that present procedures inefficient. Can hardly expect otherwise in the circumstances. When 84 Gp becomes operational and joint Cdn Army/84 Gp RAF HQ operational as such, most of your points have no business to arise. If they do, AOC and self will settle them, quickly.' He also corrected him, noting that his 'analogy [between CCRA and AOC] ... is not sound. RAF is not part of Army. "Gunners" are.'[53]

HQ staff as well as 21st Army Group's BGS Plans fleshed out the details of the air plan at a 4 August evening conference with Leigh-Mallory, Coningham and the AOCs of 84 and 83 Group, Air Vice Marshal's L.O. Brown, and Broadhurst respectively. Simonds and Crocker arrived halfway through the conference, ready for a later meeting with Crerar. The air representatives had no significant objections to the plan; however, limitations were imposed on the flexibility of the operation by their insistence that five hours, at least, was the minimum time required for notice of a postponement. Simonds tied his hands further for Phase II, agreeing that if H hour on D plus 1 was 1400 hours, no change could be made after 0900. It was also agreed that Mann, Peter Wright, Richardson, and the GSO 2 Air, 2nd Canadian Corps, would fly to the United Kingdom to arrange final details with Bomber Command, an important decision for the course of Totalize.

Crerar's most important contribution to the operation may have been the decision to send army representatives to see Harris personally; he also raised two points that would prove prescient, but were redundant, given the procedures he and Simonds had just agreed to in order to secure the bombers. First, Crerar advocated a more sophisticated approach to the preliminary bombardment. He pointed out that 'the close integration of fire and movement in [the] operation [was] most important'; the troops, particularly in view of the fact that they would be in armoured vehicles, should be brought up to 'the minimum safety distance of bombing' from the start-line. Second, Crerar observed that 'the forward troops must be prepared to move blind through the dust raised by the bombing on Targets 1 and 2.' In short, surprise was important and the momentum must be maintained. There is no record of any further discussion on these points at conference.[54]

Crerar returned to the issue of momentum in his remarks to the senior army officers the next day. His talk emphasized two themes: the historic analogy with the Canadian Corps' First World War attack of 8 August on Amiens and the importance of maintaining the momentum of the assault. Crerar was eager to replicate the decisive Battle of Amiens: 'I have no doubt but that we shall make the 8th August 44 an even blacker day for the German Armies than is recorded against the same date twenty-six years ago.' Following a summary of the Allied position, the broad objectives, and outline of the plan, the bulk of the talk was devoted to ensuring that the troops were well briefed and pressed to 'drive on, and through, and to do so with their own weapons ... the idea ... that, without a colossal scale of artillery, or air support, continued advance ... is impossible ... being far too prevalent.' He also noted that the momentum would have to be maintained through preparation, at the Command level, of plans for probable future operations and directions to 'keep the movement, and fire support, alive and nourished.' The infantry, he added, must not simply occupy objectives, but must see that as a means to an end: killing Germans.[55]

Crerar's concerns with maintaining the momentum of the attack were remembered by some in attendance.[56] Beyond the exhortations to his officers, however – which were undoubtedly undermined by his lack of experience – and the warnings he issued at the Army-Air conference on 4 August, Crerar made only one more, somewhat weak, attempt to ensure that the need to maintain the momentum of the attack was a dominant consideration before Totalize was launched.

18 The Learning Curve: Totalize and Tractable

I

Crerar faced a steep learning curve as the Allied armies prepared to break out of the Normandy bridgehead. He proved receptive to new ideas for breaking through the German lines – he was one of the few to evaluate the German reports on Allied deficiencies – and tried to address some of the problems. Yet he was still hesitant to force his conceptions on his subordinates, except in very broad terms.

On 2 August 1944, ULTRA intelligence revealed that Hitler had ordered Commander-in-Chief West General Gunther von Kluge to redeploy at least four of the nine panzer divisions on the Anglo-Canadian front for an offensive against the Americans at Avranches; by 6 August, despite Kluge's protests, the German front lines had been altered, probably for the better, by the replacement of the 1st and 9th SS Panzer divisions with 89th and 272nd Infantry divisions. Crerar passed on the information regarding 1st SS Panzer to Simonds on 5 August, troubled somewhat as to whether his army was prepared to exploit a breakthrough in the forthcoming operations. Speaking by phone to deGuingand, the army commander requested an extra division for 1 British Corps 'to give Crocker one Division in hand for emergencies.' After speaking to Monty at his Tac HQ, deGuingand gave the ambiguous reply that, while at present no formations were available, conditions might improve. In short, Crerar could 'continue to hope but not to rely on this.' After informing Crocker of Montgomery's decision, Crerar informed Simonds of the thinning of 1st SS forward positions and the 'probable thickening of [the] Breteville–St Sylvain [sic] position in rear.' He asked the corps commander how this would effect his existing plans; the exact question was not recorded, but from Simonds's answer it appears Crerar also remarked on the pause preceding Phase II. Simonds replied that the new information would affect the air plan only insofar as he would have the preponderant weight of the attack on Phase II. There was 'no prospect [of] changing timing Phase 2. Would want an interval.'[1] Crerar did not press the issue, and Simonds changed his plan for Totalize. The third phase was incorporated into the second: both the 4th Canadian Armoured and the Polish Armoured divisions would attack immediately following the bombing of the defensive lines that signalled the beginning of Phase II. Simonds's announcement to his divisional commanders was met with some shock and mild protests, particularly at the narrow frontage allotted each division, but it went through. He hoped using the armour early would maintain the forward momentum of the assault.[2]

Changing the timing of the bombing would have been difficult. The process of acquiring the bombers had taken on a life of its own. The difficulties are recounted in Stacey, and summarized in many other works. The salient point from Crerar's perspective was that Mann, as the army commander's representative, was on the spot when Harris stated on 6 August, after Simonds had issued the revised, and final, orders for Totalize, that 'he was not prepared to bomb at night as planned ... and that there was no question of deviating from this policy.' HQ First Canadian Army had been working quickly to detail the bombing plan. Following the changes in the enemy's disposition, Beament had phoned Mann at 2237 on the 5th to enquire about the implications of cancelling the proposed target schedule. Mann replied later that night, near midnight, that any cancellation must be passed through First Canadian Army to 83 Group, who would pass the alternative plan to Bomber Command; twenty-four hours' notice was required because of the process. Mann also noted that he had been asked to meet with Harris the next day to 'ensure correct detail.' Unconcerned, he sent his assistants back to the theatre.[3]

Harris's refusal to use his bombers at night in close proximity to troops without the proper marker and targeting procedure was understandable; a stunned Mann, however, quickly pointed out that the operation was proceeding on the basis of agreements reached with the SASO. He insisted that the sudden turnaround, and its implications for the entire strategic situation in Normandy, had to be explained to Montgomery and Crerar personally; strangely, Harris refused. Mann was able to bring Harris around, following assurances over the telephone from Crerar and Simonds that the army would test the use of targeting markers that could be seen by the bombers at night; otherwise the operation would have to start at 2130 hours. Simonds preferred the later start time, but had no choice but to go along. The tests were successful, however, and the operation went ahead as planned.[4]

Totalize was scheduled to begin on 7 August; however, a German offensive launched towards Avranches on the evening of the 6th initiated a series of attacks and counterattacks that would significantly alter both the objectives of the operation and its strategic importance. Kluge's 7th Army assault force made some limited gains, capturing Mortain, but by midday on 7 August it had been stopped; the successes of the British to the North and the Americans in capturing Le Mans on the 8th eliminated any chance for a renewal of the operation. The Americans' movement in the south left the Seventh German Army's flank vulnerable, with the German defenders, including Fifth German Army, in a deep pocket still trying to move east while the British bore down from the north and the U.S. forces moved southwest.

In the final hours before the offensive, Crerar was committed to working out the details of inter-army boundaries and flank support with Dempsey's Second British Army. The 12 British Corps was assigned this task through the development of operations east of the River Orne; on the 6th, the corps was on the line of the river as far south as Thury Harcourt.[5] Second British Army was to take over Falaise following Totalize, while First Canadian Army turned to the east, its operations directed on the River Seine.[6] The German assault forced Montgomery to alter this plan. He informed Crerar of the progress of the Germans and the delay it would cause the Americans. Late in the afternoon of the 7th, Crerar phoned Simonds to tell him that Falaise must 'not only be captured [but] strongly secured against any enemy attempt to regain it.' While Crerar suggested that light armoured forces be sent to the east, west, and south of Falaise, his instructions that the Polish Armoured Division be directed to assist 1 British Corps in clearing the Germans west of the River Dives rather than thrusting further east until 'the situation [was] clarified to the south' indicates that he perhaps saw the potential envelopment, but was too cautious to advocate the move.[7]

II

Once Totalize had begun, First Canadian Army HQ's influence on the course of the battle was limited. Crerar's willingness, and, to a degree, need, to concede Simonds control of the tactical battle was best signalled by his request in April that Simonds be 'put in the picture' about ULTRA intelligence.[8] The army commander's main tool to influence the battle was his control of the tactical air effort. Unfortunately, as described in the previous chapter, the circumstances of 84 Group's late arrival and the procedure developed for liaison with 83 Group proved decidedly unsatisfactory, for both reconnaissance and close support; further, despite anecdotal evidence of support from individual units – the sporadic attacks that cheered the doomed 28th Armoured Regiment (the British Columbia Regiment) on the ninth being the best known – it would appear that 2 TAF's effectiveness in these battles was greatly exaggerated. Still, Crerar had Mann provide assessments on the 11th and the 18th of 84 Group's efforts and the steps taken to improve cooperation after Totalize. Mann reported that relations were 'excellent.'[9]

An army commander could also influence the battle through his presence. During the operation, Crerar limited his visits to Simonds who was stationed at HQ 2nd Division. He spent his late afternoons coordinating operations with Dempsey and Lieutenant-General N.M. Ritchie of 12 British Corps at the latter's HQ under Montgomery's watchful eye.[10] Except for acting quickly to investigate and limit the potential fallout from the short bombing of 8 August, Crerar's was not a dynamic presence during Totalize. Montgomery, in a letter to Brooke on 9 August, characterized him as nervous.

> Harry Crerar is fighting his first battle and it is the first appearance in history of a Canadian Army HQ. He is desperately anxious it should succeed. He is so anxious that he worries himself all day!!
> I go see him a lot and calm him down. He will be much better when he realises that battles seldom go as planned, that great patience is required, that you keep on at it until the other chap cracks, and that if you worry you will eventually go mad!! He seems to have gained the idea that all you want is a good initial fire plan, and then the Germans all run away!![11]

Others remembered him differently. Correspondent Ross Munro recalled that Crerar came through 'this trying period ... with an equanimity that was something to witness.'[12] However, the image of Crerar pulling meditatively on his briar pipe was soon replaced with the reality, for some at least, of the chain-smoking, sometimes ill-tempered commander.

During the operations in August and September, Crerar's command style differed in intensity, but only moderately in substance. It was unique in some ways, however. Crerar's inexperience meant that he allowed Simonds to run the battles his way. Crerar's health was also declining, and would bottom out by September. He was also consumed, in part because he did tire easily, with learning the business of running the army during active operations. His activities at HQ First Canadian Army bear this out. He had laid out a methodical procedure for dealing with decision making during operations; the HQ began the implementation of these procedures during Totalize and Tractable – a system that would function essentially unchanged until Crerar returned to England at the end of September. He leaned heavily on his senior staff, and this approach was reflected in a practice of command that laid a heavy, if diffused, responsibility on the operations, planning, and intelligence staffs. Crerar's dictums that a 'good staff officer' was advisor, agent, and 'the servant of the troops' were the animating principles behind the procedures and organization of HQ First Canadian Army.

Once operations began, First Canadian Army headquarters was divided into Main and Rear HQs. The former was the operational brain of the army, its duties defined in principle as the 'preparation and distribution of all executive orders, appreciations, ... required to implement plans of [the] Army Commander and AOC.' The Rear HQ was responsible for the administrative implementation of the army commander's plans.[13] First Canadian Army's Tactical HQ was a temporary establishment, the forward echelon of the Main HQ commanded by Crerar, who was supported by one ADC from his personal staff (which consisted of one PA and two ADCs), staff from the operations branch, as well as liaison and signals staff to 'permit the GOC-in-C to exercise command when the tactical situation require[d] him to position himself away from Main HQ.' In practice, it allowed Crerar to follow the army as necessary without waiting for the complete movement of the Main HQ. He kept Main HQ close; his Tac HQ was rarely five miles from Main.[14]

Crerar's use of the Main HQ as his real base of operations reflected his reliance on his staff; the First Canadian Army BGS believed that the army commander viewed them all as 'good managing clerks at different levels.' He also believed that Crerar 'didn't really want a chief of staff – he wanted a good managing clerk to see that everything ran smoothly at the HQ.'[15] In comparison to Montgomery's Chief of Staff deGuingand, who acted as an alter ego for Montgomery, Mann's position was redundant in that Crerar did not maintain a completely separate tactical headquarters. The memorandum on the organization of HQ First Canadian Army narrowly defined his authority: the exercise of the Chief of Staff's authority as a deputy was not considered 'normal except in the absence of the Army Commander.'[16] Mann rarely attended conferences on Crerar's behalf; however, Mann was trusted completely and he took on more responsibility after Crerar's return from sick leave in November 1944.

Neither did Crerar use Mann to winnow operational information, although he clearly oversaw the staff and planning. Crerar was detail oriented. Awakened by his batman – who recalled waiting outside the general's door watching the second hand of his watch – who served him tea and gave him the day's weather forecast, he was briefed by Lieutenant Finlay Morrison, his ADC at 0630. Promptly at 0700, the army commander met directly with his senior staff officers, usually, but not always, including the BGS and his G1s for intelligence, air and operations. as well as the DA and QMG. They fed Crerar information on the previous night's – and the day's anticipated – developments. Crerar's own records indicate that these meetings did not begin until 17 August when operations beyond Normandy were considered, but that they were run as discussion rather than orders groups.[17] This method was seen as a weakness, one that was apparent as his health declined. There was no central authority figure or C of S for authority to devolve upon.

Paperwork, including correspondence that Crerar insisted on writing himself in longhand, usually consumed the rest of his morning. Before noon, Crerar left the HQ for the remainder of the day, going forward to stay with his corps commanders – a pattern that he followed for the duration of the campaign in northwest Europe. Contact with the HQ was maintained through an ADC; one ADC, Morrison, remained in camp while the other, Lieutenant Giles Perodeau (taken on because Crerar believed him to be French), accompanied the army commander on his daily trips to the front. Under 'normal' conditions, Main HQ was 'sited on or near main signals artery and up to 40 miles behind [the] leading Corps HQ.' During operations, the requirements of the RAF group, particularly the necessity of staying close to airfields, as well as conditions in the field, might increase this distance or that between Main and Tac HQ. Crerar used his aircraft to minimize the time lost in transit between the HQs; he also used it for recce, sometimes pressing his pilot to cross enemy lines. The BGS recalled that Crerar would contact the HQ to direct them to correct any problems he saw with administration or traffic control.[18]

Montgomery often used deGuingand in his place, particularly when he was in the midst of operations. His C of S believed it contributed to his chief's lack of understanding regarding the problems of other commanders. Montgomery was increasingly isolated from his Main HQ; in 21st Army Group, Tac HQ 'always remained a separate entity' and all staff information was transmitted through the Chief of Staff. There was no one on staff – with the possible exception of Brigadier David Belchem, Monty's GSO 1 Operations – able to argue with the Master. The impact of Montgomery's isolation was best illustrated by his determination to go forward with Operation Market Garden and the staff's acquiescence, despite their doubts.[19]

Generally at HQ First Canadian Army, Crerar laid down the day-to-day policy through his instructions to the administrative and general staff in their early morning meetings. The combination of planning by committee and his daily meetings while operations were underway involved Crerar with staff one level below his senior staff. This method suggested he was unable to discern between essential, important, and unimportant elements of command responsibility – a sign of inexperience. Crerar did not yet understand what he needed to know. It was also the product of a man whose actions were animated by the importance of the principle that underlay them. His BGS remembered Crerar's outburst at two G1s who had inserted an inaccurate map reference in the morning's intelligence summary. In contrast, his ADC recalled Crerar's response upon finding himself lost because of Morrison's map-reading error: '[Crerar] wasn't angry, he just told him that the troops couldn't be left waiting: they were 500 men and he was only one.'[20]

Crerar was not remembered for his warmth. He appeared to be all business, a 'general 24 hours a day.' His determination to maintain himself as a living example for his staff and men added to his stiffness. Both ADCs remembered examples of his consideration and understanding, however. All commented on his physical bravery; he drove his own Jeep, following Monty's example, and returned from his airborne reconnaissance with bullet holes in the wings of his aircraft. Batman Tom MacDonald recalled Crerar's dilemma on whether to wear the red-banded hat marking him as a general officer while visiting the front and risk bringing fire down on the troops or wear a beret and have the troops think he was yellow: he wore the regulation hat.[21]

Crerar's relationship with his immediate staff remained 'correct as opposed to warm'; once operations began, he made no conscious attempt to keep in touch with the lower echelons of the HQ.[22] The atmosphere in 'A' Mess was characterized as 'generally happy,' its lighter moments provided by Church Mann. Crerar, however, kept a tight rein on the members, particularly his Chief of Staff, wary of his penchant for physical humour. In this period, the mess was not lavish but they ate well off white tablecloths and silver service; wine and drinks were permitted – Crerar punctually taking a gin with lunch and two Scotches with dinner, one before and one after – but moderation was strictly observed.[23] During operations, his contact outside of 'A' Mess was minimal. This practice was typical; Dempsey spoke to his Main and Rear HQ only in late November, the first time since June, and then in order to put them in the big picture for the impending operations.[24]

The sheer size of the HQ inhibited frequent contact. During operations, the entire Main HQ of First Canadian Army was akin to a small self-contained, carefully planned city, run by a camp commandant and marked by road signs. Moving it was major task. In open country, it could encompass half a square mile or more, defined by the regulation fifty to one hundred yards between offices. Crerar's personal encampment was on the periphery of the Main camp, approximately two hundred yards distant to keep him mobile and aloof from its daily turmoil. His caravan was 'comfortable' and well designed. He emphasized personal mobility, stemming from his desire to maintain close contact with his commanders. If he did not have a high-profile style of command, he retained its substance.

First Canadian Army's relationship with the RAF is a good example of an area where Crerar's emphasis was on the maintenance of low-key personal ties and how its spirit effected implementation in practice by the staff. Organizationally, HQ First Canadian Army and HQ 84 Group RAF operated together in the field, normally from vehicles; both army and air had operation rooms about fifty yards apart. The Group Captain, Operations, worked with his opposite number, the Colonel GS (later BGS). 'He and I,' recalled Brigadier Beament, 'were in each other's pockets for the whole time.' A Joint Battle Room was the centre for coordinating and fighting the day-to-day operations 'in conformity with the Army Comd/AOC plans.'[25] Occupied by the army's Colonel GS and his GSO 1s for Operations, Air, and Intelligence and the air force's group and wing captain of Operations as well as the Group Intelligence Officer, the JBR also brought the two groups together for a daily conference – usually in the evening – in order to discuss and plan the following day's operations, implementing any specific instructions received from Crerar and the AOC, or their senior staff. There was no combined army and air intelligence room dealing with moment-to-moment information affecting air and land – a significant omission.[26]

In principle, this method kept the army and air close; in day-to-day targeting, cooperation at this level was crucial. 'The staff input to the air function,' recalled GSO 1 (Ops) Lieutenant-Colonel Anderson, 'was greater than the commander's decision-making factor.'[27] Cooperation was influenced in practice by the attitudes and actions of the army commander and the AOC. Both Air Vice-Marshal 'Bingo' Brown, an Australian, and Group Captain F.E. Rosier were anxious to cooperate with their army counterparts; their close working relationship was cemented by Crerar's merging of his 'A' Mess with that of Brown's. Air Vice-Marshall Brown was, unfortunately, so cooperative that he was replaced in November 1944 with AVM E.C. Huddleston, a man characterized as 'less cooperative.' He signalled his attitude by establishing a separate mess. Crerar was upset by this action, but tried to limit the effects by having Huddleston as a frequent guest in his mess.

III

Operation Totalize began well. The Canadian 'break-in' assault formations breached the German forward defences – Von Kluge called it 'a breakthrough ... such as we have never seen' – but the 'breakthrough' stalled on 9 August as a result of a combination of factors: Simonds's decision to wait for the scheduled bombing (another indictment of the inability to initiate or call off the bombers quickly); the inexperience of the 4th Canadian and Polish armoured divisions, exacerbated by casualties among the Poles caused by USAAF's short-bombing; superior German tanks and the strength of the hastily improvised German defences; and inadequate tank–infantry cooperation. Kitching recalled, 'We lost the momentum of the attack, the very thing General Crerar had warned against.' The pace of the advance on 9 August as well as the timely intervention of the 12th SS Panzer allowed the Germans to improvise another strong defensive line with the Canadians still some eight miles from Falaise. On the morning of 11 August, Simonds cancelled the attack and began preparing for a new set-piece assault.[28]

The strategic situation was changing rapidly, however. The success of the American drive across Brittany and the concurrent German drive towards Avranches had prompted Bradley on 8 August, with Eisenhower's support, to persuade Montgomery that the Third U.S. Army and First U.S. Army should wheel north to attempt an envelopment, west of the Seine, shorter than that envisaged by the C-in-C's original plan. Third U.S. Army would meet the Canadians at Falaise. Prompted by the limited success of Totalize, Montgomery issued a directive on 11 August to his Army Group and Army commanders detailing the new objectives. While the 12th U.S. Army Group advanced towards Argentan to the general line Sees-Carrouges, Second British Army was to 'advance its left towards Falaise.' Crerar's army was directed to 'capture Falaise ... a first priority and ... vital ... then operate with strong armoured and mobile forces to secure Argentan.' The front between Falaise and the sea was to be secured, a task left to the weakened 1 British Corps. The 2nd Canadian Corps was now charged with both taking and holding Falaise and moving to take Argentan, some twelve miles beyond the former.[29]

Despite the increased difficulties of the Canadians' new task and the strength of the American arm of the pincer, Montgomery did not strengthen the Canadian army, nor, as the battle developed, did he make the alternative move of altering the boundaries between the two army groups to allow the U.S. armies to take full advantage of their momentum. Both decisions and the resulting escape of significant numbers of German troops through the 'Falaise gap' between Falaise and Argentan has prompted an ongoing debate among historians.

Two points should be made. Montgomery was slow to react to the difficulties encountered by the Canadians; he could have reinforced them from Second British Army with 7th Armoured, but did not. But he was not asked after the operation had begun. Had he given Crerar the extra division he requested for 'emergencies,' this formation might have been useful. Fear of upsetting Canadian sensibilities or doubts about the 7th stemming from their poor performance in earlier operations have been forwarded as explanations for his failure to strengthen First Canadian Army; neither seems to mesh with Montgomery's previous actions.[30] He simply misjudged the operation and was overly optimistic about the Canadians' chances for success. Writing to Brooke on 9 August, he had commented on the problems they faced. 'The Canadians should be able to fight their way to Falaise,' he wrote. 'They will not have the easy time they fancied but they should get there; at present their forward movement is not making rapid progress.' He added that he thought the 'Germans [would] fight hard for Falaise ... it is good defensive country and we must not expect things to go too rapidly.' Similarly, he noted that the Polish Division had 'not displayed that dash we expected, and have been sticky,' and that the Eighth Air Force had caused significant casualties among the Canadians and Poles. Despite these observations, Montgomery's only action at this juncture was to tell 'Harry to give them [the Poles] a kick in the fork.'[31]

Montgomery nevertheless adapted to the flow of the battle, if not forcefully. The next day in discussions with Crerar and Dempsey, Montgomery acknowledged the fact that the main German forces faced the Canadian and British armies; following another meeting at 12 Corps HQ on the eleventh, he ordered Dempsey to 'thrust strongly in a South-Easterly direction with 12 Corps,' making it clear to both army commanders that this move was intended 'to assist Cdn Army in their task.'[32] This was the bare minimum, but it may have sated any desire for additional help on the part of the Canadian commanders. They certainly made no requests for additional forces despite the puzzlement of at least one divisional commander at the new objectives.[33]

Montgomery adapted further to the advances of the Americans and the beginnings of the German withdrawals. On the 13th, he met with Bradley and Dempsey to discuss future operations, 'particularly as regards Army Group and Army boundaries.' Crerar was not invited. According to Dempsey, the meeting resulted in the decision that so 'long as the Northward move of Third Army meets little opposition, the two leading Corps will disregard inter-Army boundaries. The whole aim is to establish forces across the enemy's lines of communication so as to impede – if not prevent entirely – his withdrawal.'[34] Montgomery, then, had used his authority to keep the army group boundaries from hindering the successful completion of the short envelopment; Bradley, who refused to allow Patton's Third Army to go beyond Argentan, must shoulder a large part of the blame for the gap, a responsibility he accepted.

Crerar's operational role became that of a functionary for Montgomery, exhorting Simonds and the commanders of 2nd Canadian Corps to greater efforts. He crisscrossed the battlefield between corps HQs, making brief appearances at Simonds's HQ, as well as Crocker's and 12 Corps', but was not a dominant presence. He and the army HQ were further limited in their ability to influence the battle by the problems in rapidly communicating requests for air support – a problem Crerar hoped would resolve itself once 84 Group was fully established. Beyond the standard recces and sorties, Crerar made limited use of the fighter-bomber wings at his disposal once the August operations started. Only once, following discussions with Simonds on 20 August, did he order the rocket-firing Typhoons to blunt a German counterattack. No other active interference was recorded. He described the situation to Stacey in 1958, noting that once the battle had begun, 'there was nothing much the Army Group Commander, the Army Commander, and even the Corps Commander could do to influence matters at that stage.'[35]

The air function Crerar was absorbed with was the short-bombing, which occurred on 8 August at the start of Phase II of the operation. He had been at the front conferring with Simonds and seeking information from his provost corps regarding POWs when he witnessed the 8 USAAF drop. He hurried back to Main HQ to 'report the matter and investigate.'[36] After conferring with Leigh-Mallory and Broadhurst, Crerar returned his attention to the operations; the next day he began finding new commanders to replace two casualties of the bombing: Brigadier Wyman of 2nd Canadian Armoured Brigade and Keller of 3rd Division. He promoted Brigadier Dan Spry to command the division, on the recommendation of Simonds and Burns.

Crerar also began damage control to limit the potential rift between air and army over the short bombing. He sent letters to Simonds and Crocker noting the positive effects and directing them to relay to 'all ranks that all possible steps are being taken, and will continue to be taken, to prevent a recurrence of such an unfortunate event.' He believed that personal errors and technical inaccuracies could 'not be completely eliminated.' Crerar took a similar line with the government.[37] He wanted to maintain solid relations with Harris.

Preparations for a new operation, Tractable, including the use of the RAF's heavy bombers, had begun on the 12th; both Simonds and Crerar concluded, unfairly, that the main problem had been lack of initiative by the divisional commanders, not lack of resources, complex plans, or the German defenders. The 2nd Canadian Corps' divisional COs bore the brunt of Simonds's wrath; accordingly when Crerar, on the basis of Montgomery's directive, instructed him on 11 August to take Falaise and Argentan, Simonds developed a plan that varied little from Totalize.[38] When formal instructions were received from Crerar on the 13th, Simonds's plan was already developed. He launched it during the day under cover of a smokescreen while the heavy bombers moved in two hours after H-Hour to destroy bypassed strong points.

Crerar was again removed from the tactical planning. The C of S, 2nd Canadian Corps, briefed Beament on the operational plans, and an air plan was formalized at a meeting of the army commander, his senior staff, Simonds, Brown and his senior staff, as well as a representative from Bomber Command. The plans were reviewed and approved by Leigh-Mallory prior to their formal acceptance.[39] On the 14th, Crerar sent a forceful message to all commanders involved in the attack, taking pains to instill the importance of momentum: 'Hit him first, hit him hard and keep on hitting him.'[40] Going forward to see the bomber attack, he was horrified to witness the repeat of the short-bombing; most of his afternoon was consumed in discussions with his staff and writing reports on the incident. It was not until late afternoon that Crerar was able to return to Simonds's corps HQ to review the day's events.

The second short-bombing during Tractable on 14 August tested his equanimity, but not his faith in bombing. 'Operation "Tractable" started off very well indeed,' Crerar wrote BGS Richardson, 'but the programme, later on in the afternoon, was somewhat upset by some bad work on the part of a proportion of heavy bombers ... [nevertheless] I still have strong hopes that we will be on our objectives by tonight.'[41] Still, Crerar quickly requested from the BGS Plans at Main HQ 21st Army Group an 'unofficial chart and note' on the chains of command air forces and armies in 21st Army Group, motivated by the desire to thoroughly investigate the short-bombing. The request also revealed the confusion regarding the lines of communication between the senior HQs in the Allied camp. Harris also initiated an investigation of the short-bombing; it was discovered that while the initial drop was a combination of technical and human errors, the bombing had continued because no one at First Canadian Army HQ, or at SHAEF, had informed Bomber Command that the yellow smoke it used as target indicators was also used by Allied troops as recognition signals for their own air forces – with devastating results on the 14th.[42]

Crerar downplayed blame on both sides. He had his Chief of Staff examine Harris's report for any statements that might be construed as defamatory towards the army, but it was largely favourable. Mann had argued that it was partially First Canadian Army HQ's responsibility to have informed Harris or his representative of the targeting procedure during the numerous discussions, but Crerar, having examined the loose chain of command, concluded that if fault could be assigned, and he was not positive that it should be, then AEAF was ultimately responsible for ensuring that RAF Bomber Command was informed of SHAEF procedures in place since March. In the end, Crerar and Mann chose to placate Harris, and emphasize the bombing's 'valuable' contribution 'to the great success of that "break-through" operation.'[43] The importance of staying on Harris's good side was crucial; Bomber Command was not sympathetic to the army's needs, and this feeling grew as the campaign continued into the fall. The correspondence between the Air Marshal of the RAF, Lord Tedder, and the Chief of the Air Staff, Air Chief Sir Charles Marshal Portal in late October revealed that they believed that the army in general – and First Canadian Army in particular – was far too dependent on heavy bombing 'when it is not essential and when its only purpose is to save casualties.'[44] It was a remarkable statement. Still, Crerar and the others retained their faith in the bomber. 'We have not forgotten how to use the guns but there is no doubt,' Crerar wrote a friend on 15 August 1944, 'that the psychological effect of several thousand tons of bombs, followed closely by determined attack, has proved very efficacious, even to the indoctrinated Hitlerite Youth!'[45] He was thus prepared to accept the risks in coordinating the support of heavy bombers, and purposefully decided not to adopt a 'critical attitude.'[46]

Despite the disruption and casualties caused by the short bombing, Tractable breached what has been characterized as 'the best-organized defensive position left to the Germans in Normandy.' The 2nd Canadian Corps moved slowly towards Falaise in the face of determined defenders who knew the cost of losing that vital road link, but gained a breakthrough by the end of the 14th. Second British Army was also encountering fierce resistance, prompting Montgomery on 14 August to order the Canadians to 'capture Falaise as well as contain it' but to do so 'as to interfere as little as possible with the secondary objective of ... seizing Trun.'[47]

Montgomery's changing orders and objectives were the defining characteristic of the next week of operations. Crerar was essentially out of the loop, for parts of the battle at least. From the 14th, for six days, Crerar continued to relay Montgomery's changing objectives to Simonds, most of which the GOC, 2nd Canadian Corps, had already anticipated or, as Crerar suspected, received direct from the C-in-C, 21st Army Group. When Montgomery met with Dempsey and Bradley on the 15th, Crerar was again ignored. Neither situation sat well with Crerar: 'He said that Monty kept phoning him to do this and that,' George Kitching wrote of a conversation on 21 August, 'and, when he was not available, he knew Montgomery was talking with Simonds directly and giving him orders.' On occasion the record of conversations suggests Simonds's exasperation at having to receive the same directions twice. Crerar still took pride in the course of the battle, writing an old friend, 'Certainly the Canadians of this generation have ...

lost none of the dash and determination possessed, in the old days, by their fathers and uncles.'[48]

Crerar had little time for reflection on this point as the battle to close the gap devolved into a series of confusing engagements with shifting objectives. The 2nd Canadian Corps bore the brunt of the fighting from 13 to 18 August as a result of Bradley's decision to halt Patton's Third Army at Argentan; on the 16th, Montgomery ordered First Canadian Army to capture Trun and hold it strongly to stop the elements of five Panzer divisions then trying to break out of the gap. Further exhortations by Monty on 17 August to move the Canadian and Polish armoured divisions quickly past Trun into Chambois – orders Crerar transmitted to Simonds – were the final operations in the battle to close the Falaise gap. Simonds and his divisional commanders were left to close the gap, holding the line Chambois–St Lambert–Trun and then linking up with the Americans closing in from the north.[49]

Crerar continued his regular visits to the front; his two main concerns were ensuring a smooth link up between his army and the Third U.S. Army, and coordinating the attacks of the air force upon whom had devolved much of the responsibility for destroying the German forces striving to blast their way through the gap. Immediate liaison became the key to both. Aware of the dangers of accidental collisions as the two forces came together, HQ First Canadian Army attempted to establish an interchange of information with HQ Third U.S. Army. From 12 August an artillery liaison officer was keeping Corps and Army Headquarters abreast of American plans.

The majority of information on the American advances came from 21st Army Group Headquarters; consequently, Montgomery's 16 August update prompted Crerar to seek a better means of having information on U.S. Third Army operations passed to his HQ. He wrote directly to Patton, informing him that he was sending a liaison officer for attachment to his headquarters to collect information; he invited Patton to do the same. Arriving in Le Mans, the liaison officer found that First U.S. Army had now taken over the sector and he presented Crerar's letter. The suggestion was rebuffed on the grounds that liaison, with the exception of corps artillery, could take place only at the Army Group level.[50]

The exchange of information took on a greater urgency on 17 August as reports poured into HQ First Canadian Army of attacks by American air forces on Canadian, Polish, and British troops. Crerar, assuming his liaison officer had successfully established himself at HQ Third U.S.

Army, wired Patton that he considered 'it essential that we have very close wireless liaison and exchange of situations at not more than hourly intervals' in order to 'curtail all avoidable occurrences of this nature.'[51] Despite the resistance by the U.S. army headquarters, First Canadian Army continued to send hourly reports on the situation, as they understood it, regarding Canadian army troops, while requesting similar information. From the 18th, reports were sent to both the U.S. Third and First armies.

The weather during this period was good, and the Germans, forced to move by day, presented tempting targets to the tactical air forces. The proximity of the Allied forces to the German troops resulted in frequent attacks by the air forces on their own armies. As already noted, Crerar had taken steps to prevent U.S. air forces from attacking Allied troops; on 18 August, he and his senior staff met with Coningham and Brown to discuss the opportunity that now presented itself while the Germans remained vulnerable. Prior to the meeting, Mann reported to him on the 'excellent' state of army–air relations that now pertained between 84 Group and First Canadian Army. Organizational problems in the Joint Battle Room had been worked out to everyone's satisfaction, and procedures for changes to the bomb lines, which theoretically guided the pilots in their attacks, had been improved. Mann pointed out that, while in practice the 'pilots undoubtedly find it hard to map read in the local terrain,' the real problem was the interchange of information at the Army Group level, a point proven, he believed, by the fact that there was no evidence of attacks by either 84 or 83 group on their own troops; U.S. aircraft were the culprits. These points were discussed at the meeting. It was decided that while 84 and 83 group were to have greater discretion in selecting targets, the increasing frequency of attacks necessitated the adoption of the preventive measures – such as extra briefings of pilots using information obtained from G(Ops) – taken by First Canadian Army. The 2 TAF and HQ 21st Army Group were also asked to take 'strong measures.'[52]

The events during this period justified the stress laid on good relations between HQ First Canadian Army and 84 Group. Crerar was quick to deflect any personal or inter-service problems that might arise from the unintended air attacks. That evening, he penned a letter to all commanders and commanding officers, 'giving the rough figures of total vehicles destroyed by 2nd Tactical Air Force during the day, as an antidote to situation which had developed during wholesale attacks by RAF, intended for enemy targets.' In it, he stressed the 'peculiar difficulties to the Allied air forces caused by the convergence of US, British and Canadian armies on a common objective, with air action against the enemy forces within that Allied circle most desirable up to the point of their surrender.' He gave the figures in order that all units and formations could judge the matter 'rationally' and thus 'obtain some idea of the tremendous military balance in their favour.' There is no evidence of the reaction to this communication.[53]

Though the fighting still raged through 18–21 August, Crerar and all the senior Allied commanders were contemplating the next stage of operations. From 17 August, Crerar began regular meetings with his senior staff to discuss both the progress of present operations and the immediate future. On 19 August, he ordered Simonds to reinforce the Polish Armoured Division with 4th Armoured Brigade in anticipation of an advance to the Seine. He had spent considerable time compiling an outline plan for the advance on Trun, which, while overtaken by events, indicated that Crerar was determined – prompted perhaps by his awareness of the marginal operational role he had played up to this point – to carve out a greater role in the planning and handling of future operations.[54] With the army headquarters now up and running, and the Normandy campaign drawing to a dramatic close as German losses reached close to half a million, he wanted a chance to command.

19 Coalition Battles

I

Major-General George Kitching was dismissed following what Simonds considered 4th Canadian Armoured Division's poor performance in Totalize and Tractable. The morning of 22 August found Kitching standing in front of Harry Crerar's desk in his caravan. 'He was kindness itself,' recalled Kitching. 'He treated me as an uncle might treat his favourite nephew except that he rarely used Christian names.' Following the appropriate pleasantries, relaxed by a cigarette, Crerar told him that he was having trouble with Montgomery. 'If it's any comfort to you,' Crerar concluded, 'it may not be long before Montgomery tries to remove me.'[1]

And it was true. By September 1944, Crerar and Montgomery's relationship deteriorated steadily, mirroring Crerar's declining health and Montgomery's erratic behaviour. It was an important command problem, one with political, coalition, and military implications as the battle for the Scheldt approaches became a critical factor in sustaining the flow of supplies to the Allied armies. Crerar's grip on the army was increasingly tenuous. By his own account, his powers of decision slipped markedly as euphoria descended on the senior officers and headquarters staffs of the British and Canadian armies in late August and early September. Further, Montgomery wanted to replace Crerar with Simonds, and tested the limits of his own influence to achieve this goal.[2]

By the end of August, the German position in Normandy had collapsed completely; the Allies had destroyed elements of thirty-seven divisions, and the Germans were in retreat. The stunning victory in

Normandy and the rapidity of the advance through France and into Belgium convinced most that the German will to resist was destroyed. The belief that the Germans were nearly finished influenced many among the Allied High Command as they planned for the crossing of the Seine. It influenced Crerar's approach to operations along the left flank as well as the reinforcement crisis that developed in August–September. Writing on 24 August, Crerar was guardedly optimistic that the war would soon end. 'I believe,' he wrote to Sherwood Lett, 'that the toughest fighting is now over. Indeed, if we were not at war with a government of fanatics, an unconditional surrender would have taken place a week or so ago.'[3]

The most immediate issue influencing Crerar's handling of operations following the Normandy battles was the greatly reduced strength of the units under his command, Canadian and Polish. He had to balance his responsibility to his troops with coalition demands. Crerar's position was delicate; he was accountable to many masters. The problem facing Crerar was exacerbated by the difficulties imposed on the Canadian Army by terrain and logistics as it turned northward to advance along the coast, and began crossing the Seine in the face of stiff German resistance.

The reinforcement crisis had been casting a shadow for several months, but moved to the forefront as casualties mounted in Normandy.[4] Through July, general duty infantry casualties of on average 120 per battalion prompted Crerar to draw CMHQ's attention to the increasingly dangerous situation. Listing the shortfalls unit by unit, he went to the heart of the problem: 'Am concerned about infantry general duty deficiencies which approximate 1900. Our ability to continue severe fighting or to exploit a break-through would be severely restricted through lack of replacement personnel ... I consider this the most serious problem of Cdn Army at the moment and to require most energetic handling.'[5]

The reply from Price Montague was not reassuring. He estimated that remustering artillery, service corps, and armoured corps would satisfy approximately 80 per cent of the army needs, until approximately mid-October. Indeed, Chief of Staff, Stuart, CMHQ, had, before his departure on 25 July, approved a staff recommendation for remustering up to 25 per cent of the artillery and up to 60 per cent of the service corps; this recommendation was based on reports from Brigadier A.W. Beament, Officer-in-Charge Canadian section GHQ, 1st Echelon, 21st Army Group – the brother of BGS, First Canadian Army, G.E. Beament – that infantry casualties were dramatically higher vis-à-vis other corps (78 per cent of infantry, against War Office estimates of 63 per cent) than had been estimated by CMHQ; this estimate had been used, despite Beament's warnings to Stuart in December 1943 that the numbers were wrong.[6] Montague suggested that the arrival of reinforcements in the theatre could be sped up if Crerar would accept personnel who had not completed their training; otherwise, he asked Crerar to affirm the present policy of withholding personnel until trained to the minimal acceptable standard. Under this policy, he estimated that 3,773 all ranks could be dispatched by 19 August.[7]

On 7 August, Crerar consulted with Simonds, who briefed him on the potential shortfall, following Operation Totalize, of up to 2,500 general duty infantry in 2nd Division alone. Crerar concluded that the reinforcements promised by Montague and Stuart were insufficient. Influenced by the success of remustering in easing the reinforcement shortages in Italy, Crerar promoted it as the quickest means of alleviating the problem in northwest Europe.[8] Instructions had already been issued on 5 August to dispatch remustered men to the 13th Infantry Brigade, the designated retraining organization. Crerar cabled his plans to CMHQ on the 8th. He estimated that the problem was 'confined to Infantry General Duty' and that operations for the balance of the month would 'likely ... involve much heavy fighting.' He went on, 'It is quite clear that only solution lies in vigorous remustering and strenuous conversion training.' To that end he requested a study of the feasibility of 'shortening conversion training by grading on entry.'[9]

Three points were notable. First, Crerar emphasized that that the problem, and therefore the remustering policy, was confined to the infantry; the remustering of officers, as well as tradesmen, remained voluntary, with the exception of those in disbanded units, not least because of the morale and political difficulties involved in reassigning the higher-paid skilled tradesmen who had volunteered under specific conditions. Second, Crerar also insisted that, regardless of the urgency, all must be trained to a 'minimum acceptable standard.'[10] Third, he was willing to risk the long-term health of the army over the possibility that a decision could be secured before the crisis became acute. He concluded that in 'view distinct possibility that operations of next four weeks may prove turning point remustering policy should be based on short view. It is vital that our offensive power be maintained and long term futures must be risked to produce early results.'[11] This was another indication of the influence of the optimism that permeated the Allied high command during the heady days of August 1944.

Reconciling the directive to maintain a minimum standard of proficiency with the need for immediate reinforcements proved difficult. By mid-August, only 1,875 men were remustered, despite assurances from Stuart to Montgomery that steps were being taken to improve the situation. Indeed, Stuart took pains to control 'alarmist' reports to Ottawa regarding the potential problem, hoping that indirect measures such as increasing pressure on volunteers to join the general service infantry would alleviate the situation. Crerar distanced himself from the 'gloves-off' effort designed to 'persuade NRMA men' to go 'GS.'[12] Stuart, at this point a very sick man, while in Ottawa painted a rosy picture of the reinforcement situation, one that delighted Mackenzie King but was not accurate.

The Deputy Chief of Staff, CMHQ, Brigadier M.H.S. Penhale, crossed over to Army Headquarters on 10 August to apprise Crerar and his staff of the limitations of supplying remustered men in the short time prescribed. Penhale's visit was not recorded in Crerar's war diary, nor was any record kept of the discussions. Soon after, however, the HQ staff considered, in Stacey's words, 'the possibility of accepting infantry reinforcements with a lower standard of training.' Neither Crerar nor his staff wanted this and so informed CMHQ; Stuart concurred, but suggested that any men competent enough to complete refresher training 'more quickly' would be sent to alleviate the immediate shortfall.[13] The shortfall continued, however. By 16 August, the deficiency was such that HQ First Canadian Army was encouraging the dispatch of men returned from hospital as soon as available, as well as 'otherwise provided' in order to add to 'bayonet' strength. The crisis peaked, statistically, on 31 August when the shortfall in other ranks was 4,318.

By the end of August, Crerar's position was increasingly difficult. Montgomery and his 21st Army Group staff were pressuring the Canadians to move faster. But his army was weakening with each passing day. He pressed for solutions within the army itself. On 31 August, he wrote Stuart that the steps towards remustering should 'soon produce amelioration [of the] existing situation' but went on to emphasize the 'urgency of the existing situation.' Following a memorandum by Simonds, which maintained that discrepancies between casualty figures and unit establishments were the result of too lenient a view of battle exhaustion, straggling, and absenteeism – the study itself a measure of how desperate the reinforcement situation was – Crerar ordered Walford to pen a harsh memorandum reminding the COs that what they were dealing with was in fact desertion. A terse reminder to the DA and QMG to 'get some speed out of the JAG section' two days later suggests his interest in this as an interim solution to the problem, as well as indicating his exasperation with a staff not adapting to mobile warfare as quickly as it might have. The result was a precisely worded memorandum to Simonds, directed to the formation commanders, that absence, cowardice, and desertion should not go unpunished. A final rejoinder to Stuart in mid-September that the reinforcement situation showed no 'general improvement over that which obtained a month ago' and 'require[d] [his] personal and urgent attention' seems to have been Crerar's last word on the subject before he went off sick.[14]

Was there more Crerar could have done? Not at this stage. There were only two options beyond remustering. He could have demanded immediate conscription of NRMA men for overseas service, but that would have solved nothing, for he would have been turned down and that would been very damaging to the war effort, and possibly army morale. He refused public comment on the situation 'on principle.'[15] He could also have accepted a shorter training or retraining period – an option that was considered but dismissed. This question plagued the higher command, even after the war. Writing in 1956 on the issue of manpower and the Canadian Army, E.L.M. Burns observed that it was worth considering whether manpower was wasted in 'trying to attain too high a standard of reinforcement training.' His conclusion was that the reverse was often true: there were complaints all through the war that reinforcements were untrained, despite the twenty-three to thirty-one weeks between enlistment and going to the front. They were more likely to be killed or wounded. His solution was to improve liaison between front-line units and base reinforcement units to enhance the actual training rather than shorten the time.[16] This again would have no short-term impact but was tried in November as Crerar assessed the post-Scheldt state of his army in general and officer corps in particular.

Crerar was doing everything possible to keep his army fighting, and had been since early August. The issue in the late summer and early autumn of 1944 was one of operational capability; in the long term, morale also loomed as a key consideration as the reinforcement problem continued and became by November the conscription crisis. While he had some responsibility for the creation of the situation, how much is debatable. In the short term, he was acting responsibly. The problem was rooted in the acceptance of earlier policies, ranging from those on proportional wastage rates, to creating too many headquarters sending formations to different theatres and then overstaffing them. CMHQ was criticized in this regard. And finally, it was a product of the intensity of the fighting in the Normandy battles.

The problem was not confined to the Canadians. The reinforcement issue also loomed as a potential area of conflict in the multi-national First Canadian Army, placing Crerar in a delicate situation. On 17 August, the Polish Commander-in-Chief General K. Sosnknowsi requested that Crerar consider the inability of the Polish Army in London to make good reinforcements when assigning tasks to the Polish Armoured Division. Crerar responded by reminding the C-in-C that the British and Canadians were also experiencing manpower problems, and he concluded with the observation that the 4th Canadian Armoured Division had a 20 per cent higher casualty rate, suggesting that neither he nor Simonds had been 'unmindful of the casualty situation in allotting operational tasks to these two Armoured Divisions.' It became more and more important as the Canadians crossed the Seine.

II

Montgomery was clearly unhappy with Crerar's handling of the operations, but clashes with Crerar over operations were only one of many problems that irritated the newly promoted field marshal through late August and early September. As the Normandy campaign ended, he was struggling to secure permission from Eisenhower to undertake his 'pencil-like' thrust to the Ruhr, an operation that Montgomery was convinced could bring about the collapse of the entire German war effort in the west; not coincidentally it would require his retention as ground forces commander. Since 15 August, he had been discussing the use of an airborne army to pave the way. On 23 August, Eisenhower rejected Montgomery's plans as neither feasible, given the logistical situation, nor desirable, given the estrangement between Montgomery and the American commanders. Their doubts about his command abilities, and his about theirs, only added to the personality problems. Accordingly, 'Ike' took over direct control of the ground forces while retaining his position as Supreme Allied Commander and continued with a 'broad front' strategy – both as previously planned. Montgomery's was left in no doubt as to his position when he was, again as intended, effectively demoted to command of 21st Army Group; his ego was not salved by his promotion to field marshal.

In late August, Montgomery's operational orders conformed to Ike's strategic concept, but begrudgingly and with an eye to developing his own plans later. On 26 August, Montgomery ordered First Canadian Army to operate northwards, cross the Seine, and secure Le Havre and Dieppe. All enemy forces 'in the coastal belt up to Bruges' were to be destroyed. On the right, Second British Army was to advance rapidly towards Amiens, but was instructed to be prepared to support airborne troops who might be dropped in the Pas de Calais to facilitate the clearance of the area and eliminate the threat of the V1 and V2 rockets then raining down on southeastern England.[17] Late on the 29th, Montgomery decided against the use of airborne troops in the Pas de Calais on the then correct assumption that the Channel ports would not be defended and that the German 15th Army would be forced to retreat eastward in the face of the rapid advance by Second British Army, which had already crossed the Somme, against opposition characterized as 'weak,' and captured Amiens. Consequently, Crerar was summoned to Monty's HQ, where he received orders to 'push' his armoured divisions north along the axis Abbeville–St Omer to safeguard the British army's increasingly exposed flank and to take over the Abbeville extension of the Somme bridgehead from 30 British Corps. Crerar, however, warned Monty that his transport and maintenance needs were such that he could not use more than two divisions north of the Somme. Monty was dubious about this assertion. Noting the difficulties arising because the 'Canadian army [was] hanging back somewhat,' he ordered deGuingand to investigate 'maintenance matters' with the First Canadian Army staff: 'It is essential,' he concluded, 'that the whole of Second Canadian Corps ... should be able to operate right up to Bruges and clear the Channel coast, but to do this Crerar says he wants more GT Companies, and if so he must have them.'[18] Crerar met with Dempsey and Monty later on the 1st, and received the latest situation report and Monty's instructions.

Crerar did as he was ordered, flying back to his HQ and meeting once more with his staff about the movement of his tactical headquarters, before he retired because of an attack of dysentery. Despite the fact that the Canadians and Poles were meeting stiff resistance from fresh German divisions and incurring heavy casualties while trying to cross the Seine, and the growing concerns over manpower, on 1 September Crerar ordered his depleted armoured divisions to race for the Somme, assured by his operations staff that there was no significant enemy resistance south of the river. Simonds consequently ordered his corps (with the exception of 2nd Canadian Division, which was, not coincidentally, to stay in the Dieppe area and reorganize) forward on the axis Abbeville–St Omer–Ypres until the line of the Somme was reached. At that point, the 4th Canadian Armoured Division – operating at half of its authorized tank establishment and promised a four-day rest – would stop to refit.[19]

These orders were in keeping with the spirit of Montgomery's orders. Neither his operations group, which reported that 4th Canadian Armoured was making good progress and over halfway between Neufchatel and Abbeville, nor Simonds had felt there was any lack of push. Nor was it unreasonable to anticipate a pause for some of the formations to absorb some reinforcements, given the heavy fighting and manpower concerns that had been growing since early August.

Montgomery disagreed with the decision to pause for a refit. On 2 September deGuingand reported that, contrary to Crerar's assertion, 'Canadian Army "Q" say their [transport] sufficient to allow Second Canadian Corps of four divs and Corps tps to operate to Bruges.' Later that day, Monty wired Crerar:

> Second Army now positioned near the Belgian frontier and will go through towards Brussels tomorrow. It is very necessary that your armoured divisions should push forward with all speed towards St. Omer and beyond. DO NOT consider this is the time for any division to halt for maintenance. Push on quickly [emphasis in original].[20]

Montgomery's message was ambiguous, and it is unclear whether his sole concern was that Crerar had stopped his armoured divisions or 'any division.'[21] Montgomery's main concern was his belief that the British forces were miles ahead of the Canadians. In either case, Crerar had before him very different information. As the Polish Armoured arrived at Abbeville, they found no British troops, but the initial reports available to the chief engineer suggested that three bridges were captured intact. By early afternoon Crerar's own flights over the battlefield had revealed that this information was wrong. Resistance had been encountered on 4th Canadian Armoured's front at Airaines, but still the Canadian army had fulfilled Monty's orders; there were also concerns about the availability of large-scale air support as the forward troops put more distance between themselves and the airstrips, but it was deemed sufficient for the resistance then being encountered. The minutes of the morning staff meetings also reflected the continued concerns over maintenance.[22]

Crerar's response reflected both this information and his testiness at Monty's barb:

> Delighted to learn that Second Army is now positioned near Belgian frontier would advise you that until late this afternoon Second Army troops have not been within 5 Miles of Abbeville and that all bridges R. Somme Ne Piquingy blown with enemy in considerable strength holding north bank. With assistance flank attack 4 British Armd. Bde. from direction Piquingy and Polish Armd. Div. attacking Abbeville across R. Somme from south Simonds hope secure crossings tonight.
>
> Not a case of more Divs. on line R. Somme but of 2 Canadian Inf. Div. Bns. down to average strength 525 and in my opinion a 48 Hr. halt quite essential in order it can absorb approx. 1000 reinforcements arriving today.
>
> You can be assured that there is no lack of push or rational speed Canadian army. St. Omer and beyond will be reached without any avoidable delay.

The Field Marshal, perceiving a lack of drive on the part of the Canadians, was not long in reporting to Brooke about Crerar's inept handling of the army.[23]

Montgomery's attitude was also creating tension between the staffs of the First Canadian Army and 21st Army Group. The Canadians were perceived as overly cautious. On 2 September, the investigation by Monty's Chief of Staff into Crerar's claims that the maintenance situation of the Canadian army was holding it back determined that the Canadians were prone to 'bellyaching about their inability to maintain their troops forward,' but that 'Walford [was] quite happy.' More damning was the perception that the Canadian army was hesitant to come to grips with the Germans. Writing to Monty on the impending operations against Le Havre, deGuingand noted that he hoped

> the Canadians do not make too much fuss about Havre [sic], as Bill Williams [21 AG Chief Intelligence Officer] says there is only an indifferent static Bde there besides flak and CD troops. I mention this because David Strangeways, whom I sent forward with a party to get into Rouen at an early stage ... found the Canadian Bde sitting around the City saying that they could not get in owing to opposition. Strangeways then got tired of waiting and drove in with his chaps, finding no-one there!

A few days later, deGuingand informed Montgomery how necessary it was to secure a port north of Dieppe, and added that he 'hoped Crerar realizes the urgency of the situation' and that he was taking it up through 'staff channels.'[24]

An unhappy Montgomery had duly informed Dempsey of Crerar's estimation of the problems in crossing the Somme. Given the possibility that 'it must be some time before Canadian army moves up your left flank,' he told Dempsey to slow his advance, suggesting he stop along the Brussels-Ghent line. Fearing the loss of momentum, Monty arranged a meeting between his army commanders for 3 September.[25] Crerar balked, citing national considerations, in this case a ceremony scheduled to commemorate the liberation of Dieppe. Anxious to attend the Dieppe ceremony, Crerar wired Montgomery that unless '[the] operational situation requires my arrival at TAC British Army at 1300 hrs, tomorrow would appreciate if meeting could take place say 1700hrs.' He explained, 'Have arranged to be present at a formal religious service and parade elements of 2 Canadian Division at Dieppe commencing about noon tomorrow and from a Canadian point of view desirable I should do so. Will however conform with your wishes.'[26] Montgomery made his wishes known before day's end on the 2nd: 'Essential you should attend meeting at Tac Second Army at 1300 hours tomorrow 3 September.'[27]

There is some evidence that Crerar, anticipating Montgomery's reply, ignored the message; he was still at his HQ when the message arrived, although he later claimed that 'no messages had been received for me from C-in-C' before he flew to meet Simonds at his Tac HQ in the early morning hours of 3 September. He also claimed to have arranged for any messages from the C-in-C to be forwarded immediately to 2nd Canadian Corps or 2nd Division.[28] He had made arrangements, but not those: Mann recounted after the war how Crerar, before he left for the Dieppe ceremony, told him that 'in no circumstance was he [Crerar] to receive any further communication from Monty until it was too late to cancel his role in the Dieppe ceremonies.' Mann recalled that when he received, on the evening of the second, Montgomery's follow-up message stating that Crerar was 'definitely required' to attend the conference, he informed the SO that there was an error in decoding and ordered the SO to send a query, 'also in code to delay things, asking for a repeat.' It was not until 1447 hours on the third that a reply was sent from First Canadian Army. It read that no reply had been received regarding the 'deferment [of the] rendevouz [sic]' and that Crerar, already in the air, was most 'anxious' to learn if this was acceptable. When the new message arrived, error-free as expected, Mann had the duty SO check the decoding. 'As time had now run past any conformity with the Monty order,' he wrote, 'I had it sent on to 2 Div.'[29]

In the days that followed, Montgomery, simmering over the delays, had Crerar investigate. Mann dutifully fulfilled his mandate to 'have full enquiries and report made by the Chief Signal Officer immediately.' Enquiries were made, Crerar spoke to the CSO, and the Tac HQ wireless arrangements were tested; no problems were discovered. Oddly, three days later on the 7th, a message from Montgomery was delayed, and an upset Crerar had the poor CSO before him once again. New wireless communication arrangements between 21st Army Group Tac HQ and First Canadian Army Tac HQ were quickly arranged.[30]

Crerar followed his itinerary on the third and claimed to have assumed that Montgomery's conference was of a 'personal' nature rather than a formal meeting between army commanders; Montgomery's wires gave no indication that anyone other than Dempsey would be in attendance. Crerar met with Simonds before departing for the Dieppe ceremony, to discuss the tactical and operational situation; at 1020, he flew to Dieppe, attended two emotional services at the Canadian Cemetery, and took the march past. Following the ceremony, Crerar climbed into his Auster and flew the fifty-five miles to Demspey's HQ; here he discovered that he had missed a formal conference attended by the C-in-C's 21st and 12th U.S. Army Group as well as the GOC of First U.S. Army. Informed of this, Crerar flew to Montgomery's HQ.

Crerar's attendance at the ceremony in Dieppe led to a well-known blow-up with Montgomery. The Field Marshal took Crerar to task for his absence and, forgetting himself, chewed him out, stating that their 'ways must part.' As Crerar reported in a lengthy memorandum written for Stuart the next day, he pointed out that he 'could not accept this attitude and judgement on his part,' having 'carried out my responsibilities as one of his two army commanders, and as the Cdn Army Comd, in what I considered to be a reasonable and intelligent way, in the light of the situation as I knew it, or appreciated it.' He had also emphasized the importance of the ceremony at Dieppe: 'I had, as previously explained, a definite responsibility to my Government and country which, at times, might run counter to his own wishes. There was a powerful Canadian reason why I should have been present with 2 Cdn Inf Div at Dieppe that day. In fact, there were 800 reasons – the Canadian dead buried at Dieppe cemetery.'

Montgomery was abrupt and 'intimated that he was not interested in my explanation – that the Canadian aspect of the Dieppe ceremonial was of no importance compared to getting on with the war.' Montgomery suggested he had investigated the signals mix-up, and concluded that even if Crerar had not received the communications, then in 'default of other agreed arrangements, I should have made it my business to be present.' He continued this hard line, intimating that Crerar would be replaced, until Crerar played the national card: "I replied that I assumed he would at once take this up through higher channels and that I, in turn, would at once report the situation to my government.' Faced with Crerar's stance, and to Crerar's surprise, Montgomery backed off, concluding that even if Crerar 'had not been able to come ... [he] should have sent [his] C of S to the meeting.' They continued to argue, Montgomery wishing to close the matter, and Crerar insisting that it be aired. In the end, Crerar satisfied himself with the report to Stuart. Crerar concluded,

> I must state that I received the impression, at the commencement of the interview, that the C-in-C was out to eliminate forcefully, from my mind that I had any other responsibilities than to him. The Canadian ceremony at Dieppe was not of his ordering, nor to his liking. It had been the cause of an interference with an instruction which he had separately issued to me – to meet him at a certain time and place. As the interview proceeded, and he found that I would not retreat from the stand I had taken – that I had a responsibility to Canada as well as to the C-in-C – he decided to 'consider the matter closed.' It was not a willing decision, nor one that I can assume will be maintained. However, though our relations have obviously been strained, I trust that the situation is temporary and I shall do what I can to ease them, though without departing from what I consider it my duty to do, or not to do, in my capacity as a Canadian.[31]

Crerar was correct. This paragraph summed up the problem caused by the ambiguity inherent in the relationship between a Dominion force commander and a British superior, when both exercised their prerogatives to the fullest extent. Crerar was accountable to the Canadian government for the fate of the army and its soldiers. And he had coalition responsibilities as well.

Was this command problem and Crerar's absence from the meeting significant from an operational point of view? Not immediately, but it did have consequences. The most significant short-term repercussion of the clash was Crerar's disinclination to question Montgomery's fixation with Market Garden and the Ruhr. Montgomery's biographer,

Nigel Hamilton, gives it more weight, characterizing the 3 September meeting as a 'Fatal Conference,' one 'as important for the final course of World War II' as Monty's conference with Eisenhower on 23 August, where the Master had been forced to accede to Eisenhower's wishes for the broad front strategy. Observing that without strong strategic direction from SHAEF and Eisenhower, the army commanders 'were being compelled to initiate their own strategy,' he lays the blame for the direction of the campaign directly at Crerar's feet: 'Crerar's failure, by his absence, to present the Canadian case for caution in assigning bold missions for the Allied armies without first ensuring priority to the seizure of the Channel ports and Antwerp, as well as the capture of the 150,000 Germans reckoned to be retreating along the coast, was to be of profound significance.' Later, he blames Eisenhower for not 'unequivocally' ordering Monty to secure the Channel ports and Antwerp. The nub of his argument, in direct contradiction to all previous characterizations of Monty, is that a hapless field marshal, bitter and confused, was allowed by both his army commanders and his superior to stumble into the operational quagmire of Market Garden.

Montgomery had shown himself to be indecisive when faced with too many strategic opportunities, but it stretches credulity to suggest that Crerar would have dissuaded Montgomery. It does raise the question of whether Crerar, in direct contradiction to Montgomery's perception about his 'bellyaching,' was forceful enough in pointing out the difficulties of seizing quickly, with his under-strength army, the Channel ports required to support 'a full-blooded Allied advance.'[32] Certainly Crerar did not make a forceful case for the difficulties involved in clearing the ports, but it is unlikely that he would have done so at this meeting, or that it would have had any effect on Montgomery. As of 3 September, intelligence reports from HQ First Canadian Army indicated that 'the enemy did not intend to defend Le Havre, and stiff resistance was not anticipated'; two days later, Crerar's intelligence officer informed the staff at their morning conference that it was 'the probable intention of the enemy to withdraw to the Siegfried Line or the Rhine before attempting to establish a def[ensive] line.'[33] The main problem facing Crerar's army was not yet that it had too many tasks, but rather it had too few men and resources, in particular bridging equipment and means of crossing the numerous canals and rivers facing the Canadians. After the war, in a letter to Stacey suggesting that he was understating in drafts of the official histories the difficulties of the coastal terrain from a tactical and administrative point of view, Crerar wrote that it seemed that the Canadian army always had 'ten more rivers to cross and many, many canals to cross as well.'[34] This was an area of concern, particularly as resources like pontoon and folding boat equipment as well as bridging companies were transferred from First Canadian Army to Second British Army. Crerar's difficulties in this period were largely caused by the fact that First Canadian Army was denuded of supplies and formations following the 3 September conference as Montgomery pursued his course. By 7 September, dissatisfied with the pace of the build-up for his own 'full-blooded thrust' for the Ruhr, Montgomery rerouted further supplies destined for First Canadian Army. It was no coincidence that on that same 7 September, Brigadier Walford observed that a '10-ton truck was now worth more than a Sherman tank.'[35]

There is no record of any further open disagreement between Crerar and Montgomery over the speed of Canadian operations. However, this seemed more a result of the strained relationship as well as Crerar's declining health than any meeting of the minds.[36]

While the immediate repercussions were minimal, the relationship between Crerar and Monty, and between their HQs, remained strained, and it preoccupied Crerar for at least the 4th, as he spent the better part of it preparing a memorandum on the incident. It was also on Montgomery's mind, as his venom spilled into his operational reports to Brooke. While such criticism of coalition and Allied partners was hardly unusual, Montgomery took the precaution, as noted by historian Stephen Hart, of using the 'rare War Office "Guard" security classification ... reserved for use by only the highest British commanders' relating 'messages of far reaching importance or controversial matters which must never be known to the United States.'[37] The use of this classification was an indication of how strongly Montgomery felt about Crerar's performance, but, as Brooke's admonishments in the summer suggested, Montgomery abused this classification not least because it gave him a secure vehicle to vent and to test the limits of his influence on strategy and command with Brooke.

Still, the temper of Montgomery's views is clear from his comments to Brooke. On 4 September he observed that the 'Canadian Army has had trouble in crossing the Somme as all bridges were blown on their front. They have now got over at Pont Remy and north of Abbeville and are now beginning to move northwards and are now about three miles north of the Somme. The operations of this Army since crossing the Seine have been badly handled and slow.'[38]

Neither was he inclined to apologize until Trumbell Warren, his Canadian PA, pointed out the potential political repercussions if Crerar took it to Ralston: 'He's [Crerar] not going to swallow.'[39] Initially hesitant, nevertheless, Montgomery reconsidered and wrote a note of apology. 'I am sorry I was a bit rude the other day, and somewhat outspoken. I was annoyed that no one came to a very important conference. But forget about it – and let us get on with the war. It was my fault.'[40]

Crerar's willingness to make it a political issue dampened Montgomery's anger, but he would not forget. Neither would Crerar. 'I've never seen a chap so mad,' recalled Warren as Crerar emerged from the field marshal's caravan. As he drove to his aircraft, he recalled that Crerar was very angry. '"That guy is not going to get away with that."'[41] In his correspondence, he minimized the clash, but was still upset: 'Monty has been pretty trying on a couple of occasions during the last few days,' he wrote Stuart on 5 September. 'He is very upset at the loss of operational command over the U.S. Armies,' Crerar continued, 'and his nomination to Field Marshal's rank has accentuated, rather than eased, his mental disturbance.'[42] It was clear that by this time he had Montgomery's measure. Stacey wrote in his memoirs, 'I remember Crerar saying Monty would always go through a yellow light; but when the light turned red, he stopped.'[43]

Montgomery's temper prompted Crerar to write Stuart an unusual note, urging him to press the minister and CGS to greater efforts to reunite the 1st Canadian Corps with First Canadian Army. Significantly, once this was accomplished, he wanted Stuart to have the political authorities take action to redefine the position of the Canadian forces to 'serving together' rather than 'in combination' with the British – a coalition partner rather than a British formation. The army commander wanted to establish the 'appropriate degree' of Canadian autonomy, to ensure some freedom of action, as he believed that the 'decisions taken [on occupation and administration of forces] will undoubtedly affect future international relations and responsibilities of Canada.' Though Crerar believed the war would be over soon, he also wanted to strengthen his position relative to Montgomery. He would have to wait another eight months.[44]

Neither did Montgomery forget the altercation. His concerns regarding Crerar had been sufficient for him to delay the employment of FCA headquarters through June, and to harshly rebuff Crerar's attempts to discuss the delay. Montgomery's note to Brooke demonstrated that the field marshal's aim was to replace Crerar, and that he recognized that this was a major issue. As events would prove, he would do his best to achieve this and make one last attempt to minimize the responsibilities of Crerar and his army. Crerar, however, would prove up to the tests.

20 First Canadian Army and the Scheldt

I

Crerar and First Canadian Army were harshly criticized for their handling of operations following the breakout from Normandy. British historians have tended, with the exception of Hart's study of 21st Army Group, to parrot Montgomery's criticisms that the operations were 'badly handled and slow.' Canadians historians have been more cognizant of the resource, manpower, and topographical challenges facing First Canadian Army. But Crerar and First Canadian Army's achievements were significant. Crerar's efforts to keep his resource-starved multinational army fighting, in the face of manpower shortages and increasingly tough resistance from the Germans, were notable. Particularly significant was the concentration of firepower of the three services in support of Canadian operations, in part as a substitute for FCA deprivation – an impressive accomplishment, given the personalities involved, but one that was overshadowed by Simonds's assumption of command and completion of the clearing of the Scheldt.

During the first week of September 1944, the most important development for both sides was the sudden capture of Antwerp, with its port facilities intact, by Second British Army on 4 September. To the Allies this achievement was symbolic of both the impressive gains all along the front – Brussels had fallen the day before – and the belief that the Germans, despite signs that their resistance was stiffening, seemed to be beaten. Montgomery, oblivious to the logistical situation, saw in Antwerp's fall an opportunity. He drafted a telegram to Eisenhower: 'I consider that we have now reached a stage where one really powerful and full-blooded thrust towards Berlin is likely to get there and thus end the

German war.' He suggested that the logistical situation could support only one such offensive; naturally, it should be his. Eisenhower agreed with Monty's concept in principle, but in practice continued to favour a version of his broad front strategy. He gave priority to the northern operations but felt that at this time operations to open Le Havre and Antwerp would allow an advance against both the Ruhr and the Saar, thus keeping both the British and Americans active, and happy. Montgomery, however, continued to stress that his offensive should be given priority, and reacted accordingly.

The momentum of the Canadian campaign through the rest of September was slowly blunted: as their tasks multiplied, or shifted, the resources allotted shrank. Unit strength continued to decline. Crerar's health also deteriorated. As well, the unwieldy inter-service command structure became more important as First Canadian Army came increasingly to depend on the firepower of Bomber Command, tactical air support, and ultimately the guns of the Royal Navy. Simultaneously, German resistance stiffened as Hitler reorganized his defences in the west in reaction to the fall of Antwerp.[1] Field Marshal Gerd von Rundstedt, dismissed in July, was appointed the new Commander-in-Chief West. The 1st Parachute Army, a mix of Luftwaffe recruits and paratroops, commanded by Colonel-General Kurt Student, was deployed in the Antwerp–Albert Canal sector. Hitler's Directive of 4 September designated Le Havre, Boulogne, and Dunkirk as well as the Scheldt approaches to Antwerp, including Walcheren Island, as 'fortresses' to be defended to the last. On 5 September, the German 15th Army, in danger of being cut off by the fall of Antwerp, began a difficult but organized retreat to a line on the Albert Canal, on the right of the Student's parachute army. For the next two and a half weeks, the 15th Army moved close to 90,000 men, 600 guns, and 6,200 vehicles, harassed only by the Allied tactical air forces; the newly reorganized and reinvigorated 15th Army implemented Hitler's orders and substantially strengthened the garrisons of the Channel ports, while creating two new fortresses, Scheldt Fortress North and Scheldt Fortress South. By the second week of September, Antwerp was effectively closed to the Allies as the Germans entrenched along the fifty-mile approach.

No one tried to stop the Germans as they prepared to deny the Allies the ports they would soon so desperately need; indeed, no one but the Germans recognized the significance of what was happening. Montgomery's eyes were firmly fixed on the Ruhr; clearing the Scheldt estuary was not yet even a secondary consideration. His M523 of 3 September directed that 21st Army Group's intention was to 'advance eastward and destroy all enemy forces encountered,' and secondly to 'occupy the RUHR, and get astride the communications leading from it into Germany and the sea ports.' Second British Army was given the most important role; he contemplated no significant task for First Canadian Army: 'Canadian army will clear the coastal belt, and will then remain in the general area Bruges-Calais until the maintenance situation allows of its employment further forward.' He issued no other formal directives for eleven days, but began to reconsider First Canadian Army objectives as the situation dictated. On 6 September, as it became obvious that the German positions along the approaches denied the Allies access to Antwerp, he asked Crerar for his 'opinion on the likelihood of early capture of Boulogne,' noting that the 'immediate opening of some port north of Dieppe [was] essential for rapid development of [his] plan.' As noted, deGuingand was also dispatched to ensure that Crerar realized the urgency of the situation.[2]

First Canadian Army had already begun to liberate the Channel ports. The forward elements of Crocker's corps had run up against Le Havre's formidable defences on the second, and it was evident that a set-piece attack, supported by Bomber Command and the Royal Navy, was necessary if losses were to be minimized. On the night of 5–6 September, the 3rd Division ran into the landward defences of Boulogne; it was clear that the Germans were also going to hold that city. This news, and reports that the Germans were preparing to defend the ports, prompted instructions to Simonds to press on with all speed. Simonds ordered the development of another set-piece attack built around the heavy bombers, medium artillery, and armoured carriers tied up in the assault on Le Havre. Planning for the operation to reduce Boulogne had thus already begun when Montgomery's enquiry reached Crerar. He was able to cable Monty on 6 September that the army was already examining the problem of securing Boulogne.[3] Crerar had been informed only that morning, during the joint conference, that Boulogne would probably require a 'treatment similar to Le Havre,' an estimate confirmed over the next few days. The operational method for capturing the ports was now settled. Operation Astonia against Le Havre began on 10 September, after which the fortress was reduced within three days, with over 11,000 prisoners reported as taken at a cost of 388 casualties. While the German garrison commander questioned the efficacy of the bombing, if there were any doubts in the minds of First Canadian Army staff and its commander, the ratio of losses to POWs put them to rest. Crerar believed that bombers were a necessary component of his operations to capture the other coastal ports. On 15 September he wrote Air Chief Marshal Arthur Harris, 'Yesterday, the C in C handed me a large and difficult job to do, in the next week or ten days, which I am now studying. I am already quite convinced, however, that I shall need to call upon you for the maximum support, if it is to be successfully accomplished.'[4]

Some critics question the decision to liberate the ports. After the war Simonds said that he tried to convince Crerar to bypass the ports completely; there is no wartime evidence for this assertion. Should Crerar have gone directly for the Scheldt? And could he have?[5] Thanks to Ultra intercepts, Crerar was aware that the Germans were preparing to defend the estuary, and so was his staff. As early as 7 September, in contrast to the intelligence report issued two days earlier suggesting the Germans would withdraw to the Rhine, the head of army intelligence informed Crerar that it was 'probable that [the Germans would] try to form a def[ensive] line along the Albert Canal,' offering 'stiff resistance with fresh divisions.'[6] Even before he received this news, Crerar was urging Simonds to hurry, as information was received on the resistance outside Boulogne. Once Montgomery's request regarding Boulogne arrived, Crerar met Simonds twice, first to instruct him on the priority for capturing the ports and then to discuss the operations to besiege Boulogne. Simonds and Crerar seem to have agreed on the operational method, which meant that the siege of Boulogne would have to await the fall of Le Havre, and the transfer of support resources some 150 miles.

If there were any doubts as to whether the Channel ports should be taken, they were stilled by successive orders from Montgomery giving priority to obtaining a harbour to support his thrust to the Ruhr. He had calculated that the ports of Dieppe, Le Havre, Boulogne, Calais, and Dunkirk would provide him with enough supplies to get to Berlin; only 'one good Pas de Calais port' would take him into the Ruhr. On 9 September, the army commanders met and Crerar was informed that the approaches to Antwerp were designated as First Canadian Army's 'last priority.' He issued a directive to his corps commanders that same day, prioritizing First Canadian Army's tasks as the capture of Le Havre, Boulogne, Dunkirk, and Calais, 'preferably in that order,' and 'secondary in importance' the 'capture or destruction of the enemy remaining North and East of the Ghent-Bruges Canal.' Reflecting Montgomery's orders, he did not mention Antwerp. On 10 September, a meeting with

Eisenhower forced Montgomery to at least pay lip service to opening the port.[7] On the twelfth, he cabled Crerar stressing the importance of moving on to Boulogne as soon as Le Havre fell, but he also, for the first time, noted that 'the early opening of Antwerp [was] daily becoming of increasing importance' and that the approaches would have to be cleared; there was, however, no urgency in his wire: 'Grateful for your views as to when you think you can tackle this problem.'[8]

Monty's enquiry prompted a detailed assessment of the operations and resources necessary to open the Antwerp approaches. First Canadian Army was already facing problems imposed by the distances between its operations; the supporting services, particularly the artillery, engineers, and the air force, were encountering difficulties in maintaining the level of support required by the Canadian army. The sieges absorbed the bulk of the army's firepower. The Royal Engineers, taxed to the limit by the crossings and the paucity of bridging equipment, were also required to build or rehabilitate the airfields required by No. 84 Group. This was in the hands of the new chief engineer, Brigadier Geoffrey Walsh, a Permanent Force officer who had served as the chief engineer for 1st Canadian Corps; characterized as cold, he was nevertheless efficient and had known Crerar at RMC.[9] The small number of airfields was important. In Crerar's directive of 9 September, No. 84 Group was instructed to deal with the Germans in the Ghent area. The first ten days of September had been devoted to constructing airfields in the St Omer area; now, on the tenth, following requests that certain construction groups be allowed a month to rest and refit, it was decided to abandon all work on these fields and find sites in the Lille area, farther from the ports, but closer to the anticipated line of 21st Army Group's advance. The impact of such delays can only be estimated, but the minutes of the headquarters conference meetings suggest that the number of sorties was severely limited by the delays in airfield construction and the priority given the ports. The crossings on the River Scheldt were, on 11 September, the third and last priority for the air operations.[10]

This was one example of how the pace of operations was taxing the resources of the army as well as the capacity of the still relatively inexperienced headquarters and commander to coordinate the allocation of those steadily shrinking resources. The problems were being addressed, and, despite his weakness, Crerar was making his presence felt: in his sorties over the battlefields, Crerar had observed heavy traffic congestion along the main routes of advance, and instructed Walford that traffic control was becoming a problem, as the distances made maintaining more than two forward and return routes an impossibility. A week later, by mid-September, the problems were identified, and included a lack of communication between the armies, corps, and line of communication troops. The HQ First Canadian Army had already addressed this particular area, making changes in the quality and quantity of inter-HQ communications, but further changes to the administration of the traffic routes were soon made. The far-flung operations were straining the headquarters movements, however. On 12 September, the HQ requested more communications aircraft to facilitate the movement of the staff and air liaisons because of 'the present distance involved between HQs and the various elements of [First Canadian Army] HQ.' Communications between the army and higher formation headquarters were also tenuous at points: on the 11th, Walford forwarded a request from 21st Army Group's Major-General in Charge of Administration (MGA) that information on the capture of the Channel ports and beaches be passed on 'as early as possible.' Beament observed that such information was being forwarded to the Tac HQ, but that on his visit that day he 'tactfully suggest[ed] that this information be passed to the MGA as soon as received from us.' Given the control exerted over army operations, or at least tasks, by 21st Army Group, the poor communications were surprising.[11]

Like his headquarters, Crerar was stretched thin. The manpower shortages required constant attention. Crerar met Stuart at army headquarters on several occasions to discuss this difficulty, as well as policy questions on the postwar shape and employment of the armed forces. Crerar was also determined to maintain a high profile as the Canadian army's representative. Consequently, official visits – some for the press, some for the local populace – to Rouen, Ypres, and the Vimy Ridge memorial were scheduled. For Crerar, these trips were also personal. 'It was evident,' he wrote in his war diary, 'that the official return of the Canadians was enthusiastically welcomed and considered an historic occasion.' He wanted to be a part of that history. He made sure as well to visit field hospitals and units regularly.[12] Close contact with his scattered forces was maintained through the air, and he was a frequent visitor to his corps' HQs as well as the C-in-C's HQ, using his personal staff for more mundane duties. The routine was taking its toll, and stressed an already fragile constitution, fragility reflected in a greater concern for his surroundings and personal living conditions. In early September 1944, however, although stretched, Crerar was able to undertake his duties.

He was passive, however, in questioning roles his army was handed and did not push hard when he requested more resources. This approach was evident on 13 September, when Montgomery reassessed the strategic situation. He implied that he had given First Canadian Army a task beyond its means in his instructions on the 12th. In a letter written the next day, he asked Crerar whether he could accelerate operations if some of the objectives were dropped or the priorities were reversed. While Montgomery suggested he was willing to 'give up' Dunkirk and Calais, his next directive, issued on the 14th, declared that he expected the approaches to Antwerp and the Channel ports, except Dunkirk, to be cleared with all speed. He had now reversed the order of operations already in progress, and pressed for a greater sense of urgency in completing them. While stressing that the 'really important thing is speed in setting in motion what we have to do' and that the army would be able to 'tackle both ... tasks simultaneously,' Montgomery now decided that the 'setting in motion of operations designed to enable us to use the port of Antwerp' was 'probably the most important.' Montgomery did not stop at issuing general instructions on how to develop operations. He also suggested Crerar use one corps HQ to control the operations against the Channel ports and the other for the action to open the approaches to Antwerp. Montgomery also arranged for heavy bomber support, for use of airborne troops against Walcheren island, and for Crerar's army to take over responsibility for Antwerp in order to develop operations 'westward along the neck of the peninsula towards Walcheren.'[13]

Here was a formidable range of tasks, beyond the army's capacity to perform speedily – an interpretation reflected in the request that emerged from Crerar's meetings with his operations and planning staff on that same day. They presented two alternatives, both of which conformed with Montgomery's conceptions, but recognized that the existing operational situation limited what was possible. The problem was to first disentangle the headquarters and formations from operations already underway, and then switch them quickly over long distances with limited routes and transportation; second, more formations were needed to effectively take over Antwerp and protect Second British Army's flank. The key was how quickly Calais could be invested and whether Montgomery would free some resources, particularly 12 British Corps and 53rd Division, already responsible for Antwerp; the former operation would determine whether 1 British Corps HQ could be moved quickly, while Montgomery's decision on resources would determine if the corps HQ would have to be switched to the right flank, allowing 2nd Canadian Corps to concentrate on the Scheldt. In either case, Crerar estimated that the operations against the Channel ports would take at least ten days and that 1 British Corps HQ could be moved in no less time. After that, Crerar agreed that the Scheldt operations were 'very tough propositions' and would require all the support suggested by Montgomery, although no detailed study had yet been conducted.[14]

Neither the request for further resources nor the assessment that such operations were beyond First Canadian Army's capacity pleased Montgomery. On 13 September, he signalled that both 12 British Corps and the 53rd Division were committed to Market Garden; instead, he ordered – no suggestions this time – Crerar to bring 1 British Corps HQ and 49th Division up to Antwerp as early as possible while grounding 51st Division. Only ninety minutes later, Montgomery offered a new solution: 'Early use of Antwerp so urgent that I am prepared to give up operations against Calais and Dunkirk and be content with Boulogne. If we do this will it enable you to speed up Antwerp business. Discuss this with me tomorrow when you come here for conference.'[15]

Crerar placed Montgomery's points before his heads of branches and advisors, who met following the usual morning conference to discuss the implications of Operation Infatuate, the plan to clear the approaches of South Beveland and capture Walcheren. The discussions at this conference illustrate another limitation imposed on First Canadian Army fighting as a coalition partner: as structured, the Allied inter-service command organization made it difficult to shift the momentum of operations already initiated. First Canadian Army, depending as it did on Bomber Command, the Royal Navy, and 21st Army Group arrangements with 2 TAF, was particularly vulnerable to the limitations these arrangements imposed. With no clear-cut priority, the interdependence of the services became as much of a handicap to assigning priorities as it was a help once they had been decided upon. Once the infantry divisions had 'peeled off' to engage the garrisons of the Channel ports and the armoured divisions were committed to the Scheldt, switching them became a proposition costly in both precious time and transport equipment.

By 14 September, from the army's perspective, the naval and heavy bomber support for the operations had become interlocked. The Naval Liaison Officer at First Canadian Army headquarters was asked to consider whether Antwerp could be used if the ports of Boulogne and Calais remained in German hands, or whether Boulogne could be used if

Calais was still in enemy hands. He concluded that Boulogne could not be used without significant losses if the guns of Calais were in German hands; Dunkirk could be masked, but the other ports, from the naval perspective, had to be taken. The decision to use Bomber Command's resources placed similar constraints on strategic flexibility. Because support by the heavy bombers required nothing short of negotiations, the preparations for their use at both Boulogne and Calais were secured at the same time; but the arrangements were not made until the 15th, after a twenty-four-hour delay because First Canadian Army HQ had to wait for the representative from Bomber Command to arrive. Even then, there was some hesitation on the part of Bomber Command to commit its full resources, until Simonds forcefully made a case that they would ensure a decisive and speedy decision. Similarly, the desire of First Canadian Army to bring to bear the full firepower at its command meant further delays as the brigadier Royal Artillery, Brigadier H.O.N. Brownfield, arranged, to good effect, for the 14- and 15-inch guns positioned at Dover to neutralize the German cross-Channel batteries in the Calais–Cape Gris Nez region. The result was a masterpiece of interservice cooperation, one not often recognized, but with the unwieldy Allied command structure, it took time.

The decision to examine the implications of whether to undertake operations at the same time against the Channel ports and the Antwerp approaches left open the question of whether to switch corps headquarters. If neither Boulogne or Calais was assaulted, it was clear to army headquarters staff that instead of implementing the 'tentatively planned' move of 1 British Corps and 49th British Division to take over on the right, both time and fuel could be saved if 2nd Canadian Division and 2nd Canadian Corps took over this responsibility. Time and fuel could also be saved if the specialized equipment destined for Boulogne from Le Havre was stopped. The advantages and disadvantages of the alternatives were laid before Crerar in time for his meeting with Montgomery later on 14 September.[16]

The meeting clarified the situation to an extent, producing two significant changes to First Canadian Army's responsibilities: Dunkirk was to be masked, thus freeing 2nd Canadian Division for operations in the Scheldt, and the army would pay more attention to Antwerp. Montgomery's directive was clear: the 'whole energies of the Army will be directed towards operations designed to enable full use to be made of the port of Antwerp.' Monty also directed 1 British Corps HQ and 49th Division to move to the right 'as soon as possible,' grounding 51st Division. Still, First Canadian Army operations remained subsidiary to Second British Army's and in support of the 'real objective': the Ruhr.

Crerar's directive to his corps commanders reflected these new priorities, but questions remained. In particular, he was unable to sort out the corps' responsibilities, in part because no one could be certain how strongly the garrisons of the Channel ports would resist, and partly because the transport shortages made any unnecessary movement a calculated risk. The 1 British Corps was thus left with two possible roles: if a deliberate siege was necessary to take Calais, then 1 British Corps would undertake it, but if resistance seemed unlikely, then Simonds's corps, already handling the operation, would finish the job before turning its full attention to the approaches to Antwerp. The ambiguity of this directive, which captures the ambiguity implicit in Montgomery's orders to attempt two major operations, was not removed until 19 September, when 1 British Corps was ordered to secure the right flank to free 12 British Corps, then supporting the flagging Operation Market Garden.

The responsibilities placed on the Canadian Army, and in particular on 2nd Canadian Corps, were enormous: First Canadian Army Headquarters directed a front that stretched some 200 miles; its resources were not only limited but decreasing, as the HQ and elements of 1 British Corps were likely to be grounded; and the operational responsibilities before it were complex inter-service operations, using specialized equipment, that required careful planning for transport over vast distances on two roads. The Canadian staff was, in short, faced with two daunting tasks: the logistical and air support challenge that maintaining the momentum of operations against the Channel ports represented, as well as planning and initiating operations to free the Scheldt.

Crerar and his staff could shape the Channel operations by the speed with which they shifted resources or obtained strategic air and naval support, but such attention kept the focus on the Channel ports while operations to open up Antwerp were only slowly developed. While much of the onus fell on the staff, Crerar maintained his regimen of daily flights to keep the staff alert to major problems. The staff itself performed magnificently; particular credit was given the transport and Service Corps as they moved the equipment used in the capture of Le Havre to Boulogne, a distance of 200 miles with, as Church Mann described it, 'limited transportation' by driving continuously for twenty-four hours. With Astonia complete, Wellhit – the attack on Boulogne – began on 17 September, later than planned but remarkably early, given the handicaps facing army and corps planners. As it was, the 3rd Canadian Division attacked with neither the firepower nor the troops – two brigades compared to two divisions – available to 1 British Corps.[17] Crerar and his headquarters did not, however, force the pace of events; indeed, a certain hesitation in the face of the conflicting tasks emerged, affecting future decisions. The location of the HQ was changed and then changed back several times during the first weeks of September until it was finally relocated nearer the coastal operations. Decisions on operations against the ports became so dependent on forces outside the control of First Canadian Army that they took on a life of their own.

Planning for the attacks against the Scheldt estuary reflected the same tendency to react to events, driven by the ponderous decision-making process among the services and the fact that the army lacked a clear-cut objective within its means. Crerar initiated formal planning for Operation Infatuate on 13 September, following Montgomery's directive; simultaneously the staff grappled with the ongoing planning for taking Boulogne and Calais. There was little urgency in Monty's exhortations regarding the Antwerp approaches. Montgomery and his staff remained preoccupied with the Ruhr, which he later admitted was a mistake. To that end, deGuingand's main concerns centred on obtaining the use of the Channel ports. First Canadian Army planning and operations staff followed suit.[18]

II

Planning for Infatuate quickly assumed the same ponderous dimensions that inter-service planning, limited resources, and minimal strategic direction had imposed on earlier schemes. Crerar's approach did nothing to minimize the delays. He assembled his staff for a special conference, led by Mann, to discuss the immediate problems of the operation for presentation to Montgomery. Despite evident concerns over inadequate resources, a shift in priorities was not considered. The alternative was a continued reliance on support from the navy and air force, but this ensured that operations would develop slowly. Montgomery's rejection of the Canadian request for greater resources only increased the army's dependence on naval and air support. Just how hard it was to produce speedy evaluations when so many parties were involved was underlined on 17 September when First Canadian Army hosted Admiral Ramsay, Allied Naval Commander Expeditionary Force, and

Brigadier-General Stuart Cutler of the Airborne Army, to discuss the plans for Infatuate.

Montgomery's changing priorities, and the increasingly stiff German resistance, upset the administrative and operational plans already in progress to clear the approaches. In mid-September, the advance of Major-General Harry Foster's 4th Canadian Armoured Division had been stopped by the unexpectedly heavy German resistance, but now turned to destroy German forces in the Breskens pocket west of the Terneuzan Canal, while the Polish Armoured mopped up to the east as far as Antwerp. Securing the south bank of the Scheldt was the aim of these operations. Expectations of their success provided the framework for the initial plans that emerged from the Plans Section, an expectation based on intelligence summaries that as late as 20 September suggested that the enemy, while offering resistance along the Leopold Canal, was withdrawing in the face of the Canadian advance.[19] They were also predicated on 3rd Canadian Division's availability, assuming its relief at Calais by 1 British Corps, if a prolonged operation was necessary. That Crerar intended to keep a tight reign on the few resources available to him was signalled in his directive of 15 September that forbade, as a result of the transport shortage, any formation movement without express consent of army headquarters. This order might also be viewed as part of Crerar's determination to take control of a battle that was becoming increasingly usurped by his corps commander, an underlying struggle that would become clearer as the plans for the Scheldt operation evolved.

Crerar's attempts to maintain his resources were shattered by the failure of Operation Market Garden, which began on 17 September. Second British Army had insufficient troops and armour to push its offensive the fifty miles towards Arnhem, so Crerar's army was stripped to support it. On the 19th, as noted, he was forced to commit 1 British Corps east of Antwerp in order to relieve 12 British Corps of responsibilities to allow it to support Market Garden. This proved a major blow for First Canadian Army plans. Crerar's plans to release 3rd Canadian Division to support 2nd Canadian Division's operations west of Antwerp and in the city were stopped, as one of his corps was effectively removed from his operational control, although the army had still to provide precious transport resources for its operations. The 3rd Canadian Division was now committed to a deliberate attack on Calais that would keep it occupied from 25 September to 1 October. Clearance of the southern Scheldt and the area north of Antwerp now loomed as a difficult operation, particularly as the Germans continued to view this as their most important defensive commitment in 21st Army Group's theatre.[20]

Crerar and his senior staff's efforts to squeeze resources out of 21st Army Group met with mixed results. At the request of 2nd Canadian Corps, the staff struggled to get two Army Group Royal Artillery units, one of which was grounded for lack of transport, and, at Crerar's suggestion, to find ways to move stores through the waterways of the Leopold Canal, in preparation for operations against the islands of the estuary. They also sought Dutch troops to relieve their already stretched army troops of guard duties in the liberated areas.[21] The results were meagre.

There was also now a danger that three headquarters would share control of the campaign. The evolution of the plans for Operations Infatuate and Switchback indicate that this was a concern. On 19 September the Plans Section issued a detailed appreciation of Operation Infatuate as a basis for the discussion between Crerar and Simonds on that same day. There is no record of their conversation; Crerar's directive to his corps commanders, written following the meeting, suggests that the decision to relocate 1 British Corps to the right flank and 2nd Canadian Corps operations against Walcheren Island were the main topics. The army plan, however, was based on three assumptions: that the Canadians would hold the southern Scheldt; Airborne troops would be available as promised Crerar by Montgomery in mid-September and reiterated by Cutler on the 17th; and Bomber Command would provide unqualified support. The planners envisioned operations developing east of South Beveland, using this area as a staging point to take in turn the South Beveland peninsula, the Walcheren causeway, and then Walcheren Island itself. Airborne troops, in conjunction with small-scale waterborne assaults and after a heavy preliminary bombardment, would be used in two brigade-sized operations to secure a bridgehead on the island as well as jumping off points for a frontal assault across the causeway. A combined arms operation against the island was ruled out. The appreciation itself was straightforward, if unoriginal, in its conception of a series of frontal assaults, and perhaps bears out the GSO 1 Plans recollection years later that the section was unnecessary and might have been broken up.[22]

On the 21st, Simonds, who did his own planning, outlined his objections to the army plan. The postwar debate over who initiated changes to the plan in outline and the idea for bombing the dykes to flood the island became enmeshed in the tension between Simonds and Crerar.[23] Simonds objected to the assumptions that underlay the Plans Section's appreciation. He believed that the ground north of the Leopold Canal would not fall easily into Canadian hands, but would be a 'preliminary and a most important part of the whole operation.' Neither did Simonds dismiss the notion of a combined assault, noting that 'after further study it occurred to me that if the dykes at West Cappelle could be breached by bombing it might provide an approach by which seaborne assault could reach the dunes on either side.' It was an idea he noted he would present at the major conference scheduled on the twenty-third to discuss the operation.[24]

On the same day as Simonds penned his memorandum, Crerar and Mann met with Admiral Ramsey (the Allied Naval Commander-in-Chief) and deGuingand to discuss future operations and plans to capture Walcheren. In a departure from his earlier written appreciation, Crerar asserted that no detailed plan could be completed until the area north of the Leopold Canal and east of South Beveland – roughly the line from Bergen op Zoom to Roosendaal – was secure and until the extent of airborne cooperation was known. According to the war diary and the attached memorandum of the meeting, he also suggested a minor combined operation, which might land only on the southwest coast of Walcheren and that 'from a military point of view,' he considered it to be highly desirable, if possible, 'to flood Walcheren.' He concluded by noting his support for 'sustained and heavy bomber attacks' to destroy the island's defences. He nevertheless accepted assurances that the latter operation would not work. After the war, both Simonds and Crerar claimed credit for the alteration of the plan to include the flooding of Walcheren; Crerar brought the memorandum of the meeting of the 21st to Stacey's attention in 1947, following a review of the one-volume official history and then again in 1952 after reading the third volume of the official history. Simonds's comments on the army appreciation of the 21st were possibly in Crerar's hands before the conference; there is no record of his having met Crerar until after the early afternoon conference between the service chiefs. Still, Crerar's proposals were very close to Simonds's objections. His quick retreat from the idea also suggests that the idea was not his alone.[25]

What is clear is that it was Simonds who sold it, but in doing so furthered the tensions between himself and Crerar, as well as between the Allied Air Force commanders and First Canadian Army. These spilled out at the inter-service conference of the 23rd and in the subsequent debate over the degree of support that the bombers should provide the Canadians throughout the campaign. Representatives from all the services and the three army HQs attended the conference – some thirty-five officers in all. It was Crerar's final contribution to the planning for the Scheldt operation. It was 'the responsibility [he] felt he must accomplish before putting [himself] in the hands of the medicals,' and the views he presented were, in outline, accepted as the operational plan.[26]

Crerar was in very poor health when the conference began; another attack of dysentery on the 21st left him severely weakened. Following opening remarks that stated simply that 2nd Canadian Corps was responsible for the operation, Crerar presented a number of possible scenarios and options for both the preliminary operations and the primary tasks. Before the army could concentrate its 'full resources' on Walcheren, the long-range batteries at Calais and Cap Gris Nez had to be silenced; it had not yet been decided whether to simply mask it or capture it, meaning that 3rd Canadian Division remained uncertain of its immediate future. A similar ambivalence framed the approach to Infatuate. He presented four 'possibilities' that appeared 'favourable for carrying out the assault': the employment of airborne troops, a land operation along the isthmus into Zuid Beveland, a waterborne operation across the West Scheldt, and a seaborne landing on Walcheren. Crerar stressed the importance of 'very' heavy bombing support, 'which should start as soon as possible and carry on until the actual assault.' He also called for an examination of the deliberate flooding of Walcheren, a possibility dependent on 'sanction by higher authority' and its feasibility, a position from which he did not waver. In summary, he described the divisional and corps movements necessary to execute the operations. Simonds's exposition was similarly sketchy, and he qualified his remarks by stating that he 'had not been able to go into [the plan] as fully as he would have like to have done.' Nevertheless, following an outline of his conception of how the operation would develop, he made a strong case for flooding Walcheren by breaching the dykes.[27]

The reaction from the other services was mixed. Brigadier Cutler from the Airborne Army reiterated the recent Supreme Allied Commander decision not to employ airborne troops. Pressure from Crerar and 21st Army Group forced the ever-pliable Ike to reconsider, and the day before the conference he left open the possibility, if not the probability, that airborne troops would still be made available. Crerar restated his hope that this option would remain open.[28]

The reaction of the Air Force was equally ambivalent. At the conference, Bomber Command's representative, Air Vice-Marshal Oxland, voiced his concerns as to whether the bombers could breach the dykes and the degree of support that the heavy bombers could give in attacking gun emplacements on the island. He was more forthcoming in his notes on the meeting. 'I find it difficult to believe that a breach of sufficient dimensions could be made [in the dykes to flood the island],' he wrote. 'I got the impression that the Engineer who was present was of the same opinion.' The negative tone continued a few paragraphs later as he reiterated both Crerar's and Simmonds's emphasis on commencing the bombing attacks on the defences as soon as possible: 'I stated that as Bomber Command could not undertake to silence the guns, although we may be lucky in one or two cases, all we could expect to do would be to affect the morale of the troops and destroy the communications.' This, he suggested, would be better effected if the bombing began closer to 'D' day, which was expected to be some three weeks away. He concluded by relating his surprise that First Canadian Army staff, specifically Mann, believed that Bomber Command was on call and all that was necessary 'was to pass [on] the detailed requirements' rather than making 'an official request.'[29]

Certainly Bomber Command refused to continue in a support role, despite the assurances given 21st Army Group by Eisenhower that both Bomber Command and 8th U.S. Air Force would be at its disposal. If the resistance to the Canadian army's request in late September did not make this clear, there was an unmistakable increase in hostility through October. Convinced that the bombing effort was better directed towards Germany, and no longer under SHAEF command, the air chiefs showed no sympathy for the plight of the army. An exchange of letters between Chief of the Air Staff Portal and Deputy Supreme Commander Marshal Tedder illustrated just how far removed they were as they pondered the demoralization caused by bomber support when it was used 'only ... to save casualties.' Both feared that the Anglo-Canadian armies in particular were 'drugged with bombs'; Tedder cited the 'repeated calls by the Canadian Army for heavy bomber effort to deal with a part-worn battery on Walcheren' as a prime example.[30] And the many intermediaries between the Canadian army and Arthur Harris show no greater understanding of the army's needs. The best indication of the growing tension between the army and its air support was sacking of the First Canadian

Army AOC, Brown in October. A disappointed Mann noted that Brown was being replaced because of a 'basic difference of outlook with [Coningham] especially as to the army/RAF relationship.' Mann, and Brown, believed that AOC's support of the army's need for improved coordination had made him 'persona non-grata' with the air marshal.[31] Neither 84 Group nor Bomber Command directed their full efforts in support of the Canadian army operations, despite Crerar's efforts to maintain a close relationship with Harris himself. Simonds had no opportunity to build such a relationship. Only the Royal Navy unreservedly supported the operation and the army's requests. Captain Pugsley, representing the navy, asked Simonds for his requirements for naval craft and enquired how best the navy could cooperate with training for the combined operations.

Three problems presented themselves as the conference ended. One was personal. After he returned to his HQ, the tension at the conference was such that Simonds felt compelled to pen a letter to Crerar to 'reassure [him] of my complete and continuing loyalty.' He went on to note that he hoped that disagreements and suggestions would not be interpreted 'as showing any disloyalty.'[32] Two further problems, and by far the more pressing, were directly related to operations: whether or not to flood the island and whether or not the heavy bombers could be secured. Crerar ordered a study of the first. Walsh was present at the conference and left the impression with at least one participant that he doubted the viability of bombers breaching the dykes. His report delivered on the 24th confirmed this impression: Walsh argued that it was unlikely that a sufficient breach could be blasted to allow naval craft a channel; neither would the subsequent flooding create a depth sufficient to allow assault craft to operate. Walsh's memorandum convinced Crerar that it was not a feasible operation, and he reported as much to Simonds. The corps commander, however, remained positive that the results would be good and argued in his submission on the 25th that nothing would be lost by trying. The latter argument and the conviction with which it was argued convinced Crerar. Mann was directed to request authority from 21st Army Group 'to arrange for a deliberate effort to breach the dykes,' which he did on the 26th.[33] The task of making the final plea to the air chiefs, however, fell to Simonds as Acting GOC-in-C.

During the period prior to the Scheldt campaign, decisive action was difficult to achieve. Crerar's style of command left him vulnerable to disagreements and conflicting agendas; his health ensured it would be so. The impression left, however, was that the HQ was increasing rudderless, with no steady hand at the tiller. Some of his staff believed, in retrospect, that Crerar lost his powers of decision. 'I don't remember any time at which the headquarters' operations were at such a low ebb as in September when he went sick,' remembered Beament. 'I don't recall any other time when we were in that kind of a situation because I think we were lacking in effective leadership.'[34]

While Monty must shoulder some blame for haphazard development of the strategic situation, Crerar was also unable to assert control over the operations; buffeted by the opinions of his staff and circumstances, he presented options not plans. He was reaching the end of his tether as he struggled to overcome his deteriorating health. The dysentery, which had racked his body periodically since mid-June, was not responding to treatment; five severe attacks and the accompanying symptoms had progressively weakened him. By mid-September, stomach and 'griping [sic] abdominal pain' had reached a point where even mild exertion left him winded and perspiring. An attack of dysentery on the 19th prompted medical personnel to recommend a thorough examination; he revealed to them that he was often tired and found it necessary to 'drive himself to do work which should normally require ordinary effort.' The diagnosis from the examination of the 19th was anemia; the report of the 25th recommended that Crerar undergo further diagnosis and treatment in England. Any inclination to resist was stilled by the severe attack of dysentery that had begun on the 21st. On the 26th, Crerar conferred with Montgomery and recommended that Simonds be made acting GOC; Montgomery, naturally – probably eagerly – concurred.[35]

III

By most accounts, Simonds's assumption of command reinvigorated the army HQ; where Crerar managed, Simonds commanded. Senior staff remembered the difference as he took control of the operational planning for the Scheldt:

> We gave him the facts, he went away to his quarters and made his own appreciation, called together a meeting of everybody involved ... and said 'Gentlemen, this is what we're going to do.' He laid it down very clearly, ABC, and everybody was so surprised at the [difference] because before all the meetings had been like tactical exercises at the staff college but with

no real conclusions. [With Simonds in command] everybody gulped a couple of times, disappeared and we got on with it.[36]

Their styles of command certainly contrasted sharply. Was there a substantive difference in army command, as measured by the course of operations? Not as much as one would expect. The decisive shift came when Montgomery gave priority to opening the approaches to Antwerp. Up to that point, despite the mutual respect and admiration between Monty and Simonds, the limits on how an army commander, particularly one in 21st Army Group, could influence a battle were clearly illustrated by the change of command. Montgomery continued to remove precious resources from First Canadian Army to support the now clearly failing Market Garden. On 27 September, he ordered 1 British Corps, which now included the Polish Armoured Division, to operate on a northward axis to free Second British Army from the dangers of a long left flank. By the 29th, it was clear that the airborne troops would not be available. His directive of the 29th stated that Antwerp remained a secondary priority – a view reconfirmed when HQ 21st Army Group overturned a naval order to give priority to securing landing craft for the Scheldt operations and bluntly conveyed the message to First Canadian Army staff begging for more resources. 'C in C has decided,' Mann told the morning joint conference, 'that first priority has to be given to the immediate ops rather than the future ops, therefore Second Brit Army has to be looked after first.' Less than a week later, the 51st Highland Division was directed to support Montgomery's final effort to reach the Ruhr. Simonds did not dispute these reallocations, use his relationship with Montgomery to postpone the operation, or call for greater support. Instead, as one author has observed, he seemed to view undertaking the operation with the three Canadian divisions as a challenge. 'There was no task which could be stated to be "impossible,"' he observed at the operational conference of the 29th, 'and that since the task ... had been assigned to us it was necessary for us to evolve the method which appeared to offer the best possibility of success.'[37] The most significant changes shaping the battle from the command perspective came not from Simonds but rather from the other services. The most important decision was to give the opening of the approaches to Antwerp priority over all other operations.

Crerar spent a week in hospital from the 29th and then for the next three weeks alternated between the hospital and convalescing with friends in Yorkshire as well as with Sir Edward Peacock. His convalescence was not uninterrupted. He instructed Mann to forward First Canadian Army Intelligence Summaries, which Mann playfully called 'Masterpieces,' and was updated regularly on the progress of the army by Simonds.[38] The final weeks of October were consumed, however, by a crisis over the renewed question of Burns's fitness for command. The British had never completely accepted Burns, although there was a definite ebb and flow to their appreciation of his command abilities. Leese's replacement by Lieutenant-General Sir Richard McCreery at the end of September 1944 had not eased the problem; rather, it had exacerbated it, as the British blamed the Canadians for the slow advance across the Gothic Line. Burns's own dour personality also had soured relations with his divisional commanders, Major-Generals Chris Vokes and Bert Hoffmeister. Brigadier E.G. Weeks, the Officer-in-Charge, Canadian Section, GHQ, was the conduit chosen to voice the complaints as he investigated the situation. Hoffmeister and Vokes informed him that their relationship with Burns had become 'intolerable,' that they had 'lost all confidence in him,' and that they were inclined to 'be insubordinate to him.' The situation had, in short, reached a point where either the divisional commanders or Burns would have to be relieved. Alexander was aware of the tension among the Canadians but had counselled McCreery to be cautious, both because he had been in command for only two weeks and because of the potential political repercussions. The Canadians were told to maintain silence while the British complaints were written down and forwarded to the War Office and CIGS.[39]

The problem was brought to Crerar's attention on the heels of Ralston's visit to the Mediterranean in September–October and paralleled the crisis unfolding over the shortages of trained infantrymen and conscription. Before it broke into a full crisis on 20 October, Crerar attacked Burns's situation in the Mediterranean. He responded cautiously, following the same reasoning and approach that had averted a change in July. Blaming the British, in particular Leese, for undermining Burns with his subordinates, he saw it as 'more a question of national and commonwealth policy than that of military interest.'[40] As such, he maintained that the key issue, as it was in the summer, was whether Burns had the confidence of his subordinates.

Crerar did not waver in his support for Burns until his hand was forced by solid evidence that such confidence was lacking. He broached the subject with Brooke when the two dined on 24 October, noting that Stuart had reported that Burns's standing had improved. To Crerar's surprise, Brooke was blunt: Burns was respected by neither his superiors nor his subordinates. While Crerar intimated that the issue might be a lack of support for Burns, he was disturbed both at the news and his own underestimation of the problem. Over the next few days, a message from Burns helped clarify the issue as did a discussion with a reluctant Brigadier J.F.A. Lister, now DA and QMG of First Canadian Army, but not long from the same post with 1st Canadian Corps. These confirmed the views that Burns's personality had 'failed to inspire affection and confidence.' There was, he added loyally, no 'deficiency in respect to technical qualifications.'[41]

Despite the growing case against Burns, Crerar wanted more information. He suggested that Stuart go to Italy, but before Stuart could leave, Alexander and McCreery's reports and the results of Weeks's own investigation were brought to Crerar's attention. Their recommendation left no room for doubt as to the extent of the loss of confidence: 'Lieutenant-General E.L.M. Burns unsuitable to command 1st Canadian Corps and should be replaced immediately.' More damning was the clear evidence that Burns could no longer work with his subordinates. Crerar withdrew his support for the appointment, but even he did not know the full extent of the crisis. 'In spite of no able direction,' wrote Vokes in a personal letter in early November, 'we have continued to bear the cross for an individual who lacks one iota of personality, appreciation of effort or the first goddam thing in the application of book learning to what is practical in war and what isn't.'[42] On 5 November 1944, Burns left amid rumours that the corps, then in reserve, might be sent to northwest Europe, or even Burma; Vokes took temporary command until Charles Foulkes arrived on 16 November. Vokes, no fan of Foulkes, was given command of the 4th Canadian Armoured, switching places with Harry Foster. The main act over, Crerar kept a careful watch on the appointment, assuring Foulkes a month later in mid-December that he would support him during the difficult transition, but to tread carefully when replacing senior commanders. 'I can fully appreciate the "air" which pervaded at the time of your arrival.' he wrote Foulkes. 'I have gone through the same experience twice in this war.'[43]

The parallels with his own situation as well as the principles he believed were at stake may also have shaped Crerar's sensitivity to Burns's displacement and his replacement by Foulkes. Montgomery was doing his best to prevent Crerar's return before the Scheldt operations were completed. His ultimate aim was to permanently scuttle Crerar's resumption of command. Montgomery wanted Simonds to remain and hoped to use Crerar's illness to raise questions about his suitability to command. He broached the subject with the defence minister in early October 1944. Ralston recorded his conversation with Montgomery: 'He said Crerar adequate but not a ball of fire. Not in same parish with Simmonds [sic] as Army Commander,' presumably because, as Monty described him, he was 'not influenced by national ideas. His one idea was to beat the Germans.' The Field Marshal observed that if Crerar did not return and Simmonds became a casualty, he would 'have to suggest as a Comdr. one of the Corps Commanders in 2nd Army'; otherwise he would find it necessary to put the Canadians in reserve. Montgomery concluded by noting that he would 'like to see Crerar back but don't have him come back till he is in shape.'[44] Ralston wisely deferred any commitment.

This was only a preliminary move. Prompted to action on 18 October by the imminent release of publicity photos of the King and Crerar that would reveal that the latter was not with First Canadian Army, Montgomery wired Brooke recommending that CMHQ announce that Crerar was temporarily absent 'on account of sickness' and that Simonds was acting commander until his return. He concluded with a request: 'I do not know what progress Crerar is making but it is highly important that he should NOT repeat NOT return here until he is able to stand up to the rigours of a winter campaign in a damp and cold climate.' Noting that he had already broached the idea with Ralston – his recon into the minefields of Canadian politics – he observed, 'We have much dirty work ahead between now and January and only very hard and tough commanders will stand up to it.' He requested Brooke personally 'investigate this matter and advise me as to the real form regarding Crerars [sic] health and stamina.'[45]

Foulkes related to C.P. Stacey in 1948 that Montgomery assured him 'he could count on remaining as Corps Commander; Crerar wouldn't be coming back.' The Field Marshal, according to Foulkes's recollection, noted he 'had "written a letter" to ensure this.'[46] If true, his bravado backfired; Peter Crerar's recollection was that Church Mann, whom he characterized as 'very loyal' to his father, became aware after a special operational conference – perhaps the same one at which Monty spoke to Foulkes – of the field marshal's intentions. Mann allegedly phoned Crerar and warned him of Montgomery's machinations.[47] Crerar must have harboured suspicions, whether warned by Mann or not. Anticipating the doubts about his health, he acquired confirmation from two specialists – a favoured approach – of his physical well-being. On the 21st, not Brooke but the VCIGS, Nye, a confidant of Montgomery's, wired the Field Marshal the apparently disappointing results of his intrigue. 'Put your point strongly about Crerar's health to Montague,' he wrote. 'He says Crerar perfectly fit now and a certificate has been produced by two specialists saying that he is fit to resume his command within the next few days.' His next line was telling: 'In these circumstances there is nothing further we can do although I know well what you would have preferred to happen.'[48]

Montgomery was unhappy that he had failed to prevent Crerar's resumption of command. On 22 October, the day after Nye informed him of Crerar's return, Montgomery ordered a study made of the implications of switching the Canadian Army, upon completion of Operation Infatuate, across the Meuse/Rhine front to the south of Second British Army. He did not want Harry Crerar and First Canadian Army HQ controlling the upcoming battle for the Rhineland; while the transfer proved impossible, his willingness to contemplate it suggests the intensity of his mistrust of Crerar's abilities and the depths to which their personal relationship had sunk.[49]

On 23 October, Crerar wired that he wanted to return on the 31st; Monty objected, correctly observing that operations would not benefit from the sudden change in command. He requested that Brooke arrange for Crerar to remain in the United Kingdom until the 7th. Brooke, who had checked for himself, believed that Crerar was 'now recovered and ... fit to go back to France.' Nevertheless, he saw the logic in Monty's request. His intervention on Montgomery's behalf prevented another messy confrontation between the C-in-C and Crerar. Reluctantly, Crerar bowed to the logic of Simonds's retention of army command until the operations were complete. 'While there are certain Canadian and personal complications,' he wrote Brooke, 'I have come to the conclusion that, in the general operational interest, I should adjust my plans to your suggestion of the other evening (and the C-in-C's desires) and delay my resumption of active command of the First Canadian Army until 7 November when the present operations to clear Antwerp should be drawing to a close and a new phase due to commence.'[50]

Montgomery tried to have the last word. Soon after his return to First Canadian Army, Crerar was promoted to the rank of full General, effective 16 November, the first officer to hold that rank in the field. On hearing of the promotion, Montgomery wired Brooke asking him not to convey the impression that it is 'in any way for distinguished service in the field.' In a note, more meaningful than intended, he added, 'Would make things awkward here if latter meaning was conveyed.'[51]

21 The Rhineland Offensive

I

The Rhineland Offensive was the high point of the commonwealth campaign in northwest Europe. The 21st Army Group had the critical task of crushing the German army on the west bank of the Rhine. However, the British and Canadian forces, and the American as well, were reaching the end of their manpower resources. Crerar, steering the planning for the upcoming offensive, dealt simultaneously – and controversially – with both the policies and politics of the reinforcement crisis, as well as the ongoing tensions with Montgomery, who was only reluctantly accepting the fact that Crerar would command FCA in the next offensive.

Crerar returned to his headquarters on 7 November, although he officially resumed command only at 1200 hours on 9 November, a result of Montgomery's desire to retain Simonds in command while the Scheldt offensive was completed. There was a certain logic to this approach, but it probably fuelled the residual tension between the two Canadians and emphasized Montgomery's antagonism towards Crerar. Still, when deGuingand visited HQ First Canadian Army on 7 November, he cabled Monty that 'Crerar is back and seems fit.'[1]

Crerar returned just as the reinforcement problem was becoming a full-blown political crisis. Major Conn Smythe's open letter in mid-September 1944 regarding the unnecessary casualties that were resulting from the use of untrained troops – a direct attack on the remustering program – had prompted a public outcry for NRMA men to be shipped overseas. From 26 September to 18 October 1944, Ralston had travelled to Italy, England, and the Continent to talk with the army's senior commanders; he heard that lives were being lost and morale was plummeting as a result of the combined effect of using untrained or half-trained troops, commitment of below-establishment units to action, and the troops' lack of hope for leave. He reported his findings to King and the Cabinet. Stuart also reported to Cabinet on the shortfalls, but it was his intimation, and Ralston's support, that conscription was necessary to avoid a crisis overseas that proved to be the catalyst for the Prime Minister's subsequent actions, and the resulting political crisis. In short order, on 1 November, King forced Ralston's resignation, appointed McNaughton as the Minister of National Defence, on the basis of his support for maintaining voluntary enlistment, and finally, on 23 November, announced the decision to conscript 16,000 'zombies,' the derisive nickname for NRMA conscripts, for overseas service.[2]

Crerar was conversant with the political developments of the conscription debates. He asked his family and friends to send news clippings, and was in touch with Stuart. Before he returned to the continent, he had spoken to Ralston and was subsequently briefed on the political fallout of the minister's report. King had also telephoned Crerar to ensure his silence, a preparatory tactic before he removed Ralston; the Prime Minister warned Crerar in a wonderfully vague statement, quoted by Stacey, that he should not 'say anything committing himself as to what he will do if certain people did certain things.' Without a hint of irony, King recorded that Crerar was 'evasive.' Crerar recorded that he told King, 'I was interested only in getting the problem solved in the right way.' And that was true, although he did not specify which was the 'right way.'[3]

The crisis was his first priority when he returned to his command. Crerar arranged a press conference, but one that was carefully orchestrated, playing fully on his solid, if mutually wary, relations with the Canadian Assistant Deputy Public Relations at 21st Army Group, Lieutenant-Colonel Richard Malone. Crerar was conscious of the fact that it was important that the war correspondents should see him as 'soon as possible after his return' both to re-establish himself and to blunt any rumours about the conscription crisis. The questions were screened and limited to Canadian military policy, a procedure that was not unusual, but underlined the delicacy of his position. Crerar met with Malone to go over exactly what he expected, and selected which answers would be off the record.[4]

The majority of the questions probed for some insights into the recent crisis, and the potential for future ones, over reinforcements; only one was asked regarding Crerar's health. The answers, in the written response, were honest, but off the record. Most would have been unpalatable for the King government, in particular Crerar's support for compulsory military training and conscription, as well as his opinion that the zombies would not be welcomed by the Canadian army; his preference was that they be sent to the Far East. These were his personal views. Crerar had little influence on the final decision, and refused to make statements on government policy.[5]

Conscription was ultimately a political decision, but the repercussions of both the debate and its introduction were very much Crerar's concern. He approached the question of integrating the conscripts by placing it in the larger context of digesting the lessons of the last months of combat, and readying the army for what promised to be a difficult campaign to clear the country up to the Rhine. The problem of manpower shortages was now one of quality rather than quantity; Crerar examined the policies on leave, reinforcements, and training as one. Here was an area where his influence was felt.

Some steps had already been taken to reshape leave policies. In September, Crerar and his HQ initiated a scheme for home leave for officers and men with five years' continuous service overseas. With Ralston's backing, they debated numbers through the fall. This was a critical issue, as a month's leave to Canada removed a soldier from his unit for three months. NDHQ preferred a quota of 250; Crerar and Montague argued for, and received, an increase to 450 per month. In practice, few went (1992) and fewer returned (53), but the debate underlined the concern at HQ First Canadian Army for the state of the troops under their command.[6]

In addition to the new policies on leave and training, Crerar quietly initiated a scheme to have formation and unit commanders from First Canadian Army lecture 'once or twice' a week to the officers, staff, and ranks of the reinforcement units. On 9 November, he wrote Price Montague, suggesting that he propose such lectures 'formally and apparently of your own initiative, as acting [sic] C of S, CMHQ.' In addition to the training value, he observed that 'incidently, and importantly to me, the occasion would permit me to allow these senior officers to obtain some two or three days in the UK and a most valuable relief from their continuous and heavy responsibilities here.' Crerar ordered that his part not be mentioned, conscious that he had to obtain Montgomery's permission for 'such special Canadian arrangements' – 'though ... this can be done, it will have to be handled very carefully.'[7]

Montague played his part and on 12 November Crerar wrote Monty that he had received a 'request' for a series of lectures to be given to the Canadian Reinforcement Units (CRU) by serving officers. The army commander expressed his support for the proposal, but he wanted Montgomery's approval of the procedure; Crerar did not 'wish to embarrass' him in any general Army Group procedures. Montgomery gave his blessing to the arrangement and Crerar ordered Simonds to proceed by giving an 'inspirational' inaugural lecture on the requirements of a leader and commander.[8]

Crerar also took steps to strengthen the reinforcement training program. To take full advantage of the experience of his officers, he informed Montague that the time had come for a 'considerable "turnover" in the senior Commanders at CRU,' citing their lack of active service. Crerar was addressing more than the substance of the training; he observed that 'this lack of practical qualification undoubtedly is regarded as a serious defect by the formation and unit commanders here, who receive the product of the CRU.' His own experience taught him that combat experience brought credibility, deserved or not.[9]

These points were brought home over the next few weeks through inspections and reports forwarded through Simonds, points that Crerar used to speed the improvements in training that were slowly working their way through the channels at CMHQ and NDHQ. The root of the problem lay in Crerar's decision taken while CGS to have unit and formation training undertaken in the United Kingdom, and not Canada. Soldiers arrived in the United Kingdom having completed Basic, Special to Arms, and possibly Trades Training, but with no collective training in units; CRU provided this training, effectively making it the responsibility of CMHQ and the overseas army to ensure that the proper level of training had been obtained before troops were sent to First Canadian Army. In the fall of 1944, NDHQ stated that it could not be assumed that reinforcements had 'reached a standard of training that would render them immediately available to First Canadian Army' without further training. In short, it wasn't their problem but CMHQ's.[10]

Steps were taken to ensure that CMHQ understood that message. Crerar brought attention to the shortfalls: in late November, he sent a terse cable to Montague regarding a recent inspection of 6th Canadian Infantry Brigade that had revealed that many of the new recruits had no night training, had not been instructed in field craft, and knowledge of their assault and platoon weapons was 'inadequate' and 'hazy.' The situation, he concluded, required 'immediate investigation and if confirmed your drastic action.' Implicit in his cable was the censure that CMHQ was not moving fast enough.

Montague, rattled, responded with a one and a half page explanation of the measures being taken to improve the standard of remustering training and those taken since the summer to improve infantry training in general. The 13th Canadian Infantry Training Brigade, formed in early 1944 to facilitate collective training up to the platoon level, had been reorganized, its training syllabus had been increased to six weeks, and there had been, in Montague's opinion, 'sweeping changes in senior appointments.' These entailed employing experienced COs removed from command in northwest Europe – Brigadier K.G. Blackader, the former CO of 8th Infantry Brigade was one example – until all of the eight training battalions and all but one of the four depot (administrative) battalions were under command of battle experienced COs. 'These,' pleaded Montague, 'are the best we can find.' He suggested that the exact origin of the drafts be sent so the problem could be traced to its source, and that the officers of the training branch could pay more frequent visits to front-line units.[11]

Crerar ordered Mann to check out the new syllabus and organization, but Montague was right: the CRU had corrected the problem as best they could at their end. Training Directive No. 1, issued by CMHQ on 3 November, emphasized the CRU's responsibility to bridge the gap between the Canadian training syllabi and the requirements of the units in the field. It incorporated the concerns raised in the field, giving priority to weapons training with the Projector, Infantry, Anti-Tank (PIAT), grenades, mines, and booby traps; field craft; and collective tactical training to fit the reinforcement into a section or equivalent subunit.[12] Much still depended on the individual commander's tactical acuity, but ultimately there was no substitute for a gradual introduction to battle, a luxury absent in the difficult months of August through October.

Simonds, while acting army commander, had also taken steps to address the problem. On 28 October, he issued a directive entitled 'Absorption of Reinforcement Personnel.' To facilitate integration, he repeated his previous instructions that each infantry battalion and armoured regiment form a 'unit reception school' directed by a core of experienced junior officers, NCOs, and ranks 'left out of battle' (LOB) to 'test and initiate the new soldiers'; and replacements, except in an emergency, would not be sent into combat until they had spent between twenty-four and forty-eight hours in the LOB 'school.'[13]

This intention proved impossible to carry out during the Scheldt campaign, but the end of the battles to clear the Scheldt allowed the changes time to work. Crerar also intervened to convince some officers who were reluctant to leave the field that it was in the interests of the army as a whole.[14] These efforts had a positive effect. When the operations to close up to the Rhine began in February 1945, there were no serious complaints about reinforcements, and Stacey reports only the occasional positive statement on the quality of replacements. And replacements did not make up the majority of battle-exhaustion cases, suggesting the effect of improvements in their training, or at least the methods by which they were absorbed into units. Battle exhaustion and shortages remained concerns until the end of the war, but never reached the same crisis point as they had in summer and fall of 1944.

For Crerar, the repercussions of the shortages went on for the next six months. In January 1945, McNaughton dispatched his former 2nd Canadian Corps GOC, Lieutenant-General Sansom, as Inspector General charged with investigating the overseas reinforcement situation. Sansom became the new minister's hatchetman, investigating the 'mutiny' of NRMA men in the Pacific Command during the political crisis. Sansom stayed abroad until the spring of 1945 and reported on the crisis in March 1945, but not before raising the hackles of the senior command overseas. Crerar, preparing for the Rhineland offensive and concerned about his own hide, was unhappy with the whole investigation as Sansom queried Crerar's subordinates. He protested to McNaughton that Sansom's mandate to assess the standards of training of reinforcements and remustered personnel was beyond the bounds of his expertise; he also saw it as an implicit threat to his prerogatives as army commander. This episode suggests that the phoenix of a struggle between DND, CMHQ, and First Canadian Army had risen again with McNaughton's appointment. Like many of his colleagues, Crerar believed that McNaughton was the wrong choice as Minister of National Defence and that McNaughton had let the army down by not supporting conscription. He also believed that McNaughton was temperamentally unsuited for politics.[15]

Crerar reacted forcefully when he read the report in March 1945. Crerar forced Sansom to excise several points that incorrectly intimated that reinforcements were available in the theatre of war during the crisis, but that lack of shipping and long lines of communication had caused 'unavoidable delays' in getting the reinforcements to the leading divisions. Clearly, this view was wrong. The offending passage was changed to read that the reinforcements had been unavailable in the theatre, thus shifting the blame away from First Canadian Army. Crerar remained sensitive to the 'unintended' slur that he committed understrength battalions to battle and that the overseas forces had mismanaged their reinforcements, not least because the report ignored the context of the summer and fall's campaigning. He and Montague were successful in having the most damning aspects of the report changed, and in registering their objections to other passages. Crerar also stubbornly resisted Sansom's suggestions, backed by senior command at CMHQ, for reducing the time spent on training in Canada by three weeks, from sixteen to thirteen weeks, thus reducing duplication in the syllabus and moving reinforcements through the system faster; Crerar reasoned it was unsound politically and psychologically, although he did not elaborate. The army commander's sensitivity aside, the old tensions and jostling for influence that had marked relations between the three main headquarters, so muted during the past few months largely as a result of Crerar's successful manoeuvres, threatened from November 1944 to split the attention of the overseas GOC once again.[16]

Crerar was safe enough, but McNaughton was clearly out for 'some scalps,' fulfilling the promise made a year earlier to Sir James Grigg, the British Secretary of State for War. His over-eager acceptance of King's approach, abandoning the Conservatives who had been courting him, suggests he sought a chance to both reaffirm his standing with the public and to have a go at men like Ralston. While Ralston deserved better, the minister's forced resignation on 1 November 1944 had pleased McNaughton, and not only because he was his replacement. McNaughton intended to make Stuart the next victim; he remembered his role in his removal. Meeting with King in secret to arrange the transition at National Defence, McNaughton insisted that Stuart, having overstepped himself by suggesting policy, and in whom he had no confidence, had to go. He also tried to be rid of Murchie, whom he saw as Stuart's man. The Prime Minister defended Murchie but allowed McNaughton to force Stuart's resignation. Stuart, exhausted, ill, and sensing what was in the wind – he characterized McNaughton's appointment as 'my Waterloo' – resigned a few days after Ralston.[17]

Stuart and Crerar had staunchly supported each other up to this point, and Stuart naturally turned to his friend Crerar for solace. McNaughton had not allowed him to return to London, so sitting at a desk in his hotel room at the Ritz-Carlton in Montreal in early November 1944, he poured out his frustration at the shabby treatment. Despite McNaughton's refusal to allow him to return to the United Kingdom, even to straighten out his personal business, he expressed his concerns over McNaughton's health, and approach. 'The whole future,' he wrote, 'looks very bleak to me.' Stuart's anguish at having to leave the army, at seeing his life's work dismantled, and his fears of McNaughton – whom he characterized as 'acting like a small Hitler' – were evident over seven handwritten pages; he asked that Crerar tear the letter up when he had read it and to 'treat it very carefully.'[18]

Crerar, as he was through the whole crisis, was wary of committing himself, although it was clear where his sympathies lay. He waited four weeks before responding, four weeks during which Stuart committed himself to the pro-conscription side, by arranging secret meetings of ministers at his home, and by feeding facts and figures to support Ralston's House of Commons critiques of the government's vacillation on conscription. Those weeks also saw the government implement, following McNaughton's failure to win favour with either the NRMA men or his former colleagues, a limited conscription. When finally sent, Crerar's letter was a model of discretion and detachment; he was 'genuinely sorry' at the state of the political issues, 'quite apart from the pain to my personal feelings caused by the effects of all this business on my personal friends,' but noted several times the limits his position placed on what he was able to say. Indeed, he already believed himself to be skating on thin ice. He wished Stuart the best of luck, thanked him for all his help, and held out the promise that they would 'talk things out, one of these days.' Crerar returned to Canada in the summer of 1945, but Stuart died soon after in November 1945. According to one source, although just one, Crerar was asked to be a pallbearer, but found an excuse to say no; Ralston, reportedly disgusted with Crerar, said yes.[19]

Crerar's distancing himself professionally was understandable, if distasteful – at this point, he was juggling Burns's displacement as well, and the issue for his army was not conscription, but reinforcements; he had been warned by King personally against jeopardizing government support, and Crerar pointed this out to all correspondents who asked. And most did. His personal distance is less understandable, but needs to be placed in the context of the emotional distance that was emerging between Crerar and most of his close professional friends, and in the context of an individual who was losing touch with his family. In short, he was isolated. Lester Pearson's correspondence was infrequent, and even then, more business than personal. Verse told his friends that he was lonely and had no one to 'send him inside stuff from home.'[20] His

Hamilton friends suffered less neglect or at least suffered it in silence; their packages of cigarettes – extras went to the troops and his mess – and letters of encouragement were welcomed as much as personal gossip, although on 'hot' topics he gave them no more of himself than he gave his colleagues. He refused comment on politics and said little of a personal nature. The years away from Verse also took their toll; he sought constant reassurances from friends and family that all was well at home. His decision to have her stay in Canada had not been completely resolved and her recent illness was a constant concern. 'Verse seems to be much better,' he wrote Shom Boswell in November 1944, 'and is certainly well enough to be quite active, socially.' He could do little; her letters were, like his, designed to comfort an absent spouse, and she was aware that he was lonely. A dozen roses at Christmas, arranged through his brother, he was aware, were no substitute. Peter was in Italy, but wrote infrequently; he worried for Peg in Canada, but she was also a source of strength for him, providing a link to Verse. He missed his grandson's childhood altogether.[21]

II

The respite following the Scheldt campaign proved more important than the measures undertaken by the senior army command in the short term to address the manpower shortages and the problems with the quality of reinforcements. 'Statistically speaking,' wrote Stacey, 'the low point had been reached on 31 August ... Improvement was rapid thereafter, though it [was] evident that, as was inevitable in all circumstances, the training of reinforcements provided by CMHQ's emergency programme left a great deal to be desired.'[22] When the Battle of the Rhineland began, the average battalion deficiency was 'nil.' Manpower concerns were also addressed at a higher level. The 21st Army Group HQ, in order to 'assist in obtaining a more economical use of manpower,' appointed the Inspector of Organization (Colonel, GS). He visited HQs, units, and installations and made recommendations for changing establishments.[23]

That appointment illustrates the point that manpower shortages and infantry reinforcement problems were not unique to the Canadian army. By 1944, all the Allied, and Axis, armies faced crises of various sorts; forecasting casualties was not an exact science. Neither was building units to meet the evolving needs of operations. The manpower shortages and the deficiencies of the replacement system in the American armies in northwest Europe illustrate just how successful the Canadian senior command was in attempting to address the problems it was encountering, although the relative scales make exact comparisons difficult. The combination of the ninety division ceiling on the U.S. army – the 'ninety division gamble' – and the underestimation of casualties among rifle companies had produced a shortage as acute as that experienced by commonwealth armies. The Americans also remustered from other arms to address the losses of riflemen, but the U.S. army remained relatively insensitive to the situation; they had no formal equivalent of the LOB school, and not until the end of 1944 did they begin to address the human side of the equation by substituting the term *reinforcement* for the morale-sapping, if brutally honest, *replacement*.[24]

Even as the political crisis subsided, the Canadian army still faced some real problems: poor morale, a shortage of French-speaking reinforcements, and the integration of the 'zombies.' By November, the army's morale was low. According to some observers, the animosity of the troops was directed at not just the government but the senior commanders as well, who were seen as distant and uncaring.[25]

Crerar understood that morale was low, but, if his correspondence is any indication, believed it was directed towards the government: 'We have all been distinctly unhappy at the turn political events have taken in Canada. It is very hard for the average man over here to appreciate what is, to him, a simple problem.'[26] News of the mutinies and disturbances in British Columbia as small groups of NRMA men armed themselves and protested the change of government policy quickly eclipsed Crerar's disgust over the political debates surrounding conscription. He found the mutinies 'unsettling and humiliating.'[27] The response to conscription in Canada forced Crerar to consider the integration of the NRMA men as a potentially explosive problem. He decided that segregation must be avoided at all costs. He consequently instructed CMHQ that draftees on arrival from Canada should be 'made' to mix with volunteers during training, 'in order to avoid trouble when [the] draft reached units in the field.' To prevent the absence of the 'General Service' shoulder flash worn by volunteers distinguishing the draftees, he insisted on uniformity of dress. He went further and, on 1 December, suggested to CMHQ that the practice of issuing NRMA distinct serial numbers be stopped. Montague argued that this was going too far, and Crerar demurred. Within a few days, however, Montague had commissioned a history of the NRMA – complete with recommendations on how to handle 'these men' once they were overseas – for distribution among First Canadian Army commanders and staff officers. The overseas army was clearly anticipating a backlash against the conscripts. Raising morale in general was another solution. In the letter of 1 December 1944, underlining Crerar's concerns about integration and morale, he asked for an improvement in the quality of films shown by the Auxiliary Services Organization and the acceleration in publishing award lists. These steps may have had some effect, or perhaps the NRMA men were not as foreign to the rank and file as they seemed to the senior command. There were no recorded incidents of problems between GS and NRMA men; few even noticed their arrival. The comments recorded were favourable. Sixteen thousand were sent overseas; over 2,400 served in field units; 69 were killed.[28]

The difficulty of maintaining the three remaining French-speaking regiments at full strength was also raised with CMHQ and DND. It was raised first by Simonds on 23 October, who noted that the deficiency had already meant assigning them 'special battle tasks.' His recommendation that French units be supplemented by one English-speaking company was politically unpalatable; the subsequent general infantry crisis and Crerar's renewed vigour provided an opportunity to tackle the issue once more. Ever the political animal, Crerar gave NDHQ three options. The first was the disingenuous suggestion that the government provide enough troops to maintain the units at fighting strength. The other alternatives were the absorption of one unit into the other two, or the use of an English-speaking company. Neither Murchie, as acting CGS, nor Montague found hope in the first option, hinting as it did that reinforcements could be found. On 7 November the Minister of National War Services, Major-General Leo LaFleche, a French Canadian and member of the Cabinet Recruiting Committee, requested the task of finding reinforcements for the French battalions. He was unsuccessful, and the shortages continued in French-speaking infantry battalions until the arrival of the NRMA men in January 1945.[29]

Replenishing the infantry units was Crerar's first priority, but improvements to headquarters organization were also set in motion on his return. Arriving at the HQ on 7 November, he had initiated, through Mann, a process of reassessment, announcing that amendments and suggestions submitted over the last few months for improvement to the organization and procedures of the HQ would now be considered; he also called for the branches to submit any further recommendations for improvement.[30] The resulting changes, as reflected in the revised HQ's 'Memorandum on Organization' indicate both First Canadian Army HQ's maturity as a fighting formation and the conclusions Crerar and his staff had drawn about the nature of the fighting so far. There were refinements in organization, and clearer descriptions of channels of command, but the most important alterations and clarifications saw a greater diffusion of responsibility from the Chief of Staff to the operational staff, particularly Beament as Colonel, GS, and the Brigadier, Royal Artillery. The army commander's role as coordinator of the staff was also stressed. The resources of 84 Group had also been increased to match its growing responsibilities. The fighters and ground-support aircraft were regrouped into the same section and layers of control were eliminated. Under the new organization, the ground troops had direct access to Forward Director Posts (FDP) and, in theory, the aircraft. The Plans section, considered by some as unnecessary, continued to have important responsibilities laid out and enlarged in the new organization. Crerar's influence was important to its survival; he handed the responsibility for coordinating the planning of the winter campaign to the Plans section.

There were concerns that the HQ was growing too large. At the end of November, there were 2,420 personnel and over 600 vehicles and trailers attached to the Army HQ; if the air force and signals personnel were included, these figures rose to 5,670 and 1,800 respectively. By January, there was sufficient concern over the numbers for Mann to issue a warning over the tendency to equate increases in establishment with increases in efficiency.[31]

Changes in command and staff were also an important element of preparing the army for the winter offensive. There had been some turnover during operations, but little time for considered appraisals. Crerar maintained a firm grip on these changes, but now proven battlefield experience eclipsed all other factors as the main measure. As late as the summer, for instance, Major-General Dan Spry's promotion to command 3rd Canadian Division after Keller had been wounded had been informed by Crerar's desire to redress a perceived preponderance of gunners in the senior command; Spry was an infantryman. When in November a new GOC was sought for 2nd Canadian Division, the appointment went to the former Commander, Corps Royal Artillery for 2nd Canadian Corps, Major-General Bruce Matthews, 'an aggressive, self-confident officer who had no doubt about his ability to command an infantry division.' Neither did Simonds and Crerar; they now had a much clearer vision of what it took to win battles in northwest Europe.[32]

Crerar's influence was also evident as he attempted to spread that battle experience throughout his command and the army in the United

Kingdom. He made the decisions on the most senior, and his approval was required before any officer ranked brigadier and above could be removed. He sent a memorandum to his corps, divisional, and armoured brigade commanders as a reminder of this fact in early January 1945.[33] Price Montague at CMHQ and the CGS, Lieutenant-General J.C. Murchie, both generally deferred to Crerar's opinions in any case.

III

While First Canadian Army absorbed infantry and lessons, plans for the campaign to clear the country west of the Rhine, code-named Operation Veritable, went forward. Allied strategy had been derailed by the strength of German resistance through October as well as the limits imposed by the logistical situation. By November, Montgomery, in consultation with Eisenhower, was developing the framework that would shape his army group's objectives for the next five months. First Canadian Army's initial role was outlined in a directive issued by Montgomery to his army commanders on 2 November in anticipation of the clearance of the Scheldt. In it, Montgomery ordered his armies to tidy up the line by clearing the Meuse pocket and 'driving the enemy back to the east side of the Meuse' in the area west of Venlo. They were also to support 12th Army Group's assault towards Cologne, both by releasing U.S. divisions under command and by developing offensive operations. To fulfill this directive, First Canadian Army was to prepare for operations 'south-eastwards from the Nijmegen area, between the Rhine and the Meuse' and 'northwards ... to secure the high ground between Arnhem and Apeldoorn with a bridgehead over the Ijssel river.' In the meantime, Crerar's army was to extend its flanks to include the Nijmegen bridgehead, transfer the divisions that had come under command to complete operations on the Scheldt, and tidy up a front that extended from Walcheren along the lower Maas, the Waal, and the Neder Cijn to Cuijk – a distance of approximately 140 miles. This would allow Second British Army the offensive strength to complete operations directed at clearing the Germans from all territory west of the River Maas.

In short, Montgomery eventually wanted the Rhineland cleared of German troops, part of Eisenhower's strategy of closing to the Rhine, while destroying German forces west of the River Maas. While a southeasterly thrust from the Maas to the Rhine had been envisioned since at least August, the preconditions for what would become Veritable were only now established by Monty's 2 November directive. It was still unclear when and by whom it would be undertaken.

The seven members of the Plans Section of First Canadian Army began a preliminary study of the operation, code-named Valediction, a study completed and passed on to Crerar on 24 November. The army commander was pleased with the results and so informed his staff, reminding them, however, to coordinate both the planning and any action taken with their counterparts at 21st Army Group HQ. On the 28th, he forwarded the results of the assessment to Montgomery.

Two points were notable about the aspects of the assessment that Crerar chose to highlight in his letter to Montgomery. One was the confidence that informed the conclusion: 'I just cannot see "Valediction" being "on" for some time, and until conditions are generally less unfavourable to its mounting.' The second notable point was how much the experiences of the previous months' campaigning, particularly the Scheldt, shaped Crerar and his staff's insistence that the operation would have to await better weather and ground conditions, and, if launched, First Canadian Army would require infantry and artillery reinforcements from Second British Army. This was a sharp change from Crerar's, and Simonds's, hesitant requests for support during the fall's campaigning.[34]

Equally sharp was Monty's reaction to Crerar's doubts. 'There is no intention of launching this operation now,' he wrote, 'and I have never expressed any wish do so.' All he had wanted was an examination, he continued. Montgomery was preoccupied with bigger matters. Attempting to take advantage of the 6th and 12th U.S. Army Group's floundering campaigns to the south, on 28 November he tried to convince Eisenhower that the best chance to achieve decisive results in closing to the Rhine was in the British sector. Once the German defences in the Rhineland were breached and the Rhine crossed, the flat terrain and the industrial prizes of the Ruhr beckoned. All he needed was Lieutenant-General William Simpson's U.S. Ninth Army and the support of Bradley's 12th U.S. Army Group. Monty's assessment, however, overlooked the preponderance of American forces (sixty-one to fifteen Anglo-Canadian divisions) and Eisenhower's preference for the more cautious and diplomatic, if ponderous, broad-front strategy. Few American generals wanted Montgomery to win the war; none wanted him to win it using American troops.

As explained to Eisenhower, Montgomery's offensive was a pincer movement on the Rhineland plain that would either destroy the German army west of the Rhine if they chose to stand and fight, or lever them out of their positions and force a retreat across the Rhine. The northern thrust, Operation Veritable, would be launched from the Nijmegen bridgehead between the Maas and the Rhine and under command of First Canadian Army. The U.S. Ninth Army would simultaneously launch the southeastern operation, code-named Grenade; Simpson's objectives were the Roer River and a linkup with the Canadian army along the Venlo-Xanten line. Second British Army would prepare to cross the Rhine once the operations were completed.

Montgomery's plan for a northern thrust was sound and this created a dilemma for Eisenhower, who was under a great deal of pressure from Bradley and Patton to launch the major offensive in the Saar region using U.S. forces. He dithered for several days, announcing on 7 December 1944 his decision to mount Montgomery's offensive in the Rhineland while allowing 12th and 6th Army Groups to undertake limited offensives. Simpson's ten-division U.S. Ninth Army would be under command of 21st Army Group for the offensive, and the operation would take place no later than 8 February 1945 to take advantage of the winter freeze.

Montgomery phoned Crerar early that evening, informing him of First Canadian Army's role. The target date for the operation was 1 January 1945. By 10 December 1944 he would have 30 British Corps, consisting of four infantry and one armoured division, for the operation, but Montgomery, while ordering 30 British Corps to take up positions on the right of First Canadian Army, suggested that Crerar make the final decision as to which corps to use. The positioning of the British corps and the planning it had undertaken in the fall made it a foregone conclusion.

That evening, through Acting Chief of Staff, Beament, Crerar gave his staff the broad outlines of Montgomery's strategy and the task before First Canadian Army. Beament then directed the staff to consider the problems involved in mounting and developing the operations. All planning was centralized in and coordinated by G Plans. The staff made detailed assessments and these were given to Crerar for his consideration. Planning began in earnest on 8 December with a conference between Crerar and his senior staff. The pattern established here was to characterize Crerar's approach to planning the battle and indeed to operations right up to the German surrender. He generally coordinated and approved the planning rather than undertaking it himself, but it was evident that Crerar's grip on the HQ and planning was much tighter than during the summer and fall.[35]

The assessments produced in early December would shape the First Canadian Army approach to the battle, despite the changing circumstances of the following months. The dominant element was that, like previous operations, Crerar worked within the strict parameters shaped by Montgomery's plans and 21st Army Group's hold on resources. Crerar at the beginning of the conference laid these out. Within that framework, however, Crerar's ability to shape the operation was much greater than during the fall, when the timing had been dictated by the speed of the German collapse and logistics.

Resources were not a problem. For the Rhineland offensive, Crerar had at his disposal a tremendous array of men and material: when the assault was launched, the ration strength of First Canadian Army was over 470,000 men, organized in two corps; 2nd Tactical Air Force, 84 and 83 Group, Bomber Command, and the medium bombers of the Eighth U.S. Army Air Force provided air support; for artillery support, there were over 1,300 medium, heavy, and anti-aircraft guns, as well as a newly organized rocket battery with almost unlimited ammunition; 1,000 tanks and armoured vehicles would, it was hoped, provide the main punch in the break-out. In the southern arm of the pincer, Ninth U.S. Army had 370,000 troops under command.

The problem that confronted Crerar and his army was the nature of the battlefield: lying between two rivers, and heavily wooded in sections, it was constricted, with limited access; it was also a flood plain of the Rhine, as well as, by February 1945, well-fortified with three defensive lines forming the northern section of the Siegfried Line. The army had to pour its massive resources into a narrow corridor and try to achieve tactical, if not strategic, surprise, while hoping that the weather held; if it did not, the terrain would become impassable – or nearly so.

In addition to weather and terrain, the immensity of the logistical requirements would also affect the launch date. Given the variables, the planning staff were ready to reconsider the practicality of launching the operation during the winter, and major modifications including frontage and the final objective. The narrow front, in particular, presented problems that the engineers feared would take time to resolve. Crerar made the tasks of his engineering chief, Geoffrey Walsh and the DA and QMG, Lister more difficult, ordering that 2nd and 3rd Canadian Division remain in place until the last minute to maximize security; movement beyond the marshalling area could take place only at night. It was agreed that the operation could be mounted twenty-eight days from 10 December, the date that 30 British Corps was redeployed.

The planners concluded, however, 'Success of the operation will depend to a large extent on the frost on the ground.'[36] The complexity of the operation soon left little room for changing the timing. Planning continued apace at the army group, army, and corps level for the next week. Crerar met with Montgomery, who reiterated the importance of Veritable as 'the British Empire contribution to the Winter Campaign,' and that for that purpose, 'First Canadian Army [was] to have complete priority on all the resources of 21 Army Group.' He noted that through 83 Group, First Canadian Army would have control of 84 Group. He hinted again that 30 British Corps would be the logical choice for the operation. He also stressed the importance of coordinating the offensive with Grenade.

The decision to leave the battle to 30 British Corps did not sit well with everyone. As Crerar prepared to outline the plan to his corps commanders, Simonds suggested that Major-General Dan Spry's 3rd Canadian Division be included in the opening operations: 'To leave the Canadians out of so important and so decisive a battle would be a bitter disappointment to the troops.' And to Simonds. Crerar agreed and the Canadians were assigned to Horrocks's corps. This change made, Crerar outlined the principles he believed governed development of the battle. The 30 British Corps would operate on the right, launching the offensive with 2nd Canadian Corps in a support role. He estimated that it would take the form of three 'highly organized and strongly supported' operations, each phase taking roughly a week. He framed it as a stage-managed, set-piece operation from the beginning, rather than the encounter battle designed to take advantage of superior Allied mobility that Monty envisioned. Given the complex organization and logistics required by the operation, this approach was logical. Crerar also stressed the importance of achieving surprise; he described operations and deployments that would keep the Germans guessing as to where the main assault would fall.[37]

Crerar's vision of a set-piece battle and the complex arrangements required to overcome the potentially disastrous congestion were at odds with Horrocks's idea of the battle, and these were the issues thrashed out over the next few days. The 30 British Corps wanted to have its two reserve divisions in the forward concentration areas to be ready to exploit any breakthrough; Mann observed that this move 'would seem to make it certain that serious congestion [would] arise and is at great variance with the conception that phase I of the operation will require at least seven days.'

Horrocks changed his view as a result of First Canadian Army's appreciation, deciding that he could not commit both his reserve divisions before Phase I was completed. He also prepared two plans: one to take advantage of hard frost and 'correspondingly good going'; the other 'where mud conditions prevail.' He called for more artillery support for the opening phases, which required a detailed program for firing the equivalent of eleven divisional artilleries. This approach would further limit the ability to alter the timetable for the assault.[38]

Crerar's idea of how the battle would develop was firmly entrenched by mid-December; Montgomery's 15 December directive that the operation would go ahead as early as possible after 1 January in order to take advantage of what he perceived as the weakened condition of the Wehrmacht, reconfirmed Crerar's conception by emphasizing that the operation must go ahead, regardless of the weather and terrain. As detailed in his remarks to the HQ staff the next day, the army commander reiterated Montgomery's agenda: First Canadian Army was being called upon to lead another 'historic' offensive, as it had in August 1944, an offensive that had the potential to be 'decisive.' The enemy could have no respite: 'This conclusion means that neither winter weather, nor bad ground conditions, must be allowed to check our offensive operations, no matter what the difficulties and acute discomfort.' He asserted that 'our operations must be of a character to force the enemy to engage in mobile operations,' a point somewhat at odds with his vision of the battle. He stressed that strategic requirements did not permit the operation to be delayed to wait for ground and air conditions more favourable to the attack. It was clear that once the timetable for the offensive was established, only a major disruption would alter it. The set-piece operational plan reinforced this rigidity: Phase I would see the clearing of the Reichswald and the line Gennep-Cleve secured; Phase II envisioned the commitment of 2nd Canadian Corps into the enlarged front and securing the line Weeze-Udem-Alt-Emmerich; in Phase III, the Hochwald defensive lines would be breached and the final objective Venlo-Orsoy secured. Crerar concluded with the observation that it was 'necessary to visualize "Veritable" as a series of operations, possibly lasting a month, or six weeks, and, in effect, being the winter campaign of 21 Army Group.'[39] The conditions for a methodical battle of attrition were clearly in place; so too was the mindset.

The timetable for the offensive was delayed, however. While Crerar spoke to his staff about the operation, the Germans launched the offensive subsequently known to history as the Battle of the Bulge, destroying several American divisions in the Ardennes and threatening the Allied line. The full impact of the offensive was not clear for several days, but by the 20th Monty was forced to delay Veritable and to redeploy his forces to meet the German threat. First Canadian Army played no part in the subsequent battles, although Crerar believed, on the basis of HQ intelligence, that the Germans were preparing for an offensive against the Nijmegan salient to support successes in the Ardennes. Postwar revelations suggested that the German army had such plans for an offensive if the Ardennes attack reached Antwerp. Crerar remained alert for any possible attempts to rub out the salient, conscious of the fact that they could expect no help from 21st Army Group and that preparations for Veritable could not be compromised. Plans were made to move the HQ on six hours' notice, and the CCRA, Major-General Plow, was placed in command of available army troops to form a perimeter defence.[40] In the end, for Crerar and his HQ, the practice manoeuvres and enemy air activity generated more entertainment than danger: 'One enemy plane passed so low over my caravan,' he wrote home on 2 January 1945, 'that I think I could have hit it with a biscuit. However, his "time over target" was so short that neither the pilot nor I had an opportunity to do anything about the situation.'[41]

As the battle raged to the south, planning for Veritable continued. The final area where Crerar had substantial input was the degree and nature of the air support. Discussions over the next month and a half centred on how best to balance the air-support needs of the break-in against the possibility of jeopardizing a breakout; in short, how to trade off the destruction and demoralization that the senior army and air command believed resulted from medium and heavy bombers, with how much the attacking forces were slowed by the cratering and debris that accompanied such bombing. Meeting with the army HQ and 84 Group HQ staff on 17 December, Horrocks made plain his preference for the heaviest air support possible; he was willing to delay launching the operation for a week in order to wait for favourable weather conditions. Crerar, however, made it equally plain that while air support for the launching and duration of Veritable would be preferable, 'in view of the uncertainty of the weather, it must be considered as a bonus.' The decision was deferred to Monty, but the elements necessary for rapid operations were becoming secondary to the need to launch and maintain the operation as quickly as possible. Stung by allegations of slowness in the fall, and despite an earlier insistence on the importance of weather and the conditions of the terrain, Crerar supported Montgomery's insistence on launching the operation as quickly as possible, which was rooted in SHAEF directives to launch coordinated attacks all along the front. Still, if support was available, Crerar and Horrocks wanted to maximize it. Despite the potential drawbacks and Horrocks's concerns, cratering was accepted, but only after a belated attempt to secure incendiary and untested liquid firebombs from 2nd Tactical Air Force. In the end, they decided that enemy strong points in villages and towns would be destroyed as long as the direction of the attack was not compromised.[42] These decisions would be revisited.

Planning for the first phase was incomplete when German successes prompted a 30 British Corps move south to assist Second British Army on 19 December 1944. It would be a full month before the operation was revived. During that time, First Canadian Army, as it had during the previous month's 'rest' on the Maas, maintained an aggressive posture shaped by Crerar's directive to his corps commanders of 13 November. The senior command planned several operations to 'tidy up' its front, and kept up an active series of patrols and raids, with no discernable effect on the enemy, although much was made of the morale-boosting and moral effects of maintaining superiority. Like the trench raids of the First World War, they were dubious exercises. This policy culminated with the costly assault on Kapelsche Veer in January 1945. Crerar's concerns regarding the need to remain alert were justified, however. On 1 December, for example, he instructed Major-General Thomas Rennie of the 51st Highland Division and, then temporary GOC of 2nd Canadian Corps, to make preparations for the possibility of a German assault on the Nijmegan bridge or an attempt to flood the Canadians out of their positions; the next day the dykes were blown.[43]

Crerar approached the tasks at hand with an energy missing in the fall. He was active on many levels and the more so when Veritable was delayed. Through December and January he paid close attention to the welfare of the troops and forged a closer relationship with the staff. Extra cigarettes were distributed to his mess and on hospital visits. He urged CMHQ to secure the newest film releases direct from the United States, complaining that the ones his troops received were dated. Tragedy struck close to Christmas, when his escort, Corporal A.B. Craig, was killed in a road accident; Crerar attended the service and sent a letter to the boy's mother describing the burial arrangements and telling her that he would 'miss him greatly.' It was not a particularly personal letter, but what it lacked in warmth, it made up for in thought.[44] Christmas and New Year's were spent on aerial reconnaissance and visiting the corps and divisional messes. In early January 1945, he paid a brief visit to London to ensure a low profile for the arrival of the conscripts in the United Kingdom. His energy was remarked upon when he lunched with Brooke: 'Crerar came during the afternoon, looking very well.'[45] He returned to his headquarters on 13 January 1945 as First Canadian Army renewed its preparations for Veritable.

Crerar, second from left, on course at the Royal Military College of Canada 1907/08. Cadet 749 would return to the RMC as an instructor and as Commandant. (Massey Library, RMC of Canada)

A young Harry Crerar in dress uniform ca. 1913. Crerar enjoyed his association with the militia, but after graduation from the RMC pursued a career with Ontario Hydro. (Massey Library, RMC of Canada)

Lieutenant Crerar of Hamilton's 4th Battery, last row, far right, at the annual militia camp, Petawawa, June 1914. Six months later, Crerar would be on his way to Europe and the western front. (Massey Library, RMC of Canada)

Crerar and his senior command, May 1945. L to R, seated: H.S. Maczek, Simonds, Crerar, Foulkes, B.M. Hoffmeister. Standing: R.H. Keefler, A.B. Matthews, H.W. Foster, R.W. Moncel, S.B. Rawlins. (Ken Bell, Canada, Dept of National Defence, LAC PA-134281)

Montgomery visits Crerar at FCA HQ Uden, Netherlands, during Operation Veritable. Montgomery had not wanted Crerar and his HQ in charge of the Rhineland operations, but more than any other, this was Crerar's battle. (Ken Bell, Canada, Dept of National Defence, LAC PA-140409)

Crerar, General Dwight Eisenhower, and Maj.-Gen. S. Maczek, GOC, Polish Armoured Division, November 1944. Fighting as part of a coalition and commanding a multi-national army were two of the challenges facing the Canadian army commander. (Canada, Dept of National Defence, LAC PA-115876)

Crerar in April 1945 with the air and ground crew of his Stinson Vigilant, his preferred means of liaising with and observing his often far-flung formations. (Ken Bell, Canada, Dept of National Defence, LAC PA-164016)

L to R, FCA Chief of Staff, Brig C. Churchill Mann, Crerar, and Air Marshal Sir Edmund Hudleston, AOC, No. 84 Group at FCA HQ in Tilburg, Netherlands, February 1945. Crerar worked hard to maintain good relations with his Air Force and Naval counterparts, his approach informed by the Canadian Corps First World War ethos of trading 'shells for lives.' (Ken Bell, Canada, Dept of National Defence, LAC PA-145766)

Crerar and the massed pipe bands pose in front of the Vimy Ridge Memorial monument during the 28th Anniversary Ceremony of the Battle of Vimy Ridge, 9 April 1945. Crerar was acutely conscious that his army's performance would be measured against that of General Sir Arthur Currie's Canadian Corps. (Canada, Dept of National Defence, LAC PA-137364)

L to R, Crerar, Foulkes, and Simonds at the memorial service in the Dieppe cemetery following liberation, 3 Sept 1944. Crerar risked Montgomery's wrath to attend. (Ken Bell, Canada, Dept of National Defence, LAC PA-116584)

Crerar addresses a press conference at First Canadian Army HQ, 7 Aug 1944. Before Operation Totalize Crerar emphasized the historic parallels with the Canadian's spearhead role in the Amien's operations in 1918. (Canada, Dept of National Defence, LAC PA-131371)

On the eve of Operation Totalize: L to R, around the map, Crerar, Air Marshal A.M. Coningham, Montgomery, and Air Chief Marshal Sir T.L. Leigh-Mallory. In the background, FCA HQ staff look on, Brig. G.E. Beament is 2nd from right, and Brig. E. Walford far right. (Ken Bell, Canada, Dept of National Defence, LAC PA-129122)

Montgomery, Prime Minister Mackenzie King, and Crerar in May 1944. Montgomery tried to convince King to minimize Crerar's right of reference to the Canadian government. He was unsuccessful, but King seriously considered it because he mistrusted his generals. (William Lyon Mackenzie King, LAC C-013234)

Crerar poses for photographer Laurie Audrian in May 1944. Crerar's assumption of command of the FCA was accompanied by a press campaign aimed to raise his profile with the Canadian public. (Laurie A. Audrian, Canada, Dept of National Defence, LAC PA-129048)

Crerar turning over command of 1st Canadian Corps to Lt.-Gen. E.L.M. Burns, 3 March 1944. Burn's appointment would prove problematic, absorbing much time and goodwill between the British and Canadian senior command, during the summer and fall of 1944. (Canada, Dept of National Defence, LAC PA-132784)

Crerar relaxing with some local children near his corps HQ at Wakehurst Place in West Sussex, April 1943. Crerar's decision that his wife Verse should remain in Canada was a difficult one, particularly after the birth of his grandchild. He would not see them for three and a half years. (Canada, Dept of National Defence, LAC PA-140413)

Montgomery, Crerar, and Ralston at British 8th Army HQ in Italy, November 1943. Montgomery was sceptical regarding Crerar's suitability to command the First Canadian Army, but Ralston returned from this fact-finding visit convinced that Crerar was the right choice. (Canada, Dept of National Defence, LAC PA-170289)

German defenders observe the aftermath of the Dieppe Raid in August 1942. (LAC C-017293)

Canadian troops practice an assault landing during an exercise in Sussex, England, May 1942. Crerar, among others, believed more realistic training and participation in small raids along the French coast were a tonic for his troop's low morale and inexperience. (Canada, Dept of National Defence, LAC PA-144598)

L to R, Crerar, Minister of National Defence J.L. Ralston, and the British Secretary of State for War, Captain David Margesson, in the UK, October 1941. Crerar, as Chief of the General Staff, pushed hard for a two-corps army formation, which Ralston, despite mistrusting Crerar's ambition, felt he had to support. (Canada, Dept of National Defence, LAC C-063112)

L to R, Crerar, Georges P. Vanier, Lt. Gen. A.G.L. McNaughton, and Brig. G.R. Turner in Paris, January 1940. Despite very different temperaments, Crerar and McNaughton worked for over a decade to promote their shared vision of Canada's army. (Canada, Dept of National Defence, LAC PA-166142)

Lt. Col. Harry Crerar in London, 1918. At the end of the First World War, Crerar was undecided about the pursuit of a career in the Permanent Forces. (Canada, Dept of National Defence, LAC PA-7162)

Crerar as Director of Military Operations and Intelligence, 1937. He later wrote that he was close to resigning so frustrated was he with the slow progress of preparing the country for a war he believed was imminent. (Massey Library, RMC of Canada)

The War of 1914-1918.

Canadian Forces.

Maj. H.D.G. Crerar.— Can. Arty.

was mentioned in a Despatch from Field Marshal Sir Douglas Haig, G.C.B., G.C.V.O., K.C.I.E. dated 9th April 1917 for gallant and distinguished services in the Field. I have it in command from the King to record His Majesty's high appreciation of the services rendered.

Winston S. Churchill
Secretary of State for War.

War Office
Whitehall, S.W.
1st March 1919.

Crerar was appointed Acting CO of his artillery brigade during the Battle of Vimy Ridge, April 1917, after the CO was killed. Crerar received a 'Mention of Despatch' for leading the brigade through the rest of April. (Massey Library, RMC of Canada)

HQ staff, the Royal Artillery, Canadian Corps in 1918. Lt. Col. Crerar sits second from left, beside the GOC, RA, Canadian Corps, Maj.-Gen. E.W.B. 'Dinky' Morrison. (Massey Library, RMC of Canada)

Crerar's official welcome back to Canada, Ottawa, 7 August 1945. L to R, Verse Crerar, Harry Crerar, Prime Minister Mackenzie King, and Peggy (Crerar) Palmer. (Canada, Dept of National Defence, LAC, C-026991)

Crerar on the eve of retirement. His influence quickly waned. (Massey Library, RMC of Canada)

22 Veritable: Crerar's Battle

I

'Probably no assault of the war has been conducted under more appalling conditions of terrain than was that one,' wrote Eisenhower in his congratulatory note to Crerar following the liberation of the Rhineland. 'It speaks volumes for your skill and determination and the valor of your soldiers, that you carried it through to a successful completion.'[1] For Operation Veritable, the plan to destroy the northern German armies east of the Rhine and an assault characterized as the British Empire contribution to the winter campaign, Crerar had under his command thirteen divisions, including nine British and an amalgam of Polish, Dutch, and Belgian units – the largest force ever commanded in operations by a Canadian. As the northern prong of 21st Army Group, First Canadian Army, would launch its offensive simultaneously with Operation Grenade; weather permitting, the Germans would be driven back in short order by the weight of Allied armour or destroyed by the 1,034 guns engaged in the bombardment. If conditions were not good, Crerar envisaged a three-stage set-piece operation, characterized by methodical preparation and overwhelming firepower – in short, a bitter set-piece battle. In either case, his army was prepared. Veritable was an operation that, as much as any could be in Montgomery's army group, was Crerar's. He kept a tight rein on the battle, flying, at considerable risk, over the battlefield and maintained a clear vision of what he wanted to achieve. The battle demonstrated the extent to which Crerar had grown into his command.

The German threat to the Allied lines was blunted by the end of December, but two more weeks passed before the bulge in the Allied lines was eliminated and the line restored. During that time, Montgomery made one last attempt to gain operational control of most of the Allied ground forces and pulled back only when indirectly threatened with dismissal. But not before he had angered the senior U.S. command with his patronizing remarks following the Ardennes battles. In mid-January 1945, he once again turned his attention to the Rhineland offensive.

On 10 January, HQ First Canadian Army was ordered to review 'the factors concerning mounting Op Veritable'; on the 16th Montgomery held a conference of his army commanders, informing them that operations to clear the Rhineland as a prelude to crossing the Rhine were once again imminent. The delay had caused no substantial alterations to the plan except to reaffirm the importance of Grenade. The Americans were now, however, reluctant to make a commitment to deploying formations under Montgomery's command. Eisenhower had to overcome the animosity of the American senior command towards Montgomery to persuade them of the necessity of diverting resources away from the Ardennes counteroffensives, and back to the Rhineland operation. As late as 15 January, Monty was telling Lieutenant-General William Simpson, GOC Ninth U.S. Army, that he should prepare to control at least four corps of sixteen divisions, information Simpson characterized as a 'bombshell.' On 21 January, SHAEF agreed to release Ninth U.S. Army, comprising twelve divisions, for Grenade, but their lack of enthusiasm was underlined by their reluctance to commit to a fixed day to facilitate coordination. Informed of SHAEF's decision, Simpson – described by one correspondent as 'a tall raw boned Texan ... lean, hard and billiard-bald' – wrote in his diary that his army's moves would be 'to the greater glory of the FM himself, since he sees fit to assume all the glory and scarcely permits the mention of an Army Commander's name.' He added that 'bitterness and real resentment' were creeping in as Monty and the British press publicized 'British Military Accomplishments won with American blood.'[2]

On 21 January, Montgomery issued a formal directive outlining an operation that was, in its essentials, the same as the one planned in December. The target date for Veritable was set for 8 February, but the launch date for Grenade remained up in the air. Despite the lack of coordination, and Montgomery's concerns about the possibility of a time lag between the two thrusts, there was no longer any question of timing. In theory, Veritable could be delayed for no more than twenty-four hours to ensure air support, but in practice the date was made virtually immobile by the strategic considerations of the whole front and the timetables of the many services and branches involved in the offensive. This became apparent in the renewed discussions over air support.

In light of the weakened state of the Luftwaffe and, it was believed, the German army following the Ardennes offensive, some of the air attacks were now deemed unnecessary. Horrocks's doubts about the usefulness of bombing resurfaced, particularly given the reduction of the enemy air forces north of the Maas and the potential for wet, muddy terrain. The air forces and Crerar preferred to use the bombers, however, even though Crerar believed that the artillery would be the decisive arm. On the question of cratering, he was pressured by the air force to accept it as the trade-off for destroying two key defence areas of the Siegfried line – Nutterden and Materborn, between the Reichswald and Cleve; Horrocks, however, feared that his ability to pass his mechanized formations through the defences once breached would be hindered by extensive cratering, particularly given the limited road access, and accepted only fighter/bomber attacks on the Nutterden section as well as 'shallow cratering' of the Materborn defences.[3] While few seemed to have questioned the value of using medium and heavy bombers to destroy the German defences and shake their morale, the possible delays that cratering had on the advance were debated. Crerar was led to believe that the air force could minimize the obstruction, using 'shallow cratering' techniques and incendiary bombs. While the weather and terrain would prove to be the main hindrances to the momentum of the advance, the full use of the Allied surfeit of airpower again potentially limited the ability to react decisively to events.

The use of the bombers was not just a question of achieving a breakthrough. Crerar also called on Horrocks to decide the fate of the historic city of Cleve. He recalled,

> One day Crerar visited me and said that, in addition to the whole of the Tactical Air Force being available to support our attack, the 'Heavies' from Bomber Command were all at my disposal. He then said, 'Do you want Cleve taken out?' ... No doubt a lot of civilians, plus women and children, were still living there. Their fate depended on how I answered Crerar's question.

It was believed that the German reserves would be fed through Cleve, and in the race to breach the defences, preventing the Germans from moving reinforcements to the battlefield was critical. Reluctantly, Horrocks said yes.[4]

During the build-up period, with the major decisions made, the burden of planning now lay with the staff and engineers, and by all accounts they performed magnificently. The achievements speak for themselves and for the quality of the staff work at HQ First Canadian Army, as well as the engineers and logisticians: to move everything into position required 100 miles of new and improved road; five new bridges were built across the Maas, using 1,880 tons of bridging equipment, including a high level bridge that at 1,280 feet was the longest pontoon bridge constructed during the war; the required building material included 20,000 tons of stones, 20,000 logs, and 30,000 pickets, all of which were transported to the front along with the 90,000 men, their equipment, 1,000 guns, 11,000 tons of ammunition, and 200,000 tons of stores that were crammed into the narrow front. Thirty-five thousand vehicles, 'travelling an average 130 miles each and using approximately 1,300,000 gallons of petrol' were kept moving by 10,000 route signs and 1,000 troops assigned to traffic control. The movements to the forward assembly area were done at night, and as D-Day loomed, the pace increased. Preparation at the headquarters included the assembly of 500,000 air photographs, 15,000 enlargements, and 800,000 special maps. This massive intelligence and logistical task had to be accomplished without alerting the Germans to the imminence of a major offensive, and for that purpose elaborate deception plans were implemented. Little wonder that Crerar instructed his staff to keep careful records and compile statistics; this was the largest force and biggest operation ever commanded by a Canadian. He understood the historic nature of First Canadian Army's achievement and wanted it recorded.

The careful and delicate timetabling required for the movement was Crerar's predominant concern in the two and a half weeks prior to D-Day, as ongoing U.S. army operations towards Bonn delayed a firm commitment to Grenade and, it was thought, might cause a postponement of Veritable. On 23 January, Montgomery suggested that if the First U.S. Army operations broke the German defences, Veritable might go in unsupported, but offered assurances that unless such 'a favourable situation did obtain,' Veritable and Grenade would be launched together. In response, Crerar noted that at least five days' notice was now required to check the forward movement and assembly if the offensive was delayed; Monty told him he would have six. The target date for Grenade became 15 February, one week after Veritable's scheduled launch date. Monty also noted that although the use of the bombers was reasonably secure, decisions made at higher levels might change that, and Crerar should be prepared to make the assault with 2nd Tactical Air only.[5]

That the timing was still equivocal illustrates one of the drawbacks of the broad front strategy. Crerar had little control over some of the most critical aspects of the battle. On 22 January, he addressed his senior officers and made that point; some recalled that such 'O' groups were thankfully few, and to them uninspiring. He spoke, he noted self-consciously, 'in terms of policies and principles – in generalities and not of details. Such is my job.' Still, Crerar addressed some specific concerns. He reminded his audience of the importance of surprise and that it would be achieved, as at Amiens and in Totalize, by an intense preliminary bombardment. Once achieved, the initiative must be maintained, 'pressed through relentlessly,' and in contrast to the German reports of the Allied tendency to occupy ground, rather than fight over it. He concluded that the 'essential requirement is to kill, or capture, Germans.' He also emphasized the importance of adequately briefing all ranks as to their part and requirements of the next two levels. He remained conscious of history, however, and described the battle as potentially decisive. He concluded, 'Conditions of ground may be tough, in the extreme. But, they must not be allowed seriously to check the momentum or to relieve the enemy of our pressure.'[6]

Little changed in the basic assumptions of the plan until 1 February. In Crerar's directive to his corps commanders on 25 January, 2nd Canadian Division was included in the initial assault, and questions about air support and timing had been settled. In response to the possibility that air support might be limited by the weather, another Army Group Royal Artillery was added, bring the total number of AGRAs to five. Planning remained predicated on the necessity of three set-piece operations, though Crerar stressed that if the 'enemy's will and means' to resist were destroyed, 30 British Corps should 'lose no opportunity of exploiting the possibilities to the full, irrespective of the Phases.'[7] On 1 February, Montgomery confirmed 8 February as the start date, a start that could be delayed by no more than twenty-four hours, even if it meant going in with no air support. Grenade was now a SHAEF priority and would be launched on 10 February.

Montgomery met his army commanders on 4 February to discuss the coordination of the two thrusts and supporting operations. The support provided for Veritable was denuded to an extent when Second British Army operations were cancelled to enable the U.S. offensives to continue, but Montgomery made it clear that the operation would go ahead, no matter what. Crerar reiterated his conception of how the battle would develop, noting the possibility of a quick breakout if everything went their way. He also observed that Grenade was an important element in that estimate. Simpson responded that he anticipated no delay as First U.S. Army intended to capture the Roer dam no later than the 10th. Even if the dam was blown, he added, he did not anticipate that the flood waters would be serious or require postponement of the operation. The conference ended on that optimistic note.[8]

The breezy optimism that characterized these last high-level meetings was ill founded and seems ironic, given that the ground had already turned to mud. The weather broke in the Germans' favour at the end of January, and as the temperatures rose, the rains came; within days, as Stacey related, 'nearly 50 companies of engineers, plus three road construction companies and 29 pioneer companies, were fully employed in maintaining the roads in the British-Canadian sector.'[9] At the end of January the BGS at HQ 21st Army Group observed that there was only a one in seven chances of another cold spell; he anticipated 'very bad ground conditions.' Montgomery, like Horrocks, had already anticipated that two alternative plans were necessary.[10] There was nothing Crerar could do to delay the offensive, but he must have known it would be a slogging match; he recorded the steady deterioration of the roads in his war diary, and wrote to Peggy that 'most of the country is underwater again, and conditions underfoot are very trying.' He hinted as much the day before the offensive began in an address to the war correspondents, when he noted that the operation might 'be protracted and the fighting tough and trying.' He was, however, privately optimistic that this would be the decisive push. 'The tremendous Russian attack, and success, is rapidly changing the strategical situation,' he wrote a friend, 'and I trust that we shall be able to do our part to speed the termination of this long and bloody business.'[11]

Crerar moved his Tactical HQ from Tilburg to Uden on 7 February; he took Walsh, his chief engineer, with him, underlining the importance of the engineering requirements for the operation. Paul Martin, the Parliamentary Assistant to the Minister of Labour and future architect of much of Canada's social welfare system, was visiting the Main headquarters and recalled the atmosphere on the eve of the battle:

I flew in a small plane, General Crerar's own, to his headquarters outside Tilburg. As we came over Holland, I could follow the never-ending line of military carriers advancing with the equipment the Canadian forces would soon need for a major battle. I was whisked into a jeep and driven past a big iron gate into a compound of brick buildings, the headquarters of the commander of the First Canadian Army. From there, I was shown to a rich, furnished railway carriage on wheels, panelled in mahogany, where I would spend the night. It was known as the 'Viper's Den.'[12]

When I was eventually taken along to meet General Crerar, I suddenly seemed to freeze up ... He was full of questions. How was Massey? How were things in London? Had I seen Ralston before I left Canada? What did I think of General McNaughton's surprising defeat in the by election in Grey North? ... After our pleasantries we had dinner with a dozen or more of his ranking officers ...

After dinner, I went back to the Viper's Den. At about ten o'clock General Crerar sent for me. 'Well,' he said, 'I must tell you that you've come at a very critical time. This could perhaps be the last push in the war. Tomorrow we shall take the offensive.' ... At about three o'clock in the morning I was awakened by the frightening noises of war. Opening the door of the Viper's Den, I saw a soldier on guard, who said, 'Well, it's started.' The sky was bright with the reflections of exploding shells; trucks were rumbling by in the darkness. It was a terrifying experience for one who did not know what war was like, and sleep was banished for the rest of the night. I had breakfast alone in my mess – everyone else was busy.[13]

Bomber Command's assault on Cleve, Goch, Weeze, Udem, and Calcar on the night of 7–8 February launched Veritable. At 0500, 1,034 guns opened fire in what was characterized as a 'concentration ... not equalled on a similar front during the entire war in the west.' It was planned as a 'battle-winning factor.' Crerar claimed credit for initiating the addition of supporting fire from anti-tank, tank, and anti-aircraft guns, known as 'Pepper Pot' tactics and developing the idea as corps commander in Italy. The evidence suggests that no British formation used – or at least defined it as – 'Pepper Pot' until Normandy, although many innovations occurred simultaneously in different formations.[14] At 0740, the barrage stopped, drawing the Germans into their defensive positions; the First Canadian Army gunners then employed their counter-battery techniques to identify the German batteries, a tactic that the Canadian Corps had used with great success at Lens in 1917. It worked again, as did so many of the tactics developed in 1917–18, and the second explosion of artillery fire was a welcome sound to the assaulting troops. The Germans defenders were stunned and demoralized by the weight of the second barrage. At 1030, under cover of an intensified barrage, the infantry of four divisions moved forward along a seven-mile front: from right to left, the 51st Highland Division, the 53rd Welsh, the 15th Scottish, and the 2nd Canadian Division. The 3rd Canadian Division was scheduled to begin its assault in the late afternoon. Armoured formations were notably absent, Crerar, Simonds, and their British counterparts having learned some lessons in Normandy about the vulnerability of armour.

Despite the conditions of the terrain, 8 February began as a clear, sunny day, and full air support was available. Tactical surprise, also critical to the success of this frontal assault, was achieved. The Germans who manned the 'West Wall' were a mixed bag: Army Group 'H' was responsible for the sector opposite 21st Army Group; directly opposite First Canadian Army was 1st Parachute Army. Among its units were the 84th Infantry Division, which was a catch-all of green troops, survivors of the Normandy battles, and a 'Stomach' battalion; they had been reinforced on the 6th by the 2nd Parachute Regiment, 2,000 men combed from the Luftwaffe, who provided the core of the resistance. Before the battle was over, four more under-strength parachute divisions would fight the Anglo-Canadian army. Their commander, General Alfred Schlemm, GOC of the 1st Parachute Army, was a veteran of the First World War and would prove a determined and skilful tactician. For support, the 84th could call on one hundred artillery pieces as well as thirty-six self-propelled guns. First Canadian Army intelligence estimated that two divisions could reinforce the Germans within six hours. The Commander-in-Chief West, Field Marshal Gert von Rundstedt, was slow, however, to appreciate that this was the main Allied thrust and the 84th was left alone for two days.

Phase I's objectives, the clearing of the Reichswald and the line Gennep-Asperden and Cleve, were secured in those two days, despite the fact that the heavy rain prevented air support on the 9th and that flooding continued to reach record heights. Crerar and Montgomery were cautiously optimistic. The C-in-C wrote Brooke that 'getting formations and units in position for this very large scale attack has been a remarkable achievement in view of very bad state of roads' but he described the day's operations as '98% successful.'[15] Crerar sounded a similar note writing his brother: 'The operation is really going better than could be expected in view of the great difficulties imposed by shocking weather and frightful ground conditions.'[16] On the tenth, Crerar forwarded to Simonds a study by 'G' Plans for an assault crossing of the Rhine at Emmerich and over the next few days initiated discussions of that operation.

They were too optimistic. The assault bogged down as Phase II was launched. Low-cloud cover and heavy rain prevented air support, and rendered already difficult terrain and roads nearly impassable. For the soldiers, the battle became a struggle against the mud, water, and the Germans. Commanders visiting the troops did so in amphibious vehicles. Supplying the troops became increasingly difficult. Forward movement was made more difficult by command mistakes. Horrocks, believing that his assaulting division (the 15th Scottish) had secured the one passable road to Cleve and the crucial Materborn defensive area, ordered the 43rd Wessex Division into Cleve. The 15th Scottish Division was still on this road, however, and the resulting tie-up delayed the assault on Cleve until the next day. Horrocks later called it 'the worst mistake I made in the war.' The urgency felt by all was understandable; the Germans were also beginning to appreciate the scope of the offensive. The 7th Parachute Division was arriving on the front. On 9 February, the Roer dams were jammed open, flooding Ninth U.S. Army's front. The next afternoon, von Rundstedt ordered his armoured reserves up. Resistance stiffened, the casualties mounted, and progress slowed. The final blow to the advance was the postponement of Grenade. The Roer River had risen by three to four feet, and was 1,000 yards across in places, moving at nine feet per second. Initially, Grenade was postponed for three successive days; on the 12th it was postponed for at least a week.

Montgomery now made a critical decision as the battle bogged down in the mud and water. Writing to Brooke of his decision to postpone Grenade, he observed that it was 'bound to have repercussions on Veritable but the more troops that Veritable [drew] up North the easier will go Grenade.' The next day, he concluded that the continued postponement 'makes it very necessary Veritable to be given all the strength that can be collected.' The Rhineland offensive now became a replay of the Normandy campaign as Montgomery envisaged the continual pressure drawing the German reserves north, away from the Ninth U.S. Army front. This was not a surprising decision; the only premise on which Veritable had been based was that the pressure must be maintained on the Germans in the north to achieve decisive results, defined as clearing the Rhineland. There would be no let-up.[17]

Once that decision was made, there was no room for manoeuvre. On the 12th, responding to Crerar's instructions of the 10th, Simonds brought forward an alternative plan that he been preparing since December 1944. The plan called for an immediate crossing over the Neder Rijn at Arnhem. This would draw reserves from the west bank of the Rhine and possibly have a great impact on Veritable. Neither Montgomery nor Crerar was interested, although Crerar suggested that Simonds keep it under consideration; he believed it was 'of secondary importance' to securing the objectives of Veritable but might be undertaken once the operation was completed.

Clearly the battle had developed a momentum of its own; short of cancelling the operation, the senior command's ability to affect the course of events was now limited. 'I was almost powerless,' recalled Horrocks, 'to influence the battle one way or another so I spent my days "smelling the battlefield."' He noted that he visited Brigade and Battalion HQs that were having a 'particularly gruelling time.' Horrocks found the battle gruelling as well, but Crerar kept him on track.

> I ... saw quite a lot of ... General Crerar, who, in my opinion, has always been much underrated, largely because he was the exact opposite to Montgomery ... he was full of common sense and always prepared to listen to the views of his subordinate commanders. Every day after the battle started ... [he] came to see me wherever I might be. I grew to like him very much, though I am afraid I must have been a terrible pain in the neck, for during part of this long drawn-out battle I was feeling very unwell ... The outward and visible sign was that I became extremely irritable and bad-tempered, yet Crerar bore with me very patiently.[18]

Crerar's paternal support for Horrocks was important, and Horrocks clearly appreciated it. The corps commander's mental fatigue and nervous temperament had been noted at the end of December 1944, when Montgomery had sent him to the United Kingdom for rest, writing to Brooke that Horrocks 'has been nervy and difficult with his staff and has attempted to act foolishly with his corps.' However, there were few commanders in the Anglo-Canadian armies who were not feeling the strain of six years of war. Crerar had visibly aged and was smoking more each day. His batman couldn't stay in the caravan because of Crerar's cough. Montgomery wanted to remove an exhausted Crocker but reinstated him after an emotional discussion. Similarly, Brooke recorded his concerns about Montgomery's fitness. It was not surprising. It is remarkable that more senior commanders were not completely worn out by these huge responsibilities. And thus the maintenance of solid working relationships became even more critical at this stage of the battle and the war.[19]

Crerar maintained a good feel for the battlefield; for the first week, he met daily with his senior staff, flew over the terrain – often dangerously low – occasionally reporting traffic snags, and then met with Horrocks to discuss the course of the battle. His most direct concern was with supplies; on the 12th, he ordered 30 British Corps to clear Gennep, and the road Gennep-Hekkens, to open a new supply route and enable his engineers to begin construction on the nearby bridge. Two days later, he ordered his engineers to convert the Groesbeek-Cleve railway into a road for tracked vehicles, and later for wheeled.[20] Limited supply routes and bottlenecks remained a major concern.

Crerar needed these new routes opened. Despite the difficulties encountered in completing Phase II of the operation, he decided on the 14th to commit 2nd Canadian Corps, although he directed that the 30 British Corps advance on the axis Goch-Geldern would be 'the main thrust of First Canadian Army ops.'[21] In the spirit of Montgomery's conception of keeping the pressure on the German defences, the main objective was to maintain the offensive at a high pitch on a slightly wider front. The original preconditions for using Simonds's corps, as laid down in the assessment by GSO 1 Ops Anderson, were the capture of Goch and the Cleve-Goch road to enable 30 British Corps to change its axis of advance to the southeast. Goch was still in German hands, but it was believed that with operations moving slowly, a two-corps front, and the regrouping it entailed, could be maintained. The 2nd Canadian Corps was powerful: under command were 2nd and 3rd Canadian Infantry and 4th Canadian Armoured divisions as well as 2nd Canadian Armoured Brigade, and, for the initial operations, 43rd Wessex Division and a brigade of 15th Scottish Division. This striking power did not matter, however, as the narrow front limited Simonds to attacking with one brigade up front.

The target, or obstacle, was Moyland Wood. The 116th Panzer Division staunchly defended it. The 46th Brigade of the 15th Scottish Division fought a bitter engagement, which it characterized as 'the worst experience ... endured since the campaign began.'[22] Spry's 3rd Canadian Division 'Water Rats' took over on the 16th, but they were stymied by the close fighting among the firs of the wood, and by fresh troops from the 6th Parachute Division. Simonds, frothing at the bit to regroup his forces for a major set-piece attack, Blockbuster Operation, pushed Spry and his commanders to clear the wood. Crerar also urged his corps and divisional commanders to maintain the pressure and clear the wood. At the height of the fighting for Moyland Wood, from the 18th to the 22nd, he constantly flew or drove to 'The Cloister' to confer with the senior commanders. On 21 February, the weather cleared and air support was sent in, with mixed results. To maintain morale, Crerar wrote a steady stream of notes encouraging and congratulating his divisions and regiments. On 17 February, the 43rd Wessex Division was praised for its efforts. On 21 February, Lieutenant-Colonel Denis Whitaker of the Royal Hamilton Light Infantry received a 'rare mid-battle' congratulatory message.[23] To most men at the sharp end, Crerar and the rest of the senior command seemed to have ignored the impact of the rain, mud, and forest.[24] There was some truth to this view, but it was not insensitivity. From the earliest inception of the operation, the senior command had stated that the offensive would be pressed, no matter what the conditions. Moyland Wood was cleared, or evacuated, on the 22nd – a result of the combined efforts of air support, Wasp flamethrowers and artillery, and the capture of the Goch-Calcar road. Nevertheless, Veritable was running out of steam.

On 21 February, Crerar outlined for Simonds and the divisional commanders the restructured operations designed to renew the momentum and complete the clearance of the Rhineland. Phase II of the operation was incomplete. At a cost of 490 officers and 8,023 other ranks, First Canadian Army had fought its way twenty miles from the start line and inflicted an estimated 24,000 casualties, half of those prisoners. They had done so without the promised support of the second arm of what had been conceived as a pincer operation. The German defences in front of First Canadian Army, while seriously weakened, were nevertheless intact. To break them, Crerar changed the main axis of advance to the north; 2nd Canadian Corps would assault the 'Hochwald layback' and break through to the final objective, the line Geldern-Xanten. It was then to take 'aggressive steps to clear the enemy from the area between the general line Udem-Sonsbeck-Xanten and the River Rhine.' Prior to this assault, 30 British Corps would clear the woods northeast of Weeze, and exploit south from Goch; its subsequent operations would support Simonds's right flank. The 2nd Canadian Corps would have priority on all available resources. Such was the basis for planning until 24 February.[25]

Why did Crerar make his main effort with 2nd Canadian Corps in the north where the enemy was strongest? The answer has its roots in the earliest conception of the operation and First Canadian Army's role: to destroy the German army west of the Rhine by the application of brute force. Both Crerar and Montgomery had stressed the importance of maintaining contact with the Germans, keeping the initiative, and 'driving on.' This was Crerar's concept of the battle. Within this framework, the combination of the exhaustion of 30 British Corps, which had borne the brunt of the casualties during the fighting, and Simonds's obvious desire to have more responsibility in the offensive, made 2nd Canadian Corps the logical choice to plan the offensive. The shifting of the weight of the offensive to the left was also part of the initial plan and, while there was a break in the fighting on the Canadian front, it continued on 30 British Corps' front. To the senior commanders, the new offensive did not appear as a dramatic break, but rather, as Horrocks described it, a 'brief pause.' Crerar continued to refer to the Veritable offensive until the Rhineland was cleared. Indeed, there was a general sense, as Simonds described it after the war, that 'Veritable had gone according to plan so far as it was able to progress. It was the general course of the operation which had not developed according to the hopes or timings previously expected.'[26]

The situation changed materially on the 23rd; that morning the Ninth U.S. Army surprised the Germans and launched Grenade before the floods had receded. Ten divisions strong, the Americans made rapid progress against fewer than 30,000 German defenders. By the 26th, they had secured a bridgehead 'twenty miles wide and ten miles deep' and were heading for the Rhine. Blockbuster was unaffected. Why? Because delaying the operation would weaken the impact of this joint Allied offensive, according to Crerar and Montgomery's conception of the battle. The army commander's rationale was explained in a letter to Maurice Pope, dated 21 February, a day when some of the most vicious fighting of the campaign was taking place in Moyland Wood:

> The alternative 'wet weather' plan is proceeding along approved lines. We have now drawn in against us, either complete or in part, no less than eleven divisions, of which four are Para and three Panzer Grenadier, and if our task has become heavier, for others it will be lighter. The situation is not unlike that which had to be met by the Army in July–August of last year.
> Casualties, on the whole, have been comparatively light and much less than one half of the total of the prisoners, alone, whom we have taken. The weather has cleared today and we are getting close support from the air,

the first time in six days. That should make a great difference in today's fighting.[27]

However it was characterized, this was a battle to defeat the German army west of the Rhine. Blockbuster would be another Totalize – or Tractable. That idea was not Crerar's alone: 'It is hoped,' wrote Dempsey in his diary on 23 February, 'that, when [Grenade] gets under way, it will enable the Reichswald battle to get on more quickly.'[28]

Still, Crerar hesitated when he saw the continued resistance in front of 30 British Corps and made an attempt to lay the framework for a controlled two-corps battle, a smaller version of the 21st Army Group battle. On 24 February, in his directive to his corps commanders regarding future operations, he noted that the development of First Canadian Army plans were 'bound to be conditioned by situations yet to be determined,' and he ordered 30 British Corps to be ready to exploit any opportunities to the south. This was an obvious reference to Grenade. The next day, with Grenade achieving spectacular results but with no discernible effect on German resistance against the 30 British Corps assault north of Weeze, he issued another directive:

> In view of the determined resistance 24/25 Feb, North of Weeze ... it will be necessary to reconsider the draft basic plan outlined to you in my memorandum of yesterday ... If by D plus 1 it is obvious that to complete Blockbuster a considerable regrouping, and a further deliberate attack is required, then a 'partial' Blockbuster will terminate the operation – i.e. the completion of Phase III and the securing of the high ground East of the Calcar-Udem road.

Crerar would maintain the offensive, but would switch the weight of the First Canadian Army advance back to 30 British Corps to enable it to gain enough room to sort out its supply problems.[29]

Blockbuster was launched in the early morning of 26 February. Simonds's plan was, in concept, simple: use massed artillery to blast a hole in the enemy's Hochwald defences across the Calcar-Udem ridge, and then unleash fresh infantry and armoured divisions through the Hochwald Gap to exploit to Xanten and Wesel. In execution, it was complex and ambitious: artificial moonlight would guide mixed battle groups along a narrow and exposed axis; they were given specific tasks tied to the artillery support. To ensure momentum once the gap had been breached, the engineers would create a new maintenance road from the Goch-Xanten railway.

The plan worked perfectly for one day. The 2nd and 3rd Canadian divisions fought through the 47 Panzer Corps and the 2nd Parachute Corps, taking the fortified town of Udem and the plateau south of Calcar. The Hochwald Gap was the next objective and Simonds was eager to press on. Schlemm, however, committed 'what were probably his best reserve units,' two fresh independent parachute battalions to the Hochwald layback, and over the next few days brought up further reinforcements from the 180th Infantry Division. The concentration of German artillery was also one of the – if not the – heaviest of the war: over 700 mortars and 1,054 guns, including large numbers of 88 mm guns, which Schlemm had diverted to the Hochwald defences. Crerar characterized it as the most 'heavily and effectively applied' firepower of the entire campaign. Schlemm, while conscious of the American forces closing in rapidly from the south, almost irrationally continued to strengthen the forces facing the Canadians. Simonds's offensive faltered and stalled; the destruction of 4th Armoured's Algonquin Carrier Platoon and the South Alberta Regiment on the night of the 27th as they moved in the Hochwald Gap signalled the beginning of five more days of bitter struggle.[30]

Rather than switch the weight to the left in the event of strong resistance as he had indicated on the 25th, Crerar continued to support Blockbuster. There is no evidence to suggest that he, Montgomery, or Simonds considered halting the offensive. Montgomery, and presumably Crerar, continued to hope that the combination of Grenade and a new major attack would enable First Canadian Army, as he told Dempsey, 'to make more progress.'[31] Crerar met with Simonds and Horrocks on the 27th and 28th to discuss the operations, but the only concern he reported to his HQ staff during this period was that ammunition situation for 30 British Corps was 'not good.' Whether this had an impact on his decision to stay with 2nd Canadian Corps is impossible to tell, though maintaining supply lines was an ongoing concern.[32] Simonds's desire to control the battle may have affected the decision to maintain the offensive; he had Monty's ear, and, for the first time, had earlier played the 'nationalist card' himself. Crerar, despite concerns about Simonds bypassing him to talk directly to Montgomery, may have desired to have Canadians play a significant role in what he himself saw as a 'historic' and 'decisive' battle. Whatever role these considerations had, continuing the operation against heavy opposition fitted with the logic that had developed since December. Crerar's earlier qualifications and conditions for launching and continuing the offensive had been consistently overridden. His correspondence suggests that he now perceived the battle as a costly but necessary fight to destroy the German army west of the Rhine. Once battle was rejoined in late February, however, the continued strength of the German resistance surprised the senior command, but rather than call a halt to Blockbuster, it only strengthened their determination to ensure that the Germans could neither slip away across the Rhine nor stiffen their resistance in front of the Americans. Blockbuster would continue.

German resistance began to show signs of breaking on 3 March 1945, but the terrain, a reduction in air support, and fatigue conspired to allow an orderly retreat to new defensive lines described as the 'Wesel Pocket.' While the Fifteenth Army on the left had crumbled in the wake of Grenade, Schlemm's army fought hard to defend a bridgehead at Wesel to cover the retirement of his forces over the Rhine. He was also charged with personal responsibility for allowing none of the bridges over the Rhine to fall into enemy hands. Schlemm nevertheless kept his best reserve units in front of First Canadian Army. Unfortunately for the Allies, bad weather hampered the air forces, limiting both the support they were able to provide the troops and their attacks against the bridges. When aircraft could fly, the concentration of German anti-aircraft guns took a heavy toll; on 1 March, 84 Group restricted the number of flights because of heavy losses. That left the Canadian and British soldiers without air support for the last week of Blockbuster.

II

The planning for and early stages of Veritable had absorbed all of Crerar's energies. Once the course of the battle was effectively decided, his attention was divided between command and policy questions once again. While the conduct of the battle remained his primary focus, Crerar's responsibilities were still broad, and he was engaged with questions of policy, old and new. In the middle of the fighting for Moyland Wood, he wrote a sharply worded letter to Burns, asserting his prerogative to control promotions throughout the army's senior command, whether under his direct command or not. This was in response to a direct communication by Burns to the commanders of First Canadian Army.[33]

Demobilization also loomed as an increasingly important issue. Questions of repatriation and discharge policy had to be settled. The CMHQ reported to Crerar on a steady increase in the number of applicants for release to the civil service and other appointments in Canada. While requesting that NDHQ review the policy, it forwarded the message to Crerar for his perusal. His approval, or agreement, was required for most questions of policy, and Montague at CMHQ made few moves without Crerar's advice.[34]

As the commander of a multinational force, Crerar also contended with the sensibilities and needs of his allies. Writing on 24 February, he observed that the Poles had begun 'to show a lack of zest for fighting,' given the Communist successes in the struggle for political control of their liberated country. 'It is hard to blame them if they begin to wonder exactly what they are fighting for. I have personally come to the conclusion that I must not count upon the 1st Polish Armoured Division as a dependable formation in tough conditions.'[35] They played a secondary role in operations to the end of the war. Crerar also showed sensitivity to the British portion of his army. Speaking to the war correspondents on the eve of the Rhineland battle, he reminded them that it was 'a matter of great importance' to give in their dispatches proper recognition to the English, Welsh, and Scottish formations. It was an issue throughout the campaign, however, as British and Canadian media continued to characterize it as a Canadian battle; Crerar did his best to restrain the excesses of senior commanders like Major-General Thomas Rennie of the 51st Highland Division, who was angered over the lack of publicity accorded his formation. For GOCs such as Rennie, fighting to restore a reputation for the division, these were important issues.[36]

Neither could Crerar forget his responsibilities to his own government and army. He wrote regular dispatches, as did Montgomery, on First Canadian Army operations. To some of his staff, this task was a heavy one and contributed to his natural caution; Geoffrey Walsh recalled,

> Monty came up to our HQ, and we had some of our divisional commanders in for dinner. Despite this, at 9 o'clock Harry Crerar got up from the table, excused himself and said he had to get his daily dispatches back to Prime Minister Mackenzie King ... It was pretty hard to lead an army in a difficult operation plus having to write to and hold the hands of the politicians back in Ottawa. I doubt if many generals could have done this as well as Crerar did.[37]

The army commander also maintained a concern for the image of his army and nurtured a close, if cautious, working relationship with Richard Malone, whom Crerar had selected as the main public relations officer at 21st Army Group. Malone kept him abreast of methods of keeping the Canadian, and British, efforts on 'the front pages of the world's press' and also keeping the troops entertained; Crerar took a keen interest in both subjects. In the winter, he vetoed a proposed series on VD and 'vulgar' stories: 'A good many copies of the paper are sent back to Canada and the result might well be more painful pondering on the part of the people at home than comparable improvement in personal hygiene on the part of Canadian troops over here.' Crerar approved nude pin-ups as long as they were tasteful. As army commander, there was little that escaped his purview.[38] While he was not now as fastidious about discipline, Crerar was always conscious of the army's image.

Though Crerar's responsibilities and contacts extended far beyond those of his contemporaries, they also isolated him. Crerar was imperturbable to many, but, in truth, he was unhappy, anxious to return home. In mid-March 1944, Maurice Pope wrote Lester Pearson to express his feelings on his recent correspondence with Crerar: 'At Verse's request I had sent him a long letter of really high-powered interesting gossip. She told me that he was lonely over there and that he had no one to send him inside stuff from home.' Pope noted 'he shot the works'; the reply was, in his words, 'pretty soulless ... And I wonder if I shall ever have the heart to send him more.' Crerar described the Rhineland battle as it raged through February and the casualties, but revealed little. The gossip was ignored. Pope felt he had been made to 'wear a hair shirt.' Crerar concluded the note, 'I must stop now as I am having an early lunch, then doing an aerial reconnaissance of the battle front and finally landing on a field near Cleve to discuss situations with my Corps Commanders.' He reminded Pope to tell 'Ambassador Pearson' that he owed Crerar a letter, and, 'as usual, he has done so for nearly a year.' Pope's philosophical conclusion: 'There are times when we can drift into the idea that we are hellers in every sense of the word, when, of course, we are not, and it is good to have the fact brought home to us from time to time.' Crerar, cut off from NDHQ, grew distant from some his closest colleagues from the 1930s and the first years of the war. His letters to family and friends grew in number, and were filled with talk of 'dreams' of his grandson, golfing, fishing, sailing, and the Muskokas.[39]

III

The Rhineland battle raged on through the first week of March 1945, but the steady stream of visitors to the battlefield also indicated that the senior command was now focusing beyond the immediate operation. In a short ceremony on 1 March, Eisenhower presented Crerar with the decoration of a Commander of the Legion of Merit. More welcome was an unexpected visit from Peter, in the theatre for a 'special job': 'He needed a haircut and his clothes were in pretty bad shape,' as all had recently been destroyed when the truck they were in ran over a mine.[40] On 4 March, Brooke and Churchill visited the front, accompanied by Monty. Crerar entertained them at his HQ and gave a short presentation on Veritable. Brooke, who had written scathing critiques of Eisenhower's, Churchill's, and Alexander's 'small-minded' displays, recorded they were 'given a very good short explanation of the fighting since the start of the operation to the present date.'[41] Crerar also recorded, as did the other senior commanders, his efforts to 'please this doughty, unpredictable leader of the free world in spite of himself, Monty or the exigencies of war. We stashed away a box of cigars and a few bottles of good sherry.' Churchill, eager 'to see active service,' was led to a heavy battery that Crerar had kept back out of shelling range. 'They trundled out a 275-pound shell on a trolley and handed Churchill a bit of chalk,' he recalled for a postwar *Toronto Star* profile. 'He bent over and printed on the casing a message to Hitler. It was, I may say, most insulting. The battery crew rammed it into the breach and Churchill, standing as directed, pulled the lanyard. The 9.45 inch went off with a great roar. Churchill beamed.'[42]

By 4 March the battle was in its final stages. The Germans withdrew to a line based on Xanten and running from just south of Veen to Mors on the Rhine, the 'Wesel Pocket.' The 30 British Corps began to move forward rapidly; on the 3rd, it had made contact with units of 16th Corps of Ninth U.S. Army. Resistance in front of the Canadian divisions remained fierce, but by the 4th, 2nd Canadian Corps was less than two miles from Xanten, key to the last remaining lateral route across the pocket.

The German retreat to the new line was picked up by First Canadian Army intelligence, and the air forces were ordered to try to destroy the bridges. The evening of the 4th, after he left Churchill, Crerar ordered renewed attacks on Balberger Wald, Veen, and Xanten. With their lines of retreat blocked and faced with new attacks, it was hoped that the Germans would surrender; they did not, and the Allied air forces were unable to knock out the bridges. This continuation of fierce resistance against hopeless odds characterized much of the final months of fighting and was a constant surprise to Allied decision makers.

It took six more days of concerted and continuous attacks all around the bridgehead – a new set-piece attack on Xanten christened Blockbuster II – and over 2,700 Anglo-Canadian casualties before the Rhineland battle was over, but Crerar and his senior command were turning their attention elsewhere. On 6 March, the German High Command gave Schlemm permission to evacuate the bridgehead. The next day, Crerar sent a directive to his corps commanders urging them to conclude Veritable 'speedily and decisively by eliminating the enemy bridgehead west of the river Rhine' and ordered Crocker at 1 British Corps to begin gathering information for assaults into Holland. On 8 March, Simonds was given command of all Anglo-Canadian forces in the reduced line, and 30 British Corps came under command of Second British Army to plan operations after crossing the Rhine; Crerar returned to his Main HQ to work on future plans. At 1040 on 10 March, the Germans blew the last bridge across the Rhine at Wesel. Montgomery made no attempt to follow up on the triumph, expressly forbidding Simpson's Ninth U.S. Army from attempting a surprise crossing of the Rhine, while the exhausted Anglo-Canadian forces stopped to prepare for a set-piece crossing. Crerar sent congratulations to his troops and gave them full credit for the victory. When Eisenhower made a point of expressing his 'admiration for the way you conducted the attack,' Crerar's reply deflected the praise: 'I believe no troops could have put up a finer exhibition of enduring gallantry and determination than was demonstrated during those weeks of bitter, bloody and muddy fighting.'[43]

In a footnote to the congratulations, Montgomery vetoed a British Ministry of National Defence suggestion that Eisenhower's note be published; he considered that the 'stress laid by the Supreme Commander on [Crerar's] personal contribution to operation makes publication somewhat unsuitable in respect to interests of AG as a whole.' Crerar agreed, but it was a petty stroke, particularly coming on the heels of Montgomery's self-serving comments following the Battle of the Bulge.[44]

The cost of the Rhineland victory was high: 1,049 officers and 14,585 other ranks. Of these, the British suffered far heavier casualties; the Canadians dead and wounded totalled 370 officers and 4,925 men. Most of these occurred after Blockbuster was launched. The Ninth U.S. Army lost 'just under 7,300.' German losses were approximately 90,000 men; they had little left to stop the Allies now. Crerar reflected on the cost when writing to a friend on 11 March: Despite the atrocious conditions 'we have accomplished the task which was set for the Canadian Army to do and, in the process, enabled other Armies to achieve striking advances with a minimum of enemy to contend with.' It was a fitting epitaph to the campaign.[45]

23 The Final Campaign

I

The final months of the war were bittersweet for Harry Crerar. The Canadian army fought an increasingly desperate enemy to liberate Holland and feed its starving people. The war was clearly over, but casualties mounted. The 1st Canadian Corps was reunited with the other Canadian formations under command of First Canadian Army. From March 1945, Crerar was enmeshed in the questions surrounding the army's future. Repatriation and the senior command appointments were two sides of the same issue: how best to preserve the legacy of the record compiled by the army during the war. It was a difficult problem. He drew heavily on the past to solve it.

Crerar took a nine-day leave on 12 March, accompanied only by Finlay Morrison and his PA, Jack Weir. Most of it was spent in Yorkshire. It was mix of business and pleasure, but policy questions were pressing. He took two days of rest before beginning meetings with Montague on promotions, changes to the headquarters establishment, and the shape of the Far Eastern Force. 'As Crerar in UK for few days I went and saw him ... ,' Montague cabled the CGS. 'He is in excellent shape.'

Crerar and Montague discussed two issues that had emerged during the final days of operations in the Rhineland. Both involved changes that Crerar wanted made, based on the experience of the campaign, but both devolved into small, if significant, power struggles with NDHQ. As the war drew to a close, tension grew between the overseas forces and Ottawa; power shifted back to Canada as the number of postwar questions increased. At the same time, Germany had not yet surrendered. Crerar fought to balance the needs of the fighting forces with the needs of the postwar army.

First, Crerar anticipated that the transition between the liberation of Holland and the end of hostilities would increase First Canadian Army's responsibilities as it became responsible for repatriation issues even as operations continued. At the end of February, he wrote Montague recommending that the Chief of Staff should carry the rank of major-general and the senior GSO of the General Staff should be placed on a par with the heads of AQ and Military Government Branches by upgrading the appointment to brigadier. Mann's staff responsibilities would increase as operations gave way to occupation and 'post-hostilities arrangements for education, welfare and demobilization of Canadian personnel.'[1] The British resisted the change on the principle that uniformity was important, but as Crerar noted, Canadian requirements required variations. The Canadian army headquarters and army commander had more responsibilities than a regular British army HQ, but the discussions indicated that those differences were not often recognized. Crerar persisted through April, however, and was at least able to upgrade Beament's appointment to Brigadier, General Staff.[2]

Crerar was also anxious to resolve command issues. Simonds wanted to remove Major-General Dan Spry as commander 3rd Canadian Division, suggesting he lacked 'quick tactical appreciation and robust drive in ... urgent tactical situations.'[3] Simonds, angry with Spry's handling of the assaults on Moyland Wood and in the Hochwald, insisted he must go; Spry was equally critical of Simonds's and Crerar's, handling of the battle: 'They really didn't understand the sharp end of battle.'[4] None of them were blameless. Moyland Wood could have been masked, but if it had to be assaulted, then it should have been attacked in strength. Crerar seemed to have some sympathy for Spry's position but he also knew that the corps commander had to have full confidence in his divisional commanders. The retirement of the commander, Canadian Reinforcement Unit, Major-General Roberts, former GOC of 2nd Canadian Division, and his subsequent appointment to the Imperial War Graves Commission, presented a solution. Montague backed Brigadier Ken Blackader to succeed Roberts; McNaughton was also promoting a candidate, further complicating the appointment. Simonds had reservations, although he characterized Spry as 'highly intelligent' and 'an excellent trainer of soldiers.' Crerar was aggressive, arguing Spry had 'done well as a divisional commander,' and he had Montague place Spry's qualifications before the CGS and the minister, noting the 'excellent results' produced by the policy of having battle-experienced officers posted to the CRU. The appointment was debated over the next month, but Crerar was able to secure Spry's appointment. Brigadier R.H. Keefler, commanding 6th Infantry Brigade, was promoted to command 3rd Canadian Division. Crerar minimized the change, refusing to submit a Change of Employment form unless it was insisted upon: 'There is a certain stigma attached to this procedure, which, in the circumstances, I should like to avoid.'[5] This also presented Crerar with the opportunity to promote a promising young French-Canadian officer, Lieutenant-Colonel Jean Allard, CO of the Van Doos – an opportunity that he seized.

Crerar's considered handling of Spry's removal was typical, but it was also related to another issue that Montague had been pressing for resolution since December: what to do with the growing number of surplus officers in the United Kingdom, while there was a glut of PF officers in Canada. The issue was never completely resolved, but grew in symbolic importance as NDHQ's authority increased as the war drew to a close. For Crerar it was the first shot in his battle to staff the postwar army with experienced overseas officers.

Crerar wanted the command changes confirmed before operations were renewed and spent a great deal of his leave in discussions with Montague. He was able to spend some time in London with friends and relatives, visits that provided him with the energy for the final push. He dined with his sister-in-law Isabel Cronyn, now a lieutenant-colonel in the Canadian Women's Army Corps and, most important, met with Brooke to discuss both personal and Canadian matters. The most immediate issue was the imminent reunification of the 1st Canadian Corps with First Canadian Army in northwest Europe. Brooke, noting their 'long and satisfactory talk,' recorded his relief: 'Thank heaven, I have at last got the whole of the Canadian Army now assembled in France.'[6]

Brooke had good reason to be relieved; reassembling the army had long been a thorn in his side. In May 1944, Crerar had encouraged the Canadian government, while drafting its directive on Crerar's command responsibilities, to propose that 1st Canadian Corps be 'unified under Canadian command' as 'soon as military considerations permit.' He later added that reunification was desirable from a national point of view and to enhance the effectiveness of the Canadian contribution. Brooke replied that he would meet the request as soon as military and shipping considerations allowed. The issue was left until, in the euphoria following the breakout from Normandy and after his blow-up with Montgomery, Crerar wrote Stuart urging him to press the minister and

CGS to greater efforts to reunite the 1st Canadian Corps with First Canadian Army.[7] Undoubtedly Crerar's faith in the British was at low ebb; he saw a unified army under his command as an important card in defining Canada's position in the postwar world, as Borden had used the achievements of the Canadian Corps in 1919.

The Canadian government subsequently renewed its campaign to bring the corps back from the Mediterranean, a campaign detailed in the official history, but it had no effect until the Combined Chiefs of Staff decided at Malta in February 1945 to reinforce the European theatre at the expense of the Mediterranean. On 5 February, CMHQ was informed that the Canadians would be united in Europe. The operation, code-named Goldflake, took place over February and March 1945. Foulkes – characterized by his superior, Lieutenant-General Dick McCreery, as 'a great improvement on Burns' – and his senior staff arrived in northwest Europe in mid-February; 1st Canadian Division came under Simonds's command on 3 April, completing the move. Most in the 1st Canadian Corps were enthusiastic about unification, but the officers and staff at Corps and Divisional HQs were wary, after the relaxed standards of the Eighth British Army, of the rigid practices insisted on by Crerar.[8]

II

Crerar took his farewell of the United Kingdom at the Beaver Club, in the basement of Canada House in Trafalgar Square, in London on 21 March, his visit prompted in part because of the news that it was struggling financially. He returned to oversee the planning for First Canadian Army's final tasks and to smooth out any rough spots as the army accommodated itself to the changes of command and structure. The army's operational mission was clarified in the midst of the usual wrangling between SHAEF and Montgomery. In a directive issued to his army commanders on 9 March at an outdoor 'informal little affair,' Montgomery outlined First Canadian Army's tasks for the future. Second British Army would be responsible for mounting the major crossings at Wesel, Xanten, and Rees, code-named Operation Plunder, planned for 23–4 March; it would have operational control of 2nd Canadian Corps while it extended the bridgehead at Rees and seized Emmerich. Ninth U.S. Army and First Canadian Army would support the assault by protecting the flanks. Monty ordered the Canadian army to pay particular attention to ensuring the security of Antwerp and the

Nijmegen bridgehead. The army was to prepare to cross at Emmerich and take command to the north and northwest. From there the C-in-C envisioned First Canadian Army operating northwards through the Ijssel defences towards Appeldorn and Arnhem to secure a flank 'facing west on some suitable line running northwards from the Neder Rijn about Renkum.' Operations would then be developed eastward, forcing the Germans out of western Holland. The Canadian Army would thus play a secondary role for the remainder of the campaign, supporting Second British Army's left flank and liberating Holland, or least part of it. To the south, the U.S. army groups had broken the Siegfried Line, forced the recall of von Rundstedt as Commander-in-Chief of West, and were also poised to cross the Rhine. The conference ended as Crerar and the others each gave 'very clear' proposals of their plans, and all were accepted, 'subject to one or two minor amendments.'[9]

On 10 March, Crerar issued a directive to his corps commanders reiterating his plans for each corps. Until Plunder began, he had no role except to ensure that close contact was maintained between FCA and Second British Army. Foulkes's HQ had, in February, assumed responsibility from HQ First Canadian Army for planning an assault out of the Nijmegen bridgehead, code-named Anger. Foulkes decided it was not feasible, given the state of the enemy defences and weather, and Crerar had backed him up.[10] They now resumed preparation for an assault to support 2nd Canadian Corps' Rhine crossing. As of 20 March, Simonds's HQ was under command of Second British Army preparing for its crossing at Rees and operations for the northern drive towards Emmerich.

Operation Plunder was launched on 23 March; its outcome was never in doubt, despite Montgomery's caution. The German army had spent itself in its defence west of the Rhine, and Patton's Third U.S. Army had already secured a bridgehead across the river at Remagen on 21 March, a success that was drawing German reserves away from 21st Army Group. Montgomery was allowed his set-piece attack in the interests of Allied cooperation, but Eisenhower could not ignore the possibilities that First and Third U.S. Army's successes presented, or the hostility of their commanders to Montgomery. On 21st Army Group's front, Plunder forged ahead. Preceded by concentrated attacks by Bomber Command and wide-ranging attacks by 8th U.S. Army Air Force, Second British Army units were well established on the eastern bank by first light. The worst casualties were taken by the airborne troops dropped in support of the operation.[11] The Canadians' initial contribution to the crossing was 3rd Canadian Division's 9th Brigade and 1st Canadian Parachute Battalion. With the crossing secure, Crerar issued a directive on 24 March to Simonds, Foulkes, and Crocker describing future operations; it was mainly a reiteration of that of 10 March. The bridgehead now enlarged, 3rd Canadian Division passed back to Simonds's 2nd Canadian Corps on 28 March. The same day, Dempsey and Crerar agreed that 2nd Canadian Corps would be handed over following the capture of Emmerich and the completion of a bridge to the town.[12]

Crerar also kept a close watch on the integration of Foulkes and 1st Canadian Corps into the army. The corps officially came under command of First Canadian Army on 15 March; Simonds and his senior staff were invited to the Corps 'A' Mess to celebrate the reunion. He had good, but not warm, relations with the returning commanders, Hoffmeister and Foster; Foster was wary of Crerar's temper and felt that Simonds 'called the shots,' but gave Crerar full credit for his national stance. Like most veterans of Eighth British Army, Foster had no time for Crerar's emphasis on rules and regulations, but saw him as 'a good solid soul, part soldier, part politician.'[13] The divisional generals were strong-willed individuals, but Crerar's attention was focused on Foulkes and Simonds, and the antipathy between them. Their paths rarely crossed, however, and Crerar's 'O' groups noticeably declined in number.

Major-General Chris Vokes observed in the fall of 1944, 'Army command has mellowed Uncle Harry.' Indeed, Crerar was more relaxed. He took simple pleasure from informing subordinates of promotion. The army commander was instrumental in Jean Allard's promotion to brigadier and he played up the drama, setting up a meeting to tell him personally. Allard spent the night in the 'Viper's Den' and was paraded before Crerar at 0700: 'The general greeted me warmly ... [and] began by congratulating me for the excellent work I had done with the R22R ... He went on to say that he had decided to make me a brigadier and to give me the 6th Brigade. Realizing that I was speechless, he burst out laughing and wished me luck.'[14] While he was more relaxed, his staff remained wary. Pangman recalled Church Mann's odd sense of humour and his joking during a planning meeting for Operation Plunder where they represented the HQ at 21st Army Group with their counterparts from Second British and Ninth U.S. armies. As the requirements of the assault were discussed, the question of using 'artificial moonlight' came up, a subject that caused some puzzlement among the Americans, who had little experience with the practice of bouncing searchlights off the clouds. Mann intervened: 'Our American cousins are quite familiar with Kentucky moonshine,' he said. 'This is another way of getting lit up.' Pangman recalled that 'the Americans just burst out into laughter [and] the British are just staring ... [Church] said don't tell the army commander though. Crerar would have been horrified.'[15]

Crerar's attempt to be an example had a personal cost.[16] His relationship with his wife was strained as he struggled to set the right tone for his subordinates. At the end of March, Verse was invited to accompany Princess Juliana of the Netherlands to England as her guest, when hostilities ended. Verse jumped at the chance to see her husband and Peter, who had been in and out of hospital with a mild recurrent attack of malaria. Crerar, as he had earlier, said no. 'To accept,' he cabled Verse, 'might have a most complicating affect on Cdn government policies re overseas personnel yet to be decided, [and] would certainly make the conduct of my professional responsibilities now more difficult and I believe would also work out to our domestic disadvantage in the not distant future.'[17] The issue would come up once more before he returned to Canada. Verse was very disappointed; Peg relayed this to her father, and he was clearly worried that his wife took it personally. 'One of these days,' he wrote Peg, 'I shall be free from these responsibilities and can be a bit more selfish, but that time has not yet arrived.'[18] A little sad perhaps but admirable when many had been away from Canada for as long or longer. He did not lose his sense of humour about it, writing Hume Wrong a few weeks later that 'I hear from so many people that Verse "never looked better" that I am beginning to wonder if my continued absence is not proving beneficial!'[19]

Crerar's personal difficulties during the transitional months between war and peace reflected the problems of the nation at large in the final stages of the war in Europe and in the Far East. Canadians had been considering the type of country, if not world, they wanted when the hostilities ended since at least 1943; the success of the Cooperative Commonwealth Federation in by-elections and in polls told the governing Liberal politicians that Canadians would not accept a return to the desperate times of the Depression. By 1945, a new idea of Canada was emerging. It was evident that there was no going back. At the same time, the government implored the population to remember that the war was not over and continue to buy Victory Bonds and avoid strikes. In Europe, the Germans were clearly finished, yet from 24 March to the end of hostilities, the Canadian army would suffer, according to the official history, 6,298 casualties, including almost 1,500 dead. Among the senior command, there was none of the intoxicating excitement so characteristic of September 1944; the end of the war was presenting challenges that required attention. The predominant feature of Crerar's actions from April through to his departure at the end of July was a sense of urgency. As he struggled to guide the army through the transition between war and peace, he was desperate to complete the mission begun in earnest in July 1940 – to prevent a return to 'the stagnant backwaters of the army's prewar existence.'[20] He was equally anxious to return home and the tension between the two goals produced an immediacy that informed the last days of his command.

III

On 27 March 1945, at Monty's Tac HQ near Venlo, Crerar was informed of the Master's plan for the final assault on Germany, a plan detailed in the Field Marshal's directive of 28 March. Having 'won the Battle of the Rhine,' Montgomery would push Second British Army and Ninth U.S. Army forward to the River Elbe. Crerar's army would develop operations to support Second British Army, as laid down in previous directives, towards the German coast. The 30 British Corps would probably be given to First Canadian Army to prevent it from being overextended. The 1st Canadian Corps should prepare for operations to clear northwest Holland, but Monty hoped that such operations would not be necessary, 'as they would tend to distract from the effort available for the main object which was the complete defeat of the German Armies in Northwest Europe.'[21]

Close to midnight on 1 April, Crerar and HQ First Canadian Army assumed command of 2nd Canadian Corps operations east of the Rhine. Crerar issued instructions to fulfil Monty's 28 March directive, ordering Simonds to continue operations northward towards the line Apeldoorn-Otterloo and directing Foulkes to secure the front across the Neder Rijn, and then take Arnhem. If western Holland was left alone, then they should be prepared to regroup on a two-corps front and drive into Germany, with the sea on their left and Second British Army on their right. Despite the uncertainty over 1st Canadian Corps future operations, Crerar intended that Simonds's offensive would be the main one, and that Foulkes's operations would depend on the German reaction to having 2nd Canadian Corps cut off their route to Germany. Crerar also said goodbye to Crocker and 30 British Corps, who returned to Dempsey's army at noon on the first. They had come a long way from their stormy beginning in July 1944 and had since established good working relations, but Crerar was happy to have all the Canadian formations under his command.

Developments at SHAEF headquarters changed the Canadians' role even before Crerar issued his directives. Montgomery's relationship with Eisenhower was at a low ebb by March, and the Field Marshal's slow, methodical preparations for crossing the Rhine had increased the already sharp criticism levelled at British operational methods. Bradley and his army commanders were champing at the bit to break out of their bridgehead, but the Supreme Commander held them back in the interests of Anglo-American relations. Once Plunder was launched, he released the American armies, and they made rapid progress; Montgomery, meanwhile, maintained that his army group should make the main thrust into Germany, though he would require American troops to do so. Accordingly, his directive of 28 March assumed Ninth U.S. Army would remain under his command. Eisenhower, however, had to acknowledge the speed of the American advance, the preponderance of U.S. troops in the theatre, and the intense dislike for Montgomery felt by the American senior command. All the U.S. commanders were increasingly critical of what he considered the glacial pace of Second British Army operations. On the 28th, Eisenhower shifted the main axis of advance to the south, directing Bradley's 12th U.S. Army Group to encircle the Ruhr and then advance on the axis Kassel-Leipzig-Dresden. Berlin would be left to the Russians, who, after the success of their offensive, were only thirty miles from it; Allied forces would stop on the Elbe. The 21st Army Group would protect Bradley's northern flank, securing the northern ports and, once on the Elbe, liberate the Danish peninsula. Montgomery was appalled, not as Churchill and Brooke were, that the political importance of Berlin was ignored, but at what he perceived as a snub to his conception of how the war should be won. He fought for three more days to keep Ninth U.S. Army, but Eisenhower was unmoved; he considered a southern thrust would provide the best opportunity to split the German forces in half, to prepare a move south to counter rumoured concentrations in a 'Southern Redoubt,' and to allow American troops to fight together for the final offensive of the war.

First Canadian Army's objectives were left relatively unchanged by Eisenhower's decision, but the resources at its disposal would be limited, particularly if Holland had to be liberated. This reality was reflected in Monty's new directive, which he outlined to Crerar in his caravan on 5 April. He gave priority on resources to 2nd Canadian Corps operations to support to 'clear the coastal belt and all enemy naval establishments up to the line of the Weser' but ordered 1st Canadian Corps to clear western Holland with at least two divisions. Crerar fleshed out this directive on 7 April. He strengthened 1st Canadian Corps, so that with the aid of 49th Division and, following discussions with the Polish Commander-in-Chief and Major-General Maczek, the reactivated 1st Polish Armoured Division (despite its reinforcement problems), Foulkes's corps could use three divisions for the liberation of Holland while 2nd Canadian Corps cleared the Frisian coast.

The Canadian operations on 1st Canadian Corps' front had begun on 2 April with the clearance of the 'island' between Nijmegen and Arnhem; the Rhine was bridged west of Arnhem several days later and the battle for the city began on the 12th. By the 15th, units of the 1st Canadian Division were on the approaches to Apeldoorn. Further east, Simonds's corps had by mid-month pushed well past Deventer and Assen on their way to Groningen, making the German defence of Apeldoorn and northeastern Holland untenable. HQ First Canadian Army moved to Delden on 14 April, its last move during hostilities. Further south, the U.S. First and Third armies encircled German Army Group B in the Ruhr; on 18 April, with over 317,000 prisoners taken, organized resistance collapsed.

Discipline now became a priority for Crerar; he believed that it was slipping as the operations drew to a close, and that he needed to put his stamp on 1st Canadian Corps, fresh from the freedoms of Eighth British Army. On 12 April, he issued a memorandum to all commanders on reports of 'slovenly turnout' and 'poor saluting.' He expected action to correct this situation: 'The standard, or customs, of personnel of the other Services, or the soldiers of other countries, is not my particular concern. I am, however, vitally interested in the reputation of those who serve in the Canadian Army.'[22]

The reputation of the army and its relationship to its future now loomed large against the backdrop of crumbling German resistance. Since February, Crerar had been swamped by CMHQ with cables and memoranda on policy and postwar problems; there were numerous political and personal visitors. This was to some degree a problem of Crerar's own making, but much of it was inevitable. In comparison, Dempsey was not involved in policy decisions at any level although he also consciously kept other intrusions to a minimum, following Monty's example. Operational concerns were still foremost in Crerar's mind, but the end of hostilities was a close second.

The government and ministry moved ahead as if the war were over. At the army's main HQ, an atmosphere of victory also pervaded. As April progressed, the number of visitors increased and administering occupied territory and 'liberated' goods became an increasingly important duty. Visitors to the HQ First Canadian Army stayed in the 'Viper's Den.' The Corps HQ also began to set up elaborate facilities for the growing stream of guests. C.P. Stacey visited the army camp in mid-April to discuss the future of the official histories; he was not impressed.

> During the tour I was struck ... by the increase in pomp and ostentation at our senior headquarters, and particularly at Army ... Army Headquarters in McNaughton's time had been a simple place; it still was in Normandy, where the Army Commander's visitors' mess at Pihem was a tent in a messy farmyard. How different now! ... Harry Crerar's 'A' mess became more and more a holy of holies; I was never invited there during my visits to the Continent ... At Delden, the last night before my return, I ate a meal in a mess tent pitched in really idyllic surroundings in a lovely Dutch park, while a band played soft music nearby. The food and drink while not sybaritic, were good. It was very pleasant; but several of us remarked that it was definitely not warlike.[23]

As the casualty figures suggest, the war was not over. The formations of 1st Canadian Corps were prepared to move into western Holland, when the need to feed a starving Dutch population prompted both sides to end the fighting. On 12 April, the corps was ordered to stop on the Grebbe Line between the Ijsslmeer and the Rijn, to await instructions on further operations in western Holland and it was denuded of all but two divisions. On the 19th, 'aggressive action' was suspended; pending formal approval of this move, Crerar turned administration of relief to the Dutch over to Foulkes. On 21 April, Crerar flew to England for discussions with Montague and for medical treatment of a 'very stiff and painful' shoulder problem that developed when it was exposed to cool air during one of his aerial reconnaissance flights. He was also keen to visit 'my Pete,' who had been readmitted to the hospital. Montgomery formally suspended operations on the 22nd. On the 28th, negotiations with the Reichskommissar, Seyss-Inquart, began and supplies were soon transported into Holland.

IV

While Crerar was in England, the main objective of the trip turned to business. The government statement on demobilization was expected soon, and Crerar wanted to be at CMHQ when it arrived: 'Only in this way could any necessary clarification mutually and quickly be obtained and decisions reached.'[24] He was willing to forego treatment for his shoulder in order to be there when the government's memorandum was received. This caution proved unnecessary. The army commander spent three days in hospital while his shoulder was examined. He met Peter, and they spent an evening in the Dorchester Hotel, discussing their postwar plans. The major part of his visit was spent at CMHQ. There was a growing concern among army planners about the problems the end of hostilities in Germany would present. The tension between NDHQ and the overseas army was palpable as Crerar and Montague pressed for decisions on the postwar army.

The pressure had begun as early as January 1944. Crerar cabled Stuart, ostensibly to find out what progress was being made on planning for the postwar army, but more likely to initiate it. Brushed off by Stuart, Crerar wrote again on 1 June.

> The matter is one which is growing in importance in the Canadian Army (Overseas) and will become acute as victory becomes obvious and imminent. It is perhaps unnecessary for me to point out that decisions taken as regards the future Canadian Army should be closely related to plans for demobilization and the organization of Canadian forces participating in the Pacific operations. Certainly, the several problems cannot be properly treated as disconnected issues.[25]

This time Stuart agreed and forwarded Crerar's comments to the CGS, Murchie. Neither the War Cabinet nor the minister would 'play.' 'Even the Minister,' wrote Murchie, 'is very careful what he puts on record about this question.' Consequently, Murchie noted, 'I have only received the usual brush-off.'[26] War Cabinet minutes suggest that the government was avoiding the issue for as long as possible.

The rapid progress made in France and Belgium in September 1944 brought the issue to the fore. It prompted Crerar's first serious examination of the post-hostilities policies for repatriation and demobilization. Stuart sent him a detailed memorandum, the product of a Demobilization Committee established in 1943, outlining the proposed system of demobilization. It advocated a 'first in, first out' system based on the principle that long-service personnel be sent home as quickly as possible and that scores would be assigned to individuals, not units. Points would be assigned for length of service, marital status, and familial responsibilities; those with the most points would be sent home first, as shipping, a precious commodity in 1945, allowed.

The application of these principles would be complicated by the possibility that Canada might commit troops to the Pacific, and had committed to forming part of the army of occupation in Germany. It was further complicated by the necessity of maintaining some key personnel overseas for administrative purposes once the hostilities ended. From Crerar's perspective, the underlying tension was between the present requirements of the army to carry out its commitments in Europe and the Pacific, the future composition and position of the army in postwar Canadian society, and the futures of the individuals who had served in the overseas army, whether that future lay in the military or in return to civilian life. Crerar struggled to reconcile these options, and the solutions he found drew extensively on his own experiences; nevertheless, the rationale with which he approached the dismantling of the army was predicated on achieving a policy that, while fair to the individual soldier, ensured that the sacrifices of the last six years were not wasted.

The British–Canadian policy towards demobilization at end of the First World War, as well as his own experience of it, shaped Crerar's initial assessment of demobilization policy in 1944. In 1918, the British Ministry for Reconstruction Plans sought to guarantee full employment by first releasing workers in important industries. The inequality of the process caused soldiers' demonstrations and riots. The Canadian government changed its approach following the British riots, and adopted a policy to disperse troops to their chosen destination, on a rough 'first in, first out' system, modified by Sir Arthur Currie's insistence on bringing the troops home by units to maintain both esprit de corps and discipline, and then further modified when priority was given to married men and widowers with children.

Crerar noted the results of inequalities of demobilization by individuals that had occurred in 1918–19 when he passed CMHQ's Demobilization Plan to Walford for study: 'The result of demobilization by individuals is a complete breakup – and breakdown of unit organization and command at a time when command and control are most important.'[27] Equally important was his personal memory of demobilization. His mother's illness had brought him an early repatriation, but he remembered the general experience very differently:

> In the late summer of 1919, I went down to the old Grand Trunk Station at Hamilton, to welcome back my old Battery – the Eleventh. When the regular train pulled in, rather late, on a wet night, about a dozen weary gunners stepped down from a second class carriage. This little party of men was all that returned to Hamilton of this fine Battery which had moved, some two hundred strong, out to war ... That episode then, put a lump in my throat and a thought in my mind, and that thought has remained with me during the years ... I was determined that no soldier in First Canadian Army would repeat that experience.[28]

In the fall of 1944, Crerar outlined the principles that he considered essential to ensure a balance between the needs of the individual and the needs of the service. 'The cohesion and control,' Crerar reasoned, 'so necessary in armed forces during a period of transition is mainly dependent upon the fact that nearly all men have great affection and pride in the unit in which they served and that they wish to retain their association with it until it returns to Canada and locality from which it came.' To Crerar, the unit was the central element for the transition: the requirements of the Pacific and the occupation forces would be met this way, and those earmarked for the war in the Far East should be the first returned to Canada.[29] Canadian formations and units should be returned in order of their departure from Canada, and individuals should be returned on a territorial basis, but in units, he wrote. The needs of the Pacific force should be met from volunteers after their return to Canada. When unit integrity conflicted with territorial priority, individuals could be transferred to relevant units. This last suggestion was, and would prove, administratively unwieldy, but it illustrates that the army's image was informing Crerar's approach to demobilization. 'The average man,' Crerar argued, 'wants to go back to Canada, and to the portion of it he hails from, as a member of a "battle-proved" unit i.e. a BC man would willingly transfer to Seaforth Highlanders from Nth NS High'er in order to return to his province in such auspices.' Crerar remembered the empty welcome in Hamilton. He also felt it was important to control the dissemination of information on repatriation to the Canadian soldiers. He agreed with the concept of a questionnaire on postwar objectives and pamphlets describing the post-hostility plans, but insisted that 'arrangements for issue to all ranks including timing should be subject my control.' 'Important that until war with Germany officially over,' he added, 'nothing should be done to take eye off ball.'[30]

In September 1944, the talks on demobilization were lent some urgency by the perception that the war was as good as won. The Demobilization Directorate had been established at CMHQ early in 1943; in September 1944, Brigadier D.K. Tow was appointed as Director of Reorganization and Demobilization, and work was begun on the scheme. As Crerar's riposte suggested, the main question was whether to use the first in, first out principle or demobilize by unit. The German recovery in mid-September delayed for months further consideration of dismantling First Canadian Army, but several decisions were taken that complicated the disbandment and repatriation of First Canadian Army. In September, the government authorized, in principle, a Canadian Army Pacific Force (CAPF, initially designated as the Canadian Far East Force) that could be employed only in an area of 'direct interest' to Canada. Through the fall and spring, the composition of the CAPF was hammered out in discussions with the British and Americans; detailed planning proceeded from 20 November 1944, when the Cabinet approved a force of one division, and ancillary troops, to a total of 30,000 men. In September, Crerar believed that since few in the overseas army would volunteer, recruiting should await the return of units to Canada. This approach proved unfeasible and in April 1945 the government announced that the force would be composed of volunteers, but complicated the demobilization plans further by taking precious shipping away to return the Pacific Force volunteers to Canada.

The requirements of the Canadian Army Occupation Force (CAOF) had to be met next. In December 1944, the government committed itself, again in principle, to an occupation force of 25,000 men, composed of volunteers and personnel who were low priority for demobilization. No term was set for the occupation force's service, however. Crerar and Montague believed this was a problem, particularly for the non-volunteers, whose future opportunities might be jeopardized, a situation that a viable future in the services might ease.

Reconciling the needs of the CAOF, the CAPF, and the desire for speedy demobilization was complex. It was complicated by the absence of any government policy or announcement on the shape of the postwar army, a critical factor in determining the army commander's approach to dismantling the overseas Canadian army. Crerar had noted in his concluding remarks on the 'Detailed Statement' that 'an early decision concerning the organization and terms of service of the Post War Regular Army' was essential to provide clarity on demobilization. In October 1944, the General Staff had submitted to the Cabinet War Committee its recommendations for the postwar army's size and structure, but no action had been taken. Through the winter and spring of 1945, he tried, without much success, to hammer out the principles that were required to bring order to the myriad pressures that threatened to reduce the army's cohesion at a critical period, but his plans for the army's future were never far from his analysis. The issue resurfaced at the end of January 1945 when CMHQ issued a 'Detailed Statement of Policy' on demobilization. Again, Crerar noted that while he accepted the principle of 'first in, first out' as the basis for demobilization, he still believed it impractical to apply it without modification. The compromise proposed was that high-score personnel, defined as those with three or more years service, should be sent home, but after that, units and formations should take priority. He argued that the issue was also a question of the common good: 'Unless the fullest practicable advantage of these cohesive influences is taken, the "reallocation" process will show all the bad features which arise when "individual rights" take the place of "collective values."'[31]

Was Crerar out of touch? He was the product a different time, but he was no fool. His belief that volunteers for the Far East would be hard to come by indicates his knowledge that individuals wanted to return to Canada as quickly as possible. He wanted to go home quickly as well. And he was not oblivious to the necessity for the perception, as well as the reality, of a fair system of repatriation. The issue wasn't just how to dismantle the army; it was how to rebuild the next one. In his comments in January, Crerar fought increased pressure – which reached a peak in the winter of 1944/5 – to obtain early releases for specific officers and other ranks who would return to key jobs in the government or industry. He resisted preferential treatment on the basis that it gave individuals an advantage in re-establishing themselves in civilian life.[32] Simonds, when acting army commander, had also advocated this view, writing to Montague in November that 'the first duty of an officer of the Canadian Army is to the army until the war is won.'[33]

In mid-February 1945, Crerar received CMHQ's revised paper on the reallocation of manpower. Crerar approved the draft in principle, but conscious of how the army would be viewed in Canada, he added, 'I think the thought might be worked in that all ranks of the Canadian army owe it not to themselves, but to the Canadian soldiers of all ranks who will never return to their families and friends, that they should go back to Canada looking, as well as feeling, worthy of the magnificent reputation which Canadian soldiers have made.' He insisted on writing the foreword to the demobilization pamphlet, and that it be distributed to every officer and man in the Canadian Army Overseas before any public statements on demobilization were made.[34]

The CMHQ worked on the information pamphlet, eventually titled *After Victory in Europe*, from February but it went uncompleted until Prime Minister King's 4 April 1945 announcement that the Pacific Force would be all-volunteer; this made the simultaneous distribution of a questionnaire imperative. The Cabinet War Committee had discussed the demobilization and repatriation schemes presented by the Chiefs of Staff in late March, but no serious consideration had been given the drafts until meetings on 11 and 19 April when they examined a revised Chiefs of Staff memorandum. King signalled the government's approach to demobilization as early as September 1944 when he emphasized to the Cabinet War Committee the 'importance of following policies aimed at the maximum expansion of national income.' Industrial reconstruction required manpower, which required speedy demobilization.[35] During the intervening months, the Chiefs of Staff, acting in concert with Crerar and Montague, had mounted a vigorous campaign to change the government's perception that the end of the war against Germany marked the beginning of general demobilization. Rather, the end of the war marked instead 'the beginning of a period of reallocation of manpower, which will result in certain personnel becoming surplus to requirements.' Control over the period of transition drove their agenda. Crerar also led the battle against the early release of NRMA men, perceiving that it would cause resentment in the overseas army. On 19 April, a Special Cabinet Committee approved the military's memorandum as reflecting government policy on reallocation following Germany's defeat, including recommendations for the use of an armoured division organization to decrease the number of infantry required to make up the establishment of the occupation force.

The government still refused, however, to comment on the postwar army. The committee asked that all reference to this force be excised. The offending paragraph dealt with the retention of benefits to attract to the CAPF, 'the younger, active, intelligent, and experienced men who have already proven themselves in operations'; they noted that those benefits might not prove enough to attract the necessary volunteers. 'A pronouncement,' they concluded, 'on the composition and size of the postwar Permanent Forces, and some encouragement as to the prospects of entry into the Services as a professional career, would strongly attract this group and greatly simplify the manning problem.'[36] It was removed, but it was natural for the services to want to begin planning for the postwar organization. For Crerar, it was particularly important, because staffing the postwar army with suitable officers and men was a critical factor in his decisions about command of the CAPF and CAOF. Both were vehicles for retaining a strong nucleus of the army's wartime experience and professionalism in the postwar army.

Crerar's efforts to ensure that, as Currie had in 1919, the experience and professionalism of the First Canadian Army would be dispersed throughout the army's postwar establishment were well documented, and in part for postwar consumption. Yet Crerar was confident enough of the army's future to encourage his son Peter to stay in the Permanent Forces: 'I believe that the Canadian Active Army of the future will be a much finer organization than the old Permanent Force of the past.'[37] While the government deliberated, Crerar took steps to secure the postwar army command and staff appointments he wanted.

Crerar's influence over promotions and appointments was naturally immense, although regulations gave a large measure of authority to formation commanders and Burns. Crerar retained the right, however, to control certain specified senior appointments, and his approval was required for proposed changes.[38] In January, he reminded his commanders of his prerogatives. In April, his authority was formalized, a change prompted by the return of 1st Canadian Corps to First Canadian Army and the desire to standardize the interchange of officers. All records of service of officers recommended for staff and command appointments were maintained, and all graded staff appointments controlled, by HQ First Canadian Army. Ultimate authority would rest with the army commander:

> I desire that in the future I be advised of all proposed appointments to Command and to Second-in-Command prior to such appointments being notified. Normally immediate concurrence will be forthcoming but I shall exercise my prerogative to make alternative suggestions in cases where, in my opinion, officers deserving of consideration may have been overlooked.[39]

Similar objectives were evident in late April when, through Montague, he tried to stop NDHQ requests for specific officers to strengthen the staff in Canada. On 20 April, Montague sent a letter to Ottawa describing how administering the 'occupied' rather than 'liberated' territory was stretching resources to the limit, and that the strain would only increase when the fighting ended. He also expressed concern that the principle of requesting individuals ran counter to the army's policy on demobilization of individuals.[40] He was right, of course, but it also allowed him to forestall decisions on staffing the postwar army until the government's policy was announced. The approval of Crerar's recommendation that all promotions and staff gradings subsequent to 'Eclipse' – the code name for Canada's participation in the occupation of Germany – be frozen ensured that his would be the predominant voice in key appointments.

There was much to be done. Crerar's visit to CMHQ in April 1945 was characterized by impatience at the lack of movement in all the areas necessary to sort out the reallocation of manpower and to begin establishing the army's postwar organization. His frustration brimmed over in his correspondence: he characterized demobilization as the 'dream word' and, noting how he 'hated untidy thinking,' vowed that he wouldn't allow the men under his command to suffer as a result of 'contradictory, or confusing, policies' that should have been 'answered weeks, or months, ago.'[41] That they were not, of course, was partly due to his interference and objectives.

In London, Crerar waited only a short time for his answer. On 25 April, NDHQ cabled the government's decisions to CMHQ, and discussions began in earnest. Over two days of meetings and transatlantic cables and calls on 27 and 28 April, the reallocation of army manpower and the finalized timing of the release of the demobilization policy to the army were hammered out. Crerar dominated the proceedings and imposed his views on amendments to, and implementation of, the Cabinet War Committee memorandum. First, Crerar stressed the importance of ensuring a fair system that balanced individual and collective needs, but one that looked after the overseas soldiers first. He supported, for example, the Khaki College, which, despite his backing, did not materialize for some months. Second, the army commander recommended many alterations aimed at regulating the army's image throughout the demobilization. As he had before, he insisted on fuller explanations in the pamphlet aimed at the troops, particularly the need to stress that 'an individual's score was only the basic factor in the determination of reallocation.' Unable to move the government on its decision on the early release of NRMA men for essential employment,

Crerar wanted it clearly explained in the pamphlet that 'responsibility for granting of such leave and direction to employment [of NRMA personnel] to most urgent needs of national economy rested solely with the government.' He also argued against the proposal that troops be dispersed as soon as they detrained in Canada; instead he stated, 'It was most desirable that personnel should detrain and march or be moved to the District Depot or at least some central point where families and friends would congregate ... it was more preferable that the [families and interested spectators] see the troops en route to a central dispersal area.'[42]

The most contentious issue discussed was the composition of the Canadian Army Occupation Force, partly because there were no government announcements on the terms of service and there were widespread doubts that volunteers would fill the ranks. It was also evident, however, that the CAOF, like the CAPF, was for Crerar an important way of maximizing control over postwar appointments. In April, 'after considerable discussion,' Crerar directed that 'consideration' be given to perpetuating existing militia and Permanent Force units in the CAOF, that its education 'training ... be limited to that presently applicable to units in the field, that there would be no rehabilitation training and that emphasis would be on military training for occupational duties.' He insisted on the right to approve the appointments of the three brigade commanders.[43] The provisions for training seemed strange, given earlier concerns that occupational duties would handicap the career prospects for those returning to civilian life, but less so if the CAOF was considered as the nucleus of a postwar professional force. This approach had some currency in the British Army; Montgomery would be an advocate of an occupied Germany as the perfect training ground for the future field army.[44]

Perhaps Crerar was influenced by this approach, but it was also an important means of ensuring that the overseas forces dominated appointments in the future professional forces. He had little faith in Ottawa's goodwill. In May 1945, he tried unsuccessfully to pressure NDHQ to 'avail itself of the services of certain experienced officers on my HQ whose responsibilities here have been greatly diminished ... and who could be spared by me.'[45] The glacial response time of DND only increased the tension between Ottawa and its overseas forces.

Crerar also took a paternal interest in the future careers of his immediate staff, both those remaining in the service and those returning to civilian life. His comments on considerations affecting the CAOF reflect his concern. He had stopped Wright from returning to regimental duty, because he was a valuable member of his headquarters staff, but also because be believed his careers were better served by remaining on staff duties. The discussions about the postwar army were further complicated when it became an issue in the June 1945 election, one to which Mackenzie King's Liberals were extremely sensitive.

24 Casting the Postwar Army

I

Crerar's last battle as army commander was with the Canadian government and, in a sense, with his memory of the Canada he left. He tried to use the formations committed to the occupation and the Pacific to retain the best and brightest of First Canadian Army for postwar service. And he wanted to ensure that the demobilization of the army was viewed not as the final chapter of wartime service, but as a transition, a stepping stone to a life of peacetime civic service. Although handicapped by the absence of government policy on the shape of the postwar forces and repatriation, Crerar fought to position the army so there would be no return to the stagnation of the interwar years.

Crerar returned to Holland on 29 April. Before he left for London, he had delegated administrative responsibility for Dutch relief to Foulkes's HQ. The 2nd Canadian Corps fought on for two more weeks, but the final fortnight of hostilities was essentially directed by Simonds, as acting army commander from 22 to 29 April, and as the main commander involved in operations until 5 May. Montgomery's directive of 22 April outlined First Canadian Army's final objectives: operations in western Holland were suspended, but 2nd Canadian Corps was to operate 'strongly' against Oldenburg while supporting the left flank of Second British Army while it engaged Bremen. Following the capture of Bremen, Simonds's corps would clear northeast Holland and northwest Germany between the rivers Ems and Weser towards Emden and Wilhelmshaven, while studying the requirements of capturing the Frisian Islands. Operations would remain constant; the Germans would get no respite.

Operations by 2nd Canadian Corps remained relatively intense and there was no signal from the higher command to slow the tempo. Indeed, two days passed before Crerar visited Simonds; the paperwork demanded in preparation for implementing demobilization kept him tied to his caravan at the end of the month. The fighting was not over, however. First Canadian Army HQ staff, in their 'Forecast of Activity' for April and May, and as part of their planning for Eclipse, anticipated no decrease in the 'enemy's will to resist'; action in front of both corps was expected to be 'intense' until at least the second week of May.[1] Crerar was surprised at the continued intensity of the fighting, but was not inclined to ease the pressure. The day he left the theatre he wrote his brother, 'The war is speeding to a conclusion although the finish may not be as tidy as we could all wish. However, with fanatics and crazy men, reason certainly does not prevail, and, for the good of the future, the more of them that are killed off, the better.' Emotions ran high as the German resistance continued.[2] Crerar's antipathy towards the Germans was heightened as Canadian casualties mounted, even as the end was obviously near. 'Casualties have not been heavy,' he wrote Hume Wrong, 'but, all the same, at this closing stage in the war, even minor numbers are extra hard to accept.'[3]

Still, operations continued. In examinations of Canada's wars, one minor historiographical trend is the desire to pinpoint exactly when the fighting should have been halted and a propensity to identify which unfortunate soldier was the last killed. Currie was accused of ordering unnecessary advances on Mons. Did a lack of control from the top during the final weeks cause unnecessary Canadian dead? No. The official historian seems to have been conscious of this question, for Stacey painstakingly detailed the final hours of the war in Europe, describing to the minute when the senior command knew that the end of hostilities were imminent.[4]

On 22 April, Monty established that operations must be continued; on the 27th, he ordered Simonds, as acting army commander, to prepare plans for further operations to capture certain Frisian Islands. Simonds had meanwhile ordered a set-piece attack on the Dutch port of Delfzijl; the fighting there raged from 23 April to 2 May before the Germans surrendered. On 2 May, the German armies in Italy capitulated; Crerar received a congratulatory message for 1st Canadian Corps from Mackenzie King, which he forwarded to Foulkes, without comment.

'This protracted and bitter struggle is rapidly drawing to a close,' Crerar wrote Peg on 3 May. 'Before this reaches you, the war in Europe may be officially declared as finished.'[5] That morning a German delegation arrived at Montgomery's headquarters to discuss terms of surrender. The field marshal issued no orders to cease operations. On 4 May, the army commander was in his caravan working on routine correspondence when Monty's BGS Operations Belchem phoned at 1355 to officially inform him that negotiations were proceeding for the 'unconditional surrender' of all German forces opposite 21st Army Group. Five minutes later, Crerar phoned Simonds with the news and instructed him 'to call off any planned assaults on the town of Jever and Aurich by 1 Polish Armd Div and 3 Cdn Inf Div pending further instructions.' In the meantime, he recorded 'reconnaissance and the improvement of positions of troops under my command could go on.' The letter of these instructions was not forwarded to 2nd Canadian Corps formations; the assaults were called off, but otherwise 3rd Canadian Division recorded it was 'permissible to do anything else.' The Poles were also cautioned, but no other formation received any instructions.[6]

Crerar finished his office work and flew to 1st Canadian Corps HQ in Apeldoorn to inform Foulkes of the negotiations. He returned to his HQ for supper, entertaining guests in 'A' Mess as he had for the last few days. Lieutenant-Colonel Cecil Merritt, the Victoria Cross–winning commander of the South Saskatchewan Regiment at Dieppe, now an aspiring politician, was among the guests, despite Crerar's concerns about the precedent. At 2035, Crerar, like thousands of others, listened as the BBC broadcast was interrupted for a special announcement by SHAEF: the Germans in northwest Germany, Holland, Denmark, and the Frisian Islands had surrendered. Minutes later, the official signal from Montgomery's HQ was received: all offensive operations were suspended and a ceasefire was in effect from 0800, 5 May.[7] Crerar issued a message to all ranks, which captured the mixed emotions engendered by the announcement:

> From Sicily to the river Senio, from the beaches of Dieppe to those of Normandy and from thence northern France, Belgium, Holland and Northwest Germany, the Canadians and their Allied comrades in this army have carried out their responsibilities in the high traditions which they inherited. The official order that offensive operations of all troops of First Cdn Army will cease forthwith and that all fire will cease from 0800 hrs tomorrow Saturday 5 May has been issued. Crushing and complete victory over the German enemy has been secured. In rejoicing at this supreme accom-

plishment we shall remember the friends who have paid the full price for the belief they also held that no sacrifice in the interests of the principles for which we fought could be too great.[8]

The next day, Foulkes accepted Colonel-General Johannes Blaskowitz's surrender; miles away, Simonds, 'coldly correct,' read aloud the surrender document before handing it to his opposite number on the German side. Crerar refused to meet any German generals. Instead he sent his subordinates. The memories of two world wars and the losses – Malcolm, Trum Warren, Hamilton friends, most of the 11th Battery, and hundreds of others, 'my boys' as he characterized his soldiers years later – would not be forgotten or forgiven. 'I saw no purpose in meeting any German generals,' he said in a press interview soon after the war, 'unless I had to on some official capacity ... I have had them in adjoining fields ... that was enough.'[9] All German forces were surrendered to Eisenhower on 7 May. The war in Europe was over.

Among the troops, the predominant feeling was, by most accounts, one of relief. At the senior levels, congratulatory cables and letters flew back and forth. Crerar sent a laudatory message to 84 Group, expressing his 'admiration and appreciation' of the 'magnificent support' afforded to First Canadian Army; he sent similar messages to all formations under his command. Even Montgomery was caught up in the moment, noting, 'No commander can ever have had a more loyal subordinate that I have had in you. And under your command the Canadian army has covered itself with glory in the campaign in Western Europe.' Among the hundreds of congratulatory messages, one stood out: 'My loving thoughts and congratulations are with you on this big day, love Verse.' His reply: 'Your message good to get. Much love and may our reunion be not long delayed.'[10]

II

'It has been a long and heavy strain ... and I badly need a few months' complete rest and a chance to relax,' Crerar wrote Peg two days before the German surrender. He did not anticipate he would have one:

> The business of getting the Canadians home will not be speedily accomplished, though I have hopes that more than half of them will be back before the end of this year. So far as I am concerned, once the organization for demobilization is well established and the flow to Canada is proceed-

ing satisfactorily, I shall ask to be relieved of my job and shall return home, leaving the remaining responsibilities for some younger General to carry out.[11]

Unlike army commanders throughout the Allied armies, whose duties became mainly ceremonial, Crerar's policy responsibilities fully occupied him until he left Europe in August. It was an anxious time.

Initiating the reorganization of the army and maintaining morale during the transition now loomed as immediate problems. On 4 May, Crerar set the machinery in motion. He drafted the cable that he wanted CMHQ to send Walford, urging that in view of the 'imminent approach of VE Day' the reallocation plans be explained to the troops and the questionnaire be distributed as quickly as possible. The NDHQ refused to move on the issue until the government announced its policy on the terms of service for the Far East; when pressed by Crerar and Montague, they agreed to release the information as soon they received the minister's permission. Authorization was received on 7 May, but distribution of *After Victory in Europe* was then delayed for at least a week. As an interim measure, Crerar ordered forty copies of the text of the pamphlet issued to each division and the complete text published in the *Maple Leaf*, which would be issued 'on a wider distribution than normally.' The questionnaire was scheduled for delivery during the week 13–19 May.[12]

The scheme to dismantle and demobilize the overseas army as outlined in *After Victory in Europe* was based loosely on the 'first in, first out' principle, but the three stages of repatriation envisioned meant that in practice individual priority was secondary to the needs of the service. The questionnaire asked each soldier to state whether he preferred service with the Pacific force, the occupation force, or a discharge. Once the preferences were established, the army would determine how many officers and other ranks it needed to meet the needs of its remaining commitments. If possible, low-priority personnel would fill these requirements. Priority was determined by a point system. One month of service in Canada counted for two points; three points were awarded for one month overseas; those with familial responsibilities had their score increased by 20 per cent. Once all ranks were categorized, the first group to be shipped home would be Pacific force volunteers. The second stage would see the repatriation of high-point personnel in excess of the army's administrative requirements. The final stage would be the return of units based on time overseas.

Crerar expected that the third stage would begin by the end of July, beginning with the leading units of 1st Canadian Division. Satisfactory progress was 'mainly dependent on shipping,'[13] he noted. Once this stage was reached, he would ask to be relieved of command.

The most pressing concern was troop morale. Within hours of the official German surrender, Crerar issued a letter advising all commanding officers of the importance of 'man-management' in the period following the ceasefire, but prior to repatriation. He encouraged the maintenance of unit esprit de corps through a balanced and imaginative program of training and recreational activities; discipline had to be maintained, but he warned against 'overdoses' of drills and exercises. 'The essential thing,' he wrote, 'is to keep all ranks mentally and/or physically active, and interested, for most of their waking hours.' It would provide, he concluded, 'a different test to Commanders and leaders to those met and overcome in operations.'[14]

Stacey describes in some detail the programmes of education and entertainment established for the troops after VE Day. A handbook titled *Rehabilitation Training and Education* was prepared. Crerar went to great lengths to put these programs into practice; on 11 May, he cabled Montague to 'accelerate' the arrival the 'Meet the Navy' show, scheduled to tour England, Paris, and Brussels before playing in areas near First Canadian Army. He threatened to take the matter up with Ottawa.[15] He pressed for immediate shipments of sports equipment and kept up a steady barrage of cables aimed at DND until his demands were met. He visited the formations under his command, setting up his personal headquarters for several days at each divisional HQ 'that I may informally see something of the officers and men of each formation.' 'It was,' as he told his brother, 'the aspect of soldiering which I mainly enjoy, but in operations, I have no time left for such pleasures.'[16] At his own headquarters, groups from the support and associated services were entertained in turn: on 14 May, Huddleston and the air force liaison staff were his guests. He tried to secure a Dakota to fly enlisted men over the battlefields. He also inspected recreation and leave facilities in adjoining towns. He ensured that 'all provinces and districts' were represented in the victory parade in Berlin.[17]

Preparing the soldiers for civilian life was handled under the Rehabilitation Training Programme. Crerar's personal interest was focused on civic education; in 1st Canadian Corps and then First Canadian Army he had always promoted studies in current affairs. In some ways, a civic religion had replaced his mother's Christian ideals. The army was a prime vehicle for spreading the gospel. He feared that politics was being diluted by the expansion of the vote without a concurrent expansion of the education system. The war, and his encounters with the political system in the decade before the war, left a deep impression; earlier in the war, he had written that he saw the result of the 'tremendous changes' in his lifetime 'in the basis on which our own particular form of democracy has rested.' The vote had been extended to 'pretty near everyone of both sexes who is not in a jail or an asylum.' This, in combination with the decision in 1910 to pay members of Parliament, had, in Crerar's opinion, 'led to a lowering in the standard of outlook expected of a Member of Parliament.' He believed that popularity and constituency politics had displaced the search for 'policies which were nationally sound, but locally disadvantageous.' The 'outstanding weakness' of the 'universal franchise we are now supposed to enjoy is that no proper efforts have been made to educate our youth in the ethics of citizenship and the absolute need to insist on the possession of those ethics by the individual whom they vote for.' The decline of religious instruction had left a vacuum: 'It was essential to substitute in its place an equal or greater amount of instruction in the humanities and principles of citizenship.'[18]

Crerar was twenty-two when MPs became salaried; he was thirty when the franchise was extended. He had watched the 'colossal power and influence of education' change the face of Germany, and he had fought the generation of Germans whose outlook had been 'warped and fanatical.' He was afraid for the future; and he was not alone. Democracy had only just triumphed in 1945. As the war ended, he encouraged his son-in-law to pursue a career at the CBC, not least because there were 'great possibilities to mould and to improve public opinion through the medium of radio.' The nation was maturing in the first fifty years of the twentieth century. Crerar was part of a generation of Canadians who found themselves having to first define and then redefine what it meant to be Canadian.[19]

After VE Day, he ordered the number of periods that focused on civic education increased from four to six; the subjects included 'Civics,' 'The Organization and Operation of Different Systems of National Government,' and 'The Place of Religion in Society.' Attendance was voluntary, but characterized as 'high'; the preponderance of social clubs and the growing concern of the Dutch about dramatic increases in the number of single mothers suggest that the average soldier preferred other forms

Casting the Postwar Army 429

of education. Crerar nevertheless saw this program as essential to encourage 'constructive social thought and the development of rational public opinion.'[20]

Despite the heavy schedule, Crerar relaxed his hold on his army and himself, putting into practice his belief that work and pleasure should be distinct and completely separate. His final months were spent in comfort at the Dutch town of Apeldoorn. The tents and caravans of the Main Headquarters were located among the woods of a city park; Crerar's personal quarters were situated on the banks of the park lake. 'The scenery,' he wrote home, 'is a sort of mixture of the Muskoka and Rideau lakes. Altogether not a bad spot to finish up in.'[21] By the end of the month, Crerar had used the enthusiasm prompted by the German surrender to massage for 'A' Mess a monthly supply of whisky from Philip Chester, chief executive of Hudson's Bay Company and former master general of ordnance. His inventory of cigarettes and cigars increased dramatically, despite liberal distribution at the headquarters. He found himself in trouble with Monty when, against 21st Army Group orders, he relaxed the regulations governing women in the messes. With his operational responsibilities complete, the more relaxed side of Harry Crerar emerged.

The end of the war also required decisions on the family affairs. Crerar saw the army as the best answer for his son; he enlisted Price Montague's help.

> Since he enlisted ... he has stood on his own feet and, I believe, has done well.
> When he stayed with me the night at the Dorchester, on 27 April, I asked him concerning his future plans ... he told me then that he was considering staying on in the service. As I believe that the Canadian Active Army of the future will be a much finer organization than the old Permanent Force of the past, I was glad to hear of this because like other youngsters of his age, while his experiences in the last four or five years should help him in a military career, they have not particularly suited fitted him for civilian activities ... I think it would be in the lad's interest if you encouraged him to stay on in the Canadian army.[22]

His concern for his son, no less than his responsibility for the welfare of his army, raised his consciousness about the need to retrain the soldiers. It was also an ironic, if unintended, comment on where he saw the military relative to society as a whole. In May, he again turned down an invitation of Princess Juliana of the Netherlands to have Mrs Crerar accompany her to England: 'As I have throughout endeavoured to share the personal difficulties, and legitimate dangers, with the officers and men under my command, it seemed to me important that I should clearly maintain this attitude until my responsibilities have ceased.'[23]

While Crerar's concern for his men and morale was evident through his actions, he could not, even at the end, connect with them. His BGS recalled suggesting that Crerar gather the Main Headquarters staff in a field for an informal address, with Crerar standing in a Jeep, thanking them for their work. '"That's a good idea," he remembered Crerar said, "you just write out what I'm to say."'[24] Crerar was at this point exhausted, physically and mentally, as were many of his contemporaries, but he always expected that his actions would speak for him. The farewells were personally difficult, however. He found the formal goodbyes easier, if not less demanding. He wrote his brother in June, 'I find myself definitely weary.'[25]

On the 13th, the Main and Administrative Headquarters staffs gathered for a memorial service; Crerar read the lesson and then took the salute at a march past of all personnel. On 20 May, he held a formal dinner at the Grand Hotel, Hilversum, for his corps, divisional commanders, and senior staff officers, as well as the GOCs of 49th (West Riding) and 1st Polish Armoured Divisions. The dinner was a prelude to the First Canadian Army Victory Parade held at The Hague the next day, Crerar's choice: he reasoned that since The Hague was 'the first capital city on the continent that Canadians have entered in the sense of a Liberating Force,' they should be properly received.[26] Crerar, Prince Bernard of the Netherlands, Simonds, and Foulkes took the salute, accompanied by the army's senior command.[27] Harry Foster remembered it differently. His diary read, 'Victory Parade in The Hague under a heavy rain ... a miserable showing by the troops ... Uncle Harry, Prince Bernhard and I took the salute. The men looked slovenly and were out of step ... discipline will become a problem. I can't blame the troops. The war is over and they want to go home.'[28]

II

An increasingly anxious Crerar awaited DND and government decisions on shipping and the postwar army, as their troops grew restless. On 19 May, Crerar cabled Montague to step up the pressure on NDHQ.

He feared a mass exodus of the best men if the uncertainty continued. Montague concurred with this assessment. The government, however, was slow to make decisions even on its commitments to the Pacific and the occupation of Germany. Mackenzie King had called an election for 11 June 1945, pledging himself to the promotion of 'world security and world prosperity in the international arena and to policies of full employment and social security' in Canada. Understandably, convincing the Canadian people of his sincerity in undertaking this ambitious program, much less his willingness to implement it, took all the Prime Minister's energies.[29] It was not until 17 May that the Cabinet War Committee approved for the Pacific an infantry division, and one armoured regiment or tank battalion, organized and equipped along U.S. Army lines. DND scheduled the force to leave Canada for training in the United States on 1 September; it was committed to engage in operations in March 1946. It was estimated that approximately 40,000 troops, a figure including reinforcements, would be required. Nothing was said of the postwar army.

This decision made, Montague called a meeting for 22 May to settle the remaining details of reallocating the Canadian army's manpower. They made one final attempt on the nineteenth to secure a decision on the composition and organization of the postwar army, but with no results. When the meeting convened, the CAPF was the first on the agenda. From First Canadian Army's perspective, the requirements were simple: only the details of number, rank, and trades were necessary. Once this information was obtained, Crerar noted that a study of the completed questionnaires would enable his headquarters to nominate individuals. He warned that most would be officers and NCOs.

The army commander also voiced his opposition to modelling Canada's postwar army organization on that of the U.S. army – a step that he felt would be 'generally unpopular' with Canadian troops. Here he was mistaken. While he had shown a willingness to follow U.S. staff organization when it proved efficient, he still believed that the British military connection was valuable. Crerar supported the maintenance of the pre-war educational troika of Royal Military College, Staff College, and the Imperial Defence College, reflecting the beliefs of many contemporaries.[30] Others, like Burns, were pragmatists, foreshadowing the tensions as the army made the transition from British to American tutelage after 1945.

Questions on manning and training the CAOF were considered next; these were not as pressing, but there were concerns that the ranks could not be filled by volunteers. Suggestions ranged from using men from other arms and services, providing minimal basic infantry training, to transporting the families of occupied men to the United Kingdom or Europe – all of them unrealistic. What was missing was information on shipping for repatriation.

Montague was without answers.[31] Shipping was the most critical factor in a speedy repatriation. The allocation of shipping depended on decisions from higher bodies. Crerar recognized that any demobilization scheme would flounder if shipping was unavailable. Mackenzie King's government had sought reassurances since March that long-service personnel, whether Canadian or American, would have first priority on shipping; the best the British War Office could promise was perhaps 90,000 Canadians would be sent home in the six months following Hitler's defeat. CMHQ and the High Commissioner pressed for commitments to bring at least 150,000 home during that period. The issue remained unresolved, however.

Not content to wait, Crerar tried to make an end run around the War Office. On 31 May, Crerar wrote directly to Eisenhower, trying to enlist his support to obtain more shipping to send Canadian troops home, surmising that the U.S. authorities could influence priorities. Ike was sympathetic but reminded him that allocation of shipping for Canadian forces was 'a matter for decision exclusively between CMHQ and the British War Office.'[32] No official policy was forthcoming through June.

Despite the lack of movement, Crerar was publicly confident that all was well. 'The morale of all ranks is very high,' he wrote privately on 9 June, 'and behaviour, on the whole, has been excellent. I hope, and believe, we shall leave Holland with as good a reputation as when we entered it.'[33] Only days earlier, however, he reissued his memorandum on the necessity of maintaining discipline and saluting as a form of respect. The overseas army also consciously distanced itself from unpopular policies. The government announcement in early June that some NRMA men in Canada would be released in order to 'meet the requirements of "critical manpower shortages in the industry and the professions"'; the policy was characterized as departmental and transcribed verbatim into a memorandum with little comment.[34]

The same government inaction that hindered the efforts to secure either shipping or firm commitments on allocation also informed consideration of command appointments for the CAPF and CAOF. When no information on postwar army organization was forthcoming, Crerar was forced to move ahead without the tidy framework that he desired.

The future of the army was Crerar's first concern, but he also wanted to position suitable candidates for careers in the postwar army. His influence in the GOC appointments for the Pacific and occupation forces was clear-cut; in the major postwar appointment – the Chief of the General Staff – his influence was less direct, but just as substantial. Crerar tried, without success, to use the three appointments to resolve the major dilemma he faced: how to reward both Simonds and Foulkes and retain them in the army. The Chief of the General Staff was the real prize, though, and all of them knew it.

The first major decision was command of the CAPF. In May, Crerar tried twice to get command of the Pacific force for Simonds, urging the Minister of National Defence to make the appointment at the rank of lieutenant-general. It would be no great reward for Simonds, but it made sense from a strictly military point of view to appoint the best field commander and would also salve the wound if Simonds did not receive the appointment of Chief of the General Staff; Crerar's assessments of Simonds to this point suggested he would not.[35]

Crerar's preference for Foulkes as the postwar CGS created the main problem. Foulkes's appointment as the postwar Chief of the General Staff was, for Crerar, a critical decision, given his concerns about the army's postwar position. Guy Simonds was, at first glance, the most obvious choice for this post, although there was no firm precedent for the outstanding wartime field commander to hold the top staff position in the Canadian or British armies. Simonds believed himself the best man for the job, but the self-assurance that made him such a brilliant tactician would not necessarily ensure his success as Chief of the General Staff. Crerar suggested as much to Mackenzie King in May 1944, telling him unequivocally that Simonds was the best man to replace him as army commander, but he that he 'might not be the best man for postwar planning.'

When formally approached by Murchie in July 1945 for advice on how best to employ Simonds and Foulkes in the future, Crerar's opinion was the same: in a long and considered reply, he praised Simonds's record in the field 'as second to none' and characterized him as an 'excellent staff officer.' Nevertheless, he suggested that Foulkes's 'particular qualities' made him 'exceptionally qualified for very senior staff appointment.' As Stacey suggested in his memoirs, 'That presumably did it.' Crerar had left little to chance. He had praised Foulkes for his drive and knowledge, and he clearly admired his stability. Foulkes had also made good in Italy as Burns's successor – an accomplishment that only enhanced his reputation with Crerar. In February 1945, following receipt of a glowing report on Foulkes's command in Italy, Crerar had suggested to the GOC in C Eighth Army that he nominate Foulkes for a CBE, an award that would enhance his reputation as an operational commander.[36] Foulkes had long been his choice for CGS – and he was right.

When he returned home to Canada, Crerar tried to distance himself from the decision. In December 1945, Crerar wrote Montgomery,

> I gather that Simonds future is the subject of some discussion. When I left Holland, he definitely preferred to stay abroad rather than take on the CGS as he didn't like the prospects of a frustrating experience in that job in this period of 'wait and see.' However, the problem is now, I gather, to find him some appointment in keeping with his rank and in which he will be satisfied ... I hope that he holds his impatience in check – he is too excellent a professional soldier for Canada to lose, permanently.[37]

It seems unlikely that Simonds actually said no to taking up the appointment as CGS, but he would never be first on Crerar's list for a political appointment. Montgomery's mixed record as the first postwar CIGS suggests that Simonds would not have been the best candidate for guiding the army through postwar retrenchment.

Foulkes's nomination also ensured that Crerar's conception of the Canadian army as a civic institution would continue beyond the war; Foulkes shared many of the army commander's beliefs in the necessity of raising the public profile of the army as a means of promoting preparedness. Their support for the official histories was a good example. In April, C.P. Stacey, anxious to sort out his future but hoping to continue his work as official historian, wrote a forceful memorandum urging the establishment of certain principles that would govern the work of the army's official historian: 'If the History is to be worth anything,' he wrote, the official historian must be independent, have full access to official documents, and be able to express opinions for which the Department of National Defence was in 'no way responsible.' Underlying these principles was the understanding, based on discussions between Crerar and Stacey, that the official histories should be aimed at the public. Stacey had also discussed the idea with Simonds, but found the 2nd Corps commander dubious about the utility of writing for the public, although he agreed that it should bring out the fundamental lessons of the war.

Crerar and Montague fully supported Stacey's ideas and believed that Stacey was the man to do it. They sent a memorandum to Defence headquarters to that effect, although Stacey believed they made a 'tactical error' by not addressing it directly to Murchie and by stating that it expressed the views of the army commander and Montague. The noncommittal response, which balked at allowing the official historian the independence Stacey requested, suggests he was correct, but Foulkes's appointment as CGS ensured that Stacey's principles would be accepted intact. This view of the role of the official histories underlined the fundamental difference between Foulkes and Simonds: Foulkes shared Crerar's sensitivity to politics and the army's position in Canadian society.[38]

The other appointments were less acrimonious, but the desire among the officers and men of the Canadian army to return home conspired to upset Crerar's hopes of playing a major role in retaining the best of First Canadian Army for the postwar army. Hoffmeister was Crerar's recommendation for command of the CAPF, a recommendation fully supported by Simonds and Foulkes. Hoffmeister's appointment was confirmed. Crerar preferred Spry for command of the CAOF, but Spry wanted to return to civilian life. Vokes was Crerar's second choice, and while he too wanted to go home, he agreed to serve. The same theme ran through the other command and staff appointments.

III

As of the end of June, Crerar had precious little to offer prospective Permanent Force officers. In response to a Burns's memorandum on the necessity of deciding upon terms of service for the CAOF, Crerar observed that 'it is not possible to comment constructively on its solution until the Canadian government has reached decisions concerning the period during which a Canadian Army Occupation Force will be maintained in Germany and, also, the composition and terms of service of the Canadian Army (Active) of the future.' He concluded, 'The CGS, Canada, should, however, be advised that there is an urgent need for these questions to be answered.'[39] Montague dissented, disagreeing with the proposal for staffing the CAOF with personnel slated for the postwar army.

Montague held the memorandum until 7 July; it made little difference. The 11 June election of Mackenzie King's Liberals might have been expected to make a difference; it did not. Crerar had encouraged the soldiers of First Canadian Army to make their voices heard, but had not supported one party or the other. He hoped for a clear-cut majority, however, and predicted that King would win, making up in Quebec what he lost in other provinces. Crerar's hopes that the 'overseas soldiers' vote' would be heavy were fulfilled; the troops exacted some measure of revenge when theirs was the vote that unseated King. McNaughton also failed to gain a seat, handicapping his position as Minister of National Defence, a result that Crerar thought was best for both McNaughton, the army, and the 'national interest.' 'While I am deeply sorry, personally, for Andy,' he wrote his brother, 'if he had remained as Minister of Defence, the opposition would have "sniped" if not "bombarded" the Canadian Army continuously, in its endeavour to do Andy down. For the sake of the Canadian Army, I am glad that this is not to be.'[40]

If Crerar believed that the election would accelerate the decision making, he was wrong. Through June, purely as a result of the unexpected availability of some shipping, 15,665 men and women were sent home; some were short-service. More might have gone had Crerar's policy not required substantial reorganization, but the increase would not have been large. Frustrated, and perhaps wary of postwar judgments, Crerar and Montague decided on 1 July to place on record their views that the shipping allotment was insufficient and urging the Minister of National Defence to explore every avenue to increase it. It was sent on 2 July, two days after Crerar had made similar enquiries into his own repatriation. Crerar then took a three-day leave.

Canadian soldiers were similarly frustrated. On 4 and 5 July, riots broke out in Aldershot – disturbances that galvanized decision makers. The riots were a product of a general dissatisfaction with the perceived unfairness of the repatriation system, boredom, and the dispatch of the short-service personnel in June. The ringleaders were, however, soldiers with previous records for misconduct. Crerar saw it as a failure of leadership and as proof that the point system was decapitating his units. He was critical of CMHQ's and the CRU's response to the first disturbances and cautioned against overreacting. 'The great majority [of soldiers],' he noted, 'are good citizens and soldiers who regard these recent or any riots with extreme disfavour.' He resisted suggestions from Montague, Massey, and Montgomery that British troops might be necessary to restore order and prevent future disturbances; the situation should be 'resolutely and speedily handled' with Canadian resources. He hinted at the turmoil caused by his own policies when he said that at present the Canadian army in Holland had no units sufficiently organized to be of help.[41]

Crerar believed his commanders could do more to improve morale. On 7 July, he reissued to all commanders and commanding officers his memorandum on 'man-management'; the following day, he sent a memorandum directing their attention to the *First Canadian Army Handbook of Rehabilitation Training and Welfare* issued in April and, in particular, to the necessity of providing information 'or guidance' on citizenship, religion, rehabilitation, and demobilization. 'Incidentally,' he added, 'from the reports you receive concerning the daily discussions, you should be kept in close understanding of the current trends of thought amongst all ranks and so be greatly assisted in carrying out your present very important administrative responsibilities.' This was a thinly veiled criticism.[42]

The Aldershot disturbances occurred as Crerar and Montague were debating how best to handle the implications of a study indicating that the shipping allotments would allow them to repatriate fewer than 126,000 army and RCAF personnel before the end of 1945. Montague suggested that he and Crerar send a forcefully worded cable that would warn of the 'grave danger of widespread discontent before end of year' if troops became disappointed, comparing it to the relatively speedy U.S. demobilization. Montague called for a 'full disclosure of all the facts' on shipping negotiations. Crerar and Lister tempered Montague's more extreme statements but stressed that morale and discipline would decline if the average rate of repatriation were established at 30,000 troops a month. They resisted a full disclosure of information to the troops. They dispatched a five-page cable to Ottawa; implicit was the message that the overseas forces did not believe that NDHQ was pulling its weight in Ottawa, whether over shipping allotments or postwar army policy. Montague was already suspect in Ottawa, so his views were not well received. In 1943, even Stuart had characterized him as 'definitely disloyal to NDHQ which he represents in England.' Neither was Crerar popular in the minister's office. NDHQ's response was to distance itself from the problem by issuing a statement on 4 July that 'in spite of strong representations in London and Washington,' they might obtain shipping to repatriate fewer than 126,000 Army and RCAF men in the second half of 1945.[43]

The events of the first week in July produced a sense that the demobilization scheme was becoming unhinged. On 7 July, Crerar received a memorandum from Burns analyzing the plans for the Canadian Armoured Corps (CAC), Royal Canadian Artillery (RCA), Corps of the Royal Canadian Engineers (RCE), and Canadian Infantry Corps (CIC) to go back as units 'while other arms and services go back as drafts.' Initiated on the 3rd, it was highly critical of the policy. Burns believed that combination of a unit system and individual repatriation split along service lines would 'give rise to discontent.' He recommended that all arms go home on a unit basis with drafts of non-essential high-score personnel and 'semi-compassionate' cases repatriated 'with, or after each divisional group.'[44] Two more days of discussions with Montague and his staff prompted Crerar to act on Burns's recommendations to prevent further disturbances and discontent.

Crerar issued two edicts to stem the flow of volunteers and long-term service personnel, using Burns's memorandum to change the system of demobilization. On the 9th, he sent a message to Montague stating that, owing to 'shortages of experienced commissioned, warrant and non-commissioned officers,' it was necessary to temporarily stop the flow of volunteers to the CAPF. The next day, he gave notice that the 'individual priority system' of repatriation had reached 'its practicable limit.' He reasoned that if the 'acute shortages' of the 'present period of "repatriation by disintegration"' continued until then, it would 'not be possible adequately to maintain and administer the troops remaining in the country.' Using the information supplied in Burns's memorandum as a starting point, Crerar reasoned, that even though the long-service, 'high point' personnel were found in the administrative services, they should be the last released, while the low-point infantry should be first. He concluded by outlining the new approach to maintaining morale as the repatriation policy was changed. Its success would depend on the 'inspiration and leadership you show to all under your command.'[45] Crerar stressed the need for all commanders to explain to all ranks the need for the change. In case explanations were insufficient, he also authorized the formation of ad hoc units to assist the Canadian Provost Corps. Canadian divisional commanders were quietly requested to consider ways that 'practical assistance' could be rendered to the Dutch in reconstruction and agriculture.

It was no secret that Crerar preferred that the soldiers return by unit; on a personal and professional level, he believed it best balanced the needs of the army and the individual. At his insistence, this view had been stressed in the information distributed to the troops. It was made clear that the point system would eventually be discontinued. In early June, it was estimated that unit repatriation would commence once the CAPF and 30,000 long-service drafts had been dispatched; 'it is hoped it will be possible to commence the repatriation of units on 1 August 1945.'[46] Shipping problems, and the reorganization required by Crerar's insistence on units returning on a territorial basis, meant that by July this neat sequence was moot, but since there was no policy on when the change would occur, Crerar had tremendous discretionary power and exercised it. The timing suggests he was also genuinely concerned that his ability to maintain discipline was being affected.

It was a controversial decision. Morale was low throughout the summer, and Crerar's seemingly abrupt shift arguably pushed it even lower. Some studies demonstrate that in fact few long-service personnel had been sent home. Nevertheless, studies also demonstrate that the Aldershot disturbances were the worst excesses and that the army provided plenty of distractions.[47] In order to combat any further deterioration of morale, Crerar created policies to entice more officers to stay overseas: one tied promotions for warrant and non-commissioned officers to remaining overseas 'until services no longer required, regardless of point score.' Commanders of brigades and higher formations would also receive pay commensurate with acting rank, but not promotion. This reversed the previous policy that all promotions following Eclipse would continue as acting only in order to 'avoid "inflation" in staff gradings.'[48]

The growing chorus of discontent with the demobilization plan reached a crisis in mid-July when the Minister of Veterans Affairs, Ian Mackenzie, criticized Crerar for breaking 'Ottawa's pledge' and denounced, in an interview with Ross Munro, the army commander's policies for creating a 'split' in the army in Holland. Crerar was furious and dispatched a series of cables urging McNaughton or the Canadian government to silence Mackenzie, and 'act quickly to correct the misunderstanding which would be created by the publication of this interview.' Mackenzie was severely chastened by Mackenzie King and denounced in the press. His ill-chosen incursion could only fuel the dissatisfaction.[49]

Crerar's efforts to secure a formal decision on his own return paralleled the repatriation tempest. 'We are all getting into a terrific state of nerves and excitement at the thought of all our menfolk coming home,' wrote Peg in June 1945. This was a sentiment echoed by Crerar's friend

Ike Perley-Robertson: 'Look forward so much to seeing you again, and hearing your voice.' Sailing and fishing at Loon Island beckoned. 'It all seems rather like a dream,' he wrote John, 'and I won't believe it until it comes true.'[50] He believed that the repatriation scheme was, in its essentials, sound and that he could do no more. On 17 July, he observed, 'All things are very healthy here, so far, and I believe that everything will go smoothly once repatriation by units, rather than by drafts, commences.' He added, 'I believe that the time has now come when I can leave the remaining responsibilities here, to someone else, with a clear conscience on my part.'[51] The government acquiesced to Crerar's insistence that the it select a firm date for his departure, prompted perhaps by the discontent with the demobilization policy; 31 July was chosen.

Crerar's imminent departure drew Guy Simonds into the repatriation policy circle. He had been against a system based exclusively on repatriation by unit and formation, but recognized that administrative and operational needs had also to be addressed. Events in July and August confirmed the need to reconfigure the scheme. The system in August was 'chaotic' as the administrators struggled to re-post long-service soldiers to the 1st and 2nd divisions to ensure their early repatriation. Simonds, who took over as army commander when Crerar returned to Canada, amended the policy to repatriate the Canadian army, based on both long-service personnel and formations – a scheme similar to that proposed by Burns in early July. Simonds was fortunate that this amendment coincided with a dramatic increase in shipping as the Pacific War ended; the numbers repatriated, already exceeding expectations, increased – 33,775 were sent home in July. According to the official history, the strength of the overseas army on VE Day was 281,757 all ranks; by 31 December 1945, 184,054 had been shipped home.

Was Crerar's policy at the root of the problem? Partially. Simonds, while critical of Crerar's approach, pointed out the basic flaw had been the over-optimistic estimates of shipping allocation: 'Whilst length of service individuals would not, I believe, have been a contentious point had the return of the army to Canada been quicker, as matters stood, with a spread of nearly a year between the first and last troops to be repatriated, it assumed marked and urgent importance.'[52] What Crerar would have done – when in August it became clear that the transfer was an administrative nightmare – is open to conjecture. It is also difficult to determine the impact of gutting the administrative and command structure of the units that remained. In the end, Crerar, having been forced in 1919 to watch the dissipation of the costly expertise of the Canadian Corps, tried to craft a demobilization policy that would prevent that, while still addressing the needs of individuals, with limited success.

This proved to be Crerar's last policy struggle. On 19 July, he and Simonds met with his divisional COs to obtain progress reports on education, recreation, and training programs.[53] On 20 July, at Prince Bernhard's castle in Spledrop he was invested with the Grand Cross of the Order of Orange (a week later he had to get the prince to intervene to have his minister, a tenant, vacate Crerar's house; he had refused to leave before 31 August). The next day Crerar handed over command of the remaining Canadian forces in the Netherlands to Simonds. The headquarters was a shell of its former self. Mann had left some days before; Lister took over as dual Chief of Staff and DA and QMG – a dubious choice, as Lister would soon be court-marshalled for his involvement in black market activities. At 0930 on 21 July, almost two years to the day since the First Canadian Army Headquarters had become operational, Crerar left his Main Headquarters. In a slightly forced show of familiarity, he waved goodbye to the camp personnel who had been 'informally' assembled along the road.[54] Crerar spent a busy ten days in London. He attended numerous official functions, including investiture by the King with the Companion of Honour and the award of the Distinguished Service Medal by President Harry Truman. Allowed to take two guests, he took his batman Tom Macdonald and his driver Corporal Stuart Watson, to their surprise and delight. More poignant were the goodbyes to friends. Brooke, Sir Edward Peacock, the Masseys, Peter and Zouch attended luncheons and dinners at Claridge's. On his last day in London, he dined with Vincent Massey before boarding the train at 'bomb-shattered' Euston Station, waved on by some curious Londoners attracted by the Canadian Provost Guard; accompanied by Montague, he travelled in a private car to Glasgow. On 30 July, he boarded the *Isle de France* for Canada, retirement – and obscurity.

25 Fading Away

I

Harry Crerar died on 1 April 1965. A photograph of Crerar in the den of his Rockcliffe home accompanied one of the obituaries; it is a snapshot of the melancholy that characterized his final years. Still dapper in a thin black tie, white shirt, and suit coat, moustache neatly clipped, he sits in front of one of the two walnut display cabinets that showcased medals and souvenirs, a lifetime of memories and accomplishments. Autographed pictures of Ike, Monty, and other generals hang next to honorary degrees. A magnifying glass in one hand and an unidentified book in the other, with pictures of Queen Elizabeth and Prince Philip to his right, he self-consciously pretends to read, surrounded by the mementoes of his military life and the honours that that flowed from it.

As far the public was concerned, Harry Crerar faded into obscurity almost immediately upon his retirement. His influence was felt through his recommendations for the postwar CGS, and through the late 1940s he was still called on for diplomatic missions, and offered some chances to play a more active role in public service. For the sake of his wife, and, he argued, to obtain a wider influence, he refused. He wanted to devote himself to wider national causes. Crerar was not interested in narrow military affairs, as he defined the term. By the mid-1950s he became, not unlike the army, a shadow of his former self, surrounded by reminders of past glories but a marginal figure in the political capital of a country he had served for nearly thirty years. He was interviewed as much for his brushes with greatness as for his own achievements. Except for a few minor diplomatic missions, Crerar was largely a forgotten figure, eventually rendered an anachronism by his public pronouncements in favour of conscription, military education, and a reverence for civic education – ideas that were out of tune with the country's development.

Crerar's return was low key. The *Isle de France*'s journey across the Atlantic from Glasgow to Halifax was notable for introducing Crerar on a personal level to thousands of Canadian troops. He was at his best: relaxed, humble, thoughtful, and open. The media played up the contrast between his stature and his humility, quoting his insights on leadership, the war, and its impact on Canadian troops; they were thirsty for anything that would allow them to describe to Canadians the man who had led their army. 'The people of Canada do not know Harry Crerar well,' wrote Lee Shapiro for his CBC broadcast. 'He was always loath to fill the spotlight and as a result no sharp facets of his character sparkled on the home front.'[1]

On board ship, Crerar exuded the persona of the citizen-soldier. He took pains to ensure that his presence on board did not interfere with the normal informality of repatriation voyages. Rumours that sunbathing would be banned because of Crerar's presence were squashed when Crerar stripped off his shirt and set up on deck. Flanked by Church Mann and Geoffrey Walsh, he took his meals in the huge mess with 2,000 other officers.

In his talks with reporters and in his one shipboard lecture, he was optimistic about the future, more optimistic than his letters suggest. He spoke of how the soldiers were returning home as better Canadians, and citizens – themes that would become a mantra in future addresses. 'When you think of how much more those chaps are Canadians,' he told Shapiro, 'how much less they are Nova Scotians or British Columbians, you can't help feel anything but good come out of it.' He also reminded his listeners that in 'the midst of our rejoicing' they should remember that 'we leave many thousands of the best of our breed buried in Europe, to the families and sweethearts of those who died, our return must revive thoughts of their own men, whom they will never be able to welcome.'[2]

On 5 August, the ship docked in Halifax. The ceremony to greet him had been organized for maximum effect. Among the assembled political and military dignitaries, stood Verse and Peg, as he had requested; reporters described the scene as Harry Crerar stood on the captain's bridge, 'high above the boat deck ... a gray, thoughtful man': 'As the hilly outline of Halifax took shape when the transport nosed into the harbour there was a tension aboard that could almost be felt ... There was no cheering at first, but that came later.'[3]

Verse and Peg came on board to greet him, followed at a respectable distance by the reception committee. A few weeks earlier, Crerar had described his anxiety that they be the first to meet him: 'It will certainly be pretty thrilling to see the two of you again.' After a brief luncheon, he walked down the gangplank, cheered by the troops aboard the ship, to receive the keys to the city. He returned to the gangplank, 'not to salute in response to continued cheering – but to doff his hat to the cheering men and women ... it was a gesture full of humility and warm friendliness.'[4]

Crerar's homecoming was overshadowed by the dropping of the atomic bomb on Hiroshima and the end of the war in the Pacific. The press praised him, although not lavishly, obviously enjoying their access to the reserved soldier. His train wound its way to Ottawa, stopping at major centres in New Brunswick and Quebec, greeted at every town by eager local dignitaries and veterans. In Moncton, he arranged a quiet visit with Mrs Boyd Anderson, the widow of a colleague since the First World War. After he arrived in Ottawa on the seventh, the plaudits continued: a guard of honour met him at Union Station, a victory parade down Wellington and Elgin, and despite the rain, curious onlookers mixed with cheering crowds. There were laudatory speeches by the Prime Minister and gathered dignitaries. He met with the press at National Defence Headquarters in the Woods Building. Reporters described him as 'genial, tanned and relaxed'; puffing on his briar, he kept the meeting light and humorous. He praised the NRMA men who had served overseas, but made no comment on conscription. He refused to be drawn into making comments on policy and past decisions but expressed himself forcefully on the potential mental and physical benefits of peacetime training, while urging his audience to remember the dead. He was, by accounts, 'charming and gracious.'[5]

The Crerars spent just one day in Ottawa before heading north to the Muskokas and the sanctuary of Loon Island, a day spent preparing for the trip and lunching at the Rideau Club with Walford, Weir, and his old friend Ike Perley-Robertson. He held an informal reception at his home in Rockcliffe, while the telegrams and letters of congratulations, later carefully documented and filed, poured in. As planned, Harry and Verse left for one month of relaxation, fishing, sailing, and golfing.

Crerar returned to Ottawa on 8 September. Both physically and professionally he was 'on the sidelines,' a general without an army or a staff appointment. He was sequestered in a small office in the Bates Building.

In December, he met with the minister to discuss the postwar army, but there is little evidence that he had any significant influence on its shape. There is evidence that the animosities between himself and National Defence Headquarters lingered: in a calculated slight, his personal caravan unit was unceremoniously dispatched to London, Ontario (where it sat for almost thirty-five years), despite his desire to showcase it as a symbol of a united Canadian army. Crerar had manoeuvred around orders from NDHQ that no personal military vehicles were to be returned to Canada, arguing disingenuously that it might be required by some future formation commander and later that as a historical artifact it could be used for publicity and then as a museum piece. According to one account, when the office of the Minister of National Defence and the CGS learned of the arrival of 'eleven tons of the General's personal vehicles ... the order to have the lot shipped to London, Ontario (CMD) for disposal was issued "before Crerar [could] get his hands on it."' Crerar was 'furious,' but it underlined the changing of the guard, and the distance between Ottawa and its overseas command.[6]

Crerar had hoped the caravan would accompany him on his last official duty: a cross-country tour. With a growing number of requests for appearances, speeches, and addresses, Crerar wrote the Minister of National Defence and, with his permission, organized a farewell tour of the country. It was intended as a goodbye to the troops before he retired, and as means of drawing attention to deeply held convictions regarding the impact of the war and its consequences for Canada. 'I am trying to plant a few ideas of mine in the minds of my fellow countrymen,' he wrote Monty in December 1945.[7] He also wanted to publicize the Canadian army's record. Several of his initiatives, including a DND-sponsored lecture series in major Canadian cities, based on Mann's report on the campaign in northwest Europe, had already been rebuffed, but Crerar was not deterred.[8]

It was an exhaustive six-week tour, particularly as it followed a packed fall schedule of addresses to clubs, universities, and veterans associations. It began in Montreal and then crept west, via London and Windsor. The Crerars – accompanied by Weir at Crerar's request – spent almost a fortnight on the West Coast, dipping into California to visit Harry's sister, before beginning the train journey back to Ottawa via Edmonton.[9] Crerar ordered it extensively documented; statistics were compiled on attendance, venues, and miles covered. 'It has been a hard grind,' he wrote Sir Edward Peacock, 'and I am relieved that it is now all over. My only hope is that it was worth the effort.' Officially, it was well received. The odd street was named in his honour, and in Toronto, the day of his visit on 7 November was declared a civic holiday; it was a half-day, however. One reporter described the crowd's reaction in Toronto: 'The 10,000 who turned out were enthusiastic to be sure, but even civic officials were a little abashed that Toronto people didn't turn out in larger numbers.' He blamed this on a breakdown by Army Public Relations, concluding that 'many in the crowd admitted that they didn't even know the general was coming until he actually drove up Bay Street.' When they saw 'who it was they let go and gave General Crerar a roar of welcome.'[10]

The ideas Crerar wanted to plant differed only in degree from his long-held views on citizenship, personal and collective responsibility, the national benefits of compulsory service, and the human condition. The titles of his talks suggest the message: 'Discipline and Democracy,' 'Character in War and Peace,' 'Civic Education and Military Preparedness,' 'Some Thoughts on War and Peace,' 'Principle and Policies of the First Canadian Army.' Having lived through two world wars, Crerar spoke passionately of the lessons he believed had emerged from the conflicts. He remained wary of humanity's capacity for 'evil' and the unceasing 'fight between good and evil'; more specifically, he believed that the Soviet Union posed an immense threat to the peace. Measures for defence had to be maintained. He returned time and time again to his view that a public, informed and educated in its civic responsibilities, was critical to supporting this policy. He pleaded with his audiences to remember the recent past.[11] He believed that in the future Canada would not have the luxury of slowly rearming. Canada's strategic position had changed. While Crerar remained an advocate of the commonwealth connection, he believed that 'Great Britain is not now able to furnish adequate military protection for itself – let alone other portions of the Commonwealth.' Time and space no longer 'insulated' Canada from the effects of European and Pacific wars.[12] Civic education was the answer to prewar 'ignorance' and 'selfishness.' He described to each audience the impact of such education on the men and women who had served in the army; he also praised the physical and mental benefits that service, and the resulting medical examinations, had brought.

In Crerar's opinion, these ex-soldiers were Canada's future and he believed it was in safe hands: 'In the men and women who previously served in the Canadian Army, Canada possesses its greatest national assets.'[13] How then could Canada safeguard itself against future aggressors, retain the initiative so evident in the returning soldiers, and continue to produce outstanding citizens who thought of the nation first and the country second? Peacetime compulsory service was the prescription for all three.[14] It would be, in short, a 'national education.'

The human cost of inadequate defence measures was the explicit motive for Crerar's position. His exposure to the nation in arms as the army commander also informed his postwar activity and thoughts, and underlined his insularity from the experience of the majority of Canadian citizens. The condition of the 'average' Canadian soldiers – their lack of education, knowledge of national and international affairs, and poor physical condition – came as a shock to his upper-middle-class sensibilities.

> Every man was medically examined ... if accepted, it was often on the basis of subsequent medical correction, or cure, of some physical defect. In many cases, the men, themselves, had no knowledge of the existence of this defect ... The amount of dental work which was found necessary to carry out on a very high proportion of enlisted men, before they could be regarded as fit, was quite staggering.[15]

He had been similarly appalled at the lack of knowledge on national and international questions that the civic education classes had revealed. During the war, for probably the first time in twenty years, Harry Crerar, having left the closed communities of Kingston and Ottawa, became familiar with average Canadians, and he hadn't liked what he saw. He was determined to use his new public profile to change it. He maintained a middle-class faith in the power of education, and these views shaped his post-retirement public life.

At first glance, it is easy to dismiss Crerar as an anachronism, but his views on citizenship were sincerely held and they had a certain appeal. 'He looked so serious,' recalled Henry Tellier after one talk in Montreal. For Crerar, a good soldier was a good citizen.[16] Many of the collective values he espoused touched a chord with a significant body of elite opinion and resonated among many who also advocated the benefits of compulsory service and civic education. The mood in the country was upbeat and buoyant, but also apprehensive that the future might be fumbled. Anything seemed possible. The media response to his tour and to Crerar himself was overwhelmingly positive. One Winnipeg city official explained that in addition to receiving him as an individual, they were also receiving him 'as a symbol of the Canadian Army.'[17] The time spent visiting veterans hospitals and individual soldiers also raised his stock. 'I think it would please you to know,' wrote one doctor in Vancouver, 'that your visit and talks with the troops pleased the latter very much and I have heard that one Navy type was surprised to find that you were "quite human."'[18]

Crerar began his retirement leave on 31 March 1946; he was struck off the strength of the Canadian Army on 27 October 1946. He had made this decision privately in February and it had been public knowledge since May 1946, but at that point it was only a question of timing. When asked by a reporter why he proposed to retire at the height of his career, Crerar replied, 'I have completed the course. There are younger men, good men, brilliant men the Canadian army has developed in this war. I don't see why I should stand as a bottleneck to their promotion in the service.'[19] This was only part of the reason, but it fitted well with Crerar's public image, or the one that was being constructed for him, at war's end.

The truth was more personal: Crerar wanted to rebuild his relationship with Verse, spend time with his family, and restore his own flagging health. He wanted a home. He had no desire to be a public figure and denied repeatedly that he wanted to enter politics or the diplomatic service. In 1946, he was Mackenzie King's third choice as lieutenant-governor of Ontario; he turned it down, as King suspected he would.[20] That same year it was rumoured that Crerar would succeed Vincent Massey as high commissioner in London; it proved untrue, but Crerar hinted that he would refuse the offer in any case. In March 1947, George Drew, then premier of Ontario, proposed that Crerar assume the chairmanship of the Ontario Hydro Commission. To work for his pre-army career employer and the creation of his beloved brother-in-law Sir Adam Beck, was the most appealing offer he received. He nevertheless turned it down. In 1953, the ambassadorship to Spain was rumoured to be his, but nothing came of it. 'The fundamental factor,' he wrote, 'is a promise to my wife, made some years ago that if I survived the recent war, I would settle down with her at long last, in Ottawa in the house which I built ... In our 30 years of married life, we never previously had a home of our own and as well, for ten years of that period, we had been separated.'[21]

Crerar's health was also precarious. He was not well when he took his leave of the army. The strain of the previous six years was evident from pictures; he had aged considerably. 'I have now reached the age of 57,' he wrote his 'best friend' Ike Perley-Robertson in May, 'and my intention is to live my remaining life under much less strenuous conditions than I have been up against during the last half dozen years.'[22]

Postwar life was very different for the Crerars. Finances and lifestyle were concerns. At the end of the war, Crerar tried to secure his retirement, but his approach to financial recognition for his services was informed by the characteristic distaste for the appearance, not the substance, of direct individual reward. He wrote Perley-Robertson, asking him to block any attempts to award him a special pension or cash payment – a British practice. He would refuse them and wanted to avoid any embarrassment to the government or himself. This was posturing, to a degree. 'On the other hand,' he wrote, 'I do not think it would be inappropriate if the Government desired to show its appreciation in certain indirect ways.'

> For instance, I would think it reasonable if the Government came to the conclusion that it would exempt my pension from Federal Income Tax. Again, the Government might show its recognition, indirectly, by maintaining my house in good repair and looking after my garden during my lifetime, along the lines its pursues in the case of Rideau Hall. Further, I believe that it is due me that the Government should look after my medical and dental care during the balance of my lifetime as I have certainly taken a good deal of health out of myself during the last few years on behalf of the country. If it is decided that I should be allotted a 'soldier-servant' during the balance of my life, this also would be reasonable and a possible great assistance – especially now when domestic servants will be so hard to come by.

He saw no irony when he added, 'I give you the above because, naturally, I do not intend to ask for anything whatsoever.'[23] Certainly the Canadian government felt no compulsion to reward its military leaders, and many of its soldiers.

Finances were, at least in Crerar's opinion, uncertain for much of the postwar period. His tax-exemption did not materialize, and the offers of directorships that he hoped would supplement his income were scattered and infrequent. The costs of his appearances were a constant preoccupation. This situation gradually improved. By 1951, he was on the boards of Barclay's Bank, Cockshutt Plow, and the Guarantee Company of North America; other less profitable directorships were turned down. His 'knowledge and experience of organization, and of Canada' heightened his appeal.²⁴ He tried to secure an appointment to the Senate, a decision prompted by economic as well as public service considerations, but was unsuccessful.

The Crerars' domestic lifestyle also reflected the new postwar realities and provided a sharp contrast with the social responsibilities of the interwar period. In the fall of 1945, the search for 'live-in domestics' proved difficult and was symptomatic of the postwar reality. 'As the house parlour-maid whom we had "walked-out" the day before the first function took place, there were certain domestic difficulties to overcome in the home, and Verse swears that it will take her another six months to recover her nerve sufficiently to have any further entertainments in the house.'²⁵

As a former army commander, Crerar faced a steady stream of requests for favours, ranging from referrals to finances. Philanthropy remained important for the Crerars, both institutional and individual, but he preferred to contribute without fanfare. He rarely refused a request and used his connections to help many. In 1947, he enlisted Tommy Burns as Assistant Deputy Minister of Veterans Affairs to help break the bureaucratic red tape that was preventing a young Polish veteran who had served in First Canadian Army from obtaining domicile status; by 1948, he had helped ten Polish veterans and their families gain admittance to Canada. Pearson noted that Crerar's 'good offices' were important in getting immigration to 'budge.'²⁶ He contributed money as well as time to a large number of youth and veterans organizations: UCC, Carleton College, the Ottawa Community Chest, the Toronto Artillery Welfare Fund – these and others were rarely refused. Compensation over and above expenses for addresses and articles was donated to charitable causes. National and local causes benefited from his fundraising abilities. He wrote references for many associated with him during the war, and before he retired, he sent a letter to the Adjutant-General urging him to look after them. One example: Finlay Morrison went on to the University of Saskatchewan where he was nominated for the Governor General's Medal; Crerar later noted Morrison was a 'first class character ... he never let me down in the two years he was with me.'²⁷

Family life, however, was Harry Crerar's number one priority. He was making up for lost time. Summers were spent with his sister at Loon Island; bass fishing, golf, and sailing – 'my favourite sport' – filled most of the time. In the summer of 1946, he proudly trumpeted his and his brother's win of the local sixteen-foot annual race. He and Verse worked clearing new trails, often going their separate ways, meeting for meals or to do some fishing. He took week-long fishing excursions with Ike Perley-Robertson, hiking and playing bridge into the night. He fussed over the slow but steady increase in his waistline and worried about Ike's health. The Maple Leafs, flourishing under Conn Smythe, regained his attention; he dropped the puck to launch their 1948–9 season. He continued to read broadly. History – on his return from Canada he ploughed through Trevelyan's *English Social History* – and politics were his favourites for serious reading, while he devoured pulp fiction at night.[28] He also became interested in the Clan Chattan, exploring his Scottish heritage and joining the clan association, prompted in part by Peter's wartime visits to Crieff. He renewed his Hamilton associations, attending 8th Field Regiment Mess dinners and visiting old acquaintances.

A favourite nearly annual trip was Nassau, while New York was a convenient stopover for shopping and the theatre. He did not see as much of his extended family as he would have liked. Summers were the times for family gatherings in the Muskokas. They became more important as the family scattered. Zouch Palmer had decided against a career in the armed forces. 'My son-in-law ... is stationed in Toronto,' he wrote an old friend in 1946, 'and has a good job in the CBC so we do not see much of that particular portion of the family. My son ... at present ... is staying with my sister in California.'[29] Harry Crerar's relationship with his son seemed strained.[30] As the war drew to a close, Crerar had urged him to stay in the service. In July 1945, Peter reluctantly wrote his father of his decision to return to civilian life: 'This was a very hard letter to write you,' he noted. After some time in Khaki University, he moved south to California to live with Violet Gallagher. This was unexpected.[31] Peter was, however, suspicious of any help from his father; he remained in the States, striking out on his own, but returning for summers in the Muskokas.

II

Crerar remained committed to public service, even if he had no desire to devote all of his time to it. At Crerar's retirement, his public profile and standing was at an all-time high. His former colleagues heaped praise on his achievements. Ralston wrote an embarrassingly glowing letter extolling his admiration for Crerar's 'character, ... thorough grounding in principles, ... power to command, and ... tidy mind.'[32] He was awarded honorary degrees by seven universities, including Queen's, McGill, Toronto, and Oxford. The usual decorations flowed in from Poland, Belgium, and France, twenty-seven in total. Even Stalin wanted to award the Canadian commander, an offer almost sunk by the Gouzenko affair. Crerar had much goodwill from the population, if only because his public image was so freshly minted.

Through the late 1940s, Crerar remained an active if marginal figure in Ottawa international affairs circles. He returned to England in June 1946 for the victory parade; in October 1946, he was invited to Czechoslovakia for investiture with three awards. The government approved the trip on the recommendation by External Affairs that a Canadian visit to a country within the Soviet sphere of influence would be 'significant.' Crerar recorded his observations for the Department of External Affairs and the Minister of National Defence. The report was brief, but suggested that Crerar had lost none of his powers of observation and insight into international affairs. He concluded that Prague should be a 'high priority for the establishment of a Canadian Legation,' as Prague was a key 'international "listening post,"' because it was there 'that all repercussions between the Soviet, US, and UK policies and ambitions [were] most quickly felt, and most closely examined.' His observations were distributed to Canadian embassies in Washington and Paris and to the High Commissioner.[33]

The available evidence suggests that Crerar's prestige remained moderately high. Pearson called on him for several minor but important diplomatic missions. In 1947, the necessity of formulating a policy on the peace settlement in the Pacific prompted a Commonwealth Conference in Canberra in August. DND and Lester Pearson, recently appointed Under Secretary of State for External Affairs, sent him to the Far East as the senior member of a Canadian Mission that included Brigadier-General Sherwood Lett, a request that Crerar accepted only reluctantly, as it 'quite upset summer arrangements for the entire family' and forced him to leave Verse at home. Pearson also sent Crerar to T.C. Davis, Canada's ambassador to China, in response to a request to send Canadian fleet units as a measure of Canada's intent to secure good relations with the Chinese: '[An RCAF Liberator] was the best we could do this year, but I think it was money well spent to send Crerar to the Far East in state ... he is having a busy and profitable time in Nanking.'[34] Crerar's detailed report on Japan was insightful and confident;

he encouraged the normalization of relations as soon as possible. His summation of the character and impact of General Douglas McArthur was masterful. He was in his element.[35]

While in China, Crerar visited Hong Kong's Sai Wan War Cemetery. He was appalled at its condition. Many of the dead remained 'unknown,' and the condition of the site contrasted sharply with that of the nearby British cemeteries. Crerar sent a scathing report to Minister of National Defence Brooke Claxton, urging that every effort be made to address the 'very unsatisfactory situation.' NDHQ responded to Crerar's letter by launching an investigation headed by the Adjutant-General E.G. Weeks, which concluded that little could be done. Crerar insisted, however, that until medical experts 'gave assurances that further identification of individual remains was impossible,' the matter should be left open. He tried to point out that the proportion of unidentified British dead was much smaller – a situation that would 'not pass unnoticed.'[36]

It was a prescient observation; in 1948, a political storm erupted when the London *Gazette* reprinted a 1945 report on the operations conducted at Hong Kong in December 1941 written by the GOC, Major-General Maltby, which was highly critical of the Canadian troops, characterizing them as 'inadequately trained for modern war.' The report, published in January, led to Opposition calls for the King government to make public the evidence used by the Duff Commission to reach its conclusions in 1942. Claxton consulted Crerar on the propriety of releasing this information, but he was largely a bystander, albeit a very interested one. He had been told of the report in the summer of 1946 when it was first brought to the attention of Foulkes as CGS; the British intended to publish it, but were convinced by Foulkes, following discussions with Montgomery, to excise the most offensive paragraphs. Maltby's interpretation of the Canadian troops was self-serving at best, and untrue according to the recollection of other imperial troops and the Japanese themselves. In 1948, Foulkes was against raising the issue once again. The report generated some controversy in Parliament but remained largely a non-issue outside of Ottawa.[37] Crerar left no evidence of his reaction, but his displeasure with the first draft of the Hong Kong chapter of the official history that emphasized the problems with the troops rather than the terrain revealed his sensitivity to the issue.

Crerar continued to represent Canada on a variety of missions. In 1948, he was the Special Ambassador at the enthronement of Queen

Juliana of the Netherlands. He was hesitant, stating that he would go only if accompanied by his wife, fulfilling a promise to take her to the scenes of the Canadians' final battles made when he had turned down her request to come over in 1945. The government accepted this condition and, in September 1948, the Crerars represented Canada at the coronation and revisited the battle sites in France and Belgium, stopping, by one account, at over thirty war graves cemeteries. 'It was very apparent that [a] feeling of friendship and admiration for Canada and Canadians is spread wide and goes deep,' he reported. 'Roars of applause for "Canada" ... developed whenever the car in which I was travelling moved slowly enough for the people to recognize the Canadian flag.' Henri Tellier, who accompanied Crerar at his request as his ADC, recalled one gathering: 'It was a standing ovation as the Canadian car circled the track. Respect and gratitude for Canadian soldiers, yes. But, also recognition and affection for General Crerar.'[38]

III

Canada was a country very different from the one that had gone to war in 1939. The war had launched Canada towards its mid-twentieth century form as an urbanized, industrial, North American nation, but the late 1940s and 1950s were a period when Canadians struggled with their new identity and position in the world. Underlying the confidence epitomized by the 'Golden Age' of External Affairs was a fear of American influence and culture. The establishment of the Massey Commission reflected the turmoil present in the transition from semi-dependence on Britain to a North American nation, and the fear for the next stage was semi-dependence on the United States.

For those interested in defence and foreign policy, the transition provided opportunities for a change in the way Canada approached defence policy; others believed that the struggle between Communist Russia and the United States left Canada little choice but to alter its ways. In the first years after the war, Crerar adhered to both views. His calls became more strident and direct as the Soviet Union became more aggressive in Europe and Asia. His trips abroad in 1947 and 1948 cemented a belief that a Third World War was possible, and even probable, if Germany and Japan were not revived economically and if the United States and Canada continued their withdrawal from Europe. His calls for peacetime military service became calls for rearmament. He characterized as folly the belief that the atomic bomb made conventional wars obsolete. Crerar believed that the unity evident during the war had given way to 'selfishness, wishful thinking and diversity.' He remained hopeful, however, that Canadians were 'inclined to be much more realistic in their international outlook than twenty-five years ago.'[39] Crerar did not think the United Nations provided the model for solving these problems. His addresses on the topic of the imperial link stressed the commonwealth connection as a model for Canada's future international relations but he acknowledged, reluctantly, that the commonwealth's time had past.[40]

By the late 1940s, he believed that public opinion must be changed through a better understanding of defence issues. He was an increasingly vocal proponent for civic education and the promotion of a better understanding of Canada.[41] In 1947, he joined the Canada Foundation, whose basic objective was to promote at home and abroad an understanding of the 'life and thought of the Canadian people.' In 1948, he accepted the chairmanship of the Canadian Citizenship Council, a voluntary organization formed in 1941 that coordinated the activities of public and private agencies dedicated to national improvement. The Sports College, directed at young Canadians, was also a favourite cause.

Crerar's opinions had no direct impact on Canadian defence policies, in part because he marginalized himself. In 1945, he removed his name from the Ottawa telephone directory. To his former colleagues, he stressed that he wanted his 'whereabouts in Ottawa a secret from the majority.' But remaining on the sidelines was a struggle. 'I am very much on the "sideline,"' he wrote Church Mann in October 1945, 'so far as the present and future plans of the Canadian Army are concerned. Perhaps the Government will request my views ... but as I have no official responsibility for the future, it is only proper that I should not now "butt in."'[42] Crerar wanted less to distance himself from the military than to seek a more suitable and less restrictive means to influence the public debate on defence policy. Crerar's correspondence files suggest that through 1945 and 1946 his contacts with Foulkes were limited to the latter's concerns that he was being 'discriminated' against for Belgian and American awards.

Yet, when opportunities arose to play an active role within the defence establishment, Crerar refused. In 1946, Church Mann proposed that Crerar take on the editorship of the *Canadian Defence Quarterly* in an attempt to revive it; he turned him down.[43] He would not speak on defence policy to the National Defence College, refusing an invitation in 1950. Similarly, Crerar generally remained aloof from the postwar efforts to reopen the Royal Military College and reshape its future. In 1947, he was critical of the compromise plan – university cadets would train at RMC over three summers, graduates of the new RCN school at Royal Roads would finish their programs at RMC, and graduates of all officer training programs could 'choose between regular and reserve commissions.'[44] But Crerar was generally quiet on the issue, although he suggested that he never doubted it would reopen when invited to address the RMC Club in 1948.[45] Despite some criticism, Crerar maintained that no policy for officer training could have been made until the government announced the size and shape of the postwar army.[46]

While publicly maintaining his distance from official policy debates, Crerar expected that 'unofficial' consultations on either military issues or those of 'national character' would be in order. When he turned down Mackenzie King's offer of public office, Crerar noted he was happy to submit his ideas in this respect, an offer that King turned aside. He made similar overtures to External Affairs in his report on his visit to Czechoslovakia.

The Canadian government was not interested in Crerar's advice on the necessity of conscription – whether presented as compulsory peacetime training or not. The high hopes that characterized the Canadian military's postwar plans for a large professional force to carry out Canada's new commitment to international peace were dashed by the King government's traditional antipathy to defence expenditures. In June 1945, the government rejected the service proposals for a permanent force of 105,788 men supplemented by nearly 300,000 reservists and auxiliaries, and conscription. There would be no compulsory military service, nor would the proposed establishment of between 45,000 and 55,000 require it. While this force was substantially larger than the prewar regular military, it symbolized the return of the Canadian military and defence policy to the margins of the political process. The Cold War changed that.

By 1947 there was an interested, if limited, constituency for Crerar's views on defence policy. In January 1947, former wartime correspondent Ralph Allan, now an editor, invited him to write an article for *Maclean's* on Canada's position in the international arena. He agreed, but insisted that the fee be paid to a disabled veterans organization. 'War Is a Prospect Canada Must Face' appeared in the 15 July 1947 issue. It was a harsh criticism of the government's defence policy, which reiterated Crerar's calls for compulsory service, stressing that this would help, not harm, a young person's future prospects. He also praised the military's attempts at administrative integration and their emphasis on weapon's development. The military needed to go further, however; a bilingual army built on the training provided by inter-service college was a crucial step. The RCAF's role should be limited to tactical support and the RCN restricted to escort and reconnaissance. The strength of the U.S. Navy and the current missile technology made a 'big ship' navy and 'big bomber' air force redundant. His statements were unlikely to win him many friends outside of the army.

The public response, measured by letters to the editor, was limited and generally negative. 'Peace is a prospect Canada must face,' wrote a Saskatchewan resident. 'We mothers do not intend raising children for cannon fodder every generation.' The magazine received more responses damning a Blair Fraser satire that hinted that Sir John A. Macdonald was gay and the use of the 'semi-nude women' in a bathing suit on the 15 July cover. The country was reluctant to think of war so soon after 1945; the juxtaposition of the *Maclean's* cover featuring a bathing suit–clad women relaxing near a pool with the corner box displaying 'War Is a Prospect Canada Must Face' as the feature article showed even the editors recognized that.[47]

Undaunted, Crerar believed that Canadians must think of war. From 1947 through 1951, Crerar launched a heavy schedule of talks and addresses on the need to rearm and compulsory service. 'I believe that if unpleasant facts are repeatedly and frankly made public there can be created a wide public support of policies suitable to solve a threatened crisis,' he wrote in 1950. 'I wasn't able to [rouse public opinion] because of my position prior to World War II but will attempt to do so now.'[48] In many cases, he was preaching to the converted. Canadian clubs and military institutes provided his main audiences. He orchestrated his schedule of addresses to maximize their impact. He sent copies of his talks to the major urban dailies, the *Montreal Gazette* for example, and national news magazines like *Saturday Night*. This ensured steady, if not enthusiastic, coverage of his position. By the outbreak of the Korean War, Crerar's virulent attacks on government defence policy masked an even deeper private pessimism. 'The international situation has gravely deteriorated since last September – and God knows it was bad enough then,' he wrote the Legion's Dominion President Alfred Watts. 'And yet we in Canada, have yet to face up to and take emphatic steps to meet this Third World War which *we are now in*' (Crerar's emphasis).[49] Crerar's efforts peaked in 1950–1. Wartime connections proved important in this respect. Ralph Allan, by 1950 an editor at *Maclean's*, encouraged Crerar to comment on conscription, but he declined, oddly citing a fear that if he spoke out too much, the public would be given the 'impression ... of me drawing attention to my own sagacity.' In 1951, the former historical officer at First Canadian Army headquarters, Eric Harrison, now a professor of history at Queen's University, secured Crerar to author 'The Case for Conscription' for *Queen's Quarterly*. Coming in the middle of the defence policy crisis prompted by the Korean War, the article attracted some limited attention. Editorial opinion was split; his harshest critics were at the *Toronto Star*, but even *Maclean's* editorials were generally opposed to 'alarmist' statements and against conscription. Others noted that his emphasis on youth and youth organizations 'put a completely new spin on [the] conscription proposal.' Despite his talks, one supporter characterized him as too 'remote from the national scene.'[50]

Crerar was more direct in his involvement with veterans. In June 1948, Crerar accepted the position of 'Grand President' of the Canadian Legion, a position he was re-elected to until his death in 1965. His crosscountry tour in 1945–6 had raised the hopes of some veterans that they had a high-level spokesman. 'The feeling [among the men] is that they have a real friend,' wrote one Legion representative describing the reaction to Crerar's address in Ottawa in 1945, 'who will always look after their interests.'[51] They may have been disappointed. Crerar used his appointment to encourage the Legion to lobby the defence establishment; indeed, he argued that this was its primary objective. Veterans' rehabilitation and friendship should be second and third priorities. While the Legion's primary responsibility remained assisting disabled veterans, the 1950 Winnipeg National Convention adopted Operation Preparedness to encourage the government to establish means for a national registration, mobilization of national resources, and compulsory military training. Crerar allowed his name and quotes to be used in the documents sent to the Prime Minister and Minister of National Defence.[52]

IV

Eric Harrison of Queen's had also been trying – unsuccessfully – to have Crerar write his memoirs, or at least to have him sanction some form of biography. Crerar was reluctant to do so, however; he believed that his actions might prejudice his efforts to change defence policy. Similarly, he refused to raise issues that might hurt any living officer. He held this view until he died. He had already declined an approach in 1946 by the London publishing company Hutchinson and Company, then aggressively courting wartime leaders, to write his memoirs; the same cloak of privacy that Crerar drew around his life informed his approach to his memoirs. As the years went on, however, the tension between his respect for the reputations of others and his desire to ensure, and shape, his place in history was evident.

As the Cold War heated up, however, he believed that his observations on the interwar years were increasingly relevant. In 1948, he asked the associate editor of the *Ottawa Journal*, I. Norman Smith, to assist him in editing his interwar papers and addresses for publication. Smith declined, citing his lack of expertise. Crerar persisted, however, in a revealing note.

> As a matter of fact, I would much prefer that it should not be another 'soldier' who would undertake an assessment of the public value of my previously written, or spoken, thoughts. The public value of these, if it exists, lies not in the technical, military expressions of opinion but, rather, in the fundamentals of policy, strategy, leadership and organization. I would much rather trust the judgement of someone such as yourself, for instance, in these matters of enduring and general importance than that of a member of my own profession![53]

Crerar tried to promote the publication of his interwar papers as a compromise solution to a memoir and tried without success to solicit funding to publish them. '[They] give a background to my thinking and the reasons for my decisions and actions in the later Second World War,' he wrote Harrison. 'I believe that a study of them would, anyway, be rather important before anything dealing with 1939–45 was actually written.'[54] He continued to resist all efforts to encourage him to write his memoirs, although the pressure mounted in the late 1940s and early 1950s, as the senior command of the Allied nations rushed their versions of the key campaigns into print. Crerar was too conscious of embarrassing any fellow officers. In 1951, Kim Beattie, a long-time admirer, reacted to the publication of Bradley's memoirs: 'I suppose you are right about refusing to do the same thing all the American generals are doing ... but it is infuriating to be forced to watch your remoteness from the national scene.' He acknowledged, however, that he agreed with Crerar's comments on Bradley's book, 'something to the effect that it only revealed "Generals should shut up."'[55]

Crerar's desire to situate his legacy increased as his influence decreased. From 1954, Harrison and Crerar worked on his papers in hopes of publishing them in some manner. Crerar felt the pressure of time as his health declined and was conscious of the historical record, but remained committed to keeping his silence while many of his colleagues were active. By 1958, the political climate and personnel had changed enough for Crerar to contemplate authorizing a biography, but nothing was done. He was actively seeking a biographer when he died. Verse, acting on his behalf, continued to restrict access to his papers. She instructed Stacey that while he and James Eayrs had full access to his papers, they should exercise caution, as Crerar 'attached particular importance to avoiding the publication of facts from his papers which might be embarrassing to ... individual officers who are still living.'[56]

Crerar was generous with his papers, despite his reservations, and they were meticulously organized – an indirect approach to shaping the historical record. Stacey and G.W.L. Nicholson both called upon Crerar, as well as the other senior commanders, to review drafts of the official histories. Crerar's main contributions to the histories were his personal papers; Stacey had full access to everything else. The army commander wanted a 'recounting of the facts,' although he admitted that going through the drafts 'makes tragic reading at times.' 'The events of that period,' he wrote Stacey in 1956, 'make painful reminiscences to a number of persons. However, it is history that you are writing and I do not see how these matters can be left out.'[57] Yet Crerar urged Stacey to remove personal references to officers still living.

Crerar hoped the official histories would elevate the Canadian army's role during the war from the marginal position it was being relegated to by the contemporary historiography and provide a substitute for his memoirs in highlighting his own contribution. He exhorted Stacey to bring out the myriad difficulties that the Canadian army encountered on the left flank throughout the northwest Europe campaign. The latter point was directed at countering the Montgomery-centred view of the campaign reflected in Chester Wilmot's 1948 book, *The Struggle for Europe*. The spate of American and British memoirs similarly, and naturally, took national stances and Crerar hoped that Stacey's work would provide a corrective to their minimization of the Canadians.

Crerar was also sensitive to his own record. Commenting on drafts, he pounced on phrases and conclusions that suggested criticism. In

1947, he questioned Stacey's characterization that 'Crerar had a special interest [in training for assault landings],' conscious of the link with Dieppe. 'I don't care for this phrase,' he wrote. 'The inference can be taken all sorts of ways.' Similarly, he drew Stacey's attention to his own contributions, particularly in cases where the written record was ambiguous. In some cases he was justified, in others not. His memory was not always accurate. He minimized, for example, his opposition to bombing Walcheren during the fall of 1944. He correctly pointed out that he had supported the operation if technically feasible, but the record indicates that he accepted the conclusion of his staff that it was not. Simonds seized the initiative in this instance. Crerar was careful here, and in other cases, to extend credit to his subordinates, but there was a consistent pattern to his comments; he sought to highlight his active role as army commander. He reacted to Stacey's description of his role prior to the employment of First Canadian Army Headquarters in July 1944 as 'merely a spectator' with unusual fervour. Detailing his activities, he concluded, 'I feel that I was something more than "merely a spectator," to be quite frank.'[58] Stacey was no fool, and wrote carefully but truthfully. Between the lines of the official histories is the unofficial story.

Crerar addressed the historical record in other forums, although infrequently. Dieppe emerged as the most controversial topic he addressed, and he spoke of the raid publicly only five times during the entire postwar period. He characterized it as 'probably the most valuable contribution of the war to final, and decisive, Allied victory.' Crerar's defence of the raid bordered on hyperbole, as he conjectured that had Dieppe been successful, a real invasion might have failed.[59] Others defended him as well. Peter Wright's review of Terrence Robertson's *The Shame and the Glory* disputed the author's claim that Crerar deserved primary responsibility for the disaster. The controversy remained, however. In 1962, he was among the senior commanders interviewed for a CBC documentary on Dieppe; Montgomery, Hughes-Hallett, and Roberts also appeared. Crerar was refreshingly blunt in his defence of the raid; he reiterated his view on its value. When asked whether he considered the basic plan a 'good one,' he replied, 'I thought it was completely feasible.' He downplayed his role in the revival of the raid. In contrast, Montgomery and Hughes-Hallett both tried to distance themselves from the decision to use Canadian troops and the planning. Crerar also showed a surprising naivete about its aftermath. Roberts indicated that he was scapegoated by Crerar, an interpretation that Crerar's annotations to the script suggest surprised him. 'I deny that he was made the scapegoat for Dieppe,' he said in one interview. 'Definitely. There may have been other reasons, but I won't go into them. But he wasn't made a scapegoat.' In the margins, he scribbled that Roberts was 'a bit bitter' about his removal in March 1943.[60]

Crerar was consistent in his refusal to become embroiled in public denunciations of his wartime colleagues, superiors, and subordinates, but his relations with his former colleagues were mixed. He and 'Brookie' maintained their friendship, keeping up a steady correspondence and the occasional combined fishing and bird-watching expeditions.[61] Montgomery continued to test his patience, snubbing him on several visits. Yet, Crerar refused to publicly criticize Montgomery. As he had during the war, Crerar felt it was 'wrong to bring Monty's name into the controversy over Dieppe'; he added, however, 'even though the basic tactical plan was his.'[62] On a personal level, they were far too different to ever mesh. One friend recalled one of Monty's postwar visits as a tense affair; as soon as Montgomery left, Crerar turned to his friend and said, 'For God's Sake get the whisky out and let's have a drink.'[63] In contrast, Freddie deGuingand was a frequent correspondent right up to Crerar's death.

Crerar mellowed in his relations with his subordinates. He used first names in his correspondence and maintained social contact with many from the army. First Canadian Army Headquarters reunions, codenamed Elbow, were first organized and held in 1952 as a VE reunion in his honour. It was attended by close to 700 former officers. He gave an 'on-air' address and was presented with a portrait. Crerar was against being the guest of honour, concerned that McNaughton, Foulkes, and Simonds might take offence. To underline his commitment to avoiding 'hurt feelings,' he kept extensive lists of headquarters personnel for mailings and cards.[64] There were two notable exceptions to the tempo of Crerar's postwar relationships: McNaughton and Simonds. The Crerars and McNaughtons never re-established their prewar closeness; Crerar seemed to distance himself from his former mentor, although there appeared to be little open animosity. McNaughton was the only person whom Crerar directly criticized in his commentary on Stacey's histories. Establishing McNaughton's wartime contribution was a ticklish subject for many. Mackenzie King fought to ensure that McNaughton received equal recognition from the British for his role in shaping the Canadian army. Crerar, sensitive to perceived slights, belatedly urged Mann to invite McNaughton to the Elbow dinners. He did not attend. Dissonance, not animosity, characterized their postwar relationship.

In contrast, Crerar's postwar relationship with Guy Simonds was characterized by hostility – most, if not all, generated by Simonds. C.P. Stacey speculates that Simonds's 'hatred' of Crerar began when he learned that Crerar had recommended Foulkes for CGS. Stacey's anecdotes regarding Simonds's ongoing attempts to attack Crerar reputation indicate that whatever the depth of jealousy between the two men during the war, the animosity came later. While Simonds 'lost no opportunity of impressing upon' Stacey 'the crimes of Harry Crerar,' Crerar, who had ample opportunity to reciprocate in reviewing Stacey's work, generally praised Simonds. He did, however, try to secure some credit for tactical decisions that were clearly his corps commander's.[65]

Crerar's health did not stand up to the rigours of the aggressive stance he took on defence policy; 1952 saw a precipitous decline. After several warnings from his doctor, he was ordered to slow down. The number of addresses given dropped off sharply; invitations soon followed suit. In part, this was a calculated change. 'If I become a public bore by speaking on this subject other than occasionally, when I have something which just *must* be said,' he wrote in response to a query regarding his limited schedule, 'my views just won't be taken seriously.'[66] Crerar's taste for polemic and moralizing, frequently indulged in his talks, seemed less and less attractive as did the virulence with which he promoted compulsory service and preparedness. His appeal peaked with the Korean War; by 1956, his criticisms of the army as 'an attractive show-window' and his predictions of the decline of the RCAF in the face of surface-to-air missiles did not endear him to his former colleagues.[67] It was also clear that he could no longer maintain the pace he set in the late 1940s. Any appointments he accepted were largely ceremonial. He served in a number of honorary positions and wrote many forewords to the spate of regimental histories produced during the 1950s.[68]

His decline was underlined when he was invited to attend the funeral of George VI in 1953, an event that also coincided with the Ninth Anniversary of the D-Day landings. In 1948 he was appointed as an aide-de-camp to King George VI, the first Canadian to receive that honour; in the spring of 1953, Crerar was called to attend George VI's funeral, but went instead as aide-de-camp to Elizabeth's coronation – a very proud moment. While in Europe, he and Verse visited the Canadian battlefields in France. Bruce West, a journalist covering the speeches and visitations that Crerar attended in France, observed how Crerar had aged. 'During the few minutes we flew along the coast,' he wrote, 'the old soldier was obviously living in another world of almost a decade ago.' It was an emotional and strenuous itinerary; at Berniere-sur-Mer, the mayor 'clamped one hand on Crerar's shoulder and shouted his speech into his ear above the wind while the other hand grimly clutched the copy of his speech.' Crerar was less kind: 'We were met by the Mayor, where in a pathetic speech of welcome, he remembered the day of liberation.' He remembered his visit to the cemetery: 'I notice how neat and orderly the cemetery is. Some 4000 of our boys, my boys, lay there. May they rest in peace.'[69] The strain of an emotional two weeks laid him up in London, where he was ordered on a special diet and rest in order to be prepared to accompany the Queen as Aide-de-Camp during her coronation.

By the mid-1950s, his health severely limited his activities. Travel was too much. Approached in 1954 to write articles for *Saturday Night* and *Maclean's*, he declined, directing the editors to earlier addresses to distill his views on military preparedness. In the spring of 1958, Queen Elizabeth requested Crerar accompany her on a state visit to Holland. 'Naturally, all of us here who know Harry Crerar,' Michael Adeane wrote the Governor General, 'hope very much that he will feel able to accept.' Crerar accepted the honour, characterized by the *Times*, as an 'imaginative gesture.' Minister of Defence George Pearkes sounded the only sour note when he refused Crerar's request for Tom Macdonald's services. The Dutch greeted Crerar's arrival enthusiastically, but the trip was too much; that fall, Crerar was forced to cancel a meeting with the Duke of Edinburgh in Ottawa when doctors ordered him to rest, as his heart 'showed signs of "lying down on the job."'[70] During the trip to the Netherlands, he picked up a chill from which he never completely recovered.

He remained publicly quiet during debates on defence policy in the late 1950s, steering clear of any direct criticism of Prime Minister Diefenbaker's Defence Minister George Pearkes. Privately, he was highly critical of Pearkes's policy and encouraged others to speak out against it.[71]

For the final years of his life, Crerar was largely confined to his home and family activities. In June 1958, he declined an invitation to dine with the Prime Minister and President Eisenhower as he was meeting with Vi; he wrote that it was likely his sister's 'last trip from California to Canada.' His heart ailment grew steadily worse. In May 1962, he was forced to forego ceremonies conferring on him the honorary Freedom of the City of Hoogeveen. In June 1962, the Queen Mother, wanting to see him, kindly offered to visit him at his home, an offer Crerar reluctantly accepted.⁷² Verse cared for him, a dependence that did not sit easily. Some national issues prompted a response. He spoke out against changing the flag that so many Canadians had died for, and he lent his name to similar causes. He was given an honorary life membership in the Canadian Military Institute in 1962. That same year he became an honorary trustee of the UCC Foundation. In 1962, he began to consider a biography or memoirs before it was too late.

Harry Crerar was hospitalized on 24 March 1965; he died quietly in his sleep on 1 April 1965, at age seventy-six, four weeks short of his birthday. Following services at Christ Church Cathedral, Ottawa, he was buried with full military honours in Beechwood Cemetery, Ottawa. McNaughton, Simonds, Foulkes, Walsh, Walford, Matthews, Mann, and Wright were the honorary pallbearers. His oak coffin, draped in the new Canadian flag, was mounted on a gun-carriage; on top lay his sword, gold braid, and 'the red-banded khaki field cap he wore in battle.'

> A black stallion, empty black cavalry boots reversed in the stirrups, pranced behind the rolling gun carriage. Three army colonels carried General Crerar's glistening insignia and medals on velvet cushions in their outstretched arms ... General Crerar's wife, son and daughter rode in a closed limousine a short distance behind the gun carriage.⁷³

An estimated thousand spectators gathered to watch the procession.

Former Supreme Commander, and by then former President, Dwight D. Eisenhower sent his condolences to Verse Crerar. In a warm and sensitive letter, Ike's eulogy was the summary of his career that Harry Crerar would have hoped for.

> Thursday I learned the shocking news of the death of your husband. Because, during the war days, he was a close and valued associate, I thought it fitting to issue a public statement immediately. However, I should like to write you a more personal note because of the respect, admiration and affection that I felt towards your late husband. General Crerar was notable not only because of his professional skill and qualities of leadership but because of his personal character, including his selflessness. He was not one to seek the limelight or command headlines; he was one of those great souls whose only ambition was to do his duty to his troops and to his country.⁷⁴

In the obituaries, he was described as 'stern,' 'quiet,' 'remote,' 'unobtrusive,' yet 'steady,' 'tough,' and 'a distinguished public servant.' In an acknowledgement of the contradictory descriptions, Ross Munro noted the difficulty during the war of capturing the essence of the man for the people back home. Yet he recalled that beneath the reserved, cold exterior was a 'warm and friendly nature.' Perhaps at the end, the epitaphs that best suited him were 'a Hamiltonian, and thoroughly Canadian.' '"Generals," Crerar once observed, "are pretty much like other people."'[75]

Notes

Abbreviations

AO	Archives of Ontario	MLA	Massey Library Archives
AP	Alanbrooke Papers	MKP	Mackenzie King Papers
BLMP	B.L. Montgomery Papers	MP	McNaughton Papers
CDC	General H.D.G. Crerar Document Collection	MTCLBS	Metropolitan Toronto Central Library Bio-graphical Scrapbook
CP	Crerar Papers		
CSB	H.D.G. Crerar Scrapbook	OHA	Ontario Hydro Central Records and Archives
CWCM	Cabinet War Committee Minutes	OLP	Oliver Leese Papers
DHH	Directorate of History and Heritage	PP	Parkin Papers
		PRC	Personnel Records Centre
EMP	Edward Morrison Papers		
GDP	Grant Dexter Papers	PRO	Public Records Office
GP	Graham Papers	QUA	Queen's University Archives
GV	George Vanier Papers		
HPL	Hamilton Public Library	RMC	Royal Military College
IDC	Imperial Defence College	RP	J.L. Ralston Papers
IMP	Ian Mackenzie Papers	SC	Special Collections
IWM	Imperial War Museum	SDD	Staff Duties Directorate
KCL	King's College, London	SP	Simpson Papers
LAC	Library and Archives Canada	USMA	United States Military Archives
LHC	Liddell Hart Centre for Military Archives	UTA	University of Toronto Archives
LPP	Lester B. Pearson Papers	VMP	Vincent Massey Papers
MDP	Sir Miles Dempsey Papers	WD, SO	War Diary, Senior Officer

Introduction

1 Ross Munro, Crerar obituary, *Toronto Star*, 2 Apr. 1965.
2 'General Crerar Returns,' *Globe and Mail*, 5 Aug. 1945.
3 Ibid.
4 Churchill Mann, 'A General 24 Hrs a Day,' quoted in Reader's Digest, *The Canadians at War 1939/45* (Toronto 1969).
5 Major-General George Kitching, *Mud and Green Fields: The Memoirs of Major-General George Kitching* (Langley, BC 1986), 117–8.
6 Claude Bissell, *The Imperial Canadian: Vincent Massey in Office* (Toronto 1986), 142.

Chapter 1

1 See Carl Berger, *The Sense of Power: Studies in the Ideas of Canadian Imperialism, 1867–1914* (Toronto 1970).
2 Marjorie Freeman Campbell, *A Mountain and a City: The Story of Hamilton* (Toronto 1966), 159. See also John Weaver, *Hamilton: An Illustrated History* (Toronto 1982).
3 Hamilton Public Library (HPL), Special Collections (SC), H.D.G. Crerar Scrapbook (CSB), RB CRERA HA, 'Famed Soldier Tells Women of Influence Mothers Exert,' *Hamilton Spectator*, 12 Oct. 1945; interview with Peggy Crerar Palmer, 16 Apr. 1991.
4 Metropolitan Toronto Central Library Biographical Scrapbook (MTCLBS), 6:39–40; 'Representative Women: Mrs P.D. Crerar,' *Globe and Mail*, 27 May 1911.
5 Thomas M. Bailey, ed., 'Thomas Stinson,' in *Dictionary of Hamilton Biography* (Hamilton 1981), 189; L.M. Shaw, 'Two Hamilton Families: The Stinson Family,' *Western Ontario Historical Notes* 16 (Mar. 1960): 10–11.
6 MTCLBS, 'Representative Women: Mrs P.D. Crerar'; HPL, SC, Herald Scrapbook, 'Mrs P.D. Crerar Called by Death This Morning,' *Hamilton Herald*, 20 May 1919; Jeffrey Wollock, 'Glimpses at a New England Family,' *Ontario History* 64 (June 1972): 105–13.
7 HPL, '31 Aug. 1864,' '13 Sept. 1864,' *Hamilton Evening Times*, vol. 6 (Hamilton 1985); '30 June 1865,' *Hamilton Evening Times*, vol. 2; Bailey, ed., 'William McGiverin,' in *Dictionary of Hamilton Biography*, 131–2; Carolyn Gray, 'Peter Duncan Crerar,' in *Dictionary of Hamilton Biography*, ed. Thomas Bailey (Hamilton 1991), 2:34.
8 MTCLBS, 'Representative Women,' *Globe and Mail*, 27 May 1911; W.R. Plewman, *Adam Beck and the Ontario Hydro* (Toronto 1947), 25; HPL, 'Mrs P.D. Crerar Called by Death This Morning,' 20 May 1919.

9 G. Mercer Adam, ed., 'John Crerar,' in *Prominent Men of Canada: Persons Distinguished in Professional and Political Life, in the Commerce and Industry of Canada* (Toronto 1892), 297; George MacLean Rose, *A Cyclopedia of Canadian Biography: Being Chiefly Men of the Time* (Toronto 1886), 45–6.
10 Rose, *A Cyclopedia*, 45–6; Adam, 'John Crerar,' 297.
11 HPL, SC, Merkworth House Scrapbook, vol. 1, 'Merkworth House,' *Hamilton Spectator*, 29 Jan. 1953; Rose, *A Cyclopedia*, 46; LAC, Crerar Papers (CP), vol. 20, D317, Personal Correspondence to 1964, C/6-9/P, Jack Pickersgill to Crerar.
12 Thomas Melville Bailey and Charles Ambrose Carter, *Hamilton Firsts* (Hamilton 1973), n.p.; MTCLBS, vol. 6, 'Mrs John Crerar Passes to the Beyond,' unnamed paper, 23 Nov. 1920.
13 LAC, CP, vol. 19, D338, Crerar to Grattan O'Leary (of the *Ottawa Journal*), 1940; HPL, SC, 'P.D. Crerar Dead,' *Hamilton Herald*, 10 June 1912; LAC, CP, vol. 20, Personal Correspondence to 1964, C/6-9/P.
14 Weaver, *Hamilton*, 64–5; Alexander H. Wingfield, ed., *The Hamilton Centennial, 1846–1946* (Hamilton 1946), 42.
15 LAC, CP, vol. 16, D275, Speech to Hamilton Sanatorium, 10 Oct. 1945; Carolyn Gray, 'Peter Duncan Crerar,' in *Dictionary of Hamilton Biography* (Hamilton 1991), 2:35.
16 G. Blaine Baker, 'Legal Education in Upper Canada, 1785–1889,' in *Essays in the History of Canadian Law*, ed. David Flaherty (Toronto 1983), 49–55.
17 MTCLSM, vol. 16, 'Lady Adam Beck,' *Saturday Night*, 22 Nov. 1921, 393; HPL, 'P.D. Crerar Dead,' *Hamilton Herald*, 10 June 1912; Plewman, *Adam Beck*, 25–7.
18 LAC, CP, vol. 16, D275, Speech to Hamilton Sanitorium.
19 LAC, CP, D275, vol. 16, The Crerar Family and Mountain Sanatorium; MTCLBS, 'Representative Women: Mrs P.D. Crerar,' *Globe and Mail*; HPL, 'Mrs Crerar Succumbed to Long Illness,' *Hamilton Spectator*, 20 May 1919; J.H. Conner, *A Heritage of Healing: The London Health Association and Its Hospitals, 1909–1987* (London 1990), 1–3.
20 Speech to Hamilton Sanatorium.
21 Palmer interview; Crerar to O'Leary, 1940; Royal Military College of Canada (RMC), Massey Library Archives (MLA), RMC and Family Photo Album 1898–1911, H.D.G. Crerar (749).
22 LAC, CP, vol. 6, D153, Crerar to Peter Crerar, 6 Nov. 1942.
23 Palmer interview.
24 Speech to Hamilton Sanatorium.
25 LAC, CP, vol. 20, D329, Crerar to Mrs Hugh MacKay, 13 Oct. 1945.
26 Palmer interview; LAC, CP, vol. 20, D329, Crerar to Mrs Hugh MacKay, 13 Oct. 1945.

27 Richard B. Howard, *Upper Canada College 1829–1979: Colborne's Legacy* (Toronto 1979), 110–15.
28 Berger, *The Sense of Power*, 33–41.
29 Howard, *Upper Canada College*, 128–9, 166–7; LAC, George Parkin Papers (PP), MG30D44, vol. 122, file: Newspaper Clippings, Education – Upper Canada College, Announcement of New Principal, 22 Aug. 1895; vol. 67, file: Speeches, Notes – UCC, Address by Dr Parkin to the Boys of Upper Canada College.
30 Howard, *Upper Canada College*, 131–4.
31 Berger, *Sense of Power*, 13–41, 196.
32 Palmer interview.
33 Queen's University Archives (QUA), S. Graham Papers (GP), box 1, file 11, Peacock on 'The British Empire'; MTCLMS, vols. 11 and 20, 'The Quiet Man from Glengarry,' *Globe*, 21 Nov. 1962.
34 LAC, CP, vol. 20, D329, Crerar to Stacey, 10 Mar. 1959.
35 Howard, *Upper Canada College*, 155–6; QUA, GP, box 1, file 6, Crerar to Gerald Graham, 7 May 1959; Peacock to Stella Hotblack, 1941–1962.
36 RMC, MLA, Stephen Leacock, 'Generals I Have Trained,' *RMC Review* (1959): 156.
37 LAC, CP, vol. 16, D273, Speech to UCC, 8 Nov. 1945; Crerar to O'Leary, 1940.
38 Robert M. Stamp, 'Empire Day in the Schools of Ontario: The Training of Young Imperialists,' *Journal of Canadian Studies* 8 (1973): 32–42; as described by Stephen Leacock in Howard, *Upper Canada College*, 139–40.
39 Howard, *Upper Canada College*, 186; RMC, MLA, Room at UCC, RMC and Family Photo Album, 1889–1911.
40 Carolyn Gossage, *A Question of Privilege: Canada's Independent Schools* (Toronto 1977), 181; HPLSC, Highfield House Scrapbook, 'Highfield,' *Hamilton Spectator*, Sept. 1935; Speech to Hamilton Sanatorium.
41 Berger, *The Sense of Power*, 235–7; Robert Page, *The Boer War and Canadian Imperialism* (Ottawa, 1987), 18–19.
42 Plewman, *Adam Beck*, 63–4; LAC, CP, vol. 17, D295, Reply to an Address of Welcome, Civic Reception, City Hall, London, Ontario, 7 Jan. 1946.
43 RMC, MLA, Regulations for the RMC, Kingston, Ontario, Mar. 1907.
44 LAC, Personnel Records Centre (PRC), General H.D.G. Crerar Personal Service Record, file A, Peter Crerar to the Secretary of the Militia Council, 2 Apr. 1906.
45 Regulations ... 1907, 31, and Regulations for the RMC, Kingston, Ontario, June 1909, 20–1; Richard Preston, *Canada's RMC: A History of the Royal Military College* (Toronto 1969), 14–24.

46 RMC, MLA, Objects of the College, in Regulations ... 1907.
47 Regulations ... 1907, 31; Regulations ... 1909, 20–3; George Stanley, 'Military Education in Canada, 1867–1970,' *The Canadian Military: A Profile*, ed. Hector Massey (Toronto 1970), 174.
48 RMC, Central Registrar Records, Descriptive Roll, Cadet 749.
49 RMC, MLA, List of Marks Obtained by 3rd Class, 1906–1907; List of Marks Obtained by 2nd Class, 1907–1908; List of Marks Obtained by 1st Class, 1908–1909; Commandant's Office, Personal File, Service Card.
50 R. Guy C. Smith, ed., *As You Were: Ex-Cadets Remember* (RMC 1984), 1:75–6; RMC, Central Registrar Records, Personal File; originally printed in *RMC Review* (Nov. 1921): 59.
51 Preston, *Canada's RMC*, 280; LAC, CP, vol. 14, D251, Commandant's Remarks to Recruit Class, Aug. 1938.
52 LAC, CP, (D251), Commandant's Speech, Closing Exercises – 1939.
53 Smith, *As You Were*, 1:76.
54 RMC and Family Photo Album, 1898–1911; Crerar to O'Leary, 1940.
55 Crerar to O'Leary, 1940.
56 LAC, CP, vol. 22, D380, Crerar to McNaughton, 26 Dec. 1919.
57 LAC, CP, vol. 16, D266, Address to Civic Stadium, Hamilton, 10 Oct. 1945.
58 HPL, H.D.G. Crerar Scrapbook, 'Crerar Is Going Overseas to Command Second Division,' *Toronto Star*, 24 Nov. 1941; Crerar to O'Leary, 1940.
59 MTCLBS, vol. 1, 'Peter D. Crerar, K.C. Dies at Hamilton,' *Globe*, 10 June 1912; HPL, 'Mrs Crerar Succumbed to Long Illness,' *Hamilton Spectator*, 20 May 1919.
60 Merrill Denison, *The People's Power: The History of Ontario Hydro* (Toronto 1960), 94–5, 184.
61 Ontario Hydro Central Records and Archives (OHA), *Sixth Annual Report of the Hydro-Electric Power Commission of the Province of Ontario for the Year Ended October 31st, 1913* (Toronto 1914), 199–200.
62 OHA, 'Canada's Crerar: Commander-in-Chief Canadian Army Overseas Was Former Head of H.E.P.C. Lab,' *Hydro News*, Feb. 1944; Denison, *People's Power*, 194; OHA, *Seventh Annual Report of the Hydro-Electric Power Commission of the Province of Ontario for the Year Ended October 31, 1914* (Toronto 1915), 2.
63 OHA, 84296, Sir Adam Beck General Correspondence, Gaby to Adam Beck, 7 Mar. 1913.
64 Plewman, *Adam Beck*, 396–400.
65 Department of National Defence (DND), Directorate of History and Heritage (DHH), Brigadier Orde Interview, 77/490, 119; LAC, CP, vol. 19, (D338), Letter of 19 Sept. 1940.

66 Crerar to Gratton O'Leary, 1940.
67 HPL, SC, Gardiner Scrapbooks, vol. 280, Canadian Artillery: Field Battery; G.W.L. Nicholson, *The Gunners of Canada* (Toronto 1967), 1:135–6.
68 LAC, RG24, vol. 1883C, Notes on the History of Military District 2; Nicholson, *Gunners of Canada*, 1:169–70.
69 R. Haycock, *Sam Hughes: The Public Career of a Controversial Canadian* (Ottawa 1986), 139.
70 LAC, RG24, vol. 284, HQ3-20-10; vol. 348, HQ 33-20-175, Date and Detail of Troops, Petawawa Camp, 1911.
71 LAC, RG24, vol. 348, HQ 33-20-189, Report Petawawa Training Camp, 26 July 1911.
72 Desmond Morton, *The Canadian General* (Toronto 1973), 313–14.
73 Nicholson, *Gunners of Canada*, 1:174.
74 His attendance record is taken from the following sources: LAC, RG24, vol. 350, Nominal Roll of Officers, Petawawa 1914, HQ 33-20-280, and Nominal Roll of Officers, Petawawa 1913, HQ 33-20-248; Crerar to O'Leary; RMC and Family Photo Album, 1898–1911.
75 LAC, RG24, vol. 349, HQ 33-2-233, Date and Detail of Troops, Petawawa Camp 1913; vol. 350, HQ 33-20-280, Nominal Roll of Officers, Petawawa 1914.
76 LAC, RG9 II B5, vol. 2, file 9, Abridged Annual Reports upon 4th Battery, 2nd Brigade, CFA, 1910–13; HPL, SC, 'Lt-Colonel Crerar Had a Splendid Record in War,' *Hamilton Spectator*, 21 Mar. 1919.
77 LAC, CP, vol. 6, D122, Crerar to D.S.G. Adam, 14 Jan. 1945.

Chapter 2

1 English-Canadian historiography of the war has traditionally portrayed it as a positive force on a national level, if not a personal one. Jonathan F. Vance, *Death So Noble: Memory, Meaning, and the First World War* (Vancouver 1997).
2 2. Peter Simkins, *Kitchener's Army: The Raising of the New Armies, 1914–16* (Manchester 1988), 40–5.
3 G.W.L. Nicholson, *The Gunners of Canada: The History of the Royal Regiment of Canadian Artillery* (Toronto 1967), 1:194; Ronald Haycock, *Sam Hughes: The Public Career of a Controversial Canadian, 1885–1916* (Ottawa 1986), 178–81.
4 Nicholson, *Gunners of Canada*, 1:194.
5 Ibid., 195; Colonel G.W.L. Nicholson, *Canadian Expeditionary Force, 1914–1919: The Official History of the Canadian Army in the First World War* (Ottawa 1962), 16–23.

6 LAC, CP, vol. 19, D338, Crerar to Grattan O'Leary, 1 Aug. 1940.
7 *The Great Adventure with the 4th Battery, C.F.A.* (1919), 5–7.
8 Quote from Marjorie Freeman Campbell, *A Mountain and a City: The Story of Hamilton* (Toronto 1966), 200; 'Artillery-Field: 2nd Brigade,' *The Quarterly Militia List of Canada: June 1914* (Ottawa 1914), 159; Library and Archives Canada (LAC), RG9 III, vol. 4683, Historical Record, 11th Battery.
9 LAC, Crerar Papers (CP), vol. 18, D381, Crerar to Lieutenant-Colonel George T. Inch, 1936.
10 Crerar to Inch, 1936; John Ellis, *Eye Deep in Hell: Life in the Trenches, 1914–1918* (Glasgow 1976), 137–8; Paul Fussell, *The Great War and Modern Memory* (Oxford 1975), 69–70.
11 LAC, CP, vol. 15, D268, World War One Diary, journal entry 31 Aug. 1914.
12 James L. Talman, 'Benjamin Cronyn,' in *Dictionary of Canadian Biography* (Toronto 1972), 2:205–10; interview with Peggy Crerar Palmer, 16 Apr. 1991.
13 Interview with Lieutenant-Colonel and Mrs Pip Nation, 1 Nov. 1990; Palmer interview.
14 LAC, CP, vol. 15, D268, Crerar to Lieut-Col Nicholson, 26 July 1964.
15 Journal entries 4–5 Sept. 1914.
16 Journal entries 1–2 Sept. 1914; quote from *The Great Adventure*, 7.
17 Journal entry 8 Sept. 1914.
18 Nicholson in *Gunners of Canada*, 1:199, states that the 4th and the 7th Battery from Hamilton were integrated to form the 7th Battery, 3rd Brigade of the CEF. This is at odds with both the recollections in Crerar's journal and the Historical Record of the 11th Battery, the unit designation in France, which state that a section of the London Battery was integrated to form the 8th Battery before the CEF went overseas; journal entry 1 Sept. 1914; Historical Record, 11th Battery.
19 Journal entry 8 Sept. 1914.
20 Journal entry 16 Sept. 1914.
21 Journal entry 5 Sept. 1914; Haycock, *Sam Hughes*, 183.
22 Journal entry 16 Sept. 1914.
23 Nicholson, *Canadian Expeditionary Force*, 29.
24 Journal entries 30 Sept.–1 Oct. 1914. The dates of the journal entries do not always correspond to the established dates for certain events. In these cases the historical date shall be taken as correct.
25 LAC, RG9 III D1, vol. 4683, folder 28.
26 Journal entry 8 Oct. 1914.
27 Journal entries 1–6 Oct. 1914.
28 Journal entry 2 Oct. 1914.
29 Journal entry 7 Dec. 1914; Historical Record, 11th Battery.

30 Journal entry 3 Nov. 1914.
31 Journal entry 19 Dec. 1914.
32 Journal entry 3 Nov. 1914.
33 Nicholson, *Gunners of Canada*, 1:204.
34 Journal entry 21 Nov. 1914.
35 Journal entry 3 Nov. 1914.
36 Journal entry 15 Jan. 1915.
37 LAC, RG9 III C4, Historical Record – 3rd Brigade; John Swettenham, *McNaughton* (Toronto 1965), 1:39.
38 Journal entry 18 Feb. 1915; Nicholson, *Gunners of Canada*, 1:207–8; Daniel Dancocks, *Welcome to Flanders Fields: The First Canadian Battle of the Great War; Ypres 1915* (Toronto 1988), 86.
39 Journal entry 20 Feb. 1915.
40 LAC, RG41, vol. 6, Flander's Field 4.
41 Journal entries 22–27 Feb. 1915.
42 Journal entries 22–27 Feb. 1915.
43 Journal entry 12 Mar. 1915.
44 Journal entries 26–28 Feb. 1915; Swettenham, *McNaughton*, 1:39–40; Nicholson, *Gunners of Canada*, 1:208–9.
45 Journal entry 26–28 Feb. 1915.
46 Journal entry 5 Mar. 1915; Ellis, *Eye Deep in Hell*, 96–100.
47 Nicholson, *Gunners of Canada*, 1:211–13.
48 Journal entry 12 Mar. 1915.
49 Nicholson, *Gunners of Canada*, 1:212; Bombardier James Logan, 39th Battery, C.F.A., in Gordon Reid, ed., *Poor Bloody Murder* (Oakville 1980), 227.
50 Journal entry 12 Mar. 1915.
51 Alan Clark, *The Donkeys* (London 1961), 48–54.
52 Journal entries 12, 21 Mar. 1915.
53 Nicholson, *Gunners of Canada*, 1:214.
54 Journal entries 18, 30 Mar. 1915; Tim Travers, 'Allies in Conflict: The British and Canadian Official Historians and the Real Story of Second Ypres,' *Journal of Contemporary History* 24 (1989): 319.
55 Fussell, *The Great War*.
56 Journal entry 21 Mar. 1915.
57 Journal entries 1, 15–16 Apr. 1915.
58 Nicholson, *Canadian Expeditionary Force*, 58–9.
59 Journal entry 20 April 1915; Nicholson, *Gunners of Canada*, 1:222; *Canadian Expeditionary Force*, 56–7.
60 Journal entry 20–21 Apr. 1915.
61 LAC, CP, vol. 26, D392, Remarks to the Red Chevron Club – 21 Apr. 1951.

62 Journal entry 29 Apr. 1915; Remarks to the Red Chevron Club; Swettenham, *McNaughton*, 1:43; Nicholson, *Canadian Expeditionary Force*, 61–2.
63 Remarks to the Red Chevron Club.
64 Nicholson, *Gunners of Canada*, 1:224–7; Journal entry 29 Apr. 1915; Remarks to the Red Chevron Club; Dancocks, *Welcome to Flanders Fields*, 118–20.
65 Nicholson, *Gunners of Canada*, 1:226–9; journal entries 28–9 Apr. 1915.
66 Journal entry 30 April and 1 May 1915.
67 Journal entries 30 Apr. and 1 May 1915; J.M. Winter, *The Experience of World War I* (New York 1989), 138; Nicholson, *Gunners of Canada*, 1:230.
68 Journal entries 30 Apr. and 1 May 1915.
69 Journal entry 29 Apr. 1915.
70 Dancocks, *Welcome to Flanders Fields*, 226–7.
71 Journal entries 2, 6 May 1915.
72 Journal entry 6 May 1915; Nicholson, *Gunners of Canada*, 1:230.
73 Journal entry 12–13 May 1915.
74 Journal entry 15 May 1915.
75 Journal entry 15 June 1915.
76 There have been attempts to lay some blame for some of the early withdrawals, which threatened disaster, at the feet of Sir Arthur Currie, then commanding officer, 2nd Infantry Brigade. See Daniel Dancocks, *Sir Arthur Currie: A Biography* (Toronto 1985), and A.M.J. Hyatt, *General Sir Arthur Currie: A Military Biography* (Toronto 1987).
77 Journal entries 19 Mar. and 27 May 1915.

Chapter 3

1 Shelford Bidwell and Dominick Graham, *Fire-Power: British Army Weapons and Theories of War 1904–1945* (London 1982), 76–7.
2 Library and Archives Canada (LAC), Crerar Papers (CP), vol. 15, D268, World War One Diary, journal entry 4 June 1915.
3 Journal entries 15 Apr. and 13 May 1915.
4 Journal entry 13 July 1915; LAC, RG9 III C4, file 5, folder 3, OC 3rd Canadian Artillery Brigade to Staff Captain, 6 July 1915.
5 LAC, RG9 III C4, vol. 4292, file 13, folder 7, Routine Orders, Brigadier-General Burstall, 29 Aug. 1915; journal entry 16 Aug. 1915.
6 LAC, RG9 III C4, vol. 4291, file 14, folder 7, Brigade Order No. 43, Command, 22 July 1915.
7 Department of National Defence, 'Corps Administration: Artillery,' *The Report of the Ministry, Overseas Forces of Canada, 1918* (London 1919), 243–4.
8 LAC, RG9 III D1, Canadian War Records, vol. 4683, file 15, folder 28, 10th

Battery Historical Records; LAC, CP, vol. 22, file: Material 1914–18, Extracts from Memorandum and Instructions on Forthcoming Operations, 20 Sept. 1915.
9 Journal entries 1–6 Nov. 1915.
10 Colonel G.W.L. Nicholson, *Canadian Expeditionary Force, 1914–1919: The Official History of the Canadian Army in the First World War* (Ottawa 1962), 119–25.
11 Journal entries 6 Sept.–18 Oct. 1915.
12 LAC, RG9 III, vol. 4278, file 2, Part II: Officers Supernumerary to Normal Establishments of Units in the Field, *Regulations Governing the Promotion and Gradation of Officers, July 1917*; LAC, CP, vol. 22, (D380), Crerar to OC, 16 Sept. 1916.
13 LAC, CP, vol. 22, D380, Letter, 20 Dec. 1915, Appointments, Transfers and Reports 1915–1931; journal entry 3 Nov. 1915; LAC, RG9 III C4, vol. 4292, file 13, Crerar to OC, 3rd Brigade, 20 Nov. 1915.
14 LAC, RG9 III C4, vol. 4292, file 13, Brigade Order, 24/12/15; LAC, Personnel Records Centre (PRC), Personal File, Mewburn to Adjutant-General, 12 Jan. 1916.
15 Hamilton Public Library (HPL), Special Collections (SC), 'Social Notes,' *Toronto Daily Star*, 12 Jan. 1916; 'In Society,' *Hamilton Spectator*, 29 Dec. 1915.
16 'Social and Personal, Crerar and Cronyn,' *Toronto Daily Star*, 14 Jan. 1916; 'In Society,' *Hamilton Spectator*, 14 Jan. 1916.
17 LAC, PRC, HQ 8648-1, Adjutant-General Cable, 4 Mar. 1916; LAC, RG9 III C4, vol. 4290, file 3, Crerar to Norton, 26 Feb. 1916.
18 LAC, CP, vol. 22, D330, Crerar to OC, 3rd Brigade, 24 Mar. 1916.
19 G.W.L. Nicholson, *The Gunners of Canada* (Toronto 1967), 1:242–4.
20 Ibid.; Bidwell and Graham, *Fire-Power*, 112–14.
21 Bidwell and Graham, *Fire-Power*, 94–117.
22 LAC, RG41, vol. 6, Flander's Fields 1: New Techniques and Old Delusions.
23 LAC, RG9 III, vol. 4292, file 13, Personnel 11-5-15 to 31-3-16, Message to O.C., 3rd Brigade 253-16; vol. 4290, file 1, Field Message, 18 Apr. 1916.
24 Gordon Reid, ed., *Poor Bloody Murder* (Oakville 1980), 116.
25 LAC, PRC, Personal File, Record of Service, 7 Mar. 1932.
26 John Swettenham, *To Seize The Victory: The Canadian Corps in World War 1* (Toronto 1965), 1:149–62; Nicholson, *Gunners of Canada*, 1:277–87, quotation from 283.
27 LAC, RG9 III C4, vol. 4283, folder 26, Historical Record: 11th Battery.
28 LAC, RG41, vol. 6, Flanders Fields 1, p. 17.
29 LAC, CP, vol. 19, Crerar to Grattan O'Leary, 1 Aug. 1940.

30 Archives of Ontario (AO), MU2051, '1915 Military Records,' *11th Battery, C.F.A., February 1915–February 1918.*
31 LAC, PRC, Record of Service, Mar. 1932.
32 LAC, CP, vol. 19, D333, Crerar to Peter Crerar, 4 Oct. 1941; D304, Crerar's Response to 'Questions for a Programme on Artillery Tactics,' Jan. 1962.
33 LAC, CP, vol. 22, D380, Brigadier-General, CRA, 3rd Canadian Division to Crerar, 26 Sept. 1916; LAC, RG9 III, vol. 872, file A-49-3, AQ 2-804, 2 Apr. 1917.
34 C.P. Stacey, 'The Staff Officer: A Footnote to Canadian History,' *Canadian Defence Quarterly* 3 (1973/4): 46–7; Stephen Harris, *Canadian Brass: The Making of a Professional Army, 1860–1939* (Toronto 1988), 127–30.
35 LAC, CP, vol. 18, D332, typewritten copies of messages, dated 28-7-17 through 31-7-17 between GOC, RA, DAAG, and 3rd Brigade; LAC, Edward Morrison Papers (EMP), MG30 E81, vol. 7, Officers Dossier; LAC, RG9 III C4, Historical Record, 11th Battery.
36 HPL, 'Flight Lieutenant Malcolm Crerar Paid the Price,' *Hamilton Daily Spectator*, 8 Aug. 1917; 'Malcolm Crerar: Appreciation of a Boy Hero,' *Hamilton Daily Times*, 13 Aug. 1917; Martin Papers, 'Died Like a Hero,' *Hamilton Herald*, n.d.; interview with Peggy Crerar Palmer, 16 Apr. 1991; LAC, RG24, vol. 4290, file 34-1-54-2.
37 Nicholson, *Gunners of Canada*, 300–1.
38 Royal Military College (RMC), Crerar's Service File, 5th Canadian Divisional Artillery Notebook; Nicholson, *Gunners of Canada*, 1:300–1; Swettenham, *To Seize the Victory*, 147.
39 LAC, RG9 III C4, vol. 4284, file 8, Operation Order No. 1, Wilford Camp, 19 Aug. 1917; Addenda to Operation Order No. 1, 19 Aug. 1917.
40 LAC, RG9 III C4, vol. 4284, file 1, M 41/9/55 Headquarters, 5th Canadian Division Artillery; Various Authors, *The Story of the Sixty-Sixth, CFA* (Edinburgh 1919), 62–72.
41 LAC, RG9 III C4, vol. 4284, file 1, Messages to Brigades, 16 Sept. 1917, 9 and 22 Jan. 1918; vol 4285, Gas File.
42 LAC, CP, vol. 21, D329, Comments on Official History, Crerar to Nicholson, June 1961; vol. 19, Crerar to Grattan O'Leary, Aug. 1940.
43 For example, LAC, RG9 III C4, vol. 4288, file 4, Fifth Canadian Divisional Artillery, G 69/2/631, 21 Mar. 1918; or see vol. 4285, 19 Mar. 1918, G 69/2/547.
44 LAC, CP, vol. 18, D332, A.F. Brooke to Crerar, 29 Dec. 1917.
45 LAC, CP, vol. 20, D313, Crerar to Lieutenant-General Sir Otto Lund, 17 Oct. 1952.

478 Notes to pages 58–63

46 LAC, RG9 III C4, vol. 4283, file 9, folder 2, series of field messages and memos 29 Oct.–18 Nov. 1917.
47 LAC, RG9 III C4, vol. 4283. For example, Defence Scheme, Copy 31 for 12 Jan. 1918.
48 Nicholson, *Gunners of Canada*, 1:323.
49 John Swettenham, *McNaughton* (Toronto 1968), 1:101; LAC, A.G.L. McNaughton Papers (MP), MG30 E133, vol. 108, Duguid to Crerar, 31 Aug. 1922; RG9 III, vol. 868, First Army: Trench Mortar Batteries, 9 Aug. 1917.
50 Quote from Crerar to O'Leary. For an example of Crerar's use of the trench mortars, see LAC, RG9 III C4, vol. 4283, file 9, G 50/17/660, 5th Can. Div. Arty., 26 Apr. 1918; Bruce I. Gudmundsson, *On Artillery* (Westport 1993), 76–84.
51 Bill Rawling, *Surviving Trench Warfare: Technology and the Canadian Corps, 1914–1918* (Toronto 1992), 179.
52 Quoted in Swettenham, *McNaughton*, 1:97; LAC, CP, vol. 19, Crerar's response to 'Questions for a Programme on Artillery Tactics,' Jan. 1962.
53 LAC, EMP, vol. 5, Personnel: Officers, Instructions and Rulings; RG9 III, vol. 872, file A-49-3, Confidential Report, 5th Canadian Divisional Artillery; CP, vol. 18, Personal Correspondence, 1914–18.
54 LAC, EMP, vol. 5, Staff Appointments – Canadian Artillery, Order M.S.9.1.73, dated 23 Feb. 1918 from the DA and QMG.
55 LAC, RG9 III, vol. 915, Confidential Report on Major D.A. White. Donald A White graduated second in the RMC class of 1909. From *The Quarterly Militia List, June 1914* (Ottawa 1914), 360.
56 King's College, London (KCL), Liddell Hart Centre for Military Archives (LHC), Alanbrooke Papers (AP), diary 1/1/11, 2 May 1918.
57 LAC, CP, vol. 20, quote from Crerar to Lt-Gen. Sir Otto Lund, 17 Oct. 1952.
58 Swettenham, *McNaughton*, 1:97, 136–9; KCL, LHC, AP, Notes on My Life, 3/A/1, vol. 1, 59.
59 LAC, CP, vol. 22, Instruction for Demonstration of 8-inch (Medium) Trench Mortar Equipment, file: Material 1914–1919.
60 LAC, EMP, vol. 7, Staff Captain, GOC, RA to Canadian Corps 'A,' P.730-3-2, 6 Sept. 1918; Nicholson, *Gunners of Canada*, 1:342–3.
61 LAC, CP, vol. 18, D332, Crerar to Canadian Corps 'G,' 20 July 1918; Crerar's notebook June to Sept 1918, General Crerar's Personal Correspondence, 1914–18: Brigade Major; RG9 III B1, vol. 941, file: E-80-3, Reorganization of Trench Mortars.
62 Nicholson, *Gunners of Canada*, 1:343.
63 Ibid., 1:338–9.
64 LAC, CP, vol. 18, D332, Memobook as A/S.O., RA.

65 Bidwell and Graham, *Fire-Power*, 140–4.
66 Crerar to O'Leary.
67 LAC, CP, vol. 20, Crerar to Lt-General Sir Otto Lund, 17 Oct. 1952; KCL, LHC, AP, 3/A/1, vol. 1, 60.
68 Nicholson, *Gunners of Canada*, 1:349–55; LAC, CP, vol. 18, Record of Service, 9 Mar. 1932.
69 LAC, RG41, vol. 6, Flander's Fields 1, 17.
70 LAC, CP, vol. 18, E.J. St John to Crerar, 20 Aug. 1918; vol. 22, file: Material 1914–1918, Artillery Notes on Operations of the Canadian Corps, Aug. 26 to Sept. 4, 1918, 0.20/20-2, 6 Oct. 1918.
71 LAC, CP, vol. 18, Canadian Corps to M.O.C.F., 23 Sept. 1918.
72 Swettenham, *McNaughton*, 1:155; Nicholson, *Gunners of Canada*, 1:358–9; LAC, CP, vol. 18, Crerar to Brooke, 19 July 1918.
73 Swettenham, *McNaughton*, 1:89, 157–8.
74 LAC, RG9 III, vol. 3922, file 10, folder 7, Organization and Procedure of Counter-Battery Office, Jan. 25, 1919.
75 LAC, CP, vol. 13, D230, file: The Capture of Valenciennes.
76 LAC, RG9 III, vol. 3923, file 4, folder 12, Notes on Counter-Battery Support in Capture of Mont Houy by the Canadian Corps, 3 Feb. 1919.
77 LAC, CP, vol. 19, D306. For the last week and a half of hostilities see RG9 III, vol. 3921, file 2, folder 4, Counter-Battery Staff Office, Weekly Summaries, 1–14 Nov. 1918; CP, vol. 7, D137, Saliez to Crerar, 8 Apr. 1945.
78 LAC, RG9 III, vol. 3922, folder 7, file 10. For the full report and appendices, Crerar to GOC, RA, 25 Jan. 1919, Organization and Procedure of Counter-Battery Office.
79 Bidwell and Graham, *Fire-Power*, 132.
80 LAC, CP, vol. 18, D332, McNaughton to Crerar, 3 Mar. 1919; HQ III Army Corps, AEF to Crerar, 27 Jan. 1919.
81 LAC, RG9 III, vol. 3922, folder 7, file 9, McNaughton's Notes on the Work of a Counter-Battery Office, Dec, 1919; and Crerar to GOC, CCHA, 9 Dec. 1919.

Chapter 4

1 Library and Archives Canada (LAC), Crerar Papers (CP), vol. 18, D332, Assistant-Secretary, Minister of Overseas Military Forces of Canada to 'Harry,' 20 Dec. 1918; General Andrew McNaughton Papers (MP), vol. 1, file: Military Correspondence 1914–1919, Crerar to McNaughton, 21 Feb. 1919.
2 LAC, Personnel Records Centre (PRC), Crerar's Personal File, Confidential

Report on Officers, 1919; Edward Morrison Papers (EMP), MG30E81, vol. 1, Demobilization.
3 LAC, CP, vol. 19, D338, Crerar to Grattan O'Leary, 1 Aug. 1940
4 LAC, CP, vol. 7, D150, Crerar to Peg Palmer, 1 July 1945.
5 LAC, CP, vol. 20, D331, Crerar to James MacBrien, 9 Nov. 1945.
6 LAC, CP, vol. 22, D380, Crerar to McNaughton, 26 Dec. 1919; , RG24, C-5046, HQ Staff, 30 June 1922.
7 LAC, MP, vol. 108, file: 1919, Currie to McNaughton, 25 Feb. 1919.
8 LAC, MP, vol. 1, Crerar to McNaughton, 21 Feb. 1919; CP, vol. 22, D380, McNaughton to Crerar, 30 Dec. 1919.
9 LAC, CP, vol. 22, D380, Letter to Crerar, Dec. 1919.
10 LAC, PRC, Crerar's Personal File, Notice to the Minister in Militia Council from the Adjutant-General, 1 June 1920; CP, vol. 22, D380; Crerar's Personal File, Adjutant-General to Minister in Militia Council, 1 June 1920, HQ 8648-1; EMP, vol. 3, Artillery Corps Organization, Morrison to Crerar, 2 Mar. 1920. See Stephen Harris, *Canadian Brass: The Making of a Professional Army, 1860–1939* (Toronto 1988), 140–7.
11 LAC, MP, series II, vol. 100, Currie to McNaughton, 25 Feb. 1919; RG24, C-5056, HQC 4451, Policy for Selection of Staff Officers, 15 Mar. 1919; RG24, Correspondence, Secretary, Military Council to Adjutant-General, 19 Mar. 1920.
12 James Eayrs, *In Defence of Canada: From the Great War to the Great Depression* (Toronto 1964), 3.
13 Desmond Morton, 'Bayonets in the Streets: The Canadian Experience of Aid to the Civil Power,' *Canadian Defence Quarterly* 20 (Spring 1991): 32.
14 Norman Hillmer and William McAndrew, 'The Cunning of Restraint: General J.H. MacBrien and the Problems of Peacetime Soldiering,' *Canadian Defence Quarterly* 8 (Spring 1979): 41–6; Harris, *Canadian Brass*, 154.
15 Department of National Defence (DND), Directorate of History and Heritage (DHH), D13/165, Civil Defence, Crerar to Colonel L. Roy, 12 May 1925.
16 DND, DHH, 77/490, R.J. Orde Interview, 119.
17 LAC, CP, vol. 6, D122, Crerar to Adams, 14 Jan. 1945.
18 G.W.L. Nicholson, *The Gunners of Canada* (Toronto 1967), 2:8–10; LAC, CP, vol. 14, D259, Crerar to Lt-Colonel W.C. Hagerty, 8 Dec. 1936.
19 LAC, PRC, Crerar's Personal File, Annual Confidential Report for 1920; Annual Confidential Report for 1921.
20 LAC, MG26 I, Sir Arthur Meighen Papers, vol. 39, Beck to Meighen, 31 May 1921.
21 Orde interview.

22 LAC, CP, vol. 22, D380, Letters to Sir Adam Beck from Arthur Meighen and H. Guthrie, 3 and 8 June 1921.
23 LAC, CP, vol. 22, D380, S.D. Form 64, 20 June 1922, Examination Marks; Crerar to Powell, 26 July 1922; John A. English, *The Canadian Army and the Normandy Campaign: A Study of Failure in High Command* (New York 1991), 51.
24 Brian Bond, *The Victorian Army and the Staff College, 1854–1914* (London 1972), 328–9; Brevet Major A.R. Godwin-Austin, *The Staff and the Staff College* (London, 1927), 273–96; Royal Military College (RMC), Crerar's Vertical File, Crerar's Exercise and Notes, Staff College, 1923–4.
25 Public Record Office (PRO), War Office Papers, W032/3098, Staff College Regulations, 1921.
26 Robin Higham, *The Military Intellectuals in Britain, 1918–1939* (New Brunswick, NJ 1966), 11–12.
27 Anthony John Trythall, *'Boney' Fuller: Soldier, Strategist and Writer, 1878–1966* (New Brunswick, NJ 1977), 53–4.
28 Colonel Roderick MacLeod and Denis Kelly, eds., *The Ironside Papers* (London 1962), 15; Trythall, *'Boney' Fuller*, 93–4, 102–3. On Fuller's affect, see Maurice A. Pope, *Soldiers and Politicians: The Memoirs of Lt-General Maurice A. Pope, CB, MC* (Toronto 1962), 58.
29 King's College, London (KCL), Liddell Hart Centre for Military Archives (LHC), Alanbrooke Papers (AP), Notes on My Life, vol. II 3/A/11, 1923–6.
30 LAC, George Vanier Papers (GV), MG32A2, vol. 4, Introductory Message by Major-General Sir Edmund Ironside, Jan. 23 1923, file: 1923 Part A, Staff College. Crerar's notes are from Staff College Notebooks, RMC Massey Library Archives.
31 PRO, W032/3098, Staff College Regulations, 1922; A.R. Godwin-Austin, *The Staff and the Staff College* (London 1927), 287–9.
32 LAC, VP, vol. 4, file: 1923: Staff College; PRO, W032/3098, Staff College Regulations, 1922.
33 LAC, CP, vol. 24, Biography – Notes.
34 LAC, VP, vol. 5, Report on Staff College Course, January–July 1924; Report on Staff College Course, Aug.–Dec. 1924, file: 1924 5–6 Part B; Godwin-Austin, *The Staff and the Staff College*, 288–9.
35 Brian Holden Reid, 'J.F.C. Fuller and B.H. Liddell Hart: A Comparison,' *Military Review* 70 (May 1990): 5, 64–73; LAC, VP, vol. 5, Report on Staff College Course, Jan.–July 1924, Aug.–Dec. 1924, file: 1924 5–6, Part B; Crerar's Staff College Notebooks, RMC Massey Library Archives.
36 LAC, CP, vol. 10, D213, Some Remarks on the Changing Techniques of War, Address to the Canadian Artillery Association, Feb. 1932; H.D.G. Crerar,

'Notes on Service Journals,' Review of *Journal of the Royal United Service Institution* in *Canadian Defence Quarterly* 10, no. 4 (1933): 517.
37 LAC, VP, vol. 5, Report on the Staff College Course, Aug.–Dec. 1924; H.D.G. Crerar, 'Notes on Service Journals,' *Canadian Defence Quarterly* 10, no. 1 (1932): 122; 'The Study of War by Junior Officers: Some Further Views and Experiences,' *Journal of the Royal United Service Institution* 77 (Aug. 1932): 527–37.
38 LAC, CP, vol. 10, D214, Canada and Empire Defence, 1923; D213, Lecture 1, 1st Class, Military History 1928; H.D.G. Crerar, 'Notes on Service Journals,' Review of *Journal of the Royal United Service Institution* in *Canadian Defence Quarterly* 8, no. 4 (1931): 585.
39 LAC, VP, vol. 4, Introductory Message by Major-General Sir Edmund Ironside, 23 Jan. 1923, file: 4-22 (1923).
40 LAC, VP, vol. 5, file: 1924 Tour of the Continent, Report and Diary; CP, vol. 10, D214, Report on the Italian Tour, Jan. 1924.
41 LAC, CP, vol. 22, D380, Toast to Dominions, 19 Dec. 1924.
42 Interview with Peggy Crerar Palmer, 16 Apr. 1991.
43 LAC, PRC, Crerar's Personal File, file C, Crerar to McNaughton, 1 Apr. 1926.
44 LAC, VP, vol. 5, file: 1925–26 Staff College Friends, Vanier to Crerar, Feb. 1926.
45 LAC, CP, vol. 22, D380, Confidential Report, Staff College, Nov. 1924, file: Appointments, Transfers and Reports, 1915–1931. Some sources indicate that officers rarely received poor reports and that Dominion officers were examined even less rigorously. Martin Van Crevald, *The Training of Staff Officers* (New York 1990), 51; Pope, *Soldiers and Politicians*, 54; LAC, VP, vol. 5, Vanier to Crerar, 20 Dec. 1925, file: Staff College Friends Correspondence.
46 LAC, CP, vol. 22, D380, McNaughton to Crerar, 5 Sept. 1924.
47 LAC, CP, vol. 22, D380, Crerar to McNaughton, 19 Dec. 1924; High Commissioner to Crerar, 10 Dec. 1924.
48 Eayrs, *In Defence of Canada*, 1:89.
49 LAC, PRC, Crerar's Personal File, Major-General, Director of Staff Duties to Aldershot Command, 31 Dec. 1924; CP, vol. 22, D380, McNaughton to Crerar, 18 Feb. 1925; CP, vol 6, D153, Crerar to Collins, 12 June 1945.
50 Richard A. Preston, *Canada and 'Imperial Defence': A Study of the Origins of the British Commonwealth's Defence Organization, 1867–1919* (Durham, NC 1967), 527–8.
51 LAC, CP, vol. 6, D153, Crerar to Major-General R.J. Collins, 12 June 1945.
52 LAC, CP, vol. 22, D380, McNaughton to Crerar, 18 Feb. 1925; Crerar to Colonel Roy, 31 May 1925; Crerar's quote from 'Canada and Empire Defence,' LAC, CP, vol. 10, D214.

53 LAC, MP, vol. 109, file: National Defence Headquarters Reorganization, 1922–4; Harris, *Canadian Brass*, 153–7; LAC, RG24, C-5075, HQC 3574, MacBrien to Minister, 26 Mar. 1926; Major W. Alexander Morrison, *The Voice of Defence: The History of the Conference of Defence Associations* (Ottawa 1982), 64–5.
54 LAC, CP, vol. 22, D380, Wavell to McNaughton, 17 Jan. 1926; Crerar's Personal File, file C, Annual Confidential Report, 23 Nov. 1925; LAC, CP, vol. 6, D153, Crerar to Collins, 12 June 1945; vol. 22, D382, Crerar to Colonel Phipps, 24 Aug. 1925; Wavell to Phipps, 31 Aug. 1925; Major-General R.J. Collins, *Lord Wavell: A Military Biography* (London 1948), 117–9; RMC, Crerar Scrapbook, from a Second World War interview with Jack Mosher, 'General Crerar Says,' n.d; DND, DHH, Interview with Brigadier Orde; PRO, WO, 196/24, Report by the War Office Standing Committee on Coast Defence, 20 Dec. 1928.
55 Crerar's Personal File, Annual Confidential Report 1925. See, for example, LAC, CP, vol. 6, D153, Problems of Canadian Defence, Lecture to Southern Command, 3 Nov. 1925.
56 LAC, CP, vol. 9, D210. Extract from The Development of Closer Relations between the Military Forces of the Empire, 31 Mar. 1926. Also published in *Journal of the Royal United Service Institution* 71 (Aug. 1926), 451–62, and *Canadian Defence Quarterly* 3 (July 1926), 423–32.
57 LAC, CP, vol. 9, D219, The Development of Closer Relations between the Military Forces of the Empire, 30 Jan. 1926.
58 LAC, CP, vol. 10, D214, Canada and Empire Defence (second version); vol. 22, D380, Appointments, Transfers and Reports 1915–1931, 'Problems of Canadian Defence' to Southern Command, Salisbury 1925; Letter to the Editor, 23 Aug. 1925.
59 LAC, Mackenzie King Papers, MG26 J2, Correspondence, 122882.
60 LAC, CP, vol. 19, D338, Crerar to Grattan O'Leary, 1 Aug. 1940; G.A. Phillips, *The General Strike: The Politics of Industrial Conflict* (London 1976), 161–2.
61 LAC, CP, vol. 22, D382 R. Whigham to CIGS, 18 May 1926; vol. 14, D232, Memorandum on Experience and Lessons of the General Strike, May 1926 with Reference to War Office Organization, 20 May 1926.
62 LAC, CP, vol. 22, D382, Personal Papers 1924–5, War Office: General Correspondence; vol. 6, D153, Crerar to Collins, 10 June 1945.
63 LAC, VP, vol. 5, Vanier to Crerar, 24 Mar. 1926.
64 LAC, CP, vol. 22, D382, Crerar to McNaughton, 25 June 1926.
65 Crerar's Personal File, Annual Confidential Report for 1926; LAC, CP, vol. 22, D380, Extracts from Confidential Reports, 1925, and McNaughton to Crerar, 15 Mar. 1926.

484 Notes to pages 82–7

66 Harris, *Canadian Brass*, 194–5; David French, *Raising Churchill's Army: The British Army and the War against Germany, 1919–1945* (Oxford 2000), 60–1.
67 Crerar's Personal File, Annual Confidential Report 1926; Recommendation, Chief of Staff MacBrien to D.C.G.S., 4 May 1927.
68 LAC, CP, vol. 22, D380, Colonel H.E. Boak to Crerar, Jan. 1928; William E.J. Hutchinson, 'Test of a Corps Commander: Lieutenant-General Guy Granville Simonds, Normandy – 1944' (unpublished MA thesis, University of Victoria, 1982), 58–64; interview with Brigadier G.E. Beament, Oct. 1990.
69 Crerar's Personal File, Annual Confidential Report 1927.
70 Hillmer and McAndrew, 'The Cunning of Restraint,' 40–7; Harris, *Canadian Brass*, 153–5.
71 DND, DHH, Orde Interview; LAC, RG24, C-5056, HQC 4451, Policy for Selection of Officers, 15 Mar. 1919; Correspondence, Secretary, Militia Council to Adjutant-General, 19 Mar. 1920.
72 DND, DHH, Orde Interview.
73 Harris, *Canadian Brass*, 155, 196–7; LAC, CP, vol. 22, D380, T.V. Anderson to Crerar, 20 Jan. 1928; Richard A. Preston, *Canada's RMC: A History of the Royal Military College* (Toronto 1969), 250–3.
74 Crerar vented his emotions in an undated rough draft. LAC, CP, vol. 22, D380, Crerar to Colonel T.V. Anderson, 17 Jan. 1928; Anderson to Crerar, 20 Jan. 1928; DND, DHH, Orde Interview; Palmer interview.
75 LAC, CP, vol. 7, D214, Lecture Notes for the First Class.
76 Beament interview; RMC, Registrar's File Cadet 749, C.F. Constantine, Report on Crerar, 24 June 1929, and K.M. Holloway, Staff Adjutant to Crerar, 14 May 1929; Crerar's Personal File, Annual Confidential Report for 1928.
77 J.L. Granatstein interviews with Sparling and Geoffrey Walsh.
78 LAC, CP, vol. 18, D379, Crerar to Bob Partiger, 10 Dec. 1929.

Chapter 5

1 Library and Archives Canada (LAC), Crerar Papers (CP), vol. 22, D380, McNaughton to Crerar, 23 Nov. 1928.
2 LAC, CP, vol. 19, D338, Crerar to Grattan O'Leary, 1 Aug. 1940; Stephen Harris, *Canadian Brass: The Making of a Professional Army, 1860–1939* (Toronto 1988), 174–82.
3 Major W. Alexander Morrison, *The Voice of Defence: The History of the Conference of Defence Associations* (Ottawa 1982), 64–5.
4 Harris, *Canadian Brass*, 155–7; Department of National Defence (DND), Directorate of History and Heritage (DHH), National Defence Headquarters: Proposed Reorganization.

5 DND, DHH, Brigadier Orde Interview, 77/490.
6 *Report of the Department of National Defence*, 1929–39 (Ottawa 1939).
7 LAC, McNaughton Papers (MP), vol. 104, series II, file: 1031-33, Return Showing Number of Officers and Number of Other Ranks on Duty with Pay on 31 December 1931, in the Several Departments at National Defence Headquarters; DND, DHH, Orde Interview; *Report of the Department of National Defence for the Fiscal Year Ending 1926* (Ottawa 1926), 7.
8 LAC, RG24, C-5046, HQC 1-1-89, Appointments to General Staff.
9 LAC, RG24, C-5046, HQC 1-1-89, McNaughton to AG, Feb. 1930; C-5056, Civilian Personnel, Organization of General Staff, AG to CGS, 19 Apr. 1929.
10 Maurice A. Pope, *Soldiers and Politicians: The Memoirs of Lt-General Maurice A. Pope, CB, MC* (Toronto 1962), 81.
11 Harris, *Canadian Brass*, 156–7.
12 McNaughton to AG, Feb. 1930; AG to CGS, 19 Apr. 1929.
13 DND, DHH, Orde Interview; Crerar's Personal Service File, file A.
14 LAC, CP, vol. 13. See, for example, The Optional Clause and the Peace Pact, D228, and files D225, D226; vol. 18, D379, Crerar to Dick Dewing, 15 Feb. 1930; Crerar to Bob Partiger, 10 Dec. 1930; LAC, RG24, C-5077, Minutes of Censorship Committee, 1929; vol. 2684, HQS 5199, JCS Minutes.
15 LAC, CP, vol. 11, D218, Memorandum on the Reorganization of the Non-Permanent Active Militia, Jan. 1931.
16 Ibid.; Harris, *Canadian Brass*, 174–7.
17 LAC, RG25, vol. 1748, file 506, Membership Lists of CIIA.
18 LAC, CP, vol. 10, D214, Empire Interests in the Near and Middle East, 1930.
19 Philip Wigley, *Canada and the Transition to Commonwealth: British-Canadian Relations 1917–1926* (Cambridge 1977), 270–2.
20 LAC, CP, vol. 18, D379. See Personal Correspondence, 1929–1930; Crerar to Robert Partiger, 10 Dec. 1929.
21 LAC, CP, vol. 11, D220, Discipline of the Armed Forces: Memo Reports 1930–31, and The Statute of Westminster in Its Bearing on the Armed Forces of the Crown, 1931.
22 H.D.G. Crerar, Review of *The Co-ordination of Imperial Defence*, by Major Walter Elliot, *Canadian Defence Quarterly* 7, no. 3 (1930): 430.
23 LAC, CP, vol. 22, D380, Crerar to McNaughton, 10 July 1931.
24 LAC, CP, vol. 12, Crerar's comments on F.R. Scott's *Canada and the Commonwealth* and Escott Reid's 'The Future of the Commonwealth in the Light of Changing World Conditions.' See letter to Robertson 5 Apr. 1933, D221 and D223.
25 LAC, CP, vol. 11, D218, Political Obligations and Military Problems of Canada, Pearson to Crerar, 12 Mar. 1931; J.L. Granatstein, *The Ottawa Men: The*

Civil Service Mandarins, 1935–1957 (Toronto 1982), 42; LAC, RG25, vol. 1850, file 922, CIIA Research Programme.
26 Vanier quote from LAC, MP, vol. 112, Vanier to McNaughton, 1 Apr. 1932; CP, vol. 18, D379, Crerar to Sutherland Brown, 12 Jan. 1932; LAC, MP, vol. 104, Disarmament, Book G.
27 LAC, CP, vol. 13, D229. Quote from LAC, vol. 13, D229, Geneva diary, April–July 1932, 12 May 1932. Crerar's views after his return are from General Staff Memorandum on the General Commissions Resolution of 23 July 1932, 12 Sept. 1932; LAC, CP, vol. 18, D379, Crerar to W.O.H. Dodds, 19 Aug. 1932; Crerar to W.A. Riddell, 2 Sept. 1932; Crerar to Grasett, 11 Jan. 1933. Dupre quote from LAC CP, vol. 1, D3, Letter to DM Sutherland, 8 Aug. 1932.
28 LAC, CP, vol. 18, D39, Crerar to W.H.P. Elkins, Commandant RMC, 8 May 1933.
29 James Eayrs, *In Defence of Canada: From the Great War to the Great Depression* (Toronto 1964), 120–1.
30 Morrison, *The Voice of Defence*, 65.
31 LAC, CP, vol. 18, D379, Personal Correspondence, 1929–1930; Crerar's Personal File, Annual Confidential Report, 1929; Colonel, DMT and SD to Brigadier Gibson, DOC, MD No. 6, 24 June 1930.
32 LAC, CP, vol. 22, Crerar to Lieutenant-Colonel F.R. Phelan, 28 Feb. 1933, file: Service Matters, 1929–1933.
33 LAC, CP, vol. 10, D213, Crerar, 'Notes on Service Journals,' *Canadian Defence Quarterly* 8, no. 2 (1931): 282; Some Remarks on the Changing Techniques of War, Address to the Canadian Artillery Association, Feb. 1932.
34 From 'Notes on Service Journals,' *Canadian Defence Quarterly* 7, no. 4 (1930): 577. See Ken Stuart's 'Editorial on "Organization, Infantry,"' *Canadian Defence Quarterly* 9, no. 1 (1931): 5; Serge M. Durflinger on the cautious approach to mechanization and armour in 'The Canadian Defence Quarterly 1933–1935: Canadian Military Writing of a Bygone Era,' *Canadian Defence Quarterly* 20 (June 1991): 46–7.
35 Harris, *Canadian Brass*, 157; John Swettenham, *McNaughton* (Toronto 1968), 1:277–8; 'Notes on Service Journals,' *Canadian Defence Quarterly* 9, no. 3 (1932): 431.
36 Quote in 'Notes on Service Journals,' *Canadian Defence Quarterly* 10, no. 3 (1933): 382–3. See also 10, no. 2 (1933): 382–3, and 8, no. 4 (1931): 517–18. First quote from 8, no. 3 (1931): 426–7. LAC, CP, vol. 18, D337, Crerar to the CGS, 4 Apr. 1938.
37 Eayrs, *In Defence of Canada*, 1:88.
38 LAC, CP, vol. 18, D379, Crerar to Haining, 28 Apr. 1933.

39 LAC, CP, vol. 18, D379, Crerar to E. Panet, 14 June 1933.
40 Crerar's Personal File, Annual Confidential Report, 1929; Report by Officer's Immediate Commander, 1930.
41 Crerar's tactical knowledge was characterized as 'sound' in place of the choices on the form: *scanty, average, excellent*. Report by Officer's Immediate Commander, 1931.
42 LAC, CP, vol. 1, D3, Matthews to Crerar, 21 Apr. 1933; Crerar's Personal File, HQ C.3523 to Militia Secretary, 1 Apr. 1933; Memorandum, H.Q. 8648-1 (on Crerar's appointment as technical advisor); Report by Superior Officer, 1932; LAC, CP, D3, Dupre to McNaughton, 8 Aug. 1932.
43 Public Record Office (PRO), W032/3878, XC8911, DMO and I to DSD, 1926; LAC, CP, vol. 10, D212, Notes on Imperial Defence College; vol. 18, D379, Reading List, Imperial Defence College; Pope, *Soldiers and Politicians*, 98–105.
44 LAC, CP, vol. 18, D379, Draft of Reply to R.H. Haining, 1934. Crerar was one of three referees for the prize-winning essay from which this quote was drawn. See 'Editorial,' 395, and 2nd Lieutenant Wm. Wallace Goforth, 'The Influence of Mechanization and Motorization on the Organization and Training of the Non-Permanent Active Militia,' *Canadian Defence Quarterly* 10, no. 4 (1933): 431.
45 LAC, CP, vol. 11, D220, draft and final version of Lecture on Canada and Imperial Defence, 1934.
46 DND, DHH, 000.8 (D5), Crerar to Maurice Pope, 2 June 1936.
47 Crerar's Personal File, Brigadier C.F. Constantine to the Secretary, High Commissioner of Canada, 24 Sept. 1934, and Secretary George Vanier to Constantine, 10 Oct. 1934; LAC, CP, vol. 1, D3, IDC Confidential Report from Admiral L.G. Preston, 13 Dec. 1934.
48 DND, DHH, 000.8 (D5), Crerar to Maurice Pope, 2 June 1936
49 C.P. Stacey, *Six Years of War: The Official History of the Canadian Army in the Second World War* (Ottawa 1955), 1:5–14; Harris, *Canadian Brass*, 181–2.
50 Quote from Pope, *Soldiers and Politicians*, 70–2; See Norman Hillmer, 'Defence and Ideology: The Anglo-Canadian Military "Alliance" in the 1930s,' *International Journal* 33 (Summer 1978): 600.
51 LAC, MP, vol. 100, ACM to McNaughton, 8 Feb. 1945.
52 LAC, CP, vol. 1, D3, Brigadier C.F. Constantine to the Secretary, High Commissioner of Canada, 24 Sept. 1934, and Secretary George Vanier to Constantine, 10 Oct. 1934; CP, vol. 10, D211, Crerar to CGS, Feb. 1935.
53 Pope, *Soldiers and Politicians*, 93.
54 Swettenham, *McNaughton*, 2:315–7; Harris, *Canadian Brass*, 158; LAC, CP, vol. 10, D211, Crerar to Vanier, 17 June 1935.

Chapter 6

1 Department of National Defence (DND), Directorate of History and Heritage (DHH), Orde Interview; DHHBIOG L, HFG Letson Interview, May 1981; LAC, MG27 III B5, Mackenzie Papers, vol. 29, X-4, The Requirements of Canadian Defence, Nov. 1935.
2 DND, DHH, Orde and Letson interviews.
3 J.L. Granatstein, *The Ottawa Men: The Civil Service Mandarins, 1935–1957* (Toronto 1982), 63–91; John Hilliker, *Canada's Department of External Affairs* (Montreal and Kingston 1990), 1:208–9.
4 LAC, CP, vol. 12, D222, latter quote from Crerar to Alan Plaunt; vol. 15, D431, see Crerar to Colonel C.H.L. Sharman, 18 Feb. 1935; Major W. Alexander Morrison, *The Voice of Defence: The History of the Conference of Defence Associations* (Ottawa 1982), 65–6.
5 J.L. Granatstein and Robert Bothwell, '"A Self-Evident National Duty": Canadian Foreign Policy, 1935–1939,' *Journal of Imperial and Commonwealth History* 2 (January 1975): 212–33; Hilliker, *Department of External Affairs*, 176–208; Norman Hillmer, 'The Anglo-Canadian Neurosis: The Case of O.D. Skelton,' in *Britain and Canada: Survey of a Changing Relationship*, ed. Peter Lyon (London 1976), 63–84.
6 LAC, CP, vol. 14, D259, Crerar to Brigadier W.H.P. Elkins, DOC, MD2, 2 Mar. 1935; vol. 11, D218, Scheme for the Re-organization of the Canadian Militia, 15 July 1935. Work had also begun on Defence Scheme No. 4, a plan to send a Canadian contingent to take part in a minor empire crisis. See LAC, RG24, vol. 2733, HQS-5718.
7 LAC, CP, vol. 14, D259, Crerar to Brigadier W.H.P. Elkins, DOC, MD 2, 2 Mar. 1935; RG24, C-5046, HQC1-1-89, Crerar to CGS, 16 Feb. 1938.
8 Granatstein, *Ottawa Men*, 68–70.
9 LAC, CP, vol. 10, D211, latter quote from Crerar to M.A. Pope, 11 Apr. 1936; Stephen Harris, 'The Canadian General Staff and the Higher Organization of Defence, 1919–1939,' *War and Society* 3, no. 1 (1985): 90–6.
10 LAC, RG24, vol. 2684, Memo: An Outline, the Function and History of the IDC, 5 Sept. 1936.
11 LAC, CP, vol. 10, D211, last quote from Crerar to Colonel W.T. Torr, 13 Jan. 1936; vol. 12, D222, Reid to Crerar, 9 Jan. 1936, D222; McNaughton Papers, vol. 103, series II, The Higher Direction of War, file: January 1935; CP, vol. 10, Christie to Crerar, 1936.
12 LAC, CP, vol. 12, D223, Crerar to Professor R.A. MacKay re Latter's 'Canada and the Empire,' 16 Sept. 1936'; Granatstein, *Ottawa Men*, 63–75.
13 LAC, CP, vol. 14, D231. See, for example, 'Appreciation of U.K. Govern-

ment Policy in the Italo-Ethiopian Dispute,' 1935, and Crerar to Bob Partiger, 12 Oct. 1935; vol. 18, D381, Crerar noted that Britain was unprepared to take action in the Rhineland crisis of 1936. Crerar to W.M. Taylor, 11 Apr. 1936; CP, vol. 11, D220, The Statute of Westminster in Its Bearing on the Armed Forces of the Crown, 1931.
14 James Eayrs, *In Defence of Canada: Appeasement and Rearmament* (Toronto 1965), 2:138–9.
15 C.P. Stacey, *Six Years of War: The Official History of the Canadian Army in the Second World War* (Ottawa 1955), 1:11–13; Stephen Harris, *Canadian Brass: The Making of a Professional Army, 1860–1939* (Toronto 1988), 181–3.
16 Public Record Office (PRO), W0196/3, Defence of Pacific Ports, and W0196/4, Defence of East Ports, 1936; LAC, RG24, vol. 2774, HQ7-6756, Report on Coast Defence Construction Committee; Stacey, *Six Years of War*, 1:7–13; LAC, CP, vol. 19, D305, Crerar to Colonel A.F. Duguid, Historical Section, 3 Jan. 1946.
17 LAC, MG27 III B5, Mackenzie Papers, vol. 37, file D-5, The Etibank Incident, Aug. 1936.
18 LAC, CP, vol. 11, D217, Lecture: 'An Appreciation, Defence Problems Confronting Canada'; RG24, vol. 2774, file: HQC 6670, Halifax Incident; CP, vol. 15, D431, Crerar to H.H. Matthews, Dec. 1936; James Eayrs, *In Defence of Canada: From the Great War to the Great Depression* (Toronto 1967), 1:101.
19 LAC, CP, vol. 12, D222, Memorandum to CGS, 10 Dec. 1936.
20 LAC, CP, vol. 9, D210, Crerar to Keenleyside, 25 Jan. 1937; LAC, MG27 III B5, Mackenzie Papers, vol. 37, D2, memorandum.
21 LAC, RG25, vol. 1789, file 318-T, Imperial Conference: Defence; DND, DHH, Pope to Crerar, 14 May 1936; LAC, RG24, vol. 2684, HQS 5199, vol. 1, memorandum, 7 Jan. 1937.
22 LAC, CP, vol. 10, D211, Crerar to Haining, 30 Mar. 1937.
23 LAC, RG24 (G1), vol. 1817, file 63, series of letters between DMND and Skelton; Mackenzie Papers, vol. 30, X-12, Correspondence between King and MND; LAC, CP, vol. 10, D211, Pearson to Crerar, 19 Mar. 1937; Mackenzie King Papers and Diary, 5 May 1937; CP, vol. 21, D329, Crerar to Stacey, 14 Sept. 1951.
24 LAC, RG25, vol. 1788, Documents on Imperial Defence Conference; CP, vol. 9, D210, Crerar to Christie, Jan. 1936, file: Correspondence with Loring Christie; Hilliker, *Department of External Affairs*, 200–9; Maurice A. Pope, *Soldiers and Politicians: The Memoirs of Lt-General Maurice A. Pope, CB, MC* (Toronto 1962), 129–30.
25 LAC, CP, vol. 18, D381, Crerar to Trappes-Lomax, 4 Nov. 1937.
26 LAC, CP, vol. 11, D218, Memorandum on a Canadian Organization for

the Higher Direction of National Defence, 8 Mar., 31 May, and 28 Dec. 1937.
27 DND, DHH, 000.8(D3), DMO and I, Liaison Letters.
28 See LAC, RG24, vol. 2646, file: HQS 3498; Harris, *Canadian Brass*, 183.
29 LAC, MG27 III B5, Mackenzie Papers, vol. 29, X-4, The Requirements of Canadian Defence, 1936 and 1937; LAC, CP, vol. 18, D381, Crerar to Pope, 19 Aug. 1937; Pope to Crerar, 24 Aug. 1937.
30 LAC, MG27 III B5, Mackenzie Papers, vol. 37, file D-8.
31 LAC, CP, vol. 9, D210, Extracts from Personal Letters to and from Colonel Partiger, M.0.2, War Office, Sept. 1937 to Feb. 1938.
32 LAC, CP, vol. 10, D211, Crerar to Sir Ronald Adam, DCIGS, 1 June 1938. Emphasis in original.
33 LAC, CP, vol. 10, D211, Liaison with Military Attaché.
34 LAC, CP, vol. 14, D231, Visit to Germany, 16–21 June 1937; vol. 10, D214, Memorandum to the CGS, 2 Oct. 1937.
35 DND, DHH, 112.3M1(D3), Study of World Political Trends, 1937.
36 LAC, RG25, vol. 1781, file 254(II), International Situation.
37 LAC, RG24, C-5067, file 33-ND-CGS, 22 June 1937; C-5075, Military Training.
38 LAC, CP, vol. 1, D3, Crerar to CGS, 30 Oct. 1937; vol. 11, D218, Crerar to Victor Sifton, 8 Aug. 1940, The Organization of the Department of National Defence; J. L. Granatstein interview with Elliot Rodgers; LAC, RG25 G1, vol. 1785, file 283, part I, Intelligence Summaries.
39 LAC, MG27 III B5, Mackenzie Papers, vol. 30, X-19, Ashton to the Minister, 14 Oct. 1937; LAC, CP, vol. 11, D218, Crerar to Victor Sifton, 8 Aug. 1940.
40 LAC, CP, vol. 10, D211, Crerar to Sir Ronald Adam, DCIGS, 1 June 1938.
41 LAC, CP, vol. 18, D337, Crerar to Lt-General Sir J.E.S. Brind, 10 Mar. 1938.
42 LAC, MG27 III B5, Mackenzie Papers, vol. 29, file: Canadian Defence Requirements, 1935–38.
43 LAC, CP, vol. 10, D211, Crerar to Pearson, 21 Dec. 1937.
44 LAC, CP, vol. 18, D381, Crerar to Major J.H.F. Pain, 12 Feb. 1935.
45 LAC, CP, vol. 18, D381, Dewing to Crerar, 18 Sept. 1937.
46 LAC, MG27 III B5, Mackenzie Papers, vol. 30, X-40, LeFleche to the Minister, 6 Aug. 1938; CGS to the Minister, 8 Oct. 1938.
47 LAC, MG27 III B5, Mackenzie Papers, vol. 30, X-40, Memorandum, Ashton to the Minister, 7 Oct. 1937.
48 Royal Military College (RMC), Registrar's File, H.Q.8648-1, vol. 4, Adjutant-General to Commandant, 23 July 1938; LAC, CP, vol. 1, D3, Crerar, Memo to CGS, 30 Sept. 1937; Crerar's Personal File, Report by Officer's Immediate Superior, 1935 and 1936.

49 LAC, CP, vol. 14, D248, H.H. Matthews to Crerar, 3 Oct. 1938; Richard Preston, *Canada's RMC: A History of the Royal Military College* (Toronto 1969), 286–7; LAC, CP, vol. 15, D262, Crerar to Lt-Colonel W.G. Wurtle, 23 June 1939; vol. 14, D254, Crerar to Sansom, 12 Dec. 1938; J.L. Granatstein, *The Generals: The Canadian Army's Senior Commanders in the Second World War* (Toronto 1993), 45.
50 Harris, *Canadian Brass*, 186; LAC, CP, vol. 14, D250, HQS 3498, FD27, Crerar to A.G., 8 Mar. 1939.
51 Eayrs, *In Defence of Canada*, 121.
52 LAC, CP, vol. 14, D243, Ashton to Crerar, 6 Sept. and 20 Sept. 1938; M.A. Hooker, 'Serving Two Masters: Ian Mackenzie and Civil–Military Relations in Canada, 1936–39, *Journal of Canadian Studies* 21 (Spring 1986): 35–9; vol. 15, D261, Crerar to Stacey, 24 Aug. 1939.
53 J.L. Granatstein interview with R.B. Bennett; author interview with P.T. Nation, 1991.
54 LAC, CP, vol. 14, D255, Crerar to Rogers, various letters 1938.
55 LAC, CP, vol. 14, D253, Crerar to MacDermot, 20 Mar. 1939.
56 LAC, CP, vol. 14, D253, Personal Correspondence.
57 LAC, CP, vol. 14, D253, Crerar to Owen Clough, 14 July 1939.

Chapter 7

1 C.P. Stacey, *Six Years of War: The Official History of the Canadian Army in the Second World War* (Ottawa 1955), 1:40–3.
2 Ibid., 38–53.
3 LAC, CP, vol. 14, D248, Crerar to Major-General H.H. Matthews, Adjutant-General, 2 Sept. 1939.
4 LAC, CP, vol. 1, D3, Crerar to Anderson, 2 Sept. 1939.
5 Crerar to H.H. Matthews, 2 Sept. 1939; LAC, CP, vol. 1, D3, Crerar to Kenneth Greene, Greene and Robertson, Insurance Brokers, n.d. (reply received 5 Sept.).
6 LAC, CP, vol. 1, D3, T.V. Anderson to Crerar, 25 Sept. 1939.
7 LAC, CP, vol. 1, D3, Anderson to Crerar, 22 and 25 Sept. 1939.
8 LAC, CP, vol. 14, D248, Matthews to Crerar, 28 Aug. 1938.
9 LAC, CP, vol. 14, D252, Crerar to Major E. Greene, 19 Sept. 1939; C.P. Stacey to Crerar, 4 Sept. 1939.
10 LAC, CP, vol. 14, D255, Crerar to Norman Rogers, Minister of Labour, 11 Sept. 1939.
11 Richard Preston, *Canada's RMC: A History of the Royal Military College* (Toronto 1969), 287.

12 LAC, CP, vol. 14, D248, Crerar to Matthews, 3 Oct. 1939.
13 LAC, CP, vol. 14, D251, first quotes from Remarks to RMC Cadets, 11 Oct. 1939, in RMC – Notes for Addresses and Lectures, 1935–1939; Preston, *Canada's RMC*, 287.
14 LAC, CP, vol. 1, D3, Memorandum [regarding Crerar's appointment]; PRC, Crerar's Personal File: H.D.G. Crerar, RMC Orders, Part II, Staff, 17 Oct. 1939; CP, vol. 15, D271, War Diary, Senior Officer (WD, SO), Sept. 1939, CMHQ.
15 LAC, CP, vol. 15, D271, WD, SO, 16–20 Oct. 1939.
16 LAC, McNaughton Papers, vol. 252, file: War Orders, Higher Organization for War; Stacey, *Six Years of War*, 1:194–203.
17 LAC, Lester B. Pearson Papers (LPP), MG26 N8, vol. 1, Pearson diary entry, 29 Oct. 1939.
18 LAC, CP, vol. 1, D9, Crerar to Minister of National Defence J.L. Ralston, 17 June 1940; D7, Crerar to Price Montague, 28 June 1941.
19 LAC, LPP, vol. 1, diary entry 29 Oct. 1939; University of Toronto Archives (UTA), Vincent Massey Papers (VMP), box 310, vol. 40, diary entry 23 Nov. 1939.
20 LAC, CP, vol. 15, D271, WD, SO, 30 Oct. 1939; Vincent Massey, *What's Past Is Prologue: The Memoirs of the Right Honorable Vincent Massey* (Toronto 1963), 320–1.
21 Jack Pickersgill, *The Mackenzie King Record* (Toronto 1960), 1:75–6; C.P. Stacey, *Arms, Men and Governments: The War Policies of Canada, 1939–1945* (Ottawa 1970), 206.
22 LAC, CP, vol. 1, D3, Adjutant-General to Crerar, 17 Oct. 1939; RMC Massey Library Archives, Major-General W.H.P. Elkins Papers, Loggie to Elkins, 28 Nov. 1939; Stacey, *Six Years of War*, 1:195.
23 LAC, CP, vol. 1, D8, Crerar to Lt-Colonel V. Dykes, 23 Nov. 1939.
24 LAC, LPP, vol. 1, quote from Pearson diary, 31 Oct. 1939.
25 Telegram 610, High Commissioner to Secretary of State for External Affairs, 4 Nov. 1939, reprinted in David R. Murray, ed., *Documents on Canadian External Relations, 1939–1941/Part I* (Ottawa 1974), 7:381.
26 Quotes from Stacey, *Six Years of War*, 1:213–4; Claude Bissell notes that Crerar had 'assigned' an important role to the high commissioner. *The Imperial Canadian*), 141–2.
27 LAC, CP, vol. 1, D2, from Memorandum on Responsibilities and Functions of Canadian Military Headquarters, 18 Apr. 1940, and Memorandum of 10 June 1940.
28 King's College, London (KCL), Liddell Hart Centre for Military Archives (LHC), General Richard Dewing Papers, Richard Dewing diary, 6 and 24 Nov. 1939.

29 LAC, CP, vol. 1, D271, WD, SO, 30 Oct. 1939; quote from L.B. Pearson, *Mike: The Memoirs of the Right Honourable Lester B. Pearson* (Toronto 1972), 1:149–50; KCL, LHC, Dewing Papers, diary entry 8 July 1940.
30 LAC, RG24, vol. 13,359, WD, 'G' Branch, entries Dec. 1939–Jan. 1940.
31 LAC, CP, vol. 15, D271, WD, SO, 4 and 5 Dec. 1939.
32 LAC, LPP, vol. 1, diary entry 18 Jan. 1940; KCL, LHC, Alanbrooke Papers, Notes on My Life, 3/A/III, 28 Jan. 1940.
33 LAC, LPP, Pearson diary, 24 Dec. 1939.
34 C.P. Stacey, *Arms, Men and Governments: The War Policies of Canada 1939–1945* (Ottawa 1970), 212.
35 LAC, CP, vol. 11, D220, The Statute of Westminster ... 1931; Stacey, *Arms, Men and Governments*, 211–3.
36 See John Swettenham, *McNaughton* (Toronto 1968), 2:30–1; Stacey also notes McNaughton's confrontational style in *Arms, Men and Governments*, 213–6.
37 LAC, CP, vol. 15, D271, WD, SO, quote from 1/Int.Sum/1, 7 Nov. 1939, Massey to External (Crerar to CGS), Appendices.
38 LAC, CP, vol. 22, D335, T.A. Crerar to Norman Rogers, 18 Nov. 1939.
39 LAC, CP, vol. 1, D271, WD, SO, 24 Nov. and 23 Dec. 1939 for discussions on McNaughton's cable. See WD, SO, 3 Apr. 1940, and Swettenham, *McNaughton*, 2:47.
40 LAC, CP, vol. 22, D335, Crerar to McNaughton, 29 Jan. 1940.
41 LAC, CP, vol. 1, D335, handwritten draft, Crerar to Norman Rogers, n.d., App't, Transfers, Reports, Oct. 1939–Mar. 1942.
42 LAC, LPP, vol. 1, Pearson diary 5–20 Apr. 1940.
43 LAC, CP, vol. 22, D335, paraphrase and notes of conversation between Crerar and Rogers, n.d.
44 LAC, CP, vol. 15, D271, WD, SO, entries for 1, 5, and 30 Apr. 1940. See WD, SO, 3 May 1940.
45 LAC, CP, vol. 1, D2, memorandum: Responsibilities and Functions of Canadian Military Headquarters, 18 Apr. 1940, and memorandum: Notes on Discussion between the Minister of National Defence and Crerar, 26 Apr. 1940; quote from Stacey, *Six Years of War*, 1:196; LAC, RG24, vol. 13,359, Entries for Feb. in War Diary, 'G' Branch (particularly 29 Feb. 1940).
46 LAC, CP, vol. 1, D8, Crerar to Norman Rogers, 2 Dec. 1939.
47 Stacey, *Six Years of War*, 1:197.
48 LAC, CP, vol. 1, D271, WD, SO, 26–27 Jan. and 26. Feb 1940.
49 DND, DHH, Orde Interview; LAC, Maurice Pope Papers, MG27 III F4, vol. 1, diary 11 Jan. 1944.
50 LAC, CP, vol. 15, D271, WD, SO, 18 Mar. 1940.

51 LAC, CP, vol. 1, D271, WD, SO, 3–4 Jan. 1940; LPP, vol. 1, Pearson diary, 7 Jan. 1940; LAC, Pope Papers, diary 11 Jan. 1944.
52 LAC, CP, vol. 15, D271, WD, SO, 13–14 Feb. 1940; Stacey, *Six Years of War*, 1:73; John A. English, *The Canadian Army and the Normandy Campaign: A Study of Failure in High Command* (New York 1991), 65–6.
53 See Pickersgill, *The Mackenzie King Record*, 1:74–6; Crerar's remarks are recorded in LAC, CP, vol. 15, D271, WD, SO, 15 Feb. 1940; Swettenham, *McNaughton*, 2:45–6.
54 RMC, Massey Library Archives, Notes on Conference, 20 Apr. 1940; LAC, CP, vol. 1, D2, Notes Discussions between the MND and Major-General Crerar, 26 Apr. 1940; Memorandum, Decisions Made by Minister of National Defence at Conference, 7 May 1940.
55 RMC, Elkins Papers, Elkins Memorandum to the Minister, 25 Apr. 1940; LAC, CP, vol. 16, D271, Memorandum to the Minister, with Suggestions for Appointments, 7 May 1940; Stacey, *Six Years of War*, 1:196–7; DND, Hist, 89/86, Record of Visit to the UK of Defence Minister, Apr. 18–May 9, 1940.
56 Quote from E.L.M. Burns, *General Mud: Memoirs of Two World Wars* (Toronto 1970), 99; Maurice A. Pope, *Soldiers and Politicians: The Memoirs of Lt-General Maurice A. Pope, CB, MC* (Toronto 1962), 148–51.
57 KCL, LHC, Dewing Papers, diary entry 16 Apr. 1940.
58 LAC, CP, vol. 15, D271, WD, SO, 15–18 Apr. 1940; RG24, vol. 13,360, War Diary, General Staff Branch, 15–20 Apr. 1940.
59 Stacey, *Arms, Men and Governments*, 111–20; Queen's University Archives (QUA), Grant Dexter Papers (GDP), series I, section C, transfer case (TC) 2, Sifton to Grant Dexter, 22 May 1940; LAC, CP, vol. 1, D9, Crerar to Norman Rogers, 15 Feb. 1940.
60 Letter to the editor, *Times*, 1 June 1940.
61 LAC, CP, vol. 15, D271, Crerar recorded draft of telegram, WD, SO, 17 June 1940; telegram GS 882, WD, SO, June, Appendix B; LAC, CP, vol. 1, D9, Crerar to Captain H.A. 'Sandy' Dyde, 24 June 1940; D271, Crerar to Norman Rogers, 10 June 1940, and Crerar to J.L. Ralston, 17 June 1940; Robert Campbell, 'James Layton Ralston and Manpower for the Canadian Army' (unpublished MA thesis, Wilfrid Laurier University, 1986), 24–5.
62 LAC, CP, vol. 1, D9, Crerar to Ralston, 17 June 1940.
63 Ibid., and LAC, CP, vol. 1, D9, Crerar to Rogers, 10 June 1940; CP, vol. 1, D9, vol. 15, D271, WD, SO, 22 June 1940. Reply did not come until 1 July. Final quote GS882, Appendix B, WD, SO.
64 See Stacey, *Arms, Men and Governments*, 67–8; QUA, GDP, series I, TC2, quote is from Grant Dexter, Memo Conversation with Major-General H.D.G. Crerar, 13 Sept. 1940.

65 LAC, CP, vol. 15, D271, GS 0421, Defensor to Canmilitary, 1 July 1940, WD, SO, July: Appendix A; WD, SO, 1 July 1940.
66 LAC, CP, vol. 15, D271, WD, SO, 17 June 1940; RG24, vol. 13,361, War Diary, General Staff Branch, 17–18 June 1940; Swettenham, *McNaughton*, 2:114.
67 LAC, CP, vol. 15, D271, WD, SO, 27 June 1940; Swettenham, *McNaughton*, 2:119–22.

Chapter 8

1 Address to the House of Commons, 26 Jan. 1942, *Debates of the House of Commons*, vol. 1, *1942* (Ottawa 1942); Library and Archives Canada (LAC), Mackenzie King Papers (MKP), King Diaries, MG26 J13, microfiche T169–170, entries 18–26 Jan. 1942.
2 Stephen Harris, 'The Canadian General Staff and the Higher Organization of Defence, 1919–1939: A Problem of Civil–Military Relations,' *War and Society* 1 (May 1985): 83–98.
3 C.P. Stacey, *Arms, Men and Governments: The War Policies of Canada, 1939–1945* (Ottawa 1970), 111–15.
4 J.L. Granatstein, *The Ottawa Men: The Civil Service Mandarins, 1935–1957* (Toronto 1982), 201–7.
5 J.L. Granatstein, *Canada's War: The Politics of the Mackenzie King Government, 1939–1945* (Toronto 1975), 102–7.
6 Stacey, *Arms, Men and Governments*, 129; Queen's University Archives (QUA), Grant Dexter Papers (GDP), 2142, series I, section C, transfer case (TC) 2, folder 18, Memo of Conversation with Major-General H.D.G. Crerar, 13 Sept. 1940; Richard S. Malone, *A Portrait of War, 1939–1943* (Don Mills 1985), 59.
7 LAC, CP, vol. 1, D15, CGS Files – Matters to App't as VCGS; Privy Council Records, RG2 7C, Cabinet War Committee Minutes, vol. 1, 4 July 1940.
8 LAC, Andrew McNaughton Papers (MP), MG30E133, vol. 230, file CC7/30-1, McNaughton to Brigadier-General Arthur Clarke, 10 July 1940.
9 LAC, CP, vol. 22, D335, Crerar to John Dill, 5 July 1940; vol. 1, D4, Letters of Congrats.
10 LAC, MP, vol. 227, file: CC7/Crerar/6, Crerar to McNaughton, 16 July 1940.
11 LAC, CP, vol. 15, D271, Crerar to CGS, 2 July 1940; AC 903, Defensor to Canmilitary, 5 July 1940, Appendices to War Diary.
12 First quote from LAC, CP, vol. 1, D4, Crerar to Colonel C.H.L. Sharman, 24 July 1940; He expressed similar sentiments to Price Montague and others; D13, Draft 'Observations on Canadian Requirements in Respect to the

Army'; vol. 23, D418, Confidential Memorandum for the Minister, 15 July 1940.
13 LAC, CP, vol. 23, D418, Memorandum; vol. 1, D13, Rough Draft of 'Observations on Canadian Requirements in Respect to the Army,' CGS Files.
14 Editorial, *Globe*, 27 July 1940; editorial, *Whig-Standard*, 29 July 1940.
15 LAC, Lester Pearson Papers (LPP), vol. 3, Crerar to Pearson, 27 July 1940; CP, vol. 1, D12, Crerar to McNaughton, 8 Aug. 1940.
16 QUA, GDP, TC2, folder 18, Memo Conversation with Major-General Crerar, 13 Sept. 1940.
17 Stacey, *Arms, Men and Governments*, 129.
18 LAC, CP, vol. 1, D12, Crerar to McNaughton, 8 Aug. 1940; figure from J.R.M. Butler, *History of the Second World War*, United Kingdom Military Series (London 1957), 2:29–32.
19 LAC, RG2 7C, vol. 1, Cabinet War Committee Minutes (CWCM), 26 July 1940.
20 LAC, RG2 7C, vol. 1, CWCM, 26 July 1940; King Diaries, T151, diary entry 26 July 1940; RG2 7C, vol. 1, Appendix to Cabinet War Committee Minutes, The Canadian Army: Memorandum for the Minister, 3 Sept. 1940.
21 LAC, CP, vol. 11, D218, Scheme for the Re-organization of the Canadian Militia, 15 July 1935; Stephen Harris, *Canadian Brass: The Making of a Professional Army, 1860–1939* (Toronto 1988), 182–3.
22 The Canadian Army: Memorandum for the Minister, 3 Sept. 1940.
23 LAC, CP, vol. 1, D1, 1942 Army Programme and the Canadian Chiefs of Staff 'Appreciation of the War Effort. Nov. 1941.'
24 Department of National Defence (DND), Directorate of History and Heritage (DHH), General H.D.G. Crerar Document Collection (CDC), 112.1(D16), draft copy of 'Appreciation – What Should Be the Nature of Canada's Military Effort during the Next Year?' 13 Sept. 1940, and handwritten comments, Crerar to ADSD, Canadian Army Programme.
25 LAC, CP, vol. 1, D12, Crerar to McNaughton, 8 Aug. 1940.
26 See LAC, RG2 7C, vol. 1, CWCM, 26 July 1940; CP, vol. 19, D338, Crerar to Pope, 4 Sept. 1940.
27 LAC, RG2 7C, vol. 1, CWCM, 'Appreciation – What Should Be the Nature ... ' 25 Sept. 1940.
28 Timothy Harrison Place, *Military Training in the British Army, 1940–1944* (London 2000), 80–101.
29 DND, DHH, Kardex Collection, Crerar, General H.D.G., 112.1(D33), file: Corps and Army Troops Policy. See Memorandum ACGS Pope to CGS, 8 Sept. 1941, and handwritten note, CGS to ACGS, 13 Sept. 1941.
30 LAC, LPP, vol. 3, Crerar to Pearson, 18 Mar. 1941.

31 LAC, RG2 7C, CWCM, vol. 1, 26 July 1940; King Diary, T151, entry 26 July 1940; Jack Pickersgill, *The Mackenzie King Record* (Toronto 1960), 1:129.
32 QUA, GDP, TC3, folder 21, Memo, Conversation with King, Feb. 28, 1942.
33 Paul Hammond, *Organizing for Defense: The American Military Establishment in the Twentieth Century* (Princeton, NJ 1961), 188–222.
34 LAC, CP, vol. 11, D218, Memorandum on a Canadian Organization for the Higher Direction of National Defence, First Draft, 8 Mar. 1937.
35 LAC, Personnel Records Centre, Crerar's Personal File, file C, press release July 1940; CP, vol. 23, D418, Memo to CGS, Re: Duties as Chief of the General Staff, 24 July 1940.
36 LAC, CP, vol. 23, D418, Memorandum to the Minister, 29 July 1940.
37 Stacey, *Arms, Men and Governments*, 124.
38 LAC, RG24, vol. 2853, HQC 8664(i), Memorandum, Creation of Staff Duties Directorate of the General Staff, 9 Aug. 1940, E.L.M. Burns; Memo to the Minister, 10 Aug. 1940.
39 LAC, CP, vol. 1, D12, Crerar to McNaughton. 9 Sept. 1940; Geoffrey Hayes, 'The Development of the Canadian Army Officer Corps, 1939–1945' (unpublished PhD thesis, University of Western Ontario 1992), 65–70.
40 QUA, GDP, TC2, folder 19, Memo: Conversation with Sifton, Mar. 25, 1941; Malone, *A Portrait of War*, 61–3; J.L. Granatstein, *The Generals: The Canadian Army's Senior Commanders in the Second World War* (Toronto 1993), 126–8.
41 See Memorandum, Creation of Staff Duties Directorate of the General Staff. Crerar expected modifications 'in ... duties, and the establishment of officers.' LAC, RG24, vol. 2853, HQ 8664, Memo to the Minister, 2 Sept. 1940; vol. 1, D12, Crerar to McNaughton, 9 Sept. 1940.
42 LAC, RG24, vol. 2853, HQC 8664(i), from Memorandum to CGS, 19 Feb. 1940.
43 LAC, CP, vol. 1, D12, Crerar to McNaughton, 9 Sept. 1940; Hayes, 'Development of the Canadian Army Officer Corps,' 65–70.
44 QUA, GDP, TC2, folder 19, Grant Dexter's Memo: Conversation with Sifton, Mar. 25, 1941; Malone, *A Portrait of War*, 61–3.
45 LAC, RG24, vol. 2853, HQC8664(i), Crerar to AQ, QMG, 17 Aug. 1940.
46 LAC, CP, vol. 23, D418, Memo to Minister, 17 Oct. 1940.
47 LAC, CP, vol. 23, D418, Memo to Minister, 2 Nov. 1940.
48 LAC, CP, vol. 23, D418, Memo to Minister, 3 Nov. 1940.
49 LAC, CP, vol. 23, D418, Memo to Minister, 29 Nov. 1941; Memo to Minister, 31 Mar. 1941.
50 LAC, LPP, vol. 3, Crerar to Pearson, 27 July 1940.
51 See Alex Danchev, 'Dill,' in *Churchill's Generals*, ed. John Keegan (New York

1991), 51–67; Ed Cray, *General of the Army: George C. Marshall, Soldier and Statesman* (New York 1990), 135–46.
52 QUA, GDP, TC2, folder 19, Memo of Conversation with Sifton, 25 Mar. 1941.
53 See, for example, QUA, GDP, TC2, folder 19, Memo 12 June 1941, and folder 20, Memo 10 Oct. 1941; Malone, *A Portrait of War*, 61–70.
54 Quote from GDP, TC2, folder 19, Memo 10 Oct. 1941; Granatstein, *Canada's War*, 106, 214; Robert Campbell, 'James Layton Ralston and Manpower for the Canadian Army' (unpublished MA thesis, Wilfrid Laurier University 1986), 19–80.
55 LAC, CP, vol. 1, D12, Crerar to McNaughton, 9 Sept. 1940; vol. 19, D338, Crerar to Pearson, 4 Sept. 1940; Pearson to Crerar, 10 Sept. 1940; Crerar to Pearson, 4 Oct. 1940; Crerar to Dick Dewing, 4 Feb. 1941.
56 J.L. Granatstein and J.M. Hitsman, *Broken Promises: A History of Conscription in Canada* (Toronto 1977), 148–9.
57 LAC, RG2 7C, vol. 1, CWCM, 1 Oct. 1940.
58 LAC, King Diaries, T153, dairy entry 1 Oct. 1940; RG2 7C, vol. 1, CWCM, 1, 3, 10 Oct. 1940.
59 LAC, CP, vol. 28, D420, vol. 28, Address to Canadian Club of Ottawa, Sept.–Nov. 1940.
60 LAC, CP, vol. 14, D258, The Military Problem: Address to the Canadian Club, 23 Oct. 1940; RG2 7C, vol. 2, CWCM, 23 Oct. 1940.
61 LAC, King Diary, T153, diary entry 23 Oct. 1940; RG2 7C, vol. 2, CWCM, 23 Oct. 1940.
62 LAC, J.L. Ralston Papers, MG27 III B11, vol. 63, English Trips Sept. 1940–Jan 1941, Ralston Notebook; CP, vol. 19, D338, Crerar to Hamilton Boswell, 11 Nov. 1940.
63 Public Record Office (PRO), W0106/4872, XC8911, Possible Employment for Canadian Formations, 25 Nov. 1940. Next two paragraphs also drawn from this document.
64 PRO, W0106/4872, Notes of Meeting Held in the War Office, 17 Dec. 1941.
65 LAC, RG2 7C, vol. 3, CWCM, 8 Jan. 1941; PRO, W0106/4872, Notes on Meeting at the War Office, 2 Jan. 1941.
66 LAC, RG2 7C, vol. 3, CWCM, 24–28 Jan. 1941; C.P. Stacey, *Six Years of War: The Official History of the Canadian Army in the Second World War* (Ottawa 1955), 1:91–2.
67 LAC, LPP, vol. 3, Crerar to Pearson, 7 Feb. 1941; CP, vol. 1, D12, Crerar to McNaughton, 4 Mar. 1941.
68 LAC, LPP, vol. 1, D12, Crerar to McNaughton, 4 Mar. 1941.
69 LAC, CP, vol. 19, D338, Crerar to Trappes-Lomax, 7 Feb. 1941.
70 LAC, CP, vol. 19, D338, Pearson to Crerar, 4 Sept. 1940.

Chapter 9

1. Library and Archives Canada (LAC), Crerar Papers (CP), vol. 19, D338, Stan Kingsmill to Crerar, 23 Jan. 1941; Lester B. Pearson Papers (LPP), vol. 3, Co-ordination of War Committees, Excerpts, Crerar to Pearson, 14 Nov. 1941.
2. LAC, CP, vol. 19, D338, Crerar to Heeney, 12 Feb. 1941.
3. LAC, CP, vol. 1, D4, Crerar to Cliff Morden, 12 Sept. 1940.
4. Terry Copp and Bill McAndrew, *Battle Exhaustion: Soldiers and Psychiatrists in the Canadian Army, 1939–1945* (Montreal and Kingston 1990), 30–1.
5. LAC, CP, vol. 1, D7, Crerar to Price Montague, 9 June 1941. This led to some dissension, particularly at . Richard Preston, *Canada's RMC: A History of the Royal Military College* (Toronto 1969), 293–5.
6. LAC, CP, vol. 23, D418, Memorandum: The Training of the Canadian Army, Sept. 1941.
7. Geoffrey Perret, *There's a War to Be Won: The United States Army in World War II* (New York 1991), 119–25.
8. Ian Hay, *The Second World War, 1939–1945: A Short Military History Series; Arms and the Men* (London 1950), 161–3.
9. John A. English, *The Canadian Army and the Normandy Campaign: A Study of Failure in High Command* (New York 1991), 70–80; C.P. Stacey, *Six Years of War: The Official History of the Canadian Army in the Second World War* (Ottawa 1955), 1:133–7.
10. Greenfield, Kent Roberts, Robert Palmer, and Bell I. Wiley, *United States Army in World War Two: The Army Ground Forces, the Organization of Ground Combat Troops* (Washington, DC 1947), 42.
11. LAC, CP, vol. 23, D418, Memo: The Training of the Canadian Army, 3 Sept. 1941. The 'fundamentals' of responsible citizenship were stressed in basic and advanced training. See Department of National Defence, *The Battle of the Brains: Canadian Citizenship and the Issues of War* (Ottawa 1941). Also vol. 26, D336, Address, Civic Education and Military Preparation.
12. LAC, CP, vol. 1, D12, Crerar to McNaughton, 16 Apr. 1941.
13. Queen's University Papers (QUA), Grant Dexter Papers (GDP), TC2, folder 20, Memo: 6 Sept. 1941; LAC, CP, vol. 1, D7, Crerar to Price Montague, 29 June 1941; Jean Pariseau and Serge Bernier, *French Canadians and Bilingualism in the Canadian Armed Forces* (Ottawa 1988), 1:113–5.
14. LAC, CP, vol. 1, D12, Crerar to McNaughton, 16 Apr. 1941; Crerar to McNaughton, 19 May 1941.
15. LAC, CP, vol. 1, D12, Crerar to McNaughton, 16 Apr. 1941; J.L. Granatstein, *Canada's Army: Waging War and Keeping the Peace* (Toronto 2002), 191–3.

16 J.L. Granatstein, *The Politics of Survival: The Conservative Party of Canada, 1939–1945* (Toronto 1970), 73–4.
17 LAC, CP, vol. 28, D419, Crerar to Ralston, 27 July 1940.
18 Ibid.; LAC, CP, vol. 14, D258, Crerar to Stuart, 8 July 1939; Department of National Defence (DND), Directorate of History and Heritage (DHH), Document Collection: Crerar, H.D.G., 112.1(D16), Recommended in Draft 3, 'Canadian Army Programme for 1940' [sic]. E.L.M. Burns claims authorship of this particular memorandum. E.L.M. Burns, *General Mud* (Toronto 1970), 102–3.
19 C.P. Stacey, *A Date with History: Memoirs of a Canadian Historian* (Ottawa 1983), 64–6.
20 J.L. Granatstein, *Canada's War: The Politics of the Mackenzie King Government, 1939–1945* (Toronto 1975), 201–5.
21 LAC, CP, vol. 1, D12, Crerar to McNaughton, 19 May 1941; RG2 7C, vol. 4, Cabinet War Committee Minutes (CWCM), 20 May 1941; J.L. Granatstein and J.M. Hitsman, *Broken Promises: A History of Conscription in Canada* (Toronto 1977), 152–3. Journalists also had it that Crerar urged the recruiting campaign on Ralston. QUA, GDP, TC2, folder 19, Memo: June 12, 1941.
22 QUA, GDP, TC2, folder 20, Memo: 12 June 1941.
23 LAC, CP, vol. 1, D12, Crerar to McNaughton, 26 June 1941; McNaughton to Crerar, 19 July 1941.
24 LAC, CP, vol. 19, D333, Letters to *MacLean's* and *Calgary Post* in Personal Correspondence, July 1941–Nov. 1941; QUA, GDP, TC2, folder 20, J.W. Dafoe to Grant Dexter, 29 July 1941.
25 LAC, CP, vol. 19, D333, Crerar to Burns, 13 July 1941.
26 QUA, GDP, TC2, folder 20, Talk with Major-General Crerar, Memo 28 July 1941.
27 LAC, CP, vol. 19, D338, Crerar to Zouch Palmer, 27 Mar. 1941; J.L. Granatstein, *The Generals: The Canadian Army's Senior Commanders in the Second World War* (Toronto 1993), 128–30.
28 LAC, RG33-120, vol. 2, file 1-44, Memo: Canadian Battalions, 24 Sept. 1941.
29 See, for example, Granatstein, *Canada's Army*, 195–200; Carl Vincent, *No Reason Why: The Canadian Hong Kong Tragedy – an Examination* (Stittsville, ON 1981). For further detail on Crerar's decision, see Paul Dickson, 'Crerar and the Decision To Garrison Hong Kong,' *Canadian Military History* (Spring 1994): 97–110.
30 LAC, RG33-120, Proceedings, vols. 1–5, 186–91, 251–3, Testimony of Major-General K. Stuart and Major-General M. Pope.
31 Malcolm H. Murfett, 'Living in the Past: A Critical Re-examination of the Singapore Naval Strategy, 1918–1941,' *War and Society* 11, no. 1 (1993): 76–9.

32 Public Record Office (PRO), War Office Papers WO106/5136, Imperial Defence College (IDC) Exercise No. 3, 1934.
33 PRO, WO 106/5136, IDC Exercise No. 3, pp. 291, 330; Royal Military College (RMC), Massey Library Archives (MLA), Crerar's Vertical File, Crerar's IDC Notebook.
34 Crerar's IDC Notebook; LAC, CP, vol. 15, D431, Confidential Address on the 'IDC,' to the Canadian Artillery Association, Feb. 1935.
35 IDC Exercise No. 3, 153–4.
36 LAC, CP, vol. 11, D217, Notes: Canada's Point of View, Japan, 1936.
37 LAC, LPP, vol. 3, file: Correspondence Crerar, 1936–1942, Crerar to Pearson; CP, vol. 12, D222, Crerar to Escott Reid, 7 Jan. 1936, Comments on Draft Report 'Canada and the Pacific.'
38 LAC, MG27 III B5, Ian A. Mackenzie Papers, vol. 29, file: Minister's Secret Letter to Cabinet, Nov. 1936.
39 LAC, LPP, vol. 3, Crerar to Pearson in Nov. 1936. In Correspondence Crerar, 1936–1942.'
40 LAC, CP, vol. 1, D7, Crerar to Montague, 9 June 1941.
41 LAC, RG33-120, vol. 3, Crerar's Testimony, Telegram 1000, Crerar to W.K. Campbell, Secretary to the Royal Commission Enquiring into Hong Kong Expedition, 11 Apr. 1942.
42 LAC, CP, vol. 21, D329, Crerar to C.P. Stacey, 23 Oct. 1953.
43 Vincent, *No Reason Why*, 25.
44 LAC, CP, vol. 15, War Dairy, London Trip, 20 Oct. 1941. According to Crerar's war diary of conversations with the British secretary of state for war, Ralston 'stated that ... the Canadian government was fully prepared to sanction employment of the Canadian Corps in any military operations which the War Office might recommend.'
45 Prime Minister Winston Churchill and the chiefs of staff vehemently opposed the idea when it was suggested in Jan. 1941. Stacey, *Six Years of War*, 1:438–9.
46 See Christopher Thorne, *Allies of a Kind: The United States, Britain and the War against Japan, 1941–1945* (New York 1978).
47 David Dilks, '"The Unnecessary War"? Military Advice and Foreign Policy in Great Britain, 1931–1939,' in *General Staffs and Diplomacy before the Second World War*, ed. Adrian Preston (Totowa, NJ 1978), 98–131.
48 Winston Churchill, 'Prime Minister to General Ismay, 7 Jan. 1941,' *The Second World War* (Boston 1985), 3:157.
49 The British VCGS recorded Churchill's optimism after his return from the Placentia Bay meeting with Roosevelt in late August 1941. Brian Bond, ed., *Chief of Staff: The Diaries of Lieutenant-General Sir Henry Pownall* (London 1974), 2:37–8.

50 Thorne, *Allies of a Kind*, 4.
51 F.H. Hinsley, *British Intelligence and the Second World War* (London 1981), 2:73–5; John Dower, *War Without Mercy: Race and Power in the Pacific War* (New York 1986).
52 Sir Llewellyn Woodward, *British Foreign Policy in the Second World War* (London 1962), 174–5.
53 Peter C. Calvocoressi and Guy Wint, *Total War* (Hammondsworth 1979), 2:292–309.
54 Ibid., 2:454.
55 LAC, RG33-120, vol. 2, file 5, exhibit 1, cypher 162, Secretary of State for Dominion Affairs to the Secretary of State for External Affairs, 19 Sept. 1941.
56 LAC, RG33-120, vol. 1, Proceedings of the Royal Commission, Testimony of C.G. Power, 269–70.
57 LAC, CP, vol. 23, D418, Memorandum to CGS, Duties as Chief of the General Staff, 24 July 1940.
58 QUA, GDP, TC3, folder 21, Memo, Conversation with King, 28 Feb. 1932; H. Blair Neatby, *William Lyon Mackenzie King, 1932–1939: The Prism of Unity* (Toronto 1976), 182–3; J.W. Pickersgill, *The Mackenzie King Record* (Toronto 1960), 1:12–14.
59 LAC, CP, vol. 15, D271, WD, SO, CMHQ, 3 June 1940.
60 LAC, RG33-120, vol. 1, Proceedings of the Royal Commission, Testimony of General K. Stuart and General M.A. Pope.
61 LAC, RG33-120, vol. 2, exhibits 1–44, PO-1, Record of Conversations on Important Subjects, 23-9-41, DMO and I, and Canadian Battalions – Hong Kong, 24 Sept. 1941; vol. 1, Proceedings of the Royal Commission, Testimony of Brigadier Gibson.
62 Testimony of Brigadier Gibson.
63 LAC, RG33-120, vol. 3, Telegram: Crerar to Campbell, 11 Apr. 1942.
64 LAC, RG33-120, vols 16–20, Proceedings of the Royal Commission, Testimony of Lt-Colonel Murray, pp. 1768–75; vol. 1, Proceedings of the Royal Commission.
65 DND, DHH, Kardex Collection, Foulkes, Lt-General C., 111.13(D66), 'Military Comment on Drew and Duff Reports, February 1948.'
66 See Hinsley, *British Intelligence*, 2:3–11; LAC, RG24, vol. 2853, HQC 8664(i) for Crerar's re-organization of the General Staff Branch of NDHQ.
67 The state of training was the nominal issue that prompted the Royal Commission Enquiry of 1942. The Duff Report cleared the General Staff of negligence. Right Honourable Sir Lyman Duff, *Report on the Canadian Expeditionary Force to the Crown Colony of Hong Kong* (Ottawa 1942).
68 LAC, RG33-120, vol. 2, file: Exhibits 1–44, Memo to the Minister, 30 Sept. 1941, Exhibit 13.

69 LAC, RG33-120, vol. 2, Exhibits 1–44, Major-General L.F. Page, GOC 4th Canadian Division, Memorandum on NDHQ File BDF, 26 Sept. 1941, exhibit 10.
70 LAC, RG33-120, vol. 2, Crerar to the Minister, 30 Sept. 1941, Exhibits 1–44, and Crerar to Campbell, 11 Apr. 1942; Stacey, *Six Years of War*, 1: 444–60.
71 English, *Failure in High Command*, 70–80; Stacey, *Six Years of War*, 1:133–7.
72 LAC, CP, vol. 23, D418, Memo to the Minister, Extension of Period of Compulsory Training to Four Months, 26 Jan. 1941; vol. 1, D55, draft of Crerar's testimony to Campbell, 11 Apr. 1942, in response to the question 'What is your opinion as to the effect on the fighting efficiency of the two battalions of the addition of the personnel mentioned [above]?'
73 LAC, RG33-120, vol. 2, Exhibits 1–44, Draft Memorandum to the Minister, exhibit 11.
74 LAC, CP, vol. 15, War Diary, London Trip, 21 Oct. 1941.
75 LAC, CP, vol. 1, D1, Army Programme, 1942–43; RG2 7C, vol. 6, Reference to Chiefs of Staff 'Monthly Appreciation,' HQS5199, 5 Nov. 1941.
76 LAC, RG33-120, vol. 3, telegram: Crerar to Campbell, 11 Apr. 1942.
77 Chan Lan Kit Ching, 'The Hong Kong Question during the Pacific War (1941–1945),' *Journal of Imperial and Commonwealth History* 11 (1973): 56–78.

Chapter 10

1 Library and Archives Canada (LAC), Crerar Papers (CP), vol. 19, D333, Crerar to Burns, 13 July 1941.
2 LAC, RG2 7C, vol. 3, Cabinet War Committee Minutes (CWCM), 29 July 1941. King preferred expanding the Air Force. H. Blair Neatby, *William Lyon Mackenzie King: The Prism of Unity, 1932–1939* (Toronto 1976), 182–3.
3 LAC, RG2 7C, vol. 3, CWCM, 15 and 29 July 1941; QUA, GDP, TC2, folder 20, Memo: Conversation with Crerar, 28 July 1941.
4 LAC, CP, vol. 1, D12, Crerar to McNaughton, 11 Aug. 1941.
5 LAC, CP, vol. 19, D333, from Crerar to Burns, 13 July 1941; C.P. Stacey, *Six Years of War: The Official History of the Canadian Army in the Second World War* (Ottawa 1955), 1:94.
6 Stacey, *Six Years of War*, 1:94–5.
7 QUA, GDP, TC3, folder 22, Memo: 4 Mar. 1942, Conversation with Ralston.
8 QUA, GDP, TC2, folder 20, Memo: 16 Sept. 1941, and Memo: Talk with Ralston, 10 Oct. 1941; Robert Campbell, 'James Layton Ralston and Manpower for the Canadian Army' (unpublished MA thesis, Wilfrid Laurier University 1986), 89.

9 LAC, CP, vol. 15, WD, London Trip, 14 Oct. 1941; King's College, London (KCL), Liddell Hart Centre for Military Archives (LHC), Alanbrooke Papers (AP), 12/XIII/8, Interview with Crerar for book on Brooke, n.d.
10 Stacey, *Six Years of War*, 1:95.
11 LAC, CP, vol. 15, WD, London Trip, 20 Oct. 1941; RG2 7C, vol. 6, CWCM, 6 Nov. 1941.
12 LAC, CP, vol. 1, D1, Army Programme, 1942–1943; RG2 7C, vol. 6, Appendices CWCM, Reference to Chiefs of Staff 'Monthly Appreciation,' HQS5199, 5 Nov. 1941.
13 LAC, RG2 7C, CWCM, 2–4 Dec. 1941.
14 QUA, GDP, TC2, folder 20, Memo: 20 Nov. 1941.
15 LAC, RG2 7C, vol. 6, CWCM, 2 Dec. 1941.
16 Stacey, *Six Years of War*, 1:417–19; LAC, Mackenzie King Papers, vol. 312, P.263720, reel C-4866; QUA, GDP, TC2, folder 20, Memo: 9 Oct. 1941.
17 LAC, LPP, vol. 3, Pearson to Crerar, 13 Aug. and 4 Sept. 1940.
18 LAC, CP, vol. 22, D335, Massey to Ralston, 5 Nov. 1941, cipher no. 2040. McNaughton told Lester Pearson he did not have faith in Pearkes or Odlum. LAC, LPP, vol. 1, Pearson diary entry 28 Apr. 1941.
19 LAC, CP, vol. 22, D335, Ralston to McNaughton, 14 Nov. 1941 and McNaughton to Ralston, 17 Nov. 1941, cipher no. 2133; KCL, LHC, AP, Diary 5/4, 10 and 21 Oct. 1941.
20 LAC, CP, vol. 22, D335, McNaughton to Minister of National Defence, 11 Nov. 1941, cipher no. 2081.
21 LAC, CP, vol. 22, D335, Ralston to McNaughton, 14 Nov. 1941 and McNaughton to Ralston, 17 Nov. 1941, cipher no. 2133.
22 LAC, RG2 7C, vol. 6, CWCM, 19 Nov. 1941.
23 Reginald Roy, *'For Most Conspicuous Bravery': A Biography of Major-General George R. Pearkes through Two World Wars* (Vancouver 1977), 166–9.
24 LAC, LPP, Pearson Diaries, vol. 1, 28 Apr. 1941.
25 LAC, CP, vol. 22, D335, McNaughton to Minister for National Defence, 29 Nov. 1941, cypher no. 2251; vol. 21, D329, Crerar to Stacey, Observations by General Crerar on Draft of Official History, 14 Sept. 1951.
26 LAC, CP, vol. 22, D335, Minister of National Defence to McNaughton, 1 Dec. 1941, and Montague to DND, 27 Dec. 1941.
27 LAC, CP, vol. 19, D333, Crerar to Burns, 8 Nov. 1941; Crerar to Mrs Herbert Gallagher, 15 Nov. 1941; William Gregg interview with Tom Macdonald. Thank you to William Gregg for providing this material.
28 LAC, RG24, vol. 13,683, War Diary, Mar. 1942, 'G' Branch, 1 Canadian Corps, Memorandum: [Discussions with McNaughton, Paget and Crerar] 25 Dec. 1941.

29 LAC, RG24, vol. 13,683, memorandum, 25 Dec. 1941; CP, vol. 1, D18, GOC Files 1941–1944, Memoranda General; Stacey, *Six Years of War*, 1:96; John Swettenham, *McNaughton* (Toronto 1968), 2:188–9.
30 Stacey, *Six Years of War*, 1:97; Nigel Hamilton, *Monty: The Making of a General, 1887–1942* (London 1984), 479.
31 Swettenham, *McNaughton*, 2:188.
32 LAC, CP, vol. 19, D333, Crerar to Donnie White, 21 Nov. 1941.
33 KCL, LHC, AP, 12/XI/4/61, Interview with Crerar, n.d.; LAC, J.L. Ralston Papers (RP), MG27 III B11, vol. 59, Overseas Trip in 1943, Substance of Conversation with [Brooke and Stuart], 15 Nov. 1943; Hamilton, *Monty: The Making of a General*, 479.
34 KCL, LHC, ABP, 3/A/V, Notes on My Life, 6–8 Jan. 1942.
35 LAC, RG24, vol. 13,683, War Diary 'G' Branch 1st Canadian Corps, General Report from Canadian Corps for the Week Ending 10 Jan. 1942; KCL, LHC, AP, 5/5, Diary, 7 Jan. 1942.
36 LAC, RP, vol. 70, Mr Ralston's Personal Notes re Personal Preliminary Enquiry; King Diaries, T171, 12 Feb. 1942.
37 LAC, RG2 7C, vol. 6, CWCM, 3 Dec. 1941.
38 Stacey, 'Appendix A: Strength and Casualties – Canadian Army,' *Six Years of War*, 1:522–3.

Chapter 11

1 Library and Archives Canada (LAC), Crerar Papers (CP), vol. 2, D182, Crerar, handwritten note, Dec. 1946.
2 LAC, CP, vol. 19, D333, Crerar to Mrs Herbert Gallagher, 4 Dec. 1941.
3 Nigel Hamilton, *Monty: The Making of a General, 1887–1942* (London 1984), 479.
4 See Timothy Harrison Place, *Military Training in the British Army, 1940–1944: Dunkirk to D-Day* (London 2000), and David French, *Raising Churchill's Army: The British Army and the War against Germany, 1919–1945* (Oxford 2000), for the disagreements over operational doctrine.
5 King's College, London (KCL), Liddell Hart Centre for Military Archives (LHC), Alanbrooke Papers (AP), Diary 5/5, 15 June 1941; Notes on My Life, 3/A/IV, Apr. 1941.
6 Hamilton, *Monty: The Making of a General*, 327; John A. English, *The Canadian Army and the Normandy Campaign: A Study of Failure in High Command* (New York 1991), 125–6.
7 C.P. Stacey, *A Date with History: Memoirs of a Canadian Historian* (Ottawa 1983), 235.

8 University of Toronto Archives (UTA), Vincent Massey Papers (VMP), box 311, folder 50, diary entry 12 Mar. 1943.
9 Reginald H. Roy, *For Most Conspicuous Bravery: A Biography of Major-General George R. Pearkes through Two World Wars* (Vancouver 1977), 168.
10 Christopher H.N. Hull, 'A Case Study of Professionalism in the Canadian Army in the 1930s and 1940s: Lieutenant-General G.G. Simonds' (unpublished MA thesis, Purdue University 1989), 41.
11 LAC, RG24, vol. 13,683, War Diary, 'G' Branch HQ Canadian Corps, Training Instruction No. 6, 25 Feb. 1942; Hamilton, *Monty: The Making of a General*, 470–81.
12 LAC, CP, vol. 7, D180, Memorandum by GOC 1 Cdn Corps on Contents of Letter Dated 15 Dec. 43 from Maj-Gen Simonds Comd 5 Cdn Armd Div, 12 Dec. 1943; vol. 2, D17, HQ Canadian Corps to BGS, Points [Raised] during Discussion with Army Commander, 11 Jan. 1942, and Notes on Corps Commanders Memorandum after Discussion with Army Commander, 12 Jan. 1942.
13 LAC, CP, vol. 6, D154, Crerar to Allen H. Bill, 9 Jan. 1942.
14 LAC, CP, vol. 2, D17, GOC/2 HQ Canadian Corps, 14 Jan. 1942.
15 LAC, CP, vol. 7, D180, Simonds to Crerar, 15 Dec. 1943; Major-General George Kitching, *Mud and Green Fields* (Langley, BC 1986), 117–9.
16 LAC, RG24, vol. 13,683, War Diary: Jan 1942, South-Eastern Command Exercise Beaver, Remarks by the Army Commander, 2 Jan. 1942.
17 Imperial War Museum (IWM), B.L. Montgomery Papers (BLMP), BLM20/5, Alanbrooke to Montgomery, 8 Jan. 1942.
18 LAC, RG24, vol. 13,683, War Diary, 'G' Branch, HQ Canadian Corps, General Report from Cdn Corps for Week Ending 10 Jan. 42, SD 10-1-2; Hamilton, *Monty: The Making of a General*, 480.
19 KCL, LHC, AP, Diaries 5/4, entry 31 Jan. 1941.
20 IWM, BLMP, BLM 20/5, Brooke to Montgomery, 8 Jan. 1942.
21 LAC, CP, vol. 2, (D17), Crerar to Montgomery, 6 Jan. 1942.
22 Interview with Henri Tellier 1992; Claude Bissell, *The Imperial Canadian: Vincent Massey in Office* (Toronto 1986), 142.
23 LAC, G24, vol. 13,683, War Diary, 'G' Branch HQ Canadian Corps, General Reports from Canadian Corps, Feb.–Apr. 1942.
24 G. Hayes, 'The Development of the Canadian Army Officer Corps, 1939–1945' (unpublished PhD thesis, University of Western Ontario 1992), 79–80; Stephen Harris, *Canadian Brass: The Making of a Professional Army, 1860–1939* (Toronto 1988), 208–9.
25 Lieutenant-General Henri Tellier in correspondence with the author, Jan. 1992.

Notes to pages 191–5   507

26 LAC, LPP, vol. 3, Crerar to Pearson, 25 Apr. 1942.
27 LAC, RG24, vol. 13,683, WD, 'G' Branch, HQ Cdn Corps, Feb. 1942; Organization of Training, GOC/4-0, 26 Feb. 1942; CP, vol. 5, D24, Crerar to Divisional Commanders, 20 Mar. 1942.
28 LAC, CP, vol. 19, D333, Crerar to Peter Crerar, 7 Oct. 1941.
29 LAC, CP, vol. 7, D152, Crerar to Major-General Turner, DA and QMG, First Canadian Army, 7 July 1942; Montague to Crerar, 25 July 1942; vol. 1, D23, Crerar to Keller, 13 Nov. 1942, and memorandum of discussions in May 1943.
30 LAC, RG24, vol. 13,683, War Diary, Crerar to Commanders and COs, 16 Mar. 1942.
31 LAC, CP, vol. 1, D23, Crerar to GOC, First Canadian Army, GOC 6-1-7, 9 Apr. 1943.
32 LAC, CP, vol. 7, D145, Crerar to Brigadier Whitehead, 19 May 1942.
33 LAC, CP, vol. 2, D21, Crerar to McNaughton, 20 Apr. 1942, and memorandum, Crerar and McNaughton Discussions, HQ 1st Canadian Corps, 13 Apr. 1942.
34 Roy, *For Most Conspicuous Bravery*, 168–71; LAC, CP, vol. 1, D23, Crerar to Pearkes, 8 May 1942, and Memo on Incident between Crerar and Pearkes, 1st Canadian Corps, 9 May 1942.
35 LAC, CP, vol. 2, (D182), Montgomery's 'Notes on Beaver III' and 'Beaver III – Notes on Commanders.'
36 Hamilton, *Monty: The Making of a General*, 498.
37 LAC, CP, vol. 21, D329, Organization of Training, GOC/4-0, 26 Feb. 1942; RG24, vol. 13,683, War Diary, 'G' Branch, HQ 1st Canadian Corps, Mar. 1942; Memorandum to Commanders, GOC/4-0, 16 Mar. 1942.
38 Kitching, *Mud and Green Fields*, 129–30.
39 LAC, RG24, vol. 13,694, War Diary, 'G' Branch, HQ 1st Canadian Corps, Army Commander's Personal Memorandum No. 2, SE/231/OPS, 21 Mar. 1942.
40 LAC, CP, vol. 19, D338, Harry to John Crerar, 16 July 1942; English, *Failure in High Command*, 112–18.
41 Quoted from circular letter issued 26 Mar. 1942, in Stacey, *Six Years of War*, 1:243.
42 LAC, RG24, vol. 13,683, War Diary, 'G' Branch, HQ 1st Canadian Corps, Apr. 1942, Crerar to All Commanders and Commanding Officers, GOC 4-0, 17 Apr. 1942.
43 LAC, CP, vol. 2, D182. See Montgomery's Notes on the Broader Aspects of Beaver III, as well as notes on exercises Beaver IV and Conqueror; English, *Failure in High Command*, 125–42.

44 LAC, RG24, vol. 13,683, War Diary, May 1942, 'G' Branch, HQ 1st Canadian Corps, General Report from 1st Canadian Corps for Week Ending 31 May 1942, SD10-1; vol. 12,301, Remarks of Army Commander, SE Army Exercise 'Tiger,' 4 June 1942.
45 LAC, CP, vol. 2, D182, Montgomery to Crerar, 30 May 1942.
46 LAC, CP, vol. 19, D305, Crerar to Colonel G.W.L. Nicholson, 5 Feb. 1952.
47 Kitching, *Mud and Green Fields*, 123.
48 LAC, RG24, vol. 12,301, Remarks of Army Commander, S.E. Army Exercise 'Tiger.'
49 IWM, BLMP, BLM49/19, Montgomery to Brooke, 28 Feb. 43.
50 LAC, CP, vol. 6, D 1153, Crerar to John Crerar, 3 June 1942.
51 LAC, RG24, vol. 13,683, War Dairy, October 1942, 'G' Branch, HQ 1st Canadian Corps, Instructions to Staff Officers, HQ 1st Canadian Corps, 21 June 1942, GOC 5-6-2.
52 Shelford Bidwell and Dominick Graham, *Fire-Power: British Army Weapons and Theories of War, 1904–1945* (London 1982), 220–9.
53 Colonel G.W.L. Nicholson, *The Gunners of Canada: The History of the Royal Regiment of Canadian Artillery* (Toronto 1972), 2:108–9.
54 LAC, RG24, vol. 12,301, Final Remarks by Army Commander; Exercise 'Tiger,' 4 June 1942.
55 IWM, BLM49/18, Montgomery to Brooke, 23 Feb. 1943; Hamilton, *Monty: The Making of a General*, 503.
56 LAC, RG24, vol. 13,683, War Diary, June 1942, 'G' Branch HQ 1st Canadian Corps, Crerar to All Commanders and Commanding Officers, GOC 4-0, 4 June 1942.
57 LAC, RG24, vol. 13,683, War Diary, Crerar to 1st Canadian Corps, GOC/4-0, 4 June 1942.

Chapter 12

1 Library and Archives Canada (LAC), Crerar Papers (CP), vol. 6, D154, Crerar to Allen Bill, 9 Jan. 1942; Lester B. Pearson Papers (LPP), vol. 3, file: Crerar, H.D.G. 1936–1942, Crerar to Pearson, 25 Apr. 1942.
2 LAC, RG24, vol. 13,683, War Diary, 'G' Branch, HQ Canadian Corps, Feb. 1942, Memorandum: Crerar to All Commanders and Commanding Officers, Canadian Corps, 5 Feb. 1942, GOC/3-6.
3 C.P. Stacey and B. Wilson, *The Half-Million: The Canadians in Britain, 1939–1946* (Toronto 1987), 16.
4 John Swettenham, *McNaughton* (Toronto 1968), 2:244–8.
5 LAC, RG24, vol. 10,765, D129, Memorandum on Visit of Lt-Gen. Paget, 6

Sept. 1941; Pearkes to Simonds, 29 Nov. 1941; vol. 10,764, D203, Personal Memoranda to Commanders, 1 Nov. 1941.
6 LAC, RG24, vol. 10,765, D124, Crerar to Montgomery, 5 Feb. 1942.
7 LAC, RG24, vol. 10,765, D124, Montgomery to Crerar, 8 Feb. 1942.
8 LAC, LPP, vol. 3, Crerar to Pearson, 25 Apr. 1942.
9 LAC, CP, vol. 1, D55, The War Office to Defensor, 11/2/42, 70012 Cipher 11/2.
10 LAC, CP, vol. 1, D55, Defensor to Canmilitary, 11 Feb. 42, GS 2173; Crerar to Ralston, 12 Feb. 42.
11 LAC, RG33 120, vol. 3, McNaughton to Duff, 16 Mar. 1942; CP, vol. 6, D153, Crerar to John Crerar, 21 Apr. 1942; Crerar to Peter Crerar, 29 July 1942.
12 LAC, RG24, vol. 10765, D124, Notes on Conference, 6 Mar. 1942; King's College, London (KCL), Liddell Hart Centre for Military Archives (LHC), AP, Diary 5/5, entries 1 Mar. and 1 Apr. 1942.
13 LAC, RG24, vol. 13,765, D182, Charles Hayden to Simonds, 11 Apr. 1942.
14 C.P. Stacey, *Six Years of War: The Official History of the Canadian Army in the Second World War* (Ottawa 1955), 1:310.
15 KCL, LHC, AP, 3/A/X, Notes on My Life, 15 Jan. 1943; Department of National Defence (DND), Directorate of History and Heritage (DHH), Crerar Document Collection, file 111.1011(D1), C.G. Power Diary Excerpt, Mission to United Kingdom, 16 Aug. 1942.
16 LAC, RG24, vol. 10,765, Small Scale Raids, 4 Apr. 1942.
17 Stacey, *Six Years of War*, 1:329; Nigel Hamilton, *Monty: The Making of a General, 1887–1942* (London 1984), 521.
18 LAC, CP, vol. 2, D182, Notes on Beaver III, 25 Apr. 1942.
19 LAC, RG24, vol. 13,683, War Diary, April 1942, 'G' Branch, HQ 1st Canadian Corps, Training Instruction No. 9, 30 Apr. 1942; Stacey, *Six Years of War*, 1:329.
20 LAC, CP, vol. 2, D21, Lt-Gen Jack Swayne, CGS, Home Forces to McNaughton, 4 July 1942.
21 LAC, CP, vol. 2, D21, Memorandum on Conversation with Lieutenant-General B.L. Montgomery, Commanding SE Army on 4 July 1942, Commencing 1800 Hrs.
22 LAC, CP, vol. 3, D67, Crerar to Stuart, 30 May 1944.
23 F.H. Hinsley, 'Appendix 13,' *British Intelligence in the Second World War: Its Influence on Strategy and Operations* (London 1981), 296–300.
24 'I should not myself have agreed to either of these changes,' Bernard Law Montgomery, *The Memoirs of Field-Marshal, The Viscount Montgomery of Alamein, K.G.* (London 1958), 76. Montgomery forgot that he chaired the meeting at which this decision was made. Hamilton, *Monty: The Making of a General*, 522–3.

25 LAC, CP, vol. 19, D338, Crerar to John Crerar, 16 July 1942; Crerar to Peter Crerar, 29 July 1942.
26 LAC, RG24, vol. 10,765, D126, Crerar to McNaughton, 11 Aug. 1942.
27 LAC, CP, vol. 20, Dieppe Interviews, Ross Munro.
28 LAC, A.G.L. McNaughton Papers (MP), vol. 135, C.B. 04244 The Raid on Dieppe: Lessons Learnt, Extract from the Dieppe Combined Report, Sept. 1942; Stacey, *Six Years of War*, 1:402; D. Whitaker, *Dieppe: Tragedy to Triumph* (Toronto 1992), 165–6.
29 Stacey, *Six Years of War*, 1:391.
30 LAC, MP, vol. 135, CB 04244(1), The Raid on Dieppe: Lessons Learnt, Extract from the Dieppe Raid Combined Report, Sept. 1942, PA 1-8-3.
31 Whitaker, *Dieppe*, 251–62.
32 Desmond Morton, *A Military History of Canada* (Edmonton 1985), 203; Brereton Greenhous, 'Review Essay: Dieppe; Tragedy to Triumph,' *Canadian Defence Quarterly* 22, no. 1 (Special No. 2/1992): 36.
33 LAC, CP, vol. 2, D21, for increasing tempo of schedule. For examples of continuity in training policy see RG24, vol. 13,683, War Diary, Aug.–Sept. 1942, 'G' Branch, HQ 1st Canadian Corps, Notes on Exercise 'Harold,' 6 Aug. 1942; GOC 4-0, Crerar to All Commanders [on Discipline, Morale and Training], 14 Aug. 1942; Training Instruction No. 16, 24 Sept. 1942.
34 LAC, RG24, vol. 13,683, War Diary, Oct. 1942, 'G' Branch, HQ 1st Canadian Corps, GOC 4-0-7, All Commanders and Commanding Officers, 16 Oct. 1942; vol. 13,684, WD Apr. 1943, 'G' Branch, HQ 1st Canadian Corps, Training Instructions No. 22, 1/Trg Instr/4, 18 Apr. 1943.
35 LAC, RG24, vol. 13,684, War Diary, Sept. 1942, 'G' Branch, HQ 1st Canadian Corps, Training Instruction No. 16, 24 Sept. 1942.
36 Training Instruction No. 22, 1/Trg Instr/4,' 18 Apr. 1943; LAC, RG24, vol. 13,685, War Diary June 1943, 'G' Branch, HQ 1st Canadian Corps, Training Instruction No. 25, 4-8-4, 23 June 1943.
37 John A. English, *The Canadian Army and the Normandy Campaign: A Study of Failure in High Command* (New York 1991), 144.
38 LAC, MP, vol. 135, GS 2972, McNaughton to CGS, 21 Aug. 1942, PA 1-8-1.
39 LAC, CP, vol. 7, D140, Crerar to McNaughton, 27 Aug. 1942.
40 LAC, MP, vol. 135, GOC 1-0-4, Crerar to All Commanders and Commanding Officers, 29 Aug. 1942; Report on Operation Jubilee, 20 Aug. 1942, PA 1-8-1.
41 LAC, CP, vol. 6, D139, Crerar to Vi, 30 Oct. and 8 Dec. 1942; J.L. Granatstein interview with William Young, son of Major-General J.V. Young, Crerar's ADC, 1942; LAC, CP, vol. 6, D153, Crerar to John Crerar, 7 Nov. 1942.
42 LAC, CP, vol. 21, D324, Crerar to Stacey, 23 July 1947; vol. 7, D150, Crerar to Major-General M.A. Pope, 27 Oct. 1942; D171, Crerar to Alanbrooke, 10 June 1944.

43 LAC, CP, vol. 1, D17, Crerar to McNaughton, 2 Sept. 1942; McNaughton to Paget, 30 Sept. 1942; vol. 2, D22, GOC 1-0, Crerar to SE Army, 13 Apr. 1943; D22, 1-1-9, Adv. HQ 1 Cdn Corps to C-in-C, First Canadian Army, Present Role 1 Cdn Corps, 16 June 1943.
44 LAC, CP, vol. 7, D172, file: Personal Correspondence with Field Marshal Montgomery; Crerar to Vincent Massey, University of Toronto Archives, Vincent Massey Papers, folder 49, diary entry 7 Nov. 1942.

Chapter 13

1 University of Toronto Archives (UTA), Vincent Massey Papers (VMP), B87-0082/311, folder 49, diary entry 7 Nov. 1942; LAC, CP, vol. 7, D172, Crerar to Montgomery, 20 Sept. 1943. Latter quote from D150, Crerar to Peg Crerar, 14 Sept. 1943.
2 UTA, VMP, folder 51, diary 12 May 1943; quote from 15 Sept. 1943.
3 LAC, CP, vol. 6, D153, Crerar to A.J. Crerar, 7 Nov. 1942; Crerar to Kerr Cronyn, 21 Jan. 1943; D139, Crerar to Mrs C. Gibson, 9 Feb. 1944; D153, Crerar to Peter, 2 May 1943; vol. 7, D150, Pope to Crerar, 15 Oct. 1942.
4 UTA, VMP, folder 50, diary 31 Mar. 1943.
5 Queen's University Archives (QUA), Grant Dexter Papers (GDP), TC3, folder 22, memo, 13 Mar. 1942; C.P. Stacey, 'Canadian Leaders of the Second World War,' *Canadian Historical Review* 66 (March 1985): 67.
6 UTA, VMP, folder 50, diary 16 Apr. 1943. Massey agreed with George McCullogh's assessment.
7 Interview with Brigadier G.E. Beament, 1990; QUA, GDP, TC3, folder 22, memo, 13 Mar. 1942.
8 UTA, VMP, folder 50, diary 31 Dec. 1942.
9 UTA, VMP, folder 50, record of conversations with McNaughton in diary 3 Dec. and 31 Dec 1942; John Swettenham, *McNaughton* (Toronto 1969), 2:234.
10 Swettenham, *McNaughton*, 2:264–5; LAC, CP, vol. 2, D21, Crerar to McNaughton, 19 Oct. 1942, and McNaughton to Crerar, 20 Oct. 1942; C.P. Stacey, *A Date with History: Memoirs of a Canadian Historian* (Ottawa 1983), 126.
11 LAC, CP, vol. 6, D153, Crerar to A.J. Crerar, 8 Dec. 1942; Crerar to Kerr Cronyn, 21 Jan. 1943; UTA, VMP, folder 48, diary 10 June 1942; folder 50, diary 12 May 1943.
12 As retold in J.L. Granatstein, *The Generals: The Canadian Army's Senior Commanders in the Second World War* (Toronto 1993), 103.
13 King's College, London (KCL), Liddell Hart Centre for Military Archives (LHC), AP, file 3/A/X, Notes on My Life, 15 Jan. 1943.

14 J.W. Pickersgill, *The Mackenzie King Record* (Toronto 1960), 1:497–8; Hugh L. Keenleyside, *On the Bridge of Time: Memoirs of Hugh L. Keenleyside* (Toronto 1981), 2:130–1; UTA, VMP, folder 51, diary 27 Aug. 1943.
15 LAC, RG24, vol. 13,684, War Diary, Dec. 1942, 'G' Branch, HQ 1st Canadian Corps, 1/Trg Instr/4, Hardening Training — Assault Courses, 27 Dec. 1942; E.L.M. Burns, *General Mud: Memoirs of Two World Wars* (Toronto 1970), 116–19.
16 William Earnest John Hutchinson, 'Test of a Corps Commander: Lieutenant-General Guy Granville Simonds, Normandy 1944' (unpublished MA thesis, University of Victoria 1982), 106–7; Swettenham, *McNaughton*, 2:239; Christopher H.N. Hull, 'A Case Study in Professionalism in the Canadian Army in the 1930s and 1940s: Lieutenant-General G.G. Simonds' (unpublished MA thesis, Purdue University 1989), 42; LAC, CP, vol. 5, D24, Crerar to McNaughton, 30 Aug. 1942.
17 LAC, RG24, vol. 13,683, War Dairy, Oct. 1942, 'G' Branch, HQ 1st Canadian Corps, GOC 5-6-2, Crerar to Commanders, 4 Oct. 1942; Burns, *General Mud*, 118.
18 RMC, Crerar Papers, GOC Admin Procedures and Systems Charts, 27 Nov. 1942.
19 Timothy Harrison Place, *Military Training in the British Army, 1940–1944* (London 2000), 79; David French, *Raising Churchill's Army: The British Army and the War against Germany, 1919–1945* (Oxford 2000), 198–9.
20 RMC, Crerar Papers, GOC Notebook, Points for Discussion, 3rd Division; French, *Raising Churchill's Army*, 254–6.
21 RMC, Crerar Papers, GOC Notebook, Points for Discussion, n.d.; Timothy Harrison Place, *Military Training in the British Army, 1940–1944: From Dunkirk to D-Day* (London 2000), 92.
22 LAC, CP, vol. 7, D171, Brooke to Crerar, 24 Feb. 1943; RG24, vol. 13,684, War Diary, Feb. 1943, 'G' Branch, HQ 1st CC 'Spartan' Appreciation by Lt-Gen H.D.G. Crerar, 2/Exercises/18, 16 Feb. 1943.
23 LAC, J.L. Ralston Papers (RP), MG27 III B11, vol. 54, Officer Assessments, ca. May 1943, Stuart to Ralston. Thanks to Terry Copp for providing a copy of this document.
24 LAC, CP, vol. 7, D171, Crerar to Brooke, 24 Feb. 1943.
25 John A. English, *The Canadian Army and the Normandy Campaign: A Study of Failure in High Command* (New York 1991), 143–7; LAC, RG24, vol. 13,684, War Diary, Feb. 1943, 'G' Branch, HQ 1st Canadian Corps, 'Spartan' Appreciation by Lt-Gen H.D.G. Crerar, 2/Exercises/18, 16 Feb. 1943.
26 Imperial War Museum (IWM), B.L. Montgomery Papers (BLMP), file: BLM 49/19, Montgomery to Brooke, 23 Feb. 1943, and file: BLM 49/18, Montgomery to Brooke, 28 Feb. 1943.

27 French, *Raising Churchill's Army*, 209.
28 Opinions on McNaughton from English, *The Canadian Army*, 144–7; John Rickard, 'The Test of Command, McNaughton and Exercise Spartan, 4–11 March,' *Canadian Military History* (Summer 1999): 22–38.
29 KCL, LHC, AP, 12/XII/5, Interview, Sir James Grigg, n.d.; KCL, LHC, AP, Diary 5/6a, 8 Mar. 1943.
30 LAC, RP, vol. 54, Officer Assessments, Stuart to Ralston.
31 QUA, GDP, TC3, folder 24, Memo 25 June 1943 — for Victor [Sifton]; UTA, VMP, folder 50, 12 May 1943; LAC, CP, vol. 7, D137, Crerar to Stacey, 25 July 1943.
32 LAC, CP, vol. 7, D145, Crerar to Worthington, 24 May 1943.
33 KCL, LHC, AP, Notes on My Life, 31 Mar. 1943, file: 3/A/VIII; ibid., Interview with Crerar, n.d. (probably Mrs M.C. Long, 1954), file: 12/XIII/8.
34 KCL, LHC, AP, Diary 5/7, 18 June 1943; AP, 2/V, vol. V, 6 Jan. 1942.
35 Both quotes from Carlo D'Este, 'Appendix L: Montgomery and the Canadians,' *Bitter Victory: The Battle for Sicily 1943* (New York 1988), 615.
36 LAC, RP, vol. 59, file: Overseas Trips in 1943, Substance of Conversations between General Sir Alan Brooke, CIGS and Lieut-General K. Stuart, CGS in Connection with Fitness of Lieutenant-General A.G.L. McNaughton To Command in the Field, 13 Nov. 1943; C.P. Stacey, *Arms, Men and Governments: The War Policies of Canada, 1939–1945* (Ottawa 1970), 231; QUA, GDP, TC3, folder 26, Memo of Conversation with Ralston, 3 Feb. 1944.
37 KCL, LHC, AP, Diary 5/7, 5 and 27 July 1943.
38 LAC, W.L. Mackenzie King Papers (KP), Mackenzie King Diary, 10 July 1943; Stacey, *Arms, Men and Governments*, 232.
39 LAC, RP, vol. 59, Talk with Crerar, 30 July 1943.
40 LAC, KP, Quote from King Diary, 10 Aug. 1943; UTA, VMP, folder 51, diary 14 July 1943; KCL, LHC, AP, Diary 5/7, 3 Aug. 1943.
41 LAC, RP, vol. 59, Talks with Brooke and Stuart, 3 Aug. 1943, and Talks with McNaughton and Stuart, 5 Aug. 1943.
42 LAC, KP, King Diary, 14 Aug. 1943.
43 Pickersgill, *The Mackenzie King Record*, 497–8.
44 LAC, KP, King Diary, 10–14 Aug. 1943; Pickersgill, *The Mackenzie King Record*, 607.
45 IWM, BLMP, BLM 1/97, Brooke to Montgomery, 29 Sept. 1943.
46 LAC, CP, vol. 6, D145, Crerar to Peg Crerar, 14 Sept. 1943; D122, Crerar to Ian Anderson, 10 Dec. 1943; RP, vol. 59, file: Overseas Trips in 1943; Stacey, *Arms, Men and Governments*, 237–47; Swettenham, *McNaughton*, 2:327–349. For McNaughton's reaction see UTA, VMP, folder 51, diary 8 Oct. 1943.
47 LAC, RP, vol. 59, Ralston, Lunch with Paget and Stuart, 8 Nov. 1943.

48 LAC, RP, vol. 59, Discussions with Stuart and McNaughton, 8 Nov. 1943; KP, King Diary, 10 Nov. 1943; Pickersgill, *The Mackenzie King Record*, 611.
49 LAC, KP, King Diary, 12 Nov. 1943.
50 Public Records Office (PRO), W0216/190, Stuart to Brooke, 9 Nov. 1943; Brooke to Stuart, 12 Nov. 1943.
51 UTA, VMP, box 312, folder 52, diary 8–10 Nov. 1943.
52 LAC, RP, vol. 59, Discussion with McNaughton, 14 Nov. 1943, and Substance of Conversations between Sir Alan Brooke ... and Stuart.
53 LAC, RP, vol. 59, Barri, Discussion with Alexander, 27 Nov. 1943.
54 LAC, RP, vol. 59, Discussion with Monty, 22 Nov. 1943.
55 LAC, CP, vol. 8, D167, Crerar to Price Montague, 1 Dec. 1943; vol. 15, D267, Comd 1st Canadian Corps War Diary, 21 Nov. 1943.
56 LAC, RP, vol. 59, Discussions with Stuart and Crerar, 30 Nov. 1943; vol. 2, D21, Crerar to McNaughton, 19 Oct. 1942.
57 LAC, CP, vol. 8, D167, Crerar to the Minister, 29 Nov. 1943; RP, vol. 59, Discussions with Crerar and Stuart, 30 Nov. 1943.
58 LAC, RP, vol. 59, Alternative Courses, App't, Army Commander, by Ralston, 12 Dec. 1943.
59 LAC, RP, vol. 59, Discussions with Nye, 13 Dec. 1943.
60 LAC, RP, vol. 59, Notes of Interview with Nye, VCIGS, 13 Dec. 1943; Notes of Interview with VCIGS, 18 Dec. 1943; No. 3226, Ralston to Prime Minister, 22 Dec. 1943.
61 KCL, LHC, AP, 14/24, Montgomery to Brooke, 28 Dec. 1943.
62 LAC, VMP, box 312, folder 52, diary 20 Jan. 1944.

Chapter 14

1 G.W.L. Nicholson, *The Canadians in Italy: The Official History of the Canadians in the Second World War* (Ottawa 1956), 2:342–4.
2 Library and Archives Canada (LAC), Crerar Papers (CP), vol. 15, D267, WD CO, 1st Canadian Corps, 29 Oct. 1943; vol. 21, D329, Crerar to Nicholson, 28 Aug. 1952, Comments on Official History; Nicholson, *The Canadians in Italy*, 2:355.
3 George Kitching, *Mud and Green Fields* (Langley, BC 1986), 176.
4 Nicholson, *The Canadians in Italy*, 2:355–6; LAC, CP, vol. 21, D329, Crerar to Nicholson, 28 Aug. 1952; C.P. Stacey, *Arms, Men and Governments: The War Policies of Canada, 1939–1945* (Ottawa 1970), 219.
5 LAC, RP, vol. 53, file: Montgomery – General, High Command in War, by General B.L.M. Montgomery, Jan. 1943, copy sent to Ralston from Charles Power, 8 May 1943.

6 LAC, CP, vol. 6, D122, Crerar to Ian Anderson, 10 Dec. 1943; Major-General Chris Vokes, *Vokes: My Story* (Ottawa 1985), 152–3; Kitching, *Mud and Green Fields*, 176.
7 LAC, CP, vol. 6, D139, Crerar to Vi, 2 Dec. 1943.
8 LAC, CP, vol. 7, D180, GOC 6-9-M, Crerar to Montgomery, 17 Dec. 1943.
9 LAC, CP, vol. 7, D180, GOC/6-9-S, Crerar to Simonds, 10 Dec. 1943.
10 LAC, CP, vol. 7, D180, Crerar to Simonds, 10 Dec. 1943; Howard Graham, *Citizen and Soldier: The Memoirs of Lieutenant-General Howard Graham* (Toronto 1987), 160–4; Nigel Hamilton, *Monty: Master of the Battlefield, 1942–1944* (London 1985), 335.
11 LAC, CP, vol. 7, D180, Montgomery to Crerar, 21 Dec. 1943.
12 William Earnest John Hutchinson, 'Test of a Corps Commander: Lieutenant-General Guy Granville Simonds, Normandy 1944' (unpublished MA thesis, University of Victoria 1982) 139–45; John A. English, *The Canadian Army and the Normandy Campaign: A Study of Failure in High Command* (New York, 1991), 186–90.
13 LAC, CP, vol. 7, D180, preceding quotes from Crerar to Simonds, 15 Dec. 1943.
14 LAC, CP, vol. 3, D178, Crerar assessment of Simonds as potential army commander, 16 May 1944.
15 Nicholson, *The Canadians in Italy*, 354; LAC, CP, vol. 7, D180, Simonds to Crerar, 15 Dec. 1943.
16 LAC, CP, vol. 7, D180, Crerar to Stuart, 13 Jan. 1944; 'Memorandum by GOC 1 Cdn Corps on Contents of Letter Dated 15 Dec. 43 from Maj-Gen Simonds Comd 5 Cdn Armd Div, 21 Dec 43; J.W. Pickersgill, *The Mackenzie King Record* (Toronto 1960), 1:689–90; LAC, CP, vol. 3, D178, file: Assessment, 16 May 1944, Higher Command – C Army Overseas.
17 J.L. Granatstein interview with Brigadier P.A.S. Todd, 1991.
18 LAC, CP, vol. 6, D122, Crerar to Ian Anderson, 10 Dec. 1943; LAC, Personnel Records Centre (PRC), Crerar's Personal File, file A, Henry Crerar: Case History Sheet, 23 Feb. 1946.
19 KCL, LHC, ABP, 14/24, Monty to Brooke, 28 Dec. 1943.
20 Dominick Graham and Shelford Bidwell, *Tug of War: The Battle for Italy, 1943–1945* (London 1986), 253–4.
21 Imperial War Museum (IWM), Sir Oliver Leese Papers, box 2, 1 Jan. 1944.
22 IWM, B.L. Montgomery Papers (BLMP), file: BLM 126/9, Montgomery to Brooke, 7 July 1944.
23 LAC, CP, vol. 7, D140, Crerar to Montague, 8 Apr. 1943; vol. 2, D21, Crerar to McNaughton, 11 Aug. 1943; Terry Copp interview with Brigadier-General J.W. Megill, 1990.

24 IWM, Leese Papers, box 2, 11 Jan. 1944.
25 LAC, CP, vol. 1, D23, Commenting on 'Pickaxe,' Crerar to Burns, 13 Aug. 1943; RG24, vol .13,685, War Diary, 'G' Branch, HQ First Canadian Corps, GOC 5-4, Crerar to All Commanders and Commanding Officers, 17 Sept. 1943.
26 See, for example, LAC, RG24, vol. 13,685, War Diary, Sept. 1943, 'G' Branch, HQ 1st Canadian Corps, 'Training Instruction No. 31, Period 15 Sept.–31 Oct. 43.
27 LAC, CP, vol. 1, D18, GOC/ 3-6, 6 Oct. 1943; J.L. Granatstein interview with Lt-Col. E.T. Winslow, 1st Canadian Corps, 1992.
28 LAC, CP, vol. 15, D267, Comd, 1st Canadian Corps War Diary, Dec. 1943, GOC 1-4-1, The Responsibilities of the Comd, the Staff and the Services HQ, 1 Canadian Corps.
29 Nicholson, *The Canadians in Italy*, 355–65. For another interpretation of the dispute over transport see John A. English, *The Canadian Army and the Normandy Campaign: A Study of Failure in High Command* (New York 1991), 189.
30 LAC, CP, vol. 7, D150, Perley-Robertson to Crerar, 25 Mar. 1944; RG24, vol. 13,686, see February and March War Diaries, 'G' Branch, HQ 1st Canadian Corps; Richard S. Malone, *A Portrait of War, 1939–1943* (Don Mills 1983), 214–5.
31 LAC, CP, vol. 6, D139, Crerar to Vi, 9 Feb. 1944.
32 Chris Vokes, *Vokes: My Story* (Ottawa 1985), 152–3; LAC, CP, vol. 15, D267, War Diary, Comd 1st Canadian Corps, GOC 3-6, Crerar to Comds 1 Cdn Div, 5 Cdn Div and 1 Cdn Armd Bde, 26 Feb. 1944; RG24, vol. 13,686, War Diary 'G' Branch HQ 1st Canadian Corps, 1 Cdn Corps Study Period, 15 Feb. 1944, and 1 Cdn Corps Training Instruction No. 1, 19 Feb. 1944; Vokes, *Vokes*, 155–6.
33 LAC, CP, vol. 15, D267, War Diary, Comd 1st Canadian Corps, GOC 3-6, 26 Feb. 1944.
34 LAC, CP, vol. 1, D18, GOC 3–6, Memorandum on Daily Routine, 24 Jan. 1944; interview with Brigadier G.E. Beament, July 1990.
35 LAC, CP, vol. 7, D156, Crerar to Jim Lister, DA and QMG, 27 June 1944.
36 Graham and Bidwell, *Tug of War*, 256–365; John Ellis, *Brute Force: Allied Strategy and Tactics in the Second World War* (New York 1990), 326–40.
37 LAC, E.L.M. Burns Papers, vol. 1, file: WWII 4-2-1, 4/Trg Policy/1/2, 1 Canadian Corps Training Instruction No. 3, 26 Mar. 1944; Lessons from Recent Fighting, 12 June 1944, file: Reports and Lessons.
38 LAC, CP, vol. 8, D167, Crerar to Stuart, 12 Feb. 1944; vol 7, D171, Crerar to Brooke, 12 Feb. 1944.
39 LAC, CP, vol. 8, D167, Stuart to Crerar, 23 Feb. 1944; vol. 7, D171, Brooke to Crerar, 22 Feb. 1944.

40 LAC, RG24, vol. 13,615, War Diary, G(Ops) Tac HQ, 9 Mar. 1944; Martin Blumenson, *The Patton Papers: 1940–45* (Boston 1957), 426–7.
41 LAC, CP, vol. 7, D145, Crerar to Wigan, 26 Mar. 1944; D150, Peg Crerar to Crerar, 5 Apr. 1944.
42 LAC, CP, vol. 15, D265, Crerar's Personal War Diary, 17 Mar. 1944; Department of National Defence (DND), Directorate of History and Heritage (DHH), 000.9(D79), Misc. Biographies of Canadian Army Personnel; Brigadier G.E. Beament interview.

Chapter 15

1 Library and Archives Canada (LAC), Crerar Papers (CP), vol. 3, D73, Crerar to Massey, 6 Apr. 1944; Massey to Crerar, 11 Apr. 1944.
2 LAC, Lester B. Pearson Papers (LPP), vol. 3, Crerar, 1944–56, Pearson to Crerar, 26 Mar. 1944; Crerar to Pearson, 5 Apr. 1944.
3 Text in Terry Copp, *Fields of Fire: The Canadians in Normandy* (Toronto 2003), 269–76.
4 King's College, London (KCL), Liddell Hart Centre for Military Archives (LHC), ABP, Diary 5/8, 29 Mar. 1944.
5 University of Toronto Archives (UTA), Vincent Massey Papers (VMP), box 312, folder 52, diary 31 Jan. 1944.
6 Carlo D'Este, *Decision in Normandy: The Unwritten Story of Montgomery and the Allied Campaign* (London 1984), 55–70.
7 Imperial War Museum (IWM), B.L. Montgomery Papers (BLMP), BLM 107/1, Directive to First Canadian Army, 1 Mar. 1944, 21 A Gp/00/91/G (Plans).
8 LAC, CP, vol. 8, D167, Crerar to Minister of National Defence, 29 Nov. 1943; C.P. Stacey, *The Victory Campaign: The Official History of the Canadian Army in the Second World War* (Ottawa 1960), 3:31.
9 LAC, CP, vol. 8, D22, Senior Appointments, First Canadian Army, May 1942–June 1943.
10 LAC, CP, vol. 6, D141, Crerar to Angela Fox, 26 Mar. 1944; C.P. Stacey, *A Date with History: Memoirs of a Canadian Historian* (Ottawa 1983), 90; Terry Copp interview with George Pangman, 19 Feb. 1987, and with Brigadier Cunningham, fall 1982.
11 Beament interview.
12 Terry Copp interview with W.A.B. Anderson, n.d; DND, DHH, Biographical Files of Personnel Decorated, 000.9(D86); Beament interview.
13 DND, DHH, First Canadian Army Documents, 312.009(D31), Notes on Operational Commitments, First Canadian Army – 5 Jan. 1944.
14 Anderson interview.

15 DND, DHH, 312.009(D31), Memo: Ops Branch GS, HQ First Canadian Army, 5 Jan. 1944.
16 KCL, LHC, ABP, Diary 5/7, 27 July 1943; Stacey, *The Victory Campaign*, 3:31.
17 Pangman interview; Beament interview; LAC, RG24, vol. 13,615, G(OPS) War Diary, 10 Mar. 1944.
18 LAC, RG24, vol. 13,617, G(OPS) War Diary, Apr. 1944; Pangman interview.
19 DND, DHH, 312.009(D12), Org and Functions (Liaison and Trg), 6 Jan. 1944; 312.009 (D31); LAC, RG24, vol. 13,617, G(OPS) War Diary, Apr. 1944.
20 LAC, RG24, vol. 13,616, GS/SD War Dairy, 13 Apr. 1944.
21 LAC, CP, vol. 8, D167, Stuart to Crerar, 22 Feb. 1944.
22 LAC, RG2 C7, vol. 3, COS1 Stuart to Ralston, 8 Mar. 1944.
23 LAC, RG24, vol. 13,615, G(OPS) Tac HQ War Diary, Mar. 1944.
24 LAC, RG24, vol 13,616, War Diary GS/First Canadian Army HQ, Apr. 1944.
25 LAC, RG24, vol. 13,616, War Diary GS/First Canadian Army HQ, Mann to 2 Canadian Corps re 2 Canadian Corps Order of Battle, 18 Mar. 1944.
26 LAC, RG24, vol. 13,616, War Diary GS/First Canadian Army HQ, Minutes of Meeting Held by Chief of Staff, 21 Army Group, 20 Mar. 1944.
27 All of above from LAC, CP, vol. 15, D265, Address by Crerar to HQ First Canadian Army on the Responsibilities of the Comd, the Staff and the Services, 31 Mar. 1944.
28 LAC, CP, vol. 6, D141, Crerar to Mrs A. Fox, 29 Mar. 1944.
29 Beament interview; correspondence with Jeffrey Williams, 15 Nov. 1989.
30 LAC, CP, vol. 8, D176, CMHQ to GOC-in-C, 29 Mar. 1944; vol. 4, D79, Crerar to Stuart, 3 Apr. 1944; Stuart to Crerar, 13 May 1944.
31 DND, DHH, 312.009(D27), Memo: Organization of Command, Functioning of the Staff, Services, Miscellaneous Appointments at HQ FCA and Certain Other Organizations Which Operate in Close Liaison with HQ,'1 June 1944; LAC, CP, vol. 4, D79, 71-1-1/SD, 11 May 1944.
32 George Forty, *US Army Handbook, 1939–1945* (New York 1979).
33 LAC, RG24, vol. 13,616, War Diary GS/SD, 72-6-1/SD, 13 Apr. 1944.
34 Anderson and Pangman interviews; LAC, RG24, vol. 13,619, War Dairy G(Ops), 1 May 1944.
35 LAC, RG24, vol. 13,619, War Diary GS/Int, Initial Plan – Exercise Flit, 102/Ex Flit/1, 27 Apr. 1944.
36 LAC, RG24, vol. 13,619, War Diary GS/Int, Chief of Staff's Conference, 3 May 1944.
37 LAC, RG24, vol. 13,617, War Diary, GS/Tac HQ, Main HQ First Cdn Army Report on Exercise Flit, 17 May 1944; DND, DHH, D27, Memorandum, 1 June 1944.
38 LAC, RG24, vol. 13,616, War Diary GS, Apr. 1944, 81-0-0/Trg, 15 Apr. 1944.

39 LAC, RG24, vol. 13,616, 31-9-0/Trg, 22 Apr. 1944.
40 LAC, RG24, vol. 13,619, War Diary SD, May 1944, 71-1-0/SD, 25 May 1944.
41 Nigel Hamilton, *Monty: Master of the Battlefield, 1942-1944* (London 1985), 547.
42 Pangman and Beament interviews; KCL, LHC, ABP, 3/B/XII, 7 Apr. 1944; Blumenson, *The Patton Papers*, 434.
43 Beament interview.
44 LAC, CP, vol. 21, D324, Crerar to Stacey, 23 July 1947.
45 LAC, CP, vol. 8, D177, Crerar to Keller, 28 Apr. 1944.
46 Stacey, *The Victory Campaign*, 3:42-3.
47 LAC, CP, vol. 8, D176, Crerar to Stuart, 23 Apr. 1944.
48 LAC, CP, vol. 3, D49, Crerar to Stuart, 3 May 1944; LAC, RG2, Records of the Privy Council, Cabinet War Committee Minutes (CWCM), vol. 15, 3 and 24 May 1944.
49 KCL, LHC, ABP, Diary 5/8, 14 Dec. 1943 and 28 Feb. 1944.
50 IWM, BLMP, BLM 107/6, 21st Army Group/1001/C-in-C, May 1944; Hamilton, *Master of the Battlefield*, 586-7.
51 For more on air power and cooperation, see Michael Bechtold, 'Close Air Support in Normandy: The Case of First US Army and IX Tactical Air Command' (unpublished MA thesis, Wilfrid Laurier University 1993).
52 LAC, CP, vol. 3, D49, Crerar to Montgomery, 8 May 1944.
53 LAC, CP, vol. 8, D176, Crerar to Stuart, 26 Apr. 1944.
54 LAC, CP, vol. 3, D49, Crerar to Stuart, 3 May 1944.
55 LAC, CP, vol. 8, D176, Crerar to Stuart, 13 May 1944.
56 KCL, LHC, ABP, Diary 5/8, 16 May 1944.
57 LAC, RG24, vol. 10,688, D7, Cabinet Instructions and Interpretations of Same by Montgomery, Stuart to Brooke, 18 May 1944.
58 LAC, W.L. Mackenzie King Papers (KP), diary, 17-18 May 1944.
59 Richard S. Malone, *A Portrait of War, 1939-1943* (Don Mills 1983), 237; LAC, W.L. Mackenzie King Papers (KP), diary 17-18 May 1944.
60 LAC, CP, vol. 8, D168, Crerar to Ralston, 30 Mar. 1944; Crerar to Ralston, 13 Apr. 1944.
61 LAC, KP, diary 17 and 18 May 1944; Jean Pariseau and Serge Bernier, *French Canadians and Bilingualism in the Canadian Armed Forces* (Ottawa 1986), 1:117; General Jean V. Allard, *The Memoirs of General Jean V. Allard* (Vancouver 1988), 49.
62 LAC, RG2 7C, vol. 15, CWCM, 24 May 1944.
63 IWM, BLMP, BLM73, diary 18 and 26 May 1944.
64 LAC, CP, vol. 3, D67, Stuart to Crerar, 29 May 1944; Crerar to Stuart, 30 May 1944.

65 LAC, CP, vol. 3, D67, Crerar to Stuart, 10 June 1944; Crerar to Stuart, 16 June 1944; Stuart to Brooke, 16 June 1944.
66 LAC, CP, vol. 8, D161, CMHQ to GOC, First Canadian Army, 21 Aug. 1944; Crerar to Stuart, 22 Aug. 1944.
67 LAC, CP, vol. 3, D178, Crerar to Simonds, 19 Apr. 1944; Burns to CMHQ, 10 May 1944.
68 LAC, CP, vol. 3, D178, Crerar to Stuart, 16 May 1944; LAC, KP, diary 17 May 1944.
69 LAC, CP, vol. 3, D178, Crerar to Stuart, 16 May 1944.
70 LAC, CP, vol. 5, D24, Recommendations for Promotion, Officers, 1 Cdn Corps, 24 Aug. 1942; LAC, J.L. Ralston Papers (RP), vol. 54, Stuart to Ralston, Apr. 1943.
71 Figures from J.L. Granatstein, *The Generals: The Canadian Army's Senior Commanders in the Second World War* (Toronto 1993), 6–7.
72 Lt-General Henri Tellier, Crerar's ADC, in correspondence with the author, Jan. 1992.
73 LAC, CP, vol. 3, D178, Crerar to Simonds, 29 Aug. 1944.
74 Granatstein, *The Generals*, 250–1.
75 LAC, CP, vol. 8, D176, Stuart to Crerar, 8 Sept. 1944.
76 Allard, *Memoirs*, 109.
77 LAC, RG24, vol. 13,619, GOps WD, Minutes, Chief of Staff's Conference, 3–13 May 1944.
78 Tellier in correspondence.
79 Ibid.; LAC, RG24, vol. 13,619, Minutes, 7 May 1944.
80 LAC, CP, vol. 8, D177, Crerar to Keller, 29 June and 3 July 1944.
81 H. Essame, *Patton: A Study in Command* (New York 1974), 124–5.
82 Ibid.; LAC, CP, vol. 8, D177, Crerar to Keller, 29 June 1944.
83 LAC, CP, vol. 7, D148, Crerar to Nation, 17 May 1944; interview with Mr and Mrs Pip Nation, Oct. 1990.
84 LAC, CP, vol. 6, D153, Crerar to Peter Crerar, 30 Apr. 1944.
85 LAC, CP, vol. 6, D148, Crerar to Peg, 5 May 1944; Crerar to Peter Crerar, 25 June 1944; interview with Peggy Crerar Palmer, 16 Apr. 1991.
86 LAC, CP, vol. 8, D168, Crerar to Ralston, 6 Apr. 1944.
87 QUA, C.G. Power Papers, box 10, James Duncan Correspondence, 7 Sept. 1944.

Chapter 16

1 Library and Archives Canada (LAC), Crerar Papers (CP), vol. 21, D329, Crerar to Stacey, 23 July 1947.

2 LAC, RG24, vol. 13,617, War Diary May 1944, Address by Crerar to Senior Commanders, First Canadian Army, 14 May 1944.
3 Carlo D'Este, *A Genius for War: A Life of General George S. Patton* (London 1996), 594–5.
4 Bernard Law Montgomery, *The Memoirs of Field-Marshal, The Viscount Montgomery of Alamein, K.G.* (London 1958), 213–4; Martin Blumenson, *The Patton Papers: 1940–45* (Boston 1957), 460–1.
5 Preceding from LAC, CP, vol. 3, D49, Crerar to Breadner, 11 July 1944.
6 Imperial War Museum (IWM), B.L. Montgomery Papers (BLMP), BLM 107/1, Neptune Directive, 1 Mar. 1944.
7 LAC, RG24, vol. 13,619, War Diary, G (Ops), Chief of Staff's Conference, 19 May 1944.
8 LAC, CP, vol. 8, D158, Operation Axehead, 12 Apr. 1944.
9 LAC, CP, vol. 8, D156, Crerar to C in C, 21st Army Group, 12 Apr. 1944.
10 Ibid.
11 LAC, CP, vol. 21, D329, Comments on Official History; Terry Copp interview with George Pangman, 19 Feb. 1987.
12 Carlo D'Este, *Decision in Normandy: The Unwritten Story of Montgomery and the Allied Campaign* (London 1984), 202–5; LAC, CP, vol. 8, D188, Williams's Intelligence Appreciation, 30 Apr. 1944.
13 LAC, CP, vol. 8, D188, deGuingand to Mann, 24 Apr. 1944.
14 LAC, RG24 C17, vol. 13,619, War Diary, 'G' Ops, Appendices to Appreciation and Outline Plan of Operation Axehead, May 1944.
15 LAC, G24, vol. 13,619, C of S Conference, 19 May 1944.
16 LAC, CP, vol. 3, D43, deGuingand to Crerar, 4 May 1944; Crerar to deGuingand, 19 May 1944.
17 LAC, CP, vol. 8, D188, Crerar to Simonds, 12 June 1944; Crerar to Simonds, 8 May 1944; Crerar to Dempsey, 4 May 1944; vol. 3, D43, Crerar to Simonds, 17 May 1944; Crerar to Simonds, 2 June 1944.
18 IWM, BLMP, BLM 119/4, Crerar to Montgomery, 14 May 1944.
19 IWM, BLMP, BLM 119/4, Montgomery to Crerar, 15 May 1944.
20 LAC, CP, vol. 8, D176, Crerar to Stuart, 4 June 1944; G.W.L. Nicholson, *The Canadians in Italy: The Official History of the Canadians in the Second World War* (Ottawa 1956), 2:479–80.
21 Public Records Office (PRO), WO216/168, Leese to Kennedy, 8 June 1944; LAC, CP, vol. 3, D176, Crerar to Stuart, 15 July 1944.
22 LAC, CP, vol. 15, War Diary, Introduction to Briefing of Officers, 7 June 1944.
23 LAC, RG24 C17, vol. 13,619, Memorandum on the Development of the Int Branch at HQ First Canadian Army, 1943–1944, 1 June 1944.

24 LAC, CP, vol. 7, D171, Brooke to Crerar, 21 June 1944; Crerar to Brooke, 27 June 1944; Brooke to Crerar, 3 July 1944.
25 LAC, CP, vol. 7, D171, Crerar to Brooke, 10 June 1944.
26 LAC, RG24, vol. 13,619, War Diary G'Ops,' Chief of Staff's Conference Minutes, 19 May 1944.
27 LAC, CP, vol. 7, D148, Crerar to Nelles, 13 June 1944.
28 LAC, CP, vol. 7, D140, Crerar to Peter Crerar, 25 June 1944; Pangman interview; LAC, RG24, vol. 13,619, 'G' Ops War Diary, 19–20 June 1944.
29 LAC, CP, vol. 15, War Diary, 19 June 1944.
30 Ibid.; LAC, J.L. Ralston Papers (RP), vol. 54, Officer Assessments, Mar. 1943.
31 C.P. Stacey, *The Victory Campaign: The Official History of the Canadian Army in the Second World War* (Ottawa 1960), 3:146.
32 LAC, CP, vol. 15, War Diary, 19 June 1944.
33 Nigel Hamilton, *Monty: Master of the Battlefield, 1942–1944* (London 1985), 675.
34 Timothy Harrison Place, *Military Training in the British Army, 1940–1944* (London 2000), 14.
35 LAC, CP, vol. 8, War Diary, Notes of Conference: C-in-C and GOC-in-C, 24 June 1944; PRO, W0205/5B, Communication between C of S and Montgomery, Note, 26 June 1944.
36 J.L. Granatstein interview with Finlay Morrison.
37 Stacey, *The Victory Campaign*, 3:152.
38 Nicholson, *The Canadians in Italy*, 2:451; E.L.M. Burns, *General Mud: Memoirs of Two World Wars* (Toronto 1970), 162–3.
39 IWM, Oliver Leese Papers (OLP), box 2, Leese to his wife, 19 Jan. and 12 Mar. 1944.
40 PRO, WO 216/168, CIGS Corr with Leese, Leese to DMO, 16 Apr. and 26 May 1944; LAC, CP, vol. 7, D156, Leese to Crerar, 28 May 1944.
41 PRO, WO 214/55, Adv AAI to CIGS, 29 June 1944.
42 PRO, WO 214/55, Brooke to Alexander, 22 July 1944.
43 PRO, WO 216/168, Leese to DMO, 8 June 1944.
44 PRO, Alexander Papers, W0214/55, Correspondence between Alexander and CIGS.
45 LAC, CP, vol. 8, D176, Crerar to Stuart, 26 June 1944.
46 LAC, CP, vol. 3, D178, Memo to the C of S, 2 July 1944; vol. 15, D265, War Diary, 1–2 July 1944.
47 LAC, CP, vol. 15, D265, War Diary, 1–2 July 1944.
48 Pangman interview; PRO, Sir Miles Dempsey Papers (MDP), WO 285/9, 8 June 1944.
49 Terry Copp and Robert Vogel, *Maple Leaf Route: Caen* (Alma, ON 1985), 98–9.
50 PRO, MDP, War Diary, WO 285/9, 4 July 1944.

51 IWM, BLMP, BLM 119/7, BLM Crocker to Dempsey, 5 July 1944.
52 IWM, BLMP, BLM 119/7, Dempsey to Montgomery, 6 July 1944; Montgomery to Crerar, 8 July 1944.
53 IWM, BLMP, BLM 126/9, Monty to Brooke, M508, 7 July 1944; BLM 97/22, Leese to Monty, 11 June 1944.
54 King's College, London (KCL), Liddell Hart Centre for Military Archives (LHC), ABP, 3/B/XII, 7 Apr. 1944.
55 IWM, BLMP, BLM 119/31, Monty to CIGS, 12 Nov. 1944.
56 LAC, CP, vol. 3, D72, Crerar to Simonds, 10 July 1944.
57 LAC, CP, vol. 3, D72, Crerar to Stuart, 10 July 1944.
58 LAC, CP, vol. 3, D72, memorandum, 14 July 1944; Crerar to Stuart, 15 July 1944.
59 PRO, WO 214/55, Stuart to Leese, 21 July 1944.
60 LAC, CP, vol. 8, D178, Crerar to Stuart, 15 July 1944.
61 IWM, BLMP, BLM 1/101, Brooke to Montgomery, 11 July 1944.
62 PRO, WO 214/55, Brooke to Alexander, 22 July 1944.
63 IWM, BLMP, BLM 126/12, Montgomery to Brooke, 14 July 1944.
64 IWM, BLMP, BLM 126/11, M51D, Directive to Army COs, General Situation, 10 July 1944.
65 LAC, CP, vol. 15, War Diary, 3–7 July 1944.
66 LAC, RG24, vol. 10,799, D8, Lessons Learned, 1 July 1944; Dominick Graham, *The Price of Command: A Biography of General Guy Simonds* (Toronto 1993), 139–40.
67 LAC, CP, vol. 7, D169, SCAO to DA&QMG, 11 July 1944; Crerar to Simonds, 13 July 1944.
68 Terry Copp and William McAndrew, *Battle Exhaustion: Soldiers and Psychiatrists in the Canadian Army, 1939–1945* (Montreal and Kingston 1991), 133; LAC, CP, vol. 7, D169, Crerar to Simonds, 15 July 1944.
69 Department of National Defence (DND), Directorate of History and Heritage (DHH), 86/544, Simonds Correspondence, Crerar to Burns, 11 Mar. 1944.
70 LAC, CP, vol. 15, D288, War Diary, Appendix 2, Notes on Meeting with CIGS, 19 July 1944.
71 LAC, CP, vol. 15, D288, War Diary, July 1944, Appendix 1, Memo on Conference, 20 July 1944.

Chapter 17

1 Terry Copp interview with George Pangman, 19 Feb. 1987.
2 Library and Archives Canada (LAC), Crerar Papers (CP), vol. 7, D156, Crerar to Lister, 2 Aug. 1944; vol. 15, D288, War Diary, 19–22 July 1944.

3 Pangman interview; John English, 'The Casting of an Army: Being a Treatise on the Bases and Conduct of the Canadian Army Operations Beyond the Normandy Bridgehead to the Closure of the Falaise Gap' (unpublished PhD thesis, Queen's University 1989), 330–2.
4 LAC, RG24, vol. 13,617, War Diary, May 1944, Address by Crerar, 14 May 1944.
5 Carlo D'Este, *Decision in Normandy: The Unwritten Story of Montgomery and the Allied Campaign* (London 1984), 60.
6 LAC, CP, vol. 21, Notes on Official Histories; C.P. Stacey, *The Victory Campaign: The Official History of the Canadian Army in the Second World War* (Ottawa 1960), 3:9–11.
7 Stacey, *The Victory Campaign*, 3:9–11.
8 Interview with Brigadier G.E. Beament, 1990; Pangman interview.
9 LAC, CP, vol. 8, D181, Memorandum by GOC, 24 July 1944; Crocker's Memorandum, 24 July 1944.
10 LAC, CP, vol. 8, D181, Comments by GOC-in-C, First Canadian Army on Memorandum ... Submitted by GOC 1st British Corps, 24 July 1944.
11 Stacey, *The Victory Campaign*, 3:169–97.
12 LAC, CP, vol. 8, D181, Crerar to Montgomery, 24 July 1944.
13 LAC, CP, vol. 8, D181, Memorandum on Meeting with C-in-C, 21 Army Group, 25 July 1944.
14 King's College, London (KCL), Liddell Hart Centre for Military Archives (LHC), ABP, Alanbrooke 14/1, Montgomery to Crerar, 26 July 1944; Crerar to Brooke, 26 July 1944; Montgomery to Brooke, 26 July 1944.
15 PRO, DP, W0285/8, Montgomery to Dempsey, 19 June 1944.
16 Major-General Sir Francis deGuingand, *Operation Victory* (New York 1947), 467–8.
17 Crerar's Personal Service Record, Medical Report, 26 Sept. 1944.
18 Beament interview.
19 LAC, CP, vol. 6, D113, Leaves to Canada, Mann to Montague, 14 Sept 1944; C.P. Stacey, *Six Years of War: The Official History of the Canadian Army in the Second World War* (Ottawa 1955), 1:429–31.
20 LAC, CP, vol. 6, D154, Personal Correspondence, 20 Aug. 1944.
21 LAC, CP, vol. 4, D85, Visits – First Canadian Army, Stuart to Crerar, 5 Sept. 1944.
22 Stacey, *The Victory Campaign*, 3:183; Terry Copp and Robert Vogel, *Maple Leaf Route: Falaise* (Alma, ON, 1985), 66.
23 Terry Copp, *Fields of Fire: The Canadians in Normandy* (Toronto 2003), 163–7.
24 Stacey, *The Victory Campaign*, 3:199.
25 LAC, CP, vol. 15, D265, War Diary, 28 July 1944.

26 Stacey, *The Victory Campaign*, 3:200.
27 Copp, *Fields of Fire*, 123–30, 196–7; Stephen Ashley Hart, *Montgomery and 'Colossal Cracks': The 21st Army Group in Northwest Europe, 1944–45* (London 2000), 156–7, 171. Hart notes that Montgomery, in the Normandy campaign, gave little weight to German views.
28 LAC, CP, vol. 7, D156, Crerar to Lister, 2 Aug. 1944.
29 LAC, CP, vol. 3, D72, G Air Drill for OPs, 24 July 1944.
30 LAC, CP, vol. 2, D41, Operations 1st British Corps, 27–29 July 1944.
31 Stacey, *The Victory Campaign*, 3:201; Reginald Roy, *1944: The Canadians in Normandy* (Toronto 1984), 147.
32 LAC, CP, vol. 15, D265, War Diary, 30 July 1944.
33 LAC, CP, vol. 15, D265, War Diary, Aug. 1944.
34 LAC, CP, vol. 15, D265, War Diary, 30 July 1944.
35 LAC, CP, vol. 2, D40, 'Op Totalize,' 1 Aug. 1944.
36 Ibid.; Copp and Vogel, *Maple Leaf Route: Falaise*, 90.
37 LAC, CP, vol. 3, D75, Appx to Tactical Directive, 22 July 1944; Terry Copp, *The Brigade: The Fifth Canadian Infantry Brigade* (Stoney Creek, ON 1992), 97.
38 LAC, CP, vol. 7, D169, Crerar to Simonds, 31 July 1944.
39 LAC, CP, vol. 21, Crerar to Stacey, 7 June 1952.
40 Hart, *Montgomery and 'Colossal Cracks,'* 157; LAC, RG24, vol. 10,635, Reports on Ops First Canadian Army, (D10), Op Report, 7–23 Aug. 1944.
41 LAC, CP, vol. 15, WD, 31 July and 1 Aug. 1944.
42 Copp, *The Brigade*, 92–3; LAC, CP, vol. 15, War Diary, 2 Aug. 1944.
43 LAC, CP, vol. 3, D75, 1 Aug. 1944.
44 Martin Blumenson, *The Battle of the Generals: The Untold Story of the Falaise Pocket—The Campaign That Should Have Won World War II* (New York 1993), 145.
45 LAC, CP, vol. 7, D156, Crerar to Lister, 2 Aug. 1944.
46 LAC, CP, vol. 2, D40, Crerar to C of S, re Operation Totalizer [sic], 2 Aug. 1944.
47 LAC, CP, vol. 15, WD, 3 Aug. 1944; PRO, 2nd Brit Army/Dempsey Diaries, 285/9, 6–16 Aug. 1944.
48 Stacey, *The Victory Campaign*, 3:210–1.
49 LAC, CP, vol. 2, D40, Memorandum of Points Arising at Conference Held at HQ FCS in the Field, 4 Aug. 1944.
50 LAC, CP, vol. 3, D72, Mann to Crerar, 11 Aug. 1944.
51 Blumenson, *The Battle of the Generals*; David Irving, *The War between the Generals: Inside the Allied High Command* (New York 1981); Copp, *Fields of Fire*, 92–5.

526 Notes to pages 302–8

52 IWM, BLMP, BLM126/9, Monty to Brooke, 7 July 1944; Irving, *The War between the Generals*, 187.
53 LAC, CP, vol. 3, D72, Crerar to Mann, 12 Aug. 1944; Copp, *Fields of Fire*, 93–4.
54 LAC, CP, vol. 2, D40, 601/Conf Gen/1, 5 Aug. 1944.
55 From LAC, CP, vol. 2, D40, GOC-in-C 1-0-7/1, 5 Aug. 1944; John A. English, *The Canadian Army and the Normandy Campaign: A Study of Failure in High Command* (New York 1991), 268.
56 George Kitching, *Mud and Green Fields* (Langley, BC 1986), 193.

Chapter 18

1 Library and Archives Canada (LAC), Crerar Papers (CP), vol. 2, D40, Precis of Conversations (Telephone or Direct).
2 George Kitching, *Mud and Green Fields* (Langley, BC 1986) 192–3; John A. English, *The Canadian Army and the Normandy Campaign: A Study of Failure in High Command* (New York 1991), 269–73.
3 LAC, CP, vol. 2, D40, C of S 1-1-0, 5 Aug. 1944.
4 LAC, CP, vol. 2, D40, Memo of Telephone Conversation between C of S First Canadian Army ... Comd First Canadian Army, 6 Aug 1944; C.P. Stacey, *The Victory Campaign: The Official History of the Canadian Army in the Second World War* (Ottawa 1960), 3:212–3.
5 Public Records Office (PRO), Dempsey Papers (DP), W0285/9, 6 Aug. 1944.
6 LAC, CP, vol. 2, D40, GOC-in-C 1-0-4, 6 Aug. 1944.
7 LAC, CP, vol. 2, D40, Notes on Telephone Conversation with Comd 2 Cdn Corps, 7 Aug. 1944.
8 F.W. Winterbotham, *The Ultra Secret* (London 1974), 193.
9 Terry Copp and Robert Vogel, 'Anglo-Canadian Tactical Air Power in Normandy: A Reassessment' (paper presented to the American Military Institute, April 1987); Stacey, *The Victory Campaign*, 3:224; LAC, CP, vol. 15, War Diary Appendices, 18 Aug. 1944.
10 LAC, CP, vol. 15, War Diary, 8–11 Aug. 1944; PRO, DP, W0285/9, 7–12 Aug. 1944.
11 King's College, London (KCL), Liddell Hart Centre for Military Archives (LHC), AP, Alanbrooke 14/29, Monty to Brooke, 9 Aug. 1944.
12 Ross Munro, Crerar obituary, *Toronto Star*, 2 Apr. 1965.
13 LAC, RG24, vol. 13,620, From Introduction to Standing Orders – Volume I – Main, 10 Aug. 1944.
14 LAC, RG24, vol. 13,620, Section XVI – Tactical Headquarters; J.L. Granatstein interview with Finlay Morrison, Crerar's ADC, May 1944–1946, .

15 Interview with Brigadier G.E. Beament, 1990.
16 Department of National Defence (DND), Directorate of History and Heritage (DHH), (D27), 'Memorandum ... '
17 Beament interview; LAC, CP, vol. 15, WD, 17 Aug. 1944; Thomas MacDonald as quoted in Reader's Digest, *The Canadians at War*, vol. 2 (Toronto 1969).
18 Interview with Giles Perodeau, Mar. 1992; interview with Finlay Morrison in discussion with the author, Mar. 1992; LAC, RG24, vol. 13,620, HQ First Canadian Army, Standing Orders; Beament interview.
19 Major-General Sir Francis deGuingand, *Operation Victory* (New York 1947), 182–93; Richard Lamb, *Montgomery in Europe, 1943–45: Success or Failure?* (London 1983), 222–6.
20 Lamb, *Montgomery in Europe*, 222–6.
21 MacDonald, in *The Canadians at War*.
22 Jeffrey Simpson, Junior Staff Officer at HQ, First Canadian Army, in correspondence with the author Jan. 1991.
23 Morrison interview; Perodeau interview; Lt-General Henri Tellier, Crerar's ADC, in correspondence with the author, Jan. 1992; MacDonald, in *The Canadians at War*.
24 PRO, DP, W0285/16.
25 PRO, W0205/20, Introduction to Tactical Air Force Air Staff Instructions, Part I: TAF Methods of Support of Armies, 17 Sept. 1943.
26 Beament interview; LAC, RG24, vol. 13,620, Standing Orders ... HQ First Canadian Army.
27 Terry Copp interview with W.A.B. Anderson, n.d.
28 Kluge quote from Roman Jarymowycz, 'General Guy Simonds: The Commander as Tragic Hero,' *Warrior Chiefs: Perspectives on Senior Canadian Military Leaders*, ed. Lieutenant-Colonel Bernd Horn and Stephen Harris (Toronto 2001), 122; Kitching, *Mud and Green Fields*, 209–11.
29 LAC, CP, vol. 2, D65, C-in-C Directive M518; Stacey, *The Victory Campaign*, 3:233–4; Terry Copp and Robert Vogel, *Maple Leaf Route: Falaise* (Alma, ON: Maple Leaf Route, 1983), 108–11.
30 Carlo D'Este, *Decision in Normandy: The Unwritten Story of Montgomery and the Allied Campaign* (London 1984), 426–7.
31 KCL, LHC, ABP, Alanbrooke 14/29, Monty to Brooke, 9 Aug. 1944.
32 PRO, DP, W0285/9, 10–11 Aug. 1944.
33 Tony Foster, *Meeting of Generals* (Toronto 1986), 371.
34 PRO, DP, W0285/9, 13 Aug. 1944.
35 LAC, CP, vol. 21, D329, Crerar to Stacey, 10 Jan. 1958.
36 LAC, CP, vol. 15, War Diary, 8–11 Aug. 1944.

37 LAC, RG24, vol. 10,635, D1A, Crerar to Ralston, 1 Sept. 1944; LAC, CP, vol. 5, D118, Crerar to Simonds, 10 Aug. 1944.
38 LAC, CP, vol. 2, D39, Handwritten Precis of Conversation, 11 Aug. 1944.
39 LAC, CP, vol. 15, War Diary, 13 Aug. 1944.
40 LAC, CP, vol. 2, D39, G0113, Crerar to All Commanders, 14 Aug. 1944.
41 LAC, CP, vol. 7, D138, Crerar to Richardson, 14 Aug. 1944.
42 LAC, CP, vol. 5, D118, Memo Regarding the Report of the AOC in C Bomber Command, Mann to Crerar, 28 Aug. 1944.
43 LAC, CP, vol. 5, D118, Crerar to Harris, 29 Aug. 1944.
44 H. Essame, *The Battle for Germany* (London 1969), 47.
45 LAC, CP, vol. 7, D145, Crerar to Brigadier-General N.W. Webber, 15 Aug. 1944.
46 LAC, CP, vol. 15, War Diary, 14 Aug. 1944; vol. 7, D145, Crerar to Webber, 15 Aug. 1944.
47 LAC, CP, vol. 2, D39, Crerar to Simonds; Terry Copp, *Fields of Fire: The Canadians in Normandy* (Toronto 2003), 232–5.
48 Kitching, *Mud and Green Fields*, 201; LAC, CP, vol. 15, War Diary, Appendix 6, 16 Aug. 1944; LAC, CP, vol. 7, D145, Crerar to Webber, 15 Aug. 1944.
49 LAC, CP, vol. 15, War Diary, Aug. 1944, Appendices 6 and 7; Copp and Vogel, *Falaise*, 111–28.
50 LAC, CP, vol. 2, D39, Liaison Signal.
51 LAC, CP, vol. 2, D39, Crerar to Patton, 17 Aug. 1944.
52 LAC, CP, vol. 3, D72, Mann to Crerar, 18 Aug. 1944; CP, vol. 15, War Diary, 18 Aug. 1944.
53 LAC, CP, vol. 15, War Diary, 18 Aug. 1944 and Appendix 8.
54 LAC, CP, vol. 2, D39, Pencil Notes, 18 Aug. 1944.

Chapter 19

1 George Kitching, *Mud and Green Fields* (Langley, BC 1986), 207.
2 For more information see Paul D. Dickson, 'Colonials and Coalitions: Canadian-British Command Relations between Normandy and the Scheldt,' in *Leadership and Responsibility in the Second World War*, ed. Brian P. Farrell (Montreal and Kingston 2004), 235–73.
3 Library and Archives Canada (LAC), Crerar Papers (CP), vol. 7, D156, Crerar to Lett, 24 Aug. 1944.
4 LAC, CP, vol. 5, D129, CMHQ to NDHQ, 10 Apr. 1944.
5 LAC, CP, vol. 5, D129, Crerar to Montague, 4 Aug. 1944; figures from Major-General E.L.M. Burns, *Manpower in the Canadian Army, 1939–1945* (Toronto 1956), 92–3.

6 C.P. Stacey, *Arms, Men and Governments: The War Policies of Canada, 1939–1945* (Ottawa 1970), 430–9.
7 LAC, CP, vol. 5, D129, Montague to Crerar, 5 Aug. 1944.
8 Burns, *Manpower in the Canadian Army*, 96–7.
9 LAC, CP, vol. 5, D129, Crerar to Montague, 8 Aug. 1944.
10 LAC, CP, vol. 5, D129, Crerar to Montague; Geoffrey Hayes, 'The Development of the Canadian Army Officer Corps, 1939–1945' (unpublished PhD thesis, University of Western Ontario, 1992), 184–8; Burns, *Manpower in the Canadian Army*, 123.
11 LAC, CP, vol. 5, D129, Crerar to Montague, 8 Aug. 1944.
12 Stacey, *Arms, Men and Governments*, 432–4.
13 Ibid., 438.
14 LAC, CP, vol. 5, D129, Crerar to Stuart, 31 Aug. and 18 Sept. 1944; vol. 4, D123, Crerar to Simonds, 2 Sept. 1944.
15 LAC, CP, vol. 6, D154, Crerar to Lt.Col W.H. Boswell, 23 Nov. 1944.
16 Burns, *Manpower in the Canadian Army*, 80–1.
17 Public Record Office (PRO), Dempsey Paper (DP), W0285/2, M520 General Operational Situation and Directive, 26 Aug. 1944.
18 PRO, DP, W0205/5B, Correspondence between Chief of Staff and Commander in Chief, Letter to C of S, 1 Sept. 1944; Terry Copp and Robert Vogel, 'No Lack of Rational Speed,' *Journal of Canadian Studies* 16 (Autumn 1981): 147.
19 LAC, RG24 C17, vol. 13,626, GOC8, 1 Sept. 1944; Minutes of Morning Joint Conference, Main HQ First Canadian Army, 1 Sept. 1944.
20 Imperial War Museum (IWM), B.L. Montgomery Papers (BLMP), BLM109/9, M141, Montgomery to Crerar, 2 Sept. 1944.
21 21. Stephen Ashley Hart, *Montgomery and 'Colossal Cracks': The 21st Army Group in Northwest Europe, 1944–45* (London 2000), 169.
22 LAC, RG24 C17, vol. 13,626, Minutes of MJM, 2 Sept. 1944.
23 IWM, BLMP, Crerar to Montgomery, 3 Sept. 1944; King's College, London (KCL), Liddell Hart Centre for Military Archives (LHC), ABP, Alanbrooke 14/30, M156 to Brooke, 4 Sept. 1944.
24 PRO, W0205/5B, deGuingand to Monty, 3 and 7 Sept. 1944.
25 PRO, DP, W0285/2, Monty to Dempsey, 3 Sept. 1944.
26 IWM, BLMP, BLM109/15, C67, Crerar to Montgomery, 2 Sept. 1944.
27 IWM, BLMP, BLM 106/16, Montgomery to Crerar, 2 Sept. 1944.
28 LAC, RG24, vol. 10,651, FN215-C1.019 D7, Notes re Situation Which Developed between C-in-C, 21 AG and GOC In C, First Canadian Army 2/3 Sept. 1944.
29 Department of National Defence (DND), Directorate of History and Heri-

530 Notes to pages 331–40

tage (DHH), 86/544, Mann to Charles Foulkes, 2 Apr. 1963; IWM, BLMP, BLM109/19, Mann to 21AG HQ, 3 Sept. 1944.
30 LAC, CP, vol. 3, D47, Intercommunication Signals, Crerar to Mann, 4 Sept. 1944; Crerar to Mann, 7 Sept. 1944; CSO to Crerar, 7 Sept. 1944.
31 Notes re Situation which Developed Between C in C 21 AG and GOC First Cdn Army, 2/3 Sep 44, 4 Sept. 1944.
32 Nigel Hamilton, *Monty: The Field Marshall, 1944–1976* (London 1986), 16–20.
33 LAC, RG24 C17, vol. 13,626, Minutes of MJC, 3–5 Sept. 1944.
34 LAC, CP, vol. 21, D329, Crerar to Stacey, 10 Mar. 1959.
35 LAC, RG24 C17, vol. 13,626, Minutes of MJC, 5 Sept. 1944; 'Muskateer,' 'The Campaign in North-West Europe III: Some Aspects of Administration,' *Royal United Service Institute Journal* 103 (Feb. 1958): 77; C.P. Stacey, *The Victory Campaign: The Official History of the Canadian Army in the Second World War* (Ottawa 1960), 3:300.
36 Interview with Brigadier G.E. Beament, 1990.
37 Hart, *Montgomery and 'Colossal Cracks,'* 168–9.
38 LAC, CP, vol. 15, War Diary, Sept. 1944; KCL, LHC, ABP, Alanbrooke 14/30, M156 to Brooke, 4 Sept. 1944.
39 Hamilton, *Monty*, 35–6.
40 LAC, RG24, vol. 10,651, Monty to Crerar, 7 Sept. 1944.
41 Hamilton, *Monty*, 35–6.
42 LAC, RG24, vol. 10,633, (D318), Crerar to Stuart, 5 Sept. 1944.
43 C.P. Stacey, *A Date with History: Memoirs of a Canadian Historian* (Ottawa 1983), 236.
44 LAC, CP, vol. 4, D104, Crerar to Stuart, 5 Sept. 1944.

Chapter 20

1 C.P. Stacey, *The Victory Campaign: The Official History of the Canadian Army in the Second World War* (Ottawa 1960), 3:306–9.
2 Imperial War Museum (IWM), B.L. Montgomery Papers (BLMP), BLM109/25, Monty to Crerar, 6 Sept. 1944; Public Record Office (PRO), W0205/5B, Communications between C of S and Montgomery, Cable C0551, 6 Sept. 1944.
3 IWM, BLMP, BLM109/28, Crerar to Monty, 6 Sept. 1944.
4 Library and Archives Canada (LAC), Crerar Papers (CP), vol. 6, D155, Crerar to Harris, 15 Sept 1944.
5 Hubert Essame and Eversley M.G. Belfield, *The North-West Europe Campaign, 1944–1945* (Aldershot 1962), 65; W. Dennis Whitaker and Shelagh Whitaker, *Tug of War: The Canadian Victory That Opened Antwerp* (Toronto 1984), 68–70.

6 LAC, RG24 C17, vol. 13,626, Minutes of JMC, 7–9 Sept. 1944.
7 Stacey, *The Victory Campaign*, 3:310.
8 Ibid., 331; IWM, BLMP, BLM109/30, Monty to Crerar, 12 Sept. 1944.
9 Department of National Defence (DND), Directorate of History and Heritage (DHH), 000.9(D93), Biographies of Canadian Army Officers; J.L. Granatstein interview with Finlay Morrison.
10 LAC, RG24 C17, vol. 13,626, Minutes of JMC, 7–13 Sept. 1944.
11 LAC, RG24 C17, vol. 12,626, 10–15 Sept. 1944; Q Mov Policy Letter Number 1, 18 Sept. 1944; Main F CA to Main 84 GP RAF re Comn Aircraft, 12 Sept. 1944; LAC, CP, vol. 15, War Diary, 7 Sept. 1944.
12 LAC, CP, vol. 15, War Diary, 8 Sept. 1944.
13 IWM, BLMP, BLM109/32, Monty to Crerar, 13 Sept. 1944.
14 LAC, CP, vol. 15, War Diary, 10–13 Sept. 1944; Stacey, *The Victory Campaign*, 3:358–9.
15 IWM, BMLP, BLM109/33, Monty to Crerar, 13 Sept. 1944.
16 LAC, RG24 C17, vol. 13,626, Conference Held To Discuss Immediate Problems of Infatuate, 14 Sept. 1944; Stacey, *The Victory Campaign*, 3:338.
17 Terry Copp and Robert Vogel, 'No Lack of Rational Speed,' *Journal of Canadian Studies* 16 (Autumn 1981): 149–50.
18 B.L.M. Montgomery, *The Memoirs of Field-Marshal, the Viscount Montgomery of Alamein* (London 1958), 297.
19 LAC, RG24 C17, vol. 13,626, Minutes of MJC, 15–20 Sept. 1944.
20 Terry Copp and Robert Vogel, *Maple Leaf Route: Antwerp* (Alma, ON 1984), 89–90.
21 LAC, RG24 C17, vol. 13,626, Minutes of MJC, 15–21 Sept. 1944.
22 Terry Copp interview with George Pangman, 19 Feb. 1987.
23 Richard Lamb, *Montgomery in Europe, 1943–45: Success or Failure?* (London 1983), 253; Whitaker and Whitaker, *Tug of War*, 80.
24 Dominick Graham, *The Price of Command: A Biography of General Guy Simonds* (Toronto 1993), 180–1.
25 LAC, CP, vol. 21, D329, Crerar to Stacey, 23 July 1947 and 7 June 1952; vol. 15, D260, War Diary 21 Sept. 1944.
26 LAC, CP, vol. 21, D329, Crerar to Stacey, 23 July 1947.
27 LAC, CP, vol. 15, D265, War Diary, Sept. Notes for Conference on Operation Infatuate, 22 Sept. 1944; DND, DHH, Air 14/911, Notes on Conference – Operation Infatuate, 23 Sept. 1944.
28 DND, DHH, Air 14/911, Notes on Conference – Operation Infatuate, SHAEF to Montgomery, 21 Sept. 1944; Stacey, *The Victory Campaign*, 3:374.
29 DND, DHH, Air 14/911, Notes on Conference – Operation Infatuate, 26 Sept. 1944 by Oxland.
30 H. Essame, *The Battle for Germany* (London 1969), 47–8.

31 LAC, CP, vol. 7, file 6-9-M, Mann to Crerar, 30 Oct. 1944.
32 LAC, CP, vol. 7, D169, Simonds to Crerar, 23 Sept. 1944.
33 DND, DHH, Air 14/911, Mann to 21st Army Group, 26 Sept. 1944; Stacey, *The Victory Campaign*, 3:375–7.
34 Beament interview.
35 LAC, Personnel Records Centre, Crerar's Personal File, Medical Report, 26 Sept. 1944.
36 Beament interview.
37 LAC, RG24 C17, vol. 13,626, Minutes of MJC, 30 Sept. 1944; DND, DHH, Air 14/911, Minutes of Conference, 29 Sept. 1944; Terry Copp and Robert Vogel, *Maple Leaf Route: Scheldt* (Alma, ON 1985), 18.
38 LAC, RG24 C17, vol. 13,626, Minutes of MJC, 29 Sept. 1944.
39 LAC, CP, vol. 4, D178, Weeks to CMHQ, MGA205, 1 Nov. 1944. For a more comprehensive version see J.L. Granatstein, *The Generals: The Canadian Army's Senior Commanders in the Second World War* (Toronto 1993), 133–43.
40 LAC, CP, vol. 4, D178, Weeks to CMHQ, MGA205, 1 Nov. 1944.
41 Ibid.; KCL, LHC, AP, Diary 5/10, 24 Oct. 1944.
42 LAC, MG31 G21, Penhale Papers, vol. 1, Vokes to Penhale, 2 Nov. 1944.
43 LAC, CP, vol. 3, GOC-in-C/6-10-3, Crerar to Foulkes, 19 Dec. 1944.
44 LAC, J.L. Ralston Papers (RP), vol. Notes of Conversation, 8/10/44, Eindhoven, F.M.M.
45 IWM, BLMP, BLM115/64, Montgomery to Brooke, 18 Oct. 1944.
46 C.P. Stacey, *A Date with History: Memoirs of a Canadian Historian* (Ottawa 1983), 236f.
47 Interview with Peter Crerar, summer 1991.
48 IWM, BLMP, BLM115/69, VCIGS to Montgomery, 21 Oct. 1944.
49 PRO, 21st Army Group HQ Papers, W0205/18, Notes for the Chief of Staff, 22 Oct. 1944.
50 IWM, BLMP, BLM115/74, Montgomery to Brooke, 23 Oct. 1944; LAC, CP, vol. 7, D171, Crerar to Brooke, Nov. 1944; AP, Diary 5/10, 24 Oct. 1944.
51 IWM, BLMP, BLM119/35, Montgomery to CIGS, 17 Nov. 1944.

Chapter 21

1 Public Record Office (PRO), W0205/5B, Communication between C of S and Montgomery, COS/S5, 7 Nov. 1944.
2 C.P. Stacey, *Arms, Men and Governments: The War Policies of Canada, 1939–1945* (Ottawa 1970), 441–51.
3 Ibid., 457.
4 Library and Archives Canada (LAC), Crerar Papers (CP), vol. 3, D31, Weir to Malone, 2 Nov. 1944.

5 LAC, CP, vol. 3, D31, Notes for Press Conference.
6 C.P. Stacey, *The Victory Campaign: The Official History of the Canadian Army in the Second World War* (Ottawa 1960), 3:430.
7 LAC, CP, vol. 5, D107, Crerar to Montague, 9 Nov. 1944.
8 LAC, CP, vol. 5, D107, Correspondence, 12–23 Nov. 1944.
9 LAC, CP, vol. 4, D178, Crerar to Montague, 14 Nov. 1944.
10 LAC, CP, vol. 3, D36, Murchie to Montague, 31 Oct. 1944; Montague to Crerar, 11 Nov. 1944.
11 LAC, CP, vol. 3, D36, Montague to Crerar, 25 Nov. 1944; C.P. Stacey, *Six Years of War: The Official History of the Canadian Army in the Second World War* (Ottawa 1955), 1:204.
12 LAC, CP, vol. 3, D36, Training Directive No. 1, 3 Nov. 1944.
13 Dominick Graham, *The Price of Command: A Biography of General Guy Simonds* (Toronto 1993), 171–2.
14 LAC, CP, vol. 16, War Diary, Nov. 1944.
15 LAC, CP, vol. 6, D153, Crerar to John Crerar, 15 June 1945; D154, Crerar to Warren Bickersteth, June 1945.
16 LAC, CP, vol. 6, D154, Correspondence between Crerar, Sansom, and McNaughton, 5 Mar.–4 Apr. 1944.
17 LAC, McNaughton Papers, vol. 267, Appointment to Cabinet; Granatstein, *The Generals*, 232–5.
18 LAC, CP, vol. 7, D137, Stuart to Crerar, 7 Nov. 1944.
19 Ibid.; Crerar to Stuart, 2 Dec. 1944; Granatstein, *The Generals*, 232–5.
20 LAC, Lester B. Pearson Papers (LPP), vol. 11, Pope to Pearson, 15 Mar. 1945; Crerar to Pope, 21 Feb. 1945.
21 LAC, CP, vol. 6, D154, Crerar to Boswell, 23 Nov. 1944; Crerar to John Crerar, 18 Nov. 1944.
22 Stacey, *The Victory Campaign*, 3:632.
23 PRO, W0205/64, Memo: Inspector of Organization, 6 Jan. 1945.
24 Ed Cray, *General of the Army: George C. Marshall; Soldier and Statesman* (New York 1990), 483; Geoffrey Perret, *There's a War to Be Won: The United States Army in World War II* (New York 1991), 372–6.
25 Terry Copp and William McAndrew, *Battle Exhaustion: Soldiers and Psychiatrists in the Canadian Army, 1939–1945* (Montreal and Kingston 1991), 144–5.
26 LAC, CP, vol. 6, D139, Crerar to Greene, 5 Dec. 1944.
27 LAC, CP, vol. 7, D156, Crerar to Sherwood Lett, 2 Dec. 1944.
28 Stacey, *Arms, Men and Governments*, 470–9; Stacey, *The Victory Campaign*, 3:632–3; LAC, CP, vol. 4, Crerar to Montague, 1 Dec. 1944.
29 LAC, CP, vol. 5, D129, Montague to Murchie, 15 Nov. 1944; Stacey, *Arms, Men and Governments*, 462–81.
30 LAC, CP, vol. 4, Memo on the Org of HQ First Cdn Army, 8 Nov. 1944.

31 DND, DHH, Memorandum on the Organization of Command, etc., 1 Feb. 1945; LAC, CP, vol. 4, Memorandum on Organization, 29 Nov. 1944; Mann to HQ, 10 Jan. 1945.
32 LAC, CP, vol. 4, D179, Appointments; Terry Copp and Robert Vogel, *Maple Leaf Route: Victory* (Alma, ON 1988), 28.
33 LAC, CP, vol. 4, D179, AAG on Senior Appointments, 4 Jan. 1945.
34 LAC, CP, vol. 2, D25, Crerar to Mann, 27 Nov. 1944; Crerar to Monty, 28 Nov. 1944.
35 Interview with Brigadier G.E. Beament, 1990.
36 LAC, CP, vol. 15, Minutes of a Special Conference to Discuss Future Ops, 7 Dec. 1944; Operation Veritable: Points Arising from Planning Conference, 8 Dec. 1944.
37 LAC, CP, vol. 15, Notes of Remarks of C in C 21 Army Group, 9 Dec. 1944; Principles Governing Operation Veritable, for Corps Commanders, 10 Dec. 1944.
38 LAC, CP, vol. 2, D25, Notes Regarding Basic Plan, 12 Dec. 1944; Notes of a Meeting of Comd 30 Brit Corps with Army Comd, 13 Dec. 1944.
39 LAC, CP, vol. 2, D25, Remarks to Staff Officers, HQ First Canadian Army, 16 Dec. 1944.
40 LAC, CP, vol. 21, Crerar to Stacey, 27 Aug. 1958; Stacey, *The Victory Campaign*, 3:442–2.
41 LAC, CP, vol. 7, Crerar to W.M. Taylor, 2 Jan. 1945.
42 LAC, CP, vol. 2, D25, Operation Veritable: Air Support, 17 Dec. 1944.
43 LAC, CP, vol. 15, War Diary, Dec. 1944, Crerar to Rennie, 1 Dec. 1944.
44 LAC, CP, vol. 6, D153, Crerar to Ira Craig, 22 Dec. 1944.
45 LAC, CP, vol. 16, War Diary, Jan. 1945; AP, Diary 5/10, 10 Jan. 1945.

Chapter 22

1 Library and Archives Canada (LAC), Crerar Papers (CP), vol. 6, D142, Ike to Crerar, 26 Mar. 1945.
2 Imperial War Museum (IWM), B.L. Montgomery Papers (BLMP), BLM138/5-9, Monty to SHAEF, 12–21 Jan. 1945; United States Military Archives (USMA), Simpson Papers (SP), box 11, Personal Calender, HQ Diary, 15–19 Jan. 1945.
3 Public Record Office (PRO), AIR14/912, Operation Veritable: Air Plan, Revised 29 Jan. 1945.
4 Sir Brian Horrocks with Eversley Belfield, *Corps Commander* (London 1977), 183–4.
5 LAC, CP, vol. 2, D25, Notes on Conference, 23 Jan. 1945.

6   LAC, CP, vol. 2, D25, Address to Senior Officers, 22 Jan. 1945.
7   LAC, CP, vol. 2, D25, Crerar to Corps Commanders, 25 Jan. 1945.
8   LAC, CP, vol. 2, D25, Notes on Conference, 4 Feb. 1944.
9   C.P. Stacey, *The Victory Campaign: The Official History of the Canadian Army in the Second World War* (Ottawa 1960), 3:458.
10 PRO, Dempsey Papers, 21 Army Group Papers, W0205/9, 21 Army Group General Situation, 21 Jan. 1945; Considerations Concerning Operations Veritable and Grenade, 31 Jan. 1945.
11 LAC, CP, vol. 6, D153, Crerar to Ned Cape, 25 Jan. 1945; vol. 16, War Diary, February Appendices, Remarks by GOC-in-C to War COs, 7 Feb. 1945.
12 The HQ First Canadian Army visitors' VIP caravan, the 'Viper's Den,' believed to have housed a brothel for the German High Command near Breda in Holland, was acquired in November 1944. It was fitted with chandeliers, mauve curtains, and rosewood panelling.
13 Paul Martin, *A Very Public Life* (Ottawa 1983), 1:354–5.
14 LAC, CP, vol. 21, D329, Crerar to Stacey, 27 Aug. 1958; David French, *Raising Churchill's Army: The British Army and the War against Germany, 1919–1945* (Oxford 2000), 268.
15 King's College, London (KCL), Liddell Hart Centre for Military Archives (LHC), Alanbrooke Papers (AP), 14/6, Montgomery to CIGS, 8 Feb. 1945.
16 LAC, CP, vol. 6, D153, Crerar to John, 11 Feb. 1945.
17 KCL, LHC, AP, Alanbrooke 14/6, Montgomery to CIGS, 10–11 Feb. 1945.
18 Sir Brian Horrocks with Eversley Belfield, *Corps Commander* (London 1977), 183.
19 IWM, BLMP, BLM 119/47, Monty to CIGS, 27 Dec. 1945; 119/71, Monty to CIGS, 15 Feb. 1945; 19/73, Monty to CIGS, 18 Feb. 1945.
20 LAC, RG24 C17, vol. 13,634, HQ War Diaries, Minutes of Morning Conference, 13 Feb. 1945.
21 LAC, RG24 C17, vol. 13,643, Minutes of Morning Conference, 16 Feb. 1945.
22 H. Essame, *The Battle for Germany* (London 1969), 160–1.
23 LAC, CP, vol. 16, War Diary, 18–22 Feb. 1945; LAC, RG24 C17, vol. 13,634, Army War Diaries, 16–22 Feb. 1945; Brigadier-General Denis Whitaker and Shelagh Whitaker, *Rhineland: The Battle to End the War* (Toronto 1989), 171.
24 Whitaker and Whitaker, *Rhineland*, 144–7.
25 LAC, CP, vol. 2, D25, Crerar's handwritten notes.
26 LAC, RG24, vol. 10,798, 011(D1), Memo of Interview with Simonds, 8 Feb. 1947.
27 LAC, Lester B. Pearson Papers (LPP), vol. 11, Crerar to Pope, 21 Feb. 1945.
28 PRO, Dempsey's Diary, W0285/11, 23 Feb. 1945.
29 LAC, CP, vol. 2, D25, Directives to Corps Commanders, 24 and 25 Feb. 1945;

Dominick Graham, *The Price of Command: A Biography of General Guy Simonds* (Toronto 1993), 202–3.
30 Stacey, *The Victory Campaign*, 3:508–22.
31 PRO, Dempsey's Diary, W0285/11, 27 Feb. 1945.
32 LAC, RG24 C17, vol. 13,634, Minutes of Morning Conference, 26 Feb. 1945.
33 LAC, CP, vol. 6, D154, Crerar to Burns, 15 Feb. 1945.
34 LAC, CP, vol. 16, War Diary, Feb. 1945.
35 LAC, CP, vol. 7, D140, Crerar to McCreery, 24 Feb. 1945.
36 LAC, CP, vol. 16, War Diary Appendices, Remarks by GOC-in-C to WarCos, 7 Feb. 1945.
37 Quoted in Whitaker and Whitaker, *Rhineland*, 32.
38 LAC, CP, vol. 3, D74, Malone to Crerar, 22 Nov. 1944; Crerar to Malone, 8 Jan. 1945.
39 LAC, PP, vol. 11, file: Pope, M ... 1944–46, Pope to Pearson, 15 Mar. 1945.
40 LAC, CP, vol. 6, (D141), Crerar to Gweneth Fisher, 1 Mar. 1945.
41 KCL, LHC, AP, Diary 5/10, 4 Mar. 1945.
42 LAC, CP, vol. 20, D320, Correspondence with Jim Nichols, Profile, 1960.
43 LAC, CP, vol. 6, D142, Crerar to Ike, 30 Mar. 1945.
44 LAC, CP, vol. 6, D142, MND to Crerar, 1 April 1945; Crerar to MND, 5 Apr. 1945.
45 LAC, CP, vol. 7, D156, Crerar to HFG Letson, 11 Mar. 1945.

Chapter 23

1 Library and Archives Canada (LAC), Crerar Papers (CP), vol. 4, D179, Crerar to Montague, 28 Feb. 1945.
2 LAC, CP, vol. 4, D179, Cables and letters, Mar. 1945.
3 LAC, CP, vol. 4, D179, Montague to Murchie, 10 Mar. 1945.
4 Whitaker and Whitaker, *Rhineland*, 145.
5 LAC, CP, vol. 4, D179, Crerar to Montague, 6 Mar. 1945.
6 King's College, London (KCL), Liddell Hart Centre for Military Archives (LHC), Alanbrooke Papers (AP), Diary 5/10, 19 Mar. 1945.
7 LAC, CP, vol. 4, D104, Crerar to Stuart, 5 Sept. 1944.
8 G.W.L. Nicholson, *The Canadians in Italy: The Official History of the Canadians in the Second World War* (Ottawa 1956), 2:661–2; LAC, CP, vol. 7, D140, McCreery to Montgomery, 16 Feb. 1945.
9 Public Record Office (PRO), Dempsey Papers (DP), W0285/2, 21st Army Group Papers, Orders for the Battle of the Rhine, 9 Mar. 1945; Nigel Hamilton, *Monty: The Field Marshal, 1944–1976* (London 1986), 409.
10 LAC, RG24 C17, vol. 13,609, Army War Diaries, Operation Plunder, 21 Feb. 1945.

11 PRO, Dempsey Papers, WO 285/11, Dempsey's War Diaries, 23–30 Mar. 1945.
12 Ibid., 28 Mar. 1945.
13 Tony Foster, *Meeting of Generals* (Toronto 1986), 340, 394–5.
14 General Jean Allard, *The Memoirs of General Jean V. Allard* (Vancouver 1988), 109.
15 Terry Copp interview with George Pangman,19 Feb. 1987.
16 LAC, CP, vol. 7, D152, Crerar to Turner, 7 July 1942.
17 LAC, CP, vol. 6, D153, Crerar to Verse, via CGS, 30 Mar. 1945.
18 LAC, CP, vol. 7, D150, Crerar to Peg, 3 May 1945.
19 LAC, CP, vol. 7, D145, Crerar to Hume Wrong, 19 Apr. 1945.
20 LAC, CP, vol. 1, D13, Rough Draft of 'Observations on Canadian Requirements in Respect to the Army,' CGS Files.
21 LAC, CP, vol. 16, March War Diary, Notes on Conference with C-in-C, 27 Mar. 1945.
22 LAC, CP, vol. 16, April War Diary, GOC-in-C 5-4, 12 Apr. 1945.
23 C.P. Stacey, *A Date with History: Memoirs of a Canadian Historian* (Ottawa 1983), 165–6.
24 LAC, CP, vol. 4, D179, Montague to Murchie, 20 Apr. 1945.
25 LAC, CP, vol. 5, D98, Crerar to Stuart, 1 June 1944.
26 LAC, CP, vol. 5, D98, Murchie to Stuart, 10 June 1944.
27 LAC, CP, vol. 4, D106, handwritten note to DA and QMG, 1 Sept. 1944.
28 LAC, CP, vol. 16, D285, Western Trip Papers, Discipline and Democracy, 1946.
29 LAC, CP, vol. 5, D94, Crerar to Stuart, 5 Sept. 1944.
30 LAC, CP, vol. 5, D94, C66, Crerar to Stuart, 2 Sept. 1944.
31 LAC, CP, vol. 5, D94, Crerar to C of S, CMHQ, 30 Jan. 1945.
32 LAC, CP, vol. 5, D94, Crerar to Montague, 14 Jan. 1945.
33 LAC, CP, vol. 5, D129, Montague to Murchie, 15 Nov. 1944.
34 LAC, CP, vol. 5, D94, Crerar to C of S, CMHQ, 17 Feb. 1945.
35 LAC, RG2 7C, vol. 16, CWCM, 23 Sept. 1944.
36 LAC, RG2 C7, vol. 17, CWCM, 19 Apr. 1945, and Chiefs of Staff Memorandum for Cabinet War Committee, 10 Apr. 1945.
37 LAC, CP, vol. 8, D176, Crerar to Price Montague, 15 May 1945.
38 LAC, CP, vol. 4, D179, J.W. McCLain on Senior Appointments, 4 Jan. 1945.
39 LAC, CP, vol. 4, D179, Appointments and Promotions: Interchange of Personnel, 8 Apr. 1945.
40 LAC, CP, vol. 4, D179, Montague to Murchie, 20 Apr. 1945.
41 LAC, CP, vol. 9, D154, Crerar to J.B. Bickersteth, 9 June 1945.
42 LAC, CP, vol. 4, D106, Minutes of Conf ... Reallocation of Canadian Army Manpower, 28 Apr. 1945.
43 Ibid.

44 Hamilton, *Monty: The Field Marshal*, 608.
45 LAC, CP, vol. 4, D179, Crerar to Montague, 11 May 1945.

Chapter 24

1 Library and Archives Canada (LAC), RG24 C17, vol. 13,609, Forecast 'O' Activity, G Plans, 1 Apr. 1945.
2 LAC, Crerar Papers (CP), vol. 6, D153, Crerar to John Crerar, 22 Apr. 1945.
3 LAC, CP, vol. 7, D145, Crerar to Wrong, 19 Apr. 1945.
4 John Swettenham describes Currie's libel trial in *To Seize the Victory: The Canadian Corps in the First World War* (Toronto 1965), 1–20.
5 LAC, CP, vol. 7, D150, Crerar to Peg, 3 May 1945.
6 LAC, CP, vol. 16, War Diary, July, Appendix C, 4 May 1945.
7 LAC, CP, vol. 4, D85, Series of Cables, 28 April to 1 May 1945.
8 LAC, CP, vol. 4, D85, Appendix D.
9 LAC, CP, vol. 8, D160, Press Interview, Aug. 1945; vol. 17, D438, Journal of Events, UK and Europe Visit, 1953.
10 LAC, CP, vol. 6, D153, Cables, 8 May 1945.
11 LAC, CP, vol. 7, D150, Crerar to Peg, 3 May 1945.
12 LAC, CP, vol. 4, D104, Demobilization.
13 LAC, CP, vol. 16, War Diary, May 1945, GOC-in-C, 3–6, 8 May 1945
14 Ibid.
15 LAC, CP, vol. 6, D135, Crerar to Montague, 11 May 1945.
16 LAC, CP, vol. 4, D84, First Canadian Army Local Visits.
17 Public Record Office (PRO), W0205/5C, Part I, Chief of Staff Correspondence, Note, May 1945.
18 LAC, CP, vol. 19, D338, Crerar to Zouch Palmer, 27 Mar. 1941.
19 LAC, CP, vol. 6, D145, Crerar to Zouch Palmer, 20 Mar. 1941.
20 LAC, CP, vol. 26, D390, Civic Education and Military Preparation.
21 LAC, CP, vol. 6, D154, Crerar to J.B. Bickersteth, 9 June 1945.
22 LAC, CP, vol. 8, D176, Crerar to Montague, 15 May 1945.
23 LAC, CP, vol. 6, D154, Crerar to Prince Bernhard of the Netherlands, 15 May 1945.
24 Interview with Brigadier G.E. Beament, 1990.
25 LAC, CP, vol. 3, D75, Crerar to John Crerar, 15 June 1945.
26 LAC, CP, vol. 5, D112, Crerar to Lister, 7 May 1945.
27 C.P. Stacey, *The Victory Campaign: The Official History of the Canadian Army in the Second World War* (Ottawa 1960), 3:614–5.
28 Tony Foster, *Meeting of Generals* (Toronto 1986), 446.
29 Quote from 'Mackenzie King's Opening Address, 16 May 1945,' in *Histori-*

cal Documents of Canada, ed. C.P. Stacey (Toronto 1972), 121; C.P. Stacey, *A Date with History: Memoirs of a Canadian Historian* (Ottawa 1983), 5:154.
30 LAC, CP, vol. 3, D35, Postwar Staff Training Policy, 5 Apr. 1945; vol. 5, D101, Office Routine and Instructions, Staff Organization.
31 LAC, CP, vol. 4, D106, Minutes of Conference Held by GOC-in-C, Reallocation, 22 May 1945.
32 LAC, CP, vol. 6, D142, Crerar to Ike, 31 May 1945; Ike to Crerar, 9 June 1945.
33 LAC, CP, vol. 6, D154, Crerar to Bickersteth, 9 June 1945.
34 LAC, CP, vol. 5, D94, Lister Memorandum, 10 June 1945.
35 LAC, CP, vol. 4, D179, Crerar to Montague, 18 and 27 May 1945.
36 LAC, CP, vol. 7, D140, Crerar to McCreery, Feb.–Mar. 1945; vol. 4, D179, Crerar to Murchie, 5 July 1945; J.L. Granatstein, *The Generals: The Canadian Army's Senior Commanders in the Second World War* (Toronto 1993), 165.
37 LAC, CP, vol. 20, D331, Crerar to Montgomery, 22 Dec. 1945.
38 Stacey, *A Date with History*, 164–78.
39 LAC, CP, vo. 4, D179, Crerar to Murchie, 5 July 1945.
40 LAC, CP, vol. 6, D153, Crerar to John Crerar, 15 June 1945.
41 LAC, CP, vol. 4, D123, Cables in Discipline File.
42 LAC, CP, vol. 4, D106, Demobilization File.
43 LAC, CP, vol. 4, D106, Cables and Amendments, 1–3 July 1944; LAC, Ralston Papers, vol. 54, Stuart to Ralston.
44 LAC, CP, vol. 4, D106, Burns to Crerar, 7 July 1945.
45 LAC, CP, vol. 4, D106, Crerar to All Commanders, 10 July 1945.
46 LAC, CP, vol. 5, D94, Lister on Repatriation, 8 June 1945.
47 Dean Oliver, 'Awaiting Return: Life in the Canadian Army's Overseas Repatriation Depots, 1945–1946' (paper delivered to The Veterans Charter and Post–World War II Canada Conference, Oct. 1995).
48 LAC, CP, vol. 16, War Diary, July 1945, Message C257; vol. 5, D96, Operation Eclipse, Crerar to Chief of Staff, 26 Mar. 1945.
49 LAC, CP, vol. 4, D104, Copy of *The Maple Leaf*, 19 July 1945; Cable, Montague to Crerar, July 1945.
50 LAC, CP, vol. 7, D150, Peg Crerar to Crerar, 20 June 1945, and Perley-Robertson to Crerar, 15 May 1945; vol. 6, D153, Crerar to John Crerar, 15 June 1945.
51 LAC, CP, vol. 7, D150, Crerar to Ike-Perley Robertson, 17 July 1945.
52 Dominick Graham, *The Price of Command: A Biography of General Guy Simonds* (Toronto 1993), 218.
53 LAC, CP, vol. 16, D266, War Diary, July 1945, Appendix.
54 Jeffrey Williams in correspondence with the author, 15 Nov. 1989.

Chapter 25

1 From Library and Archives Canada (LAC), Crerar Papers (CP), vol. 25, D350, 'Broadcast by Lee Shapiro over CBC Network,' 5 Aug. 1945.
2 Ibid.
3 'Crerar Returns to Canada,' *Globe and Mail*, 5 Aug. 1945.
4 LAC, CP, vol. 7, D150, Crerar to Peg, 1945.
5 LAC, CP, vol. 8, D160, Return to Canada, 1945; vol. 21, D331, Martin to Crerar, 23 Nov. 1945.
6 Thanks to William Gregg for this material. William Gregg, 'General Crerar's Caravan,' *Wheels and Tracks: The International Review of Military Vehicles* 7 (1984): 16–17.
7 LAC, CP, vol. 20, D314, Crerar to Montgomery, 22 Dec. 1945.
8 LAC, CP, vol. 8, D176, Crerar to Montague, 26 June 1945.
9 LAC, CP, vol. 16, D285, Western Trip, 1945–46.
10 LAC, CP, vol. 20, D317, Crerar to Peacock, 17 Feb. 1946; 'General Crerar Visits Toronto, *Globe and Mail*, 7 Nov. 1945.
11 LAC, CP, vol. 26, D366, Civic Education and Military Preparedness, Dec. 1945.
12 LAC, CP, vol. 27, D401, Address to RMC Club, May 1948.
13 LAC, CP, vol. 26, D364, The Canadian Soldier as Citizen.
14 LAC, CP, vol. 26, D391, The Need for Canadian Military Preparation.
15 LAC, CP, vol. 19, D303, Crerar to Goforth, 8 Jan. 1946.
16 Lt-General Henri Tellier, Crerar's ADC, in correspondence with the author, Jan. 1992. See LAC, CP, vol. 19, D303, Crerar to Goforth, 8 Oct. 1948.
17 LAC, CP, vol. 16, D287, Visit to Winnipeg, 8 Jan. 1946.
18 LAC, CP, vol. 20, D319, Personal Correspondence, 5 Feb. 1946.
19 LAC, CP, vol. 25, D350, Lee Shapiro Broadcast Transcript.
20 J.W. Pickersgill and D.F. Forster, *The Mackenzie King Record* (Toronto 1970), 3:54.
21 LAC, CP, vol. 19, D305, Crerar to Drew, 9 Mar. 1947.
22 LAC, CP, vol. 7, D150, Crerar to Perley-Robertson, 12 May 1945.
23 LAC, CP, vol. 7, D150, Crerar to Perley-Robertson, 12 May 1945.
24 LAC, CP, vol. 24, D430, Personal Correspondence, Directorships.
25 LAC, CP, vol. 19, D308, Crerar to Greene, 14 Nov. 1947.
26 LAC, CP, vol. 20, D320, Crerar to Burns, 23 Jan. 1947; D313, Acting Under-Secretary of State, 29 Sept. 1948; D314, Pearson to Crerar, Jan. 1948.
27 LAC, CP, vol. 20, D331, Reference Letter for Morrison, 1947.
28 LAC, CP, vol. 19, D304, Letter of 17 Dec. 1945.
29 LAC, CP, vol. 20, D309, Crerar to Bill Hynes, 16 Feb. 1946.

30 LAC, CP, vol. 20, D317, Crerar to Mrs H.Z. Palmer, 17 Nov. 1945.
31 LAC, CP, vol. 20, D314, Crerar to Murchie, 28 Oct. 1945.
32 LAC, CP, vol. 20, D319, Ralston to Crerar, 8 Aug. 1945.
33 LAC, CP, vol. 16, D278, Crerar to Secretary of State for External Affairs, 21 Oct. 1946.
34 LAC, Lester B. Pearson Papers (LPP), vol. 3, Nominal Files, 1942–57, Pearson to Davis, 22 Aug. 1947.
35 For more information see LAC, RG25, vol. 3104, China Dispatches.
36 LAC, CP, vol. 17, D286, Visit to Japan.
37 Kenneth Taylor, 'The Challenge of the Eighties: World War II from a New Perspective; The Hong Kong Case,' in *Men at War*, ed. Tim Travers and Christon Archer (Chicago 1982), 197–211; LAC, CP, vol. 24, D330, Mann to Crerar, Aug. 1946.
38 LAC, CP, vol. 17, D301, Report on Visit to Netherlands; interview with Henri Tellier.
39 Quote from LAC, CP, vol. 26, D388, International Affairs and National Responsibilities.
40 LAC, CP, vol. 19, D308, Correspondence between Gault and Crerar, Oct. 1950.
41 LAC, CP, vol. 21, D343, Personal Correspondence, Canadian Citizenship Council.
42 LAC, CP, vol. 20, D314, Crerar to Mann, 19 Oct. 1945.
43 LAC, CP, vol. 24. D330, Mann to Crerar, 7 Aug. 1946.
44 Richard A. Preston, *To Serve Canada: A History of the Royal Military College Since the Second World War* (Ottawa 1991), 23–5.
45 LAC, CP, vol. 27, D401, Address to RMC Club 1948.
46 Preston, *To Serve Canada*, 23.
47 'War Is a Prospect Canada Must Face,' *Maclean's*, 15 July 1947; letters to the editor, *Maclean's*, 1 Oct. and 15 Dec. 1947.
48 LAC, CP, vol. 20, D309, Crerar to Honourable W.D. Herridge, 16 Jan. 1950.
49 LAC, CP, vol. 21, D344, Canadian Legion – BESL, 1946–64.
50 LAC, CP, vol. 19, D303, Kim Beattie to Crerar, 19 Sept. 1949; D306, Beattie to Crerar, 9 July 1951.
51 LAC, CP, vol. 21, D331, Carew Martin to Crerar, 23 Nov. 1945.
52 LAC, CP, vol. 25, D345, Address by General Crerar to Dominion Convention, 1 Aug. 1954; vol. 16, D285, Some Thoughts Concerning Veteran's Associations.
53 LAC, CP, vol. 24, Letter to Norman Smith, 1 Sept. 1948.
54 LAC, CP, vol. 24, D334, Biography File, Crerar to Harrison, 22 Jan. 1954.
55 LAC, CP, vol. 19, D306, Beattie to Crerar, 9 July 1951.

56 LAC, CP, vol. 24, D458, Verse Crerar to Stacey, 5 Aug. 1965.
57 LAC, CP, vol. 21, D329 Crerar to Stacey, 10 Mar. 1959; Crerar to Stacey, 24 Oct. 1956.
58 LAC, CP, vol. 21, D329, Crerar to Stacey, 23 July 1947.
59 LAC, CP, vol. 16, D285, The Contributions of the Canadians at Dieppe.
60 LAC, CP, vol. 26, D378, Dieppe – Script.
61 LAC, CP, vol. 19, D302, Personal Correspondence 'B.'
62 LAC, CP, vol. 3, D88, Preliminary Narrative on Dieppe and Normandy, Letter to Stacey, 10 June 1944.
63 Terry Copp interview with Brigadier P.A.S. Todd, 1991.
64 LAC, CP, vol. 21, D372, Personal Correspondence, VE Dinner.
65 Stacey, *A Date with History*, 233–4.
66 LAC, CP, vol. 21, D344, Personal Correspondence – BESL.
67 See *Globe and Mail*, 17 Mar. 1956.
68 He was the honorary colonel of the Stormont, Dundas, and Glengarry Highlanders, 1952–6; the honorary colonel commandant of the Canadian Military Intelligence Association, honorary life member of the Royal Canadian Artillery Association.
69 LAC, CP, vol. 17, D438, Journal of Events, UK and Europe Visit, 1953.
70 LAC, CP, vol. 17, D450, British Royal Visit to Netherlands, March 1958.
71 LAC, CP, vol. 20, D314, Crerar to Macklin, 28 Sept. 1959.
72 LAC, CP, vol. 24, D432, Visit of Queen Mother; D443, Honorary Freedom.
73 'Crerar Laid to Rest,' *Globe and Mail*, 5 Apr. 1965.
74 LAC, CP, vol. 24, D455, Eisenhower to Verse Crerar, 6 Apr. 1965.
75 Various articles, University of Guelph, Obit File.

Bibliography

Primary

Archives of Ontario, Toronto

Frederick Gaby Collection, MU7692
Hydro-Electric Inquiry Commission, RG18 B67, Volumes 1–2
Misc. Military Records, 11th Battery, MU2051

Directorate of History and Heritage, Department of National Defence, Ottawa

Biographical Files
Document Collection: Army Co-op RCAF; Crerar, Gen. H.D.G.
First Canadian Army Documents
General Staff Documents
Kardex Collections: Army Council Minutes; Crerar; Foulkes; Staff Organization, Canadian Army
R.J. Orde Interview (protected)

Hamilton Public Library (Special Collections)

Assessment Rolls, 1867, 1878, 1882, 1884, 1890, 1899
Christ's Church Cathedral Scrapbook, Volume 1
H.D.G. Crerar Scrapbook
Gardiner Scrapbooks

544   Bibliography

Hamilton – Social Life and Customs Scrapbook (Mrs P.D. Crerar)
Herald Scrapbook, Volume 1: Obituaries, Part 1; Volume J1
Martin Papers, Archives File
Merkworth House Scrapbook

Imperial War Museum, London, United Kingdom

General Sir F. deGuingand Papers
General Sir Richard Haining Papers
Lieutenant-General Sir Oliver Leese Papers
FM Viscount Montgomery Papers
Lieutenant-Colonel Trumbell Warren Papers

Liddell Hart Centre for Military Archives, King's College, London, United Kingdom

FM Viscount Alanbrooke Papers and Diaries
General Richard Dewing Diaries
Field Marshal Ismay Papers

Library and Archives Canada, Ottawa

E.L.M. Burns Papers, MG31 G6
H.D.G. Crerar Papers, MG30E157
H.W. Foster Papers, MG30E383
Ian Mackenzie Papers, MG27 III B5
Mackenzie King Papers, MG26 J13, Diaries, 1938–44
C.C. Mann Papers, MG30E384
Andrew McNaughton Papers, MG30E133
A. Meighen Papers, MG26 I
E. Morrison Papers, MG30E81
Victor Odlum Papers, MG30E300
G.R. Parkin Papers, MG30D44
L.B. Pearson Papers MG26 N1; MG26 N8
Penhale Papers, MG31 G21
M. Pope Papers, MG27 III F4
J.L. Ralston Papers, MG27 III BII
Escott Reid Papers, MG31 E46 (closed)
Georges Vanier Papers, MG32 A2
RG2 7C, Volumes 1–7, Privy Council, Minutes of the Cabinet War Committee
RG9 II B5, Volume 2, Annual Inspection Reports, Art
RG9 III B1 Volumes 866–8, 872, 915 Staff Courses, 972

RG9 III D1
  Volume 2740, Training Officers, WW1
  Volumes 3919–23, C.B.S.O., R.A.
  Volume 4278, 4th Div. Artillery, Officers
  Volumes 4283–5, 5th Div. Artillery
  Volumes 4288–92, 3rd Brigade, C.F.A.
  Volume 4310, War Diary, 10th Battery
  Volumes 4682–3, Historical Records
RG24
  Volume 284, 4th Battery, Hamilton
  Volume 304, DMO and I
  Volumes 348–50, Petawawa 1911–14
  Volume 1883C, Notes on M.D.2
  Volumes 2650–1, Defence Scheme No. 3
  Volume 2684, JCS
  Volumes 2733, 4465
  Volume 2774, Halifax Speech
  Volume 2853, JCS
  Volume 4290, Mrs P.D. Crerar, Homes
  Volumes 10,635–8, FCA
  Volume 10,651, Monty Correspondence
  Volume 10,668
  Volume 10,765
  Volume 10,768 Dieppe
  Volume 10,794, Foulkes
  Volumes 10,797–9, 2nd Cdn Corps
  Volume 10,878
  Volumes 11,001–2, War Diaries
  Volume 12,301, Exercise 'Tiger'
  Volumes 13,359–13,362, CMHQ G.S. War Dairies
  Volume 13,609, HQ FCA GS Plans
  Volumes 13,616–13,629, HQ FCA
  Volumes 13,634–13,635
  Volumes 13,654–13,655
  Volumes 13,683–13,686, HQ 1st Cdn Corps, War Dr.
RG33/120, Volumes 1–3, Royal Commission/Hong Kong
RG41, Volume 6, CBC Flanders Fields Interviews

National Personnel Records Service, Ottawa

General Crerar's Personal Service File

546 Bibliography

Ontario Hydro Central Records and Archives, Toronto

Annual Reports: 1913, 1914
Archives Biographical: Crerar, H.D.G.
Sir Adam Beck General Correspondence, Nos. 4–6

Public Record Office, London, United Kingdom

CAB12	Committee of Imperial Defence
WO32	Military Education
WO106	DMO and I
WO196	Directorate of Artillery
WO205	21 Army Group HQ Papers
WO214	Alexander Papers
WO216	CIGS Papers
WO282	Dill Papers
WO285	Dempsey Papers, 2nd British Army

Queen's University Archives, Kingston

Grant Dexter Papers, 2142
  Series I, Transfer Cases 1–4
  Series II, Transfer Case 8
Gerald S. Graham Papers (Sir E.R. Peacock), 2170
  Box 1, Files 1–16
C.G. Power Papers, 2150
  Boxes 5, 7, 10

Royal Military College of Canada, Kingston

Massey Library Archives
  List of Marks Obtained, Cadets 1907–9
  Memorandum on the Organization, the Functioning of the Staff, Services
  Miscellaneous Appointments at HQ First Canadian Army, February 1945
  Miscellaneous Scrapbooks
  Papers, Notebooks 1939–61
  Photograph Album, 1898–1911
  RMC Review
  SC Exercises and Notes
  Tape Recording, Crerar Address to Hamilton Civic Arena, 1945

Central Registrar
  Personal File
  RMC Descriptive Roll

University of Toronto Archives

Vincent Massey Papers, Volumes 310–312 and Diaries

Interviews and Correspondence

Beament, Brigadier G.E. (Brigadier, General Staff FCA HQ)
Crerar, Peter (General Crerar's son)
Morrison, Finlay Angus (Crerar's ADC, May 1944–6) (courtesy of J.L. Granatstein)
Nation, Colonel (Officer Cadet, RMC), and Mrs P.T.
Palmer, H.Z. (son-in-law, Officer Cadet, RMC)
Palmer, Margaret Crerar (General Crerar's daughter)
Perodeau, Giles (Crerar's ADC, Aug. 1944–Mar. 1945) (courtesy of J.L. Granatstein)
Preston, Richard (Official Historian, RMC)
Tellier, Lt-General Henri (Crerar's ADC, 1940–2)
Todd, Brigadier P.A.S. (courtesy of Terry Copp)
Warren, Trumbull (Personal Assistant, Field Marshal Montgomery)
Williams, Jeffery (Junior Staff Officer, FCA HQ/Historian)

Printed

Alexander of Tunis, Field Marshal Earl. *The Alexander Memoirs 1940–1945.* Edited by John North. London: Cassell, 1962.
Allard, General Jean V. *The Memoirs of General Jean V. Allard.* With Serge Bernier. Vancouver: UBC Press, 1988.
Burns, Lieutenant-General E.L.M. *General Mud: Memoirs of Two World Wars.* Toronto: Clarke, Irwin, 1970.
Canada. Ministry of Overseas Forces. *Report of the Ministry, Overseas Military Forces of Canada, 1918.* London: Overseas Forces, 1919.
Crerar, General H.D.G. 'The Case for Conscription.' *Queen's Quarterly* 58 (1951): 1–13.
deGuingand, Major-General Sir Francis. *Operation Victory.* New York: Scribner's, 1947.
Graham, Howard. *Citizen and Soldier: The Memoirs of Lt-General Howard Graham.* Toronto: McClelland and Stewart, 1987.

Horrocks, Lieutenant-General Sir Brian. *Corps Commander*. With Eversley Belfield. London: Sidgwick and Jackson, 1977.
- *Escape to Action*. New York: St Martin's, 1960.
Kitching, Major-General George. *Mud and Green Fields*. Langley, BC: Battleline Books, 1986.
Lovat, Lord. *March Past: A Memoir by Lord Lovat*. London: Weidenfeld and Nicholson, 1978.
Massey, Vincent. *What's Past Is Prologue: The Memoirs of the Right Honourable Vincent Massey*. Toronto: Macmillan, 1963.
Malone, Richard S. *Missing from the Record*. Toronto: Collins, 1946.
- *A Portrait of War, 1939–1943*. Don Mills, ON: Totem Press, 1985.
McNaughton, Major-General A.G.L. 'The Capture of Valenciennes: A Study in Co-ordination.' *Canadian Defence Quarterly* 10 (April 1933): 279–94.
Montgomery, Bernard Law. *The Memoirs of Field-Marshal, The Viscount Montgomery of Alamein, K.G.* London: Collins, 1958.
- *Montgomery of Alamein*. 2 vols. London: Corgi Books, 1974.
Murray, David R., ed. *Documents on Canadian External Relations, 1939–1941/Part I*. Vol. 7. Ottawa: Department of External Affairs, 1974.
O'Leary, Grattan. *Grattan O'Leary: Recollections of People, Press and Politics*. Toronto: Macmillan, 1977.
Pearson, L.B. *Mike: The Memoirs of the Right Honourable Lester B. Pearson*. Vol. 1. *1897–1948*. Toronto: University of Toronto Press, 1972.
Pope, Maurice A. *Soldiers and Politicians: The Memoirs of Lt-General Maurice A. Pope, CB, MC*. Toronto: University of Toronto Press, 1962.
Power, Chubby. *A Party Politician: The Memoirs of Chubby Power*. Edited by Norman Ward. Toronto: Macmillan, 1966.
Roberts, James Alan. *The Canadian Summer: The Memoirs of James Alan Roberts*. Toronto: University of Toronto Press, 1981.
C.P. Stacey. *A Date with History: Memoirs of a Canadian Historian*. Ottawa: Deneau, 1983.
Simonds, Peter. *Maple Leaf Up, Maple Leaf Down: The Story of the Canadians in the Second World War*. New York: Island Press, 1946.
Vokes, Major-General Chris. *Vokes: My Story*. Ottawa: Gallery Books, 1985.

Secondary

Unpublished

Campbell, J.R. 'James Layton Ralston and Manpower for the Canadian Army.' Unpublished MA thesis, Wilfrid Laurier University, 1986.
English, Lieutenant-Colonel J.A. 'The Casting of an Army: Being a Treatise on

the Bases and Conduct of Canadian Army Operations beyond the Normandy Bridgehead to the Closure of the Falaise Gap.' Unpublished PhD thesis, Royal Military College, 1989.
Eyre, Kenneth Charles. 'Staff and Command in the Canadian Corps: The Canadian Militia 1896–1914 as a Source of Senior Officers.' Unpublished MA thesis, Duke University, 1967.
Hayes, Geoffrey. 'The Development of the Canadian Army Officer Corps, 1939–1945.' Unpublished PhD thesis, University of Western Ontario, 1992.
Hooker, Martia Ann. 'In Defence of Unity: Canada's Military Policies, 1935–1944.' Unpublished MA thesis, Carleton University, 1985.
Hull, Christopher H.N. 'A Case Study in Professionalism in the Canadian Army in the 1930s and 1940s: Lieutenant-General G.G. Simonds.' Unpublished MA thesis, Purdue University, 1989.
Hutchinson, William Earnest John. 'Test of a Corps Commander: Lieutenant-General Guy Granville Simonds, Normandy 1944.' Unpublished MA thesis, University of Victoria, 1982.

Selected Secondary Sources

The following list represents a list of secondary sources that have been most useful in the writing this biography. Some others have been used, and were useful; these are listed in the footnotes.

Bailey, Thomas M., ed. *Dictionary of Hamilton Biography*. Hamilton: Griffin, 1981.
Beloff, Max. 'Britain and Canada between Two World Wars: A British View.' In *Britain and Canada: Survey of a Changing Relationship*, edited by Peter Lyon, 50–60. London: Cass, 1976.
Bercuson, David J., and S.F. Wise, eds. *The Valour and the Horror Revisited*. Montreal and Kingston: McGill-Queen's University Press, 1994.
Berger, Carl. *The Sense of Power: Studies in the Ideas of Canadian Imperialism, 1867–1914*. Toronto: University of Toronto Press, 1970.
Bidwell, Shelford, and Dominick Graham, *Fire-Power: British Army Weapons and Theories of War, 1904–1945*. London: Allen and Unwin, 1982.
Bissel, Claude. *The Imperial Canadian: Vincent Massey in Office*. Toronto: University of Toronto Press, 1986.
Blumenson, Martin. *The Battle of the Generals: the Untold Story of the Falaise Pocket: The Campaign That Should Have Won World War II*. New York: Morrow, 1993.
Bond, Brian. *British Military Policy between the Two World Wars*. Oxford: Clarendon, 1980.

- *The Victorian Army and the Staff College, 1854–1914*. London: Eyre Methuen, 1972.
Bothwell, Robert. *C.D. Howe: A Biography*. Toronto: McClelland and Stewart, 1979.
Bryant, Arthur. *Triumph in the West, 1943–1946: Based on the Diaries and Autobiographical Notes of Field Marshal The Viscount Alanbrooke*. London: Collins, 1959.
- *The Turn of the Tide, 1939–1943: Based on the Diaries and Autobiographical Notes of Field Marshal The Viscount Alanbrooke*. London: Collins, 1957.
Burns, Major-General E.L.M. *Manpower in the Canadian Army, 1939–1945*. Toronto: Clarke, Irwin, 1956.
Butler, J.R.M. *History of the Second World War: United Kingdom Military History Series: Grand Strategy*. Vol. 2. *September 1939–June 1941*. London: Her Majesty's Stationery Office, 1957.
- *History of the Second World War: United Kingdom Military History Series: Grand Strategy*. Vol. 3. Part II: *June 1941–August 1942*. London: Her Majesty's Stationery Office, 1964.
Campbell, John P. *Dieppe Revisited: A Documentary Investigation*. London: Cass, 1993.
Campbell, Marjorie Freeman. *A Mountain and a City: The Story of Hamilton*. Toronto: McClelland and Stewart, 1966.
Collins, Major-General R.J. *Lord Wavell: A Military Biography*. London: Hodder and Stoughton, 1948.
Copp, Terry. *The Brigade: The Fifth Canadian Infantry Brigade, 1939–1945*. Stoney Creek, ON: Fortress, 1992.
- *Fields of Fire: The Canadians in Normandy*. Toronto: University of Toronto Press, 2003.
Copp, Terry, and Bill McAndrew. *Battle Exhaustion: Soldiers and Psychiatrists in the Canadian Army, 1939–1945*. Montreal and Kingston: McGill-Queen's University Press, 1990.
Copp, Terry, and Robert Vogel, *Maple Leaf Route: Antwerp*. Alma, ON: Maple Leaf Route, 1984.
- *Maple Leaf Route: Caen*. Alma, ON: Maple Leaf Route, 1983.
- *Maple Leaf Route: Falaise*. Alma, ON: Maple Leaf Route, 1983.
- *Maple Leaf Route: Scheldt*. Alma, ON: Maple Leaf Route, 1985.
- *Maple Leaf Route: Victory*. Alma, ON: Maple Leaf Route, 1988.
- '"No Lack of Rational Speed": 1st Canadian Army Operations, September 1944.' *Journal of Canadian Studies* 16 (Fall–Winter 1981): 145–55.
Cray, Ed. *General of the Army: George C. Marshall; Soldier and Statesman*. New York: Norton, 1990.

Dancocks, Daniel G. *Welcome to Flanders Fields: The First Canadian Battle of the Great War; Ypres, 1915.* Toronto: McClelland and Stewart, 1988.

D'Este, Carlo. *Bitter Victory: The Battle for Sicily, 1943.* New York: Dutton, 1988.

– *Decision in Normandy: The Unwritten Story of Montgomery and the Allied Campaign.* London: Pan Books, 1984.

– *A Genius for War: A Life of General George S. Patton.* London: Harper Collins, 1996.

Dixon, Norman. *On the Psychology of Military Incompetence.* London: Cape, 1976.

Douglas, W.A.B., and Brereton Greenhous. *Out of the Shadows: Canada in the Second World War.* Toronto: Oxford University Press, 1977.

Durflinger, Serge M. 'The Canadian Defence Quarterly 1933–35: Canadian Military Writing of a Bygone Era.' *Canadian Defence Quarterly* 20, no. 6 (June 1991): 43–8.

Dziuban, Colonel Stanley W. *United States Army in World War II.* Special Studies: Military Relations between the United States and Canada, 1939–1945. Washington, DC: Office of the Chief of Military History, 1959.

Eayrs, James. *In Defence of Canada.* Vol. 1, *From the Great War to the Great Depression.* Toronto: University of Toronto Press, 1964.

– *In Defence of Canada.* Vol. 2, *Appeasement and Rearmament.* Toronto: University of Toronto Press, 1965.

Ellis, Chris, and Peter Chamberlain, eds. *Handbook on the British Army, 1943.* London: Military Book Society, 1974.

Ellis, John. *Brute Force: Allied Strategy and Tactics in the Second World War.* New York: Viking, 1990.

Ellis, L.F. *Victory in the West.* Vol. 2. *The Defeat of Germany.* London: Her Majesty's Stationery Office, 1968.

English, John. *Shadow of Heaven: The Life of Lester Pearson.* Vol. 1. *1897–1948.* Toronto: Lester and Orpen Dennys, 1989.

English, John A. *The Canadian Army and the Normandy Campaign: A Study of Failure in High Command.* New York: Praeger, 1991.

– 'Great War, 1914–1918: The "Riddle of the Trenches."' *Canadian Defence Quarterly* 15 (Autumn 1985): 41–7.

– *On Infantry.* New York: Praeger, 1981.

Foster, Tony. *Meeting of Generals.* Toronto: Metheun, 1986.

Fraser, David. *Alanbrooke.* New York: Atheneum, 1982.

French, David. *Raising Churchill's Army: The British Army and the War against Germany, 1919–1945.* Oxford: Oxford University Press, 2000.

Gibbs, N.H. *History of the Second World War, United Kingdom Series: Grand Strategy.* Vol. 1, *Rearmament Policy.* London: Her Majesty's Stationery Office, 1976.

Godwin-Austin, Brevet Major A.R. *The Staff and the Staff College.* London: Constable, 1927.
Graeme-Evans, Alex. 'Field Marshal Bernard Montgomery: A Critical Assessment.' *Army Quarterly and Defence Journal* 104, no. 4 (1973–4): 412–26.
Graham, Dominick. *The Price of Command: A Biography of General Guy Simonds* Toronto: Stoddart, 1993.
Graham, Dominick, and Shelford Bidwell. *Tug of War: The Battle for Italy, 1943–1945.* London: Hodder and Stoughton, 1986.
Granatstein, J.L. *Canada's Army: Waging War and Keeping the Peace.* Toronto: University of Toronto Press, 2002.
– *The Generals: The Canadian Army's Senior Commanders in the Second World War.* Toronto: Stoddart, 1993.
– *The Ottawa Men: The Civil Service Mandarins, 1935–1957.* Toronto: Oxford University Press, 1982.
– *Canada's War: The Politics of the Mackenzie King Government, 1939–1945.* Toronto: Oxford University Press, 1975.
Granatstein, J.L., and Robert Bothwell. '"A Self-Evident National Duty": Canadian Foreign Policy, 1935–1939.' *Journal of Imperial and Commonwealth History* 3 (January 1975): 212–33.
Granatstein, J.L., and J.M. Hitsman. *Broken Promises: A History of Conscription in Canada.* Toronto: Oxford University Press, 1977.
Gray, Carolyn. 'Peter Duncan Crerar'; 'Marion Elizabeth (Crerar) Stinson'; 'Thomas Henry Stinson.' In *Dictionary of Hamilton Biography.* Vol. 2. Editor-in-chief Thomas Bailey. Hamilton: Griffin, 1991.
The Great Adventure with the 4th Battery C.F.A., B.E.F. N.p., 1919.
Greenfield, Kent Roberts, Robert Palmer, and Bell I. Wiley. *United States Army in World War Two: The Army Ground Forces, the Organization of Ground Combat Troops.* Washington, DC: Historical Division, United States Army, 1947.
Greenhous, Brereton. 'Dieppe: Tragedy to Triumph.' *Canadian Defence Quarterly* 22, no. 1 (Special no. 2, 1992): 34–5.
Griffith, Paddy. *Battle Tactics of the Western Front: The British Army's Art of Attack 1916–1918.* London: Yale University Press, 1994.
Gudmundsson, Bruce I. *On Artillery.* Westport, CT: Praeger, 1993.
Hamilton, Nigel. *Monty: The Making of a General, 1887–1942.* London: Hodder and Stoughton, 1984.
– *Monty: Master of the Battlefield, 1942–1944.* London: Hodder and Stoughton, 1985.
– *Monty: The Field Marshal, 1944–1976.* London: Hamilton, 1986.
Hampden, Gorden. *The War Office.* London: Westminster, 1935.

Harris, Stephen. *Canadian Brass: The Making of a Professional Army, 1860–1939.* Toronto: University of Toronto Press, 1988.
- 'The Canadian General Staff and Higher Organization of Defence, 1919–1939.' *War and Society* 3 (May 1985): 83–98.
- 'Or There Would Be Chaos: The Legacy of Sam Hughes and Military Planning in Canada, 1919–1939.' *Military Affairs* (October 1982): 120–6.
Hart, Stephen A. *Montgomery and 'Colossal Cracks': The 21st Army Group in Northwest Europe.* Westport, CT: Praeger, 2000.
Hay, Ian. *The Second World War, 1939–1945: A Short Military History Series; Arms and the Men.* London: Her Majesty's Stationery Office, 1977.
Haycock, Ronald. *Sam Hughes: The Public Career of a Controversial Canadian 1885–1916.* Canada: Wilfrid Laurier University Press and Canadian War Museum, 1986.
Hillmer, Norman. 'The Anglo-Canadian Neurosis: The Case of O.D. Skelton.' In *Britain and Canada: Survey of a Changing Relationship*, edited by Peter Lyon, 61–84. London: Cass, 1976.
- 'Defence and Ideology: The Anglo-Canadian Military "Alliance" in the 1930s.' *International Journal* 33 (Summer 1978): 588–612.
Hillmer, Norman, and William McAndrew. 'The Cunning of Restraint: General J.H. MacBrien and the Problems of Peacetime Soldiering.' *Canadian Defence Quarterly* 8 (Spring 1979): 40–7.
Hinsley, F.H. *British Intelligence in the Second World War: Its Influence on Strategy and Operations.* Vol. 2. London: Her Majesty's Stationery Office, 1981.
Horn, Lieutenant-Colonel Bernd, and Stephen Harris, eds. *Warrior Chiefs: Perspectives on Senior Canadian Military Leaders.* Toronto: Dundurn, 2001.
House, Captain Jonathon M. *Towards Combined Arms Warfare: A Survey of 20th Century Tactics, Doctrine and Organization.* Fort Leavenworth, KS: US Army Command and Staff College. Combat Studies Institute, August 1984.
Howard, Richard B. *Upper Canada College, 1829–1979: Colbourne's Legacy.* Toronto: MacMillan, 1979.
Hunter, T. Murray. *Canada at Dieppe.* Canadian War Museum Publication No. 17. Ottawa: Canadian War Museum, 1982.
Huntington, Samuel P. *The Soldier and the State: The Theory and Politics of Civil–Military Relations.* Cambridge, MA: Harvard University Press, 1985.
Hyatt, A.M.J. 'Canadian Generals of the First World War and the Popular View of Military Leadership.' *Histoire sociale/Social History* 24 (November 1979): 418–430.
- *General Sir Arthur Currie: A Military Biography.* Toronto: University of Toronto Press and the Canadian War Museum, 1987.
- 'Sir Arthur Currie and the Politicians: A Case Study of Civil–Military Rela-

tions in the First World War.' In *Swords and Covenants*, edited by Adrian Preston and Peter Dennis, 147–63. London: Croom Helm, 1976.

Irving, David. *The War between the Generals: Inside the Allied High Command*. Don Mills, ON: Nelson, 1982.

Janowitz, Morris. *The Professional Soldier: A Social and Political Portrait*. New York: Free Press, 1961.

Katz, Michael B. *The People of Hamilton, Canada West: Family and Class in a Mid-Nineteenth Century City*. Cambridge, MA: Harvard University Press, 1975.

Keegan, John, ed. *Churchill's Generals*. New York: Grove Weidenfield, 1991.

Kingseed, Major Cole C. 'The Falaise-Argentan Encirclement: Operationally Brilliant, Tactically Flawed.' *Military Review* 12 (December 1984): 3–11.

Kitching, Major General George. 'General Guy Simonds: In Appreciation.' *Canadian Defence Quarterly* 4 (Autumn 1974): 9–10.

Lamb, Richard. *Montgomery in Europe, 1943–45: Success or Failure?* London: Buchan and Enright, 1983.

Lewin, Ronald. *Montgomery as Military Commander*. New York: Stein and Day, 1971.

Lutz, James H. 'Canadian Military Thought, 1923–39: A Profile Drawn from the Pages of the Old Canadian Defence Quarterly.' *Canadian Defence Quarterly* 8 (Autumn 1979): 40–9.

MacLeod, Colonel Roderick, and Denis Kelly, eds. *The Ironside Diaries, 1937–1940*. London: Constable, 1962.

McAndrew, William J. 'Fire or Movement? Canadian Tactical Doctrine, Sicily 1943.' *Military Affairs* 51 (July 1987): 140–5.

– 'Stress Casualties in Italy, 1943–1945.' *Canadian Defence Quarterly* 17 (Winter 1987/88): 47–56.

Macquire, Eric. *Dieppe: August 19*. London: Corgi Books, 1974.

Montgomery, Field Marshal the Viscount. *The Path to Leadership*. New York: Putnam, 1961.

Morton, Desmond. *When Your Number's Up: The Canadian Soldier in the First World War*. Toronto: Random House, 1993.

Neatby, H. Blair. *William Lyon Mackenzie King: The Prism of Unity, 1932–1939*. Toronto: University of Toronto Press, 1976.

Nicholson, G.W.L. *Canadian Expeditionary Force, 1914–1919: The Official History of the Canadian Army in the First World War*. Ottawa: Queen's Printer, 1962.

– *The Canadians in Italy: The Official History of the Canadians in the Second World War*. Vol. 2. Ottawa: Queen's Printer, 1956.

– *The Gunners of Canada: The History of the Royal Regiment of Canadian Artillery*. Vol. 1. *1534–1919*. Toronto: McClelland and Stewart, 1967.

- *The Gunners of Canada: The History of the Royal Regiment of Canadian Artillery.* Vol. 2. *1919–1967.* Toronto: McClelland and Stewart, 1972.
Pariseau, Jean, and Serge Bernier. *French Canadians and Bilingualism in the Canadian Armed Forces.* Vol. 1. *1763–1969: The Fear of a Parallel Army.* Ottawa: Department of Supply and Services, 1986.
Perret, Geoffrey. *There's a War to Be Won: The United States Army in World War II.* New York: Random House, 1991.
Pickersgill, J.W. *The Mackenzie King Record.* Vols. 1 (*1939–1943*) and 2 (*1944–1945*). Toronto: University of Toronto Press, 1960.
Place, Timothy Harrison. *Military Training in the British Army, 1940–1944: From Dunkirk to D-day.* London: Cass, 2000.
Plewman, William Rothwell. *Adam Beck and Ontario Hydro.* Toronto: Ryerson, 1947.
Preston, Adrian. 'The Higher Study of Defence in Canada.' *Journal of Canadian Studies* 3 (August 1968): 17–28.
Preston, Richard A. *Canada and 'Imperial Defence': A Study of the Origins of the British Commonwealth Defence Organization, 1867–1919.* Durham, NC: Duke University Press, 1967.
- *Canada's RMC: A History of the Royal Military College.* Toronto: University of Toronto Press, 1969.
- *The Defence of the Undefended Border: Planning for War in North America, 1867–1939.* Montreal and Kingston: McGill-Queen's University Press, 1977.
- 'Military Education, Professionalism and Doctrine.' *Revue internationale d'histoire militaire* 51 (1982): 273–301.
- 'The Military Structure of the Old Commonwealth.' *International Journal* 17 (Summer 1962): 98–121.
- *To Serve Canada: A History of the Royal Military College of Canada since the Second World War.* Ottawa: University of Ottawa Press, 1991.
Rawling, Bill. *Surviving Trench Warfare: Technology and the Canadian Corps, 1914–1918.* Toronto: University of Toronto Press, 1992.
Rickard, John Nelson. 'The Test of Command: McNaughton and Exercise Spartan, 4–12 March 1943.' *Canadian Military History* (Summer 1999): 27–36.
Rogers, Peter G., ed. *Gunner Ferguson's Diary: The Diary of Gunner Frank Byron Ferguson, 1st Canadian Siege Battery.* Hantsport, NS: Lancelot, 1985.
Roy, Reginald. 'Black Day for the Black Watch.' *Canadian Defence Quarterly* 12 (Winter 1982/3): 34–40.
- *For Most Conspicuous Bravery: A Biography of Major-General George Pearkes.* Vancouver: University of British Columbia Press, 1977.
Shaw, L.M. 'Two Hamilton Families: The Stinsons.' *Western Ontario Historical Society Notes* 16 (March 1960): 10–17.

Sheppard, Alan. *Sandhurst: The Royal Military Academy Sandhurst and Its Predecessors.* London: Hamlyn, 1980.
Smith, R. Guy C., ed. *As You Were: Ex-Cadets Remember.* Vols. 1 and 2. Royal Military College: RMC Club of Canada, 1984.
Stacey, C.P. *Arms, Men and Governments: The War Policies of Canada, 1939–1945.* Ottawa: Queen's Printer, 1970.
– *Canada and the Age of Conflict.* Vol. 1. *1867–1921.* Toronto: University of Toronto Press, 1984.
– 'Canadian Leaders of the Second World War.' *Canadian Historical Review* 66 (March 1985): 64–72.
– *Six Years of War: The Official History of the Canadian Army in the Second World War.* Vol. 1. Ottawa: Queen's Printer, 1955.
– 'The Staff Officer: A Footnote to Canadian History.' *Canadian Defence Quarterly* 3 (Winter 1974): 43–7.
– *The Victory Campaign: The Official History of the Canadian Army in the Second World War,* Vol. 3. Ottawa: Queen's Printer, 1960.
Stacey, C.P., and Barbara M. Wilson. *The Half-Million: The Canadians in Britain, 1939–1945.* Toronto: University of Toronto Press, 1987.
Stamp, Robert M. *The Schools of Ontario, 1876–1976.* Toronto: University of Toronto Press, 1982.
Stanley, George. 'Military Education in Canada, 1867–1970.' In *The Canadian Military: A Profile,* ed. Hector Massey, 168–77. Toronto: Copp Clark, 1970.
Swettenham, John. *McNaughton.* Vol. 1. *1887–1939.* Toronto: Ryerson, 1968.
– *McNaughton.* Vol. 2. *1939–1943.* Toronto: Ryerson, 1969.
– *To Seize The Victory: The Canadian Corps in World War I.* Toronto: Ryerson, 1965.
Thorne, Christopher. *Allies of a Kind: The United States, Britain, and the War against Japan, 1941–1945.* New York: Oxford University Press, 1978.
Travers, Tim. *The Killing Ground: The British Army, the Western Front and the Emergence of Modern Warfare, 1900–1918.* London: Unwin Hyman, 1990.
Villa, Brian Loring. *Unauthorized Action: Mountbatten and the Dieppe Raid.* Toronto: Oxford University Press, 1989.
Vincent, Carl. *No Reason Why: The Canadian Hong Kong Tragedy – an Examination.* Stittsville, ON: Canada's Wings, 1981.
Weaver, John C. *Hamilton: An Illustrated History.* Toronto: Lorimar and National Museum of Man, 1982.
Wigley, Phillip. *Canada and the Transition to Commonwealth: British – Canadian Relations, 1917–1926.* Cambridge: Cambridge University Press, 1977.
Whitaker, Brigadier-General Denis, and Shelagh Whitaker. *Dieppe: Tragedy to Triumph.* Toronto: McGraw-Hill Ryerson, 1992.

- *Rhineland: The Battle to End the War.* Toronto: Stoddart, 1989.
- Whitaker, Brigadier-General Denis, and Shelagh Whitaker, *Tug of War: The Canadian Victory That Opened Antwerp.* Toronto: Stoddart, 1984.

Whitaker, Brigadier-General Denis, and Shelagh Whitaker, with Terry Copp. *The Soldier's Story: Victory at Falaise.* Toronto: Harper Collins, 2000.

Woodward, Sir Llewellyn. *British Foreign Policy in the Second World War.* London: Her Majesty's Stationery Office, 1962.

Worthington, Larry. *'Worthy': A Biography of Major-General F.F. Worthington.* Toronto: Macmillan, 1961.

Young, Lieutenant-Colonel F.W., ed. *The Story of the Staff College, 1858–1958.* Aldershot: Gale and Polden, 1958.

Ziegler, Philip. *Mountbatten.* New York: Harper and Row, 1985.

Index

Alanbrooke. *See* Brooke, Field Marshal Sir Alan
Alexander, General Sir Harold, 223–4, 231–2, 266, 271–3, 276–7, 356–7
Anderson, Major-General T.V., 115, 119–20, 125, 130, 135, 139–41
Antwerp, 333, 337–8, 339, 340–1, 343–8, 355, 359, 378, 404
Army Council, 25, 150, 290
Ashton, Major-General E.C., 99–101 *passim*, 108, 115
Astonia, Operation (Le Havre), 240, 263–4, 265, 327, 329, 333, 338–9, 340–1, 345, 346
Axehead, Operation, 240, 243, 247, 263–6, 268

B battery (RCHA), 83–4, 241
Beament, Brig. A.W., 323–24
Beament, Brig. G.E., 83–4, 213, 235, 241–2, 245–6, 248, 285, 290, 300, 305, 311, 315, 354, 371, 374, 402
Beattie, Kim, 459
Beaver, Exercise, 188
Beaver II, Exercise, 190
Beaver III, Exercise, 190, 193–4, 203
Beaver IV, Exercise, 194

Beck, Sir Adam, 5, 8, 20–1, 69, 73, 448
Beck, Lady Lillian, 5–6, 8, 14
Bennett, R.B., 87, 99, 214
Blackader, Brig. Ken, 364, 402
Blockbuster I, Operation, 392, 393–6
Blockbuster II, Operation, 399–400
Borden, Sir Robert, 21, 25
Boulogne, 201, 338, 339–41, 344–5, 346–7
Bradley, Gen. Omar N., 248, 262, 293, 298–9, 312, 314, 317–18, 373–4, 409, 459–60
British army, 35–6, 74, 76, 77, 80, 91, 143–4, 158, 187, 196, 253, 273, 279, 402
 First World War, Formations:
  First, 33, 35, 59, 61; Second Army, 32, 33, 38; Fourth Army, 62; 3rd Corps, 32, 33
 Second World War, Formations:
  21 Army Group, 223, 238–9, 241, 242, 243, 244, 249, 251, 253, 258, 260, 263, 264–5, 270, 279, 283, 288–9, 293, 297, 300, 302, 310, 316–19 *passim*, 322, 324, 326, 329, 331, 337, 339, 341–2,

344, 349, 351–5 *passim*, 360–1, 368, 373–7 *passim*, 381, 386, 388, 394, 397, 405–6, 409, 424; Second British Army, 231, 239, 262, 264, 265, 273, 278, 281–2, 284, 292, 294, 297, 299, 300, 302, 306, 313, 317, 327, 330, 334, 337, 339, 348, 355, 359, 372–4, 379, 386, 400, 404–9 *passim*, 422; Eighth British Army, 250, 271, 404, 406, 410; 1 British Corps, 239, 244, 265, 273–4, 278, 282, 283, 284–6, 292, 294, 296, 304, 306, 313, 343–4, 345–7, 348–9, 355, 400; 8 British Corps, 279; 12 British Corps, 187, 244, 291, 296, 306, 307, 314, 343, 344, 346, 348; 30 British Corps, 248, 275, 327, 374, 376, 379, 385, 391–5 *passim*, 399, 400, 408; 3rd British Infantry Division, 195, 295, 297; 6th Airborne Division, 286; 7th British Armoured Division, 275, 292; 15th Scottish Division, 388–9, 391; 3rd Wessex Division, 389, 391, 392; 49th West Riding Division, 286, 344–5, 410, 430; 51st Highland Division, 286, 295, 344–6 *passim*, 355, 379, 388, 397; 53rd Welsh Division, 343–4, 388; Army Group Royal Artillery (AGRA), 349, 385

British Expeditionary Force (BEF), 61, 126, 133–4

Broadhurst, Air Marshal Sir Harry, 302, 315

Brooke, Field Marshal Sir Alan: Crerar and command of FCA, 231, 235–6, 239, 241, 250–1, 253, 268, 271–2, 274–81, 288, 329, 334–5, 356; Crerar's return, 358–9, 380; First Canadian Army, 126, 178–82 *passim*, 185–9 *passim*, 201, 215; First World War 54, 57–8, 60–1, 63–4; McNaughton 218–25 *passim*; Rhineland 388–90, 399, 403, 409, 453; Staff College, 74

Brown, Air Vice Marshal Sir Leslie H., 302, 312, 315, 319, 353

Brown, Brig.-Gen. J. Sutherland, 83, 88, 89, 93

Browne, Maj.-Gen. A.W. (Adj.-Gen.), 148–9, 158–9

Brussels, 328, 330, 337, 427

Bucknall, Lt.-Gen. G.C., 248, 275, 285–6

Bulge, Battle of the, 377, 400

Burns, Lt. Gen. E.L.M., 123, 124, 125, 132, 147, 148, 158, 163, 180, 235, 254, 266, 271–3, 275–7, 279, 280, 315, 356–7, 396, 404, 418, 431, 438, 440, 450, 500n18

Burstall, Lt.-Col. H., 23, 26

Cabinet War Committee, 135, 138–40, 143, 146, 152, 155, 162, 169, 174, 177–9, 252, 416–17, 419, 431

Canadian Army Occupation Force (CAOF), 415, 418, 420, 431–2, 435–6

Canadian army (Permanent), 21–4, 28–9, 30–3, 69, 77, 101, 123, 140, 144–5, 153, 159, 161, 164, 182, 189, 191–3, 213–14, 233, 249–50, 276, 361, 368–71, 401, 403–4, 412, 416, 418, 422, 425, 429, 431, 434–5, 438, 455–6, 460

Formations:

First Canadian Army. *See* First Canadian Army

1st Canadian Corps, formation of,

128–9, 131–2, 136, 143, 144, 152, 158, 162, 167, 175; active, 158, 179, 181, 184–5, 187, 188–90, 193, 195–7, 198–9, 210–17 *passim*, 221–36 *passim*, 241, 254, 256, 261, 271–2, 285, 293, 335, 341, 357, 401, 403–4, 406, 408, 410, 411, 418, 423–4, 427
2nd Canadian Corps, 137, 191, 193, 215, 218, 238, 240, 243, 247–8, 265–6, 270, 279, 282, 289, 291–2, 294, 295, 302, 313–15, 317–18, 330, 344, 345–6, 349, 351, 365, 371, 376–7, 379, 391–3, 395, 399, 404–6, 408, 410, 422–4
1st Canadian Infantry Division, 123–4, 130, 201, 226, 227, 230, 234, 255, 276, 404, 410, 427
2nd Canadian Infantry Division, 129, 131, 178–9, 192, 195, 198, 202–3, 204, 208, 265, 278–9, 330, 345, 348, 371, 385, 388, 402
3rd Canadian Infantry Division, 185, 192, 194, 219, 223, 238–9, 248, 250, 266, 269, 270–1, 273, 286, 292, 295, 347–8, 351, 371, 375, 376, 388, 391, 395, 403, 406, 424
4th Canadian Armoured Division, 171, 270, 283, 295, 305, 312, 321, 326, 328, 357, 391
5th Canadian Armoured Division, 221, 228, 230, 232, 255, 266, 276
1st Polish Armoured Division, 305–6, 312, 313, 318, 320, 322, 326, 328–9, 348, 355, 381, 397, 410, 424, 430, 450
2nd Canadian Armoured Brigade, 239, 266, 269, 315, 391
1st Canadian Parachute Battalion, 406

6th Infantry Brigade, 256, 363, 403
Royal Hamilton Light Infantry, 14, 207, 209, 392
Royal Rifles of Canada, 163, 171–2
Winnipeg Grenadiers, 163, 171–2
See also General Staff
Canadian Army Pacific Force (CAPF), 415, 418, 420, 431–2, 433, 435, 438–9
Canadian Defence Committee, 101–2, 103, 105
Canadian Defence Quarterly, 80, 81, 95, 105, 455
Canadian Institute of International Affairs (CIIA), 91, 93, 101, 105, 116
Canadian Military Headquarters (CMHQ), xiii, 118, 122, 123–7, 130–3, 135, 139, 141, 154, 162, 183, 224, 240, 242, 245, 271–2, 290, 322–4, 326, 358, 362, 363–4, 365–6, 369–70, 372, 379, 396–7, 404, 410, 412, 415–17, 419, 426, 432
Canadian Military Institute, 93, 105, 465
Channel Ports, 327, 333, 338–40, 342–5, 346–7
Chief of the Air Staff (CAS), 106, 138, 148, 150, 153
Chief of the General Staff (CGS): Crerar as, xiii, xix, 136, 138–83 *passim*; goals, 140–2, 143–6, 147, 154–6, 174–9, 180–3; Hong Kong (*see* Hong Kong); publicity, 153, 160–3, 174; relations, 148–51, 158–9, 162; role, 137–9, 142, 146–8, 150, 178–9
Chief of the Naval Staff (CNS), 90, 138, 148, 150, 153
Chester, Peter, 149, 429

562 Index

Christie, Loring, 102, 106–8, 120
Churchill, Sir Winston, 81, 167–8, 214, 248, 262, 399, 409, 501n45
Cochrane, Lt.-Col. J., 241, 242, 246
Conference of Defence Associations, 94
Coningham, Air Marshal Sir Arthur, 301–2, 319, 353
conscription crisis, 221, 325, 356, 361–2, 365, 367–9. *See also* reinforcements
Constantine, Maj.-Gen. C.C., 84, 105
Crerar, Alaister John, 9–10, 69, 113, 194, 196, 203, 204, 210, 212, 214, 368, 379, 423, 427, 430, 436, 451
Crerar, General H.D.G. 'Harry'
   airpower, views on, 95, 106, 128, 143, 153, 177, 195, 243, 250, 261–2, 283–4, 289, 293–6, 299–303 *passim*, 305, 307, 311–20 *passim*, 338, 340–1, 347, 352–3, 283, 392–3, 396, 457, 463
   ambition, xiv, xvii, 3, 10, 20, 46–7, 69, 75–6, 82, 84, 92, 140, 150–1, 175, 178, 185, 211, 452, 466
   artillery, views on, 17–18, 21–2, 36, 40, 44, 46–7, 50–1, 52, 54, 56–68 *passim*, 72–3, 75, 95, 216–18, 232, 233, 247, 261, 279, 303, 373, 375, 383, 387, 394
   awards and honours, 18, 54, 441, 449, 452
   battle drill, views on, 194, 216, 217
   battle exhaustion, views on, 324–5, 364
   Bomber Command, views on. *See* Crerar, airpower; Crerar, bombing; Harris; *and under* RAF
   bombing, 67, 204–5, 299, 301–3, 305, 307, 312–17 *passim*, 339, 349–52, 375, 378, 383, 461
   British, views on the, xiv–xv, 3, 12, 14, 20, 26, 31, 36–7, 57–8, 76–7, 80, 89, 91, 96–7, 103, 109, 112, 125–7, 169, 189–90, 203, 248, 253, 272–7 *passim*, 281, 356, 397, 404, 428–9, 431
   Burns, relations with, 123, 132, 147, 158, 163, 235, 254, 271–3, 275–7, 356–7, 418, 431, 450
   Canadian army, views on, xiv–xv, 69, 86, 141, 98, 123, 161, 164, 191–2, 245, 407–8, 412, 416, 429, 434–5, 446, 455
   Canadian autonomy, views on, 89, 91, 97, 109, 126, 131, 146, 169, 188–9, 199, 203, 223, 248–9, 250–1, 255, 302, 335
   Canadian Corps, shadow of, xvi, 128, 140, 144, 233, 261, 303, 317–18, 385
   childhood, 9–15
   civic responsibilities, views on, xiv–xv, 3, 258, 422, 427, 428, 434, 443, 446–7, 455
   command, army, xiii, xvi, 218–19, 220–5, 227, 231, 235–47 *passim*, 253–9, 261–3, 276–8, 281–2, 287–8, 306–8, 309–12, 319, 324–6, 334, 337, 342–4, 350–9 *passim*, 397–8, 402–4, 406, 410–12, 420, 441
   command, battery, 47–8, 49, 50–1, 52, 53, 55, 57
   command, corps, xiii, 184–5, 188–90, 11–13, 195–7, 198, 210, 212, 215, 217, 226, 229–31, 233–5, 261
   command, style, xvi–xviii, 31, 48–9, 58–9, 67, 72, 77, 83, 97, 132–3,

184–5, 188, 190, 191–3, 216, 290–1, 358, 398, 407
command, views on, 75–6, 117, 159, 178, 191–2, 194, 196, 258
conscription, views on, 137, 139, 146, 151, 160–2, 174, 176, 178, 192, 220–1, 252, 325, 356, 361–2, 365, 367, 369, 443–4, 456, 458
counter-battery methods, 47, 59, 60, 61, 65, 67, 233, 234, 247, 387
demobilization, 69, 396, 402, 412–14, 415–17, 419, 422, 423, 425, 432, 437–8, 439–41
democracy, views on, xv, 75–6, 427–8, 436, 442–3, 446
deputy minister of defence, views on, 71, 79, 105, 111, 112, 115, 116, 138, 157, 249
Dieppe. *See* Dieppe
disarmament, views on, 91, 93–4
education, views on. *See* education
father, husband, and grandfather, as, xiv, 9–10, 70, 77, 95–6, 107, 113–14, 151, 162–3, 180, 212, 227–8, 368, 398, 407, 450–1
French Canadians, views on, 18, 30, 160, 172, 252, 256, 309, 369–70, 403
Germans, views on, 30, 34, 37, 44, 45, 152, 303, 317, 322, 385, 423, 425
health, xvii, 18, 90, 150–1, 178–9, 190, 219, 289, 308–9, 321, 334, 338, 351, 353–4, 358–9, 362, 411–12, 448–9, 460, 463–4
imperialism, views on, 12, 17, 19–20, 76, 78, 80, 91–2, 96–7, 102, 106, 110, 112, 164, 204, 431, 455
international relations, views on, 84, 90–4, 98–106, 110, 114, 204, 335, 447, 452, 455–7
King, Mackenzie, relations with, 104, 146, 169, 221, 230, 249, 251–3, 254, 361, 367, 433, 436, 441, 448, 456
leadership, on, xvi, 13, 17, 19, 75–6, 117, 150–1, 160, 190–3, 194, 196, 208, 256–7, 258, 436, 438, 443, 459
McNaughton, relations with, 60, 79, 82, 86, 93, 96, 126–7, 129, 140, 160, 176, 178–80, 210, 211–15, 217, 219, 220–5, 227, 238, 281, 436, 462, 465
memoirs, xiv, xviii, 458–60, 465
militia (Non-Permanent Active), views on, 5, 14, 21, 24, 68, 71, 80, 82, 90–1, 105, 115, 160–1, 182, 420
Montgomery, relations with, 184, 186, 187, 188–90, 193, 195, 203–4, 211, 217–18, 224–31 *passim*, 239, 249–53, 260, 268–70, 274–8, 281, 286–9, 307, 321, 329–35, 357–9, 390, 400, 425, 434, 461–2
morale, 31–2, 59, 76, 157, 162–3, 173, 186, 198–9, 201, 202, 204, 208, 210, 214–19 *passim*, 224, 232–3, 242, 244, 247, 258, 260, 270, 276, 293, 323, 325, 352, 361, 369–70, 379, 383, 392, 426–7, 430, 432, 437, 438, 439
operational art, views on, 62, 65–6, 79, 94–5, 145, 154, 159–60, 184, 190–1, 192–3, 196, 198–9, 208, 210, 216–18, 226, 229–34 *passim*, 238, 245, 248, 261–2, 266, 284–6, 293, 296–7, 309, 339–40, 346–8, 377, 409, 505n4
personality, 10, 15, 76–7, 84, 97, 117, 129, 132–3, 150–1, 192, 290, 452

preparedness, views on, 86, 100, 105, 112, 434, 446, 458, 463-4
promotion, views on, 49, 50, 54, 95-6, 119, 128-9, 132, 140, 150, 175, 179, 227
Ralston, relations with, 135-6, 140, 142, 147-8, 150-1, 161-2, 181, 200-1, 214-15, 222, 224-5, 227, 238, 249, 335, 358, 367, 387, 452
recreation (and fitness), xvii, 9, 19, 84, 151-2, 257, 398, 440, 444, 450
Simonds, relations with, 188, 228-30, 349-50, 353, 354, 395, 400, 402, 433-5, 462-3
Stuart, relations with, 121, 158, 215, 221, 223-4, 235, 240-53 *passim*, 275-6, 291, 335, 366-7
tanks (armour), views on, 75, 95-6, 112, 116, 145, 197, 204, 216-17, 233, 261, 264, 295, 381, 388
Crerar, John (uncle), 5-7, 9
Crerar, Malcolm, 8, 10, 55-6, 68, 425
Crerar, Margaret (Peggy) (daughter), 69, 70, 77, 96, 112-14, 117, 151, 154, 163, 180, 212-15 *passim*, 222, 236, 259, 368, 386, 407, 439-40, 443, 465; Zouch Palmer, 117, 180, 259, 418, 441, 451
Crerar (Stinson), Marion (mother), xiv-xv, 4-5, 6, 8-9, 10, 11, 14, 20, 26, 55-6, 69
Crerar, Peter (father), 6-7, 9-10, 20
Crerar, Peter (son), 77, 93, 95-6, 107, 112-14, 163, 180, 191, 201, 212-13, 215, 219, 227, 258, 358, 368, 399, 407, 412, 418, 441, 451
Crerar, Verse (wife), xiv, 27, 49, 55, 64, 70, 77, 93-5, 98, 107, 109, 112-14, 116, 119, 122, 152, 154, 180, 194, 212, 227, 231, 236, 258, 267-8, 407, 425, 444-5 *passim*, 448, 450, 451, 454-5, 460, 464-5
Crerar-Gallagher, Violet (sister), 8, 110, 113-14, 163, 176, 180, 189, 209-10, 212, 445, 450, 451
Crerars, in Scotland (Alexander and Margaret), 5-6, 451
Crocker, Gen. Sir John T., 274-5, 284-98 *passim*, 302, 304, 314-15, 339, 390, 400, 406, 408
Cunningham, Brig. D.G., 275-6
Currie, Sir Arthur, 70-1, 82, 277, influence of 418, 423, 475n76
Currie, Col. G.S., 139, 249

Defence Council, 88, 101, 129, 135-6, 138, 147-8
Defence Scheme No. 3, 99, 102, 108, 116, 119, 128, 143
deGuingand, General Sir Frederick, 262, 264-5, 289, 300, 304, 308, 310, 327, 328, 329-30, 339, 350, 360, 462
Dempsey, Lt.-Gen. Miles, 231, 239, 248, 262, 265, 269-75 *passim*, 281, 284, 289, 291, 301-2, 306, 307, 311, 314, 317, 327, 330, 331, 394-5, 406, 409, 410
Dewing, Gen. Sir Richard, 115, 125, 133, 136
Dexter, Grant, 133, 142, 146, 150-1, 178, 213, 218
Dieppe, xix, 209-10, 339-40, 424; campaign for experience, 161-2, 169, 184, 198-9, 201-3; ceremony and return, 328-32; constitutional issues, 203-4; impact, 206-9, 210-11, 248, 264, 267-8; planning, Crerar's role, 204-6; postwar view, Crerar on, 461-2
Dill, Field Marshal Sir John, 140, 176

Index 565

Director/Directorate of Military Operations and Intelligence (DMO and I), 78, 88–90, 98–101 *passim*, 108, 110, 111–12, 115, 125, 165, 169–70
Dunkirk, 134, 338, 340, 343–5

education, Crerar's early: Highfield, 13–14, 15; Royal Military College of Canada (*see* Royal Military College of Canada); Upper Canada College, 11, 13, 15, 24, 114, 465
Eisenhower, Gen. Dwight D., 236, 249, 251, 262, 291–2, 301, 326, 333, 337, 338, 341, 352, 372, 373–4, 381, 382, 398, 400, 405, 409, 425, 432, 465
External Affairs, Department of, 81, 90–3, 99–100, 102–3, 106–10, 118, 123–4, 139, 452, 454, 456

Falaise, 291–2, 294, 299, 306, 312–13, 315, 317, 318
Falaise Gap, 313, 318
First Canadian Army (FCA), 218, 250–3, 272–3, 292, 298, 299–301, 322, 324, 341, 352, 361–3, 365, 377, 404–5, 415, 436, 446, 448; formation of, 123, 137, 144–5, 175–6, 177–83; headquarters, 193, 213, 215, 221, 235, 236, 240–3, 246–7, 263, 268–70, 278–9, 281–2, 283–4, 295, 302–3, 309–12, 316, 318–19, 327–33 *passim*, 341–2, 345–6, 370, 374–6, 382, 384–7, 402, 441, 462
First World War, Crerar and: 4th Battery, 21, 22, 23, 26–7, 28; 10th Battery, 26, 31, 47, 48–9; 11th Battery, 30, 32, 36, 39, 41, 44, 50, 52, 53, 414, 425, 473n18; 1st Canadian Division, 54; 2nd Canadian Division, 57; 3rd Canadian Division, 55; 4th Canadian Division, 59; 5th Canadian Division, 55–6, 59; 48th Highlanders, 35, 40, 42, 44; Amiens, Battle of, xiii, 62, 63–4, 303, 385; Brigade Major, 54, 55–6, 57, 60; Canadian Corps, xvi, xx, 46, 48, 51–2, 57, 59, 60–1, 62, 64, 65, 71, 80, 122, 126, 128; Counter-Battery Staff Officer, 59, 63, 65; Currie, Sir Arthur (*see* Currie, Sir Arthur); experience of, 30–68 *passim*; French army, 34, 38, 39, 40, 42–3, 52, 62, 74; Hughes, Sir Sam (*see* Hughes, Sir Sam); Last Hundred Days, battles of, 64–7; Neuve Chapelle, battle of, 30; Salisbury Plain, 30–2; Somme, Battle of, 51–2; professional development, 25, 47, 52, 55, 58–9, 61, 63, 67; Valenciennes, 65–6; Vimy Ridge, Battle of, xx, 43, 52, 53–4, 57, 58, 342; Ypres, Second Battle of, xiii, 38–47. *See also* Brooke; McNaughton; *and* Ypres
Flit, Exercise, 245–6, 250
Foster, Maj.-Gen. H.W., 357, 406, 430
Foulkes, Gen. Charles, 232, 254–5, 278, 357, 358, 404–5, 406, 408, 410, 411, 422–5 *passim*, 430, 433–5, 453, 455, 462–3, 465
French, Sir John, 22

General Staff (Canadian), 70–2, 78, 79, 81, 83, 87–8, 93–4, 99, 101–2, 103, 105, 107, 110, 119, 138–40, 146, 147–51, 153, 156, 162, 165, 170, 174, 176, 416
German army, 51, 63
First World War, Formations:

566   Index

Fourth Army, 38; Sixth Army, 53
Second World War, Formations: Army Group B, 410; 1st Parachute, 338, 388; 7th Army, 306; 15th Army, 327, 338, 345; 1st Panzer, 304; 9th Panzer, 298, 304; 12th SS Panzer, 298, 312; 84th Infantry, 388; 89th Infantry, 304; 116th Panzer Division, 391; 272nd Division, 304
Germany, 21, 76, 94, 98–9, 103, 106, 143, 152, 161, 166, 172, 183, 249, 262; Crerar visit to, 110, 118; final campaign in, 339, 352, 401, 408–9, 412, 413, 415, 417, 420, 422, 424, 428, 431, 435, 454
Goodwood, Operation, 279, 286
Gothic Line, 235, 256
Grant, W.L., 11–12
Greene, Ken, 113, 119
Grenade, Operation, 374, 376, 381–2, 384–5, 386, 389, 393–4, 395–96
Guthrie, Hugh, 73

Haig, General Sir Douglas, 33
Halifax, incident, 105–6
Hamilton, xiv, 3, 4–11, 13–15, 17, 20, 21–2, 26, 28, 32, 47, 49, 68, 113, 190, 209–10, 368, 414, 425, 451, 466
Harris, Marshal Sir Arthur 'Bomber,' 301–2, 305, 315, 316–17, 340, 352–3
histories, official, 120, 218–19, 264, 268, 285, 297, 315, 333–4, 350, 423, 434–5, 460, 461–3
Hitler, Adolf, 94, 98, 134, 304, 317, 338, 367, 399, 432
Hitler Line, 271, 272
Holland, liberation of, xiii, xix–xx, 134, 387, 400–2, 405, 408–11, 422–4, 432, 434, 437, 439, 464
Hoffmeister, Maj.-Gen. Burt, 255–6, 406, 435
Hong Kong, xiii, xix, 137, 157, 163–4, 182, 453, 500n29; background in, 164–6, 198; decision to dispatch troops, 166–70; Royal Commission, 200–1, 205; state of training, 171–3, 453–4
Horrocks, Lt.-Gen. Sir Brian, 377–9, 383–4, 386, 389–91, 393, 395
Hughes, Sir Sam, 21–2, 25, 29–30

Imperial Defence College, 88, 95–7, 99, 103, 115, 164–5, 431
Imperial General Staff, 78, 136
Infatuate, Operation, 344, 347–9, 350–3, 359
Italy, 76, 93–4, 110, 237, 240; Italian Campaign, 222–5, 226–7, 231–4, 242, 266, 271–3, 280, 283, 289–90, 323, 357–9, 360, 387, 423, 433
Interdepartmental Committees, 79, 85, 90, 91, 102, 106, 111–12
Ironside, Field Marshal Edmund, 74, 76, 77, 125, 126

Japan, 105, 110, 165–6, 167–8, 171, 453–4
Joint Staff Committee, 90, 104, 106, 107, 165
Journal of the Royal United Service Institute, 80, 95

Keefler, Brig. R.H., 403
Keller, Maj.-Gen. Rod, 192, 239, 248, 255, 257–8, 269, 271, 273–7, 279, 280–1, 315, 371
King, William Lyon Mackenzie, 81,

Index 567

99, 100, 102–3, 104, 107, 109, 112, 120, 123, 137, 145–6, 152, 153, 169, 174, 182, 220–5 *passim*, 230, 249, 251–3, 254, 262, 324, 358, 361–2, 366–7, 397, 417, 423, 431, 433, 436, 439, 441, 448, 453, 456, 462
Kingston, ON, 19, 116–17, 447
Kitching, Maj.-Gen. George, 193, 227, 255, 295, 312, 317, 321
Kluge, Gen. Gunther von, 304, 306, 312

Leacock, Stephen, 11, 13
Leigh-Mallory, Air Chief Marshal Trafford, 205, 262, 301, 302, 315–16
Leese, Sir Oliver, 231–3, 261, 270–4, 276–7, 280, 356

MacBrien, Maj.-Gen. J.H., 70, 71, 77, 79, 82
Macdonald, Angus L., 138, 155
Macdonald, Tom, 180, 310, 441, 448
Mackenzie, Ian, 101, 104, 107, 108, 109, 111, 439
Maclean's, 162, 456, 457, 458, 464
Malone, Lt.-Col. Richard, 361–2, 397–8
Mann, Maj.-Gen. Churchill, xvi, 195, 204–5, 215, 232, 240, 242–6, 256, 268, 283–4, 290, 299–302, 305, 306–7, 309, 311, 316, 319, 330–1, 346–7, 350, 352–3, 355–6, 258, 364, 370–1, 376, 402, 406–7, 441, 443, 445, 455, 462, 465
Market Garden, Operation, 310, 332–3, 344, 346, 348, 355
Massey, Vincent, 123, 124–5, 126, 186, 212, 213–14, 219, 220, 238–9, 259, 291, 387, 436, 441, 448
Matthews, Maj.-Gen. Bruce, 371, 465

Mathews, Maj.-Gen. H.H., 89, 90, 96, 115, 119, 120–1
Mazcek, Maj.-Gen. S., 410
McNaughton, General A.G.L., xv
 army command, 199, 200, 203–6, 210, 211–15, 217–19, 220–5, 230, 232; conscription crisis, 361, 365–6, 367; 402, 436, 439, 462, 465
 divisional command, 126–7, 128–9, 130–1, 133, 135–6, 140, 141, 142, 143, 145, 148, 149, 151, 160, 162
 First Canadian Army, view on, 174–86 *passim*, 192, 193, 195
 First World War, 59–60, 61, 63, 65, 66, 67
 interwar, 70, 72, 77, 81, 82, 83
 Chief of General Staff, 86–8, 90, 91, 92, 93–5, 96, 98–100
 return to Canada, 237, 238, 240, 242, 244–5, 281
 See also under Crerar, relations with McNaughton
militia, 15–6, 21–4, 25–6, 71–3, 79, 80, 87, 90–1, 94–5, 98, 99, 101–2, 104–5, 115, 119, 124, 139, 160–1, 182, 255, 420. *See also* Canadian army; *and under* Crerar, militia, views on
Militia Council, 15, 73, 87
Mitchell, Lt.-Col. J.H., 24, 28, 30, 41, 43, 47
Montague, Lt.-Gen. Price J., 124, 128, 132, 141, 162, 166, 192, 224, 236, 290, 322, 323, 359, 362, 363–4, 366, 369–70, 397, 401–3, 411–12, 415–16, 417, 418–19, 426, 427, 431–2, 435–8, 441
Montgomery, Field Marshal B.L.M., xx; 21st Army Group, 237–9, 243, 247–9, 260–71 *passim*, 274–5, 277–

84 *passim*, 286–9, 291, 293–5, 297–9, 301–8 *passim*, 310, 312–15, 317–18, 321, 324, 326–41 *passim*, 343–5, 347–50; Italy, 226, 227–30, 231, 232, 236; Mackenzie King and, 250–3; postwar, 442, 445, 453, 460, 461, 462; Rhineland, 354–9 *passim*, 360, 362–3, 372, 373–6, 377, 378, 381–6 *passim*, 388–91, 393, 395, 397, 399, 400, 403–5, 408–11, 420, 422, 423–5, 429, 434, 436; South-Eastern Army, 184, 185–9, 191, 192, 193–7, 199–200, 202–4, 210, 211, 214–18 *passim*, 221, 222, 224–5

Morrison, Maj.-Gen. Sir Edward, 57, 60, 61, 63, 70, 72–3

Morrison, Finlay, 309, 310, 401, 450

Murchie, Lt.-Gen. J.C., 220, 366, 370, 372, 412, 433, 435

Muskokas, 9, 20–1, 113, 398, 429, 444, 451

National Defence Headquarters (NDHQ), 83, 88–9, 96, 102, 107, 119, 123–35 *passim*, 139, 141, 146, 148–9, 152, 170, 211, 213, 362–3, 370, 396, 398, 401, 412, 418–9, 420, 426, 431, 437, 444–5, 453

National Resources Mobilization Act (NRMA), 135, 160, 420

Normandy Campaign, xix–xx, 205, 247, 284–304, 387–8; landings, 268–70, 273, 276, 278–80, 283–4; planning, 226, 235, 239–40, 242–3, 248, 250, 260–1, 264, 267. *See also* Axehead; Totalize; and Tractable

NRMA conscripts (zombies), 142, 160–1, 324–5, 360, 361–2, 365, 367, 369–70, 380, 417, 419, 420, 432, 444

Nye, Lt.-Gen. Archie, 201, 225, 358–9

Odlum, Maj.-Gen. Victor, 129, 132, 178

Ontario Hydro-Electric Commission, 20–1, 69, 448

Orde, Brig. R.J., 21, 72, 79, 84, 88, 101, 148

Otter, Brig.-Gen. William Otter, 23.

Overlord, Operation. *See* Normandy

Overseas Military Forces of Canada, Ministry of, 122

Paget, Gen. Sir Bernard, 180–1, 186, 194, 202, 203, 217–18, 221, 222, 224

Pangman, Lt.-Col. J.E., 242, 269, 283–4, 406–7

Parkin, George, 11–12

Pas de Calais, 327

Patton, General George S. Jr, 236, 258, 262, 270, 291, 298, 314, 318–19, 374, 405

Peacock, Sir Edward, 11–13, 76, 110, 236, 355, 441, 445

Pearkes, Lt.-Gen. George, 102, 179, 185–6, 187, 191, 192–4, 199, 203, 464, 504n18

Pearson, Lester B., 92, 93–4, 99, 102–3, 109, 113, 114, 123, 124–5, 126, 131, 142, 146, 150, 151–2, 156, 178, 179, 238, 367, 398, 450, 452

Penhale, Brig. M.H.S., 324

Perley-Robertson, Ike, 113, 440, 444, 449, 451

Permanent Force. *See* Canadian army

Petawawa, camp, 22–3, 26

Plunder, Operation, 404–5, 406, 409

Pope, Lt.-Gen. Maurice, 98–9, 102,

103, 106, 108, 111–12, 130, 132, 144, 145, 149, 158, 169, 213, 393, 398
Portal, Air Chief Marshal Sir Charles, 317, 352
Power, Charles G., 138, 169, 223, 259

Queen Elizabeth II, 442, 463, 464

Ralston, J.L., 87, 126, 135–6, 138, 139–40, 142, 147–8, 150–1, 152, 153–5, 161–2, 166, 167, 169, 172, 174–5, 176, 177–80, 181, 182, 200, 211, 213–14, 217, 220–5, 227, 238, 249, 252–3, 297, 335, 358, 360–2, 366, 452, 510n44. *See also under* Crerar
Reid, Escott, 92–3, 94, 102
reinforcement crisis, 130, 266, 290–1, 322–6, 360, 362–5, 368–9, 402, 410
Rhine River, 333, 340, 359, 360, 362, 365, 372–3, 374–5, 381, 382, 389–90, 392, 393–4, 396, 399, 400, 405, 408–9, 410
Roberts, Maj.-Gen. G.P. 'Ham,' 178, 192, 195, 203–4, 205, 209, 402, 461–2
Robertson, Norman, 93
Royal Air Force (RAF), 74, 205, 302, 311, 317, 319, 353; Formations: Bomber Command, 299, 301–2, 305, 316–17, 338, 339, 344–5, 349, 352–3, 375, 383, 405; Second Tactical Air Force (2 TAF), 284, 300, 301, 302, 307, 319, 338, 344; 83 Group, 262, 284, 294, 300, 301–2, 305, 307, 319, 375, 376; 84 Group, 243, 246, 250, 263, 283, 294, 299, 300, 302, 307, 311, 314, 319, 341, 353, 371, 375–6, 378, 396, 425
Royal Canadian Air Force (RCAF), 106, 262–3, 437, 452, 463

Royal Canadian Artillery (RCA), 71, 438; 2nd Canadian AGRA, 293
Royal Canadian Horse Artillery (RCHA), 72, 82
Royal Military College of Canada (RMC), 15–20 *passim*, 22, 24, 61, 75–6, 83, 113, 115, 116–17, 120, 191, 241, 254, 286, 341, 431, 456; Commandant, Crerar as, 18, 115–19, 120–1; instructor of tactics, Crerar as, 83–5; student, Crerar as, 14–19
Royal Navy, 338, 339, 344, 353
Rundstedt, Field Marshal Gert von (Commander-in-Chief West), 338, 388, 389, 405

Sansom, Lt.-Gen. H.L.N., 365
Saturday Night, 106, 457, 464
Scheldt Campaign, 321, 325, 337, 46–61; operations, 354–5, 365, 373; planning, 338–46, 350–4
Schlemm, Gen. Alfred, 388, 395, 396, 400
Schmidlin, Maj.-Gen. E.J.C., 105, 148, 149
Scott, F.R., 93
Seine, River, operations, 239–40, 263–5, 278, 299, 306, 313, 320, 322, 326–9, 333–4
Sicily, 226, 227–8, 261, 289, 424
Sifton, Victor, 133, 139, 149, 151, 162, 178
Simonds, Lt.-Gen. Guy, xx; clash in Sicily, 228–30; corps command, 272, 275–6, 279–81, 283, 289, 292, 294–8, 299, 302, 304, 305–7, 312, 314, 315–18, 320, 321, 323–6, 327–31 *passim*, 339–40, 345; divisional command, 227, 231, 234, 238, 239, 241, 243, 248, 251, 254–5, 256, 261,

266; pre-division command, 83, 184, 186, 187–8, 201, 206, 215, 224, 226; Rhineland, 360, 363–4, 370, 376, 388, 389, 390–3, 395, 400, 402, 406, 408, 416, 422, 423, 424–5, 430, 433–5, 440, 441, 462–3; Scheldt and army command, 349–50, 353, 354–6, 358

Simpson, Lt.-Gen. W.H. 'Bill,' 373–4, 382, 386, 400

Skelton, O.D., 81, 102–3, 106–8, 120, 122, 130

Somme, River, 327–9, 330, 334

South-Eastern Command (Army), 185–6, 187, 197, 199

Spartan, Exercise, 215, 217–18, 219–20

Spring, Operation, 291–2, 295

Spry, Maj.-Gen. D., 315, 371, 392, 402, 435

Stacey, C.P., xviii, xix, 116, 120, 142, 161, 186, 219, 260, 268, 285, 290, 293, 297, 305, 315, 324, 333–5 *passim*, 350, 358, 361, 365, 368, 386, 411, 423, 427, 433–5, 460–2, 463

Staff College (Camberley), 55, 73–7, 84, 98, 119, 125, 155, 164, 176, 241

Staff Duties Directorate (SDD), 148

Stinson, Elizabeth, 4–5

Stinson, John, 5

Stinson, Thomas, 4–5

Stuart, Lt.-Gen. Ken: CMHQ, as, 220–5, 230, 235, 240–2, 245, 249, 251–4 *passim*, 267, 271–3, 275, 280, 291, 322–5, 331, 332, 335, 342, 348, 357, 361, 366–7, 404, 412, 437; CGS, as, 182, 213, 215, 217; Commandant RMC, as, 121; General Staff, 149, 158, 169, 178

Student, Gen. Kurt, 338

Sussex, 185, 187, 207, 219

Switchback, Operation, 349

Tedder, Marshal of the RAF, Arthur, Lord, 301, 317, 352

Tellier, Lt.-Gen. Henri, 191, 256–7, 447, 454

Thacker, Maj.-Gen. H.C., 83, 87

Tiger, Exercise, 193–7

Timberwolf, Operation, 222, 230

Todd, Brig. P.A., 230

Totalize, Operation, 295–7, 299–300, 302, 305–8, 312–15, 321, 323, 385, 394

Tractable, Operation, 308, 315–8, 321, 394

training policy and practice, 125–6, 128; Army, 238, 242, 246–9, 261, 285, 323–5, 362, 363–5, 369, 420, 437, 441, 444, 456, 458, 461; Chief of General Staff, 137, 140, 143, 145, 151, 152–3, 155, 158–60, 161, 162, 171, 175; Corps, 181–90 *passim*, 192, 194, 197, 199–200, 203, 205–6, 208, 215–18, 222, 231, 235

Trun, 317–18, 320

ULTRA, 304, 307, 340

Undergo, Operation (Calais), 339, 340, 343–5, 346–7, 348, 351

United States army, 109, 146, 369, 384, 405, 431; Formations: 6th U.S. Army Group, 374; 12th U.S. Army Group, 298, 299, 313, 331, 373, 374, 409; First U.S. Army, 278, 294, 298, 299, 312, 318, 331, 384, 386; Third U.S. Army, 258, 298, 312–13, 318–19, 405; Ninth U.S. Army, 375, 382, 389, 393, 399–400, 404, 406, 408–9

United States Army Air Force, Formations: 8th Air Force, 352, 405

Vanier, Georges, 75–6, 77, 82, 93, 235, 259
Veritable, Operation, 372, 374–6, 377–80, 381–96, 398–400
Victor Two, Exercise, 190
Vigilant aircraft, 262–3, 279
Viper's Den, 387, 406, 411, 442, 445, 535n12
Visiting Forces Act, 92, 126–7
Vokes, Maj.-Gen. Chris, xviii, 132, 234, 255, 256–7, 406, 435

Walcheren, 338, 343–4, 348–51, 352, 372, 461
Walford, Maj.-Gen A.E., 236, 241, 256, 268, 283, 329, 334, 341–2, 343, 414, 426, 444, 465
War Office (British), 31, 74, 76–82, 98–9, 103, 107–9, 111, 114, 123–5, 128–33, 136, 143, 148, 154–5, 159, 167, 174, 176, 181, 185, 214, 238, 266, 323, 334, 356, 432
Warren, Lt.-Col. Trumbell, 335
Wavell, Maj.-Gen. A., 78–80
White, Maj. Don, 61
Winnipeg Free Press, 133, 139, 142
Wright, Lt.-Col. Peter, 241, 268, 283, 302, 421, 461, 465
Wyman, Brig. R.A., 266, 315

Ypres, xiii, xx, 32–3, 34, 37–8, 40–5, 50, 328, 342